.NET Internationalization

Microsoft .NET Development Series

John Montgomery, *Series Advisor*
Don Box, *Series Advisor*
Martin Heller, *Series Editor*

The Microsoft .NET Development Series is supported and developed by the leaders and experts of Microsoft development technologies including Microsoft architects. The books in this series provide a core resource of information and understanding every developer needs in order to write effective applications and managed code. Learn from the leaders how to maximize your use of the .NET Framework and its programming languages.

Titles in the Series

Brad Abrams, *.NET Framework Standard Library Annotated Reference Volume 1: Base Class Library and Extended Numerics Library*, 0-321-15489-4

Brad Abrams and Tamara Abrams, *.NET Framework Standard Library Annotated Reference, Volume 2: Networking Library, Reflection Library, and XML Library*, 0-321-19445-4

Keith Ballinger, *.NET Web Services: Architecture and Implementation*, 0-321-11359-4

Bob Beauchemin and Dan Sullivan, *A Developer's Guide to SQL Server 2005*, 0-321-38218-8

Bob Beauchemin, Niels Berglund, Dan Sullivan, *A First Look at SQL Server 2005 for Developers*, 0-321-18059-3

Don Box with Chris Sells, *Essential .NET, Volume 1: The Common Language Runtime*, 0-201-73411-7

Keith Brown, *The .NET Developer's Guide to Windows Security*, 0-321-22835-9

Eric Carter and Eric Lippert, *Visual Studio Tools for Office: Using C# with Excel, Word, Outlook, and InfoPath*, 0-321-33488-4

Eric Carter and Eric Lippert, *Visual Studio Tools for Office: Using Visual Basic 2005 with Excel, Word, Outlook, and InfoPath*, 0-321-41175-7

Mahesh Chand, *Graphics Programming with GDI+*, 0-321-16077-0

Krzysztof Cwalina and Brad Abrams, *Framework Design Guidelines: Conventions, Idioms, and Patterns for Reusable .NET Libraries*, 0-321-24675-6

Len Fenster, *Effective Use of Microsoft Enterprise Library: Building Blocks for Creating Enterprise Applications and Services*, 0-321-33421-3

Sam Guckenheimer and Juan J. Perez, *Software Engineering with Microsoft Visual Studio Team System*, 0-321-27872-0

Anders Hejlsberg, Scott Wiltamuth, Peter Golde, *The C# Programming Language*, Second Edition, 0-321-33443-4

Alex Homer, Dave Sussman, Mark Fussell, *ADO.NET and System.Xml v. 2.0—The Beta Version*, 0-321-24712-4

Alex Homer and Dave Sussman, *ASP.NET 2.0 Illustrated*, 0-321-41834-4

Alex Homer, Dave Sussman, Rob Howard, *ASP.NET v. 2.0—The Beta Version*, 0-321-25727-8

Joe Kaplan and Ryan Dunn, *The .NET Developer's Guide to Directory Services Programming*, 0-321-35017-0

Mark Michaelis, *Essential C# 2.0*, 0-321-15077-5

James S. Miller and Susann Ragsdale, *The Common Language Infrastructure Annotated Standard*, 0-321-15493-2

Christian Nagel, *Enterprise Services with the .NET Framework: Developing Distributed Business Solutions with .NET Enterprise Services*, 0-321-24673-X

Brian Noyes, *Data Binding with Windows Forms 2.0: Programming Smart Client Data Applications with .NET*, 0-321-26892-X

Fritz Onion, *Essential ASP.NET with Examples in C#*, 0-201-76040-1

Fritz Onion, *Essential ASP.NET with Examples in Visual Basic .NET*, 0-201-76039-8

Ted Pattison and Dr. Joe Hummel, *Building Applications and Components with Visual Basic .NET*, 0-201-73495-8

Dr. Neil Roodyn, *eXtreme .NET: Introducing eXtreme Programming Techniques to .NET Developers*, 0-321-30363-6

Chris Sells and Michael Weinhardt, *Windows Forms 2.0 Programming*, 0-321-26796-6

Chris Sells, *Windows Forms Programming in C#*, 0-321-11620-8

Chris Sells and Justin Gehtland, *Windows Forms Programming in Visual Basic .NET*, 0-321-12519-3

Guy Smith-Ferrier, *.NET Internationalization: The Developer's Guide to Building Global Windows and Web Applications*, 0-321-34138-4

Paul Vick, *The Visual Basic .NET Programming Language*, 0-321-16951-4

Damien Watkins, Mark Hammond, Brad Abrams, *Programming in the .NET Environment*, 0-201-77018-0

Shawn Wildermuth, *Pragmatic ADO.NET: Data Access for the Internet World*, 0-201-74568-2

Paul Yao and David Durant, *.NET Compact Framework Programming with C#*, 0-321-17403-8

Paul Yao and David Durant, *.NET Compact Framework Programming with Visual Basic .NET*, 0-321-17404-6

For more information go to www.awprofessional.com/msdotnetseries/

.NET Internationalization

The Developer's Guide to Building Global Windows and Web Applications

■ **Guy Smith-Ferrier**

♦Addison-Wesley

Upper Saddle River, NJ • Boston • Indianapolis • San Francisco
New York • Toronto • Montreal • London • Munich • Paris • Madrid
Cape Town • Sydney • Tokyo • Singapore • Mexico City

Many of the designations used by manufacturers and sellers to distinguish their products are claimed as trademarks. Where those designations appear in this book, and the publisher was aware of a trademark claim, the designations have been printed with initial capital letters or in all capitals.

The .NET logo is either a registered trademark or trademark of Microsoft Corporation in the United States and/or other countries and is used under license from Microsoft.

The author and publisher have taken care in the preparation of this book, but make no expressed or implied warranty of any kind and assume no responsibility for errors or omissions. No liability is assumed for incidental or consequential damages in connection with or arising out of the use of the information or programs contained herein.

The publisher offers excellent discounts on this book when ordered in quantity for bulk purchases or special sales, which may include electronic versions and/or custom covers and content particular to your business, training goals, marketing focus, and branding interests. For more information, please contact:

U. S. Corporate and Government Sales
(800) 382-3419
corpsales@pearsontechgroup.com

For sales outside the U. S., please contact:

International Sales
international@pearsoned.com

This Book Is Safari Enabled

The Safari® Enabled icon on the cover of your favorite technology book means the book is available through Safari Bookshelf. When you buy this book, you get free access to the online edition for 45 days.

Safari Bookshelf is an electronic reference library that lets you easily search thousands of technical books, find code samples, download chapters, and access technical information whenever and wherever you need it.

To gain 45-day Safari Enabled access to this book:

- Go to http://www.awprofessional.com/safarienabled
- Complete the brief registration form
- Enter the coupon code ZHLY-L6CN-XBLI-W1N1-GTCH

If you have difficulty registering on Safari Bookshelf or accessing the online edition, please e-mail customer-service@safaribooksonline.com.

Visit us on the Web: www.awprofessional.com
Library of Congress Cataloging-in-Publication Data:
Smith-Ferrier, Guy.
  .Net internationalization : the developer's guide to building global Windows and Web applications / Guy Smith-Ferrier.
    p. cm.
  ISBN 0-321-34138-4 (pbk. : alk. paper)
1. Microsoft .NET. 2. Microsoft .NET Framework. 3. Application software. I. Title.
  QA76.76.M52S65 2006
  005.2'768—dc22
                    2006013165

ISBN 0-321-34138-4
Text printed in the United States on recycled paper at R.R. Donnelley in Crawfordsville, IN.
First printing, August 2006

For Sandy, Samuel and Eloise

Contents at a Glance

Contents

Foreword

I'VE BEEN WORKING IN LOCALIZATION my entire career, and I've seen countless examples of how amazingly hard it can be to create a world-ready Windows product. The early days of 32-bit Windows saw a definite lack of support for international products. Since then, so many APIs related to internationalization have been added, duplicated, replaced, and deprecated in various products and platforms that almost nobody can acquire the skills needed to know for certain if their product is properly adapted to an international market.

Of course, nobody was feeling the pain of the situation that Microsoft created more than Microsoft itself. And true to form, the company created a grand vision: a brand new development framework and runtime environment, where support for all things painful and bug-causing—including such areas as memory management, security, and even internationalization—were considered from the start. We now know the result of this effort as the .NET Framework.

And what a result it is! The difference between creating internationalized applications in .NET and Win32 is like night and day. There simply is no comparison! The amount of minute details that are abstracted away by the .NET Framework is absolutely staggering.

Still, as it turns out, Visual Studio .NET does not provide a "Make My Application World-Ready Wizard." Nor will it anytime soon. Despite the complexity hidden by the .NET Framework, the software architect and developer still requires a good understanding of the issues involved in creating a culture-independent and localizable product. There simply hasn't been any one single, overviewable source of the most essential information.

That's exactly why I'm proud of my involvement in the effort behind this book. I hope that this book can have the same impact on world-ready applications as Code Complete has had on producing quality code in general or Writing Secure Code has had on producing trustworthy applications. If this work fulfills my hope, well, time will tell. The potential is certainly there. Now it's up to you to read, learn, practice, and deliver.

Jesper Holmberg,
International Project Engineer,
Core Operation Systems Division, Microsoft Corporation

Preface

IT IS OFTEN SAID THAT THE WORLD is getting smaller every day. Cheap, fast air travel; the global economy; the global climate; the insatiable desire for standards; and, perhaps, most important of all, the Internet all play a part in the homogenization of our world. It is ironic, therefore, that this shrinking effect is not a benefit to developers—in fact, it has the opposite effect. As the world community achieves greater awareness and greater tolerance, the demand for culturally aware software increases. Within the U.S. and Canada, for example, significant Hispanic, French, and Chinese populations exist.

At best, English-only Windows applications and Web sites are difficult for these cultures. At worst, these applications and Web sites exclude or even offend these populations. Such Web sites also are potentially illegal. For example, France and Quebec, Canada, both have laws prohibiting the hosting of English-only Web sites. Many countries (Wales, for example) also require that public services always be available in the native language, in addition to English. From marketing and financial viewpoints, English-only applications—and particularly Web sites—represent a massive lost market. By their very nature, Web sites are global, but an English-only Web site loses marketing opportunities to people who do not speak English. From a marketing point of view, such a lost opportunity is a criminal waste.

Good news exists, however. The .NET Framework has arguably the most comprehensive support for internationalizing .NET applications of any development platform. The .NET Framework provides a significant infrastructure for globalizing applications, and Visual Studio 2003 and 2005 provide excellent functionality for localizing Windows applications. Although Visual Studio 2003 offered little help for ASP.NET developers, rest assured that Visual Studio 2005 has thorough support for localizing Web applications.

What This Book Covers

This book covers the internationalization of .NET Windows Forms and ASP.NET applications. It covers both versions 1.1 and 2.0 of the .NET Framework, and both Visual Studio 2003 and Visual Studio 2005. Although the main focus of the book is on the .NET Framework 2.0 and Visual Studio 2005, it highlights differences between them and the .NET Framework 1.1 and Visual Studio 2003. Visual Studio 2003 developers can read this book by skipping the sections on Visual Studio 2005, but I advise against this. Visual Studio 2005 offers many useful new facilities—many of which can be retrofitted to Visual Studio 2003—to provide guidance on how to design Visual Studio 2003 applications with a clear migration path to Visual Studio 2005. For a list of the new internationalization features in the .NET Framework 2.0 and Visual Studio 2005, see Appendix A, "New Internationalization Features in the .NET Framework 2.0 and Visual Studio 2005."

Chapter 1, "A Roadmap for the Internationalization Process," provides a general overview of what is involved in internationalizing an application, and includes more specific information on why some of the more advanced chapters will be of more interest to you and what solutions can be found in them. Chapter 2, "Unicode, Windows, and the .NET Framework," lays down the foundation of what Unicode is and what you can expect from the operating system and the .NET Framework. The essential mechanics of internationalization are covered in Chapter 3, "An Introduction to Internationalization," and this should be considered a prerequisite for all other chapters. From here, Windows Forms developers should read Chapter 4, "Windows Forms Specifics," and ASP.NET developers should read Chapter 5, "ASP.NET Specifics." Chapter 6, "Globalization," covers the concept of globalization in depth, along with the .NET Framework globalization classes and some solutions for globalization issues that are not covered by the .NET Framework classes. Chapter 7, "Middle East and East Asian Cultures," covers issues that are specific to right-to-left cultures (Arabic, Divehi, Farsi, Hebrew, Syriac, and Urdu) and Asian cultures (Chinese, Korean, and Japanese). Chapter 8, "Best Practices," provides internationalization guidance on a more general level, including issues such as the choice of fonts. Chapter 9, "Machine Translation," provides solutions for automatically translating your resources into other languages. Chapter 10, "Resource Administration," describes a number of utilities included in the source code for this book, to help with the administration of resources.

As applications grow beyond the simplistic examples used to illustrate concepts, the maintenance and management of applications' resources demand more dedicated solutions. Chapter 11, "Custom Cultures," describes how to create your own cultures and integrate them into the .NET Framework 2.0 and Visual Studio 2005. Custom cultures are useful for creating pseudo translations, supporting unsupported cultures, creating commercial dialects, and supporting languages outside their normal country (e.g., Spanish in the U.S., Chinese in Canada, and Urdu in the United Kingdom). Chapter 12, "Custom Resource Managers," describes how the existing resource managers work internally, and how to write new resource managers and use them in Windows Forms applications and ASP.NET applications. Custom resource managers are the solution to numerous developer issues, from changing the origin of resources (to, say, a database) to changing the functionality of resource managers (to, say, standardize specific properties throughout an application). Chapter 13, "Testing Internationalization Using FxCop," shows how to use FxCop to apply internationalization rules to your assemblies. It covers the existing FxCop globalization rules, introduces new globalization rules based on the issues raised throughout this book, and shows how to write these rules to enable you to write your own rules. Chapter 14, "The Translator," discusses the issues and solutions involved in including the translator in the internationalization process. As noted already, Appendix A, "New Internationalization Features in .NET Framework 2.0 and Visual Studio 2005," includes a list of the new features in the .NET Framework 2.0 and Visual Studio 2005. Most of these features are covered throughout the book, so this appendix is mostly a list of pointers to chapters within the book. Appendix B, "Information Resources," is a list of books, resources, Web sites, magazines, online machine-translation Web sites, blogs, conferences, organizations, and commercial machine-translations products that will raise your awareness of the internationalization community.

Who Should Read This Book

This book is aimed at developers, team leaders, technical architects—essentially, anyone who is involved in the technical aspects of internationalizing .NET applications. The book uses C# examples, but the content is equally relevant to Visual Basic.NET developers and anyone who uses Visual Studio. The book expects that Visual Studio will be the main development environment, but many chapters focus solely on the .NET Framework. As such, the information contained within has equal value if you use an alternative development environment such as SharpDevelop or Borland Delphi 2005.

What You Need to Use This Book

To get the most from this book, you need the .NET Framework 2.0 and Visual Studio 2005. Alternatively, you can follow a large part of this book using the .NET Framework 1.1 and Visual Studio 2003. You can follow a lesser part of this book using the .NET Framework 1.1 or 2.0 and an alternative development environment.

Source Code

The complete source code for this book is available for download at http://www.dotneti18n.com. You will also find errata, updates to the code, new code examples, and additional information.

Acknowledgments

I WOULD LIKE TO THANK Jesper Holmberg, Ken Cox, Mark Blomsma, Douglas Reilly, Jason Nadal, Martin Peck, Shaun Wilde, and the Microsoft Globalization Team for their excellent help in reviewing this book; the better three quarters of 4 Chaps From Blighty (Brian Long, Steve Scott, and especially Steve Tudor, at http://www.4chapsfromblighty.com) for their excellent technical expertise and their readiness to help a friend in need; everyone who worked on this book at Addison-Wesley but notably Joan Murray, Jessica D'Amico, Curt Johnson, Antje King, Marie McKinley, Andy Beaster, and Lara Wysong for their dedication to the cause; many people at Microsoft especially "Dr. International" for their specific help and their general contribution to the internationalization world; Roy Nelson for his problem-solving skills; and Yae Nobuto for her linguistic skills. Special thanks to my brother, Paul, for too many reasons to list.

Finally, for the avoidance of doubt, the fictional character Frodo Potter does not appear anywhere in this book.

About the Author

Guy Smith-Ferrier is an author, developer, trainer, and speaker with more than 20 years of software engineering experience. He has internationalized applications in four development platforms, including the .NET Framework. He has spoken at numerous conferences on three continents and been voted Best Speaker twice. He is the author of C#/.NET courseware and the official Borland courseware for COM and ADO. He has written articles for numerous magazines, has co-authored an application-development book, and is the author of the ADO chapter of *Mastering Delphi 6* (Sybex, 2001). He lives in the U.K. with his wife and two children. His blog is at http://www.guysmithferrier.com.

1

A Roadmap for the Internationalization Process

L EARNING IS LIKE CLIMBING a mountain. When you stand at the bottom of a
mountain, you cannot actually see the top; the side of the mountain gets in the
way. What you see is the first peak on the horizon. As you climb over that peak, you
see the next peak on the horizon. You keep doing this until the last peak is the summit and your climb is over. I have always felt that technical subjects seem simple
when I don't know anything about them. As I climb each peak, I see the other
subjects behind my initially imperfect view and realize that there is more to climb.
Each peak reveals new peaks that I was not aware of.

Internationalization is like a mountain. From the outside, the subject might seem
simple—you just translate all the text, don't you? But as each problem is solved, it
allows us to see other problems on the horizon. From the bottom of the mountain,
it is difficult to see all the peaks before we reach the top. The purpose of this chapter is to provide an aerial view of the mountain. Its goal is to help project managers
and developers appreciate some of the higher-level decisions that must be made in
the internationalization of an application. It poses many questions and leaves most
unanswered. The answers lie in the subsequent chapters of this book. If you are a
developer, lend your copy of this book to your project manager (or buy him or her
a new copy) and ask him or her to read this chapter; with this overview, managers
should get a broad grasp of your world.

The Operating System

Your choice of the version of Windows to use for your application has a significant impact upon the functionality of your application. As always, the most recent operating systems provide the best support; this is especially true in internationalization. A clear distinction exists between Unicode versions of Windows (Windows NT 3.51, Windows 2000, Windows XP, and above) and non-Unicode versions of Windows (Windows 95, 98, and Me); I advise using a Unicode version of Windows, at the very least. The version of the operating system also affects support for mirroring, which is used in right-to-left cultures (such as Arabic, Hebrew, and Persian [Farsi]), font availability and font functionality, the number of supported cultures (languages and regions), and support for complex scripts (some writing systems such as Thai require considerably more complex support for rendering than comparatively simple Latin languages).

The .NET Framework and Visual Studio

Your choice of which version of the .NET Framework to use has perhaps the greatest impact of any decision under your control. Obviously, the .NET Framework 2.0 has significantly better internationalization support than the .NET Framework 1.1. Take a look at Appendix A, "New Internationalization Features in the .NET Framework 2.0 and Visual Studio 2005," for a complete list of the differences. Some of these new features can be retrofitted into the .NET Framework 1.1 (e.g., strongly typed resources and IDN mapping); others can be simulated with varying degrees of success (e.g., WinRes Visual Studio File Mode and custom cultures). However, others are solely the domain of the newer version of the framework (for example, `TableLayoutPanel`).

The version of the .NET Framework (i.e., 1.1 or 2.0) dictates the version of Visual Studio (2003 or 2005, respectively). The functionality of Visual Studio 2005 is obviously superior to that of Visual Studio 2003. The Resource Editor has greater functionality; support for strongly typed resources is built into the IDE; and Windows Forms support a new property reflection model. Of greatest significance to ASP.NET applications is that Visual Studio 2005 supports localizing ASP.NET applications. In Visual Studio 2003, localizing an ASP.NET application is all your own work.

Languages

The languages that your application supports dictate many of the considerations that arise when internationalizing your application. Latin languages, such as French, German, and Spanish, make the fewest demands on your application and require a relatively low level of technology to support. The further you go from Latin languages, the greater awareness you need of issues that Latin languages do not require.

Right-to-left languages (such as Arabic, Hebrew, and Persian [Farsi]) require support for reading text right to left (instead of left to right) and mirroring. In a mirrored form or Web page, controls are repositioned from one side of a form to the other. In addition, controls are rendered right to left (e.g., scrollbars are on the left of a control, and menus start from the right and expand to the left).

Your choice of operating system affects the level of font technology available to support your languages. Chinese, Japanese, and Korean (often abbreviated to CJK) languages use glyphs that are not present in most fonts. Windows 2000 and above support font linking. This allows a font, such as MS Mincho, to be linked to another, such as Microsoft Sans Serif, so that when a glyph is required that is not found in the base font, the other linked fonts are searched for the required glyph. This technology takes away much of the burden of choosing a suitable font because you can stay with a single font, such as Microsoft Sans Serif, and rely on font linking to find the missing glyphs. Similarly, other languages (e.g., Devanagari) use scripts that require complex rendering, which is not found in Latin scripts. This complex rendering is achieved automatically if your operating system supports font fallback (which Windows 2000 and above do) and this support is installed.

East Asian languages (Chinese, Japanese, and Korean) make further demands on the application. These languages have considerably more characters than are available on a QWERTY keyboard (there are 5,000-odd Japanese Kanji characters), so a software component called an Input Method Editor (IME) is used to enter characters. Typically, this issue is more relevant to Windows Forms applications than ASP.NET applications: IMEs are used with both Windows Forms applications and ASP.NET applications, but Windows Forms applications can optionally offer help in controlling the IME. The question in terms of development is, do you offer help in controlling the IME, and, if so, how much help do you offer?

The languages that you need to support also dictate whether you need to use custom cultures. A custom culture is a language or a language and region (or a replacement of an existing language or language and region) that is not already known to the .NET Framework. For example, if you wanted to support Bengali in Bangladesh, you would have to create a custom culture. Similarly, if you wanted to support a known language outside of its "known" region (e.g., Spanish in the United States), then you would have to create a custom culture. Although custom cultures can be created in the .NET Framework 1.1, support for this is very low and you are strongly advised to use the .NET Framework 2.0.

The languages that you need to support also affect your testing process. For accurate testing, you must test your application on the version of the operating system that your users will be running. The "version" means not only the release (Windows 2000, XP, 2003, and so on), but also the language. If your users will be running German Windows XP Professional, then your testing is not complete if you test it in English Windows XP Professional. You should consider two testing scenarios: Windows Multiple User Interface and Virtual PC. Both are covered in Chapter 2, "Unicode, Windows, and the .NET Framework."

Resource Formats

The strings, bitmaps, icons, audio, and other files that can be translated or localized in your application are collectively called *resources*. During development, these resources are moved out of the source code and into a separate location. One of the fundamental decisions that you must make is what format these resources will be stored in. This decision has far-reaching implications. The most commonly used format, and the one offered by default in Visual Studio 2003 and 2005, is resx files. A resx file is an XML file. The .NET Framework 2.0 offers resx, resources, txt, and restext as choices, but you can choose a completely new format as well.

A common alternative to these is to use a database to store all resources, but you could equally use XLIFF (XML Localization Interchange File Format, a format used to exchange localization data between tools). As with all decisions, you must weigh the pros and cons. The .NET Framework and Visual Studio lend themselves to using resx files. Their support for this format is complete. resx files can be manipulated using all .NET Framework SDK tools and all parts of Visual Studio, including, notably, Visual Studio's Resource Editor. All other formats have less support to some degree and involve some additional effort to support. This does not mean that a database, for example, cannot be used. In Chapter 12, "Custom Resource Managers," we create a resource manager for a database. In the same chapter, we create a utility for creating strongly typed resources, for resources in any format. In Chapter 10, "Resource Administration," we create a Resource Editor replacement that, among other uses, enables you to read and write resources in any format.

One of the benefits of storing resources in a database is that resources can be changed easily at runtime. (By contrast, unless you are writing an ASP.NET 2.0 application, changes to resx files require a recompilation for the changes to be seen.) Thus, a database offers a great solution for translators because they can immediately see the results of their translation. In addition, a database is suitable if the strings of an application are rapidly changing, making a recompilation of the application unsuitable.

Languages and Cultural Formatting

One of the first decisions that you must make is how users will specify what language or language and region they want the application to use. This question involves several parts.

First, .NET Framework applications make a distinction between the language and region used for the user interface and the language and region used for cultural formatting. The user interface refers to the text and images that are shown to the user. Cultural formatting refers to issues such as the formatting of dates, numbers, and currencies. The first part of this decision involves whether you should allow your users to make a distinction between these two settings. If they can make a distinction between these two settings, it would be possible to have the user interface in, say, Spanish but use cultural formatting for the U.S. This would be useful for the millions of Spanish-speaking people who live and work in the U.S. (although you might argue that creating a custom culture is a better solution).

Second, you should be aware that languages vary from region to region. English as spoken in the United States is not exactly the same as English as spoken in the U.K. The same is true for French in Canada compared with French in France, and, perhaps more important, Portuguese in Brazil compared with Portuguese in Portugal. One of the decisions you must make is how specific your translations will be. If you translate from English to French, will you use a single French translation for all French-speaking countries, regardless of their region? Imagine that you had to use an application in which the phrase, "The bank has not honored this check," is displayed as "The bank has not honoured this cheque" (which uses the British English spelling). In the United States, you would probably get support calls complaining of spelling errors in the application.

Windows Forms Applications

Windows Forms applications have their own considerations. You must decide whether users are allowed to specify which language and region the application should use. Certainly, giving users a choice is always good from a functionality point of view. If you use the .NET Framework dialog controls (including `MessageBox`), however, you might not be able to deliver on this promise. These controls draw resources from the operating system and the .NET Framework Language Packs. Consequently, if your application is running on a Spanish version of Windows with a Spanish .NET Framework Language Pack, the dialogs will be in Spanish. This is a great time saver if your application's user interface should be in Spanish. However, if you have given users a choice of what language the application should use, they could choose a different language from the operating system (say, French), making the user interface schizophrenic (part would be in French, and part would be in Spanish).

If you decide to give your users a choice, you will also need to decide how users specify that choice. You might choose to let users specify this in the Regional and Language Options Control Panel applet. This is convenient, but you should also consider what would happen if they change this setting while the application is running. An alternative is to offer some menu setting inside the application. If you do this, you should consider whether a change to the language here means that the setting applies immediately or when the application next starts. If it applies immediately, you will need a way of refreshing the entire application's user interface (see Chapter 4, "Windows Forms Specifics," for a number of solutions).

If your application is a Windows Forms 2.0 application and you intend to use `ClickOnce` to deploy and update your application, you should also consider whether the `ClickOnce` user interface should be localized. The question here is this:

Is the user interface of the deployment and update mechanism separate from that of the application? For example, if you write a Spanish application, should the ClickOnce interface also be in Spanish? If the answer is yes you will also need to localize ClickOnce (see Chapter 4).

ASP.NET Applications

The single biggest factor affecting the internationalization of ASP.NET applications is whether you use Visual Studio 2003 or Visual Studio 2005. Visual Studio 2005 has considerable support, whereas Visual Studio 2003 offers no support beyond what the .NET Framework already offers. That is not to say that you cannot internationalize ASP.NET 1.1 applications, just that such internationalization is a manual process with no additional help from the tools.

You also must decide how users will specify their language and region. A common approach to this problem is to adopt users' language preferences from their browser (this information is passed in the HTTP header of all requests). A refined variation on this theme is to adopt users' initial settings from the browser and then let the user override the settings in a user profile. You should also decide whether users should be allowed to specify a different language and region for the user interface to the language and region for their cultural formatting. In an ASP.NET application, such different settings will lead to a schizophrenic user interface if you use the Calendar control. For example, if the user specifies that the user interface is in Spanish, but the cultural formatting is United States, a page would display in Spanish but a Calendar control on the same page would display in English.

You also need to consider exactly what gets handed over to your translator to translate. Do you give the translators just the resources or the aspx pages as well? Handing over the aspx pages introduces new problems, not the least of which is that these critical files have to be locked while with the translator (which could be days or weeks). A better solution is to ensure that all static text has been removed from your aspx pages and placed in resources. Of course, this means that the issue of formatting is now outside the hands of the translator and in the hands of the developers.

If your application caches pages (for better performance), your caching process must be language/region–aware. If it is not, the first user to access a page will have the page cached, and subsequent users will get the same cached page even if they use a different language.

You also must decide whether to use absolute or relative positioning of controls. By default, Visual Studio 2003 uses absolute positioning and Visual Studio 2005 uses relative positioning. Pros and cons exist for both approaches, but in internationalization terms, consider that absolute positioning causes significant problems for localization; this is not only because controls do not automatically reposition and resize, but also because mirroring does not work when controls are absolutely positioned. As a general rule, you should use relative positioning in internationalized applications; if you intend to use mirroring (for right-to-left languages such as Arabic, Hebrew, and Persian [Farsi]), you should consider this a requirement.

Globalization

Globalization is the process of adapting an application so that it does not have cultural preconceptions. The most common example is the different date formats used throughout the world. An application that displays dates as "MM/dd/yy" assumes the U.S. date format. Globalization is not limited to dates, however, and covers many lesser-known subjects. How many of the following, for example, do you know?

Not all languages have a concept of upper case.

A conversion to upper case does not result in the same string in all cultures.

Not all regions use the Gregorian calendar.

Some regions use a 13-month calendar.

"AM" and "PM" suffixes are not "AM" and "PM" in all languages.

In some languages, month names take a different form when the month can be said to "own" a day.

Several regions have more than one way of sorting data.

Thai does not use spaces to separate words (words are not separated at all).

The Windows Program Files folder isn't always called "Program Files" on non-English versions of Windows.

The good news is that the .NET Framework understands all these issues (and many more), and the advice is quite clear: Always use the .NET Framework classes. This will solve a very large part of the globalization issues of your application. You need a very good reason to use your own classes instead of those provided by the .NET Framework. For more details, see Chapter 6, "Globalization."

One decision that you might need to make early in the development of your application is how to refer to cultures. A culture is a language or a language-and-region combination. If you need to store a culture or a list of cultures (for, say, a user's preferred settings), you must decide whether to store them as names or as numbers. If you are using the .NET Framework 2.0, the answer is simple: Always store culture identifiers as strings (because strings can identify all cultures, regardless of whether they are custom cultures, cultures for alternate sort orders, or any other culture). Unfortunately, if you are using the .NET Framework 1.1, there is no easy answer to this; your decision will depend upon the functionality your application requires. If you use alternate sort orders, you must store these cultures as numbers. If you don't use alternate sort orders, you should store cultures as strings. Of course, you could store alternate sort orders as numbers and all other cultures as strings; in that case, you would need to be able to read and write cultures as both names and numbers.

Localization

Localization is the process of creating resources for a given language or a language and region. When you create a French version of your application, you have *localized* it. Localization brings with it some more decisions.

You must decide what language you want your exceptions to be thrown in. You might at first think that exceptions should be in the same language as the user interface. Alternatively, you might take the approach that all exceptions should be handled by an application-wide handler, with the exception logged and sent to the support team, and a different (localized) message displayed to the user. In this scenario, you might decide that all exceptions should be in the original developer's language. After all, if your developers are English, how much use is an error message in German? In an ASP.NET application, you might opt for this second approach. In a Windows Forms application, you might adopt both approaches. Consider that an "Unable to find the specified file" exception might be of immediate use to the user, so it could be argued that it should be localized. However, a "Value does not fall within the expected range" exception is of no value to the user (unless the application is a developer tool) and is intended for the developer, so it should probably not be localized.

You also must consider how much or how little your translator will do. Primarily, should the translator redesign forms or Web pages? When text is translated, it is often larger than the original text. You need to decide how to cope with this expansion. The traditional approach has been to let translators redesign forms (moving controls out of the way and resizing controls, for example) so that collisions do not occur. An alternative approach is to design forms with room for expansion. The .NET Framework 2.0 offers an additional solution that allows Windows Forms applications to behave in a similar way to HTML, and bump controls out of the way or wrap text as necessary.

Yet another consideration is how to translate hotkeys. Many controls have hotkey assignments to allow users to jump to controls using a set of keystrokes. For example, Alt+C might jump to a "Country" text box. If the form is localized and the prompt is now, for example, "Pays" instead of "Country," clearly, a hotkey of Alt+C is meaningless. The decision that you need to make is whether to ask your translator to make these hotkey assignments or whether to automate assignments of hotkeys in code. The problem with placing this in the hands of the translator is that the translator might not always be able to see hotkey assignment clashes if he or she cannot see the form on which the text lies. The problem with automating this process is that the most logical hotkey is not always the hotkey that gets assigned.

Machine Translation

Machine translators are programs that translate text. They can be Windows programs, Web services, or Web sites. They provide a way of automating the translation of your application. You must decide whether to use them, and, if so, how much to use them. Start with the premise that machine translation will not be perfect. It will make mistakes. If you use a machine translation, you must also follow up the machine translation with a review by a human translator who can catch all the machine's translation mistakes. That said, many of the translations will be correct, and this approach can significantly reduce the amount of time that it takes for the overall translation effort (and, therefore, the cost of that effort). In addition, this approach is very useful for getting a demo version of the application up and running with little or no translation cost. Consider that if you demo the Greek version of your application using a machine translation, it will be indistinguishable from a human translation to someone who cannot read Greek.

Another very important use for machine translation is to create a pseudo translation of your application. A pseudo translation is a translation to a pseudo language that looks very similar to the original language but that can also be identified as not the original language. The benefit of a pseudo translation is that it allows developers to test that the application is localizable while still being able to read the prompts in the application so that it can be used without having to learn another language. This approach is a very useful strategy in testing an internationalized application. However, it requires you to choose a culture that is used for the pseudo translation. If you are using the .NET Framework 2.0, the best solution to this is to create a custom culture specifically for this purpose (this is one of the examples in Chapter 11, "Custom Cultures"). If you are using .NET Framework 1.1, then the best solution is to hijack an existing culture.

Resource Administration

The basic process of maintaining resources—that is, adding, editing, and deleting text and images—is simple. Visual Studio provides a Resource Editor (with lesser functionality in Visual Studio 2003) to maintain resources. However, in a large application, the maintenance of these resources is a significant part of the development process. The problem is that if you delete an entry from one language, you will probably want to delete the same entry from all the others. The same can also be true for adding and editing resources. It is easy for resources to get out-of-synch with each other. A tool is needed to help manage the numerous changes made to resources and to keep those resources in synch. Chapter 12 provides the Resource Administrator for this purpose. In addition to this, unlike the Visual Studio Resource Editor, it is not restricted to using resx files. Furthermore, it can automatically translate resources as they are added. So if you add a new string for a MessageBox for "Collect additional company information?", the French resource is also updated with a string for "Rassemblez l'information additionnelle de compagnie?"

Testing

I have already pointed out that the most accurate testing is performed only by running the application on the language version of the intended operating system, and also that using a pseudo translation is a great way to find localizability issues before the application is released beyond the developers. Another tool in the testing armory is FxCop. Throughout this book, I make various recommendations or point out choices that you might want to adopt in the internationalization of your application. FxCop is a static analysis tool included with Visual Studio 2005 Team System and available for download for the .NET Framework 1.1 and 2.0. It enables you to create rules that enforce the decisions and choices you have made. Chapter 13, "Testing Internationalization Using FxCop," contains a collection of rules that enforce the recommendations made in this book. You can enable or disable individual rules according to your decisions.

Translation

One of the decisions you must make with regard to translating your application is how to provide immediate (or very fast) visual feedback of the translator's translations. For translators to achieve a speed of translation that is financially viable, they will sometimes translate long lists of strings one after another. This gives good productivity for the translator, but the translations occur out of context. That is, the translator does not see the context in which the strings are used. Often the context in which the string is used (not to mention its length) can change the vocabulary or grammar used in the translation. If the translator simply translates a list of strings and does not get to see the translations used within the application until the strings are returned to the developers, reintegrated into the application, and sent back to the translator, there can be an unnecessarily high number of translation iterations. One solution is to provide feedback to the translator as soon as possible, or even to allow the translator to translate text in context.

To provide feedback as soon as possible, you have a number of strategies, which are investigated at length in Chapter 14, "The Translator." Clearly, using a database for resources is a good solution in this respect because the resources are held in only a single format and do not need to be converted from one format to another (as resx files do). However, Chapter 14 investigates other solutions.

In a Windows Forms application, you can use the Windows Resource Localization Editor (WinRes). This is a forms designer that has similar functionality to the Visual Studio Forms Designer, which your translator can use to translate strings and redesign forms. This tool has the benefit that it allows translators to see their translations in context. WinRes has pros and cons (see Chapters 4 and 14)—you must decide whether the pros outweigh the cons.

Where Are We?

We are looking down on the mountain with a high-level map in our hands. I have presented many of the issues on which decisions must be made. The details behind those decisions are found in the remaining chapters of this book. The technical issues that get us from the bottom of the mountain to the summit can also be found within these chapters. Good luck on your ascent.

■ 2 ■

Unicode, Windows, and the .NET Framework

O UR INDUSTRY HAS A HUMBLE BEGINNING. The American Standard Code for Information Interchange (ASCII) character set that underlies the American National Standards Institute (ANSI) upon which DOS was built included upper and lower characters for the English language alone. We have come a long way since then. In this chapter, you will learn about the operating environment in which your .NET application will run, including Unicode, Microsoft Windows support for Unicode, different language versions of Microsoft Windows, and different language versions of the .NET Framework.

Unicode

In the words of the Unicode Consortium (see http://www.unicode.org), Unicode provides a unique number for every character, regardless of platform, program, or language. This means that if you use Unicode to represent characters in your application, there is no ambiguity over what a character should be in the application's user interface, in the application's input devices, or in the application's data. It's a simple concept, but it is a fundamental building block for an international application. The good news for .NET developers is that the .NET Framework and Visual Studio use Unicode throughout, so Unicode is a given.

The numbers that identify characters are called *code points*. Unicode groups these code points into 17 blocks of numbers, called *planes*, which consist of 64KB code points each. The first plane is plane 0 (also called the Basic Multilingual Plane, BMP) and includes the most commonly used languages. The 16 other planes include languages that are not in current use (e.g., Gothic and Old Italic), mathematical and musical symbols, and characters for more languages. The mapping of characters to code points is an ongoing process (Unicode 3.0 has more than 50,000 code points, Unicode 4.0 has more than 94,000), and although the Unicode Consortium will eventually catch up with all the existing characters in the world, new characters and symbols will arise, and Unicode will need to be updated to include these. For this reason, the Unicode specification has a version that identifies the features that are covered within that release. Because code points are just numbers, the .NET Framework can read and write any code point without requiring previous knowledge of the code point. Note, however, the limit to which such unknown code points can be handled. When the .NET Framework has no information about a code point, it cannot know how to sort, case, or render it. So although the .NET Framework 1.1 was released before the most recent version of Unicode, it can still read and write all the new code points, although it cannot make decisions about how to process these code points. Fonts, however, are another matter, but they fall outside the .NET Framework.

Unicode mapping tables are tables that map legacy code pages (covered in the next section) to their Unicode equivalents. Table 2.1 shows the Unicode Mapping Table versions that the .NET Framework supports.

Table 2.1 .NET Framework Support for Unicode Mapping Tables

Framework	Unicode Mapping Tables
.NET Framework 2.0	4.0
.NET Framework 1.1	3.0

Code Pages

Before Unicode, there was darkness. The darkness was code pages, and they provided a poor solution to the problem that ASCII was inadequate. ASCII uses the first 7 bits of a byte to define 128 characters, which include Latin characters, numbers, punctuation, and control characters. With these 128 characters taken, there were only 128 possible values remaining to represent all the other characters in the world in a single byte. This was clearly impossible, so the solution of code pages was created.

A code page defines one possible set of characters for these remaining 128 characters. Each character is identified by a number called a code point. For example, the Windows code page 1252 is "Western Europe" and includes many Latin accented characters. Similarly, the Windows code page 1256 includes Arabic characters. This solves the problem of representing a single character in a single byte, but it is a disaster for data integrity. To know what character a code point is trying to represent, you have to know what code page it uses. A file that was created for code page 1252 is meaningless (for the upper 128 characters) if it is represented using code page 1256. Even worse, not all scripts (e.g., including Armenian and Geez [Ethiopia]) have a code page, so representing such characters without Unicode support ranges from difficult to impossible. Mercifully, if your application does not interact with legacy systems and your application does not use the console, you will be spared from having to use code pages because the .NET Framework is based upon Unicode, not code pages.

Unicode Windows

The level of internationalization support that you can expect from the operating system depends upon the version of the operating system running on your client machines. Windows NT 3.51, NT 4.0, 2000, XP, 2003, and Vista (formerly code-named "Longhorn") are all 32-bit Unicode platforms and support Unicode natively. ANSI functionality (which, in the Windows world, equates to Windows code page functionality) is also supported, but in most cases, ANSI functions "transcode" (translate from one character set to another) inputs to Unicode, call the Unicode API, and then convert the return value to ANSI before returning it to the caller.

Code Page Windows

Windows 95, 98, and Me are 16-bit versions of Windows that are based on code pages instead of Unicode. After the invention of Unicode, these versions of Windows became known as "non-Unicode" Windows. In practical terms, these operating systems have very low support for Unicode (see http://msdn.microsoft.com/archive/ default.asp?url=/archive/en-us/win9x/ chilimit_5alv.asp for a complete list of supported Unicode Win32 APIs). The .NET Framework adds a level of Unicode support to these operating systems. It is important to note that the limitations of the operating system still exist. For example, Unicode-only scripts (such as Armenian, Devanagari, Georgian, and Tamil) are not available on 16-bit Windows. Some controls (`Date-TimePicker`, `ImageList`, `ListView`, `ProgressBar`, `StatusBar`, `TabControl`, `ToolBar`, `TrackBar`, `TreeView`) inherit their support from the common control library and do not support Unicode on 16-bit Windows. The consequence is that these controls process data as ANSI, so Unicode characters (such as Japanese characters) won't display (unless the application is running on a language version of Windows specifically designed to support those characters, e.g., Japanese Windows 98). If it is within your control, you are well advised to avoid using these operating systems for international applications. If you cannot avoid them, proceed with caution.

Virtual Machines

At some point during your application's testing phase, you will need to run your application on the target environment. This might be a different version of Windows to the development platform, and/or it might be a different language of Windows than the developer's language. It is not sufficient to test an application by simply switching the application's culture to the target culture. Throughout this book, you will find numerous differences that are a consequence of the version of Windows or the language of Windows; consequently, you must test the application using the target environment. The traditional approach to this problem is to install the target environment on a new machine. This is as close to an absolute solution as you can get, but it is costly in terms of hardware if you are testing multiple versions of Windows, each with its own language. A simpler solution is to use virtual machine software, such as Microsoft's Virtual Server, Microsoft's Virtual PC, or VMWare's VMWare Server and WorkStation. These software packages create "virtual machines" that run as guests within a host operating system. The guest operating systems can be any operating system, including Windows, Linux (for testing Mono .NET applications), and DOS. Figure 2.1 shows Virtual PC hosting the Japanese version of Windows XP Professional Service Pack 2, testing a translated .NET Windows Forms application.

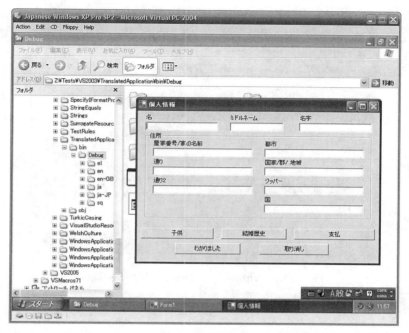

Figure 2.1   Virtual PC Hosting Japanese Version of Windows XP Professional

Virtual PC Tip

If you are using Virtual PC, you can easily share a path on the host machine as a new drive on the guest machine. You might use this to share your development output folder with the guest operating system so that each time you do a build, you can test the application immediately without any copying of files. To do this, start the virtual machine, click the Virtual PC Console Settings button, and select the Shared Folders icon on the left side of the dialog box (see Figure 2.2). Click the "Share Folder…" button to share a folder with the guest operating system. The shared folder becomes a new drive in the guest operating system.

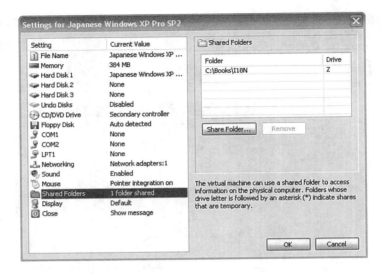

Figure 2.2   Virtual PC Virtual Machine Settings

Windows Multilingual User Interface Pack

Windows Multilingual User Interface (MUI) Pack is a collection of resource files that can be added to the English version of Windows 2000, XP, and 2003. Windows MUI is installed after the installation of a regular English-language version of Windows. You can choose as many languages as you want from any of the localized languages (33 languages in Windows XP MUI). Once the languages are installed, you can switch between the languages using Regional and Language Options in the Control Panel. An additional "Language used in menus and dialogs" combo box on the Languages page is present only after Windows MUI has been installed (see Figure 2.3).

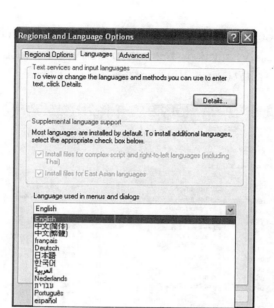

Figure 2.3   Enhanced Regional and Language Options in Windows MUI

Click OK, and then log off and log back in again to see the user interface in the new language. In Figure 2.4, you can see `WordPad.exe` running in Windows MUI using the Japanese language.

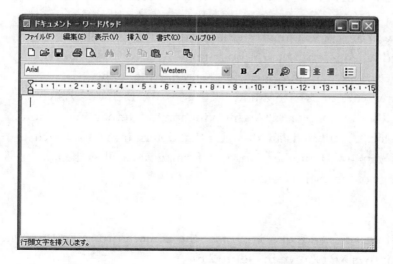

Figure 2.4   `WordPad.exe` in Windows MUI Using Japanese

The Japanese resources are loaded from a resource file with the same name as the executable, with a ".mui" suffix, in the %WINDOWS%\mui\FALLBACK\ <LCID> folder (see Figure 2.5). The LCID (locale ID) for "Japanese (Japan)" is 1041 (x0411).

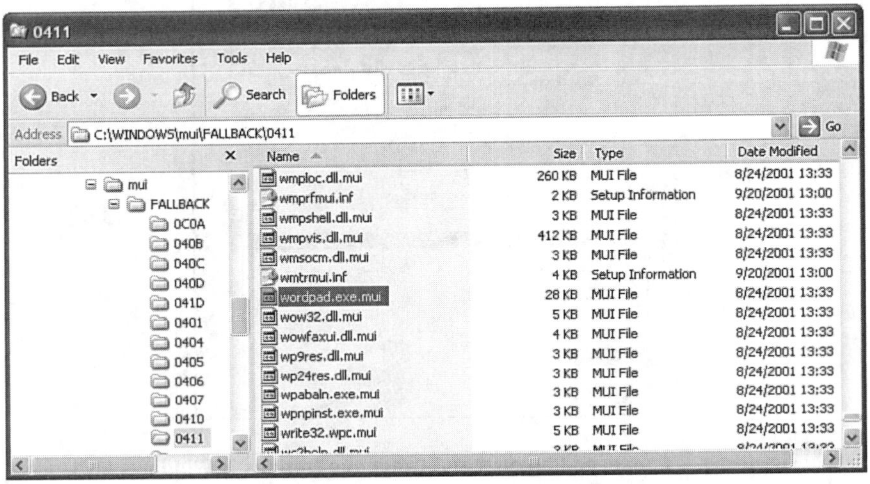

Figure 2.5   Windows MUI User Interface Resource Files

A "locale" and a "culture" are the same. Both refer to a combination of a language in a specific country or region and, optionally, a script—for example, "French (Canada)." The difference is only in the context in which the words are used. A "locale" is used when referring to the operating system or to Win32 API functions. A "culture" is used when referring to the .NET Framework or .NET Framework classes and methods. As you shall see in Chapter 3, "An Introduction to Internationalization," the locale/culture is an identifier that determines issues such as date/time and number/currency formats, as well as the language of the user interface.

The resulting WordPad.exe is almost the same as running WordPad.exe in Japanese Windows XP (shown in Figure 2.6).

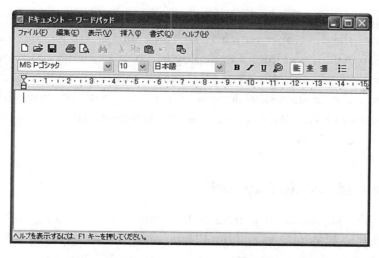

Figure 2.6 `Wordpad.exe` in Japanese Windows

However, some important differences exist. These are either advantageous or disadvantageous, depending on what you want to use Windows MUI for. First, the default fonts shown are the defaults for English Windows XP, not Japanese Windows XP. Second, the Input Method Editor (IME, software that allows the user to type ideographic or phonetic characters on a keyboard that does not have such characters) is not enabled by default. Although you can easily add IME support (see Chapter 7, "Middle East and East Asian Cultures"), this isn't something that a developer who is unfamiliar with Japanese would think to do.

Windows MUI has pros and cons for international development. In terms of deployment and support, it can be a valuable asset. The infrastructure team can deploy an English version of Windows, install Windows MUI, and let users choose their language. The support team knows that, regardless of the interface, the underlying operating system is English; at the very least, the user interface can be switched back to English, changes can be made, and the user interface can be switched back to the user's language. In development terms, less effort is required to globalize the application because the underlying operating system is English. So not all locale-specific assumptions (such as the program files folder always being called "Program Files") get revealed as bugs. However, the converse can also be true; some globalization issues are more likely to occur on Windows MUI than on localized versions of Windows.

You might also argue that it is useful for testing purposes. Windows MUI certainly provides the developer with an easy route into viewing behavior in a target language. However, if you intend to deploy to a non-English version of Windows, globalization testing using Windows MUI can provide a false sense of security. The only legitimate test in such situations is to test using both Windows MUI and the localized version of Windows. Of course, limited resources might force you into choosing between the two.

Language and Locale Support

Microsoft invests significant resources in developing and localizing the 33 languages for client versions of Windows and the 19 languages for server versions of Windows. In addition, the number of locales supported increases with each new version (see Table 2.2).

Table 2.2 Number of Locales Supported for Each Windows Version

Windows Version	Locales Supported
Windows Vista	200+
Windows XP Service Pack 2	160
Windows Server 2003	135
Windows XP	135
Windows 2000	125
Windows NT 4.0	105
Windows NT 3.51	45
Windows Millennium Edition	114
Windows 98	114
Windows 95	105

Supporting and maintaining these languages involves a significant effort, so it is not surprising that there are still many languages for which no version of Windows is available. Sometimes this is a reflection of the business case for the given language (demand vs. significant development effort), but sometimes it is a consequence of Microsoft being bound by U.S. export law and being unable to support certain languages in certain locales. In response to the former, Microsoft created Windows Language Interface Packs (LIPs). A LIP is a partial localization of a language or a language in a specific region. It is a localization of the 20% of the features that are used 80% of the time (the "20/80" rule). Typically, this includes the desktop, Control Panel applications, Windows Explorer, Internet Explorer, Outlook Express, and other commonly used user interfaces. The result is that Microsoft is capable of providing partial support for many more languages and locales. The release of new LIPs is not limited to the release of platforms and service packs. At the time of writing, the number of LIPs stands at 27 (including Bulgarian, Catalan, Latvian, and Thai); for an up-to-date list, see http://www.microsoft.com/globaldev/DrIntl/faqs/lipfaq.mspx#EWB.

Despite the success of this approach, LIPs cannot provide support for all languages and locales by themselves. LIPs are limited to the functionality included in the operating system's National Language Support (NLS). If the NLS functionality to support a language is missing, the language cannot be supported. In response to this, Microsoft created Enabling Language Kits (ELKs). ELKs add NLS support to allow LIPs to be created for a language. An ELK can add new fonts, shaping engines (which shape characters according to their context), keyboards, sorts, and locale information, to allow a LIP to be created for a given language/region. ELKs in Windows XP SP2 include Bengali, Bosnian, Maori, Maltese, Quechua, Sami, and Welsh.

.NET Framework Languages and .NET Framework Language Packs

The .NET Framework 2.0 is available in 24 languages. The .NET Framework 1.1 supports the same list of languages, with the exception of Arabic and Hebrew. You can download the .NET Framework from http://www.microsoft.com/downloads (search on ".NET Framework Redistributable Package").

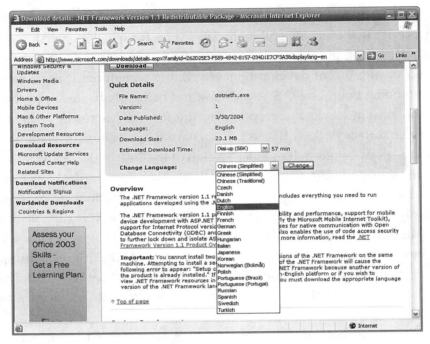

Figure 2.7   .NET Framework 1.1 Download Page

The .NET Framework redistributable is packaged differently for the .NET Framework 1.1 and the .NET Framework 2.0. We start by looking at the .NET Framework 2.0. The .NET Framework 2.0 redistributable package, `dotnetfx.exe`, is a single package that supports all languages. The `dotnetfx.exe` that you download from the English page is 100% identical to the `dotnetfx.exe` that you download from the French page. The difference lies only in the fact that the English page has instructions in English and the French page has instructions in French. The package itself, however, contains the complete user interface resources for all supported languages. The setup user interface adapts to the language version of Windows on which it is being run, so if you run `dotnetfx.exe` on French Windows, the installation dialogs are in French. The important point to grasp here is that the .NET Framework that is installed is always *the English version of the .NET Framework.*

The .NET Framework 1.1 redistributable package (see Figure 2.7) has some similarities and some differences to the .NET Framework 2.0 redistributable package. The package itself, `dotnetfx.exe`, is different for different languages. The "Change

Language" combo box of the download page determines not only the language in which instructions are displayed on the download page, but also the language of setup dialogs used during installation. So the `dotnetfx.exe` that you download from the English page is not the same as the `dotnetfx.exe` that you download from the French page. If you run the `dotnetfx.exe` that you download from the French page, the language of the setup dialogs will be French (regardless of the language version of Windows that it is being run on). Despite this, the result of the installation is the same as for the .NET Framework 2.0. The .NET Framework that is installed is always *the English version of the .NET Framework.* Consequently, if your deployment team performs the setup process itself, there is no value in deploying a different language version of `dotnetfx.exe`.

You might wonder how you can get localized versions of all the text in the .NET Framework. Enter .NET Framework Language Packs. .NET Framework Language Packs include text and other resources for languages other than English. You can download Language Packs from http://www.microsoft.com/downloads (search on ".NET Framework Language Packs") as shown in Figure 2.8.

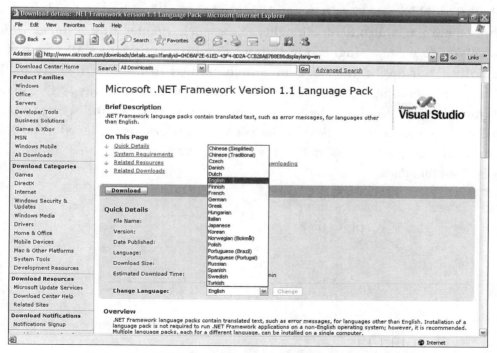

Figure 2.8   .NET Framework 1.1 Language Packs Download Page

Select a language other than English (there is no language pack for English because the .NET Framework includes the original English) and click Go. As with the ".NET Framework" download, a similar page is displayed in the chosen language with an obvious "Download" button. The language pack files have the same name for each language, so you must create separate directories or rename them. You can install as many language packs on the same machine as you need. Your .NET application will use the resources from the language pack according to the current setting of the `System.Threading.Thread.CurrentThread.CurrentUICulture` property. We cover this essential property in the next chapter.

Where Are We?

In this chapter, we laid down the foundation for all .NET applications. .NET applications are based on the .NET Framework, which is based on Unicode. Unicode enables us to support most of the languages in the world and many character sets for other purposes using a single unconfused system. The .NET Framework runs on both 32-bit Unicode Windows and 16-bit code page Windows, and adds back an approximation of Unicode functionality to these legacy operating systems, which allows you to write a single-source application that runs across all versions of Windows. Your applications are, of course, limited to the functionality of the underlying operating system and for this reason, you should always strive to use not only Unicode Windows, but also the most recent releases and service packs. Finally, language resources used by the .NET Framework are retrieved from .NET Framework Language Packs, not by the language version of the .NET Framework Redistributable Pack.

■3■
An Introduction to Internationalization

I N THIS CHAPTER, YOU WILL LEARN THE fundamental implementation of inter-
nationalization. The examples are based on a Windows Forms application using
Visual Studio 2005 and the .NET Framework 2.0, but very little in this chapter is spe-
cific to Windows Forms or to the version of Visual Studio or the .NET Framework.
The information in this chapter is equally relevant to ASP.NET applications and to
Visual Studio 2003 and the .NET Framework 1.1. For information on Windows
Forms, see Chapter 4, "Windows Forms Specifics;" for information on ASP.NET, see
Chapter 5, "ASP.NET Specifics."

Internationalization Terminology

Throughout this book, I use various internationalization terms to describe different
parts of the internationalization process. In this section, I identify these terms and
describe their meaning. Figure 3.1 shows the hierarchy of internationalization terminology as adopted by Microsoft. It shows the term *internationalization* as an
umbrella for the various stages in the process: world-readiness, localization, and customization. Let's take a look at each term in turn.

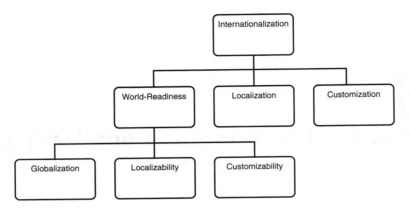

Figure 3.1   Microsoft's Internationalization Terminology

The terms *internationalization, globalization,* and *localization* are often abbreviated to *"I18N," "G11N,"* and *"L10N,"* respectively. The abbreviations take the first and last letters and the number of letters between them, so *internationalization* starts with an "I," has 18 more letters, and then ends in an "N." The naming convention originates from DEC, when they used to abbreviate long e-mail names using this convention. The naming convention spread beyond e-mail names and on to internationalization. Although you could apply the same convention to *customization* to get *C11N*, no one would recognize the abbreviation because it is not in common use.

World-Readiness

World-readiness is an umbrella term for all the functionality that developers must provide to complete their part of the internationalization process. This includes globalization, localizability, and customizability.

Globalization

Globalization is the process of engineering an application so that it does not have cultural preconceptions. For example, an application that converts a `DateTime` to a string using this code has a cultural preconception that the date format should be MM/dd/yyyy:

```
DateTime dateTime = new DateTime(2002, 2, 13);
string dateTimeString = dateTime.ToString("MM/dd/yyyy");
```

These preconceptions must be eliminated from the code. Many of these preconceptions are obvious, such as the date/time format, but many are not so obvious. Globalization issues include date/time formats, number formats, currency formats, string comparisons, string sort orders, calendars, and even environmental conditions. Do you assume, for example, that the Program Files folder is always "\Program Files"? (It isn't.) Or that the first day of the week is Sunday, or that everyone uses a 12-hour clock? The subject of globalization is fully covered in Chapter 6, "Globalization," but the bottom line is that if you always use the .NET framework globalization classes and you always use them properly, you will greatly diminish the number of globalization problems in your applications.

Localizability

Localizability is the process of adapting an application so that its resources can be replaced at runtime. *Resources*, in this context, are primarily the strings used in your application, but also include the bitmaps, icons, text files, audio files, video files, and any other content that your users will encounter. In this code, there is a hard-coded, literal use of a text string:

```
MessageBox.Show("Insufficient funds for the transfer");
```

To make the application "localizable," we must rewrite this code to make this resource load at runtime. You will see how to achieve this later in this chapter.

Customizability

Customizability is the process of adapting an application so that its functionality can be replaced at runtime. For example, taxation laws vary considerably from location to location; California sales tax, for example, is not the same rate and does not follow the same rules as, say, Value Added Tax in the U.K. (or in the Netherlands, for that matter). A "customizable" application is one that is capable of having critical parts of its functionality replaced. Often this means using a plug-in architecture, but it might be sufficient to store a set of parameters in a data store. You will encounter customizability less than localizability—or, indeed, never. Customizability is also referred to as *marketization*, especially on Microsoft Web sites.

All these steps (globalization, localizability, customizability) together make up the work that developers must complete as they refer to adapting the application's source code to make it ready for localization and customization.

Localization

Localization is the process of creating resources for a specific culture. Primarily, this involves translating the text of an application from its original language into another language, such as French. Often the translation process is performed by a translator, but it might also be performed by a machine (known as machine translation, or "MT") or by a bilingual member of staff. In addition, the localization process might or might not include the redesign of forms and pages so that translated text doesn't get clipped or truncated and so that the form or page still looks correct in the target culture. It also involves translating other resources into culturally correct resources for the specific culture. A classic example of a culturally unaware resource is the first Windows version of CompuServe's e-mail program. The Inbox was represented by an icon for a U.S. metal mailbox with a flag indicating that mail had arrived. This icon is specific to the U.S. and had little or no meaning outside the U.S. In this case, the entire icon needed to be changed, but in other cases, localization might simply require changing a color. For example, a red "Stop" sign doesn't convey a warning in China or Japan, where red can indicate prosperity and happiness.

Customization

Customization is the process of creating a specific implementation of functionality. Whereas customizability gives an application the potential to be customized, customization is the implementation of a specific case. If your application supports customization through a plug-in architecture, this step will likely be performed by developers. The developers might be your own developers, but in highly customizable applications that offer an open plug-in architecture, these developers could be anyone.

Internationalization Terminology Confusion

The terminology described so far and the terminology used throughout this book use the interpretations used by Microsoft. This makes sense because this book focuses on a Microsoft technology as implemented by Microsoft. You should be aware, however, that the rest of the industry does not adhere to these definitions. Primarily, the meanings of *"internationalization"* and *"globalization"* are transposed. Figure 3.2 shows the broad hierarchy of internationalization terminology according to the rest of the industry.

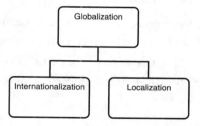

Figure 3.2   Internationalization Terminology as Used by the Rest of the Industry

The term *"globalization"* is used to describe the entire process. whereas the term *"internationalization"* is used to describe sometimes world-readiness and sometimes globalization. Unfortunately for us, the rest of the industry has the upper hand in this issue. In the mid-1990s, Microsoft transposed the meanings of *internationalization* and *globalization,* and it stuck. All Microsoft documentation (including namespaces in the .NET Framework) uses the Microsoft interpretations of these terms. So if you read documentation from non-Microsoft sources, be aware that it might use the same words but have different meanings.

Cultures

Cultures are the fundamental building block of internationalization in the .NET Framework. Every issue that you will encounter in this subject has a culture at its heart. As such, this is clearly where we must begin. A culture is a language and, optionally, a region. In the .NET Framework, it is represented by the `System.Globalization.CultureInfo` class. Typically, a culture is created from a culture string, although we look at other possibilities in Chapter 6. The culture string is specified in the RFC 1766 format:

```
languagecode2[-country/regioncode2[-script]]
```

`languagecode2` is an ISO 639-1 or 639-2 code, `country/regioncode2` is an ISO 3166 code, and `script` is the writing system used to represent text in the country/region (e.g., Latin, Cyrillic). For example, the following code creates a `CultureInfo` object for the English language:

```
CultureInfo cultureInfo = new CultureInfo("en");
```

(`CultureInfo` is in the `System.Globalization` namespace, so you must add a "`using System.Globalization;`" directive to the source.) This object simply represents neutral English, not English in the U.S. or English in the U.K., so it does not represent a specific region. To identify a specific country or region, you extend the string:

```
CultureInfo cultureInfo = new CultureInfo("en-GB");
```

This object represents English in the U.K. (written as "`English (United Kingdom)`" so that the region is in brackets after the language) and all that this includes. For example, the object includes information about the date patterns used in the U.K.:

```
string shortDatePattern =
    cultureInfo.DateTimeFormat.ShortDatePattern;
```

The value assigned to `shortDatePattern` is "dd/MM/yyyy". Similarly, this next assignment assigns the U.K. pound sign (£) to `currencySymbol`:

```
string currencySymbol = cultureInfo.NumberFormat.CurrencySymbol;
```

Here are a few more examples of culture strings:

"`en-US`" (English in the U.S.)

"`en-AU`" (English in Australia)

"`fr`" (French, no specific country)

"`fr-FR`" (French in France)

"`fr-CA`" (French in Canada)

"`es`" (Spanish, no specific country)

"es-ES" (Spanish in Spain)

"es-MX" (Spanish in Mexico)

"sr-SP-Latn" (Serbian in Serbia and Montenegro using the Latin script)

"sr-SP-Cyrl" (Serbian in Serbia and Montenegro using the Cyrillic script)

Typically, the language code is 2 characters (but not always) and the country/region code is 2 characters.

CultureInfo objects are classified as either invariant, neutral, or specific, and operate in the simple hierarchy shown in Figure 3.3.

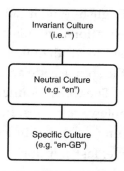

Figure 3.3 CultureInfo Hierarchy

The *invariant culture*, represented by an empty string, is intended to represent the absence of any given culture (in reality, the invariant culture has much in common with the English culture, but this is not the same as it being the English culture, and you should not write code that depends upon this). This quality of not being a particular culture makes the invariant culture ideal for streaming data in a culturally-agnostic format. A *neutral culture* is a representation of a language but is not specific to a particular region—for example, the "en" culture represents English in general, not English in a specific region. In particular, neutral cultures do not include region-specific globalization information because they are not specific to a region. A *specific culture* represents a language in a specific region—for example, the "en-US" culture represents English in the United States and includes region-specific information such as date/time and number formats.

`CultureInfo` objects have a `Parent` property so that the "en-US" specific culture knows that its parent is the "en" neutral culture—which, in turn, knows that its `Parent` is the invariant culture. This hierarchy is essential for the fallback process described later in this chapter.

Localizable Strings

To illustrate how the essential internationalization process works, here we localize a single string. Let's return to the hard-coded string you saw earlier:

```
MessageBox.Show("Insufficient funds for the transfer");
```

Clearly, this line of code is in English—and it can only ever be in English. We need to go through two phases to internationalize this code: First, we need to make this code localizable. Second, we need to localize it. To make the code localizable, we need to remove the string from the source code and place it in some other container that can be changed at runtime. The .NET Framework and Visual Studio have a ready-made solution to this problem: resx files. In Chapter 12, "Custom Resource Managers," we look at maintaining resources in locations other than resx files; for now, however, we use this simple, fast solution that Visual Studio naturally lends itself to. resx files are XML files that contain resources such as strings and bitmaps. To create a resx file in Visual Studio 2005, right-click the project in Solution Explorer; select Add, New Item…; and select Resource File (see Figure 3.4).

The name of the resx file is important because it is used in the code to identify the resources. It can be any name that does not conflict with a name that Visual Studio has or will automatically create. For example, `Form1.resx` is not acceptable in a Windows Forms application that has a form called `Form1`. It is always wise to adopt a file-naming convention. I follow this convention:

The resx file always has the same name as the source file to which it relates, and is suffixed with "`Resources`." For example, `TaxCalc.cs` has an associated resx file called `TaxCalcResources.resx`. The suffix is important for two reasons. First, Visual Studio 2003 and 2005 automatically add resx files for Windows Forms (e.g., `Form1.cs` already has a `Form1.resx`), and this resx is considered to be under the control of Visual Studio. Second, Visual Studio 2005 can automatically create a strongly-typed class corresponding to a resx file, and this class is given a name that corresponds to the resx file. For example, if the `TaxCalc.cs` resources were placed in `TaxCalc.resx`, Visual Studio 2005 would create a corresponding strongly-typed resources class called `TaxCalc`, which would conflict with the existing `TaxCalc` class.

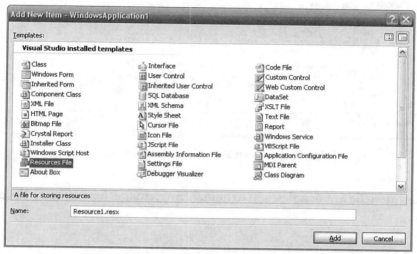

Figure 3.4   Adding a Resource File to a Project

Visual Studio 2005 Windows Forms applications have a default resource file called `Resources.resx`. This resource file is for your own use; Visual Studio 2005 will not add or remove resources from it. The resource file itself is no different than a resource file that you create yourself, but it is present in every Visual Studio 2005 Windows Forms application. To maintain resources in it, either expand the Properties entry in the project in Solution Explorer and double-click Resources.resx, or double-click Properties and select the Resources tab. It is possible to delete or rename this file, but if you do so, the Resources property page will assume that the project no longer has a default resource file and will provide a warning to this effect.

After the resource file has been created, Visual Studio presents the Resource Editor (see Figure 3.5).

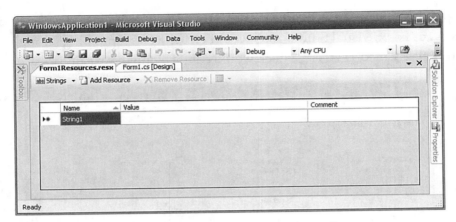

Figure 3.5   Visual Studio 2005 Resource Editor

The Resource Editor enables you to enter string, image, icon, audio, file, and other resources.

The Visual Studio 2003 Resource Editor enables you to enter string resources and, with a little effort, can be used to enter images. See the section entitled "Adding Images and Files in Visual Studio 2003" for details.

For Name enter a name by which this string resource will be identified (e.g., "InsufficientFunds"). You can find resource key name guidelines in the .NET Framework 2.0 help by looking for "Resource Names" in the index, but essentially, names should use Pascal case and should be descriptive but not verbose. For Value, enter the string itself (i.e, "Insufficient funds for the transfer"). Comment is used to hold additional information that the translator or other developers can use. Be aware, however, that the comment is maintained solely within the resx file. For reasons that will become clear shortly, the comment is not included in your compiled assemblies and is not shipped with your application. Enter a comment. The content of the comment depends upon who the comment is intended for. Mostly likely, it is a message to the translator/localizer and would contain instructions about the string's use, such as "InsufficientFunds is used in a MessageBox".

Visual Studio requires that resources must be saved for their changes to be included in the generated assembly.

How It Works

Let's stop for a moment to consider what will happen to this resource. Select the `Form1Resources.resx` file in Solution Explorer and take a look at it in the Properties Window. The `Build Action` property says that it is an Embedded Resource. This means that Visual Studio will identify the correct compiler for this resource type, compile it, and embed the result in the generated assembly. The correct compiler for resx files is a built-in version of `resgen.exe`. This compiler has many purposes, but one of them is to compile XML resx files into "resources" files. A "resources" file is a binary version of an XML resx file. You can perform this step manually if you want to see the command-line tool in action. Enter "`resgen Form1Resources.resx`" at the command prompt in the application's folder (make sure that you have saved the resx file in Visual Studio first):

```
Read in 1 resources from "Form1Resources.resx"
Writing resource file...  Done.
```

The result is a file called "`Form1Resources.resources`" that contains the compiled resources. You can open this file in Visual Studio (select File, Open, File... and enter the filename). Visual Studio uses its Binary Editor to show the file; you can see that the comment is nowhere in the file.

Visual Studio embeds the compiled output in the generated assembly using a build task that is a wrapper for the Assembly Linker (`al.exe`; see Chapter 14, "The Translator," for more details). You can see this using IL DASM (.NET's IL Disassembler). Open the generated assembly (i.e., `WindowsApplication1.exe`) and double-click the `MANIFEST` entry. Scroll down until you come to the following line:

```
.mresource public WindowsApplication1.Form1Resources.resources
```

"`.mresource`" identifies that it is an embedded resource. As mentioned before, the name is important. Notice that it is prefixed with the application's namespace, "`WindowsApplication1`," and it is suffixed with ".`resources`" (because that was the resulting name after the resx file was compiled). Although there is little value in doing so, you could perform the same steps as Visual Studio manually by maintaining the resx files outside Visual Studio, compiling them into binary resources manually using `resgen.exe`, and embedding the resources in the generated assembly using the Assembly Linker (`al.exe`) tool.

At this stage, we have a `WindowsApplication1.exe` assembly that has an embedded resource called "`WindowsApplication1.Form1Resources.resources`," which contains a single string called "`InsufficientFunds`," which has a value of "`Insufficient funds for the transfer`." We need a way to retrieve this string from the embedded resource. For this, we need a Resource Manager.

Resource File Formats

Before we look into resource managers, let's take a brief look at the possibilities for resource file formats. Four resource file formats are used for resources. The `.resx` file format that you have already encountered is an XML format. The `.resources` format that you have also already encountered is a binary format representing a compiled `.resx` file. The `.txt` file format is simply a text file with key/value pairs. So `Form1Resources.txt` would simply be:

```
InsufficientFunds=Insufficient funds for the transfer
```

The `.restext` file format (introduced in the .NET Framework 2.0) is the same as the `.txt` file format; the only difference is the extension. The new extension enables developers to make a clearer distinction between a text file that might contain any freeform text and a text file that is used explicitly for resources. Table 3.1 compares the file formats.

When choosing a file format, weigh the relative benefits of each. `.resx` files are recognized by Visual Studio and are human readable. They also have explicit classes for their manipulation (`ResourceManager`, `ResXResourceReader`, `ResXResourceWriter`). `.resources` files are not human readable and must originate from a `.resx`, `.txt`, or `.restext` file. `.txt` files are human readable but are not recognized as resource files by Visual Studio, and are not so easily manipulated programmatically as resources.

Table 3.1 Resource File Formats

File Extension	Supports String Resources	Supports Other Resources	Supports Comments	Supports File References	Has Direct Support in the .NET Framework	Extension Recognized by ResGen
.resx	Yes	Yes	Yes	Yes	Yes	Yes
.resources	Yes	Yes	No	No	Yes	Yes
.txt	Yes	No	No	No	No	Yes
.restext	Yes	No	No	No	No	In 2.0 only

Resource Managers

Resource managers retrieve resources. The .NET Framework versions 1.1 and 2.0 include two resource-manager classes, `System.Resources.ResourceManager` and its descendant, `System.ComponentModel.ComponentResourceManager`. The former is used in all .NET applications, whereas the latter is typically used only in Visual Studio 2005 Windows Forms applications. We return to the latter in Chapter 4. We create new and exciting resource managers in Chapter 12.

We start by taking a high-level view of how `System.Resources.ResourceManager` retrieves resources. When an attempt to load a resource entry is made (using `ResourceManager.GetString` or `ResourceManager.GetObject`), the `Resource Manager` looks through its internal cache of resources to see if the request can be supplied from the cache. If not, a `ResourceSet` is loaded from a resource embedded in an assembly. A `ResourceSet` is a collection of resource entries and is equivalent to an in-memory copy of a single resx file (you can think of a `ResourceSet` as a `DataTable` for resource entries). The `ResourceSet` is added to the `ResourceManager`'s internal cache. Finally, the `ResourceSet` is searched for the resource entry that matches the requested key. The `ResourceManager` class is covered in depth in Chapter 12.

The `System.Resources.ResourceManager` class retrieves resources either from a resource embedded in an assembly or from stand-alone binary resource files. To retrieve resources from a resource embedded in an assembly, we create a `Resource-Manager` using the class constructor. To retrieve resources from stand-alone binary resource files, we use the static `CreateFileBasedResourceManager` method. For the purposes of this example, we focus on the former. To retrieve the string, we need to create a `ResourceManager` object and call its `GetString` method. Add a couple of `using` directives to `Form1.cs`:

```
using System.Resources;
using System.Reflection;
```

Add a `private` field to the `Form1` class to hold the `ResourceManager`:

```
private ResourceManager resourceManager;
```

Instantiate the `ResourceManager` at the beginning of the `Form1` constructor:

```
public Form1()
{
    resourceManager = new ResourceManager(
      "WindowsApplication1.Form1Resources",
      Assembly.GetExecutingAssembly());

    InitializeComponent();
}
```

The first parameter to the `ResourceManager` constructor is the fully qualified name of the resource that we want to retrieve. Recall from the assembly's manifest that the resource was called "`WindowsApplication1.Form1Resources.resources`." The `ResourceManager` class adds the "`.resources`" suffix so that it should not be included in the name passed to the constructor. The second parameter to the `ResourceManager` constructor is the assembly in which this resource can be found. In this example and most others like it, we are saying that the resource can be found in the assembly that is currently executing: i.e., `WindowsApplication1.exe`. The `ResourceManager` class supports three public constructor overloads:

```
public ResourceManager(string, Assembly);
public ResourceManager(string, Assembly, Type);
public ResourceManager(Type);
```

We have just covered the first. The second is a variation on the first and specifies the type to be used to create new `ResourceSet` objects. The third specifies the Type for which resources should be retrieved. This is also a variation on the first constructor because it uses the Type's Name for the resource name and the type's assembly as the assembly where the resource can be found.

All that remains is for us to retrieve the string using the `ResourceManager`. Change the original hard-coded line from this:

```
MessageBox.Show("Insufficient funds for the transfer");
```

to this:

```
MessageBox.Show(resourceManager.GetString("InsufficientFunds"));
```

The `ResourceManager.GetString` method gets a string from the resource: `"InsufficientFunds"` is the key of the resource, and `GetString` returns the value that corresponds to this key.

At this point, we have a localizable application; it is capable of being localized, but it has not yet been localized. There is just the original English text. From the user's point of view, our application is no different from when the text was hard coded.

Localized Strings

To reap the rewards of our work, we need to offer a second or third language. In this example, we add French to the list of supported languages. This is where the culture strings that we discussed earlier come in. The culture string for neutral French is "fr." Create a new Resource File using the same name as before, but use a suffix of ".fr.resx" instead of just ".resx" so that the complete filename is `Form1Resources.fr.resx`. Into this resource file, add a new string, using the same name as before, "`InsufficientFunds`"; into the Value field this time, though, type the French equivalent of "`Insufficient funds for the transfer`" (i.e., "`Fonds insuffisants pour le transfert`").

Compile the application and inspect the output folder. You will find a new folder called "`fr`" beneath the output folder. If the output folder is `\WindowsApplication1\bin\Debug`, you will find `WindowsApplication1\bin\Debug\fr`. In this folder you will find a new assembly with the same name as the application, but with the extension "`.resources.dll`" (i.e., `WindowsApplication1.resources.dll`).

The `Form1Resources.fr.resx` file has been compiled and embedded in this new assembly. This new assembly is a resources assembly, and it contains resources only. This assembly is referred to as a satellite assembly. If you inspect the manifest of this satellite assembly using IL DASM (`<FrameworkSDK>\bin\ildasm.exe`), you will find the following line:

```
.mresource public WindowsApplication1.Form1Resources.fr.resources
```

In this way, you can support any number of languages simply by having sub-folders with the same name as the culture. When you deploy your application, you can include as many or as few of the subfolders as you want. For example, if your application gets downloaded from a Web site or server, you can supply a French version that includes only the French subfolder. Similarly, you can offer an Asian version that includes Chinese, Japanese, and Korean subfolders. In addition, if you update one or more resources, you need to deploy only the updated resource assemblies, not the whole application.

CurrentCulture and CurrentUICulture

Of course, our work is not quite done yet. The problem with the solution so far is that the French resources exist but are not being used. For reasons that will become clear in a moment, the only time the French version of the application will be seen is when it is run on a French version of Windows. Apart from usability considerations, this makes testing your application unnecessarily difficult.

Two properties determine the default internationalization behavior of an application are: `CurrentCulture` and `CurrentUICulture`. Both properties can be accessed either from the current thread or from the `CultureInfo` class, but they can be assigned only from the current thread. Assuming that the following directives have been added to `Form1.cs`:

```
using System.Globalization;
using System.Threading;
```

The first two lines provide the same output as the second two lines:

```
MessageBox.Show(Thread.CurrentThread.CurrentCulture.DisplayName);
MessageBox.Show(Thread.CurrentThread.CurrentUICulture.DisplayName);
MessageBox.Show(CultureInfo.CurrentCulture.DisplayName);
MessageBox.Show(CultureInfo.CurrentUICulture.DisplayName);
```

CurrentCulture represents the default culture for all classes in System.Globalization and thus affects issues such as culture-specific formatting (such as date/time and number/currency formats), parsing, and sorting. CurrentUICulture represents the default culture used by ResourceManager methods and thus affects the retrieval of user interface resources such as strings and bitmaps. CurrentCulture defaults to the Win32 function GetUserDefaultLCID. This value is set in the Regional and Language Options Control Panel applet, shown in Figure 3.6. Consequently, in a Windows Forms application, the user has direct control over this setting. In an ASP.NET application, the value is set in the same way, but because it is set on the server, its setting applies to all users and a more flexible solution is required (see Chapter 5).

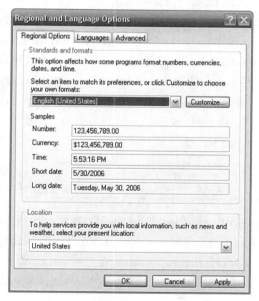

Figure 3.6   Regional and Language Options

Bear in mind that the CurrentCulture is culture-specific, not culture-neutral. That is, the value includes a region as well as a language. If you consider that this value determines issues such as date/time formats and the number and currency formats, you can understand that it is meaningless to assign a "French" culture to `CurrentCulture` because French in Canada has completely different globalization values to French in France. In general, your application should strive to acquire a specific culture for the `CurrentCulture`, but there is an option to manufacture a specific culture, which can be considered a last resort. The `CultureInfo.CreateSpecificCulture` method accepts a culture and returns a specific culture from it. So if you pass it "`fr`" for French, you get a culture for French in France. Similarly, for Spanish you get Spanish (Spain), and for German you get German (Germany). You can forgive the people of England for being a little surprised that the specific culture for English is not England; it is the United States.

The `CurrentUICulture`, however, defaults to the Win32 function `GetUserDefaultUILanguage`. This value is usually determined by the user interface language version of the operating system and cannot be changed. So if you install the French version of Windows, `GetUserDefaultUILanguage` returns French; therefore, `CurrentUICulture` defaults to French. However, if you install Windows Multiple User Interface Pack (Windows MUI; see Chapter 2, "Unicode, Windows, and the .NET Framework"), the user can change the language version of the user interface through a new option that appears in the Regional and Language Options. The `CurrentUICulture` can be culture-neutral, culture-specific, or the invariant culture.

Armed with this knowledge, you can see why on a typical machine running in the U.K., the following code results in "`English (United States)`," followed by "`English (United Kingdom)`":

```
MessageBox.Show(Thread.CurrentThread.CurrentCulture.DisplayName);
MessageBox.Show(Thread.CurrentThread.CurrentUICulture.DisplayName);
```

To see the French resources in our example application, we need to provide a means by which the user can select a language. This facility is simplistic in the extreme; see Chapters 4 and 5 for more advanced solutions. Add a `RadioButton` to the form, set its `Text` to "French," and add a `CheckChanged` event with this code:

```
Thread.CurrentThread.CurrentUICulture = new CultureInfo("fr");
```

This line creates a new `CultureInfo` object for neutral French and assigns it to the `CurrentUICulture` of the current thread. This affects all `ResourceManager` methods on this thread, which default to the `CurrentUICulture` from here on. You can also set the `CurrentCulture` in a similar fashion:

```
Thread.CurrentThread.CurrentCulture = new CultureInfo("fr-FR");
```

Notice that, in this example, the culture is a specific culture ("`fr-FR`"), not a neutral culture ("`fr`"). Add another `RadioButton`, set its `Text` to `English`, and add a `CheckChanged` event with this code:

```
Thread.CurrentThread.CurrentUICulture = CultureInfo.InvariantCulture;
```

This line doesn't actually use the English resources as the `RadioButton`'s `Text` implies it does. Instead, it sets the `CurrentUICulture` to the invariant culture. Although the effect will be the same and the user will see English resources, the setting simply causes the `ResourceManager` to use the resources that are embedded in the main assembly instead of a satellite assembly. Now you can run the application, select one of the `RadioButtons`, and see the `MessageBox` use the correct resource string according to your selection.

We have made our application localizable, and we have localized it. To add new languages, we need only add new versions of `Form1Resources.resx` (e.g., `Form1Resources.es.resx` for Spanish), add a `RadioButton` to set the `CurrentUICulture` to the new language, and compile our application to create the new satellite assembly (e.g., `es\WindowsApplication1.resources.dll`).

CurrentCulture, CurrentUICulture, and Threads

I mentioned in the previous section that the `CurrentCulture` and `CurrentUICulture` properties are set on a thread. The full implication of this might not be immediately apparent. This means each thread must have its `CurrentCulture` and `CurrentUICulture` properties explicitly and manually set. If you create your own threads, you must set these properties in code. The important point to grasp here is that new threads do not automatically "inherit" these values from the thread from which they were created; a new thread is completely new and needs to be reminded of these values. To create a new thread, you could write this:

```
Thread thread = new Thread(new ThreadStart(Work));
thread.CurrentCulture   = Thread.CurrentThread.CurrentCulture;
thread.CurrentUICulture = Thread.CurrentThread.CurrentUICulture;
thread.Start();
```

This solves the problem, but it is cumbersome and relies on every developer remembering to set these properties (developers will eventually forget). A better solution is to create a thread factory:

```
public class ThreadFactory
{
  public static Thread CreateThread(ThreadStart start)
  {
    Thread thread = new Thread(start);
    thread.CurrentCulture   = Thread.CurrentThread.CurrentCulture;
    thread.CurrentUICulture = Thread.CurrentThread.CurrentUICulture;
    return thread;
  }
}
```

Of course, now you are relying on your developers to remember to use the `ThreadFactory` instead of creating threads manually. See Chapter 13, "Testing Internationalization Using FxCop," for the "Thread not provided by `ThreadFactory`" rule, which ensures that new threads are not created using the `System.Threading.Thread` constructor.

The Resource Fallback Process

The `ResourceManager` class has built-in support for resource fallback. This means that when you attempt to access a resource that doesn't exist for the given culture, the `ResourceManager` attempts to "fall back" to a less specific culture. The less specific culture is the `Parent` of the culture, so recall from Figure 3.3 that a specific culture falls back to a neutral culture, which falls back to the invariant culture. You can think of this as inheritance for resources. This behavior ensures that you do not duplicate resources and that as your application's resources get more specific, you need to detail only the differences from the "parent," just as you would with class inheritance.

Consider how this works with string resources. Let's add another string resource to `Form1Resources.resx` in our main assembly (also called the fallback assembly). The Name is "`ColorQuestion`" and the Value is "`What is your favorite color?`". Add a similar string resource to `Form1Resources.fr.resx` with the Value "`Quelle est votre couleur préférée?`". Now consider that not all versions of English are the same. The spelling of English in the United States often differs from the spelling of the same words in the United Kingdom, Canada, and Australia: *Color* is the one that everyone seems to remember. So "What is your favorite color?" will not go down well in the United Kingdom because two of the words are spelled "incorrectly." Add a similar string resource to `Form1Resources.en-GB.resx` (where "en-GB" is "`English (United Kingdom)`") with the Value "`What is your favourite colour?`". Figure 3.7 shows the relationship between the resources.

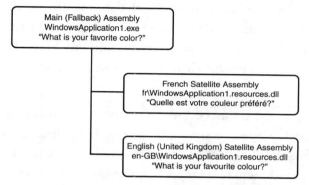

Figure 3.7   String Resources in Fallback and Satellite Assemblies

So let's consider what will happen when the `CurrentUICulture` is set to various cultures and `ResourceManager.GetString` is called to get the "`ColorQuestion`" string. If `CurrentUICulture` is French, `ResourceManager.GetString` looks for the string in the `fr\WindowsApplication.resources.dll` satellite assembly. It finds the string immediately and returns it, and that is the end of the process. If `CurrentUICulture` is French in France ("`fr-FR`"), `ResourceManager.GetString` looks for `fr-FR\WindowsApplication1.resources.dll` and fails to find it. It then falls back to the `Parent` of `fr-FR` culture, which is neutral French, and finds the string there. The benefit of this approach is that if the `CurrentUICulture` is French in Canada ("`fr-CA`"), the same steps would happen, with the same result. In this way, we can deploy the neutral French satellite assembly and have the French language covered, regardless of where it is used.

Now consider what happens to English. If the `CurrentUICulture` is English in the United Kingdom ("`en-GB`"), `ResourceManager.GetString` looks for the string in `en-GB\WindowsApplication1.resources.dll`. It finds it, and the people in the United Kingdom get a string that gives them a warm and loved feeling. If the

CurrentUICulture is English in the United States ("en-US"), ResourceManager.
GetString looks for enUS\WindowsApplication1.resources.dll and doesn't
find it. It falls back to neutral English ("en") and looks for en\WindowsApplica-
tion1.resources.dll—but it doesn't find that, either. It falls back to the parent of
"English", which is the invariant culture. It looks for the resource in the main assembly and finds it there. Similarly, if the CurrentUICulture is German, for example,
ResourceManager.GetString falls back all the way to the main assembly and
returns the original English (United States) string. Only if the string is not present in the main fallback assembly is an exception thrown; this makes sense because to
ask for a string that doesn't exist is clearly a programmer error.

> It should be noted that because of the way in which the .NET
> Framework probes for assemblies, if you have installed your
> satellite assemblies in the Global Assembly Cache (GAC), they
> will be found there first before the application's folders are
> probed.

The fallback process enables you to create only those resources that are different
from their parent. In the case of strings, it is highly likely that almost every string in
every language will be different from the original English, but that regional variations are much fewer and farther between. After all, the majority of U.S. English is
the same as U.K. English. The fallback process behaves the same way for other
resources such as bitmaps, but the number of differences is likely to be fewer. A wise
approach to using bitmaps in your application is to strive to create bitmaps that are
as culturally neutral as possible. If you can create a bitmap that does not include
words, does not use colors to convey meaning, and does not rely upon culturally-
specific references (such as the U.S. mailbox), the bitmap will have a broader appeal.
If you follow this approach, the main assembly will naturally have every bitmap
required by the application. However, unlike string resources that almost always
need to be translated to other languages, it is unlikely that the satellite assemblies
will contain many differences.

NeutralResourcesLanguageAttribute and UltimateResourceFallbackLocation

As wonderful and helpful as the fallback process might sound, the previous expla-nation might provoke the question, "If the `CurrentUICulture` is `en-US`, won't every call to `ResourceManager.GetString` take longer than necessary because it is looking first for the `en-US` resource (and failing to find it) and second for the `en` resource (and failing to find it) before finally trying the main assembly?" The answer is, yes, it will take longer. For this reason, we have `System.Resources.Neutral-ResourcesLanguageAttribute`. The `NeutralResourcesLanguage` attribute enables you to declare the culture of the main assembly. The purpose of this is to save unnecessary searching for resource assemblies. You use it like this:

```
[assembly: NeutralResourcesLanguageAttribute("en-US")]
```

This line can go anywhere (for example, at the top of `Form1.cs`), but it is best placed with other similar assembly attributes in `AssemblyInfo.cs`. With this attrib-ute in place when `CurrentUICulture` is `en-US`, `ResourceManager.GetString` looks in the main assembly immediately without performing unnecessary lookups in the `en-US` or `en` folders. In Visual Studio 2005, you can set this same attribute in the Assembly Information dialog (click the Assembly Information... button in the Application tab of the project's properties).

The .NET Framework 2.0 introduces an overloaded `NeutralResources LanguageAttribute` constructor that accepts an additional parameter, which is an `UltimateResourceFallbackLocation`. This enumeration has two members, shown in Table 3.2.

Table 3.2 `UltimateResourceFallbackLocation` **Enumeration**

Member	Description
MainAssembly (default)	Resources are located in the main assembly
Satellite	Resources are located in a satellite assembly

You can use this enumeration to specify that the fallback resources are not in the main assembly but are instead in a satellite assembly:

```
[assembly: NeutralResourcesLanguageAttribute("en-US",
  UltimateResourceFallbackLocation.Satellite)]
```

In this scenario, your main assembly contains no resources, and all resources are placed in satellite assemblies. In our example, there would be no `Form1Resources.resx` file; instead, there would be a `Form1Resources.en-US.resx` file from which the `en-US\WindowsApplication1.resources.dll` assembly gets generated. Before adopting this approach, you might consider that Visual Studio does not have any facility for not generating a default resource. For example, Visual Studio always generates `Form1.resx` for `Form1`, and this resource is placed in the main assembly. You would then have to create a second similar resource for `en-US`, making the resource in the main assembly redundant. (Unfortunately, Visual Studio 2005's Assembly Information dialog does not allow you to set the `UltimateResource-FallbackLocation`, so you must set this value manually in `AssemblyInfo.cs`). Of course, the command-line tools don't have this preconception, so you can create your own build script to build the main assembly without the redundant resources. In this scenario, you would let Visual Studio 2005 create redundant resources, and the final build process would simply ignore them. The only minor downside is that you should keep the redundant resources in synch with the fallback resources so that there is no difference between the Visual Studio–developed application and the final build application.

Image and File Resources

The Visual Studio 2005 Resource Editor maintains string, bitmap, icon, audio, file, and other resources in a resx file. You've seen how to add a string to a resource file. To add an image, select "Images" from the Categories combo box (entries in the combo box are bold when there are one or more entries of that type). The main part of the Resource Editor showing the strings is replaced with an area that shows all the image resources. It is blank at this stage. To add an image from an existing file, drop down the Add Resource button and select Add Existing File…; use the "Add existing file to resources" file open dialog to locate the image you want to add. Let's say that you want to show the national flag of the selected culture as the form's background so that the user has very clear feedback of the currently selected culture. Add the U.S. national flag to `Form1Resources.resx` and ensure that the image is called "NationalFlag" (see Figure 3.8).

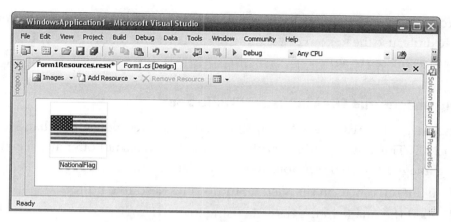

Figure 3.8   Adding an Image Using the Visual Studio 2005 Resource Editor

Repeat the process and add the French national flag to `Form1Resources.fr.resx`; ensure that it is called "`NationalFlag`". Thus, all resources have an image entry with the same name. If you give the images country-specific names, such as `USNationalFlag` and `FrenchNationalFlag`, the resource names will not be polymorphic. To use the bitmap as the form's background, set `Form1.BackgroundImageLayout` to `Stretch` and add the following line to the end of the `Form1` constructor:

```
BackgroundImage = (Bitmap) resourceManager.GetObject("NationalFlag");
```

`ResourceManager.GetObject` retrieves an object resource in the same way that `ResourceManager.GetString` retrieves a string resource. We know that the resource is a bitmap, so we cast it to a `Bitmap` and assign it directly to the form's `BackgroundImage`. Of course, when the current thread's `CurrentUICulture` changes, there is no `CurrentUICultureChanged` event that we can hook into to get notification that it has changed, so we need to add this same line immediately after any line that changes the `CurrentUICulture`—that is, we have to add it to the end of both radio buttons' `CheckChanged` events. Now the form will always show the national flag of the selected `CurrentUICulture`.

To add a text file as opposed to an image, you follow a similar process. If the file already exists, click the Add Resource button in the Resource Editor, select Add Existing File…, and enter the text file to add. If the file does not already exist, click the Add Resource button, select Add New Text File, and enter a name for the resource. To edit the text file, double-click its resource icon. To retrieve the contents of the text file, use the `ResourceManager.GetString` method, just as you would for getting a resource string.

Adding Images and Files in Visual Studio 2003

Adding images to a resx file in Visual Studio 2003 requires more effort than for Visual Studio 2005. The Visual Studio 2003 Resource Editor does not offer any facilities for reading image files. Two solutions to this problem exist:

1. Use file references in the Visual Studio 2003 Resource Editor
2. Embed the image in the resx file using `ResEditor.exe`

The first solution lies in manually mimicking the functionality of the Visual Studio 2005 Resource Editor. The Visual Studio 2005 Resource Editor creates "file references" to the image files that it adds to resx files. That is, the image file is referenced by the resx file (instead of the image being embedded in the resx file). The reference is achieved using the `ResXFileRef` class, which is present in both the .NET Framework 1.1 and 2.0. To add the `NationalFlag` image to a resx file using the Visual Studio 2003 Resource Editor, add a new resource entry called "`NationalFlag`" and set its type to "`System.Resources.ResXFileRef, System.Windows.Forms, Version= 1.0.5000.0, Culture=neutral, PublicKeyToken=b77a5c561934e089`". This indicates that the value of the resource entry is a file reference, not the actual value. Now set the value to "`C:\Books\I18N\Tests\VS2003\Windows Application1\NationalFlag.bmp;System.Drawing.Bitmap, System.Drawing, Version=1.0.5000.0, Culture=neutral, PublicKeyToken=b03f5f7f11d50a3a`". The value includes the filename and the type of the resource (i.e., `System.Drawing. Bitmap`). The entry in the resx file looks like this:

```
<data name="NationalFlag" type="System.Resources.ResXFileRef,
System.Windows.Forms, Version=1.0.5000.0, Culture=neutral,
PublicKeyToken=b77a5c561934e089">
    <value>
    C:\Books\I18N\Tests\VS2003\WindowsApplication1\NationalFlag.bmp;
    System.Drawing.Bitmap, System.Drawing, Version=1.0.5000.0,
    Culture=neutral, PublicKeyToken=b03f5f7f11d50a3a
    </value>
</data>
```

In this example, the file includes an absolute path. This isn't strictly necessary, but you might find it helpful. Without an absolute path, both Visual Studio 2003 and `Res-Gen` assume the current folder. For Visual Studio 2003, this is the `devenv.exe` folder, which is typically `\Program Files\Microsoft Visual Studio .NET 2003\Common7\IDE`. Consequently, without an absolute path, you must place the referenced files in this folder, which is a poor choice for files that are specific to a single application.

The second solution is to embed the image in the resx file using one of the examples in the .NET Framework SDK, `ResEditor.exe`, which allows all objects in resx and resources files to be maintained. The source for `ResEditor` is in `<SDK>\v1.1\Samples\Tutorials\resourcesandlocalization\reseditor` (where `<SDK>` is the location of the SDK, probably `\Program Files\Microsoft Visual Studio .NET 2003\SDK`). Build `ResEditor` using the `build.bat` file found there. Run `ResEditor.exe`; select File, Open; and open `Form1Resources.resx`. In the TextBox to the left of the Add button, enter "`NationalFlag`" and click Add. Now click the ellipses in the `PropertyGrid` and enter the name of the file. The bitmap is added to the resx file (see Figure 3.9).

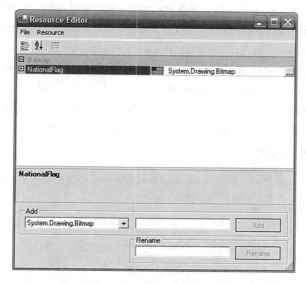

Figure 3.9 **Adding an Image Using the .NET Framework 1.1 SDK** ResEditor.exe

Strongly-Typed Resources in the .NET Framework 2.0

Recall the code that retrieves the resource string:

```
MessageBox.Show(resourceManager.GetString("InsufficientFunds"));
```

This line is fragile. It relies upon a string, `"InsufficientFunds"`, to identify the resource string. If this string includes a typo, the code will still compile successfully, but it will throw an exception at runtime. The problem is that this string cannot be verified at compile time, so it is a fragile solution. A better solution is one that the compiler can verify. To solve this problem Visual Studio 2005 introduces Strongly-Typed Resources. A strongly-typed resource is to resources what a strongly-typed dataset is to `DataSets`; it is a generated class that includes the resource key names as properties. The line of code can be rewritten to use a strongly-typed resource:

```
MessageBox.Show(Form1Resources.InsufficientFunds);
```

`Form1Resources` is a strongly-typed resource class in which each resource entry is represented by a property (i.e., `"InsufficientFunds"`, in this example). The `Form1.resourceManager` field is no longer needed and can be removed completely. When a resource file is created in Visual Studio 2005, a corresponding file with the extension ".`Designer.cs`" is also created, so `Form1Resources.resx` has a corresponding file called `Form1Resources.Designer.cs`. You can see this in Solution Explorer by expanding the resx node. As you add, edit, or delete entries in the resx file, the designer file is updated. If you double-click the file, you will see the generated class. Here is the `Form1Resources` class with the comments stripped out (and formatted to fit this page):

```
[global::System.Diagnostics.DebuggerNonUserCodeAttribute()]
[global::System.Runtime.CompilerServices.
CompilerGeneratedAttribute()]
internal class Form1Resources {

    private static global::System.Resources.ResourceManager
        resourceMan;

    private static global::System.Globalization.CultureInfo
        resourceCulture;

    [global::System.Diagnostics.CodeAnalysis.
        SuppressMessageAttribute("Microsoft.Performance",
        "CA1811:AvoidUncalledPrivateCode")]
```

```
    internal Form1Resources() {
    }

    [global::System.ComponentModel.EditorBrowsableAttribute(
        global::System.ComponentModel.EditorBrowsableState.Advanced)]
    internal static global::System.Resources.ResourceManager
        ResourceManager {
        get {
            if (object.ReferenceEquals(resourceMan, null)) {
                global::System.Resources.ResourceManager temp =
                    new global::System.Resources.ResourceManager(
                    "WindowsApplication1.Form1Resources",
                    typeof(Form1Resources).Assembly);
                resourceMan = temp;
            }
            return resourceMan;
        }
    }

    [global::System.ComponentModel.EditorBrowsableAttribute(
        global::System.ComponentModel.EditorBrowsableState.Advanced)]
    internal static global::System.Globalization.CultureInfo
        Culture {
        get {
            return resourceCulture;
        }
        set {
            resourceCulture = value;
        }
    }

    internal static string InsufficientFunds {
        get {
            System.Resources.ResourceManager rm = ResourceManager;
            return rm.GetString(
                "InsufficientFunds", resourceCulture);
        }
    }

    internal static System.Drawing.Bitmap NationalFlag {
        get {
            System.Resources.ResourceManager rm = ResourceManager;
            return ((System.Drawing.Bitmap)
                (rm.GetObject("NationalFlag", resourceCulture)));
        }
    }
}
```

The class encapsulates its own `ResourceManager` object in a private static field called `resourceMan`. `resourceMan` is wrapped in a static `ResourceManager` property, which initializes `resourceMan` to this:

```
new System.Resources.ResourceManager(
  "WindowsApplication1.Form1Resources",
  typeof(Form1Resources).Assembly);
```

Not surprisingly, this is very similar to the line that we wrote earlier to initialize our `resourceManager` private field. For each entry in the resx file, a static property is created to return the resource's value. You can see in the `InsufficientFunds` property that it calls `ResourceManager.GetString` and passes the `"Insufficient`cientFunds"` key. The `resourceCulture` private static field is initially null (therefore, `ResourceManager` uses `Thread.CurrentThread.CurrentUICulture`). You can set its equivalent static property, `Culture`, to specify that it should retrieve resources for a different culture. Although this is rare, you might, for example, want to display more than one culture at the same time.

In the "Localizable Strings" section of this chapter, I mentioned that the .NET Framework 2.0 help includes a set of resource key naming guidelines. If you follow these guidelines, you will encounter an apparent mismatch between this advice and the designer's warnings. One of the guidelines recommends that resource keys with a recognizable hierarchy should use names that represent that hierarchy in which the different elements of the hierarchy are separated by periods. For example, menu item resource keys might be named `Menu.File.New` and `Menu.File.Open`. This is good advice, but Visual Studio 2005 reports the warning "The resource name `'Menu.File.New'` is not a valid identifier". This is a consequence of the strongly-typed resource class that is generated from the resource. It is not possible to have a property called "`Menu.File.New`" because the period is an invalid character for an identifier. Instead, the periods are replaced with underscores, and the property is called "`Menu_File_New`". Despite this, I recommend that you continue to follow the resource key naming guidelines and ignore the warnings that result from the use of the period in resource key names.

If you prefer not to use strongly-typed resources but are concerned that the strings passed to `ResourceManager.GetString` might or might not be valid, look at the "Resource string missing from fallback assembly" rule in Chapter 13.

ResGen

Visual Studio 2005's solution of automatically maintaining strongly-typed resources is very convenient and will be sufficient for many developers. However, if it does-n't meet your requirements because, say, you generate or maintain your own resources using a utility outside Visual Studio 2005, you need the `resgen.exe` com-mand-line utility. You've seen that `resgen.exe` can generate binary resource files from resx XML resource files. It can also generate strongly-typed resources using the `/str` switch. The following command line uses the `/str:C#` switch to indicate that the generated file should be written in C#:

```
resgen Form1Resources.resx /str:C#
```

The output is:

```
Read in 2 resources from "Form1Resources.resx"
Writing resource file...  Done.
Creating strongly typed resource class "Form1Resources"...  Done.
```

This example creates `Form1Resources.cs`, which isn't the same as the Visual Studio–generated file. The syntax of the `str` switch is:

```
/str:<language>[,<namespace>[,<class name>[,<file name>]]]]
```

To get the same output with the same filename as Visual Studio, use the follow-ing command line:

```
resgen Form1Resources.resx /str:C#,
WindowsApplication1,Form1Resources,Form1Resources.Designer.cs
```

You can ignore the "RG0000" warning that resgen emits; the resgen-generated code is identical to the code generated by Visual Studio 2005. Another resgen command-line parameter of interest is `publicClass`. This parameter causes the generated class to be public instead of internal so that it can be accessed by a different assembly.

StronglyTypedResourceBuilder

Both Visual Studio 2005 and `resgen.exe` use the `System.Resources.Tools.StronglyTypedResourceBuilder` class to generate strongly-typed resources. This documented .NET Framework 2.0 class is at your disposal in case you need to generate strongly-typed resources when the two existing utilities don't meet your requirements. Two such possibilities are encountered in Chapter 12 and are solved using `StronglyTypedResourceBuilder`:

- Visual Studio accepts only resx files as input, and resgen accepts only resx, resources, restext, and txt files as input. If you maintain resources in another format, such as a database, you cannot generate strongly-typed resources.
- The generated code uses the `System.Resources.ResourceManager` class to get resources. If you maintain resources in another format, such as a database, the generated class will be using the wrong resource manager class to load the resources.

The `StronglyTypedResourceBuilder.Create` method has four overloads, two of which accept a resx filename and two of which accept an `IDictionary` of resources to generate code for. The strategy for using a `StronglyTypedResourceBuilder` directly is to load your resources into an object that supports the `IDictionary` interface and pass this to the `StronglyTypedResourceBuilder.Create` method. The `Create` method returns a `CodeDomCompileUnit` object, which is the complete `CodeDom` graph for the generated code. You would pass this to the `CodeDomProvider.GenerateCodeFromCompileUnit` method to generate the equivalent code and write it to a `StreamWriter`. Chapter 12 has a complete example.

> In the .NET Framework 1.1, the `GenerateCodeFromCompileUnit` method is not available directly from the `CodeDomProvider`. Instead, create an `ICodeProvider` using `CodeDomProvider.CreateGenerator` and call the same method with the same parameters from the resulting `ICodeProvider`.

Strongly-Typed Resources in the .NET Framework 1.1

Strongly-typed resources are a new feature in the .NET Framework 2.0 and Visual Studio 2005. As such, the .NET Framework 1.1 and Visual Studio 2003 do not support this feature. However, as you can see, this is a worthwhile feature and there is no technical reason why you shouldn't benefit from strongly-typed resources in Visual Studio 2003. To that end, I have written an equivalent to the `StronglyTyped ResourceBuilder` class for the .NET Framework 1.1, an equivalent utility to `resgen.exe` called `ResClassGen.exe`, and a custom tool that integrates this functionality into the Visual Studio 2003 IDE. These are available in the source code for this book. The generated code is almost the same as the generated code in the .NET Framework 2.0, so you can port the code to Visual Studio 2005 when necessary.

Where Are We?

In this chapter, we laid down the foundation of the internationalization process in .NET. We discussed the terminology used in this process; introduced the `Culture-Info` class upon which the whole internationalization process rests; presented the hierarchy of invariant, neutral, and specific cultures; used resx files to hold string resources; used the `ResourceManager` class to retrieve resources; localized resources; identified the purposes of the `CurrentCulture` and `CurrentUICulture` properties; and illustrated how to use strongly-typed resources to improve the reliability of applications. These issues represent the cornerstone of .NET internationalization. You can now move on to Chapters 4 and 5, on Windows Forms and ASP.NET specifics.

4

Windows Forms Specifics

I N THIS CHAPTER, WE COVER SUBJECTS that are relevant only to Windows Forms applications.

Localizing Forms

In the previous chapter, you saw how strings and bitmaps can be localized using `ResourceManager` and satellite assemblies. The same process could be used to localize forms, but it would be extremely tedious. Every string and bitmap would need to be manually loaded, but the job wouldn't stop there. Numerous other properties, such as `Size`, `Location`, `RightToLeft`, and `ImeMode`, might also need to be localized. This would amount to a significant amount of additional, repetitive code. Fortunately, Visual Studio has functionality for localizing forms in a neat and simple manner. Here we will follow an example of localizing a form. This example is deliberately simplistic, to focus on the details of localizing a form instead of providing a real-world example.

Create a new Windows Forms application, add a button in the bottom-right corner, and set its `Text` to "`Close`" (see Figure 4.1).

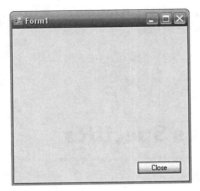

Figure 4.1   Simple Form Localization Example

Here's the first part of the InitializeComponent code generated by Visual Studio 2005 in the Form1.Designer.cs file:

```
private void InitializeComponent()
{
    this.button1 = new System.Windows.Forms.Button();
    this.SuspendLayout();
    //
    // button1
    //
    this.button1.Location = new System.Drawing.Point(205, 231);
    this.button1.Name = "button1";
    this.button1.Size = new System.Drawing.Size(75, 23);
    this.button1.TabIndex = 0;
    this.button1.Text = "Close";
    this.button1.UseVisualStyleBackColor = true;
    // etc.
    // etc.
```

Visual Studio 2003's generated code (in Form1.cs) differs by the inclusion or exclusion of properties that are specific to a version of the .NET Framework. Notice the assignment to the button's Text property; clearly, the "Close" text is hard-coded and cannot be localized in its current form.

Property Assignment Model

Now set Form1.Localizable to True (in the Properties Window) and look at the code again. What you see depends on whether you are using Visual Studio 2003 or

Visual Studio 2005. Regardless of the version of Visual Studio, I recommend that you follow the explanation for both versions—Visual Studio 2005 developers will learn why Visual Studio 2005 works the way it does, and Visual Studio 2003 developers will learn what they can look forward to. In Visual Studio 2003, you will see this in the Form1.cs file:

```
private void InitializeComponent()
{
    System.Resources.ResourceManager resources =
        new System.Resources.ResourceManager(typeof(Form1));
    this.button1 = new System.Windows.Forms.Button();
    this.SuspendLayout();
    //
    // button1
    //
    this.button1.AccessibleDescription =
        resources.GetString("button1.AccessibleDescription");
    this.button1.AccessibleName =
        resources.GetString("button1.AccessibleName");
    this.button1.Anchor = ((System.Windows.Forms.AnchorStyles)
        (resources.GetObject("button1.Anchor")));
    this.button1.BackgroundImage = ((System.Drawing.Image)
        (resources.GetObject("button1.BackgroundImage")));
    this.button1.Dock = ((System.Windows.Forms.DockStyle)
        (resources.GetObject("button1.Dock")));
    this.button1.Enabled =
        ((bool)(resources.GetObject("button1.Enabled")));
    this.button1.FlatStyle = ((System.Windows.Forms.FlatStyle)
        (resources.GetObject("button1.FlatStyle")));
    this.button1.Font = ((System.Drawing.Font)
        (resources.GetObject("button1.Font")));
    this.button1.Image = ((System.Drawing.Image)
        (resources.GetObject("button1.Image")));
    this.button1.ImageAlign = ((System.Drawing.ContentAlignment)
        (resources.GetObject("button1.ImageAlign")));
    this.button1.ImageIndex = ((int)
        (resources.GetObject("button1.ImageIndex")));
    this.button1.ImeMode = ((System.Windows.Forms.ImeMode)
        (resources.GetObject("button1.ImeMode")));
    this.button1.Location = ((System.Drawing.Point)
        (resources.GetObject("button1.Location")));
    this.button1.Name = "button1";
    this.button1.RightToLeft = ((System.Windows.Forms.RightToLeft)
        (resources.GetObject("button1.RightToLeft")));
    this.button1.Size = ((System.Drawing.Size)
        (resources.GetObject("button1.Size")));
```

```
this.button1.TabIndex = ((int)
    (resources.GetObject("button1.TabIndex")));
this.button1.Text = resources.GetString("button1.Text");
this.button1.TextAlign = ((System.Drawing.ContentAlignment)
    (resources.GetObject("button1.TextAlign")));
this.button1.Visible = ((bool)
    (resources.GetObject("button1.Visible")));
// etc.
// etc.
```

This code is significantly longer than the original, unlocalizable code. Let's look at the important differences. First, and most important, the first line creates a new `ResourceManager` object, passing in the type of `Form1`, and assigns the new object to a local variable called `resources`:

```
System.Resources.ResourceManager resources =
    new System.Resources.ResourceManager(typeof(Form1));
```

The subsequent code uses this resource manager to retrieve all the string, bitmap, and other resources that are necessary to localize this form. Take a look at the assignment to the button's `Text` property. It has changed from this:

```
this.button1.Text = "Close";
```

to this:

```
this.button1.Text = resources.GetString("button1.Text");
```

In the localizable form, a `"button1.Text"` string resource is being loaded from the resource manager. In Solution Explorer, click the Show All Files button, expand the `Form1.cs` node, and double-click `Form1.resx` (see Figure 4.2).

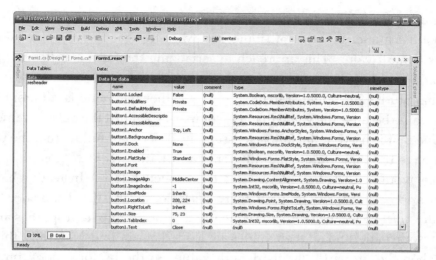

Figure 4.2   Form1.resx in Visual Studio 2003 after Localizable Is Set to True

You can see that the "button1.Text" entry has a value of "Close". So the approach used to associate each property with its localized value is to load a resource whose name is made from the name of the object plus a period, plus the name of the property. Simple and effective. Now take a look at the button's Location property. It has changed from this:

```
this.button1.Location = new System.Drawing.Point(205, 231);
```

to this:

```
this.button1.Location = ((System.Drawing.Point)
    (resources.GetObject("button1.Location")));
```

The Location property is of type System.Drawing.Point, so the code uses ResourceManager.GetObject to retrieve the value and then casts the resulting object to a System.Drawing.Point.

The next difference between the unlocalized and localized code is that, whereas the button on the unlocalized form includes 6 properties (4 properties in Visual Studio 2003) to assign values to, this localized version includes 20. In the unlocalized form, Visual Studio 2003 has simply listed every property that has a different value than its default value. In the localized form, Visual Studio 2003 has listed every property that has a `Localizable` attribute, regardless of whether its value is different than its default value. This approach to serializing the form is called the *property assignment model*.

Visual Studio 2003 deliberately ignores whether the value is different than its default value because the value that it is comparing against the default value is only the value that is used in the fallback assembly. It does not follow that the property would have the same value in a different culture (the `RightToLeft` property, for example, would clearly be different in a right-to-left culture). Instead, it has had to take the approach that any property that *could* be localizable (i.e., has a `Localizable` attribute) *must* be localizable. Consequently, all `Localizable` properties are saved to the resource file, and all their values are loaded at runtime. Naturally, this occurs even when the property has its default value. So the buttons' `Dock` property is assigned its default value from the `button1.Dock` resource.

In this example, this redundancy occurs for 16 properties for Visual Studio 2003. It is possible to argue that this is an unnecessary performance hit. Visual Studio 2005 addresses this issue, but if you are using Visual Studio 2003 and do not intend to upgrade in the near future, you should consider two points. The first is that, accepting that all performance judgments are relative, this problem possibly sounds worse than it actually is. The fear for a developer is that a lot of unnecessary resource accesses and property assignments are going on that will affect performance. Clearly, these *will* affect performance, but, to borrow a tenet from Extreme Programming, don't engineer solutions to problems that you don't know you have. Start by proving that you actually *do* have a problem. In the tests that I have performed, in which I continually have opened and closed an unlocalized form and then continually opened and closed the same localized form, I cannot see a difference. Clearly, there *is* a difference, but remember that we are looking at this problem from the user's perspective, and users can't measure in clock cycles. Of course, this is a scaling issue; if you see the issue at all, you are likely to see it only on forms with a very large number of components.

The second point is that if this issue still bothers you and you can't upgrade to Visual Studio 2005, you should take a look at the Localization Filter (http://windowsforms.net/articles/localizationfilter.aspx), from Brian Pepin, who works in Microsoft's development tools group. The Localization Filter is a design-time component that enables developers to specify which properties should be localized (and which should not). As a consequence, it reduces the number of properties on a localized form and improves the performance of localized forms. This is also an interesting example of how to interfere with the form's serialization process.

Property Reflection Model

Visual Studio 2005 is used in the same way (i.e., you set `Form1.Localizable` to true), but the way in which properties are loaded differs. Take a look at the `InitializeComponent` method:

```
private void InitializeComponent()
{
    System.ComponentModel.ComponentResourceManager resources = new
      System.ComponentModel.ComponentResourceManager(typeof(Form1));
    this.button1 = new System.Windows.Forms.Button();
    this.SuspendLayout();
    //
    // button1
    //
    resources.ApplyResources(this.button1, "button1");
    this.button1.Name = "button1";
    this.button1.UseVisualStyleBackColor = true;
    //
    // Form1
    //
    resources.ApplyResources(this, "$this");
    this.AutoScaleMode = System.Windows.Forms.AutoScaleMode.Font;
    this.Controls.Add(this.button1);
    this.Name = "Form1";
    this.ResumeLayout(false);

}
```

The first line creates a `System.ComponentModel.ComponentResourceManager` instead of a `System.Resources.ResourceManager`. `ComponentResourceManager` inherits from `ResourceManager`, so it has all the same properties and methods. `ComponentResourceManager`, which is part of both the .NET Framework 1.1 and 2.0, adds a single method, `ApplyResources`, and does not override any methods. You can see the `ApplyResources` method being used in `InitializeComponents`:

```
resources.ApplyResources(this.button1, "button1");
this.button1.Name = "button1";
this.button1.UseVisualStyleBackColor = true;
```

The 20 assignments used in Visual Studio 2003 have been reduced to just these 3 assignments in Visual Studio 2005. The `ApplyResources` method looks through every entry in the resource for a key that meets the following criteria:

- The key has the same name as the object (i.e., "`button1`").
- The key has a property that matches the property name in the key (e.g., "`Text`" in "`button1.Text`").
- The property type is the same as the resource value's type.

For each such entry, it assigns the value in the resource to the object's property. This model is called the *property reflection model* because it uses reflection to probe the object for corresponding properties. If you take a look at `Form1.resx` in Visual Studio 2005, you will see that only those `Localizable` properties that do not have the same value as their default are included in the resource file. When the form is localized for a different culture and more or fewer properties are localized, the properties will still be assigned their values, and the resources need to be only as large as is necessary for that culture. The intention is that the performance savings of assigning only those properties that need to be localized is greater than the performance loss of having to use reflection to probe the object and assign its value. With a smaller number of properties, such as we have with the button in the example, the gain outweighs the loss. You should be aware, however, that in the unlikely event that the number of localized properties approaches the number of localizable properties, the loss will outweigh the gain. However, this scenario is rather unlikely.

The .NET Framework 2.0 supports both the property assignment model used by Visual Studio 2003 and the property reflection model used by Visual Studio 2005. If you write your own form designer or need to generate form-serialization code yourself, you can specify which model you want to use with the `CodeDomLocalizationModel` enumeration, shown in Table 4.1.

Table 4.1 `CodeDomLocalizationModel` **Enumeration**

Member Name	Description
`None`	`Localizable` **properties are not written.**
`PropertyAssignment`	**All** `Localizable` **properties are written.**
`PropertyReflection`	**Only** `Localizable` **properties that are not the default are written.**

You pass the desired `CodeDomLocalizationModel` enumeration to the `Code-DomLocalizationProvider` constructor to tell it how to serialize forms. However, Visual Studio 2005 does not have any facility for setting this value; although the framework supports the capability to change the model, the IDE does not surface this capability, so you cannot choose the property assignment model.

Localizing a Form

Now that our form is localizable, we can localize it. Select the form and, in the Properties Window, drop down the Languages combo box. The list is populated using `CultureInfo.GetCultures`. This method accepts a parameter specifying what kind of cultures to get. The parameter value that is passed is `CultureTypes.All-Cultures`. In Visual Studio 2003, this returns a list that is hard-coded in the .NET Framework 1.1. In Visual Studio 2005, this returns the list of cultures available to the .NET Framework, the operating system, and the user-defined cultures. Note that the combo box does not support an incremental search, so if you type "`Fr`", you will get "Romanian" instead of "French" (because the "`F`" goes first to "French" and the "`r`" then goes to "Romanian").

Select French from the list. In Visual Studio 2005, the Form Designer caption changes to show that you are designing the French version of this form (see Figure 4.3). In Visual Studio 2003, there is no visual indication of which form you are localizing, except for the `Languages` property in the Properties Window.

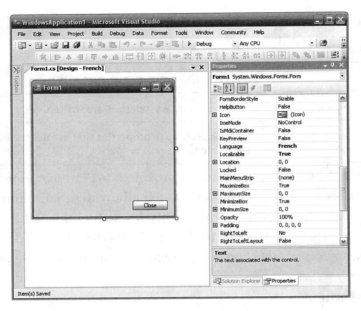

Figure 4.3　Visual Studio 2005 Localizing a Form

Change `Button1.Text` to "`Fermer`" (the French for "Close"). In the Solution Explorer, expand the `Form1.cs` node; you will see a new file, `Form1.fr.resx`, which holds the French resources for this form. Currently, this resx file has an entry for `Button1.Text` but no entry for `Button1.Size` because this property does not differ from the fallback resource (`Form1.resx`). Recall from the previous chapter that if a resource is not found in a neutral culture (i.e., `WindowsApplication1.Form1.fr.resources`), `ResourceManager` falls back to the default resources (`WindowsApplication1.Form1.resources`), so it is necessary to list only the differences from the parent. If you build the solution now, you will find a new folder ("`fr`") beneath the output folder that holds the French resources ("`WindowsApplication1.resources.dll`").

Visual Studio 2003 Form.Language Gotcha

The `Form.Language` combo box can be a little too enthusiastic in its role. If you accidentally select a language, the corresponding resx file is automatically created and added to the project. Changing the language back to "`(Default)`" or to another language does not delete the new resx file and does not remove it from the project. You must perform these steps manually (in Solution Explorer, right-click the resx file and select Delete). This problem doesn't occur in Visual Studio 2005 because Visual Studio 2005 doesn't save the resx file until the first property is changed.

Finally, to illustrate a point, move the button to a different location and change its size. In the `Form1.Language` combo box, select "`(Default)`"; Visual Studio shows the fallback resource. You can alternate between the different languages, modifying the localized form(s) as necessary. You can save your project with any language version of your form loaded in the editor; the selected language has no effect at runtime. Despite this, I recommend that you return `Language` to "`(Default)`" when you are finished making changes. In Visual Studio 2003, this is essential because there is no immediate visual feedback on which form you are editing; it is easy to save the project with a specific language visible and open it again later (or for a different developer to open it), and forget or not realize that the default is not selected before you start making changes to a language-specific version of the form instead of to the default.

The important point to grasp from moving the button is that the resources behave according to the rules of inheritance. Because of the way the `ResourceManager` falls back to more generalized resources when specific resources are missing, you can think of this as inheritance for resources. So the French resource is a more specific kind of the default resource. It is simply a list of differences from its base, just as all classes are simply a list of differences from their base. This relationship is reflected in the French resource file, `Form1.fr.resx`.

```
<data name="button1.Location" type="System.Drawing.Point,
System.Drawing">
  <value>170, 12</value>
</data>
<data name="button1.Size" type="System.Drawing.Size, System.Drawing">
  <value>110, 32</value>
</data>
<data name="button1.Text" xml:space="preserve">
  <value>Fermer</value>
</data>
```

These elements are the only entries that refer to `button1` after the `Location`, `Size`, and `Text` properties have been changed.

This demo is fine as far as it goes, but it doesn't cover the fundamental truth of development; everything changes. It is a certainty that we will change this form at some point in the future. How does this model hold up when the form is changed?

With `Language` set to "`(Default)`", add a `Label` and a `TextBox` to the form and set `label1.Text` to "`Company name`". Now set `Language` to `French`, and you can see that the French version of the form includes the newly added components. If you go back to the default version and increase the size of the `TextBox`, for example, the change is reflected in the French form. However, if you change the size of the `TextBox` on the French form, the link with the default form is lost, and changes to the `TextBox`'s `Location` on the default form are not applied to the French form. Changes to other properties, such as `Font` and `Size`, are still linked and are applied to the French form.

One final piece of the localization jigsaw is missing. If you modify a property on a culture-neutral or culture-specific form by mistake and you want to revert to the default form's property, how can you do this? Simply changing the property on the culture-neutral or culture-specific form to be the same value as the property on the default form doesn't have the right effect. Sure, they will have the same value, but they are not linked; if you change the property on the default form again, the property on the culture-neutral or culture-specific form will not change. The answer is to dive into the culture-neutral or culture-specific resx file, find the entry for the offending property, and delete it.

Adding and Deleting Components

You can easily delete components on a form in the normal way by selecting them and then pressing the Del key. If you delete the newly added `TextBox` and then select the

French form, you will see that the TextBox has been deleted from all versions of the form. This rule holds true even if the currently selected Language is not the default, so if you delete the newly added Label from the French form, it will be deleted from the default and all other forms. We've also seen that when components are added to the default form, they are added to all versions of the forms. If you add a component to a form other than the default form, the behavior you see depends on the version of Visual Studio you are using. In Visual Studio 2003, you get the dialog in Figure 4.4, stating that the component will be added to all versions of the form. In Visual Studio 2005, you get a dialog stating that controls cannot be added in localization mode, and you will have to change the language back to the default.

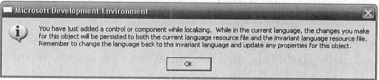

Figure 4.4 Visual Studio 2003 Warning Explaining the Effect of Adding Components to Specific Language Forms

From this adding and deleting behavior, you can conclude that components either exist or do not exist on all versions of the form; only the properties can differ, not the existence of a component. Whereas this makes life much easier in terms of localization, it can make customization more difficult. What do you do if you want a button to appear on the French form but not on any other form (including the default)? The answer is that you employ a little trickery. Add the button to the default form and set its Visible property to False. In the French form, set its Visible property to True. Problem solved.

Setting the CurrentUICulture

Now that we have made our form localizable and have localized it, our user needs a way to see the French form. Recall from Chapter 3, "An Introduction to Internationalization," that the user interface of our application is determined by the resources loaded by the ResourceManager, and that the GetString and GetObject methods default the culture to `CultureInfo.CurrentUICulture`, and that `CurrentUICulture` gets its default from the Win32 `GetUserDefaultUILanguage` function, which is normally the language version of Windows installed on the machine (except in Windows MUI, where it can be set by the user). So the only time we would see the French version of our application is when it is run on a French version of Windows. This is standard Windows behavior, but in some situations, you might need a more flexible solution.

In Chapter 3, you also learned that `CurrentUICulture` has a sister property, `CurrentCulture`, which determines the defaults for the .NET Framework's globalization classes. The user does have direct control over this value by setting the culture in the Regional and Language Options control panel applet. Though Microsoft recommends keeping these settings distinct, a common approach is to use the Regional and Language Options dialog to set both the `CurrentCulture` and the `CurrentUICulture`. To do this, add the following line as early in the application's startup process as possible (in our simple example, this would be in the application's main form's constructor, before the call to `InitializeComponent`).

```
Thread.CurrentThread.CurrentUICulture =
    Thread.CurrentThread.CurrentCulture;
```

(This assumes that there is a suitable `using System.Threading` in the file.) This solves the problem but might be inefficient in your scenario. If you offer only neutral cultures in your application (e.g., `French`, `German`, `Spanish`) and do not offer specific cultures (e.g., `French (Canada)`, `German (Germany)`, `Spanish (Mexico)`), the previous line will result in unnecessary checking for the missing specific resource. A better approach would be to use the specific culture's parent:

```
Thread.CurrentThread.CurrentUICulture =
    Thread.CurrentThread.CurrentCulture.Parent;
```

Notice that we don't need to check whether `CurrentCulture` has a parent because `CurrentCulture` is always culture specific.

Of course, if the user is using Windows MUI, the user already has control over this problem because he can set the user interface in Regional and Language Options. Despite this, the user might be confused or annoyed by having to specify the culture twice in the Regional and Language Options (once for the `CurrentCul-ture` and once for the `CurrentUICulture`), so you might like to make one setting the dominant setting and use it for both. If this is the case, you should still use the globalization setting instead of the language setting because `CurrentCulture` must include a region, whereas the language setting in Regional and Language Options does not require this.

If using Regional and Language Options doesn't suit your needs, there are alternatives. You could accept a command-line switch. You could load the setting from a configuration file or database. You could let the user specify the language of choice in a menu option (see the section "Changing the Culture During Execution").

If you are using Visual Studio 2005, the simplest solution is to maintain the user's setting in the application's settings file. In Solution Explorer, right-click the Windows Forms project, select Properties, and select the Settings tab. Enter a name for the setting (e.g., `UICulture`) and a value (e.g., "`fr-FR`"). The settings are stored in an XML file called `Settings.settings`. Visual Studio 2005 automatically maintains a strongly typed `Settings` class for this file in `Settings.Designer.cs`. The values can be accessed using the `Settings` class in the application's `Properties` namespace. The previous example for setting the `CurrentUICulture` now looks like this:

```
AppSettingsReader reader = new AppSettingsReader();

Thread.CurrentThread.CurrentUICulture =
    new CultureInfo(Properties.Settings.Default.UICulture);
```

Changing the Culture During Execution

In some applications, it might be helpful to allow the user to switch between different cultures while the application is running. This kind of application is great to demo because it provides immediate visual feedback on the act of changing the language. Figure 4.5 shows an application that offers a menu of languages.

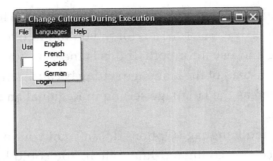

Figure 4.5   Windows Forms Application Offering a Choice of Languages

Figure 4.6 shows the same application after the user has selected Spanish as the language of choice.

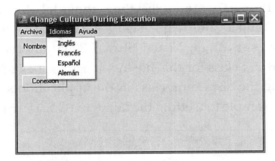

Figure 4.6   Windows Forms Application after Selecting Spanish

To achieve this result, we need to solve two problems. First, we need to be able to get a list of all forms in the application. Second, we need to be able to reapply the new resources to each form.

The first problem is easy to solve if you are using the .NET Framework 2.0. The `System.Windows.Forms.Application` class has a static property called `OpenForms`, which is a `FormCollection`. To solve our problem, we create a new class that looks like this:

```
public class ChangeFormCulture
{
    public static void ChangeAllForms(string culture)
    {
        FormCollection forms = Application.OpenForms;
```

```
        foreach (Form form in forms)
        {
            ChangeForm(form, culture);
        }
    }
}
```

The static `ChangeAllForms` method iterates through each form in the `Application.OpenForms` collection, calling the `ChangeForm` method.

Getting a List of Open Forms in the .NET Framework 1.1

The `Application.OpenForms` property is new in the .NET Framework 2.0, so it is not available in the .NET Framework 1.1. However, with reflection, we can do anything (almost). The .NET Framework 1.1 does maintain a collection of open forms, but it doesn't expose it. The collection is maintained in the `System.Windows.Forms.Application.ThreadWindows.windows` private field. To access this field, we need to construct a new `ThreadWindows` instance. The `windows` property contains an array of `IntPtrs`. The array has gaps in it, so not all of the elements are used. The following `OpenForms` property returns an array of `Form` objects by getting the value of the `windows` field, removing the gaps, and converting the `IntPtrs` to `Form` objects.

```
public static Form[] OpenForms
{
    get
    {
        Module MSCorLibModule = typeof(Form).BaseType.Module;

        Type threadWindowsType =
            MSCorLibModule.GetType(
            "System.Windows.Forms.Application+ThreadWindows");

        ConstructorInfo constructorInfo =
            threadWindowsType.GetConstructor(
            BindingFlags.Instance |
            BindingFlags.NonPublic,
            null, CallingConventions.HasThis,
```

```
            new Type[] {typeof(Control),
            typeof(Boolean)},
            null);

        if (constructorInfo == null)
            return null;

    Object threadWindow = constructorInfo.Invoke(
        new object[] {null, (Object) false});

    FieldInfo windowsFieldInfo =
        threadWindowsType.GetField("windows",
        BindingFlags.NonPublic |
        BindingFlags.Instance);

    if (windowsFieldInfo == null)
        return null;

    IntPtr[] windows = (IntPtr[])
        windowsFieldInfo.GetValue(threadWindow);

    ArrayList forms = new ArrayList();
    foreach(IntPtr window in windows)
    {
        Control control =
            Control.FromHandle(window);
        if (control != null)
            forms.Add((Form) control);
    }
    return (Form[]) forms.ToArray(typeof(Form));
    }
}
```

The second problem, applying the new resources to each form, has two solutions, each with pros and cons. The first solution is simply to use `ComponentResource Manager` to apply the new resources to each control. The `ChangeForm` method shows how to do this:

```
public static void ChangeForm(Form form, string culture)
{
    Thread.CurrentThread.CurrentUICulture =
        new System.Globalization.CultureInfo(culture);

    ComponentResourceManager resourceManager =
        new ComponentResourceManager(form.GetType());
```

```
    // apply resources to each control
    foreach (Control control in form.Controls)
    {
        resourceManager.ApplyResources(control, control.Name);
    }

    // apply resources to the form
    int X = form.Location.X;
    int Y = form.Location.Y;
    resourceManager.ApplyResources(form, "$this");
    form.Location = new Point(X, Y);

    ApplyMenuResources(resourceManager, form);
}
```

ChangeForm starts by changing the CurrentUICulture to the desired culture. It then gets a ComponentResourceManager for the given form and iterates through every control, reapplying its resources. It then saves the form's position, applies the new resources to the form, and restores the form's position. So far, so good. At the end of the method is a call to ApplyMenuResources. The problem with MenuItems is that they are components, not controls; as such, their Name property returns an empty string. The name is essential because it is the key by which the corresponding resource entries are found. The form's InitializeComponent method gets around this limitation because it knows the name of each component on the form and can generate code that uses a literal string:

```
resources.ApplyResources(this.menuItem1, "menuItem1");
```

To load the resources for the menu item, we need to find the menu item's name. The ApplyMenuResources method uses reflection to iterate through all the private fields on the form, looking for fields that have a type of MenuItem. Having found such a field, the name of the corresponding resources can be found from the name of the field, and ComponentResourceManager.ApplyResources can be called:

```
private static void ApplyMenuResources(
    ComponentResourceManager resourceManager, Form form)
{
    if (form.Menu != null)
    {
        FieldInfo[] fieldInfos = form.GetType().GetFields(
            BindingFlags.Instance | BindingFlags.NonPublic);
```

```
        foreach (FieldInfo fieldInfo in fieldInfos)
        {
            if (fieldInfo.FieldType ==
                typeof(System.Windows.Forms.MenuItem))
            {
                MenuItem menuItem =
                    (MenuItem)fieldInfo.GetValue(form);
                resourceManager.ApplyResources(
                    menuItem, fieldInfo.Name);
            }
        }
    }
}
```

This solution works well, but it does not work with all components. Some components inject additional code into the form's serialization code (in the Initialize Component method). Because the InitializeComponent method is not called when the form's culture is changed, this code will not be executed. Whether this is important depends upon the nature of the injected code. If it is important, you need the second solution to this problem. The ChangeFormUsingInitializeComponent method uses reflection to get a MethodInfo object for the form's private Initialize Component method. It deletes all the controls on the form, saves the form's position, invokes the InitializeComponent method, and restores the form's position.

```
public static void ChangeFormUsingInitializeComponent(
    Form form, string culture)
{
    // get the form's private InitializeComponent method
    MethodInfo initializeComponentMethodInfo =
        form.GetType().GetMethod("InitializeComponent",
        BindingFlags.Instance | BindingFlags.NonPublic);

    if (initializeComponentMethodInfo != null)
    {
        // the form has an InitializeComponent method
        // that we can invoke

        // save all controls
        List<Control> controls = new List<Control>();
        foreach (Control control in form.Controls)
        {
            controls.Add(control);
        }
        // remove all controls
```

```
    foreach (Control control in controls)
    {
        form.Controls.Remove(control);
    }

    int X = form.Location.X;
    int Y = form.Location.Y;

    Thread.CurrentThread.CurrentUICulture =
        new System.Globalization.CultureInfo(culture);

    // call the InitializeComponent method to add back controls
    initializeComponentMethodInfo.Invoke(
        form, new object[] { });

    form.Location = new Point(X, Y);
    }
}
```

If you are using the .NET Framework 1.1, you can use an `ArrayList` instead of the generic `List` collection (i.e., `List<Control>`) in this example.

So in this strategy, all the controls are destroyed and then rebuilt. This solves the original problem of ensuring that injected code is run, but it creates two new problems: The current values of controls are lost (e.g., `TextBox.Text`, `CheckBox.Checked`, `ListBox.SelectedIndex`), and the controls' events might fire, affecting the behavior or appearance of the form. You must decide which evil you can live with.

With our solution in place, each language menu item (e.g., `English`, `French`, `Spanish`, `German`) needs only to call the `ChangeAllForms` method, passing the correct culture:

```
ChangeFormCulture.ChangeAllForms("es");
```

Using Regional and Language Options to Change the Culture

A variation on the previous theme is to do away with the menu in the application altogether. Assume that the user controls the application's current culture using the Regional and Language Options dialog. Thus, whenever the user changes the setting in this dialog, the application should adapt to the changed setting. Unfortunately, the `CultureInfo` class does not surface a .NET event for this purpose, but the form can still trap this event by overriding the `WndProc` method and looking for a `WM_SETTINGSCHANGE` event, where the message's `LParam` is `intl`:

```
[DllImport("kernel32.dll")]
protected static extern int GetUserDefaultLCID();
private const int WM_SETTINGSCHANGE = 0x001A;
protected override void WndProc(ref Message message)
{
    switch (message.Msg)
    {
        case WM_SETTINGSCHANGE:
        {
            if ((int) message.WParam == 0 &&
                message.LParam != IntPtr.Zero &&
                Marshal.PtrToStringAuto(message.LParam) == "intl")
            {
                if (Thread.CurrentThread.CurrentCulture.LCID !=
                    GetUserDefaultLCID())
                {
                    Thread.CurrentThread.CurrentCulture =
                        new CultureInfo(GetUserDefaultLCID());

                    Thread.CurrentThread.CurrentUICulture =
                        Thread.CurrentThread.CurrentCulture;

                    ChangeFormCulture.ChangeAllForms(Thread.
                        CurrentThread.CurrentUICulture.Name);
                }
                else
                {
                    Thread.CurrentThread.
                        CurrentCulture.ClearCachedData();

                    Thread.CurrentThread.
                        CurrentUICulture.ClearCachedData();
                }
```

```
            }
          break;
        }
    }
    base.WndProc(ref message);
}
```

With the "culture change" event trapped, we check to see whether the new culture is the same as our current culture. This implementation assumes that the application's `CurrentCulture` and `CurrentUICulture` are the same, and that `CurrentUICulture` has been initialized to the `CurrentCulture` when the application started. If the culture has changed, we change the `CurrentCulture` and `CurrentUICulture` and call `ChangeFormCulture.ChangeAllForms` to change all the forms. If the new culture is the same culture as our current culture, the user has simply modified the settings for the existing culture (e.g., they have changed the date/time formats). In this case, we need to only clear our cached version of the culture so that the updated information is reread.

Although this solves the immediate problem, I must advise caution with this approach. For an application simply to rebuild all its forms, no matter what state it is currently in or what it is currently doing, is disturbing and might lead to unpredictable results.

Dialogs

The .NET Framework includes many dialog components and a `MessageBox` class, all of which display dialog boxes. These dialog boxes are part of the user interface and, therefore, require some localization. The support offered to you is either a curse or a blessing, depending upon your requirements. All the dialog components in the .NET Framework have built-in support for localization. Table 4.2 shows the components and classes, and the source of their support.

Table 4.2   Classes and Components, and Their Localization Support

Class/Component	Localization Support Provided By
ColorDialog	Operating system
FolderBrowserDialog	Operating system
FontDialog	Operating system
MessageBox	Operating system
OpenFileDialog	Operating system
PageSetupDialog	Operating system
PrintDialog	Operating system
PrintPreviewDialog	.NET Framework Language Pack
SaveDialog	Operating system

Most of these components offer their localization support courtesy of the operating system, and this is because these components are wrappers around Win32 dialogs. So on the German version of Windows, the OpenDialog component is shown in German (see Figure 4.7).

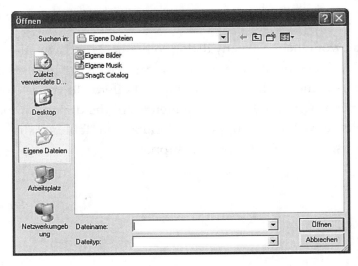

Figure 4.7 OpenDialog **on German-Language Windows**

One component, `PrintPreviewDialog`, is specific to the .NET Framework and has no equivalent dialog in the operating system; it is supplied wholly by the .NET Framework. Figure 4.8 shows `PrintPreviewDialog` running on English Windows.

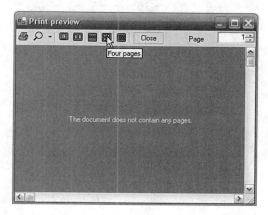

Figure 4.8   `PrintPreviewDialog` **on English Windows**

Because the localized version is dependent upon the .NET Framework Language Packs installed—and, therefore, the current setting of `CurrentUICulture`—if you open the dialog on German Windows without a German .NET Framework Language Pack installed, you get a mostly English dialog. In Figure 4.9, notice that the ToolTip is in German, whereas the rest of the dialog is in English.

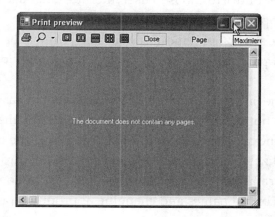

Figure 4.9   `PrintPreviewDialog` **on German Windows with No .NET Framework Language Pack**

To get the fully localized German dialog (see Figure 4.10), you must install the German .NET Framework Language Pack.

Figure 4.10 `PrintPreviewDialog` **on German Windows with the German .NET Framework Language Pack**

This is where the curse or the blessing comes in. If you want the user interface in your application to be dictated by the operating system (i.e., on French Windows, your application always runs in French), this approach is a blessing because you do not need to do anything; the work has already been done for you. If you don't want the user interface in your application to be dictated by the operating system (i.e., the user should have the control to choose a user interface language that is different than the language of the operating system), this approach is a curse. In this scenario, your application will have a schizophrenic user interface; part will be in the language chosen by the user, and part will be in a different language provided by the operating system.

Unfortunately, the only solutions to this problem are not easy. The most straightforward solution is not to use the built-in components for these purposes and to write your own identical classes from scratch that mimic the behavior completely but that have a localizable user interface. A less straightforward solution is to let the dialogs load as normal but then iterate through all the controls on the dialog looking for known control names and changing appropriate properties to localized versions.

If you choose to abandon the .NET Framework dialog components, you might like to use the "Dialog culture dictated by operating system" and "Dialog culture dictated by .NET Framework" FxCop rules, in Chapter 13, "Testing Internationalization Using FxCop," to ensure that you do not accidentally use one of these dialogs.

Windows Resource Localization Editor (WinRes)

As the name implies, the Windows Resource Localization Editor (WinRes) is a localization editor for Windows Forms resources (i.e., `.resx` and `.resources`, but not `.restext` and `.txt`). It is intended to be used by localizers to localize forms without the need for Visual Studio. WinRes is part of the .NET Framework SDK, so it is free; in comparison, only the Express editions of Visual Studio are free, and it would be impractical to insist that localizers install Visual Studio solely to localize forms. WinRes is essentially a cut-down version of the Visual Studio Forms Designer. In Figure 4.11, you can see WinRes being used to edit a form's resx file. The Properties Window on the right side is the same `PropertyGrid` component that Visual Studio uses. The Form Designer that occupies most of the window behaves in mostly the same way as the Form Designer in Visual Studio. The localizer needs to have the application's forms' resx (or resources) files, but at no point is the source code required. So for an external party to localize your forms, he would need to install the .NET Framework and the .NET Framework SDK; then you would need to send the localizer your application's forms' resx files. The localizer would localize these resx files and return them to you for reintegration into your application.

The idea is a good one, and if you are using the .NET Framework 2.0, you will probably find WinRes a useful tool. We return to WinRes in the .NET Framework 1.1 later. Figure 4.11 shows WinRes after it has opened an original, default form resource (say, `Form1.resx`). From here, the localizer can translate text, move and resize controls, and change fonts and other properties. The localizer cannot add new controls, delete existing controls, or add, edit, or delete events or source code.

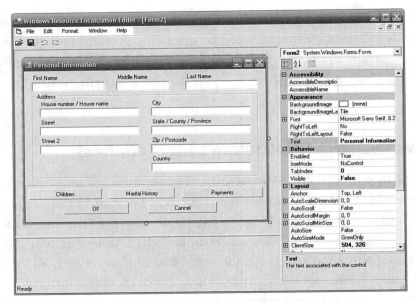

Figure 4.11   WinRes Editing a Default Resource

When the localizer has finished with one target language, he can select File, Save As (see Figure 4.12) and save the work as a new culture (say, `Form1.fr.resx`). We return to the File Mode combo box in a moment.

Figure 4.12   WinRes File, Save As Dialog

Once saved (see Figure 4.13), WinRes shows the language in the title bar. The localizer can open any or all of the fallback resx, culture-neutral resx, or culture-specific resx files. The localizer also can create new culture versions of the resx files, so they are not limited to the cultures that developers originally supplied them with.

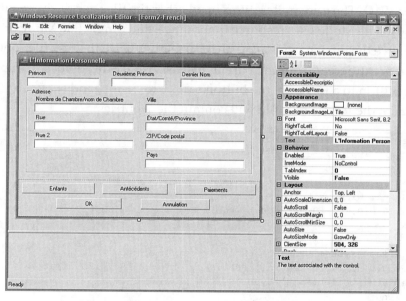

Figure 4.13   WinRes Editing a Culture-Neutral Resource

WinRes 1.1 Exception Messages

If you are using the .NET Framework 1.1 WinRes, you should be aware that its exception-reporting functionality is extremely limited. Most of the exception messages are not likely to be of much help in diagnosing the problem, and you are often left trying to work out by trial and error what WinRes is objecting to. Unlike WinRes in the .NET Framework 2.0, WinRes 1.1 also fails to load an entire form if a single control or property on the form cannot be processed. If you are stuck, check out Raghavendra Prabhu's blog entry at http://blogs.msdn.com/rprabhu/archive/ 2003/08/21/56536.aspx. Raghavendra is part of the .NET Client Team and has had to track down many WinRes problems.

Resource File Mode

The File, Save As dialog offers a File Mode combo box (see Figure 4.12). File Mode defaults to Visual Studio File Mode (VSFM) in the .NET Framework 2.0. No File Mode option exists in the .NET Framework 1.1, where WinRes can use only Single File Mode (SFM). The two modes differ in whether the files use resource inheritance: Visual Studio File Mode uses resource inheritance, and Single File Mode does not. So when you save the French version of the form using VSFM, the resx file contains only entries that are different from the parent, just as Visual Studio does. For example, if you add a button to a form, set the button's `Text` to `Close`, and set `Form.Localizable` to `true`, the form's resx file will contain these entries:

```
<data name="button1.Text" xml:space="preserve">
  <value>Close</value>
</data>
<data name="&gt;&gt;$this.Type" xml:space="preserve">
  <value>System.Windows.Forms.Form, System.Windows.Forms,
  Version=2.0.0.0, Culture=neutral, PublicKeyToken=b77a5c561934e089
  </value>
</data>
<assembly alias="System.Drawing" name="System.Drawing,
Version=2.0.0.0, Culture=neutral, PublicKeyToken=b03f5f7f11d50a3a" />
<data name="$this.ClientSize" type="System.Drawing.Size,
System.Drawing">
  <value>292, 266</value>
</data>
<data name="&gt;&gt;button1.Parent" xml:space="preserve">
  <value>$this</value>
</data>
<data name="button1.Size" type="System.Drawing.Size, System.Drawing">
  <value>75, 23</value>
</data>
<assembly alias="mscorlib" name="mscorlib, Version=2.0.0.0,
Culture=neutral, PublicKeyToken=b77a5c561934e089" />
<data name="button1.TabIndex" type="System.Int32, mscorlib">
  <value>0</value>
</data>
<data name="&gt;&gt;button1.ZOrder" xml:space="preserve">
  <value>0</value>
</data>
<data name="$this.Text" xml:space="preserve">
  <value>Form1</value>
</data>
<data name="button1.Location" type="System.Drawing.Point,
System.Drawing">
```

```
      <value>205, 231</value>
</data>
<data name="&gt;&gt;button1.Type" xml:space="preserve">
  <value>System.Windows.Forms.Button, System.Windows.Forms,
  Version=2.0.0.0, Culture=neutral, PublicKeyToken=b77a5c561934e089
  </value>
</data>
<data name="&gt;&gt;button1.Name" xml:space="preserve">
  <value>button1</value>
</data>
<data name="$this.AutoScaleDimensions" type="System.Drawing.SizeF,
System.Drawing">
  <value>6, 13</value>
</data>
<data name="&gt;&gt;$this.Name" xml:space="preserve">
  <value>Form1</value>
</data>
<metadata name="$this.Localizable" type="System.Boolean, mscorlib,
Version=2.0.0.0, Culture=neutral, PublicKeyToken=b77a5c561934e089">
  <value>True</value>
</metadata>
```

If you open the resx file in WinRes, change the button's `Text` to "Fermer", and save it to a new resx file using Visual Studio File Mode, the new resx will contain just a single entry:

```
<data name="button1.Text" xml:space="preserve">
  <value>Fermer</value>
</data>
```

As you would expect, these VSFM resx files are completely compatible with Visual Studio and can be exchanged between Visual Studio and WinRes without issue. Bear in mind, though, that because the resx "inherits" from its parent resx, WinRes must have access to the parent resx as well; otherwise, WinRes cannot open it (the actual error message is "Error - File : 'Form1.fr.resx' The default culture file for the current culture not found. Please add the default culture file."). I recommend using VSFM because the files are compatible with Visual Studio.

Visual Studio File Mode can be used only with `.resx` files; it cannot be used with `.resources` files because Visual Studio does not support editing of resources in `.resources` files.

The alternative File Mode is Single File Mode, and this is the only option available to the .NET Framework 1.1 WinRes. In Single File Mode, the resource file contains the complete resource information, which is necessary to render the form. No other resource files are necessary. So if you open a default form resource created by Visual Studio in WinRes and then save it using Single File Mode, the resource file will contain all the entries in the original resx with the values for the new culture, regardless of whether those values are the same as or different from the original resource. If you had saved the previous example using Single File Mode instead of Visual Studio File Mode, the entries would have been as follows:

```
<data name="$this.Text" xml:space="preserve">
  <value>Form1</value>
</data>
<assembly alias="System.Drawing" name="System.Drawing,
Version=2.0.0.0, Culture=neutral, PublicKeyToken=b03f5f7f11d50a3a" />
<data name="$this.ClientSize" type="System.Drawing.Size,
System.Drawing">
  <value>292, 266</value>
</data>
<data name="&gt;&gt;$this.Name" xml:space="preserve">
  <value>Form1</value>
</data>
<data name="&gt;&gt;$this.Type" xml:space="preserve">
  <value>System.Windows.Forms.Form, System.Windows.Forms,
  Version=2.0.0.0, Culture=neutral, PublicKeyToken=b77a5c561934e089
  </value>
</data>
<assembly alias="mscorlib" name="mscorlib, Version=2.0.0.0,
Culture=neutral, PublicKeyToken=b77a5c561934e089" />
<data name="button1.TabIndex" type="System.Int32, mscorlib">
  <value>0</value>
</data>
<data name="button1.Size" type="System.Drawing.Size, System.Drawing">
  <value>75, 23</value>
</data>
<data name="button1.Text" xml:space="preserve">
  <value>Fermer</value>
</data>
<data name="button1.Location" type="System.Drawing.Point,
System.Drawing">
  <value>205, 231</value>
</data>
<data name="&gt;&gt;button1.Name" xml:space="preserve">
  <value>button1</value>
</data>
```

```
<data name="&gt;&gt;button1.Type" xml:space="preserve">
  <value>System.Windows.Forms.Button, System.Windows.Forms,
  Version=2.0.0.0, Culture=neutral, PublicKeyToken=b77a5c561934e089
  </value>
</data>
<data name="&gt;&gt;button1.Parent" xml:space="preserve">
  <value>$this</value>
</data>
<data name="&gt;&gt;button1.ZOrder" xml:space="preserve">
  <value>0</value>
</data>
```

Although the entries are in a different order than in the default resx file, they are all there, except for "$this.Localizable", which is assumed to be true.

WinRes 2.0 and Cultures

The list of cultures that the .NET Framework 2.0 supports depends on both the operating system on which the framework is running and the custom cultures that are installed on that machine. WinRes 2.0 cannot open resx files for unknown cultures, so if you develop using Windows XP Professional Service Pack 2 and create, say, a culture for Welsh (United Kingdom), but your localizer uses Windows Professional 2000, they will not be able to open the cy-GB.resx files for this culture. The same is true for any custom cultures that you create (e.g., Spanish (United States)). The latter problem can be solved simply by installing the required custom culture. The former problem can be solved either by creating a dummy custom culture for the missing culture and installing that culture on the target operating system, or hijacking a culture that you do not use that is known to be present on all operating systems. For example, imagine that you do not use the Malay (Malaysia) culture. You would rename all the cy-GB.resx files to ms-MY.resx files before sending the resx files to the localizer, and you would rename them all back again upon their return.

WinRes 1.1 and Visual Studio 2003 Compatibility

As has already been noted, the WinRes that ships in the .NET Framework 1.1 SDK does not offer a choice of File Modes because it supports only one: Single File Mode. This means that the culture-neutral and culture-specific files that WinRes creates are incompatible with Visual Studio, and vice versa. So if the localizer uses WinRes to open a default resx file and create a culture-neutral or culture-specific file, Visual

Studio cannot open that file. And if developers create culture-neutral or culture-specific resx files using Visual Studio, WinRes cannot open those resx files. This implies that your development strategy must be an "either/or" approach in which you should commit either wholly to Visual Studio or wholly to WinRes with regard to culture-neutral and culture-specific resx files. However, with a little bit of ingenuity, this obstacle can be overcome.

Recall the earlier discussions on resource inheritance in this chapter. WinRes wants to "flatten" the resource inheritance so that each resx file is wholly contained. Visual Studio wants culture-neutral and culture-specific files to contain only the differences from their parent and, therefore, be dependent upon their parent file. The conclusion is that you *can* use both Visual Studio and WinRes to maintain the same resources, provided that you convert between Single File Mode and Visual Studio File Mode. The strategy works like this: The developers maintain all the resx files as part of the source code in whatever version control system you use. These resx files are used in the normal development process. When it is time to ship the resx files to the localizer to be translated, the resx files are put through a conversion process to convert them from Visual Studio File Mode to Single File Mode. The resulting files are then shipped off to the localizer. When the updated versions come back from the localizer, the files are converted back from Single File Mode to Visual Studio File Mode, and are incorporated back into the development process. This strategy is implemented in Chapter 14, "The Translator."

WinRes and Visual Form Inheritance

Visual form inheritance is a natural and obvious application of object-oriented programming; it applies the concept of class inheritance to forms. Inheritance is just as essential to form development as it is to class development. A good practice is to create a base form from which all other forms in the application inherit. This acts as a placeholder to which modifications can subsequently be made. The benefit is that to change all forms in an application, you need to make only a single change to the base form. The idea is often extended to create, say, a generic maintenance form from which all specific maintenance forms (e.g., a customer maintenance form and a contact maintenance form) inherit. There are several recommendations throughout this book for placing common code in a base form.

Using WinRes 2.0 with forms that use form inheritance requires an additional step. Before we can understand this step, we must look at the problem that WinRes 2.0 has with form inheritance. Assume that we have a form called `BaseForm` and a form that inherits from `BaseForm`, called `MaintenanceForm` and a form that inherits from `MaintenanceForm`, called `CustomerMaintenanceForm`. Assume also that we have French versions of each of these forms (i.e., `BaseForm.fr.resx`, `MaintenanceForm.fr.resx`, and `CustomerMaintenanceForm.fr.resx`). To localize the French `BaseForm`, the WinRes command is this:

```
WinRes BaseForm.fr.resx
```

This works just as you expect it to, and there is nothing special to report here. The problem comes when you try to localize the form that inherits from `BaseForm`:

```
WinRes MaintenanceForm.fr.resx
```

WinRes reports that it cannot load `MaintenanceForm`, and it uses a placeholder instead. WinRes shows all the controls that are specific to `MaintenanceForm`, but none of the controls that are inherited from `BaseForm`. To understand the problem (and the solution), we need to look inside the resx files. In `BaseForm.resx`, you find the definition for the `BaseForm`'s Type:

```
<data name="&gt;&gt;$this.Type" xml:space="preserve">
  <value>System.Windows.Forms.Form, System.Windows.Forms,
    Version=2.0.0.0, Culture=neutral,
    PublicKeyToken=b77a5c561934e089</value>
</data>
```

From this entry, we learn that `BaseForm` inherits from `System.Windows.Forms.Form`, which is what we expect. In `MaintenanceForm.resx`, you find a similar entry for the `MaintenanceForm`'s Type:

```
<data name="&gt;&gt;$this.Type" xml:space="preserve">
  <value>FormInheritanceExample.BaseForm, FormInheritanceExample,
    Version=1.0.0.0, Culture=neutral, PublicKeyToken=null</value>
</data>
```

From this entry, we learn that `MaintenanceForm` inherits from `BaseForm`, which we already know. However, if you consider what this entry means, you will see that `MaintenanceForm` inherits from the `BaseForm` in the `FormInheritanceExample` assembly. From this, you should learn that, as far as the resx file is concerned, `MaintenanceForm.resx` does *not* inherit from the `BaseForm.resx` file; it inherits from the `BaseForm` class in the assembly. WinRes requires original assembly in addition to the `MaintenanceForm.resx` file to render the form correctly. When WinRes complains that it cannot load the type for the `MaintenanceForm`, it is complaining that it cannot find the assembly that contains the `BaseForm` (i.e., `FormInheritanceExample.exe`, in this example).

There are several solutions to this problem. Either add the assembly to the Global Assembly Cache (GAC) so that WinRes can find it, or copy the assembly into the same location as `WinRes.exe`. The former approach requires that you strong name your assemblies; if this is not acceptable, you must take the latter approach. The latter approach suffers from the problem that the .NET Framework SDK's bin directory rapidly becomes littered with erroneous application assemblies that have nothing to do with the .NET Framework SDK. A better solution is to turn the problem around and copy `WinRes.exe` to the assemblies' location and run WinRes from there.

> Neither Visual Studio 2005 nor WinRes 2.0 displays localized versions of inherited controls. So when you view, say, the French form in Visual Studio 2005 or WinRes 2.0, you will see the French localized versions of all the controls introduced on that form, but the inherited controls will be shown using the fallback resources. The appearance for the developer and translator/localizer can be confusing. The resources, however, are correct, despite appearances.

WinRes 1.1 does not suffer from this issue because WinRes 1.1 does not support form inheritance. As has been noted previously, WinRes 1.1 supports Single File Mode only; as such, all resx files must contain the complete definition of the form. To localize forms that use form inheritance using WinRes 1.1 the resx files must be flattened. For example, to localize `MaintenanceForm.fr.resx`, a new `MaintenanceForm.fr.resx` file must be created that is the sum of `BaseForm.resx` plus `BaseForm.fr.resx` plus `MaintenanceForm.resx` plus `MaintenanceForm.fr.resx`.

WinRes Pros and Cons

WinRes is a great localization tool that has a number of pros and cons. On the pros side, WinRes provides localization facilities for a form in context. This means that the localizer sees the context in which translations are made and gets immediate feedback on the suitability of choices. They can see clipping problems, overlapping problems, and hot key clashes, and can decide whether the translation is correct within the context that it is being used. Don't underestimate the importance of this immediate visual feedback. From the localizer's point of view, WinRes is a great tool because the localizer can move and resize components, and change fonts, `RightToLeft` and `ImeMode` properties, and, indeed, any localizable property. Localizers like to be in control of these issues; after all, these issues make the difference between their jobs being localizers as opposed to merely translators.

On the cons side, developers might not want localizers to be able to change all the properties that they have access to. For example, developers might feel that the default resource should be designed to cope with all cultures and might adopt practices such as ensuring that controls set their `AutoSize` property to `true` and that the `Font`, `ImeMode`, and `RightToLeft` properties are set on an application-wide basis instead of on an individual control basis. You must establish who controls nontext properties in your resources (i.e., the developers or the localizer) before you get too far into your development. If you decide that these issues should be under developer control, there is no way you can prevent WinRes from allowing localizers to change properties. The solution is to write a utility to read in specific properties (such as `Text`) from the resx files coming back from the localizers, and apply them to the existing developer's resx files. In this way, only the localizer's translations are used; all other changes are dumped. Regardless of who has control over these properties, you might like to adopt the approach of applying the localizer's changes to the developers' "master" resx files so that the developers can continue to add and delete components to resx files while the localizer is working on the remote copy. See the "Reintegrating Resources" section of Chapter 14 for solutions to these problems.

Staying on the cons side, WinRes reads and writes only resx and resources files. If you have chosen to store your resources in a database (see Chapter 12, "Custom Resource Managers") or to use a different resource format, WinRes cannot be made to use it. Two possible solutions to this problem exist. One is to rewrite WinRes yourself. This is significantly more achievable in the .NET Framework 2.0 than in the

.NET Framework 1.1, but it still represents a reasonable piece of work with specialized knowledge. If you were to rewrite WinRes, an additional benefit would be that you can specify which properties the localizer can see and change in the `Property-Grid`. The other possibility is to translate back and forth between the resx file format. So when you ship your application to the localizer, you export your resources to resx files; when the localizer returns the resx files, you import them back into your own resource source.

Another issue that might or might not bother you is that WinRes is a stand-alone executable. If you intend to invoke WinRes from within your application (see Chapter 14) so that the localizer can localize while wandering around the application, a better solution for WinRes is for it to be a component. The WinRes component would be part of the application instead of a separate executable. Apart from the neatness of this solution, this would mean that the localizer wouldn't have to install the .NET Framework SDK.

Another problem with WinRes is that if you are using the .NET Framework 1.1, you are stuck with Single File Mode and you have to write a translation facility to translate to and from Visual Studio File Mode, to allow both tools to coexist.

WinRes is revisited in Chapter 14, which covers some translator-specific issues. For a list of commercial alternatives to WinRes see Appendix B, "Information Resources."

ClickOnce

Visual Studio 2005 and the .NET Framework 2.0 introduce a new deployment model for Windows Forms and Console applications called ClickOnce. ClickOnce is the successor to the .NET Framework 1.1's No Touch Deployment (also called Zero Touch Deployment, HREF Deployment, and HTTP Download) and the Patterns and Practices Group's Updater Application Block. If you are using the .NET Framework 1.1 and like the look of ClickOnce functionality, take a look at the most recent Updater Application Block, which offers similar functionality to ClickOnce for .NET Framework 1.1 applications. ClickOnce brings the ease and reliability of Web deployment to Windows Forms applications. It allows developers to publish applications to a Web server, file server, or CD-/DVD-ROM from which the client can run the application online or offline. An *online application* is one that is available only by connecting to the server containing the application and, as such, is similar in behavior to a Web application. An *offline/online application* (also called an *installed application*) is one that is installed locally on the client machine and, once it has been installed, can be run without a connection to the server containing the application. A significant benefit to this deployment model is that clients have a simple application-upgrade path. As new versions of the application are published, the client can optionally automatically receive the new upgrade.

This powerful new technology breathes new life into Windows Forms applications. This section is not intended to provide a complete introduction to ClickOnce. For further reading on ClickOnce, consult the following:

Smart Client Developer Center Home: ClickOnce
(http://msdn.microsoft.com/smartclient/understanding/windows-forms/2.0/features/clickonce.aspx)
Essential ClickOnce, by Brian Noyes (Addison-Wesley: 2006)

Instead, this section covers ClickOnce issues that are specific to internationalization. If you are new to ClickOnce, read the section entitled "A Brief Introduction to Click-Once." If you are already familiar with ClickOnce, you can skip this section. Subsequent sections discuss publishing applications with a single culture using first Visual Studio 2005 and then msbuild, localizing the ClickOnce user interface, and publishing applications with multiple cultures using first Visual Studio 2005 and then msbuild.

> If you are using the .NET Framework 2.0 but are not using Visual Studio 2005, you can still use ClickOnce. The Manifest Generation and Editing Tool (MAGE), included in the .NET Framework 2.0 SDK, provides the same ClickOnce functionality as Visual Studio 2005.

A Brief Introduction to ClickOnce

To get started with ClickOnce, create a Windows Forms application—say, WindowsApplication1—and, within Visual Studio 2005, select Build, Publish WindowsApplication1. In the "Where do you want to publish the application?" dialog, accept the offered URL (i.e., `http://localhost/WindowsApplication1`). This option publishes your application to the local Web server, so you need IIS installed.

If you don't have IIS installed on any machine, you can publish to a file location. Click Next. In the "Will the application be available offline?" dialog, accept the "Yes, this application is available online or offline" radio button. This means that when the client first connects to the Web server, the application will be installed into the Click-Once cache on the client machine. Each time the application is run, ClickOnce will check that the application is the latest version and check whether it is the application that will be run from the cache. If a newer version has been published, the user will be given an opportunity to upgrade the application. Click Next. Click Finish. When Visual Studio has finished publishing the application, the `publish.htm` Web page is displayed, showing a button to install WindowsApplication1.

From here, you assume the role of the user. If you click the Install button, the WindowsApplication1 application is installed on your computer in the ClickOnce cache. An item is added to the Start menu, and an item is added to Add/Remove Programs to allow the user to remove the new application or to revert to the previous version. If you subsequently modify the application, all you need do is publish it again. When users run their application again, they will be prompted to upgrade it. You now have the basics of ClickOnce.

Bear in mind that ClickOnce is a powerful and flexible technology, and this description skims the surface of this significant subject. Numerous options exist for changing ClickOnce behavior from within Visual Studio. Also be aware that the tools offered in Visual Studio are built using the ClickOnce API and simply represent just one way of assembling this functionality. If you find that one part of this technology is not to your liking, it is likely that your requirements can be met by using the tools or API at a lower level.

Deploying a Single Culture Using Visual Studio 2005

The first issue that you will notice when you publish an application with satellite assemblies is that none of the satellite assemblies are published. Let's assume that you now localize `Form1` in the simple Windows Forms application created in the previous section, and that you create a French version of `Form1`. When you build the application, there will obviously be a new folder called `fr` that contains a satellite assembly called `WindowsApplication1.resources.dll`. When you publish the application, however, this assembly will not be published, and all recipients will get the fallback resources only.

You can solve this problem in two ways. The first solution is to specify that the resource assemblies should be included. In the application's Properties page, select the Publish tab and click the Application Files… button. You should see just the main application, not the French satellite assembly. Check the "Show all files" check box, and the French satellite assembly appears (see Figure 4.14).

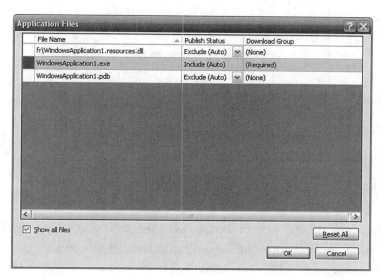

Figure 4.14   ClickOnce Application Files Dialog Showing Satellite Assemblies

You can see from this dialog that the French satellite assembly is excluded. To include the French satellite assembly, drop down the Publish Status combo box on the `fr\WindowsApplication1.resources.dll` line and click Include. Problem solved.

The second solution is to set the ClickOnce publish language (also called the target culture). (If you intend to use this option, you should return to the ClickOnce Application Files dialog first and click the Reset All button to undo the previous change.) From the Publish tab of the application's Properties page, click the Options… button to see the ClickOnce Publish Options (see Figure 4.15).

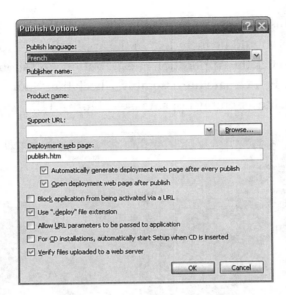

Figure 4.15　ClickOnce Publish Options

In the "Publish language" combo box, select French. If you return to the Application Files dialog now, you will see that the `fr\WindowsApplication1.resources.dll` assembly's Publish Status has been set to "`Include (Auto)`". This is not quite the same as simply "`Include`". This means that the inclusion of the satellite assembly depends on the Publish language. If you had both French and Spanish resources, for example, and you changed the Publish language to Spanish, the French satellite assembly would be excluded and the Spanish satellite assembly would be included.

When you publish the application after changing the target language, you receive the warning shown in Figure 4.16. The warning simply notes that the culture of the previously published version of the application is not the same as the culture of the version that you are now publishing. Answer Yes to overwrite the previous version of the application.

Figure 4.16   ClickOnce Published Culture Change Warning

In addition, if you do not have the .NET Framework 2 Language Pack installed for the target language, you will receive the following warning:

```
Could not match culture 'fr' for item '.NET Framework 2.0'. Using culture 'en'
instead.
```

You can ignore this warning for now. The relevance of the presence or absence of a corresponding .NET Framework 2 Language Pack is discussed in the section entitled "The ClickOnce User Interface."

Note that the Publish language automatically includes resources specifically, not generically. This means that if you add French (France) and French (Canada) versions of Form1, then setting the Publish language to French includes *only* the French satellite assembly; it does not also include the French (France) and French (Canada) satellite assemblies. So using the Publish language to automatically include satellite assemblies is not suitable if you want to publish a "generic" French version of your application that includes generic French and all specific versions of French. (Incidentally, if you set the Publish language to French (France), ClickOnce is intelligent enough to include the culture-neutral French satellite assembly.)

The Publish language is used for two purposes: the automatic inclusion of satellite assemblies and also the language of the ClickOnce bootstrapper. We cover the latter in the next section.

The ClickOnce User Interface

So far, we have simply specified what assemblies are included in the published application. An important part of internationalizing the ClickOnce deployment process is the localization of the ClickOnce user interface. All the dialogs from the publish.htm Web page onward (such as security warnings, installing and updating dialogs, and the add/remove program dialog) are all used by the recipient of your application and must all be localized. The localization of each dialog depends on the origin of the dialog (see Table 4.3).

Table 4.3 The Origin of ClickOnce Dialogs

Dialog or Page	Origin
`publish.htm`	Visual Studio 2005
`setup.exe` dialogs	ClickOnce bootstrapper resources
"Launching Application" dialog	.NET Framework Language Pack
"Security Warning" dialog	.NET Framework Language Pack
"Installing" dialog	.NET Framework Language Pack
"Update Available" dialog	.NET Framework Language Pack
"Updating" dialog	.NET Framework Language Pack
Add/Remove Programs dialog	.NET Framework Language Pack

The `publish.htm` Web page that starts the ClickOnce process going (if you are using IIS) originates from Visual Studio 2005. The language used in the dialog is determined by the language that Visual Studio 2005 uses, the presence of a corresponding .NET Framework Language Pack and the language of the operating system. For example, if you are developing using the English version of Visual Studio 2005, you will always get the English `publish.htm`. If you are developing using the Japanese version of Visual Studio 2005 (which includes the Japanese .NET Framework Language Pack) on a Japanese version of Windows, you will always get the Japanese `publish.htm`. There is no way to tell Visual Studio to generate `publish.htm` using a different language, so the English Visual Studio 2005 cannot generate a French `publish.htm`. In all likelihood, however, you would replace `publish.htm` with your own branded version of `publish.htm`, so even if such functionality existed, you might not use it anyway. To replace `publish.htm` with your own branded version, first publish your ClickOnce application as normal; when publishing is complete, then copy your branded `publish.htm` over the generated `publish.htm`. Simple, low-tech, and effective.

The ClickOnce bootstrapper (`setup.exe`) is used to install the application's prerequisites (e.g., the .NET Framework and the .NET Framework Language Packs). Whether your users see dialogs from `setup.exe` depends on whether they need to install the application's prerequisites. The ClickOnce bootstrapper's user interface is determined by the application's Publish language. The support files for the ClickOnce bootstrapper are installed in `%FrameworkSDK%\Bootstrapper` (see Figure 4.17).

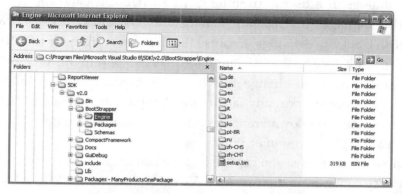

Figure 4.17   ClickOnce Bootstrapper Support Files

The `Engine` folder contains `setup.bin` and a collection of folders that are culture names. Each culture folder contains a localized `setup.xml` with Win32 resource strings, so the `fr` folder's `setup.xml` contains the French resource strings. When the application is published, a custom `setup.exe` is created by combining `setup.bin` with the resources in the `setup.xml` that corresponds to the publish language. This means that the ClickOnce bootstrapper that you create is for a single language. If you want to support more than one language, you must publish the application once for one language and then again for the second language. A number of localized `setup.xml` files are included in the .NET Framework SDK, but you are not restricted to this list. To add a new language, simply create a new folder, copy over the `setup.xml` from the English folder, and translate all the strings.

The remaining dialogs (i.e., the dialogs that are certain to be seen by all users who use a ClickOnce-deployed application) are all supplied by a .NET Framework Language Pack. The ClickOnce engine, `dfsvc.exe`, is a .NET Framework application. It uses a `ResourceManager` to get its resources and obeys the resource-fallback behavior that we already know. `ResourceManager` uses `CurrentUICulture` to determine which culture to load resources for, and we know that `CurrentUICulture` defaults to the language version of the operating system. So the language that the user sees in the ClickOnce dialogs is determined by the language of the operating system and the availability of a corresponding .NET Framework Language Pack. So if a user is running German Windows and has the German .NET Framework Language Pack installed, all ClickOnce applications will show German ClickOnce dialogs. If a user is running German Windows and the German .NET Framework Language Pack has not been installed, all ClickOnce applications will show English ClickOnce dialogs (because the fallback culture for the .NET Framework itself is English). The Publish language plays no part in this process. Also note that it is not possible to change this behavior because the ClickOnce engine, `dfsvc.exe`, does not support any facility for changing its `CurrentUICulture`. For example, you cannot deploy a French application and use a French ClickOnce user interface on an English version of Windows.

From these explanations, you can see that the language of the complete ClickOnce user experience comes from three sources: Visual Studio, the ClickOnce bootstrapper, and the .NET Framework Language Packs. A well-designed deployment scenario would ensure that the language does not change as the user progresses from one stage of deployment to the next. Obviously, it is undesirable to have the `publish.htm` in English, the bootstrapper in French, and the ClickOnce dialogs in German. Your ClickOnce strategy will be determined by those elements that you have control over and those elements that you do not. You have control over the `publish.htm` file because this is simply HTML that you can rewrite. You have control over the ClickOnce bootstrapper language because you can create new `setup.xml` files for your required languages. You do not have control over .NET Framework Language Packs because you are limited to the languages supported by Microsoft. You probably do not have control over the language version of the operating system that your users are running. Based on a lowest-common-denominator approach, you should restrict yourself primarily to the language version of the operating systems on which your application will run, and then to languages for which a .NET Framework Language Pack exists.

Deploying a Single Culture Using msbuild

Visual Studio is great for interactive development, but the .NET Framework 2.0 msbuild command-line utility is more appropriate for automating builds and automating publishing. To build a project from the command line, open a .NET Framework SDK Command Prompt (from the Microsoft .NET Framework SDK v2.0 program group), change directory to your application's source folder, and enter this:

```
msbuild
```

The default target for msbuild is "`build`", so this is the same as the following:

```
msbuild /target:build
```

To publish your application (i.e., deploy it using ClickOnce), enter this:

```
msbuild /target:publish
```

To override a setting in the application's project file (i.e., the values set in the Publish page of the project's properties), use the `/property` switch:

```
msbuild /target:publish /property:ProductName=TimeZones
```

Note that not all settings in the project file are applied when building from the command line. For example, the "Automatically increment revision with each release" check box does not apply when building using the command line, so no matter how many times you build using the command line, the revision number will not change. You can specify the full version number using the `ApplicationVersion` property, or, if this property ends in a "*" you can specify just the revision number (which is substituted for the "*") using the `ApplicationRevision` property.

ClickOnce applications are published to a folder called "`<Application>.publish`" beneath the application's output folder. So if your project file is in `\WindowsApplication1`, the application will be published to `\WindowsApplication1\bin\Debug\WindowsApplication1.publish`. After the application has been published to this location, Visual Studio 2005 copies the published files to their deployment location. If you are publishing using IIS, this is something like: `\INetPub\wwwroot\WindowsApplication1`. Note that, unlike Visual Studio 2005, msbuild does *not* copy the published files to the deployment location when publishing is complete. If you use msbuild directly, you assume responsibility for copying the published files to the deployment location.

To publish your application using msbuild, open a .NET Framework SDK Command Prompt and, from your application's folder, run msbuild and specify the `TargetCulture`:

```
msbuild /target:publish /property:TargetCulture=fr
/property:PublishUrl=http://localhost/WindowsApplication1/fr
```

When the publish is complete, copy the files from the temporary publish directory to the publish destination (e.g., `\inetpub\wwwroot\WindowsApplication1`).

Another localization issue to consider is that your publisher name and product name form part of the installation process and are used in the Start menu item and Add/Remove Programs item. If these differ in different cultures, you must include these differences in your language-specific publishing. You can specify the publisher name in msbuild using the `PublisherName` property, and you can specify the product name using the `ProductName` property.

Deploying All Cultures Using Visual Studio 2005

The scenario that we have looked at so far deploys a single-culture version of the application. If your application has more than one culture, you might like to deploy all cultures together. This scenario matches the typical Windows Installer deployment model used prior to ClickOnce. To deploy all cultures, you open the ClickOnce Application Files dialog (see Figure 4.14) and set all satellite assemblies' Publish Status to `Include`. This solves the immediate problem but introduces two new problems. First, the Publish language is no longer very meaningful and should not be used. Recall that the Publish language has two purposes: to automatically include and exclude satellite assemblies, and to specify the ClickOnce bootstrapper culture. The first use is now obsolete because we have taken direct control over the inclusion or exclusion of satellite assemblies. The second use is not meaningful anymore because no single language works for all users of the application. If the Publish language is left as "(`Default`)", it defaults to the Visual Studio language. Whatever decision you make for the language of `publish.htm` and the ClickOnce bootstrapper, remember that it is a single language for all users, and that the language the ClickOnce dialogs use depends on the client's machine and might not necessarily be the same.

The second problem that this scenario introduces is unnecessary downloads during updating. When you update your application and republish it, all users get the updated version of the application (according to your update policy). The problem is that they get all satellite assemblies, regardless of whether they want them. So the French users will also get the updates to the German satellite assemblies. Whereas each individual user might not be overly concerned about the extra download time, the cumulative effect on your server might not be so easily overlooked.

Deploying All Cultures Using msbuild

Deploying all cultures using msbuild is a relatively simple matter because the `TargetCulture` property supports the "*" wildcard:

```
msbuild /target:publish /property:TargetCulture=*
/property:PublishUrl=http://localhost/WindowsApplication1
```

Deploying All Cultures Individually Using Visual Studio 2005

Perhaps the optimum ClickOnce solution in internationalization terms is to deploy all cultures individually. Each culture (or group of cultures) is deployed to a separate location, so the French group of cultures (e.g., French, French (France) and French (Canada)) is deployed to, say, `\inetpub\wwwroot\WindowsApplication1\fr` and the Spanish group of cultures (e.g., Spanish, Spanish (Spain), and Spanish (Mexico)) is deployed to, say, `\inetpub\wwwroot\WindowsApplication1\es`. The French deployment would use a French `publish.htm` and a French ClickOnce bootstrapper, and the Spanish deployment would use a Spanish `publish.htm` and a Spanish ClickOnce bootstrapper. Certainly, this demands the greatest deployment (and maintenance) effort, but it provides the best user experience and best update performance (because users download only those satellite assemblies that are relevant to them).

Deploying all cultures individually in Visual Studio 2005 is a laborious process. You should start by considering whether to uncheck the "Automatically increment revision with each publish" check box in the Publish properties. If you uncheck this check box, all language versions will have the same publish version. This might be convenient at first, but it might not last. Bear in mind that the publish version is not the same as the build version. The build version refers to the application, whereas the publish version refers to the version of the publish operation. If you intend to update satellite resources independently of the application itself (so that typos can be fixed, for example), you will not want to republish every language when only one language changes. If this is the case, there is no value in keeping the publish version in step for all languages.

The effort involved in publishing each culture depends on whether you publish groups of cultures or individual cultures. The latter is the simplest approach because you can simply leave the Publish Status of all satellite assemblies as "Auto" and set the Publish language to the culture to be published. Finally, set the publishing location (on the main Publish properties page) to a specific location, e.g., http://localhost/WindowsApplication/fr. Then repeat the process for each culture, changing the Publish language and Publish location appropriately.

However, if you want to publish groups of cultures, you cannot rely on the inclusion or exclusion of satellite assemblies using the "Auto" Publish Status. Instead, you must explicitly set each satellite assembly to either Include or Exclude each time before you publish. So, for example, you would set the Publish Status of the French, French (France), and French (Canada) satellite assemblies to Include and the Publish Status of all other satellite assemblies to Exclude, and then set the Publish language to French and the Publish location to http://localhost/Windows Application/fr, and publish. Then repeat the process for the Spanish group of cultures, and so on. The result is a lot of error-prone work.

Deploying All Cultures Individually Using msbuild

To publish all cultures individually using msbuild, open a .NET Framework SDK Command Prompt and, from your application's folder, run msbuild:

```
msbuild /target:publish /property:TargetCulture=fr
/property:PublishUrl=http://localhost/WindowsApplication1/fr

msbuild /target:publish /property:TargetCulture=es
/property:PublishUrl=http://localhost/WindowsApplication1/es
```

These two commands publish first the French culture and then, separately, the Spanish culture. For these commands to work correctly, the satellite assemblies'

Publish Status must be set to `Auto` so that they can be included or excluded using the `TargetCulture` property. This works well for including a single culture in a publish operation. Unfortunately, it is not possible to set the Publish Status of a satellite assembly from the msbuild command line. This means that it is not possible to specify whether a satellite assembly should be included or excluded from a given publish operation, so there is no built-in capability to publish a group of related cultures (e.g., `French`, `French (France)`, and `French (Canada)`) in a single operation. You have two choices: either publish every specific culture individually (i.e., publish the `French` culture and then the `French (France)` culture and then the `French (Canada)` culture) or else write a utility to modify the `.csproj` file before each build. The `.csproj` file contains a list of all the files that can be published and, most important, their Publish Status. Here is the entry for the French satellite assembly:

```
<PublishFile Include="fr\WindowsApplication1.resources">
  <InProject>False</InProject>
  <Group>
  </Group>
  <TargetPath>
  </TargetPath>
  <PublishState>Exclude</PublishState>
  <FileType>Satellite</FileType>
</PublishFile>
```

Such a utility would change the `PublishState` element to `Include` for the given `PublishFile`.

Download On Demand

Another publish and deployment scenario that you could consider is to let the user delay the decision on their choice of language until runtime. In this scenario you publish the entire application with all languages to a single location. However, in the Application Files dialog (see Figure 4.18) you set all satellite assemblies to Include. In addition you assign a Download Group name to each of the assemblies. I recommend using the culture identifier (e.g. fr, es) to identify the file group but this is only a convention; you could just as easily use the full name (e.g. French, Spanish).

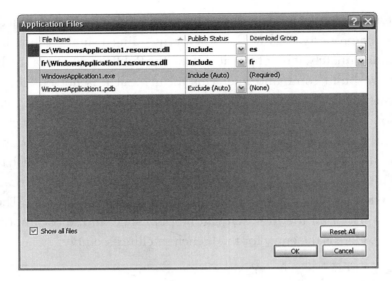

Figure 4.18   ClickOnce Application Files Dialog Showing Satellite Assemblies in Download Groups

Any file that is part of a Download Group is not automatically downloaded by the client. Instead these files are downloaded on demand. This means that when your users download your application they will receive only the fallback assemblies initially. Your application would include a means by which the user can select their choice of language. Let's say you provide a menu with French and Spanish menu items then the French menu item would include the following code:

```
if (!ApplicationDeployment.CurrentDeployment.
IsFileGroupDownloaded("fr"))
    ApplicationDeployment.CurrentDeployment.DownloadFileGroup("fr");
```

The IsFileGroupDownloaded returns True if the given file group has already been downloaded for this version. The DownloadFileGroup downloads the files in the given file group.

This solution has pros and cons. On the upside it is simple to configure and publish the application. In addition there is a single publish location that is shared across all languages and the download demand on your servers is as low as possible. On the downside the use of the ClickOnce API demands that your application is installed with Full Trust. In addition this solution is slightly intrusive in that the application must be modified in order to support the solution. A further problem is that the ClickOnce application does not automatically download previously down-loaded groups when a new version of the application is downloaded. This problem can be solved by persisting the user's language preference and adding this code to the application's startup code:

```
if (ApplicationDeployment.CurrentDeployment.IsFirstRun)
{
    Properties.Settings settings = new Properties.Settings();
    if (settings.UICulture == "fr")
        ApplicationDeployment.CurrentDeployment.
        DownloadFileGroup("fr");
    else if (settings.UICulture == "es")
        ApplicationDeployment.CurrentDeployment.
        DownloadFileGroup("es");
}
```

This code checks that the application is being run for the first time (which it will be if a new version has been downloaded), gets the user's UICulture from the application's settings and uses DownloadFileGroup to get the file group that corresponds to the user's language preference.

The final problem with this solution is that there is no automated way to install a corresponding .NET Framework Language Pack on the user's machine. The problem here is that the relevant .NET Framework Language Pack can only be installed by the ClickOnce bootstrapper and the user's choice of language isn't made until the application is running, which is after the bootstrapper has run.

.NET Framework Language Packs and ClickOnce Prerequisites

ClickOnce enables you to add prerequisites to your deployment that are installed by the ClickOnce bootstrapper before your application is installed. Primarily, this includes the .NET Framework 2.0, but ClickOnce recognizes many other prerequisites and enables you to add your own prerequisites. An obvious prerequisite for an internationalized application is one or more .NET Framework Language Packs. By default, these do not appear in the ClickOnce prerequisites dialog (click the Prerequisites… button in the project's properties Publish tab). However, after downloading a .NET Framework Language Pack, you can add it as a custom prerequisite. To make a custom prerequisite available to Visual Studio 2005 you need to create a new folder in the `%FrameworkSDK%\Bootstrapper\Packages` folder containing a `product.xml` file and a culture specific folder containing a package.xml. You could learn the format of these files and write them by hand but a simpler solution would be to download the Bootstrapper Manifest Generator (http://www.gotdotnet.com/workspaces/workspace.aspx?id=ddb4f08c-7d7c-4f44-a009-ea19fc812545) and use it to create these files and build the resulting custom prerequisite.

There are two approaches that you can take to build a custom pre-requisite product and we will cover both in this section. The first is to build a single custom pre-requisite product that includes a .NET Framework Language Pack for each culture (see Figure 4.19).

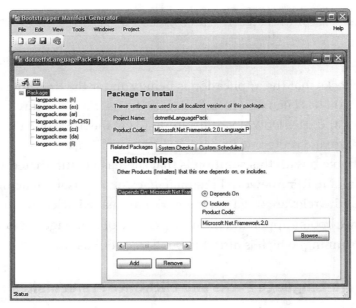

Figure 4.19　Bootstrapper Manifest Generator Showing One Product that Includes Many Packages

In Visual Studio 2005 the pre-requisites dialog shows a single product: the .NET Framework Language Pack (see Figure 4.20).

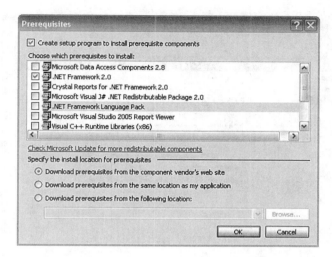

Figure 4.20   Visual Studio 2005 ClickOnce Prerequisite Showing One Product
that Includes Many Packages

The product is used as a group name for all of the .NET Framework Language Packs that you have included in the product. When you publish your application just one of these language packs will be included in the ClickOnce bootstrapper. The selection is made by matching the Publish language with a package for the same culture. This approach works well if you want to deploy a single .NET Framework Language Pack with your application and you use the Publish language to drive the language selection process.

The second, less likely, approach is to build a separate custom pre-requisite product for each .NET Framework Language Pack. Figure 4.21 shows a single product containing the French .NET Framework Language Pack. In this example the product has a single package that is not specific to a culture. You would create a separate product for each language.

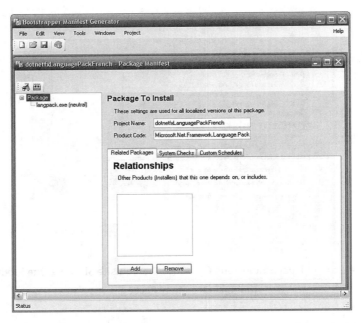

Figure 4.21   Bootstrapper Manifest Generator Showing One Product that Includes One Package

In Visual Studio 2005 the prerequisites dialog shows a product for each language (see Figure 4.22).

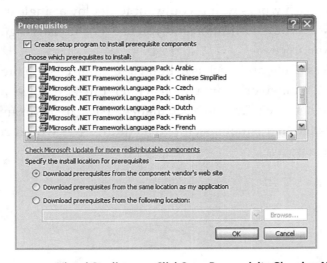

Figure 4.22   Visual Studio 2005 ClickOnce Prerequisite Showing Many
Products that Includes a Single Package Each

In this scenario each language-specific .NET Framework Language Pack product must be selected explicitly and the Publish language plays no part in the selection process. This approach requires greater configuration during the publish stage but it allows you to select more than one .NET Framework Language Pack should this be necessary for your application.

Thread.CurrentThread.CurrentCulture and ClickOnce Security

Internationalized applications also have security considerations when deployed as ClickOnce applications. You should consider how the application's `Thread.CurrentThread.CurrentCulture` is set because the application requires the `ControlThread` flag security permission to set this property. ClickOnce applications adopt their security settings from the zone they were installed from. So if you install the application from a remote Web server, the application uses the Internet security zone settings. Similarly, if you install from a path on a file server, the application uses the Local Intranet security zone settings. Neither the Internet nor the Local Intranet security zones include the necessary permission for the application to change the `Thread.CurrentThread.CurrentCulture` property. Only if the application is installed using Full Trust (i.e., it is installed from a local path or from a CD, or it demands Full Trust) or if the application has a Trust License (see "Trusted Application Deployment" in the .NET Framework SDK Help) will the application have the necessary permission to allow this property to be set. The `Thread.CurrentThread.CurrentUICulture` does not require security permissions to set its value. You can configure your application's security requirements from the project's properties Security tab (see Figure 4.23).

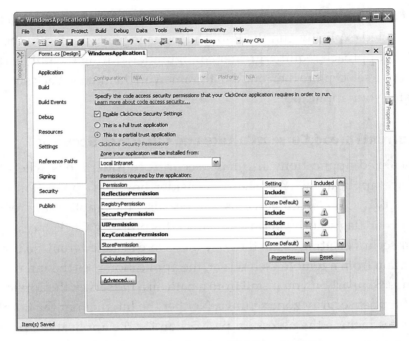

Figure 4.23   Configuring ClickOnce Security

If you click the Calculate Permissions button (positioned just below the "Permissions required by the application" grid), Visual Studio 2005 runs `permcalc.exe` to calculate the security permissions that your application requires and then sets those permissions in the grid above the button. Notice the warning yellow triangle with the exclamation mark in the `SecurityPermission` line. Select this line, click the Properties... button (see Figure 4.24), and note the status of the "Enable thread control" permission. This permission is required when the `CurrentCulture` is set in code such as this:

```
Thread.CurrentThread.CurrentCulture =
    Thread.CurrentThread.CurrentUICulture;
```

The same issue applies to file-based resource managers created using `Resource-Manager.CreateFileBasedResourceManager` because these resource managers require `FileIOPermission`.

Figure 4.24   ClickOnce Permission Settings

Where Are We?

In this chapter, we covered the internationalization issues that are specific to Windows Forms applications. You learned how to use Visual Studio to make forms localizable and to localize them, and you saw that this rests on the resource technology we discussed in the previous chapter. We looked at the different serialization models used by Visual Studio 2003 and Visual Studio 2005, and we compared their relative merits and implementations. We looked at how the user can specify the user interface culture, and how an application can cope with its culture changing without having to restart the application. We saw that the .NET Framework's dialog components and classes depend on the operating system or .NET Framework Language Pack for their resources, and that this can be either a curse or a blessing, depending on your application. We looked at the Windows Resource Localization Editor and saw that it is a great tool that can be made to work with a little thought. Finally, we looked at the way ClickOnce deploys localized applications and saw that localized applications need some additional attention to get the most from this powerful technology.

■5■
ASP.NET Specifics

W EB APPLICATIONS DEMAND INTERNATIONALIZATION perhaps more than any other type of application. Their very medium, the World Wide Web, is by definition global. Access is often available to any person with a browser anywhere in the world. Despite this, ASP.NET started life with very low support for internationalization. In contrast, ASP.NET 2 is a quantum leap forward. In this chapter, we start by looking at the internationalization story in ASP.NET 1.1. This forms a bedrock upon which the new support in ASP.NET 2 rests. Even if you intend to jump straight into internationalization in ASP.NET 2, I recommend that you cover the basics first. The second half of this chapter is devoted exclusively to the new enhancements in ASP.NET 2; if you are using ASP.NET 1.1 and do not intend to upgrade (although you would be missing out on considerable internationalization support) you can skip this half.

Localizability in .NET 1.1

Making an ASP.NET application localizable in the .NET Framework 1.1 is all your own work. Visual Studio 2003 offers no facilities to help you with this process, and the .NET Framework 1.1 offers no facilities beyond what we have seen so far. This means that your ASP.NET application handles this problem "manually" at every stage using the basic functionality that we saw in Chapter 3, "An Introduction to Internationalization." In this section, we localize an ASP.NET application. In subsequent sections, we add processing to handle the user's language preference.

To show how to localize an ASP.NET 1.1 application, we work through an example. Create a new ASP.NET Web Application and add a table, two labels (User Name and Password), two TextBoxes, and a Button (Login) so that the resulting page looks like Figure 5.1.

Figure 5.1   Example ASP.NET 1.1 Web Form before Localization

Add a new resource file to hold the page's resources. (In Solution Explorer, right-click the project; select Add, Add New Item…; select Assembly Resource File.) Call the resource file WebForm1Resources.resx. For each property that should be localized, add an entry to the resource file. Figure 5.2 shows the Resource Editor with the Text properties for the labels and button.

name	value	comment	type	mimetype
Label1.Text	User Name	(null)	(null)	(null)
Label2.Text	Password	(null)	(null)	(null)
Button1.Text	Login	(null)	(null)	(null)

Figure 5.2   Resource Editor with Entries for the Web Form's Controls

Add a private field to the page to hold a ResourceManager:

```
private ResourceManager resourceManager;
```

Add the following assignment to the page's Load event:

```
resourceManager = new ResourceManager(
    "WebApplication1.WebForm1Resources",
    System.Reflection.Assembly.GetExecutingAssembly());
```

If your application is not called `WebApplication1`, you should change the name-space used in the `ResourceManager` constructor's first parameter. Now we need to load each of the resources. Add the following code to the page's `Load` event after the previous line:

```
Label1.Text  = resourceManager.GetString("Label1.Text");
Label2.Text  = resourceManager.GetString("Label2.Text");
Button1.Text = resourceManager.GetString("Button1.Text");
```

> Note that for this solution to be effective, all controls that have localizable content must have an ID and have `runat="server"`.

At this stage, the application is localizable, but it has not yet been localized. Copy the `WebForm1Resources.resx` file to `WebForm1Resources.fr.resx` and translate each of the items into French. The application has now been localized, but so far users are unable to specify that they want to see the French version. The application's culture will be determined by the default values for `CurrentCulture` and `Current UICulture`. In other words, they will be determined by the language version of Windows on which the application is running and the culture set in the Regional and Language Options dialog for the user account on which ASP.NET is running. These settings are likely to be of use to your user only by coincidence.

Automating Resource Assignment

The previous example shows the mechanism of retrieving resources and applying them to their respective properties of their respective controls. It is easy to under-stand and is useful for demonstrating how the process works. However, as far as production code goes, it is lacking. The problem is that it is fragile. It requires the developer to remember to add an assignment for every property that should be localizable. On a form with many controls, the maintenance of this block of code is time-consuming and error prone. A better solution is a solution that does not require the code to be modified. This section explains this solution.

Remove the three property assignments and replace them with the following single call:

```
ApplyResources(resourceManager, this);
```

ApplyResources is a protected static method that you would add to a base page class. It is included in the downloadable source code for this book and is shown shortly. The essential strategy is that it iterates through all of the resources for the CurrentUICulture looking for controls that have the same name as the controls in the resources, and properties of those controls that have the same name as the properties in the resources, and assigns the resource value to those properties. ApplyResources is implemented like this:

```
protected static void ApplyResources(
    ResourceManager resourceManager, Page page)
{
    HtmlForm htmlForm = GetHtmlForm(page);
    if (htmlForm != null)
    {
        ResourceSet resourceSet = resourceManager.GetResourceSet(
            CultureInfo.CurrentUICulture, true, true);

        IDictionaryEnumerator enumerator =
            resourceSet.GetEnumerator();

        while (enumerator.MoveNext())
        {
            ApplyResources(htmlForm,
                enumerator.Key.ToString(), enumerator.Value);
        }
    }
}
```

ApplyResources gets the HtmlForm from the page using the following method:

```
private static HtmlForm GetHtmlForm(Page page)
{
    foreach(Control control in page.Controls)
    {
        if (control is HtmlForm)
            return (HtmlForm) control;
    }
    return null;
}
```

ApplyResources gets the ResourceSet (the set of resource entries) for the CurrentUICulture. It iterates through each of the entries, calling an overloaded

`ApplyResources` method to apply the resource entry to the form. The overloaded `ApplyResources` is this:

```
protected static void ApplyResources(
    HtmlForm htmlForm, string key, object value)
{
    int periodIndex = key.IndexOf(".");
    if (periodIndex > -1)
    {
        string controlID = key.Substring(0, periodIndex);
        Control control = GetControl(htmlForm, controlID);
        if (control != null)
        {
            string propertyName = key.Substring(periodIndex + 1);

            PropertyInfo propertyInfo =
                control.GetType().GetProperty(propertyName);
            if (propertyInfo != null)
                propertyInfo.SetValue(
                    control, value, new object[] {});
        }
    }
}
```

The overloaded `ApplyResources` method splits the key (e.g., `Label1.Text`) into its control ID (i.e., `Label1`) and its property name (i.e., `Text`). It calls `GetControl` to get a control that corresponds to the control ID:

```
protected static Control GetControl(
    HtmlForm htmlForm, string controlID)
{
    foreach(Control control in htmlForm.Controls)
    {
        if (String.Compare(control.ID, controlID, true,
            CultureInfo.InvariantCulture) == 0)
            return control;
    }
    return null;
}
```

The overloaded `ApplyResources` method uses reflection to get a `PropertyInfo` for the named property and calls its `SetValue` method to assign the value from the resource to the control's property.

Static Text

Static text represents a fundamental problem for an internationalized application: It cannot easily be localized. Type any text directly onto a Web form, and this text is stored as static text in the aspx page. At compile time, the static text is converted to a `LiteralControl` in the page's control tree. The `LiteralControl` is not a server-side control and can be accessed only by walking through the `HtmlForm`'s Controls. The best solution is to replace the static text with either a server-side `Label` control or a server-side `Literal` control (do not confuse a "`Literal` control" with a "`LiteralControl` control"). A `Label` control differs from a `Literal` control only in that a `Label` control can have a style and a `Literal` control cannot.

> There is a performance penalty to pay for placing all text in `Label` or `Literal` controls as opposed to typing it directly onto a page. Unfortunately, this is a penalty that you will have to endure if you want your application to be localized.

If you are unable to convert all the static text in your application to `Label`s or `Literal`s, a considerably poorer solution would be to search for known unlocalized strings and replace them with localized strings. For example, assume that a page contains "Here is some static text." The following call to `ReplaceStaticText` (included in the downloadable source code for this book) attempts to localize it:

```
ReplaceStaticText(
    "Here is some static text",
    "Voici un certain texte statique");
```

Of course, in practice you would create a resource called, say, `HereIsSomeStaticText`, and read it using a `ResourceManager`:

```
ReplaceStaticText (
    "Here is some static text",
    resourceManager.GetString("HereIsSomeStaticText"));
```

The `ReplaceStaticText` method is this:

```
private void ReplaceStaticText (
    string fallbackString, string localizedString)
{
    HtmlForm htmlForm = GetHtmlForm(this);
    foreach(Control control in htmlForm.Controls)
    {
        if (control is LiteralControl)
        {
            LiteralControl literalControl =
                (LiteralControl) control;

            literalControl.Text = literalControl.Text.Replace(
                fallbackString, localizedString);
        }
    }
}
```

The `ReplaceStaticText` method looks for every `LiteralControl` and searches for the original fallback text, replacing it with the translated text. You might prefer to break out of the loop having found a successful match, but this assumes that each string is unique to a page, and that is not necessarily true. Furthermore, the code assumes that no text is a substring of another text. So, for example, you don't have a string of `"Go"` and a second string of `"Going, Going, Gone"`. The `String.Replace` method is used because the `LiteralControl`'s `Text` value is almost certainly not exactly equal to `"Here is some static text"`. In practice, it is more likely to be something like this:

```
</P>\r\n\t\t\t<P> </P>\r\n\t\t\t<P>Here is some static text
</P>\r\n\t\t\t<P></P>\r\n\t\t\t
```

All the text and HTML immediately before and after the string is also added to the `LiteralControl`. Hopefully when you look at this "solution," you will decide that the effort involved in working around the problem (not to mention its inherent inaccuracy) is greater than solving the problem properly.

Calendar Control

Another ASP.NET control that you might consider in the internationalization of your Web application is the `Calendar` control. The good news is that the `Calendar` control is automatically localized without you having to take any action. The `System.Web.UI.WebControls.Calendar` control uses the .NET Framework's `System.Globalization.Calendar` classes (see Chapter 6, "Globalization") to load its display information. The .NET Framework includes all of the day and month names for all supported cultures, so no .NET Framework Language Packs need to be installed on the Web server to fully localize this control.

Potentially, there is also some bad news. Because the `WebControls.Calendar` class uses the `Globalization.Calendar` classes, the control is dependent upon the `CurrentCulture` to draw its localized resources. This is contrary to what you might have expected because the user interface normally uses the `CurrentUICulture` to draw its resources. In practice, this will not make any difference to your application if your application does not make a distinction between `CurrentCulture` and `CurrentUICulture`, and these values are always kept in synch. However, if you allow them to be set independently of each other and you use the `Calendar` control, your application will have a schizophrenic user interface, with the majority of the application using one culture and the `Calendar` controls using another.

Setting and Recognizing the Culture

Users need a means of specifying what culture they would like the application to use. You can provide support for this in several ways. You could detect the user's culture from the browser; you could provide an option to set the culture in your application; or you could provide a combination of both, in which you detect the initial setting from the browser and let the user change the setting in the application. Over the next few sections, we look at different options for allowing users to set the culture and recognizing the culture that they have set.

Setting the Culture in Internet Explorer

In this section, we look at allowing the user to specify the culture in Internet Explorer.

A small switch of terminology occurs here because what the .NET Framework refers to as a culture, HTTP refers to as a language.

The user's language preference is set in the `HTTP_ACCEPT_LANGUAGES` request header. This value is reflected in the `Request.UserLanguages` property, which is an array of strings. The HTTP request header doesn't make a distinction between a language used for globalization and a language used for retrieving resources for the user interface, so its single setting is typically used for both purposes. A user sets the language preference in Internet Explorer by selecting Tools, Internet Options… and clicking on the Languages… button (see Figure 5.3).

Figure 5.3   Setting the Culture in Internet Explorer

The user can set any number of language settings here. The implication is that the first language (i.e., the language at the top of the list) is the most preferred language, and subsequent languages are acceptable, but each is less preferable.

Recognizing the User Culture

The next step is to recognize and use the user's language setting. Several ways exist for achieving this, and we examine each. The first and simplest is to set the culture in the page's `Load` event:

```
private void Page_Load(object sender, System.EventArgs e)
{
    if (Request.UserLanguages != null &&
        Request.UserLanguages.GetLength(0) > 0)
    {
        CultureInfo cultureInfo =
            new CultureInfo(Request.UserLanguages[0]);
```

```
        Thread.CurrentThread.CurrentUICulture = cultureInfo;
        Thread.CurrentThread.CurrentCulture =
            CultureInfo.CreateSpecificCulture(cultureInfo.Name);
    }
etc. etc.
```

This code gets the user's language preference from the first element of the `Request.UserLanguages` array. If the user's settings are those shown in Figure 5.3, `Request.UserLanguages[0]` will be "en-US". We create a new `CultureInfo` object and assign it to `CurrentUICulture`. The next line uses `CultureInfo.CreateSpecificCulture` to create a specific culture from a potentially neutral culture. In this example the culture will be no different (i.e., it will be "en-US"), but if the original language preference was "en", the specific culture would be "en-US". Recall that this step is necessary because `CurrentCulture` must be culture-specific. Later in this chapter, we implement a more sophisticated version of this first attempt that iterates through each of the language preferences looking for a language that matches the application's supported languages.

Of course, the implementation given here is very trusting. It makes the assumption that the language chosen by the user is one that the .NET Framework recognizes. Users are free to enter a language that is not supported by the .NET Framework (e.g., Bengali is not supported by the .NET Framework 1.1), or users can enter a custom language that they type in (e.g., "xx"). In these circumstances, the `CultureInfo` constructor will throw an exception and the application will stop. A sensible enhancement to the previous code, therefore, is to trap exceptions:

```
private void Page_Load(object sender, System.EventArgs e)
{
    if (Request.UserLanguages != null &&
        Request.UserLanguages.GetLength(0) > 0)
    {
        try
        {
            CultureInfo cultureInfo =
                new CultureInfo(Request.UserLanguages[0]);

            Thread.CurrentThread.CurrentUICulture = cultureInfo;

            Thread.CurrentThread.CurrentCulture =
                CultureInfo.CreateSpecificCulture(cultureInfo.Name);
        }
```

```
        catch (ArgumentException)
        {
        }
    }
etc. etc.
```

This solution works fine for the example that we have been working with, but it suffers from two problems. First, the solution is a page-wide solution and not an application-wide solution. Second, the solution occurs a little too late in the request pipeline for some code. The first problem could be solved easily by putting the code in a page base class and ensuring that all pages inherit from the page base class; this is not a difficult problem to solve. But the second problem requires moving the code out of the page class altogether. The `HttpApplication.BeginRequest` method is the first application method to be called in the ASP.NET pipeline, and setting the culture here ensures that all subsequent code uses the correct culture. Open `Global.asax.cs` and add the following code. (If you don't have a Global Application Class, then in Solution Explorer, right-click the project; select Add, Add New Item…; select Global Application Class; and click Open):

```
protected void Application_BeginRequest(Object sender, EventArgs e)
{
    SetCultureFromUserLanguage();
}
private void SetCultureFromUserLanguage()
{
    if (Request.UserLanguages != null &&
        Request.UserLanguages.GetLength(0) > 0)
    {
        try
        {
            CultureInfo cultureInfo =
                new CultureInfo(Request.UserLanguages[0]);

            Thread.CurrentThread.CurrentUICulture = cultureInfo;

            Thread.CurrentThread.CurrentCulture =
                CultureInfo.CreateSpecificCulture(cultureInfo.Name);
        }
        catch (ArgumentException)
        {
        }
    }
}
```

Unfortunately, this solution is not without its own problems. The `BeginRequest` method occurs too early in the pipeline for the `Session` variable to be available. This means that if you allow users to set their own preferences independently of the browser's language preference and you store their preference in the `Session` variable, the `BeginRequest` method occurs too early to make use of the setting. A compromise is to use the `HttpApplication.AcquireRequestState` event, which occurs after the `Session` variable has been initialized but before the `Page.Load` event. Assuming that you have a page that sets `Session["Culture"]` to a culture string, change the Global `HttpApplication` constructor to this:

```
public Global()
{
    InitializeComponent();

    AcquireRequestState +=
        new EventHandler(Global_AcquireRequestState);
}
```

Now add the `Global_AcquireRequestState` method:

```
private void Global_AcquireRequestState(object sender, EventArgs e)
{
    if (Session["Culture"] != null)
    {
        Thread.CurrentThread.CurrentCulture =
            new CultureInfo(Session["Culture"].ToString());

        Thread.CurrentThread.CurrentUICulture =
            Thread.CurrentThread.CurrentCulture;
    }
    else
        SetCultureFromUserLanguage();
}
```

This solution has the following benefits:

- It can be applied to all requests in the application.
- It occurs earlier in the pipeline than `Page.Load`.
- It respects the user's preference if any has been set in the `Session` variable.
- It defaults the culture to the user's browser setting if there is no preference in the `Session` variable.

Setting the Culture in Configuration Files

You can, of course, ignore the user's language preference altogether and hard-code the culture. Both `machine.config` (which applies to all Web sites on the machine) and `web.config` (which applies to a single Web site) have a globalization element that allows the `Culture` and `UICulture` to be specified. The following globalization element sets the `CurrentCulture` to French (France) and `CurrentUICulture` to French:

```
<globalization culture="fr-FR" uiCulture="fr"/>
```

This setting initializes the culture for the Web site but does not prevent it from being changed subsequently. You might want to use this setting to provide a default for users who do not have a language preference set in their browser. This is preferable to relying on the default values of `CurrentCulture` and `CurrentUICulture` because these values are set in the operating system under the user account under which ASP.NET is running and apply to all Web sites that run under the same user account. As such, you might not have control over these settings. In this scenario, you would set the default culture in `web.config` and attempt to get the user's language preference in either the `Page` or `HttpApplication` class.

Caching Output by Culture

ASP.NET's caching mechanism makes a considerable difference to an application's performance. When a page is requested for the first time, a copy of the page is placed in a cache. Subsequent requests for the same page get the page from the cache without having to regenerate the page again. Caching is important from an internationalization viewpoint because your caching mechanism needs to respect the culture of the cached page. However, by default, the caching mechanism does not. Consider what happens in an application that caches pages without respect for the page's culture. Let's say the page's script includes the following line to cache the page for 5 minutes:

```
<% @Outputcache Duration=300 VaryByParam=none%>
```

When the first user requests this page, it will be added to the cache. Let's say that the first user has a language preference of French (France). From here on, all users requesting this page will receive the cached page—i.e., the French (France) page—regardless of their own language preference. This is not helpful. We need to cache the page by culture. The solution is to cache by culture using a custom string:

```
<% @Outputcache Duration=20 VaryByParam=none
VaryByCustom="CurrentUICulture"%>
```

The `VaryByCustom` attribute enables us to specify a custom string that we can use to identify the criteria by which the page is cached. This string is passed to the `HttpApplication.GetVaryByCustom` method. We override this method (in `global.asax`) and check the custom string:

```
public override string GetVaryByCustomString(
    HttpContext context, string custom)
{
    if (String.Compare(custom, "CurrentUICulture", true,
        CultureInfo.InvariantCulture) == 0)
        return CultureInfo.CurrentUICulture.Name;
    else
        return base.GetVaryByCustomString (context, custom);
}
```

The `GetVaryByCustomString` method returns a string that identifies the version of the page. In the previous example, the first user to access the page would have a `CurrentUICulture` of "fr-FR". Their copy of the page would be cached as the "fr-FR" page. If the second user to access the page had a language preference of English (United States), the cache would be searched for the requested page with a custom `CurrentUICulture` of "en-US". Because no such page would be in the cache at this point, the page would be generated and added to the cache. Subsequent requests for "fr-FR" or "en-US" pages within 5 minutes would receive the appropriate cached page.

Localizability in Visual Studio 2005

The localization story in Visual Studio 2005 is significantly more advanced than in Visual Studio 2003. To see this in action, create a new ASP.NET Web site and add a table, two labels (User Name and Password), two TextBoxes, and a Button (Login) so that the resulting page looks like Figure 5.4.

Figure 5.4   Example ASP.NET 2.0 Web Form before Localization

Make a note of the page directive:

```
<%@ Page Language="C#" AutoEventWireup="true"
CodeFile="Default.aspx.cs" Inherits="_Default" %>
and also the script for the table:-
<table>
    <tr>
        <td style="width: 100px">
            <asp:Label ID="Label1" runat="server"
            Text="User name"></asp:Label></td>
        <td style="width: 100px">
            <asp:TextBox ID="TextBox1" runat="server">
            </asp:TextBox></td>
    </tr>
    <tr>
        <td style="width: 100px">
            <asp:Label ID="Label2" runat="server"
            Text="Password"></asp:Label></td>
        <td style="width: 100px">
            <asp:TextBox ID="TextBox2" runat="server">
            </asp:TextBox></td>
    </tr>
    <tr>
        <td colspan="2" style="width: 100px">
            <asp:Button ID="Button1" runat="server"
            Text="Login" Width="264px" /></td>
    </tr>
</table>
```

Notice that the text is hard-coded and, therefore, not localizable. To make this Web form localizable, select the Design view and then select Tools, Generate Local Resource. The output window displays a couple progress messages:

```
Start creating resource content and adding 'meta:' attributes to server controls
and directives.
```

```
Finished creating resource content and adding 'meta:' attributes.
```

The Generate Local Resources option performs the following steps:

1. It adds a local resource file.
2. It modifies the page source.

We start by looking at the resource file. If the `App_LocalResources` folder does not already exist, it is created. Into this folder, a resx resource file is added in which the name is the same as the page name, but with an additional "resx" extension. So if the page is `Default.aspx`, the resource file is called `Default.aspx.resx`. For each property of each control where the property is marked with the `Localizable(true)` attribute, a new entry is added to the resource. The entry key is the name of the control plus "Resource1." plus the name of the property (e.g., "`Button1Resource1.Text`"). The entry value is the value of the property at the time the Generate Local Resources menu item was invoked. Figure 5.5 shows the contents of the resx file in Visual Studio 2005's Resource Editor. We can see from this part of the process that all the localizable values have been copied from the source into a resource.

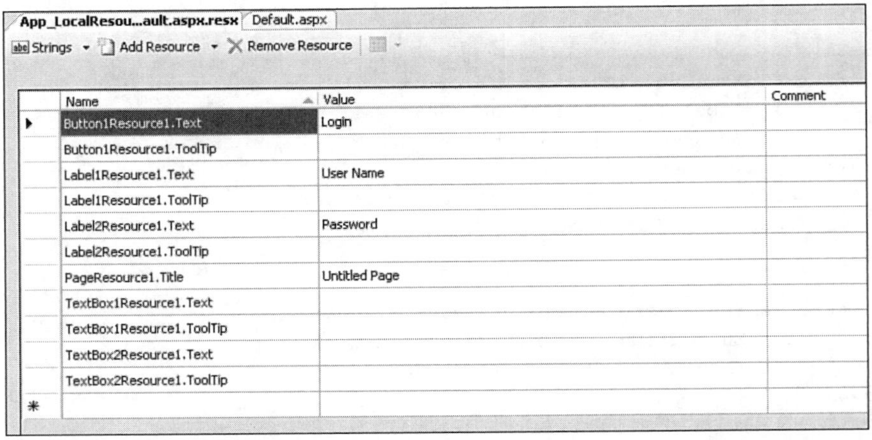

Figure 5.5   Resource Editor Showing Resources Generated by Generate Local Resources

The Generate Local Resources process is dependent upon properties being marked with the `Localizable(true)` attribute. The `Localizable` attribute is used throughout `WebControls`, but it is used considerably less freely in `HtmlControls`. Of all of the `HtmlControls`, only `HtmlAnchor`, `HtmlImage`, `HtmlInputImage`, and `Html Title` have any properties marked with `Localizable(true)`. For this reason, the majority of `HtmlControls` will not be included in the localization process by Generate Local Resources. You should change these controls to their `WebControls` equivalents.

The `WebControls` `Label.Text` and `Literal.Text` properties are marked as localizable in Visual Studio 2005, so static text placed in these controls is easily localizable.

The next change that Generate Local Resources makes is to modify the page source to reference the newly created resources. The first line that is modified is the page directive:

```
<%@ Page Language="C#" AutoEventWireup="true"
CodeFile="Default.aspx.cs" Inherits="_Default"
Culture="auto" meta:resourcekey="PageResource1" UICulture="auto" %>
```

You can see that three attributes (`Culture`, `meta:resourceKey`, and `UICulture`) have been added. We return to the `Culture` and `UICulture` attributes later. The `meta:resourceKey` attribute is the code part of an implicit expression. An implicit expression is the combination of the resources we have already seen and this key. The `meta:resourceKey` attribute specifies the name that is used to identify the resources from which the control's properties are loaded. So the Page's Title is loaded using the `PageResource1.Title` key. Generate Local Resources also adds a `meta:resourceKey` attribute to each of the controls for which resources were extracted:

```
<table>
    <tr>
        <td style="width: 100px">
            <asp:Label ID="Label1" runat="server"
            Text="User Name"
            meta:resourcekey="Label1Resource1">
            </asp:Label></td>
        <td style="width: 100px">
            <asp:TextBox ID="TextBox1" runat="server"
            meta:resourcekey="TextBox1Resource1">
            </asp:TextBox></td>
    </tr>
    <tr>
        <td style="width: 100px">
            <asp:Label ID="Label2" runat="server"
            Text="Password"
            meta:resourcekey="Label2Resource1">
            </asp:Label></td>
        <td style="width: 100px">
            <asp:TextBox ID="TextBox2" runat="server"
            meta:resourcekey="TextBox2Resource1">
            </asp:TextBox></td>
    </tr>
    <tr>
        <td colspan="2" style="width: 100px">
            <asp:Button ID="Button1" runat="server"
            Text="Login" Width="264px"
            meta:resourcekey="Button1Resource1" /></td>
    </tr>
</table>
```

Notice that the original Text attributes (and any other attributes for which a resource was extracted) remain in the source with their original value. At runtime, these values are no longer used. Their only benefit lies in providing a value at design time. This is further reflected in the Properties Window (see Figure 5.6), where properties that are bound by implicit expressions are identified with a pink icon (with an appropriate ToolTip). This serves as a warning that modifying these values here in the Properties Window (or in the source) affects only the appearance at design time, not the appearance at runtime.

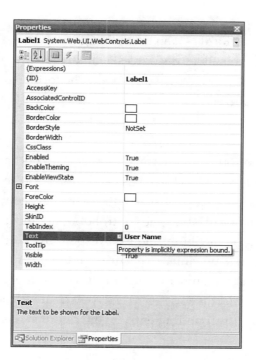

Figure 5.6   The Properties Window Showing Properties with Implicit Expressions

Note that it would be confusing to have a different design-time experience than the runtime experience, so whenever you change the resource value, you should also change the property value to keep them in synch.

At this point, the Web form is localizable but has not yet been localized. To localize the Web form, copy the resx resource file in the `App_LocalResources` folder to a new file in the same folder, and change its name to include a culture name. For example to create a French version of the Web form, copy `Default.aspx.resx` to `Default.aspx.fr.resx`. Now open the French resources in Visual Studio 2005 and translate all of the text into French. If you change your browser's language preferences to French and run the application, you will see the French version of the Web form.

The Visual Studio 2005 Web Form Designer always displays forms using the fallback resources. Unlike the Windows Forms Designer, it does not allow you to view the form using a different set of resources.

Visual Studio 2005's Web Form Designer does not remember that Generate Local Resource has been run on a Web form. When you add a new control to a form, the new control is not automatically localizable. The control does not include the `meta:resourcekey` attribute, and a corresponding entry is not added to the resource file. To ensure that the control is localizable, you must remember to either rerun Generate Local Resources or add the `meta:resourcekey` attribute to the control and create a corresponding entry in the resource file.

You can prevent Generate Local Resources from localizing individual controls by including a `meta:localize` tag in the control and setting its value to `false`:

```
<asp:Label ID="Label1" runat="server" Text="Label"
meta:localize="false"></asp:Label>
```

In this example, the `Label1` control will not be included in the Generate Local Resources process.

How It Works

It is not necessary to know how implicit expressions work in order to use them, so if you are just looking for results, you can skip this section. But for the curious, read on. One of the ways in which you can find out what ASP.NET is actually doing is to look at the source code that it generates. Include the `Debug="true"` attribute in the page directive. Add a `Label` called `LocationLabel` and add the following code to the page's `Load` event:

```
LocationLabel.Text =
    System.Reflection.Assembly.GetExecutingAssembly().Location;
```

When the application is run, the `Debug` attribute ensures that the generated code is saved to disk. The label shows the location of the generated code. Figure 5.7 shows the result when the application is run.

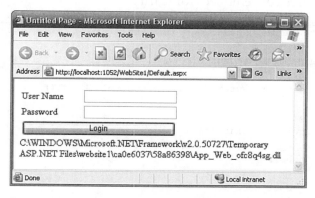

Figure 5.7   Showing the Location of Generated Source Code

Make a note of the name of the DLL (i.e., "`App_Web_ofc8q4sg.dll`" in this example). In the same folder as the DLL, you will find the generated source. The source filenames begin with "`App_Web_`" and use the suffix of the DLL (i.e., "`ofc8q4sg`") with a numbered `.cs` extension (i.e., "`App_Web_ofc8q4sg.0.cs`", "`App_Web_ofc8q4sg.1.cs`"). The "`.0.cs`" is the generated source and the "`.1.cs`" file is your own partial class (i.e., "`Default.aspx.cs`").

In the generated source code, you will find a method called `@__BuildControlform1`. (`@__BuildControlform1` is called by `@__BuildControlTree`, which is called by `FrameworkInitialize`, which is called by the worker process when the page is requested). The following is a heavily edited extract from `@__BuildControlform1`:

```
@__ctrl1 = this.@__BuildControlLabel1();
@__parser.AddParsedSubObject(@__ctrl1);

@__ctrl2 = this.@__BuildControlTextBox1();
@__parser.AddParsedSubObject(@__ctrl2);

@__ctrl3 = this.@__BuildControlLabel2();
@__parser.AddParsedSubObject(@__ctrl3);
```

```
@__ctrl4 = this.@__BuildControlTextBox2();
@__parser.AddParsedSubObject(@__ctrl4);
```

Each control is built up using a method in the generated class, and the resulting object is added to the page's parser. The @__BuildControlLabel1() method is representative of the behavior of all the "BuildControl" methods. Here is the code with the #line directives removed, for clarity:

```
private global::System.Web.UI.WebControls.Label
    @__BuildControlLabel1() {
    global::System.Web.UI.WebControls.Label @__ctrl;

    @__ctrl = new global::System.Web.UI.WebControls.Label();

    this.Label1 = @__ctrl;
    @__ctrl.ApplyStyleSheetSkin(this);

    @__ctrl.ID = "Label1";

    @__ctrl.Text = "User Name";

    @__ctrl.Text = System.Convert.ToString(
        this.GetLocalResourceObject("Label1Resource1.Text"),
        System.Globalization.CultureInfo.CurrentCulture);

    @__ctrl.ToolTip = System.Convert.ToString(
        this.GetLocalResourceObject("Label1Resource1.ToolTip"),
        System.Globalization.CultureInfo.CurrentCulture);

    return @__ctrl;
}
```

Toward the bottom of the method are two assignments to the Label's Text property and one assignment to the Label's Tooltip property. The first assignment to the Label's Text property assigns the value that is set in the IDE. This assignment is redundant because the next line makes an assignment to the same property overwriting the previous value. The second assignment to the control's Text property uses the page's GetLocalResourceObject method to retrieve a resource value using the "Label1Resource1.Text" key. The GetLocalResourceObject in this example ultimately makes a call to ResourceManager.GetObject to retrieve the resource. However, ASP.NET 2.0 is built on a provider model, and, as we see in Chapter 12, "Custom Resource Managers," it is possible to replace the existing model, which uses the `ResourceManager` class, with a different model that potentially uses a different class. In addition, `GetLocalResourceObject` goes to some lengths to identify the location of the resource assemblies. This is particularly necessary if you do not precompile your Web sites and the assemblies have pseudorandom names and are placed in folders with pseudorandom names.

If you previously read Chapter 4, "Windows Forms Specifics," you can see that ASP.NET 2's approach is similar to Windows Forms 1.1's Property Assignment Model, as opposed to Windows Forms 2.0's Property Reflection Model. The Property Assignment Model reads a property value for every property in which its `Localizable` attribute is `true`. The downside to this approach is that every localizable property is pushed to a resource file "just in case" it might be localized. The Property Reflection Model reverses the problem and examines what resources exist and then applies those resources to corresponding properties. Consequently, the Property Reflection Model is more scalable than the Property Assignment Model. ASP.NET does not support an equivalent to the Property Reflection Model in ASP.NET 2.0, but it could be argued that the need for such a model in ASP.NET is not as high as it is in Windows Forms. The main reason for this is that considerably fewer properties are marked with `Localiz-able(true)`. Instead of implying any lesser potential for localization, the problem of needing to localize properties that are less frequently localized is solved a different way. It is solved using Explicit Expressions, which we come to later in this chapter.

Resx Files, Application Domains, and Session State

One of the new features in ASP.NET 2 is that ASP.NET applications watch for changes to resx files. A change to an application's resx file has the same effect as a change to `web.config`: The application domain is unloaded and the application is restarted. There are several consequences to this. First, this makes it easy to change resx files and have their changes incorporated into the application immediately. Second, all state in the application is lost as the application domain is unloaded. Certainly, this is an excellent feature during development and can help your translator/localizer considerably, but for obvious reasons, you should avoid taking advantage of this feature in a production environment if your application state is maintained in the application domain (i.e., the default). You can store your application's state in a separate process using the `Web.config sessionState` element (set the `mode` attribute to either `StateServer` or `SQLServer`).

Automatic Culture Recognition for Individual Pages

In the previous example, you might be wondering why the French form was displayed when we didn't write any code to check the user's language preference and assign a value to the CurrentCulture or CurrentUICulture, as we had to do with the .NET Framework 1.1. Here's where the Culture and UICulture attributes that were added to the page directive by Generate Local Resources come in. The page directive now looks like this:

```
<%@ Page Language="C#" AutoEventWireup="true"
CodeFile="Default.aspx.cs" Inherits="_Default"
Culture="auto" meta:resourcekey="PageResource1" UICulture="auto" %>
```

The Culture and UICulture attributes are set to "auto," a special value indicating that the culture should be set from the first element of the request's User-Languages array. The Culture and UICulture attributes are simply initializers for the Page's Culture and UICulture properties. Contrary to what you already know about the nature of CurrentCulture, the Culture attribute does not have to be a specific culture (e.g., "fr-FR"). If it is assigned a neutral culture (e.g., "fr"), a specific culture (e.g., "fr-FR") is created from the neutral culture using Culture-Info.CreateSpecificCulture. The Culture and UICulture properties have built-in exception handling. If the culture is not recognized by the .NET Framework, the user's language preference is ignored and the culture is unchanged. So if the user's language preference is "xx" (i.e., an invalid culture) or "cy-GB" (Welsh (United Kingdom)), which is available only in Windows XP SP2 and above) and the server does not recognize the "xx" or "cy-GB" culture, no exception escapes the Page's Culture or UICulture properties set methods and the application continues unharmed. You are at liberty to change the value of the Culture and UICulture attributes (or remove them altogether). You can change them to an explicit culture (e.g., "fr", "fr-FR"), which has the effect of ignoring the user's settings and running the page using a hard-wired culture. This can be useful if the nature of the Web site dictates a given culture and the default values for the CurrentCulture and CurrentUICulture for the operating system on which the Web site is running are not suitable for the Web site. Alternatively, a compromise between the "auto" value and an explicit value is to use "auto" with a default. "auto:fr-FR" specifies a default culture ("fr-FR") to fall back to if the user's language preference is either missing or invalid. Note that in this explicit use of a culture name, the `Culture` property must be a specific culture and not a neutral culture.

How It Works

In the Web form's generated class (see the previous "How It Works" section for details on viewing the generated class) is a method called `@__BuildControlTree`. `@__BuildControlTree` is called by `FrameworkInitialize`, which is called by the worker process when the page is requested. The following is the first few lines of the `@__BuildControlTree` method (with the `#line` directives removed, for clarity):

```
private void @__BuildControlTree(Default_aspx @__ctrl) {

    @__ctrl.Culture = "auto";

    @__ctrl.UICulture = "auto";
```

The `@__ctrl` parameter passed to the `@__BuildControlTree` method is the Web form itself (i.e., `this`). The `Page.Culture` and `Page.UICulture` properties recognize the strings `"auto"` and `"auto:<culture>"` to mean that the culture should be taken from `Request.UserLanguages[0]`. `Page.Culture` ensures that a specific culture is created using `CultureInfo.CreateSpecificCulture`.

> Note that this initialization of the `CurrentCulture` and `CurrentUICulture` occurs during the `FrameworkInitialize` method. This method is called *before* any of the page's events fire, so the page's events can assume that the culture is correct.

Manual Culture Recognition for Individual Pages

ASP.NET's automatic culture recognition is very helpful, but there are some situations that it does not cater to. In these circumstances, you need to take a more active role in initializing the culture. As you saw earlier in ASP.NET 1.1, you had to choose a suitable moment in the initialization of the application to set the culture by overriding a method or adding an event that occurred soon enough in the request pipeline. In ASP.NET 2, you are given a method that you can override solely for the purpose of initializing the culture: the `Page.InitializeCulture` method. One of the problems with the automatic culture-detection process is that it looks at only the first of the user's languages preferences. If the preference is bad, it doesn't check subsequent, alternative language choices. The `InitializeCulture` method is overridden like this:

```
protected override void InitializeCulture()
{
    if (Request.UserLanguages != null &&
        Request.UserLanguages.GetLength(0) > 0)
    {
        foreach (string userLanguage in Request.UserLanguages)
        {
            CultureInfo cultureInfo =
                GetCultureInfo(userLanguage, true);
            if (cultureInfo != null)
            {
                Thread.CurrentThread.CurrentUICulture = cultureInfo;

                Thread.CurrentThread.CurrentCulture =
                    CultureInfo.CreateSpecificCulture(
                    cultureInfo.Name);
                break;
            }
        }
    }
}

protected virtual CultureInfo GetCultureInfo(
    string userLanguage, bool useUserOverride)
{
    int semiColonIndex = userLanguage.IndexOf(";");
    if (semiColonIndex != -1)
        userLanguage = userLanguage.Substring(0, semiColonIndex);
    try
    {
        return new CultureInfo(userLanguage, useUserOverride);
    }
    catch (ArgumentException)
    {
        return null;
    }
}
```

This `InitializeCulture` method gets the user's preference from the `Request` object and calls `GetCultureInfo` to get a culture from the user's language preference. The `GetCultureInfo` method strips any weighting setting from the user's language string (the weighting is specified after the semicolon) and then attempts to create a `CultureInfo` from the string, ensuring that `true` is passed for the `useUserOverride` parameter. The attempt to create the new `CultureInfo` is enclosed in a `try/catch` block to smother any exception that might result from a bad culture name.

> `Page.InitializeCulture` is called immediately after the assignment of the `Culture` and `UICulture` properties. This means that (1) `InitializeCulture` can be supplementary to the page's `Culture` and `UICulture` attributes, and (2) `InitializeCulture` is called during the `FrameworkInitialize` method and, therefore, *before* all page events.

Another variation of the previous theme would be to search through the user's language preferences for one of the languages supported by the application. So if the user's language preferences are Japanese, then French, and then English, and the application supports German, French, and English, the user should get French because this is the supported language that mostly closely matches the user's preferences. ASP.NET applications do not have a global store of the languages supported by the application, so you would need to hard-wire this list in code or in the `web.config`, or discover it programmatically by probing directory names (e.g., "de", "fr," and "en," in this example). The code to implement this is the same as in the previous example, with the addition of an `if` to determine whether the user's language preference matches a supported language.

Yet another reason why you might want to override the `InitializeCulture` method is to set the culture based upon an LCID instead of culture name. See the "Alternate Sort Orders" section of Chapter 6 for more details.

The examples in this section make an implicit assumption that the `Culture` and `UICulture` attributes are `auto`. It should be noted that there is no facility in ASP.NET to determine the value of the `Culture` and `UICulture` attributes. Recall from the "How It Works" section that the values of the `Culture` and `UICulture` attributes are built into the page's generated class and assigned to the `Culture` and `UICulture` properties.

These properties translate this temporary value (i.e., "auto") into a `CultureInfo` object. The fact that the attribute is "auto" is lost in this translation process, and it is not possible to interrogate these properties to determine what actual value was assigned to them.

Application-Wide Automatic Culture Recognition

You can see from the "Automatic Culture Recognition for Individual Pages" section that adding `Culture` and `UICulture` attributes to the page directive is clearly a page-wide solution and does not apply to other pages. You might prefer to apply an application-wide solution. Before you do, however, consider for a moment that if every page in your site has "Generate Local Resources" on it, every page will already include a page-level solution, and applying an application-wide solution would be redundant. With that said, let's look at an alternative solution. Earlier in this chapter, we saw that `Web.config` has a globalization element that has `culture` and `uiCulture` attributes to control the `CurrentCulture` and `CurrentUICulture` for all requests that come into the application. In ASP.NET 2, these attributes can be set to "auto":

```
<configuration
    xmlns="http://schemas.microsoft.com/.NetConfiguration/v2.0">
    <appSettings/>
    <connectionStrings/>
    <system.web>
        <globalization culture="auto" uiCulture="auto"/>
    </system.web>
</configuration>
```

You might be wondering why the page directive uses `Culture` and `UICulture` attributes, whereas the globalization section of the `Web.config` uses `culture` and `uiCulture` attributes for the same purpose (there is a difference in the case of the attribute names). It is a question of naming conventions. HTML attributes (used in the page directive) are Pascal cased, and XML attributes (used in `Web.config`) are Camel cased. Note that you are at liberty to change the case of the page attributes, but changing the case of the `Web.config` attributes will result in a runtime exception.

The initialization of `CurrentCulture` and `CurrentUICulture` from the `Web.config`'s globalization section occurs before the first event in the request pipeline (i.e., the `HttpApplication.BeginRequest` event), so all application code is influenced by this setting.

This solution has similar benefits to using the page's `culture` and `uiCulture` attributes, but it also has the same limitations. Recall that we overrode the page's `InitializeCulture` method to implement more sophisticated initialization of the culture. However, `global.asax` does not have a direct equivalent to the page's `InitializeCulture` method, so to provide the same enhancements across the application, we have to use the `HttpApplication.BeginRequest` event in the same way as we did in the .NET Framework 1.1.

Session/Profile vs. Page-Level Attributes

In ASP.NET 2, you can store the user's preferences in a Profile as an alternative to the Session. The difference is that profiles are persisted. However, regardless of whether you store the user's preference in the Session or the Profile, these mechanisms clash with the new page `Culture` and `UICulture` attributes. The problem is that `Profile` and `Session` information is restored before the page is initialized. If the page has `Culture` and `UICulture` attributes, when the page is initialized those attributes will set the `CurrentCulture` and `CurrentUICulture`, undoing the settings that were drawn from the Profile and Session. The solution is to either remove the `Culture` and `UICulture` attributes from the page, or restore the `CurrentCulture` and `CurrentUICulture` in the `Page.InitializeCulture` method (i.e., *after* the page's `Culture` and `UICulture` attributes have been processed).

Explicit Expressions

Another of the new features in ASP.NET 2 is explicit expressions. We have already seen implicit expressions and how property values are implicitly linked to a resource value. An explicit expression serves a similar purpose, with the difference being that a property value is explicitly linked to a resource value. Whereas implicit expressions bind resources to properties that are marked with `Localizable(true)`, explicit expressions bind resources to any property whatsoever.

Colors are one of the subjects that often change from culture to culture. Developers often use colors to convey meaning, but different colors convey different meanings to different cultures. Consequently, color properties are ripe for localization. However, you might have noticed that no color properties of Web controls are marked as `Localizable(true)`. This is where explicit expressions come in. Let's say we want to have a definition for a color that we will call `WarningColor`. The purpose of this color is to convey a warning to the user. We want to give buttons with a potentially dangerous activity this color to convey some kind of seriousness to the user. Start by adding a new string resource to the page's fallback resource file. The new string resource should have a key of `WarningColor` and a value of `Red`. Add the same resource key with a different value to any culture-neutral or culture-specific resource that should have a different color. Now select a button (I have called mine Sell Stock, which I feel is not an action that should be taken lightly), select its "`(Expressions)`" property in the Properties Window, and click on the ellipses to show the Explicit Expressions Dialog. Select a property (e.g., `BackColor`) that you want to apply the explicit expression to. In the Expression Type combo box, you can select either `AppSettings`, `Connection-Strings`, or `Resources`. The `WarningColor` resource is a local resource, so select `Resources`. In Expression Properties, select `ResourceKey` and drop down the list of resources. Select `WarningColor` (see Figure 5.8) and click OK.

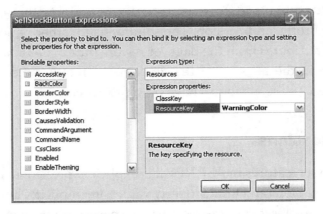

Figure 5.8   Assigning an Explicit Expression to a Property

The button's `BackColor` property is now explicitly bound to the `WarningColor` resource. This is confirmed in the Properties Window (see Figure 5.9) by the small blue icon next to the property and the ToolTip associated with this icon.

Figure 5.9   Explicit Expressions in the Properties Window

It is further confirmed by the change to the button's definition:

```
<asp:Button ID="SellStockButton" runat="server"
meta:resourcekey="SellStockButtonResource1"
Text="Sell Stock" BackColor="<%$ Resources:WarningColor %>" />
```

The `BackColor` property is assigned an explicit resource (i.e., "<%$ Resources:WarningColor %>"). You can, of course, bypass the Explicit Expressions Dialog completely and type this same text into the button's definition to achieve the same result. Similarly, you can delete this expression to unbind the property, or, alternatively, you can use the Properties Window to assign a new value to `BackColor` (which breaks the link to the explicit expression).

Notice that the `WarningColor` resource is a string, but the `BackColor` property is a `System.Drawing.Color`. The .NET Framework performs an implicit conversion from string to `Color` when the resource is applied. Also note that this is one of those occasions when you should be sure to write a comment next to the resource explaining what its purpose is. Without the comment, the translator may well translate the `WarningColor` from `Red` to, say, `Rouge` (i.e., the French for "red"), which would cause the application to fail.

This feature provides many localization opportunities. Clearly, the essential fact is that it enables us to localize any property, but these properties are not limited simply to appearance. Consider that you might have functionality that is appropriate for one culture but not for others. It may be that this culture requires an extra button—say, for calculating some local tax—that other cultures do not want. You could, of course, write code that adds this button to the control tree at runtime, but a better solution would be to use explicit expressions. In this scenario, you would add the button to the fallback page as normal. You would add a Boolean resource called, say, `SpecialTaxFunctionality` to the fallback resource and give it a value of `false`. You would bind the button's `Enabled` or `Visible` property to the `SpecialTax-Functionality` resource to ensure that it was either disabled or invisible by default. In the resource file for the culture that needs the button, you would add the `Spe-cialTaxFunctionality` resource with a value of `true`. Now the cultures for which the button is appropriate can use the button, and the cultures for which it is not appropriate either cannot see it or cannot use it.

It is worth pointing out the architectural implication of explicit expressions. Explicit expressions enable us to strike the right balance between making too many properties localizable and making too few properties localizable. In Windows Forms 1.1, all properties that could conceivably be different in a different culture are localized. This results in numerous properties being localized "just in case." This is wasteful because most of these properties are often not localized. The alternative is to provide a subset of properties that is too restrictive and prevents critical properties from being set in certain cultures. The combination of implicit expressions and explicit expressions enables developers to localize only those properties that need to be localized on a case-by-case basis. Thus, implicit expressions provide support for properties that are likely to be localized in the majority of cases (e.g., `Text`), and explicit expressions provide support for all other cases.

Global Resources

The previous example used a resource called `WarningColor`. This resource was local to the page, but in all probability, the same resource should be available throughout the application. For this reason, ASP.NET supports global resources. Global resources are available globally throughout an ASP.NET application. To change the previous example to use a global `WarningColor` resource, start by adding an `App_GlobalResources` folder. In Solution Explorer, right-click the Web site, and select Add, Add ASP.NET Folder, `App_GlobalResources`. Add a new resource file to this new folder and call the resource file `GlobalColors.resx`. Add a new entry for `WarningColor` with a value of `Red`. Select the button and open the `Expressions` property from the Properties Window. Change the `ClassKey` to `GlobalColors` (see Figure 5.10).

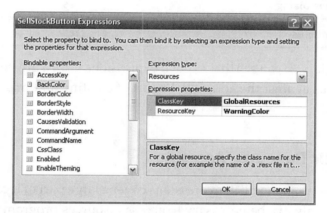

Figure 5.10   Assigning a Global Explicit Expression to a Property

The button's `BackColor` property is changed to this:

```
BackColor="<%$ Resources:GlobalColors, WarningColor %>"
```

Implicit Expressions vs. Explicit Expressions

Implicit expressions and explicit expressions have some functional overlap and some functional differences. Often there will be no choice of which to use (e.g., Generate Local Resources always uses implicit expressions), but when you write your own code, you will have to choose between the two. Table 5.1 provides a comparison between implicit and explicit expressions.

Table 5.1   Comparison Between Implicit Expressions and Explicit Expressions

	Implicit Expressions	Explicit Expressions
Access Local Resources	Yes	Yes
Access Global Resources	No	Yes
Created by Generate Local Resources	Yes	No
Use on Localizable Properties	Yes	Yes
Use on non-Localizable Properties	Yes	Yes
Use in Expressions Dialog	Yes	Yes
Use in HTML Attributes	No	Yes

From this table, you can see that explicit expressions have a greater scope, but you should weigh this against the additional effort of creating and maintaining explicit expressions.

Programmatic Resource Access

Implicit expressions and explicit expressions cover a large part of localizing an application, but it will always be necessary to access resources programmatically. In the ASP.NET 1.1 half of this chapter, we saw that we can create a `ResourceManager` and call its `GetString` or `GetObject` method to access these resources. In ASP.NET 2, you could adopt this same approach, but this would bypass ASP.NET 2's resource provider mechanism. ASP.NET 2 enables you to replace its default resource provider with a different resource provider (see Chapter 12, for example). If you were to use a `ResourceManager` directly, your application would not be capable of taking advantage of this feature effectively. Instead of using `ResourceManager.GetObject`, we can use `Page.GetLocalResourceObject`. Let's say we have a page with a `Label` called `LoggedInTimeLabel`, and we want to access a local string resource called `LoggedInTime`, which is this:

```
You first logged in at {0}
```

In the page's `Load` event, we can initialize the `Label` like this:

```
LoggedInTimeLabel.Text = String.Format((string)
    GetLocalResourceObject("LoggedInTime"),
    Session["LoggedInTime"].ToString());
```

`GetLocalResourceObject` gets the `LoggedInTime` resource object from this page's resources. Note that there is no requirement to specify where the resources are. This is in preference to the `ResourceManager` constructor, which demands this information and is consequently slightly more fragile. In the same vein, you can access global resources using the page's `GetGlobalResourceObject`:

```
string warningColor = GetGlobalResourceObject(
    "GlobalColors", "WarningColor").ToString();

ColorConverter colorConverter = new ColorConverter();

SellStockButton.BackColor =
    (Color) colorConverter.ConvertFromString(warningColor);
```

This example gets the `WarningColor` from the `GlobalColors` global resource and converts it from a string to a `System.Drawing.Color` before assigning it to the `SellStockButton`. The drawback to using `GetGlobalResourceObject` in this way is that it identifies the resource entry using a string identifier. Such access is fragile and subject to error. A better alternative to using `GetGlobalResourceObject` is to use the automatically generated, strongly-typed resource class that corresponds to the global resx file. This automatically generated class is created in a `Resources` namespace and is given the same name as the resx file (without the extension). So the first line of the previous example could be rewritten as follows:

```
string warningColor = Resources.GlobalColors.WarningColor;
```

Not only is this syntax neater, but it is checked at compile time instead of runtime.

Localizing ASP.NET 2 Components

ASP.NET 2 adds many new controls to ASP.NET. In this section, we look at the localization implications of these controls.

Login Controls

Of all the new controls, the Login controls have the greatest textual content. Figure 5.11 shows a selection of Login controls, illustrating their high textual content.

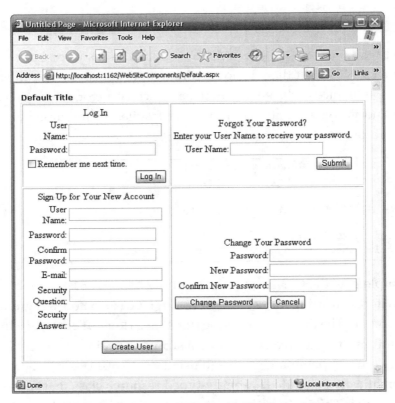

Figure 5.11   Login Controls with High Textual Content

The text used in these controls is not hard-coded. Instead, the text is maintained in properties that have been marked with the Localizable(true) attribute. As such, when Generate Local Resources is run on a page that has one of these controls, the text is copied to a resource and the properties are implicitly bound to those resources. The localization process for these controls, therefore, is the same for any other control (except that the volume of text is higher).

When template controls are added to a form, the controls initially contain text for the language version of Visual Studio. So if you are using the Japanese Visual Studio, the controls will draw from Japanese resources. Visual Studio 2005 does not provide a means by which you can specify a different default language for resources, even if you have the appropriate .NET Framework Language Pack installed.

The `LoginName` control, however, deserves a special mention. The `LoginName` control shows the name of the user who is logged in. Often this control is used to display welcome messages such as "Welcome, Rose Tyler, to the Gallifrey Medical Database." The danger here in localization terms is that a developer would build this string by concatenating bits of text. So the text might be built up from "Welcome, "; "Rose Tyler"; and ", to the Gallifrey Medical Database." Not only is this difficult for a translator to translate (because the string has been broken into pieces), but it also will not be acceptable in languages in which the order of the phrases is different than that of the developer's language. For this reason, the `LoginName` has a property called `FormatString`. By default, this is "{0}", which acts as a placeholder for the user's name. For this prompt to be correctly localizable, change the `FormatString` to `"Welcome, {0}, to the Gallifrey Medical Database"`.

SiteMap Control

The `SiteMap` control is a great new control that is at the heart of ASP.NET's navigation support. The `SiteMap` itself is simply a description of the nodes in the Web site:

```xml
<?xml version="1.0" encoding="utf-8" ?>
<siteMap xmlns=
"http://schemas.microsoft.com/AspNet/SiteMap-File-1.0" >
    <siteMapNode url="default.aspx" title="Home"
    description="Home page">

        <siteMapNode url="Login.aspx" title="Login"
        description="Login page" />
```

```
            <siteMapNode url="CreditHistory.aspx" title="Credit History"
            description="Complete Credit History Details" />

        </siteMapNode>
</siteMap>
```

These nodes include the `Title` and `Description` of each page, and, clearly, this text must be made localizable. The first step is to create resources from all of the text in the `SiteMap`. Start by creating a new `App_GlobalResources` folder, if one does not already exist. Add a new resource file—say, `Web.sitemap.resx`—to this folder and add a resource entry for each of the titles and descriptions. Next enable localization of the `SiteMap` by adding the `enableLocalization` attribute with a value of `true`:

```
<siteMap enableLocalization="true"
xmlns="http://schemas.microsoft.com/AspNet/SiteMap-File-1.0" >
```

Finally, change the `siteMapNode Titles` and `Descriptions` to use implicit expressions:

```
<siteMapNode url="default.aspx"
title="$resources: Web.sitemap, DefaultTitle"
description="$resources: Web.sitemap, DefaultDescription">

    <siteMapNode url="Login.aspx"
    title="$resources: Web.sitemap, LoginTitle"
    description="$resources: Web.sitemap, LoginDescription" />

    <siteMapNode url="CreditHistory.aspx"
    title="$resources: Web.sitemap, CreditHistoryTitle"
    description=
    "$resources: Web.sitemap, CreditHistoryDescription" />

</siteMapNode>
```

The `SiteMap` is now localizable.

Localizing the Website Administration Tool

As the name implies, the Website Administration Tool is a convenient tool for administering ASP.NET Web sites. It is, in itself, an ASP.NET 2 application and adheres to the same patterns for localizing Web site applications that are offered in ASP.NET 2.

The files and folders that make up the Website Administration Tool are located in `%FrameworkDir%\%FrameworkVersion%\ASP.NETWebAdminFiles`, complete with standard `App_GlobalResources` and `App_LocalResources` folders containing resx files. The resx files contain the `English (United States)` resources for the Website Administration Tool. The installation of a .NET Framework 2 Language Pack adds new corresponding culture-neutral resx files to the various `App_Global Resources` and `App_LocalResources` folders (there is an `App_LocalResources` folder in each application folder). So if you install the French .NET Framework 2 Language Pack, then the `App_GlobalResources\GlobalResources.resx` file will have a French sibling, `GlobalResources.fr.resx`. The Website Administration Tool does not change the default values for `CurrentCulture` and `CurrentUICulture`. This means that, by default, the user interface that you see is dictated by the language of the operating system (and the presence of a corresponding .NET Framework 2 Language Pack). You are at liberty, however, to change the Website Administration Tool's `web.config`. To change the `CurrentCulture` and `CurrentUICulture` to `French (France)` and `French`, respectively, you would add the following element:

```
<globalization culture="fr-FR" uiCulture="fr"/>
```

The Website Administration Tool shows off the benefits of ASP.NET's internationalization model excellently. Imagine that you want a localized version of the Website Administration Tool, but there is no .NET Framework Language Pack for the language that you want to use. (The .NET Framework does, after all, support considerably more languages than there are .NET Framework Language Packs.) Simply add the corresponding resx files to support your language, set the `culture` and `uiCulture` in the `web.config`, and refresh your browser. The Website Administration Tool will use your new language.

Where Are We?

ASP.NET 2 offers considerable support for internationalization. Whereas it is possible to internationalize ASP.NET 1.1 applications, the lack of direct support in the framework and IDE make this process a significant investment of hand-crafted code and resources. If at all possible, upgrade to ASP.NET 2 before internationalizing your application.

6

Globalization

I T IS RARE THAT AN ENTIRE CHAPTER CAN BE summarized in a single sentence, but this chapter can almost be summed up in this way:

Always use the appropriate .NET Framework `Globalization` class, and a large part of the globalization of your application will be taken care of for you.

To recap from Chapter 3, "An Introduction to Internationalization," globalization is the process of engineering an application so that it does not have cultural preconceptions. The .NET Framework includes many classes in its `System.Globalization` namespace designed for this purpose. This chapter explores these classes and also covers a few globalization issues that are not covered by these classes.

The CultureInfo Class

The `CultureInfo class`, introduced in Chapter 3, is the single most important class in .NET's internationalization story. It encapsulates a language; optionally, a country or region; and, in some cases, a script. In this section, we look beyond the introduction given in Chapter 3.

The `CultureInfo` class has four constructors:

```
public CultureInfo(int culture);

public CultureInfo(int culture, bool useUserOverride);

public CultureInfo(string name);

public CultureInfo(string name, bool useUserOverride);
```

Two of the constructors accept an LCID (locale identifier) and two accept a culture string. The LCID constructors are useful for constructing new `CultureInfo` objects when the culture string is not immediately available (for example, when using Win32 APIs). In addition, they are useful for constructing `CultureInfo` objects that cannot be distinguished by their culture strings (e.g., "es-ES" (Traditional Sort) and "en-ES" (Modern Sort)). See the section entitled "Alternate Sort Orders" for more details. An alternative to using the `CultureInfo` constructors in the .NET Framework 2.0 is to use the `CultureInfo.GetCultureInfo` method, which has the following overrides:

```
public static CultureInfo GetCultureInfo(int culture);

public static CultureInfo GetCultureInfo(string name);

public static CultureInfo GetCultureInfo(
    string name, string altName);
```

Two differences exist between the `CultureInfo` constructor and the `CultureInfo.GetCultureInfo` method:

- `CultureInfo` objects returned by the `GetCultureInfo` method are cached, and, therefore, subsequent hits on the same culture are returned faster.
- `CultureInfo` objects are read-only.

`CultureInfo` has a similar method called `GetCultureInfoByIetfLanguageTag` that performs the same operation but accepts an IETF language tag instead of a culture name.

The culture string used in the `CultureInfo` constructor and `GetCultureInfo` method accepts a string in the RFC 1766 format:

```
languagecode2[-country/regioncode2[-script]]
```

`languagecode2` is an ISO 639-1 or 639-2 code, and `country/regioncode2` is an ISO 3166 code. The ISO 639-1 standard specifies the two-letter code used to identify a language. Sometimes there is no two-letter code for a language, so the three-letter ISO 639-2 code is used instead. In the .NET Framework 1.1. and 2.0, this applies to just three cultures:

```
div (Divehi)
kok (Konkani)
syr (Syriac)
```

Correspondingly, the `CultureInfo.TwoLetterISOLanguage` property returns three letters instead of two letters for these cultures.

Some cultures support more than one writing system (script). Table 6.1 shows the cultures that have a script tag suffix of "Cyrl" (for Cyrillic scripts) or "Latn" (for Latin scripts).

Table 6.1   Cultures with Scripts

Culture Name	DisplayName	.NET 1.1	.NET 2.0
az-AZ-Cyrl	Azeri (Cyrillic, Azerbaijan)	Yes	Yes
az-AZ-Latn	Azeri (Latin, Azerbaijan)	Yes	Yes
bs-BA-Latn	Bosnian (Bosnia and Herzegovina)	No	Yes
sr-BA-Cyrl	Serbian (Cyrillic, Bosnia and Herzegovina)	No	Yes
sr-BA-Latn	Serbian (Latin, Bosnia and Herzegovina)	No	Yes
sr-SP-Cyrl	Serbian (Cyrillic, Serbia and Montenegro)	Yes	Yes
sr-SP-Latn	Serbian (Latin, Serbia and Montenegro)	Yes	Yes
uz-UZ-Latn	Uzbek (Latin, Uzbekistan)	Yes	Yes
uz-UZ-Cyrl	Uzbek (Cyrillic, Uzbekistan)	Yes	Yes

Two cultures use nonstandard culture string formats: zh-CHS (Chinese (Simplified)) and zh-CHT (Chinese (Traditional)). Looking at these strings, you would expect them to represent specific cultures ("zh" being a language and "CHS"/"CHT" being a country), but they do not. Instead, they are both neutral cultures and are parents to zh-CN (Chinese (People's Republic of China)) and zh-TW (Chinese (Taiwan)), respectively. For this reason, you should take care to use the `CultureInfo.IsNeutralCulture` property to determine whether a culture is neutral instead of making an inference by parsing the culture's name. This property is similarly important when considering custom cultures because there is no requirement that the name of a custom culture follow a strict `<language>`-`<region>` format. Note that there is no `CultureInfo.IsSpecificCulture` property, so the implication is that if `IsNeutralCulture` is `false`, the culture is specific. This is true for all cultures except `CultureInfo.InvariantCulture`, which is neither neutral nor specific (although it can behave like a specific culture). You can test a culture to see if it is the invariant culture by making a comparison with `CultureInfo.InvariantCulture`.

Two `CultureInfo` constructors accept a second Boolean parameter, `useUserOverride`. This parameter specifies whether the user should be able to override the culture's number, currency, time, and date default settings (used in the `DateTimeFormatInfo` and `NumberFormatInfo` classes) in the Customize Regional Options dialog (in the Regional and Language Options dialog, click on the Customize… button) (see Figure 6.1). (Prior to Windows XP Professional, these same tabs are included in the Regional and Language Options dialog, so there is no need for a Customize button.) When the `useUserOverride` parameter is `true`, the user's settings override the culture's default settings.

Figure 6.1   The Customize Regional Options Dialog Currency tab

If this parameter isn't specified, the default is `true`, so the user's own settings override the default settings. In an ASP.NET 2.0 application where `Culture` and/or

UICulture is "auto", the useUserOverride parameter is not specified; if you don't want to accept the user's settings, you need to override the InitializeCulture method to change this behavior (see Chapter 5, "ASP.NET Specifics"). In addition, the CultureInfo.GetCultureInfo method does not have a useUserOverride parameter, so this method always returns CultureInfo objects where useUserOverride is false.

The recommended practice is to accept the user's overrides. There are many reasons why the user's settings would be considered essential. For example, when a country changes its currency, the currency symbol needs to be updated. This happens frequently: in the past with France changing from francs to euros, more recently with Turkey changing from TL (Türk Lirasi) to YTL (Yeni Türk Lirasi), and possibly in the future with the English pound changing to euros. Whereas the most recent versions of the operating system are updated with such changes, they cannot predict future events, and older operating systems (e.g., Windows 98 and Windows NT, in the case of the French franc) remain out-of-date. (Windows XP SP2 was released before the introduction of the new Turkish Lira on January 1, 2005, so it became out-of-date when the old Turkish Lira was removed from circulation at the end of 2005.) A simple solution to this problem is to ensure that your users run Windows Update on a regular basis, as Windows Update keeps culture information up-to-date. The problem itself, however, is lessened by using the .NET Framework 2.0 as opposed to 1.1. The culture information provided by the .NET Framework 2.0 has been updated with known changes, so whereas the .NET Framework 1.1's tr-TR (Turkish (Turkey)) culture reports that the currency symbol is "TL", the .NET Framework 2.0's same culture reports that the currency symbol is "YTL".

In addition, typically you should trust the user's good intentions and accept their overrides. The alternative is to reject the user's overrides and either create new custom cultures with the updated information (see Chapter 11, "Custom Cultures") or create a CultureInfoProvider:

```
public class CultureInfoProvider
{
    public static CultureInfo GetCultureInfo(string name)
    {
        CultureInfo cultureInfo = new CultureInfo(name);
        ApplyKnownUpdates(cultureInfo);
        return cultureInfo;
    }
}
```

```
public static CultureInfo GetCultureInfo(int LCID)
{
    CultureInfo cultureInfo = new CultureInfo(LCID);
    ApplyKnownUpdates(cultureInfo);
    return cultureInfo;
}
public static void ApplyKnownUpdates(CultureInfo cultureInfo)
{
    if (cultureInfo.Name == "fr-FR")
        cultureInfo.NumberFormat.CurrencySymbol = "€";
    else if (cultureInfo.Name == "tr-TR")
        cultureInfo.NumberFormat.CurrencySymbol = "YTL";
    else if (cultureInfo.Name == "en-GB")
        cultureInfo.NumberFormat.CurrencySymbol = "€";
}
}
```

The problem with this solution is that you have to catch every situation that creates a `CultureInfo` and furthermore be able to change the code to create the `CultureInfo` using the new `CultureInfoProvider` class. FxCop can help with this. See the "CultureInfo not provided by Provider" rule in Chapter 13, "Testing Internationalization Using FxCop." A more sophisticated version of this `CultureInfoProvider` (which creates the `CultureInfoEx` objects shown in the section entitled "Extending the `CultureInfo` Class," later in this chapter) is included in the source code for this book.

CultureInfo.GetCultures and CultureTypes Enumeration

The static `CultureInfo.GetCultures` method gets a list of cultures that match a `CultureTypes` enumeration (see Table 6.2). So `CultureInfo.GetCultures(CultureTypes.NeutralCultures)` returns an array of culture-neutral `CultureInfo` objects:

```
foreach (CultureInfo cultureInfo in
    CultureInfo.GetCultures(CultureTypes.NeutralCultures))
{
    listBox1.Items.Add(cultureInfo.DisplayName);
}
```

The invariant culture is included in the list of neutral cultures even though `CultureInfo.InvariantCulture.IsNeutralCulture` is `false`. This inclusion in the list of neutral cultures represents a bug that was present in the .NET Framework 1.0. It persists in later versions of the .NET Framework for backward compatibility.

You can see from the enumeration value in Table 6.2 that `CultureTypes` can be added together, so `CultureInfo.GetCultures(CultureTypes.NeutralCultures | CultureTypes.InstalledWin32Cultures)` returns an array of cultures that are either neutral or known to the operating system.

Table 6.2 `CultureTypes` **Enumeration**

Name	Value	Description	.NET 1.1	.NET 2.0
AllCultures	7	All cultures known to the .NET Framework (and, in .NET 2.0, the operating system and custom cultures)	Yes	Yes
FrameworkCultures	64	All cultures known to the .NET Framework	No	Yes
InstalledWin32Cultures	4	All cultures known to the current operating system	Yes	Yes
NeutralCultures	1	Neutral cultures (language part only)	Yes	Yes
ReplacementCultures	16	Custom cultures that replace existing cultures	No	Yes
SpecificCultures	2	Specific cultures (language and country/region)	Yes	Yes
UserCustomCulture	8	Custom cultures installed on this machine	No	Yes
WindowsOnlyCultures	32	Cultures known to the operating system but not to the .NET Framework	No	Yes

The `UserCustomCulture` element is singular (i.e., it does not have an *s* at the end), whereas all the other elements are plural (i.e., they do have an *s* at the end). The naming of this element is inconsistent with its siblings. Unfortunately, the issue was not caught until it was too late in the testing cycle, and compatibility won over consistency. The singular name stays.

The `InstalledWin32Cultures` value deserves a special mention. This represents all of the cultures that are known to the current version of the operating system. For each version of the operating system, this is a different number, with Windows XP Service Pack 2 including the highest number of cultures at the time of writing. What is especially useful about this is that when new cultures are subsequently added in later versions of the operating system, they will be included in the list returned by `GetCultures` and they will be recognized without requiring a new version of the framework. In fact, some cultures either exist or not, depending upon how the operating system has been configured. The `Bengali (India)`, `Hindi` and `Malayam (India)` cultures are added to the list of cultures when complex script support is installed (see the "Supplemental Language Support" section in Chapter 7, "Middle East and East Asian Cultures"). This adaptable behavior is new in the .NET Framework 2.0, and, as the .NET Framework 1.1 doesn't support this option, it is unaware of new cultures and uses its own hard-coded culture list.

The order in which the cultures are returned is unsorted. As the culture list in .NET Framework 1.1 is fixed, the order is a constant and most similar cultures are loosely grouped together, but they are not alphabetically sorted by any criteria. The culture list in the .NET Framework 2.0 is variable, and cultures are returned in a different order than that of the .NET Framework 1.1; however, the order is still, nonetheless, unsorted.

A few of the Windows-only cultures (e.g., `cy-GB`) have an incorrect `DisplayName` in Windows XP Professional Service Pack 2. The `DisplayName` is missing the region (e.g., "`Welsh`" should be "`Welsh (United Kingdom)`"). This is a fault in the ELK resources for these cultures and should be fixed in a later Service Pack or release of the operating system. The workaround is to use the `EnglishName` or `NativeName`.

The Relationship Between CultureInfo and Other Globalization Classes

The `CultureInfo` class frequently represents the focal point of the `System.Globalization` namespace. It is supported by, and references, many other `System.Globalization` classes. The relationship between its properties and those classes can be seen in Figure 6.2.

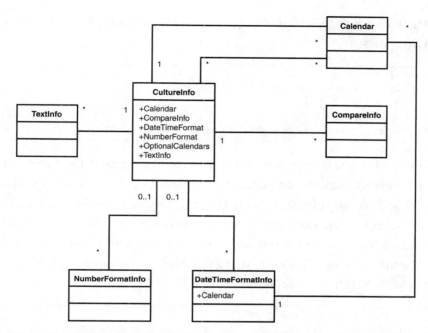

Figure 6.2 The Relationship between CultureInfo and Other System.Globalization Classes

(The properties listed in the diagram are only those properties that relate to other classes; this is not a complete list.) We explore these classes throughout this chapter.

The RegionInfo Class

As you know, the `CultureInfo` class can relate to a language by itself or a language in a country/region. However, it cannot relate to just a country/region alone. This is the purpose of the `RegionInfo` class. The `RegionInfo` class describes a country/region regardless of its language. This can be especially useful in Country combo boxes that allow you to select your country from a list of all countries, although it is worth pointing out that a region does not always have a one-to-one mapping with a country. Hong Kong, for example, is a region but not a country. `RegionInfo` supports two constructors: One accepts an LCID (locale ID), and the other accepts a region code or culture code. It should be noted, however, that an LCID refers to a specific language in a specific country; thus, there is often more than one LCID that refers to the same country/region. The `CultureInfo` class does not have a `Region` property that identifies the culture's region, but one can easily be created by either of the following lines:

```
RegionInfo regionInfo =
    new RegionInfo(Thread.CurrentThread.CurrentCulture.Name);

RegionInfo regionInfo =
    new RegionInfo(Thread.CurrentThread.CurrentCulture.LCID);
```

Of the two choices, the constructor that accepts a name is the safer of the two. `RegionInfo` objects cannot be constructed from LCIDs of custom cultures (see Chapter 11) because supplementary custom cultures all have the same LCID.

The `RegionInfo` class does not have a `GetRegions` method corresponding to the `CultureInfo`'s `GetCultures` method, but the following `GetRegions` method provides the same results. (If you are using the .NET Framework 1.1, replace `cultureInfo.Name` with `cultureInfo.LCID`.)

```
public static RegionInfo[] GetRegions()
{
    Hashtable regionInfos = new Hashtable();
    foreach (CultureInfo cultureInfo in
        CultureInfo.GetCultures(CultureTypes.SpecificCultures))
    {
        RegionInfo regionInfo = new RegionInfo(cultureInfo.Name);
        if (regionInfos[regionInfo.ThreeLetterISORegionName] == null)
            regionInfos.Add(
                regionInfo.ThreeLetterISORegionName, regionInfo);
    }
    RegionInfo[] regionInfoArray = new RegionInfo[regionInfos.Count];
    regionInfos.Values.CopyTo(regionInfoArray, 0);
    return regionInfoArray;
}
```

The `GetRegions` method uses the `CultureInfo.GetCultures` method to get a list of specific cultures (because neutral cultures do not have a country/region) and creates a new `RegionInfo` from the culture's name (or the culture's LCID in the .NET Framework 1.1). As there can be many cultures that refer to the same country/region, we search the `Hashtable` to see if the country/region is already in the list by looking for a country/region with the same `ThreeLetterISORegionName`.

The `RegionInfo` properties are listed in Table 6.3. Notice that the static `Current Region` property refers to the value retrieved by the Win32 `GetUserDefaultLCID` API, which is the value set by the user in the Regional and Language Options dialog. This property is not affected by changes to the `CurrentCulture` or `CurrentUICulture`. Also note that the `DisplayName` property gets its resources from the .NET Framework Language Pack; whereas for Windows-only cultures, the `NativeName` property gets it resources from the operating system. If you do not have an appropriate .NET Framework Language Pack installed, you will get a mismatch if the language is not English. Finally, notice the inadequacies of the Boolean type in the `IsMetric` property. This property indicates whether the country/region uses the metric system. There are no shades of gray in the Boolean type, so the United States and the United Kingdom report `False` and `True`, respectively, where neither is entirely correct nor entirely incorrect.

Table 6.3   `RegionInfo` **Properties**

Property Name	Description	.NET 1.1	.NET 2.0
CurrencyEnglishName	The English name of the currency	No	Yes
CurrencyNativeName	The native name of the currency	No	Yes
CurrencySymbol	The currency symbol	Yes	Yes
CurrentRegion	The region set in Regional and Language Options when the application started	Yes	Yes
DisplayName	The localized region name (from the .NET Language Pack for framework cultures)	Yes	Yes
EnglishName	The English region name	Yes	Yes
GeoId	A unique number identifying the geographical region	No	Yes
IsMetric	Whether the region uses the metric system	Yes	Yes
ISOCurrencySymbol	The three-character ISO 4217 currency symbol	Yes	Yes

Table 6.3 `RegionInfo` **Properties   continued**

Property Name	Description	.NET 1.1	.NET 2.0
`Name`	The name of the region	Yes	Yes
`NativeName`	The localized region name (from the operating system for Windows-only cultures)	No	Yes
`ThreeLetterISORegionName`	The three-letter ISO 3166 code	Yes	Yes
`ThreeLetterISOWindowsName`	The three-letter Windows code	Yes	Yes
`TwoLetterISORegionName`	The two-letter ISO 3166 code	Yes	Yes

Geographical Information

One of the new `RegionInfo` properties in the .NET Framework 2.0 is `GeoId`. The geographical ID is an integer that identifies a geographical region. As it uniquely identifies a geographical region, it can be used as a primary key in a database (Microsoft uses `GeoId`s to support products such as `MapPoint`). The numbers themselves are defined by Microsoft and can be referenced in the Table Of Geographical Locations (http://msdn.microsoft.com/library/default.asp?url=/library/enus/intl/nls_locations.asp). Apart from the `GeoId`'s value as a unique identifier, it can be used to retrieve information about a geographical region (as opposed to a locale). Unfortunately, the .NET Framework does not have a `GeoInfo` class to store or retrieve this information, but we can write one. Geographical information is retrieved using the `GetGeoInfo` Win32 function:

```
[DllImport("kernel32")]
protected static extern int GetGeoInfo(
    int GeoId,
    SYSGEOTYPE GeoType,
    StringBuilder lpGeoData,
    int cchData,
    int language
);
```

The `GeoId` comes straight from the `RegionInfo.GeoId` (if you are using the .NET Framework 1.1, you could use the information in the "Table Of Geographical

Locations" to build a static lookup of GeoIds from their names). The GeoType identifies the type of information you are getting and is a SYSGEOTYPE. lpGeoData is a buffer into which the returned information is placed. cchData is the size of the buffer. language is the language identifier that you want the information to be returned in (1033 is English (United States)). SYSGEOTYPE is an enumeration:

```
public enum SYSGEOTYPE
{
    GEO_NATION = 0x0001,
    GEO_LATITUDE = 0x0002,
    GEO_LONGITUDE = 0x0003,
    GEO_ISO2 = 0x0004,
    GEO_ISO3 = 0x0005,
    GEO_RFC1766 = 0x0006,
    GEO_LCID = 0x0007,
    GEO_FRIENDLYNAME = 0x0008,
    GEO_OFFICIALNAME = 0x0009,
    GEO_TIMEZONES = 0x000A,
    GEO_OFFICIALLANGUAGES = 0x000B,
};
```

To retrieve information using GetGeoInfo, you should call it once to get the buffer size and then a second time to retrieve the information itself. The following method is a convenient wrapper around the GetGeoInfo method:

```
protected virtual string GetGeoInfoString(SYSGEOTYPE sysGeoType)
{
    // find out the length of the geo information
    int length = GetGeoInfo(geoId, sysGeoType, null, 0, language);
    if (length == 0)
        return null;
    else
    {
        StringBuilder lpGeoData = new StringBuilder(length);
        // get the geo information
        int result = GetGeoInfo(
            geoId, sysGeoType, lpGeoData, length, language);
        if (result == 0)
            return null;
        else
            return lpGeoData.ToString();
    }
}
```

The full `GetInfo` class is part of the source code for this book, but here is a cut-down version showing just the `OfficialName` property:

```
class GeoInfo
{
    private int geoId;
    private int language = 1033;

    public GeoInfo(int geoId)
    {
        this.geoId = geoId;
    }
    public GeoInfo(int geoId, int language)
    {
        this.geoId = geoId;
        this.language = language;
    }
    public string OfficialName
    {
        get
        {
            string geoInfo =
                GetGeoInfoString(SYSGEOTYPE.GEO_OFFICIALNAME);
            if (geoInfo != null)
                return geoInfo;
            else
                throw new GeoInfoException(
                    "Failed to retrieve Geo Information",
                    SYSGEOTYPE.GEO_OFFICIALNAME, geoInfo);
        }
    }
}
```

You use the `GeoInfo` class like this:

```
RegionInfo regionInfo = new RegionInfo("en-US");
GeoInfo geoInfo = new GeoInfo(regionInfo.GeoId);
MessageBox.Show("Official Name: " + geoInfo.OfficialName);
```

The GEO_TIMEZONES and GEO_OFFICIALLANGUAGES enumerations always return empty values. The reason is that the time zone and official language data have not been included in any version of Windows to date.

String Comparisons

Comparing the equality of two strings is typically considered a simple matter. Programmers vary in their preference among five choices:

- The equality operator (==)
- `String.Equals`
- `String.CompareTo`
- `String.Compare`
- `String.CompareOrdinal` (and `String.Compare` used with `StringComparison.Ordinal`)

The first two choices are essentially the same choice. If the compiler detects that both sides of the equality operator are strings, the operation equates to `String.Equals`. `String.Equals` performs a case-sensitive, culture-insensitive comparison:

```
string s1 = "Bob";
string s2 = "BOB";
if (String.Equals(s1, s2))
    textBox1.Text += "Equal" + System.Environment.NewLine;
else
    textBox1.Text += "Not Equal" + System.Environment.NewLine;

string s3 = "Bob";
string s4 = "Bob";
if (String.Equals(s3, s4))
    textBox1.Text += "Equal" + System.Environment.NewLine;
else
    textBox1.Text += "Not Equal" + System.Environment.NewLine;
```

In this example, "Bob" does not equal "BOB" because they are different cases. "Bob" does equal "Bob" because their values are the same. This shows that `String.Equals` tests the values of strings, not the references of string, so although s3 and s4 have different references, they have the same value.

The third, fourth, and fifth choices are also the same if a test for equality is your only desire. These three methods return an integer, where 0 means that the two strings are equal. Although the return results will vary according to the given culture if the strings are not equal, the results will not vary, regardless of culture, if the two strings are exactly equal. Consequently, a comparison with 0 will always be accurate, regardless of cultural considerations. The difference between these methods and the meaning of nonzero return results are covered in the section entitled "Sort Orders."

Casing

Latin script languages have a concept of upper and lower case, which all developers are familiar with. However, not all languages have this concept or implement it in the same way. Some languages (e.g., Japanese) are case-less. Others exist only as upper case (e.g., Khutsuri) or lower case (e.g., Nushkuri). For these languages, no case conversions should occur. If you intend to support Azeri or Turkish, you should be aware of the special case of the letter *I*. Most Latin script languages have two I characters: a Capital Letter *I* (without a dot on top) and a Small Letter *i* (with a dot on top). Azeri and Turkish have two more *I* characters: a Capital Letter *İ* (with a dot on top) and a Small Letter *ı* (without a dot on top). You need to be aware of this because the rules for conversion between upper and lower case among these four letters are different for Azeri and Turkish cultures than they are for other cultures. (These special rules are known as Turkic Casing Rules.) Tables 6.4 and 6.5 show the effects of converting each of the four letters between upper and lower case using the "en" and "tr", cultures respectively.

Table 6.4   Upper- and Lowercasing I Using English Culture

Character Name	Character	Unicode Code Point	Upper Character	Upper Unicode Code Point	Lower Character	Lower Unicode Code Point
Latin Capital Letter	I	U+0049	I	U+0049	i	U+0069
Latin Small Letter	i	U+0069	I	U+0049	i	U+0069
Latin Capital Letter With Dot	İ	U+0130	İ	U+0130	i	U+0069
Latin Small Letter Without Dot	ı	U+0131	I	U+0049	ı	U+0131

Table 6.5   Upper- and Lowercasing I Using Turkish Culture

Character Name	Character	Unicode Code Point	Upper Character	Upper Unicode Code Point	Lower Character	Lower Unicode Code Point
Latin Capital Letter	I	U+0049	I	U+0049	ı	U+0131
Latin Small Letter	i	U+0069	İ	U+0130	i	U+0069
Latin Capital Letter With dot	İ	U+0130	İ	U+0130	i	U+0069
Latin Small Letter Without Dot	ı	U+0131	I	U+0049	ı	U+0131

From these two tables, it can be seen that the Turkish lowercase equivalent of Latin Capital *I* is not the same as the English lowercase equivalent, and the Turkish uppercase equivalent of Latin Small *I* is not the same as the English uppercase equivalent. The problem is illustrated in the following code fragment:

```
CultureInfo cultureInfo = new CultureInfo("en");
string test = "Delphi is in italics";
string testUpper = "DELPHI IS IN ITALICS";
if (test.ToUpper(cultureInfo).CompareTo(testUpper) == 0)
    Text = "Equal";
else
    Text = "Not equal";
```

The two strings are equal if the culture is "en", but they are not equal if the culture is "tr". How you handle this difference in code is dependent upon the nature of the strings being compared. If you were comparing a company name typed by a user, a case-less conversion using `String.Compare` and passing the `CurrentCulture` would be the safest comparison. If, however, you were comparing a string that could be considered a programmatic element against a known string—say, an XML tag name—you should use the invariant culture to perform the comparison, to ensure that culture-specific casing rules do not change the success of the comparison.

Sort Orders

Sorting (also called collation) has numerous differences from culture to culture. It is one of those many areas that the .NET Framework handles correctly with very little intervention on behalf of the developer, other than to specify what culture should be used for sorting. Table 6.6 provides a number of examples of characters and character combinations that sort differently in one language to another.

Table 6.6   Examples of Characters with Different Sort Behaviors in Different Languages

In some languages, letters with diacritics are treated as wholly separate characters:
In Swedish, *Ä* (U+00C4, Latin Capital Letter A With Diaeresis) is a separate character after *Z*
In German (phone book sort), *Ä* (U+00C4, Latin Capital Letter A With Diaeresis) sorts like *ae*
In Czech, *Č* is a separate character between *c* and *d*
In Czech, *Š* is a separate character between *s* and *t*
In Czech, *ž* is a separate character after *z*
In some languages, two characters sort as a single character:
In Czech, *ch* sorts as a single character between *h* and *i*
In Traditional Spanish, *ch* sorts as a single character between *c* and *d*
In Traditional Spanish, *ll* sorts as a single character between *l* and *m*
In Danish, *Æ* sorts as a single character after *Z*
In some languages, letters have the same sort as other letters:
In Lithuanian, *y* is sorted as *i*
In Swedish, *w* is sorted as *v*

Fortunately, developers do not need to remember or even know these differences—only that there are differences. Take, for example, the `Array.Sort` method. This method accepts an `IComparer` interface to sort elements of an array. If the

`IComparer` is null, `Array.Sort` uses each element's `IComparable` interface to determine the order of a sort. `IComparable` has a single method, `CompareTo`. The `String` class supports the `IComparable` interface and includes the `CompareTo` method. The `String.CompareTo` method uses the `CultureInfo.CurrentCulture.CompareInfo.Compare` method to perform a culture-sensitive comparison between two strings. In the following code snippet, the `en-US` culture is used to sort two strings:

```
string[] strings = new string[] {"eé", "ée"};
Thread.CurrentThread.CurrentCulture = new CultureInfo("en-US");
Array.Sort(strings);
foreach(string s in strings)
{
    listBox1.Items.Add(s);
}
```

The output is "eé" and then "ée". If we change the culture to `French in France` (`fr-FR`), in which diacritics (e.g., the acute accent above the *e*) are evaluated from right to left instead of left to right, the order is reversed. The point is that the sort order will respect the local culture's sort behavior without you having to know what that behavior is.

This returns us to the `String.CompareTo`, `String.Compare` and `String.CompareOrdinal` methods that we saw earlier in the "String Comparisons" section. The single difference between `String.CompareTo` and `String.Compare` is that the former is an instance method and the latter is a static method. As we have seen, the `String.CompareTo` method exists so that the `String` class can support the `IComparable` interface. In nearly all cases, `String.CompareTo` and `String.Compare` call `CompareInfo.Compare` to perform string comparisons. The various overloads either accept an explicit culture or, like most globalization methods, default the culture to `CultureInfo.CurrentCulture`. The return result is an integer indicating the relative order of the two strings:

> Negative if the first string is sorted before the second
>
> 0 if the first string is equal to the second
>
> Positive if the first string is sorted after the second

In most cases, the negative value will be -1 and the positive value will be +1. The exception is the `String.Compare` overload in the .NET Framework 2.0, which accepts a `StringComparison` enumeration where the value is `Ordinal` or `Ordinal` `IgnoreCase`. In this scenario, the "magnitude" of the difference is expressed in the same way as for `String.CompareOrdinal`.

`String.CompareOrdinal` is similar to `String.Compare`, but it performs the comparison based upon the Unicode code points of each character in the string and returns the "magnitude" of the difference. For example, `String.CompareOrdinal("a", "á")` returns `-128`. The Unicode code point of the letter "a" is U+0061 (97), and the Unicode code point of the letter "á" is U+00E1 (225). The result is 97 – 225 (i.e., –128). There are several benefits to using `String.CompareOrdinal`: It is culture-insensitive (because it uses Unicode code points) and it is faster than other comparison methods. It should also be noted that `String.CompareOrdinal` compares all characters in a string, whereas other comparison methods are dependent upon characters being defined in the .NET Framework's sorting tables. This means that if a comparison is performed using `String.Compare` and is passed the invariant culture, characters that are not in the .NET Framework's sorting tables will simply be ignored.

For these reasons, Microsoft recommends using an ordinal comparison for culture-insensitive comparisons. Additionally, it should be noted that although the actual sort itself is unlikely to yields results that are culturally significant for any particular culture, it can still be useful for maintaining ordered lists that require fast searching.

Alternate Sort Orders

The discussions on sort orders so far have assumed that each culture has a single method of sorting. However, a few cultures have more than one way of sorting the same data. All existing .NET Framework cultures have a default sort order, and a few have a single alternate sort order in addition to their default. Spanish, for example, has two sort orders: Modern/International (the default sort order that is typically used in Spain and the U.S.) and the Traditional alternate sort order (used less frequently in some situations in Spain). Each `CultureInfo` object has a single `CompareInfo` class that it uses for sorting. Using a different sort order requires creating a different culture. To use the Traditional sort order for Spanish, you must create a new `CultureInfo` object or create a `CompareInfo` object using `Compare-Info.GetCompareInfo`. The `CultureInfo` object for the alternate sort order is identical in every way to the CultureInfo object for the default sort order, with the exception of its CompareInfo object. This means that the culture's name is also the same. This presents a problem, then, in creating the CultureInfo object:

```
CultureInfo cultureInfo = new CultureInfo("es-ES");
```

This code is ambiguous to the reader because there are two cultures that have the name "es-ES". When you use a string in the format <language>-<region> to identify a culture, you get the culture with the default sort order. Both the .NET Framework 1.1 and 2.0 enable you to create a culture for an alternate sort order using a locale ID (LCID):

```
CultureInfo cultureInfo = new CultureInfo(0x0000040A);
```

In addition, the .NET Framework 2.0 supports the creation of cultures for an alternate sort order using a language and region suffixed with the alternate sort order:

```
CultureInfo cultureInfo = new CultureInfo("es-ES_tradnl");
```

The same name can be used with the new CultureInfo.GetCultureInfo method to get a cached read-only CultureInfo. The following two examples of the CultureInfo.GetCultureInfo result in the same CultureInfo object:

```
CultureInfo cultureInfo1 =
    CultureInfo.GetCultureInfo("es-ES", "es-ES_tradnl");

CultureInfo cultureInfo2 =
    CultureInfo.GetCultureInfo("es-ES_tradnl");
```

This capability to specify a culture including an alternate sort order by name is an important enhancement to the .NET Framework because it means that all cultures can now be represented as strings. In contrast, to be able to represent all cultures (including cultures with alternate sort orders), code written for the .NET Framework 1.1 must support representing cultures using both strings (e.g., "es-ES") and also integers (e.g. 0x0000040A).

Table 6.7 is a list of all of the alternate sort orders recognized by the .NET Framework 1.1 and 2.0.

Table 6.7 Cultures with Alternate Sort Orders

Culture Name	Culture English Name	Default Sort Name	Alternate Sort Name	Alternate Sort LCID	CompareInfo Name
es-ES	Spanish (Spain)	International	Traditional	0x0000040A	es_ES_tradnl
zh-TW	Chinese (Taiwan)	Stroke Count	Bopomofo	0x00030404	zh-TW_pronun
zh-CN	Chinese (China)	Pronunciation	Stroke Count	0x00020804	zh-CN_stroke
zh-HK	Chinese (Hong Kong SAR)	Stroke Count	Stroke Count	0x00020c04	zh-HK_stroke
zh-SG	Chinese (Singapore)	Pronunciation	Stroke Count	0x00021004	zh-SG_stroke
zh-MO	Chinese (Macau SAR)	Pronunciation	Stroke Count	0x00021404	zh-MO_stroke
ja-JP	Japanese (Japan)	Default	Unicode	0x00010411	ja-JP_unicod
ko-KR	Korean (Korea)	Default	Korean Xwansung—Unicode	0x00010412	ko-KR_unicod
de-DE	German (Germany)	Dictionary	Phone Book Sort DIN	0x00010407	de-DE_phoneb
hu-HU	Hungarian (Hungary)	Default	Technical Sort	0x0001040e	hu-HU_technl
ka-GE	Georgian (Georgia)	Traditional	Modern Sort	0x00010437	ka-GE_modern

> Although the Japanese and Korean alternate Unicode sorts exist, they are unlikely to be used for any real purpose for sorting Japanese or Korean data. They are almost identical to the default sort, with the exception of one or two code points (e.g., Korean Won, Japanese Yen). They exist for compatibility.

The `CompareInfo` class has a `Name` property in the .NET Framework 2.0 (but not 1.1), which is the same as the `CultureInfo.Name` (e.g. "es-ES") for all default sort orders. This name can be used to specify cultures for alternate sort orders in the .NET Framework 2.0.

It is worth noting that, regardless of the data type (i.e., string or integer) used to create a `CultureInfo` object, the resulting `CultureInfo.Name` is the same as the name of the default sort order. The following example outputs "es-ES", "es-ES", and "es-ES":

```
CultureInfo cultureInfo1 = new CultureInfo("es-ES");
CultureInfo cultureInfo2 = new CultureInfo(0x0000040A);
CultureInfo cultureInfo3 = new CultureInfo("es-ES_tradnl");
listBox1.Items.Add(cultureInfo1.Name);
listBox1.Items.Add(cultureInfo2.Name);
listBox1.Items.Add(cultureInfo3.Name);
```

To distinguish between the different cultures, you should use either the LCID (in the .NET Framework 1.1 and 2.0) or, preferably, the `CompareInfo.Name` (in the .NET Framework 2.0).

Unfortunately, the .NET Framework does not support any facility for programmatically discovering alternate sort orders. However, the Win32 `EnumSystem Locales` function accepts a parameter of `LCID_ALTERNATE_SORTS`, which does provide this functionality and enables you to offer a choice of sort orders to a user. The following class is a wrapper around this function, and the `GetAlternative SortOrders` method returns an array of LCIDs of alternate sort orders:

```
public class AlternateSortOrders
{
    public static int[] GetAlternateSortOrders()
    {
        const uint LCID_ALTERNATE_SORTS = 4;

        alternateSortOrders = new List<int>();

        EnumSystemLocales(new LocaleEnumProc(AlternateSortsCallback),
            LCID_ALTERNATE_SORTS);

        int[] alternateSortOrdersArray =
            new int[alternateSortOrders.Count];

        alternateSortOrders.CopyTo(alternateSortOrdersArray);
```

```
        return alternateSortOrdersArray;
    }

    protected delegate bool LocaleEnumProc(string lcidString);

    [DllImport("kernel32.dll")]
    protected static extern bool EnumSystemLocales(
        LocaleEnumProc lpLocaleEnumProc, uint dwFlags);

    protected static List<int> alternateSortOrders;

    protected static bool AlternateSortsCallback(string lcidString)
    {
        int LCID;
        if (Int32.TryParse(lcidString,
            NumberStyles.AllowHexSpecifier, null, out LCID))
            alternateSortOrders.Add(LCID);

        return true;
    }
}
```

The GetAlternateSortOrders method calls EnumSystemLocales and passes a method (AlternateSortsCallback) to call back for each alternate sort order and a flag (LCID_ALTERNATE_SORTS) specifying that only the alternate sorts should be enumerated. The AlternateSortsCallback method simply converts the LCID string to an integer and adds it to an internal list. When the EnumSystemLocales function has completed enumerating locales, the GetAlternateSortOrders method converts the list of integers to an array of integers and returns the array.

As an alternative, the user can specify the preferred sort order in the Regional and Language Options dialog by clicking on the Customize button and selecting the Sort tab (see Figure 6.3).

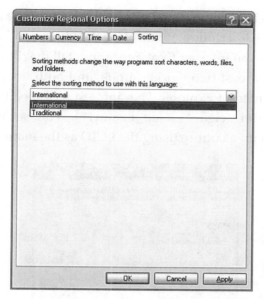

Figure 6.3   Using Customize Regional Options to Specify a Sort Order

Although this applies to all .NET Framework applications, it is unlikely to be useful in ASP.NET applications because the culture setting is more likely to arrive from the user's language preferences on their own machine. Figure 6.4 shows that the Spanish (International Sort) and Spanish (Traditional Sort) language preferences appear to be distinct.

Figure 6.4   Internet Explorer Language Preferences Dialog Showing Different Sort Orders

Unfortunately, this is just smoke and mirrors, as you can see from the "[es]" language code next to the description. If you close this dialog and reopen it (see Figure 6.5), you will see that even Internet Explorer cannot tell the difference between "es" and "es". There are at least two workarounds, and both involve defining a User-Defined language in Internet Explorer. The simplest is to specify a culture name that includes the sort order (e.g., "es-ES_tradnl"). The second, more complex, workaround is to specify a culture using the LCID as the name (see Figure 6.6).

Figure 6.5 Internet Explorer Language Preferences Dialog Showing Same Sort Orders

Figure 6.6 Internet Explorer Language Preferences Dialog with User-Defined LCID

Unfortunately, the `Culture="auto"` and `UICulture="auto"` tags used in ASP.NET 2.0 localized forms do not recognize LCIDs as valid culture identifiers, so you have to read the `Request.UserLanguage[0]` value and set the

`CurrentCulture` and `CurrentUICulture` in code. In ASP.NET 2.0, you can override the `Page.InitializeCulture` method to initialize the culture from the LCID:

```
protected override void InitializeCulture()
{
    if (Request.UserLanguages.GetLength(0) > 0)
    {
        string userLanguage = Request.UserLanguages[0];
        if ((userLanguage.StartsWith("0x") ||
            userLanguage.StartsWith("0X"))&&
            userLanguage.Length > 2)
        {
            // Int32.Parse requires that hex numbers do not
            // start with "0x" or "oX"
            string LCIDString = userLanguage.Substring(2);

            int LCID;
            if (Int32.TryParse(LCIDString,
                NumberStyles.AllowHexSpecifier, null, out LCID))
            {
                try
                {
                    Thread.CurrentThread.CurrentCulture =
                        new CultureInfo(LCID);

                    Thread.CurrentThread.CurrentUICulture =
                        Thread.CurrentThread.CurrentCulture;
                }
                catch (ArgumentException)
                {
                    // the LCID was not a valid LCID
                }
            }
        }
        else
        {
            try
            {
                int LCID = Convert.ToInt32(userLanguage);

                Thread.CurrentThread.CurrentCulture =
                    new CultureInfo(LCID);

                Thread.CurrentThread.CurrentUICulture =
                    Thread.CurrentThread.CurrentCulture;
            }
            catch (ArgumentException)
```

```
        {
            // the LCID was not a valid LCID
        }
        catch (FormatException)
        {
            // the LCID was not an integer
        }
    }
  }
}
```

This method accepts LCIDs either as hex values (prefixed with "0x") or as integers. Notice that the method deliberately ignores exceptions that result from an invalid user language, in keeping with ASP.NET's default behavior.

Persisting Culture Identifiers

There will be occasions when it will be necessary to persist a culture identifier. It may be to store a culture in a config file for a user preference, or in a database to maintain a list of selected cultures, or in an XML document for consumption by another process. The method of persistence of the culture identifier requires a moment's thought. We saw in the previous section that simply using a culture's name is insufficient to distinguish between a culture with a default sort order and a culture with an alternate sort order (because both cultures have the same name). The following method is suitable for persisting culture identifiers in the .NET Framework 2.0:

```
public static string GetPersistentCultureName(
    CultureInfo cultureInfo)
{
    if ((CultureTypes.UserCustomCulture & cultureInfo.CultureTypes)
        != (CultureTypes)0)
        return cultureInfo.Name;
    else
        return cultureInfo.CompareInfo.Name;
}
```

The if statement determines whether the culture is a custom culture (see Chapter 11). If the culture is a custom culture, the culture's name uniquely identifies the culture in all cases. If the culture is not a custom culture, the culture's CompareInfo name uniquely identifies the culture. The CompareInfo name is used instead of the culture's name because this value respects the culture's sort order. We cannot use the

`CompareInfo` name for custom cultures because custom cultures use `CompareInfo` objects from existing cultures, and such names do not uniquely identify the custom culture.

The following method is suitable for persisting culture identifiers in the .NET Framework 1.1:

```
public static string GetPersistentCultureName(
    CultureInfo cultureInfo)
{
    if (cultureInfo.LCID == 0x0000040A ||
        cultureInfo.LCID == 0x00030404 ||
        cultureInfo.LCID == 0x00020804 ||
        cultureInfo.LCID == 0x00020c04 ||
        cultureInfo.LCID == 0x00021004 ||
        cultureInfo.LCID == 0x00021404 ||
        cultureInfo.LCID == 0x00010411 ||
        cultureInfo.LCID == 0x00010412 ||
        cultureInfo.LCID == 0x00010407 ||
        cultureInfo.LCID == 0x0001040e ||
        cultureInfo.LCID == 0x00010437)
        return cultureInfo.LCID.ToString();
    else
        return cultureInfo.Name;
}
```

The .NET Framework 1.1 does not support custom cultures, so there is no need to write code for them. However, the .NET Framework 1.1's `CompareInfo` class doesn't have a name property, and its `CultureInfo`'s constructors do not accept `Compare Info` names to create cultures with alternate sort orders. The result is that cultures with alternate sort orders must be persisted using their locale IDs instead of their names. Any code that subsequently constructs a `CultureInfo` object from the resulting string must first check whether the string contains a name or number. If it contains a number, the string must first be converted to an integer.

Calendars

The calendar system known and used in most English-speaking countries is known as the Gregorian calendar. Started in 1582, it replaced the previous Julian calendar system, which had become increasingly inaccurate. Like other globalization issues, you can support any number of alternative calendar systems in use throughout the world without being aware of their differences by using the calendar classes provided. You can create new calendar objects directly from their class constructors (e.g., `new GregorianCalendar()`), but you will also encounter calendars through the use of the `CultureInfo.Calendar`, `CultureInfo.OptionalCalendars` and `DateTimeFormatInfo.Calendar` properties. For the "en-US" culture, `CultureInfo.Calendar` is a `GregorianCalendar` object. For the "ar-SA" (Arabic (Saudi Arabia)) culture, `CultureInfo.Calendar` is a `HijriCalendar` object. In fact, it is only the Arabic, Divehi and Thai cultures for which `CultureInfo.Calendar` is not a `GregorianCalendar`. The `CultureInfo.Calendar` property represents merely the "default" calendar used by the culture. Cultures can support any number of calendars (although the current maximum is seven) through the `OptionalCalendars` property. This array's first element contains the default calendar object, so `CultureInfo.Calendar` is equal to `CultureInfo.OptionalCalendars[0]`. The list of `OptionalCalendars` for the `Arabic (Saudi Arabia)` culture is shown in Table 6.8.

Table 6.8   Arabic Culture Optional Calendars

Calendar Class	Gregorian Calendar Type
HijriCalendar	
UmAlQuraCalendar **(.NET Framework 2.0 only)**	
GregorianCalendar	USEnglish
GregorianCalendar	MiddleEastFrench
GregorianCalendar	Arabic
GregorianCalendar	Localized
GregorianCalendar	TransliteratedFrench

As you can see, the last five calendars are all `GregorianCalendars`. `GregorianCalendars` have a `CalendarType` property (see Table 6.9) that determines the language used in date/time strings, but it does not affect the values of `Gregorian Calendar` properties.

Table 6.9 `GregorianCalendarTypes` **Enumeration**

Value	Description
`Arabic`	**Arabic**
`Localized`	**Language is determined by the** `CultureInfo`
`MiddleEast`	**Middle East French**
`TransliteratedEnglish`	**Transliterated English**
`TransliteratedFrench`	**Transliterated French**
`USEnglish`	**U.S. English**

For cultures that support more than one calendar, you can change the culture's calendar to one of the `OptionalCalendars` by assigning a new calendar to the culture's `DateTimeFormat.Calendar`:

```
CultureInfo cultureInfo = new CultureInfo("ar-SA");
// change the calendar to the second optional calendar
cultureInfo.DateTimeFormat.Calendar =
    cultureInfo.OptionalCalendars[1];

// change the calendar to the Gregorian(MiddleEastFrench) calendar
cultureInfo.DateTimeFormat.Calendar =
    new GregorianCalendar(GregorianCalendarTypes.MiddleEastFrench);

// Throws an ArgumentOutOfRangeException
cultureInfo.DateTimeFormat.Calendar = new JapaneseCalendar();
```

The complete set of calendar classes is shown in Figure 6.7. The classes typically differ in the following ways:

- The value of their properties (see Table 6.10)
- The name of their calendar-specific static era field (e.g., `ADEra` for `GregorianCalendar`, `HebrewEra` for `HebrewCalendar`)
- The logic used in their methods that are dependent upon calendar-specific calculations (e.g., `AddMonths`, `AddYears`, `GetDayOfYear`, `GetDaysInMonth`, `GetLeapMonth`, `GetWeekOfYear`, `IsLeapYear`)

Methods that perform day, week, and time arithmetic (such as `AddDays`, `AddHours`, `AddSeconds`, `AddWeeks`) are implemented in the base `Calendar` class.

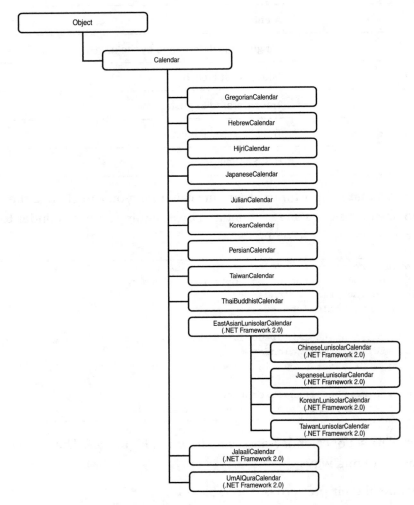

Figure 6.7   .NET Framework `Calendar` **Class Hierarchy**

Table 6.10   Calendar Property Values

Calendar Class	AlgorithmType	TwoDigit YearMax	MinSupported DateTime	MaxSupported DateTime
GregorianCalendar	SolarCalendar	2029	01 January 0001	31 December 9999
HebrewCalendar	Lunisolar Calendar	5790	01 January 1583	09 September 2239
HijriCalendar	LunarCalendar	1451	18 July 0622	31 December 9999
JapaneseCalendar	SolarCalendar	99	08 September 1868	31 December 9999
JulianCalendar	SolarCalendar	2029	01 January 0001	31 December 9999
KoreanCalendar	SolarCalendar	4362	01 January 0001	31 December 9999
PersianCalendar	SolarCalendar	1410	21 March 0622	31 December 9999
TaiwanCalendar	SolarCalendar	99	01 January 1912	31 December 9999
ThaiBuddhist Calendar	SolarCalendar	2572	01 January 0001	31 December 9999
ChineseLunisolar Calendar	Lunisolar Calendar	2029	19 February 1901	28 January 2101
JapaneseLunisolar Calendar	Lunisolar Calendar	99	28 January 1960	22 January 2050
KoreanLunisolar Calendar	Lunisolar Calendar	4362	26 January 0928	10 February 2051
TaiwanLunisolar Calendar	Lunisolar Calendar	99	18 February 1912	10 February 2051
JalaaliCalendar	SolarCalendar	1410	21 March 0622	31 December 9999
UmAlQuraCalendar	LunarCalendar	1410	18 July 0622	31 December 9999

The logic behind the calendar calculations is determined mostly by the `Algo-rithmType` property, which is a `CalendarAlgorithmType` enumeration (see Table 6.11). Although this property and its enumeration are new in the .NET Framework 2.0, it is still useful for categorizing the calendar classes in a discussion involving any version of the framework.

Table 6.11 `CalendarAlgorithmType` **Enumeration**

Value	Description
LunarCalendar	A lunar-based calendar
LunisolarCalendar	A luni-solar calendar
SolarCalendar	A solar calendar
Unknown	An unknown calendar

Table 6.12 shows some of the differences that you can expect from the calendars based on the different algorithms. The table shows the different possible values for the `Calendar GetDaysInMonth`, `GetMonthsInYear`, and `GetDaysInYear` methods. If there was any doubt about whether you should hard-code these values based on a North American/European background or use the .NET Framework's globalization classes, this table should remove that doubt.

Table 6.12 **Examples of** `CalendarAlgorithmType` **Differences**

CalendarAlgorithmType	GetDaysInMonth	GetMonthsInYear	GetDaysInYear
SolarCalendar	28, 29, 30, 31	12	365, 366
LunisolarCalendar	29, 30	12, 13	353, 354, 355, 356, 383, 384, 385
LunarCalendar	29, 30	12	354, 355

Calendars classes are often used in `DateTime` constructors to work with dates based on a given calendar, so in the following example, the year/month/day has a different meaning to each of the three calendars:

```
DateTime dateTime1 =
    new DateTime(2000, 1, 1, new GregorianCalendar());
```

```
DateTime dateTime2 =
    new DateTime(2000, 1, 1, new HijriCalendar());

DateTime dateTime3 =
    new DateTime(2000, 1, 1, new JapaneseCalendar());

listBox1.Items.Add(dateTime1.ToString("dd MMM yyyy"));
listBox1.Items.Add(dateTime2.ToString("dd MMM yyyy"));
listBox1.Items.Add(dateTime3.ToString("dd MMM yyyy"));
```

The result is:

```
01 Jan 2000
07 Jan 2562
01 Jan 3988
```

In this example, the year (2000), month (1), and day (1) mean a different day in time to different calendars.

Calendar Eras

The Calendar class has a read-only Eras integer array that lists the era numbers that can be used with the calendar. For all calendars except the JapaneseCalendar and JapaneseLunisolarCalendar, Eras has a single element containing the value 1. For the GregorianCalendar, this means that the calendar covers a single era—namely, AD (Anno Domini), also called CE (Current Era). The previous era, BC (Before Christ), also called BCE (Before Common Era), is not covered by the GregorianCalendar. The JapaneseCalendar has four eras, which are numbered 4, 3, 2, and 1 in elements 0, 1, 2, and 3 of the Eras array. The JapaneseLunisolar-Calendar has two eras, which are numbered 2 and 1 in elements 0 and 1. The only information that is available about these eras is the era name (in Kanji) and the era's abbreviated name (in Kanji). No further information is available about these eras programmatically, so you need to know that they refer to the eras of the Japanese Modern Period. Each era corresponds to the reign of a different emperor. Information about these eras, such as the Romaji names of the eras (Meiji, Taisho, Showa, and Heisei), the names of the emperors, and the periods of the eras are all unavailable, and you would have to manually hard-code such information into your application if you needed to make reference to it. The two references to the Eras property in the Calendar class are by the GetEras method and the CurrentEra field. The GetEras method accepts a `DateTime` and reports the era number (not the `Era` array element number), so the era for January 1, 2005, is 4. The `Calendar.CurrentEra` field is a read-only static constant with the value 0 and refers to the element number of the `Eras` array. Unfortunately, whereas `GregorianCalendar` has a static constant field (`ADEra`) that identifies its single era number, the `JapaneseCalendar` and `JapaneseLunisolarCalendar` classes do not have equivalent constants (e.g., `MeijiEra`, `TaishoEra`, `ShowaEra`, and `HeiseiEra`) to make programmatic comparisons with era numbers meaningful.

Calendar.TwoDigitYearMax

The `Calendar.TwoDigitYearMax` property is used to identify the century of two-digit years when date strings are parsed. For example, is "1/1/30" January 1, 0030, or January 1, 1930, or January 1, 2030 ? The `TwoDigitYearMax` represents the maximum year that is used for interpreting the century. Two-digit years that are higher than the last two digits of the year are assumed to be 100 years earlier than the `TwoDigitYearMax`. The following example uses the `English(US)` culture, which uses the `GregorianCalendar`, which has a `TwoDigitYearMax` of 2029:

```
Thread.CurrentThread.CurrentCulture = new CultureInfo("en-US");
listBox1.Items.Add(DateTime.Parse("1/1/29").ToLongDateString());
listBox1.Items.Add(DateTime.Parse("1/1/30").ToLongDateString());
cultureInfo.Calendar.TwoDigitYearMax = 2050;
listBox1.Items.Add(DateTime.Parse("1/1/29").ToLongDateString());
listBox1.Items.Add(DateTime.Parse("1/1/30").ToLongDateString());
```

The result is:

```
Monday, January 01, 2029
Wednesday, January 01, 1930
Monday, January 01, 2029
Tuesday, January 01, 2030
```

The user can change the `TwoDigitYearMax` (see Figure 6.8) by clicking the Customize button in the Regional Settings tab of Regional and Language Options.

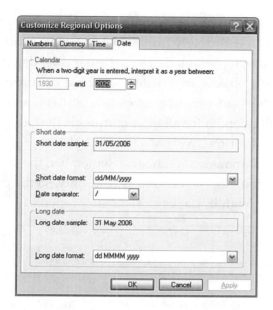

Figure 6.8   Customizing the Calendar.TwoDigitYearMax

For the value to be used, the `CultureInfo`'s `UseUserOverride` parameter must be `true`, which, by default, it is.

DateTimes, DateTimeFormatInfos, and Calendars

The relationship between the `DateTime` structure and `DateTimeFormatInfo` and `Calendar` classes warrants some explanation. The `DateTime` structure holds date/time information as a culture-agnostic point in time in the form of ticks (a long type). Regardless of how a `DateTime` structure is created, the point in time is not dependent upon any given culture, so January 1, 2000, refers to a fixed point in time, regardless of the calendar system used to create it or represent it. The `DateTime` structure accepts calendar objects in its constructor for the sole purpose of interpreting the year, month, and day passed to the constructor. (Recall from the previous section that the year 2000, month 1, and day 1 is open to interpretation depending upon the calendar system in use.) After the meaning of the year, month, and day has been established, the `DateTime` is not directly related to any given calendar.

The `DateTimeFormatInfo` class contains date-/time-formatting information. It has a read/write `Calendar` property from which it can draw information about how any given point in time is represented in a particular calendar. In the following code example, `CultureInfo` objects are created for three cultures: "en-US" (English (United States)), "ar-SA" (Arabic (Saudi Arabia)), and "ja-JP" (Japanese (Japan)). The default calendar for all three cultures is the `GregorianCalendar`, but the calendar is changed for the "ar-SA" culture to the `HijriCalendar` and for the "ja-JP" culture to the `JapaneseCalendar`. (Remember, the `CultureInfo.Calendar` property is the default `Calendar` and is read-only, so the only way to change a culture's calendar is through its `DateTimeFormat` property.)

```
CultureInfo englishCultureInfo = new CultureInfo("en-US");

CultureInfo arabicCultureInfo = new CultureInfo("ar-SA");
arabicCultureInfo.DateTimeFormat.Calendar = new HijriCalendar();

CultureInfo japaneseCultureInfo = new CultureInfo("ja-JP");
japaneseCultureInfo.DateTimeFormat.Calendar = new JapaneseCalendar();

DateTime firstJan2000 =
    new DateTime(2000, 1, 1, new GregorianCalendar());

listBox1.Items.Add(firstJan2000.ToString(englishCultureInfo));
listBox1.Items.Add(firstJan2000.ToString(arabicCultureInfo));
listBox1.Items.Add(firstJan2000.ToString(japaneseCultureInfo));
```

A single variable, `firstJan2000`, is shown three times, once for each calendar, giving the following results:

```
1/1/2000 12:00:00 AM
25/09/20 12:00:00 ص
平成 12/1/1 0:00:00
```

Although the representations of January 1, 2000, show different days, months, and years (and different AM/PM notation), it is the same point in time, as should be obvious by the fact that the variable does not change its value. The calendars are simply used to provide a human point of reference to the underlying ticks. You could draw an analogy with temperature in which the freezing point of water represents a single absolute temperature value (like a single point in time), and Fahrenheit,

Celsius, and Kelvin are simply different ways of representing the same value—so Fahrenheit, Celsius, and Kelvin act like the calendars of the temperature world.

The `DateTimeFormatInfo` class has several methods that provide access to the localized names of days, months, and eras (see Table 6.13).

Table 6.13 `DateTimeFormatInfo` **Localized Name Methods**

Method	Description	English (United States) Example
GetAbbreviatedDayName	Gets the abbreviated day name from a `DayOfWeek` **value**	`"Sun"`
GetAbbreviatedEraName	Gets the abbreviated era name from a `0`-based era number	`"AD"`
GetAbbreviatedMonthName	Gets the abbreviated month name from a `1`-based month number	`"Jan"`
GetDayName	Gets the day name from a **DayOfWeek** value	`"Sunday"`
GetEraName	Gets the era name from a `0`-based era number	`"A.D."`
GetMonthName	Gets the month name from a `1`-based month number	`"January"`

It should go without saying that you should always use these methods to iterate through day and month names instead of hard-coding them, but the following code should give you even more reason to use the `GetMonthName` method:

```
CultureInfo cultureInfo = new CultureInfo("he-IL");
DateTimeFormatInfo dtfi = cultureInfo.DateTimeFormat;
dtfi.Calendar = new HebrewCalendar();
for(int monthNumber = 1; monthNumber <=
    dtfi.Calendar.GetMonthsInYear(5345); monthNumber++)
{
    listBox1.Items.Add(dtfi.GetMonthName(monthNumber));
}
```

In this example, we use the "he-IL" (Hebrew (Israel)) culture and assign to its `DateTimeFormatInfo.Calendar` a new `HebrewCalendar` object. The Hebrew calendar has 13 months in leap years, and the Hebrew year 5345 is one such year.

We use the `Calendar.GetMonthsInYear` method to get the number of months in the given year (13, in this example), and then use the `DateTimeFormatInfo.Get-MonthName` to get the name of each month.

> In most cases, the `System.Windows.Forms.MonthCalendar` and `System.Windows.Forms.DateTimePicker` controls respect the calendar of the `CurrentUICulture`. The exception is the `HijriCalendar`, which is the default calendar for the `Arabic (Saudi Arabia)` and `Divehi (Maldives)` cultures. In this case, `MonthCalendar` and `Date-TimePicker` simply display a partially localized `GregorianCalendar` (day names are in Arabic/Divehi, and month names are in English).

DateTime.ToString, DateTime Parsing, and DateTimeFormatInfo

The `DateTime.ToString` method provides myriad formatting options for formatting date and times. You are at liberty to devise your own date/time formatting by assembling the basic building blocks of format patterns (d, M, y, g, h, H, m, s, f, t, z for the day, month, year, era, 12 hour, 24 hour, minute, second, fractions of a second, am/pm designator, and time zone offset, respectively), such as this:

```
new DateTime(2005, 1, 2).ToString("MM/dd/yy");
```

> It should be obvious that these format patterns are not localizable strings and should not be placed in resources. If they are placed in a resource, you run the risk of a translator translating them. So in French, the same string might be accidentally translated to "MM/jj/aa" (*year* is *année*, *Month* is *Mois*, and *day* is *jour*), resulting in a runtime exception.

The problem with this approach, however, is that it is almost certainly culturally biased. Whether the resulting string ("01/02/05") means January 2, 2005, or February 1, 2005, or February 5, 2001, depends on whether you come from the U.S., the U.K., or the People's Republic of China. The locale-aware solution is to let the .NET Framework worry about the format and use format characters instead of constructing your own format patterns. Format characters are single letters that indicate a completed pattern without forcing a specific implementation of that pattern. So, for example, the following conversion to the short date time character "d":

```
new DateTime(2005, 1, 2).ToString("d");
```

results in these strings in English (United States), English (United Kingdom), and Chinese (People's Republic Of China), respectively:

```
1/2/2005
02/01/2005
2005-1-2
```

The full list of format characters, their equivalent methods, and associated Date-TimeFormatInfo pattern properties is shown in Table 6.14. There is no functional difference between the format character and its associated method, so the following two lines are functionally identical:

```
new DateTime(2000, 1, 1).ToString("d");
new DateTime(2000, 1, 1).ToShortDateString();
```

However, the former accepts an optional IFormatProvider parameter (see the next section), whereas the latter does not, so it could be considered more versatile but equally, by FxCop standards (also see next section), more ambiguous.

Table 6.14   DateTime Format Character and Methods, and DateTimeFormatInfo Patterns

Format Character	Equivalent Method	Associated DateTimeFormatInfo Pattern Property
d	ToShortDateString	ShortDatePattern
D	ToLongDateString	LongDatePattern
f		

Table 6.14   DateTime Format Character and Methods, and `DateTimeFormatInfo`
Patterns   continued

Format Character	Equivalent Method	Associated `DateTimeFormatInfo` **Pattern Property**
F		`FullDateTimePattern`
g		
G		
m, M		`MonthDayPattern`
r, R		`RFC1123Pattern`
s		`SortableDateTimePattern`
t	`ToShortTimeString`	`ShortTimePattern`
T	`ToLongTimeString`	`LongTimePattern`
u		`UniversalSortableDateTimePattern`
U		
y, Y		`YearMonthPattern`

So you should conclude from this that when displaying a date/time to the user, you should always use the format character or its associated method, and should avoid building your own formats. If you want to enforce this approach in your code, take a look at the "DateTime.ToString() should not use a culture-specific format" rule in Chapter 13.

The `DateTime` structure in the .NET Framework 1.1 supports two methods for parsing date/time strings into dates/times: `Parse` and `ParseExact`. The .NET Framework 2.0 adds two new methods: `TryParse` and `TryParseExact`. The `Parse` method is very forgiving in its parsing of date/time strings and works hard to attempt to recognize numerous variations on string formats. So "12/31/01", "December, 31 01", and "31 December 01" are all parsed (using `English (United States)`) to mean December 31, 2001. This flexibility can be very handy but has a necessary performance hit and can be fooled. The `ParseExact` method, however, demands the date/time format string that should be used to parse the string. There are no gray areas; if the string doesn't match the format, an exception is thrown. The `TryParse` and `TryParseExact` .NET Framework 2.0 methods simply try the same operations but do not throw an exception if the parse attempt fails.

Genitive Date Support

If ever you needed any more reasons to let the .NET Framework do your globalization for you, then there is the issue of genitive dates. The good news is that the .NET Framework understands this problem and deals with it accurately. This is especially good news because it is unlikely that most English-only developers will know what a genitive date is or what the problem is. The issue is that, in some languages, when a month can be seen to "own" or "possess" a day, the month name changes. Table 6.15 shows English month names, Polish month names, and their genitive forms.

Table 6.15   Polish Month Names and Their Genitive Forms

English Month Name	Polish Month Name	Polish Genitive Month Example
January	styczeń	1 stycznia 2000
February	luty	1 lutego 2000
March	marzec	1 marca 2000
April	kwiecień	1 kwietnia 2000
May	maj	1 maja 2000
June	czerwiec	1 czerwca 2000
July	lipiec	1 lipca 2000
August	sierpień	1 sierpnia 2000
September	wrzesień	1 września 2000
October	październik	1 października 2000
November	listopad	1 listopada 2000
December	grudzień	1 grudnia 2000

You can see that the month name is different when it is used to "possess" a day. In the list of cultures that the .NET Framework supports, Czech, Greek, Latvian, Lithuanian, Mongolian, Polish, and Slovak all use genitive dates. The moral of the story, as usual, is to let the framework build date strings instead of taking the problem into your own hands. In both the .NET Framework 1.1 and 2.0, the `DateTimeFormatInfo` class understands how to use genitive dates, so the `Date-Time.ToString` method always returns correct strings. In the .NET Framework 2.0, you can gain programmatic access to the genitive month names using the `AbbreviatedMonthGenitiveNames` and `MonthGenitiveNames` array properties.

DateTime.ToString and IFormatProvider

The `DateTime.ToString` method has four overloads, which ultimately all boil down to a single signature:

```
public string ToString(string format, IFormatProvider provider);
```

This method simply returns the following value:

```
DateTimeFormat.Format(
    this, format, DateTimeFormatInfo.GetInstance(provider));
```

If the provider parameter is null, `DateTimeFormatInfo.GetInstance` uses `CultureInfo.CurrentCulture`.

The `IFormatProvider` interface has a single method:

```
public interface IFormatProvider
    {
        object GetFormat(Type formatType);
}
```

There are just three classes in the .NET Framework that support the `IFormatProvider` interface:

```
CultureInfo
DateTimeFormatInfo
NumberFormatInfo
```

The `GetFormat` method accepts a `Type` and returns an object of that `Type`. So if the `CultureInfo.GetFormat` method is called with the `DateTimeFormatInfo`

`Type`, then it returns the value of its `CultureInfo.DateTimeFormat` property. As the name implies, the `IFormatProvider` implementation provides formatting information. In this example, a German `CultureInfo` object provides the `IFormatProvider` interface:

```
DateTime firstJan2000 = new DateTime(2000, 1, 1);
CultureInfo cultureInfo = new CultureInfo("de-DE");
listBox1.Items.Add(firstJan2000.ToString("D", cultureInfo));
```

The following string is added to the list box:

```
Samstag, 1. Januar 2000
```

The `CultureInfo` object provides the `DateTimeFormatInfo`, which includes the date-/time-formatting patterns and also the `Calendar` required to represent the date. The FxCop "Specify IFormatProvider" rule (see Chapter 13) enforces that the `IFormatProvider` parameter is always passed to `DateTime.ToString`. The idea behind this rule is to ensure that there is no ambiguity in the way the date is represented and that the developer has been forced to consider the globalization issues of the code.

Numbers, Currencies, and NumberFormatInfo

Numbers and currencies follow a similar pattern to date/times and `DateTimeFormatInfo`, but without the additional complexity of calendars:

- Numbers and currencies are formatted using the `NumberFormatInfo` class.
- The `CultureInfo` class has a `NumberFormatInfo` property called `NumberFormat`.
- It is possible to build your own culture-unaware format strings from primitives such as #, the comma, the period, and zero (e.g., `"###,###.00"`).
- It is possible to specify culture-aware formats (see Table 6.16) using a format specifier, which draws on information in a `NumberFormatInfo` object.
- Number types that overload `ToString` methods accept an `IFormatProvider` that can be either a `NumberFormatInfo` or a `CultureInfo` (from which the `NumberFormatInfo` is extracted) .
- The FxCop "Specify IFormatProvider" rule catches number types that overload `ToString` methods, which are not called with an `IFormatProvider`.

Table 6.16　Standard Number Format Specifiers

Format Specifier	Name	Uses NumberFormatInfo
c, C	Currency	Yes
d, D	Decimal	No
e, E	Exponential (Scientific)	No
f, F	Fixed point	Yes
g, G	General	No
n, N	Number	Yes
p, P	Percent	Yes
r, R	Round-trip	No
x, X	Hexadecimal	No

As we saw with date/times, it should be obvious by now that predicting the myriad cultural differences across the world is very difficult, but to remove any doubt, have a look at the examples in Table 6.17, which show the number –20000.15 formatted for currency in a selection of different cultures. Notice the use of commas and periods to indicate sometimes a thousands separator and a decimal separator, and sometimes vice versa; the positioning of the currency symbol; the positioning of the negative sign; the expression of negatives using parentheses; and the exclusion of decimals altogether.

Table 6.17　Examples of Formatted Currencies

Culture Name	Culture DisplayName	Example Formatted Currency
ar-SA	Arabic (Saudi Arabia)	20,000.15.ر.س-
bg-BG	Bulgarian (Bulgaria)	-20 000,15 лв
ca-ES	Catalan (Catalan)	-20.000,15 €
zh-CN	Chinese (People's Republic of China)	□-20,000.15
zh-HK	Chinese (Hong Kong S.A.R.)	(HK$20,000.15)

Culture Name	Culture DisplayName	Example Formatted Currency
da-DK	Danish (Denmark)	kr -20.000,15
de-DE	German (Germany)	-20.000,15 €
de-AT	German (Austria)	-€ 20.000,15
en-US	English (United States)	($20,000.15)
en-GB	English (United Kingdom)	-£20,000.15
es-AR	Spanish (Argentina)	$-20.000,15
es-CL	Spanish (Chile)	-$ 20.000,15
ja-JP	Japanese (Japan)	**-¥20,000**
id-ID	Indonesian (Indonesia)	(Rp20.000)

International Domain Name Mapping

When the World Wide Web was first developed, the Domain Name Service upon which it is based was rooted firmly in the ASCII character set. This meant that all domain names had to conform to 7-bit ASCII. This tiny range (U+0000 to U+007f) covers the English language and very few others. The problem faced by the rest of the world was how to create domain names that used characters outside of this range yet still worked with the antiquated ASCII DNS.

Before we look at the solution, let's be a little clearer about what the problem is from the developer's point of view. Open Internet Explorer 6 or earlier and navigate to www.i18ncafé.com. Internet Explorer will be unable to navigate to this page because the domain name cannot be resolved; it contains an "e" with an acute accent (é), which is outside of the 7-bit ASCII range. If you use Internet Explorer 7, FireFox, Mozilla, Opera, or Safari, you will be able to successfully navigate to this page because all of these browsers support international domain names (IDN). Developers need to care about this problem because if your application needs to navigate to such a page using Internet Explorer 6 or earlier, or to send an e-mail to a person on such a domain name, or interact with such a domain in any way that uses DNS, you will need to know how to convert the name to its ASCII equivalent.

In 2003, the IETF published the "Internationalizing Domain Names in Applications (IDNA)" standard (RFC 3490) to provide an interim solution until DNS fully supports Unicode. Remember that the Internet is the world's largest legacy system, so upgrading it is not a fast process. IDNA is an encoding mechanism that converts Unicode domain names into ASCII domain names that can be recognized by Domain Name Servers everywhere. The .NET Framework 2.0 includes the `IdnMapping` class, which is an encapsulation of the IDNA encoding mechanism. Figure 6.9 shows a Windows Forms application that illustrates the IDN problem and solution.

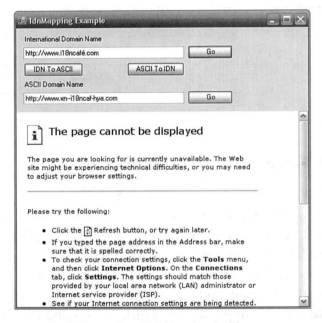

Figure 6.9   IDN Mapping Problem

The "Go" button next to the International Domain Name TextBox contains the following code:

```
webBrowser1.Navigate(textBoxIDN.Text);
```

When the button is pressed, the WebBrowser at the bottom of the form fails to navigate to the domain. The IDN To ASCII button contains the following code:

```
IdnMapping idnMapping = new IdnMapping();
textBoxASCII.Text = idnMapping.GetAscii(textBoxIDN.Text);
```

When the button is pressed, the ASCII TextBox is filled with the encoded domain name "http:// www.xn—i18ncaf-hya.com". The second "Go" button contains the following code:

```
webBrowser1.Navigate(textBoxASCII.Text);
```

The browser can successfully navigate to the ASCII domain name. To convert in the other direction, from ASCII to Unicode, you use the `IdnMapping.GetUnicode` method:

```
IdnMapping idnMapping = new IdnMapping();
textBoxIDN.Text = idnMapping.GetUnicode(textBoxASCII.Text);
```

The strategy is that, in your application, you use the `IdnMapping` class to show the Unicode domain names in the user interface, but the ASCII domain names in any programmatic operation (such as navigating to a page or sending an email).

Table 6.18 shows a number of examples of Unicode domain names and their ASCII-encoded equivalents. You should be able to appreciate from the list that Anglicizing all domain names is an unacceptable solution to people who do not use English as a primary language. It is also worth noting that names that do not need any conversion do not get any conversion, so it is safe to use the `IdnMapping` class everywhere without fear of it breaking existing code.

Table 6.18 International Domain Name Examples

Unicode Domain Name	Non-ASCII Characters	ASCII Domain Name
www.microsoft.com	None	www.microsoft.com
www.Bodenschätze.de	German	www.xn—bodenschtze-s8a.de
www.münchhausen.at	German	www.xn—mnchhausen-9db.at
www.金銭.com	Japanese	www.xn—5m4ayq.com
www.부산항.com	Korean	www.xn—or3bi2dc4z.com
www.gulvmiljø.no	Norwegian	www.xn—gulvmilj-d5a.no
www.españa.com	Spanish	www.xn—espaa-rta.com

International Domain Names and Visual Spoofing

One of the concerns that you will often see raised with regard to international domain names is visual spoofing. Table 6.19 illustrates the problem.

Table 6.19   Visual Spoofing Using International Domain Names

Original Domain Name	Spoofed Domain Name	ASCII Spoofed Domain Name
www.microsoft.com	www.microsoft.com	www.xn—mirsft-koebo8i.xn—m-rmb3ob
www.gotdotnet.com	www.gotdotnet.com	www.xn—gtdtnt-ioec87h.xn—m-rmb3ob
www.cnn.com	www.cnn.com	www.xn—nn-nmc.xn—m-rmb3ob
www.addisonwesley.com	www.addisonwesley.com	www.xn—ddisnwsly-t1g25j6bc.xn—m-rmb3ob

Can you see a difference between the original domain name and the spoofed domain name? No, neither can I—but they are different, as you can see by the ASCII domain name of the spoofed domain. The difference is that certain letters have been replaced with different letters that are visually identical in certain fonts. The Latin Small Letter *O* (U+006F), for example, has been replaced with the Greek Small Letter Omicron (U+03BF). In general, spoof characters are drawn from Cherokee, Cyrillic, or Greek characters. The problem is that people see links to Web sites and e-mail addresses (often in spam emails), and trust them to be genuine because they look genuine. The problem itself isn't new, but international domain names make the scope of the problem much wider. The problem itself doesn't have any impact on the steps you need to take when internationalizing your applications, but you should be aware of this security issue (see http://www.unicode.org/reports/tr36/ for more details).

Environment Considerations

It is good practice to avoid hard-coding references to specific file locations in any application, but international applications have an additional consideration: The names of special folders are localized in some language versions of Windows. So, if you make a direct reference to the program files folder using "\Program Files", the folder you actually find (if it exists) may or may not be the program files folder you are expecting to find. In the German version of Windows, for example, the program files folder is "\Programme". You can avoid hard-coding references to specific file locations using the Environment.GetFolderPath method. Replace code like this:

```
string programFilesFolder = @"\Program Files";
```

with code like this:

```
string programFilesFolder =
    Environment.GetFolderPath(
    Environment.SpecialFolder.ProgramFiles);
```

Extending the CultureInfo Class

As sophisticated as the CultureInfo class and its supporting classes are, it does not cover every globalization issue that your application will encounter. There are more globalization issues that you might need to address that are outside of the scope of the existing CultureInfo class. Such issues include:

- Postal code formats differ from country to country (not all countries even use a postal code).
- Address formats differ from country to country.
- Preferred paper sizes differ from country to country. (Imagine how irritating it would be to users in the United States if their .NET application defaulted to A4 every time it printed.)
- Units of measure differ from country to country (temperature, distance, volumes, etc.).

Furthermore, the CultureInfo class includes only basic information about the language/country. Information about the following is absent:

- The country's continent
- The IANA Top Level Domains used by the country
- The time zones that span the country
- The country's International Olympics Committee (IOC) code
- The International Distance Direct Dialing code used by the country

- The country's demographics (such as population, literacy, religions)
- The bumper sticker code used on vehicles of that country
- The country's capital city (in English and native language)

These examples would all extend a `RegionInfo` class instead of a `CultureInfo` class, but you can see that the need exists; it is probably only a matter of time before you find your own reasons why you want to extend the `CultureInfo` class, so we tackle this issue here. We extend the `CultureInfo` class in two stages: First we create a new `CultureInfoEx` class that can be extended. Then we extend it using an example of attaching postal code formats to a culture.

Initially, extending the `CultureInfo` class looks simple. Simply inherit from `CultureInfo` and implement the same constructors as the `CultureInfo` class:

```
public class CultureInfoEx: CultureInfo
{
    public CultureInfoEx(int culture): base(culture)
    {
    }
    public CultureInfoEx(string name): base(name)
    {
    }
    public CultureInfoEx(int culture, bool useUserOverride):
        base(culture, useUserOverride)
    {
    }
    public CultureInfoEx(string name, bool useUserOverride):
        base(name, useUserOverride)
    {
    }
}
```

The problems lie with culture's parents and the invariant culture. Whenever you use the `CultureInfo.Parent` property, it returns a new instance of a `CultureInfo` object. So in this example, we start with a new `CultureInfoEx` object, but when we get its parent, we get a `CultureInfo` object, not a `CultureInfoEx` object:

```
CultureInfoEx cultureInfo = new CultureInfoEx("en-GB");
CultureInfo parentCultureInfo = cultureInfo.Parent;
```

To solve this problem, we need to implement a new `Parent` property in our `CultureInfoEx` class:

```
public new CultureInfoEx Parent
{
    get
    {
        CultureInfo parent = base.Parent;
        if (CultureInfo.InvariantCulture.Equals(parent))
            return CultureInfoEx.InvariantCulture;
        else
            // change the type of the parent to CultureInfoEx
            return new CultureInfoEx(parent.Name, UseUserOverride);
    }
}
```

The `get` method starts by getting the base class's `Parent`. This will be a regular `CultureInfo` object. We check to see whether this is the invariant culture; if it is, we replace it with our own `CultureInfoEx` invariant culture (more on this in a moment). If it isn't the invariant, we need to build a new `CultureInfoEx` object from the name of the original parent `CultureInfo` object. We also pass the `UseUserOverride` property to the new `CultureInfoEx`'s constructor, to ensure that it adopts the user's settings if it should do so.

The second problem is the invariant culture. `CultureInfo.InvariantCulture` returns a `CultureInfo` object, not a `CultureInfoEx` object. We want our `CultureInfoEx` objects to be polymorphic, so the invariant culture must be changed to be a `CultureInfoEx` object as well. For this, we implement a new static `Invariant Culture` property:

```
private static CultureInfoEx invariantCulture;
public new static CultureInfoEx InvariantCulture
{
    get
    {
        if (invariantCulture == null)
        {
            invariantCulture = new CultureInfoEx(0x7f, false);
        }
        return invariantCulture;
    }
}
```

0x7F is the locale ID of the invariant culture. The InvariantCulture property is simply a wrapper and initializer for the private static invariantCulture field. Unfortunately, in this case, Microsoft is very fond of encapsulation, and encapsulation is opposed to inheritance. Our new invariant culture is not quite the same as CultureInfo.InvariantCulture (apart from the obvious difference in classes). The difference is that the CultureInfo.InvariantCulture is read-only, whereas CultureInfoEx.InvariantCulture is read/write. The field that holds the read-only state is internal and, therefore, prevents inheritance from working effectively. One solution to this problem would be to use Type.GetField to get the FieldInfo for the internal m_IsReadOnly field, and call its SetValue method to set it to true. It is aesthetically unpleasing, but encapsulation often presents inheritors with no other choice.

Now that our Parent and InvariantCulture properties have been implemented, there is one more issue that we should look at. Consider the following code, which starts with a specific culture ("en-US") and walks through its parents ("en" and then the invariant culture), adding the culture names to a list box:

```
CultureInfoEx cultureInfo = new CultureInfoEx("en-US");
listBox1.Items.Add(cultureInfo.Name);
while (! CultureInfo.InvariantCulture.Equals(cultureInfo))
{
    cultureInfo = cultureInfo.Parent;
    listBox1.Items.Add(cultureInfo.Name);
}
```

Notice that the while loop checks to see if the current culture is the invariant culture. More specifically, it checks to see if it is the CultureInfo invariant culture and not the CultureInfoEx invariant culture. You might expect this to either enter an infinite loop or else crash when you get the parent of the invariant culture (although that wouldn't happen because the parent of the invariant culture is the invariant culture). In fact, this code works just the way that you want it to because the test for equality is based on object references and the culture name in the .NET Framework 2.0 and the locale ID (only) in the .NET Framework 1.1. So when you compare a CultureInfo.InvariantCulture with a CultureInfoEx.InvariantCulture, the result is true because the object references/culture names (in the .NET Framework

2.0) or locale IDs (in the .NET Framework 1.1) are the same. This simple fact is essential in successfully extending the `CultureInfo` class because this test is exactly what the `ResourceManager` class does when it goes through its resource fallback process: The fallback process stops when it reaches the invariant culture. If the `CultureInfoEx.InvariantCulture` wasn't equal to the `CultureInfo.InvariantCulture`, the `ResourceManager` would enter an infinite loop.

The replacement of the `CultureInfo` class with the extended `CultureInfoEx` class lends more weight to the suggestion earlier in this chapter to use a `CultureInfoProvider` class to provide culture objects. In this case, the overloaded `CultureInfoProvider.GetCultureInfo` methods would create `CultureInfoEx` objects instead of `CultureInfo` objects.

The second stage of extending the `CultureInfo` class is to provide some new functionality. The example I use is to attach postal code format information to the culture. The `PostalCodeInfo` class is a simple example that enables us to focus on the model of extending the `CultureInfo` class instead of the details of postal codes. Postal code formats vary from country to country. The .NET Framework 2.0 `MaskedTextBox` control has a property called `Mask` that can be set to a mask to restrict input. This kind of control is ideal for helping with data such as postal codes, which obey a fixed format. The `MaskedTextBox` even has an Input Mask dialog that offers a set of input masks based upon the current culture of the development machine. Unfortunately, the correct input mask can be determined only at runtime, not at development time. Consequently, we need to have some facility that we can interrogate to get the right format for a culture. Enter the `PostalCodeInfo` class. This class and its supporting infrastructure in the `CultureInfoEx` class are loosely modeled on the `DateTimeFormatInfo` class and its supporting structure in the `CultureInfo` class. In its simplest form, the `PostalCodeInfo` class can be used like this:

```
PostalCodeInfo postalCodeInfo = new PostalCodeInfo("en-US");
maskedTextBox1.Mask = postalCodeInfo.Mask;
```

> If you are using Visual Studio 2003, there are at least two controls that offer a similar functionality to the .NET Framework 2.0's `MaskedTextBox`. The first is Microsoft's Masked Edit Control in `msmask32.ocx`. To add the control to your toolbox, right-click your toolbox, select Add/Remove Items…, select the COM Components tab, scroll down to the Microsoft Masked Edit Control component, check it, and click OK. The second is the `MaskedEditTextBox` C# control, which offers similar functionality using regular expressions at http://msdn.microsoft.com/vcsharp/downloads/samples/23samples/default.aspx. See the link entitled "Creating a Masked Edit Control using .NET Framework Regular Expressions with C#."

An overloaded `PostalCodeInfo` constructor accepts a culture name, and the `Mask` property contains the correct postal code mask for the locale (a US ZIP code, in this example). This isn't how it is expected to be used, but for now we will just look at how it is implemented and come back to a more common usage in a moment. The `PostalCodeInfo` class looks like this:

```
public class PostalCodeInfo
{
    protected static Hashtable masks;

    static PostalCodeInfo()
    {
        masks = new Hashtable();
        masks.Add("en-US", "00000-9999");
        masks.Add("en-GB", "L?90? 9??");
        masks.Add("en-AU", "LLL 0000");
    }
    public static string GetMask(string cultureName)
    {
        if (masks.ContainsKey(cultureName))
            return (string) masks[cultureName];
        else
            return null;
    }
    public static void SetMask(string cultureName, string mask)
    {
```

```
        if (masks.ContainsKey(cultureName))
            masks[cultureName] = mask;
        else
            masks.Add(cultureName, mask);
    }

    public PostalCodeInfo()
    {
    }
    public PostalCodeInfo(string cultureName)
    {
        this.mask = GetMask(cultureName);
    }
    private string mask;
    public string Mask
    {
        get {return mask;}
        set {mask = value;}
    }
}
```

It has a protected static field called `masks`, which is a `Hashtable` of all the masks for every culture. The field is initialized by the static constructor to the "known" values of postal code formats. The list can be modified using the static `SetMask` method to change incorrect values or to add new cultures that are not part of the original list. This last issue is important for supporting custom cultures that this class cannot know about at design time. The `PostalCodeInfo` constructor accepts a culture name and performs a lookup in its mask's `Hashtable` to find the corresponding postal code for the culture name. It assigns this mask to its private `mask` field, which has a public `Mask` property wrapper. The class itself is not overly complex. The next step is to make the `CultureInfoEx` class aware of it in the following addition to `CultureInfoEx`:

```
private PostalCodeInfo postalCodeInfo;
public PostalCodeInfo PostalCode
{
    get
    {
        CheckNeutral(this);
        if (postalCodeInfo == null)
            postalCodeInfo = new PostalCodeInfo(Name);
        return postalCodeInfo;
    }
```

```
    set {postalCodeInfo = value;}
}
protected static void CheckNeutral(CultureInfo culture)
{
    if (culture.IsNeutralCulture)
    {
        throw new NotSupportedException(
            EnvironmentEx.GetResourceString(
            "Argument_CultureInvalidFormat",
            new object[1] { culture.Name }));
    }
}
```

The private `postalCodeInfo` field holds a reference to the `PostalCodeInfo` object associated with the culture. The public `PostalCodeInfo` property's `get` method initializes this field. First it calls `CheckNeutral` to assert that the culture is not neutral. I have taken the approach that a postal code cannot belong to just a language—it can be associated only with a country/region. Then the field is initialized from a `PostalCodeInfo` object matching the culture name (the `CultureInfo.Name` property) of the culture.

The normal use of the `PostalCodeInfo` class, therefore, is more akin to this:

```
CultureInfoEx cultureInfo = new CultureInfoEx("en-US");
maskedTextBox1.Mask = cultureInfo.PostalCode.Mask;
```

From this simple postal code model, you should be able to extend the `Culture-Info` class to meet your own globalization requirements.

Where Are We?

We started this chapter with the basic premise that a large part of your globalization issues are handled for you if you use the .NET Framework globalization classes. The conclusion is no different. Of course, the basic premise does require that you know what the classes are, what their properties and methods are, and how and when you should use them, but you should be reassured from the examples in this chapter that the .NET Framework is going to considerable lengths on your behalf to relieve you of the burden of having to know every detail about every culture.

7

Middle East and East Asian Cultures

T HE EXAMPLES WE HAVE USED IN THIS BOOK up to this point have been based on Latin "left-to-right" languages and languages based on simple scripts. The conclusions we have drawn have been sufficient for most northern European languages, such as French, German, and Spanish. In terms of world population, however, we have not yet covered a large part of the world. Middle Eastern languages such as Arabic, Hebrew, and Persian (Farsi), and East Asian languages such as Chinese, Japanese, and Korean all have additional considerations that we need to make to correctly internationalize our applications. This chapter covers these considerations.

Supplemental Language Support

If you are using Windows Vista, you can skip this section because supplemental language support is always installed in Windows Vista. If you are using a Latin-based language version of Windows (such as `English (US)`) prior to Windows Vista that does not include support for Middle East and East Asian languages, you will need to install support before you continue. If you are using Windows 2000, Windows XP, or Windows Server 2003, open the Control Panel, select Regional and Language Options, and select the Languages tab (see Figure 7.1). Check the "Install files for complex script and right-to-left languages (including Thai)" check box to install Supplemental Language Support for Arabic, Armenian, Georgian, Hebrew, Indic, Thai, and Vietnamese. Check the "Install files for East Asian languages" check box to install Supplemental Language Support for Chinese, Japanese, and Korean. The former requires 10Mb of disk space, and the latter requires 230Mb. In addition to installing necessary fonts, the "Install files for complex script and right-to-left languages (including Thai)" check box adds three Windows-only cultures (`Bengali (India)`, `Hindi`, and `Malayam (India)`) to the .NET Framework 2.0.

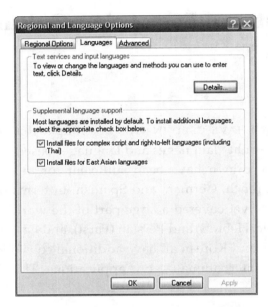

Figure 7.1   Installing Supplemental Language Support

If you are using a non–East Asian version of Windows 98, Me, or NT4 and you have not installed a Chinese-, Japanese-, or Korean-language version of Office XP, you will need to install the Microsoft Global IME with Language Packs to view Chinese, Japanese, or Korean characters. The Language Packs include the necessary fonts to render these characters and are available only as part of the Microsoft Global IME. If you have already installed Office XP, download the Microsoft Global IME from http://office.microsoft.com/en-gb/assistance/HA010347361033.aspx. If you have not installed Office XP, download the Microsoft Global IME from http://www.microsoft.com/windows/ie/downloads/recommended/ime/install.mspx.

Right-to-Left Languages and Mirroring

Right-to-left (RTL) languages are languages that read from right to left, as opposed to English, which reads from left to right (LTR). The right-to-left languages recognized by the .NET Framework 1.1 and 2.0 are Arabic, Divehi, Hebrew, Persian (called Farsi in the .NET Framework 1.1), Syriac, and Urdu. Figure 7.2 shows a simple Windows Forms application with a left-to-right `TextBox` and a right-to-left `TextBox`. Your experience when using these two `TextBox`es depends upon whether you are typing in a left-to-right language or a right-to-left language. Let's start with a left-to-right, such as English. When you type into a left-to-right `TextBox`, the characters are added to the right of the existing characters and the insertion point or I-beam moves toward the right with each new character. When you type into an RTL `TextBox`, the characters are added to the right of the existing characters, but the insertion point remains on the rightmost point of the `TextBox`.

The behavior changes if you type characters from a right-to-left language such as Arabic. You can try this by adding an Arabic keyboard. Open the Regional and Language Options Dialog, select the Languages tab, click the Details… button, click the Add… button, select a right-to-left language (e.g., `Arabic (Saudi Arabia)`) from the Input language combo box, click OK and click OK again. To use the Arabic keyboard, click the language bar on the taskbar and select "AR" from the list. Your keyboard will now type Arabic characters. When you type into a left-to-right `TextBox`, the characters are added to the left of the existing characters and the insertion point remains on the left with each new character. When you type into a right-to-left `TextBox`, the characters are added to the left of the existing characters and the insertion point remains on the leftmost point of the `TextBox`. The granularity of this behavior is at the word level, not at the control level, so if you write words in both English and Arabic within the same `TextBox`, you will see the behavior switch back and forth, depending on whether the insertion point is on a left-to-right word or a right-to-left word.

Figure 7.2   Left-to-Right and Right-to-Left TextBoxes

The reading direction doesn't affect only the direction of the text; it also affects the flow of the document. A right-to-left book is read from the rightmost page, perceived as the back of the book by left-to-right readers, to the leftmost page. This flow direction must also be reflected in applications. So the form in Figure 7.3 is unacceptable even if all of the TextBoxes support right-to-left input.

Figure 7.3   Unmirrored Windows Form

For this form to flow correctly, it must be "mirrored." Imagine that you hold up a mirror to the side of the form and look into the mirror; the image in the mirror is what the form should look like to flow correctly. Figure 7.4 shows the same form mirrored. (I have deliberately not translated the form, to allow a clearer comparison between the two forms, but it should be noted that it is very confusing to lay out a form in a right-to-left flow while using a left-to-right language.)

Figure 7.4   Mirrored Windows Form

You can see from the mirrored form that mirroring involves more than just relocating the controls. It also involves changing the appearance of the controls and the appearance of forms. Figure 7.5 shows Windows Explorer running on the Arabic version of Windows XP. In the desktop, notice that the Start menu is on the right and that the taskbar extends from right to left. Also notice the direction of all the arrows. Not only have the controls moved, but the images indicating directions have changed.

Figure 7.5   Windows Explorer on Arabic Windows XP

The concepts of right to left and mirroring are separate, but in practice, you will often find them lumped together because it is rare to use one without the other. This is reinforced in ASP.NET 1.1 and 2.0 applications, where there is usually no distinction. Windows Forms 1.1 applications support right-to-left input but no mirroring. Windows Forms 2.0 applications include support for both right-to-left and mirroring, and, unlike ASP.NET, make a distinction between the two, as you will see shortly.

Detecting a Right-to-Left Culture

In most applications, you will want to write a single code base and use separate satellite assemblies to support additional languages. In this scenario, your application must determine whether the chosen culture is a left-to-right culture or a right-to-left culture. In the .NET Framework 2.0, this is a simple matter of checking the `CultureInfo.TextInfo.IsRightToLeft` Boolean property:

```
if (System.Threading.Thread.
    CurrentThread.CurrentUICulture.TextInfo.IsRightToLeft)
```

Not only is this the simplest solution, but it is also the safest solution because it respects custom cultures (see Chapter 11, "Custom Cultures"), whereas a hard-coded dependency upon a known right-to-left culture (e.g., `if (cultureInfo.Name.StartsWith ("ar")))`) does not.

The `TextInfo.IsRightToLeft` property is new in the .NET Framework 2.0. In the .NET Framework 1.1, there is no way to ask a `CultureInfo` object if it is a right-to-left culture, so a hard-coded solution is needed:

```
public static bool CultureInfoIsRightToLeft()
{
    return CultureInfoIsRightToLeft(CultureInfo.CurrentUICulture);
}
public static bool CultureInfoIsRightToLeft(CultureInfo cultureInfo)
{
    if (cultureInfo == null ||
        cultureInfo.Equals(CultureInfo.InvariantCulture))
        return false;

    string cultureInfoLanguage =
        cultureInfo.TwoLetterISOLanguageName;

    return
        cultureInfoLanguage == "ar"  || // Arabic
        cultureInfoLanguage == "div" || // Divehi
        cultureInfoLanguage == "fa"  || // Farsi
        cultureInfoLanguage == "he"  || // Hebrew
        cultureInfoLanguage == "syr" || // Syriac
        cultureInfoLanguage == "ur";    // Urdu
}
```

This `CultureInfoIsRightToLeft` method uses the `CultureInfo`'s `TwoLetterISOLanguageName`. Remember that this property can return either two or three letters, contrary to what the property name implies, so this approach works just as well with "`div`" (Divehi) and "`syr`" (Syriac).

Right-to-Left Languages and Mirroring in Windows Forms Applications

In this section, we look at right-to-left and mirroring issues that are specific to Windows Forms applications. If you are interested in only ASP.NET applications, you can skip this section.

Right-to-left support is controlled by a public virtual property, `RightToLeft`, in the .NET Framework 1.1 and 2.0, and additionally `RightToLeftLayout` in the .NET Framework 2.0. We return to `RightToLeftLayout` shortly. The `RightToLeft` property is implemented in the `Control` class, which is consequently surfaced in all controls, including `System.Windows.Forms.Form`. The `Control.RightToLeft` property is a `RightToLeft` enumeration that has the values `No`, `Yes`, and `Inherit`. The behavior of this property can be confusing if you are not familiar with it. By default, all controls inherit their `RightToLeft` value from their parent control. The ultimate parent is a `Form`. A control that has no parent defaults its `RightToLeft` value to `No`, so by default, `Form.RightToLeft` is `No`. If `Form.RightToLeft` is changed to `Yes`, all the controls on the form adopt this new setting.

Controls can break their `RightToLeft` "inheritance" by having an explicit value of either `Yes` or `No`. A control can revert to its parent's value by setting a value of `Inherit`. The potentially confusing part of this relationship is that no control ever reports its `RightToLeft` value as `Inherit`. The property always reports what its current state is (after it has adopted its value from its parent and so on). Thus, you can assign `Inherit` to a `RightToLeft` property, but it will never be equal to `Inherit`. You can see this in Visual Studio by setting `RightToLeft` to `Inherit` in the Properties Window and observing that it immediately changes to `No` or `Yes`. Consequently, there is no way that you can tell in code whether a control has a value because it was explicitly assigned the value or because it is inheriting its value.

The `Control.RightToLeft` property is related to the `TextAlign` property, which is implemented in many controls, including `TextBox` and `Label`. The `TextAlign` property is a `TextAlign` enumeration that has the values `Left` and `Right`. The trick to understanding the behavior of the `TextAlign` property is that the terms *left* and *right* are notional and are not absolute; the enumeration values would be better renamed "Nearside" and "Farside," respectively. So when you set `RightToLeft` to `Yes` in a `TextBox`, its `TextAlign` property does not change from `Left` to `Right`. The text in the `TextBox` is indeed aligned to the right, but the interpretation of the "Left" value is that the text is aligned to the nearside of the control, where the nearside is determined by the `RightToLeft` property. The upshot of all of this is that the control behaves correctly without you having to change the `TextAlign` property whenever the `RightToLeft` property is changed.

RightToLeftLayout

Mirroring is controlled in the .NET Framework 2.0 by the `RightToLeftLayout` property. Unlike the `RightToLeft` property, which is implemented in the `Control` class and, therefore, is present in all controls, the `RightToLeftLayout` property is implemented by the following controls only: `DateTimePicker`, `Form`, `ListView`, `MonthCalendar`, `PrintPreviewDialog`, `ProgressBar`, `TabControl`, `ToolStrip-ProgressBar`, `TrackBar`, and `TreeView`. The level of support for mirroring in Windows Forms applications depends on whether you are using the .NET Framework 1.1 or 2.0 and also on the version of Windows that the client is running on; as always, the latest and greatest offers the best support (see Table 7.1).

Table 7.1   Support for Mirroring in Microsoft Windows

Operating System	Mirroring Support
Windows 98 and Me	Available only in the Arabic and Hebrew versions of Windows
Windows 2000 and above	Available in all language versions of Windows

The form in Figure 7.4 is a .NET Framework 2.0 Windows Forms form that has had its `Form.RightToLeft` property set to `Yes` and also its `Form.RightToLeft-Layout` property set to `true`. The original unmirrored form is shown in Figure 7.3. The `RightToLeftLayout` property affects the repositioning of the controls and the layout of the form's title bar. First, notice that the form's caption and System Menu have moved from the left to the right, and also that the Close, Maximize, and Minimize buttons have moved from the right to the left. Second, notice that the layout of the `Phone TextBoxes` and the hyphen `Label` between them has been preserved, including their respective alignments to the sides of the `TextBoxes` above them.

> Unlike the `RightToLeft` property, the `RightToLeftLayout` property is not inherited by child controls, so setting `Form.RightToLeftLayout` to `true` does not affect the `RightToLeftLayout` property of any other controls.

The .NET Framework 2.0 `TableLayoutPanel` and `FlowLayoutPanel` container controls illustrated in Chapter 8, "Best Practices," respect the right-to-left setting and perform the same mirroring of the controls contained within them. This makes them ideal for form layout in a scenario in which the size and position of controls change but their relative positions must remain constant.

The operation of the `Control.RightToLeft` property in the .NET Framework 1.1 is no different than that of the .NET Framework 2.0. However, the `Form.RightToLeftLayout` property is not present in the .NET Framework 1.1, and there is no equivalent functionality. Figures 7.6, 7.7, and 7.8, respectively, show a .NET Framework 1.1 form with `Form.RightToLeft` set to `false`, the same form with `Form.RightToLeft` set to `true`, and the same form mirrored in the .NET Framework 2.0, with `Form.RightToLeft` set to `true` and `Form.RightToLeftLayout`.

Figure 7.6   A .NET Framework 1.1 Form with Form.RightToLeft Set to False

Figure 7.7   A .NET Framework 1.1 Form with Form.RightToLeft Set to True

Figure 7.8   A .NET Framework 2.0 Form with Form.RightToLeft Set to True and Form.RightToLeftLayout Set to True

Two differences exist. First, the .NET Framework 1.1 does not move the System Menu, Close, Maximize, and Minimize buttons. Second, the locations of the controls on the form do not change so that sides are not aligned to the right side of other controls. To provide this same relocation behavior, you would have to write the appropriate mirroring behavior and put it into the form's `RightToLeftChanged` event.

Setting RightToLeft and RightToLeftLayout Across the Application

To support an RTL culture, you need to set the `RightToLeft` property to `Yes` and the `RightToLeftLayout` property to `true` on every form in the application. Then all the controls will adopt the `RightToLeft` property and the form will be mirrored. The question remains, "How do you set the `RightToLeft` property to `Yes` and the `RightToLeftLayout` property to `true` for every form?" Three possibilities exist.

The most flexible solution is to make this problem part of the localization process. The localizer/translator must set the `RightToLeft` and `RightToLeftLayout` properties for every form. The benefit of this approach is flexibility, in that it is possible to have some forms or some controls in which `RightToLeft` is set to `No` and `RightToLeftLayout` is `false` because the values of `Yes` and `false` would be incorrect in the given context.

Another solution is to use the `StandardPropertiesResourceManager` in Chapter 12, "Custom Resource Managers." This resource manager ensures that certain properties (e.g., `Font` and `RightToLeft`) are always given the same value across the application. In this scenario, control is moved from the localizer to the developer. The benefits of this approach are that it is easy to make application-wide changes and that it provides a high degree of continuity. The downsides are that it lacks flexibility and that if you weren't planning to use a custom resource manager, you must take additional steps to employ its use throughout your application (see Chapter 12 for more details).

The third solution is to set the `RightToLeft` and `RightToLeftLayout` properties in the form's constructor based upon whether the culture is an RTL culture (see the section entitled "Detecting a Right-to-Left Culture"). The simplest way to ensure that all forms use this approach is to create a "base" form from which all forms inherit and place the necessary code in the base form. The base form's constructor would be something like this:

```
public BaseForm()
{
    InitializeComponent();

    CheckRightToLeft();
}
```

The `CheckRightToLeft` method is this:

```
protected virtual void CheckRightToLeft()
{
    if (CultureInfo.CurrentUICulture.TextInfo.IsRightToLeft)
    {
        RightToLeft = RightToLeft.Yes;
        RightToLeftLayout = true;
    }
    else
    {
        RightToLeft = RightToLeft.No;
        RightToLeftLayout = false;
    }
}
```

It is good practice to create a base form from which all forms inherit at the start of a project so that code snippets, such as this one, can be introduced into the application at a later stage without touching every form in the project.

You might occasionally see references to using the Win32 `SetProcessDefaultLayout` function to set the right-to-left setting for an entire application. This function achieves its result for Win32 GDI applications only; it has no effect on .NET Framework applications because they are based on GDI+.

MessageBox

If you use the .NET Framework `MessageBox` class in your application, you will need to take additional steps for the `MessageBox` to display correctly in a right-to-left application. The `MessageBox` implementation ultimately comes from the operating system, but the default layout is still left to right, regardless of whether the application is running on an RTL version of Windows. In addition, but not surprisingly, your form's `RightToLeft` property is ignored. Figure 7.9 shows the result of the following call to `MessageBox.Show` on Arabic Windows XP:

```
MessageBox.Show("No MessageBoxOptions", String.Empty,
    MessageBoxButtons.OKCancel);
```

Figure 7.9   Right-to-Left MessageBox on Arabic Windows XP

(If you can't read Arabic, the button on the left is the OK button and the button on the right is the Cancel button.) The `MessageBox.Show` method accepts a `Message-BoxOptions` parameter in which you can specify that the `MessageBox` should align the text to the right and should be mirrored:

```
MessageBox.Show(
    "RightAlign and RtlReading MessageBoxOptions",
    String.Empty, MessageBoxButtons.OKCancel,
    MessageBoxIcon.None,
    MessageBoxDefaultButton.Button1,
    MessageBoxOptions.RightAlign | MessageBoxOptions.RtlReading
    );
```

You can see the result in Figure 7.10. The Close button has moved from the right to the left, the OK and Cancel buttons have been transposed, and, although it cannot be seen when the text is wider than the two buttons, the text is right-aligned instead of left-aligned.

Figure 7.10   Left-to-Right MessageBox on Arabic Windows XP

This presents a minor challenge if you want to use a single code base for all cultures, regardless of whether they are left to right or right to left. For the code to be generic, you would have to surround each call to `MessageBox.Show` with an `if` statement:

```
if (CultureInfo.CurrentUICulture.TextInfo.IsRightToLeft)
    MessageBox.Show(
        "Do you get wafers with it ?",
        String.Empty, MessageBoxButtons.OKCancel,
```

```
            MessageBoxIcon.None,
            MessageBoxDefaultButton.Button1,
            MessageBoxOptions.RightAlign |
            MessageBoxOptions.RtlReading
            );
else
    MessageBox.Show(
        "Do you get wafers with it ?",
        String.Empty,
        MessageBoxButtons.OKCancel,
        MessageBoxIcon.None,
        MessageBoxDefaultButton.Button1,
        (MessageBoxOptions) 0);
```

(The second `MessageBox.Show` casts 0 to a `MessageBoxOptions` enumeration to pass no `MessageBoxOptions` for this parameter.) This solves the problem, but it is simply too cumbersome. A better solution is to move the `MessageBoxOptions` problem off to a utility method, `GlobalizationUtilities.RtlMessageBoxOptions`, so that the previous code becomes this:

```
MessageBox.Show(
    "Do you get wafers with it ?",
    String.Empty, MessageBoxButtons.OKCancel,
    MessageBoxIcon.None,
    MessageBoxDefaultButton.Button1,
    GlobalizationUtilities.RtlMessageBoxOptions()
    );
```

Here, `GlobalizationUtilities.RtlMessageBoxOptions` is this:

```
public static MessageBoxOptions RtlMessageBoxOptions()
{
    return RtlMessageBoxOptions(CultureInfo.CurrentUICulture);
}
public static MessageBoxOptions RtlMessageBoxOptions(
    CultureInfo cultureInfo)
{
    if (cultureInfo.TextInfo.IsRightToLeft)
        return
            MessageBoxOptions.RightAlign |
            MessageBoxOptions.RtlReading;
    else
        return (MessageBoxOptions) 0;
}
```

If you want to ensure that you always use `MessageBoxOptions`, take a look at the FxCop rule that exists for this purpose. See Chapter 13, "Testing Internationalization Using FxCop," for more information.

Right-to-Left Languages and Mirroring in ASP.NET Applications

In an ASP.NET application, the concepts of right-to-left reading order and mirroring are handled as one by the HTML `dir` attribute. The `dir` attribute, introduced in HTML 4.0 and supported by Internet Explorer 5.0 and Navigator 6.0, can be applied to the HTML and BODY elements and individual HTML controls. The values are "`ltr`" (left to right, the default) and "`rtl`" (right to left). For example:

```
<HTML dir="rtl">
<body dir="rtl">
<asp:TextBox id="TextBox1" runat="server" dir="rtl">
```

> Do not confuse the `dir` attribute with the HTML DIR element for directory listings.

Where no `dir` attribute is specified, controls inherit their `dir` attribute from their parent (i.e., DIV, BODY, or HTML), so you can set the `dir` attribute for an entire page by setting the attribute in the HTML or BODY elements. You can set the `dir` attribute in the BODY in Visual Studio by selecting the DOCUMENT object and setting the `dir` property to "`rtl`" in the Properties Window. This simple approach is probably a little too simple because it sets the direction to right to left regardless of the page's culture. A better approach is to set the `dir` attribute conditionally. Three solutions exist for this problem:

- Set the `dir` attribute programmatically in the HTML element
- Set the `dir` attribute programmatically in the BODY element
- Set the `dir` attribute using an explicit expression (i.e., set it in a resource)

Setting the dir Attribute in the HTML or BODY Elements

To set the `dir` attribute programmatically in the form's HTML element, you must add the `runat` and `id` attributes to the HTML element. Change to Source view, find the HTML tag, and change it to this:

```
<html xmlns=http://www.w3.org/1999/xhtml runat="server" id="html">
```

I have given my HTML element the id of "html". Visual Studio 2005 automatically adds a corresponding protected field called "html" to the form class. If you are using Visual Studio 2003, you must add the following declaration manually:

```
protected HtmlGenericControl html;
```

You now have programmatic access to the form's HTML element. You can set the dir attribute in the Page_Load event:

```
void Page_Load(object sender, EventArgs e)
{
    if (CultureInfo.CurrentUICulture.TextInfo.IsRightToLeft)
        html.Attributes["dir"] = "rtl";
}
```

This code checks to see if the culture is an RTL culture and, if it is, sets the HTML element's dir attribute to "rtl". Remember that in Visual Studio 2005, the current culture is automatically set to the browser's first language setting if the page has been localized (and, therefore, the Page directive includes UICulture="auto").

You could use the same technique for setting the body's dir attribute (i.e., include the runat and id attributes in the body's element and set the dir attribute in the Page_Load event). Although this is possible, it doesn't achieve quite the same effect as setting the dir attribute in the HTML element because frames and captions do not inherit their dir attribute from the BODY element.

Setting the dir Attribute Using an Explicit Expression

Of course, setting the dir attribute in either the HTML or BODY elements is a programmatic solution and, therefore, places control over this issue in the hands of the developer. An alternative is to place the dir setting in a resource and hand over control to the localizer. Visual Studio 2005 lends itself to this solution in the form of Explicit Expressions. Explicit Expressions enable you to set a value for a property from a resource (see Chapter 5, "ASP.NET Specifics"). The idea is that you add an entry, such as html_dir, to a global resource and, in the HTML element, add a dir attribute that gets its value from the resource.

Let's do an example. If your Web site doesn't already have an `App_GlobalResources` folder, create one now (right-click the project in Solution Explorer and select Add Folder, `App_GlobalResources` Folder). Add a new global resource file (right-click the `App_GlobalResources` folder, select Add New Item..., select Assembly Resource File, enter `Global.resx` as the Name, and click the Add button). Add a new entry to `Global.resx` and give it the name "html_dir" and the value "ltr". Now create a new global resource file and call it "`Global.ar.resx`". This resource will be used for Arabic cultures. Add an entry and give it the name "html_dir" and the value "rtl". Now open the page's `Source` and add the `dir` attribute to the HTML element:

```
<html xmlns="http://www.w3.org/1999/xhtml"
    dir= "<%$ Resources: Global, html_dir %>" />
```

The `dir` attribute is set to an Explicit Expression. "`$Resources`" indicates that it is an explicit expression, "`Global`" is the name of the resource, and "`html_dir`" is the name of the entry. When the application runs, the resource manager determines whether the "rtl" value is read from `Global.ar.resx` or the "ltr" value is read from `Global.resx`.

Setting Right-to-Left Encoding in Internet Explorer

Yet another way to view pages as Right To Left is to set the page encoding in Internet Explorer. Open any page in Internet Explorer, right-click the page, and select Encoding, Right-To-Left Document (see Figure 7.11). (You must install Supplemental Language Support for this option to be present.) Whereas this option is available only to the end user and, therefore, would be tedious and unfeasible to use as a permanent solution, it enables a developer to assess the impact on a Web site of changing the `dir` attribute without having to perform the work.

Figure 7.11   Setting Right-to-Left Encoding in Internet Explorer

Setting the dir Attribute Across the Application

Having chosen a solution to set the `dir` attribute, you must apply this solution to the whole Web site. Visual Studio 2005 makes this easy in the form of Master Pages. A Master Page is a page from which other pages in the Web site adopt their layout and characteristics. Consequently, if you are using Visual Studio 2005, you should place your `dir` solution in your master page. If you are using Visual Studio 2003, you must apply your solution to every page manually or adopt one of the popular Master Page imitations for Visual Studio 2003.

Mirroring and Absolute Positioning

As mentioned previously, the right-to-left reading order and the mirroring of a page are both handled by the same attribute and are, therefore, inseparable. Furthermore, both are handled by the browser. However, the effectiveness of mirroring in a Web application is determined by the way the controls are laid out on the page. In Visual Studio 2003, this is controlled by the form's `pageLayout` setting, which can be either `FlowLayout` or `GridLayout` (the default). `FlowLayout` lays out a form according to HTML layout rules. `GridLayout` uses absolute coordinate positioning. By default in Visual Studio 2005, all controls are laid out using what Visual Studio 2003 calls `FlowLayout`. However, you can change the layout for newly added controls in Tools, Options…, HTML Designer, CSS Positioning, Positioning Options. In addition, you can position individual controls absolutely by right-clicking the control in the designer and selecting Style…, Position, and then selecting "Absolutely position" in the Position Mode combo box (see Figure 7.12).

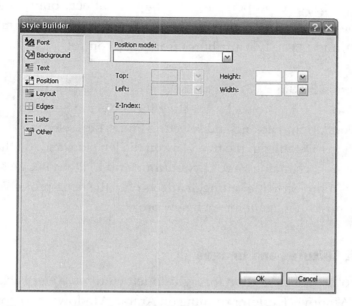

Figure 7.12   Using the Style Builder to Absolutely Position Controls

So the following HTML is generated from absolutely positioning a `Label`, `TextBox`, and `Button`:

```
<asp:label id="Label1" style="Z-INDEX: 101; LEFT: 16px;
POSITION: absolute; TOP: 16px" runat="server">Label</asp:label>

<asp:textbox id="TextBox1" style="Z-INDEX: 102; LEFT: 16px;
POSITION: absolute; TOP: 40px" runat="server"></asp:textbox>

<asp:button id="Button1" style="Z-INDEX: 103; LEFT: 16px;
POSITION: absolute; TOP: 72px" runat="server" Text="Button">
</asp:button>
```

You can see in the style attributes the `TOP` and `LEFT` values determining the absolute position of the controls. One of the problems with absolutely positioning controls is that mirroring has no effect on the controls because they cannot be relocated. The conclusion is simple: If you want your pages to be automatically mirrored, you should use `FlowLayout` in Visual Studio 2003 or avoid using the Absolutely Position style in Visual Studio 2005. If you want to convert your Visual Studio 2003 `GridLayout` forms to `FlowLayout` forms, remember that changing the DOCUMENT's `pageLayout` property to `FlowLayout` affects only controls that are added after the change. To change all the existing controls, you must delete the POSITION, TOP, and LEFT style attributes from each control.

> In Visual Studio 2003, you can set the `pageLayout` default to `FlowLayout` for a project by selecting the project in Solution Explorer, right-clicking and selecting Properties, selecting Designer Defaults in the tree view on the left side, and, on the right side, changing Page Layout from Grid to Flow. Because this is a project-wide setting, it affects only the open project and you must set it again for each new project.

Right-to-Left Cultures and Images

Images are another consideration for right-to-left cultures. Refer back to Figure 7.5, which shows Windows Explorer running on Arabic Windows, and you will see several images. Some images have been reversed, or "flipped," and others have not. For example, notice that the Windows icon on the Start menu, the Recycle Bin, and the folder images are all the same as for left-to-right Windows, whereas any image that indicates a left-to-right or right-to-left direction, such as the Back and Forward buttons in Windows Explorer, has been reversed. You must inspect each image in your application individually and decide whether the image needs to be flipped or, in a worst-case scenario, re-created. As a general rule of thumb, you can apply the following guidelines:

- Images that indicate a left-to-right or right-to-left direction should be reversed.
- Images that indicate an up or down direction should not be reversed.
- Images that include a logo, textual trademark, or flag should not be reversed.
- Images such as a check mark (a tick) are unidirectional and should not be reversed.

- Images that include text should be re-created using the translated text.
- Images that do not indicate a direction should not be reversed.

If your image is used in a `ToolStripItem` control (i.e., the parent of several `ToolStrip` controls), you can easily flip images on a case-by-case basis by setting the `ToolStripItem.RightToLeftAutoMirrorImage` property to `true`. This property takes effect only when `ToolStripItem.RightToLeft` is set to `Yes`.

Programmatic solutions to these issues also exist in GDI+ and HTML. If you use the GDI+ `Graphics.DrawString` method to draw strings onto a bitmap, you should pass the `StringFormatFlags.DirectionRightToLeft` flag as the `StringFormat` parameter (this takes care of the direction of the text but does nothing for the remainder of the image). In an ASP.NET application, you can include "`filter:flipH`" in the image control's `Style` attribute to "flip" the image.

Input Method Editors

When Christopher Sholes invented the QWERTY typewriter in the late 1860s, he wasn't overly concerned with being able to type any characters other than those used in the United States. Although some keyboards are designed for other character sets, they are not in widespread use in the Windows world, and the primary text input for Windows-based PCs remains the QWERTY keyboard. Imagine that you want to type one of the 5,000-odd Japanese Kanji characters, and you will understand that the QWERTY keyboard doesn't cut it. For some languages (e.g., Arabic, Hebrew), the problem can be solved by installing new keyboards. For others, there are simply too many characters to be input effectively using a QWERTY keyboard.

Enter Input Method Editors. An Input Method Editor (IME) is a program that enables the user to type characters that are not available on the QWERTY keyboard. The user types several letters to make up a single character. Often the same combination of letters can resolve to more than one combination of characters in the target language, so the IME uses a combination of dictionaries and user preferences to help resolve ambiguities. IMEs exist for most languages that need one (including Devanagari, Gujarati, Bangla, Gurumukhi, Oriya, Tamil, Telugu, Kannada, Malayalam, Urdu, and Vietnamese). Windows offers IMEs for Chinese, Japanese, and

Korean. In this section, we look at how to install these IMEs, how to use an IME from the user's point of view, and what you need to do to use an IME in your application.

This subject is of interest mainly to Windows Forms developers because Windows Forms applications have some control of the active IME. However, ASP.NET developers might still find this section interesting because, although HTML (and, therefore, ASP.NET) has no control over IMEs, users will still use them to enter text in Web applications.

> The level of support offered by IMEs depends upon the version of the operating system. Windows 2000, XP, and Server 2003 offer full support, so IMEs will work in all applications. Windows 98, Me, and NT 4 offer partial support, so IMEs will work only in supporting applications.

Installing an IME

If you are using a Chinese-, Japanese-, or Korean-language version of Windows, you already have an IME appropriate for your language. If you are using Windows 2000 or XP, start by following the steps in the "Supplemental Language Support" section, earlier in this chapter, to install the necessary language support for these languages. Next, open Regional and Language Options from the Control Panel, select the Languages tab, and click the Details... button to show the Text Services and Input Languages dialog (see Figure 7.13). Click the Add... button and, in the Add Input Language dialog (see Figure 7.14), select either Chinese, Japanese, or Korean and click OK. For the examples in this chapter, I use the Japanese language and the Microsoft IME Standard 2002. Back in the Text Services and Input Languages Dialog, click OK.

Figure 7.13   Text Services and Input Languages Dialog

Figure 7.14   Add Input Language Dialog

If you are using Windows 98, Me, or NT 4, the steps that you followed in the section "Supplemental Language Support," earlier in this chapter, to install the Microsoft Global IME with Language Pack will have been sufficient, and you do not need to take further steps.

How to Use an IME

If you ask nontechnical users of a Chinese-, Japanese-, or Korean-language version of Windows what an Input Method Editor is, they will probably tell you that they don't know what it is and have never used one. They will, however, be thoroughly familiar with that little thing that helps them enter characters in their own language. Watch them use the Input Method Editor, and you will be amazed at the speed at which such a tool can be used in the hands of someone who uses it as part of their everyday Windows experience. At times like these, it is helpful to be humble. So it is for monolingual English developers everywhere that this section presents a basic introduction to how to use an IME.

Open NotePad and type in `konnichiwa`, the Japanese Romaji for "Hello." You shouldn't be surprised to see the characters represented "as is" using the Roman alphabet. On the taskbar at the bottom of the screen, you should see a little "EN" symbol indicating that the current keyboard is English. Click the EN symbol, and you will see a menu of keyboard languages for which you have installed support (see Figure 7.15).

Figure 7.15   Keyboard Language Selection

Select JP (Japanese). To get a better idea of what the IME looks like, also select the Show the Language bar option. Figure 7.16 shows the Language Bar with Japanese selected.

Figure 7.16   Language Bar with Japanese Selected

The Language Bar respects the language that was selected for each application, so if you select an application that was opened (and remained open) before you switched to Japanese, you will see the Language Bar snap back to English when that application is selected. Switch back to NotePad, where Japanese was selected, and you will see the Language Bar change back to Japanese. In the Language Bar, open the Input Mode menu and select Hiragana (see Figure 7.17).

Figure 7.17   Selecting Hiragana Input Mode

Now we will type "konnichiwa" again, but first here's a quick lesson in how to type it properly. *konnichiwa* is made up of three syllables: *kon, nichi*, and *wa*. When a syllable ends in an *n* in Romaji, it must be typed with an additional *n* to terminate the syllable. *wa* is correct only in the spoken form of *konnichiwa*; it is written as *"ha"*. So to type *konnichiwa* properly, you should type "**konn**", "**nichi**" and "**ha**". When you have finished typing, press Enter to confirm the word. You should see "こんにちは". As you type "**k**" you will see a "**k**" with a dotted underline, indicating that the IME is waiting for one or more additional characters to make up a Hiragana character. Type "o", and the "ko" is replaced with "こ". Similarly, "**nn**", "**ni**", "**chi**", and "**ha**" are replaced with "ん", "に", "ち", and "は" (respectively). This is the Hiragana form of *konnichiwa*. You can convert this to Katakana or Kanji using the spacebar (known in Japanese as the *Henkan* key, the "change" key). The first time you press the spacebar, you will see the IME's first guess: "コンニチハ", which is Katakana. The same combination of Hiragana can have different conversions, so the first guess is not necessarily the correct one. Press the spacebar a second time to see a list of alternatives. Select "今日は" (which is Kanji). The IME remembers your choice so that the next time you convert the same Hiragana, it will use your preferred choice the first time.

An alternative to typing characters using the keyboard is to use the IME Pad. The IME Pad offers a selection of alternative input methods. Select IME Pad from the Japanese Language Bar and, in the drop-down menu, select Soft Keyboard (JA). Click the keyboard icon on the left side and select Hiragana/Katakana (JIS layout) (see Figure 7.18). Using the mouse, you can click on different Hiragana/Katakana characters and they will be entered into the application. Close the window to finish using the IME Pad. The IME Pad offers further alternative input methods in the form of handwriting recognition, character lookups, character recognition by their combination of strokes, individual radical selection, and, finally, speech recognition.

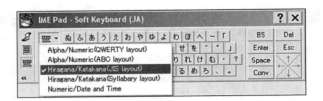

Figure 7.18   Selecting the Hiragana/Katakana (JIS layout)
Soft Keyboard in the Japanese IME Pad

To return your Windows to its original state, drag the Language Bar back onto the taskbar. You might also find that the "EN" shown in the taskbar has more icons on view than it had before. You can change the display back by right-clicking the Language Bar and selecting "Additional icons in taskbar."

Using an IME in a Windows Forms Application

Now that you know how to install and use an IME, let's look at what you need to do to make use of an IME in your application. At the simplest level, you don't need to do anything. The user can continue to use an IME with your Windows Forms application without any change to the application. Users can set the keyboard language to, say, Japanese, and when they need to enter text in a control such as a `TextBox`, they need only set the Input Mode to a suitable value and start typing. Of course, if the keyboard layout used with your application is not the default keyboard layout, they will need to set the required keyboard layout every time the application starts.

Setting the Keyboard Layout Programmatically

Your application can programmatically set the keyboard layout using the `System.Windows.Forms.InputLanguage` class. The following `SetInputLanguage` method sets the keyboard input language to a culture corresponding to the `CurrentUICulture`:

```
public static bool SetInputLanguage()
{
    return SetInputLanguage(CultureInfo.CurrentUICulture);
}

public static bool SetInputLanguage(CultureInfo cultureInfo)
```

```
{
    foreach(InputLanguage inputLanguage in
        InputLanguage.InstalledInputLanguages)
    {
        if (cultureInfo.Equals(inputLanguage.Culture) ||
            cultureInfo.Equals(inputLanguage.Culture.Parent))
        {
            InputLanguage.CurrentInputLanguage = inputLanguage;
            return true;
        }
    }
    return false;
}
```

The overloaded `SetInputLanguage` method iterates through all the installed keyboard input languages, looking for one in which the given culture matches the input language's culture or the input language culture's parent. If such a keyboard input language is found, the `CurrentInputLanguage` is set. You would add a call to `SetInputLanguage` after the `CurrentUICulture` is changed (probably in your application's start up code). You can see the effect of this method by running this from a button on a form. In the form's constructor, force the `CurrentUICulture` to be `Japanese (Japan)`:

```
System.Threading.Thread.CurrentThread.CurrentUICulture =
    new CultureInfo("ja-JP");
```

Before the button is pressed, the keyboard input layout will be EN on `English (US)` Windows. Press the button and watch the keyboard input layout change to JP. The `CurrentInputLanguage` is specific to each thread, so if you create a new thread, you must set the keyboard input layout for the new thread. Because the `System.Threading.Thread` class does not have a `CurrentInputLanguage` property of its own, you can set the `CurrentInputLanguage` only in the thread's `ThreadStart` method:

```
Thread thread = new Thread(new ThreadStart(Work));
// the new thread adopts the CurrentUICulture of the current thread
thread.CurrentUICulture = Thread.CurrentThread.CurrentUICulture;
thread.Start();
```

The `ThreadStart` method starts by initializing the `CurrentInputLanguage` just as the current thread had to do:

```
public void Work()
{
    SetInputLanguage();
    // do some work
}
```

The solution to this problem lies in the `ThreadStart` method, so the problem is not solved by using a thread factory (as suggested in Chapter 3, "An Introduction to Internationalization"). Unfortunately, because the `Thread` class is sealed, the problem also cannot be solved by subclassing the `Thread` class. Consequently, you must code the solution manually for every thread.

Control.ImeMode and the ImeMode Enumeration

Of course, you can provide greater direct control over the IME in your application. The `System.Windows.Form.Control` class has an `ImeMode` property, which is an `ImeMode` enumeration that enables you to specify the IME's Input Mode. You can see the behavior of this property in a simple Windows Forms application. Figure 7.19 shows a Windows Forms application with three `TextBox` controls and corresponding `Labels` showing each `TextBoxes`' `ImeMode`. The first and third `TextBox` controls' `ImeMode` properties are unchanged from their default and are `NoControl`. The second `TextBoxes`' `ImeMode` is `Hiragana`.

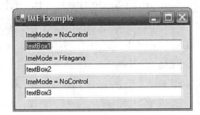

Figure 7.19   Windows Form with TextBox.ImeMode Set to Hiragana

As you tab through the `TextBox` controls, watch the Language Bar. Figure 7.20 shows the state of the IME when the focus is on the first or third `TextBoxes`. Notice the character next to the Input Mode. If you opened the Input Mode menu, you would see that this character indicates Direct Input.

Figure 7.20   Japanese Language Bar Indicating Direct Input

When you tab onto the second `TextBox`, the Language Bar shows the new Input Mode (see Figure 7.21).

Figure 7.21   Japanese Language Bar Indicating Hiragana

So the `Control.ImeMode` property simply controls the Input Mode of the IME. It doesn't do anything that users couldn't do themselves, but it does make their life easier by automatically selecting the right mode for a given context. The language you are supporting will most likely determine whether you can make an application-wide `ImeMode` setting. If you are supporting Korean, for example, you might be able to set the `ImeMode` to Hangul for every control in the application. If you are supporting Japanese, however, it is unlikely that an application would use the same `ImeMode` throughout the application because Japanese text often consists of a combination of Romaji, Hiragana, Katakana, and Kanji. If an application-wide setting is suitable, consider using the `StandardPropertiesResourceManager` in Chapter 12 to apply the same `ImeMode` throughout the application. If an application-wide setting is not suitable, you will probably need a localizer to determine which controls should use which input modes. Caution is advisable when taking such direct control of the IME, however. One of my general rules of development is that anything that is designed to be helpful to one person will nearly always end up being unhelpful to another. For each control that explicitly sets the `ImeMode` to a specific character set, the possibility exists that this character set is the wrong choice for some users in some contexts, and this will rapidly become an annoying experience for those users.

Table 7.2 shows the `ImeMode` enumeration values. Some of the values are specific to one or more IMEs. `ImeMode.Disable` disables the IME so that it cannot be used. This is appropriate for numeric input for which an IME is not required. Do not read more into this value than there is. Whereas the IME would be disabled, the regular keyboard is still fully functioning and capable of entering alphanumeric characters. As such, if the control should accept only numeric input, this should be handled within the control itself; do not set the `ImeMode` to perform this kind of validation. Disabling the IME simply provides additional feedback to the user that it is inappropriate in the current context.

Table 7.2   ImeMode Enumeration Values

ImeMode	IME Support	Description
Alpha	Japanese, Korean	Alphanumeric single-byte characters
AlphaFull	Japanese, Korean	Alphanumeric double-byte characters
Disable		The IME is disabled and cannot be turned on
Hangul	**Korean**	Hangul single-byte characters
HangulFull	**Korean**	Hangul double-byte characters
Hiragana	Japanese	Hiragana double-byte characters
Inherit		Inherits the IME mode of the parent control
Katakana	Japanese	Katakana double-byte characters
KatakanaHalf	Japanese	Katakana single-byte characters
NoControl		None (default)
Off	Chinese, Japanese	The IME is off
On	Chinese, Japanese	The IME is on

`ImeMode.Inherit` behaves in the same way as `RightToLeft.Inherit` does (see "Right-to-Left Languages and Mirroring in Windows Forms Applications," earlier in this chapter). So `Control.ImeMode` defaults to `Inherit` for controls that have a parent, and defaults to `NoControl` for controls that do not have a parent (e.g. `Form`, in this example).

The behavior of the `On`, `Off`, and `NoControl` values needs a little more explanation. Figure 7.22 shows a Windows Form with several `TextBox` controls with different settings for `ImeMode` (indicated by their corresponding labels).

Figure 7.22   Behavior of ImeMode On, Off, and NoControl Values

ImeMode.On means that the IME's input mode is switched to the value that the user was last using to enter native characters. So if the user had manually selected Katakana in textBox1, when the user entered textBox3 (ImeMode.On), the IME would switch to Katakana. This would remain true even if the user approached textBox3 from textBox5 (textBox5 forces the ImeMode to Hiragana). When the user arrives in textBox3, the input mode is simply an input mode that the user had previously manually selected. ImeMode.Off means that the input mode is always changed to Direct Input. ImeMode.NoControl means that the application does not control the input mode, and it remains as whatever the user was using on the previous control that was set to ImeMode.NoControl. The IME tries to help the user by remembering the individual settings for the user within the same form. So if the user is on textBox3 (ImeMode.On) and the user changes the input mode to Half-width Katakana, the IME will remember this setting for the duration of the form. This setting will override the user's active setting, so if the user changes the input mode on a different control and then revisits textBox3, the IME will remember that textBox3 has a specific setting and will change the input mode to accommodate textBox3. As such, the ImeMode.On value represents a compromise between wanting to help the user and overhelping the user by making decisions that are too specific about how an IME should be used.

Where Are We?

In this chapter, we looked at right-to-left languages and input method editors. Right-to-left languages require special considerations in both Windows Forms and ASP.NET applications, and require some forethought in the design and layout of forms—and potentially in code as well. Input method editors are an end-user tool for entering characters that cannot normally be entered using a QWERTY keyboard. ASP.NET applications can afford to be oblivious to this subject. The level of support that Windows Forms applications offer for IMEs is a matter of choice, ranging from no direct support to comprehensive control of the IME.

■8.
Best Practices

I N THIS CHAPTER, WE LOOK AT A NUMBER OF issues on which you will need to make development decisions—namely, fonts, string formatting, exception messages, hot key assignments, and form layout. We look at the technology behind the issues and the factors that will affect your decisions.

Font Selection

One of the many decisions you will have to make in the internationalization of your application is what font to use for your controls. Your choice will be dependent upon the languages you want to support and the functionality of the operating system your application will be running on. In this section, we look at the various font technologies that will affect your decision, to help you arrive at a conclusion.

Font Terminology and the Font Class

All developers have used fonts to a greater or lesser degree. The terminology used to describe fonts, however, is often not what developers have come to use in their everyday use of Windows; it is for this reason that a brief overview of font terminology is advisable. If you open the Fonts control panel applet, you will see the fonts that have been installed on your computer (see Figure 8.1).

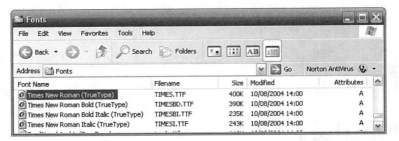

Figure 8.1   The Fonts Control Panel Applet in Details View

You can see from this figure that there is not one, but four Times New Roman font files on this computer. Times New Roman is a typeface; it describes the way characters are drawn. Each of the font files contains the characters drawn in a different style (regular, bold, bold and italic, italic). The collection of font files for a given typeface is referred to as a font family. So Times New Roman, Times New Roman Bold, Times New Roman Bold Italic, and Times New Roman Italic are all members of the same font family. The font family is given the same name as the typeface (e.g., Times New Roman), so the terms are often used interchangeably. In the .NET Framework documentation, the term *typeface* is often replaced with the term *family name*. A font is simply a typeface plus a font size, so 8 point Times New Roman Bold is a font.

> You may notice that some font families do not include bold or italic font files (e.g., Century). It is still possible to use bold and italic styles even when no font file specifically exists for that style. In these cases, the fonts are thickened or slanted to give a bold or italic impression.

The .NET Framework `Font` class is a wrapper around a specific font and can be created like this:

```
Font font1 = new Font("Times New Roman", 8);

Font font2 = new Font("Times New Roman", 8, FontStyle.Bold);
```

```
Font font3 = new Font("Times New Roman", 8, FontStyle.Bold |
    FontStyle.Italic);

Font font4 = new Font(font1, FontStyle.Bold);
```

The fonts that are installed on a machine are called physical fonts. You can request any font name with any style, and the operating system will give you the closest match to that font. The process of relating a logical font to a physical font that most closely matches the logical font is called font mapping. The font-mapping process cannot fail (unless you specify an unreasonable font size, such as infinity), so the following code does not throw an exception on any version of Windows:

```
Font font = new Font("FontDoesNotExist", 8);
```

On English Windows XP Professional SP2, this results in the Microsoft Sans Serif font. The font-mapping mechanism allocates a score to each font based upon nearly 30 criteria, and the font with the best score wins. The only useful criteria that the font mapper has to go on in this example is the font size. This will almost certainly match many TrueType or OpenType fonts, and several will have equal weights. In this scenario, as far as the application is concerned, the choice is arbitrary, as it is based upon issues such as the order of fonts during initialization.

Font Properties Extension

The Font Properties Extension is a free tool from Microsoft (http://www.microsoft.com/typography/FreeToolsOverview.mspx) that adds new tabs to the Font Properties dialog for OpenType and TrueType fonts. In the Fonts control panel applet, right-click a font file and select Properties. Normally, this dialog just has General and Summary tabs (and, on some versions, of Windows a Security tab). The new tabs contain a wide variety of information about a font. In particular, the CharSet/Unicode tab enables you to explore the "Supported Unicode Ranges" (see Figure 8.2).

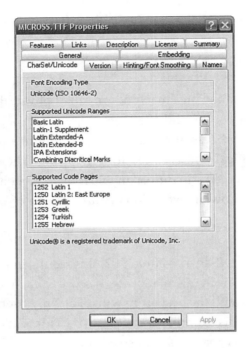

Figure 8.2   Charset/Unicode Tab of Font Properties Extension for Microsoft Sans Serif

You can get more information about Unicode code point ranges (detailing which ranges include which scripts) at http://www.unicode.org/charts/.

Using this tab, you can determine whether a font will be suitable for the languages you need to support. In terms of code point range coverage, Arial Unicode MS (installed with some Microsoft Office applications) has one of the largest. One of the limitations of the Font Properties Extension is that it cannot show additional tabs for Font Collections. A Font Collection (.TTC) is a file that is a collection of fonts. You can overcome this limitation by breaking down collections into individual font files using BREAKTTC.EXE (from the Microsoft TrueType Font SDK). The Font Properties Extension simply works with font files anywhere, so you don't have to extract the files to the system's font directory.

Getting Font Information Programmatically

You can obtain some information about a font programmatically. The Font class has a property called GdiCharSet that indicates the character set that the font supports. Unfortunately, it is mostly useless, as it can only ever be set to a value other than 1 using the following Font constructor:

```
public Font(string familyName, float emSize, FontStyle style,
    GraphicsUnit unit, byte gdiCharSet, bool gdiVerticalFont)
```

In all other cases, GdiCharSet is 1. Even when the previous constructor is used, GdiCharSet is relatively meaningless because the caller must decide what the character set is and then must tell the Font object what the font's character set is. Instead, you should use the Font.ToLogFont method to gain this and other information:

```
Font font = new Font("Simplified Arabic", 12);
LOGFONT logFont = new LOGFONT();
font.ToLogFont(logFont);
int gdiCharSet = logFont.lfCharSet;
```

The Font.ToLogFont accepts a new LOGFONT object and initializes its properties. The LOGFONT class doesn't exist in the .NET Framework, so you have to define it yourself:

```
[StructLayout(LayoutKind.Sequential, CharSet=CharSet.Auto)]
class LOGFONT
{
    public int lfHeight;
    public int lfWidth;
    public int lfEscapement;
    public int lfOrientation;
    public int lfWeight;
    public byte lfItalic;
    public byte lfUnderline;
    public byte lfStrikeOut;
    public byte lfCharSet;
    public byte lfOutPrecision;
    public byte lfClipPrecision;
    public byte lfQuality;
    public byte lfPitchAndFamily;
    [MarshalAs(UnmanagedType.ByValTStr, SizeConst=32)]
    public string lfFaceName;
}
```

The `lfCharSet` field contains a number for the character set that the font supports. The numbers are defined in `WINGDI.H` (in `%ProgramFiles%\Microsoft Visual Studio 8\Vc\PlatformSDK\Include` or `%ProgramFiles%\Microsoft Visual Studio .NET 2003\Vc7\PlatformSDK\Include`, depending on your version of Visual Studio). Search for `ANSI_CHARSET`. In the previous example, the Simplified Arabic font returns a value of `178`, which is the value defined by the `ARABIC_CHARSET` in `WINGDI.H`.

Windows Forms Controls

All Windows Forms controls inherit from `System.Windows.Forms.Control`, where the `Font` property is implemented. If the control's `Font` property is not explicitly set, it inherits its value from its parent control's `Font` property. This continues up to the ultimate parent, which gets its value from the static read-only `Control.DefaultFont` property. The implementation of the `Control.DefaultFont` property differs slightly between the .NET Framework 1.1 and 2.0. In the .NET Framework 2.0, `Control.DefaultFont` simply uses the `SystemFonts.DefaultFont` font. The `SystemFonts.DefaultFont` pseudo code is:

```
if the operating system is Japanese Windows NT4
    font = MS UI Gothic, 9 point
else if the language version of the operating system is Arabic
    font = Tahoma, 8 point
else
    font = GetStockObject(DEFAULT_GUI_FONT)
    if GetStockObject does not return an OpenType or TrueType font
        font = Tahoma, 8 point
```

The `Control.DefaultFont` value is cached, so you can refer to it continuously without a performance overhead. The .NET Framework 1.1 doesn't have the `SystemFonts` class, but similar logic is built directly into the `Control.DefaultFont` property. Here's the pseudo code:

```
if the operating system is Japanese Windows NT4
    font = MS UI Gothic, 9 point
else
    font = GetStockObject(DEFAULT_GUI_FONT)
    if GetStockObject does not return an OpenType or TrueType font
        font = Tahoma, 8 point
```

The difference in functionality is that the .NET Framework 2.0 has additional logic for handling Arabic Windows as a special case, whereas the .NET Framework 1.1 does not. So on Arabic Windows, `Control.DefaultFont` is 8 point Tahoma using the .NET Framework 2.0, and Microsoft Sans Serif 8.25 using the .NET Framework 1.1. Some example values of `GetStockObject` and `Control.DefaultFont` for different operating systems and different languages can be seen in Table 8.1.

Table 8.1 `GetStockObject` **and** `Control.DefaultFont` **Examples**

Windows Version	Language Version	GetStockObject	Control.DefaultFont (.NET 2.0)	Control.DefaultFont (.NET 1.1)
Windows XP Pro SP2	English	Microsoft Sans Serif	Microsoft Sans Serif	Microsoft Sans Serif
Windows XP Pro SP2	Arabic	Microsoft Sans Serif	Tahoma	Microsoft Sans Serif
Windows XP Pro SP2	French	Microsoft Sans Serif	Microsoft Sans Serif	Microsoft Sans Serif
Windows XP Pro SP2	German	Microsoft Sans Serif	Microsoft Sans Serif	Microsoft Sans Serif
Windows XP Pro SP2	Japanese	MS UI Gothic	MS UI Gothic	MS UI Gothic
Windows 2000 Professional	English	Microsoft Sans Serif	Microsoft Sans Serif	Microsoft Sans Serif
Windows 98 SE	English	Not OpenType/ TrueType font	Tahoma	Tahoma
Windows 98 SE	Japanese	MS UI Gothic	MS UI Gothic	MS UI Gothic

In both versions of the framework, the `Font` property is serialized on localized forms only if the `Font` property has been changed from the default on the development machine. So if the `Font` property is not changed, the `Control.DefaultFont` will be calculated at runtime and this will be on the user's machine. The moral of the story is that if you want the functionality provided by `Control.DefaultFont`, leave the font default alone at design time.

ASP.NET Controls

All ASP.NET Web controls inherit from `System.Web.UI.WebControls.WebControl`, where the `Font` property is implemented. Unlike `System.Windows.Forms.Control.Font`, `WebControl.Font` is a `FontInfo` object. The `FontInfo` object simply sets HTML attributes of a control. Figure 8.3 shows the expanded `Font` property of a `Label` control. The resulting HTML is:

```
<asp:Label id="Label1" runat="server" Font-Names="Tahoma,Arial"
Font-Size="Larger" Font-Bold="True">Label</asp:Label>
```

Figure 8.3   Properties Window Showing Expanded Label.Font Property

If the control's `Font` property is not explicitly set, it does not inherit its value from its parent or any other control; instead, the property remains blank and it is left to the browser to select a font. Setting an explicit font name on a control is bad practice unless there is something specific about the individual control that demands it. If a font must be set, it can be set in a Cascading Style Sheet (CSS). To create a CSS file, open Solution Explorer; right-click the project; select Add, New Item...; click the Style Sheet icon; and click Open. Add a definition for the body element either by typing or by using the Style Builder (in CSS Outline, expand elements, select body, right-click, and select Build Style...):

```
body
{
    FONT-FAMILY: Tahoma,Arial;
}
```

To use the CSS file, add a `LINK` element to the aspx's `HEAD` element:

```
<LINK href="StyleSheet1.css" type="text/css" rel="stylesheet">
```

This assumes that the style sheet is called `StyleSheet1.css`.

However, the simplest and most effective solution is to leave the problem of font selection to the browser. Obviously, this support is dependent upon the browser on the client, but in Internet Explorer, it can be configured by selecting Tools, Internet Options… and clicking on the Fonts… button (see Figure 8.4).

Figure 8.4   Internet Explorer Font Configuration

This dialog allows the user to specify which fonts are used for which languages. The "Language script" combo box allows the user to select a language, and the two list boxes below allow the user to specify which fonts are used for Web pages and plain text, respectively. If the user is running on Windows, all of the same issues covered in the next few sections (font substitution, font linking, font fallback) apply equally to an ASP.NET application as they do to a Windows Forms application.

The SystemFonts Class

The `SystemFonts` class, introduced in the .NET Framework 2.0, is a collection of read-only static properties and one method that represent intelligent wrappers around the system's font properties set by the user in the Display control panel applet. Table 8.2 shows the properties of the `SystemFonts` class and some example values.

Table 8.2 `SystemFonts` **Properties and Example Values**

Name	Description	Example on English Windows XP Pro SP2
CaptionFont	The font that an application can use to display text in the title bars of windows	Trebuchet MS
DefaultFont	The default font that an application can use for dialogs and forms	Microsoft Sans Serif
DialogFont	The font that an application can use for dialogs and forms	Tahoma
IconTitleFont	The font that is used for icon titles	Tahoma
MenuFont	The font that an application can use for menus	Tahoma
MessageBoxFont	The font that is used for message boxes	Tahoma
SmallCaptionFont	The font that is used to display text in the title bars of small windows, such as tool windows	Tahoma
StatusFont	The font that an application can use to display text in the status bar	Tahoma

The properties include the kind of intelligence seen in the `Control.Default-Font` discussion earlier in this chapter, so you can expect different results on Windows 98 and Me, for example. You can change the system fonts from the Display control panel applet by selecting the Appearance tab and clicking on the Advanced button to get the Advanced Appearance dialog (see Figure 8.5).

Figure 8.5   Use the Advanced Appearance Dialog to Set Properties of SystemFonts

You can use the `SystemFonts` class as part of the localization process by setting a form's `Font` to `SystemFonts.DialogFont`. This is best done in the form's constructor:

```
public Form1()
{
    Font = SystemFonts.DialogFont;
    InitializeComponent();
}
```

To apply this behavior across your application, create a `Form` base class, set the `Font` in the base class, and ensure that all forms inherit from the base class. In this way, you can abstract the problem of choosing a font, and your application can use a font that is appropriate for the machine that it is running on.

Font Substitution

One of the older font technologies is font substitution (introduced in Windows 3.1). Font vendors often copyright their font names and, consequently, the names become unique. Font substitution allows one font name to be replaced with another. So, for example, you could map a font face name of Helvetica to the physical font Arial. Whenever the Helvetica font is requested, an Arial font would be returned. Font substitutions are set in the Registry in Windows NT and above at `HKEY_LOCAL_MACHINE\Software\Microsoft\Windows NT\CurrentVersion\FontSubstitutes` (see Figure 8.6).

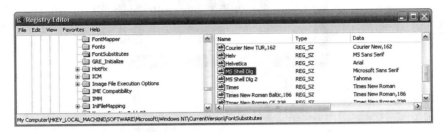

Figure 8.6   Font Substitution Registry Entries

In Windows 98 and Me, they are set in the `FontSubstitutes` section of `WIN.INI`:

```
[FontSubstitutes]
Helv=MS Sans Serif
Tms Rmn=MS Serif
Times=Times New Roman
Helvetica=Arial
MS Shell Dlg=MS Sans Serif
MS Shell Dlg 2=MS Sans Serif
Monotype.com=Andale Mono
```

So in the following code snippet, where a Helvetica font is not installed and Helvetica has been mapped to Arial:

```
new Font("Helvetica", 12).Name;
```

the `Name` property is "`Arial`".

MS Shell Dlg and MS Shell Dlg 2

Font substitution is of interest in the localization process because of two font face names: MS Shell Dlg and MS Shell Dlg 2. These font face names are set to different fonts for different versions of Windows and different language versions of Windows (see Table 8.3).

Table 8.3   MS Shell Dlg and MS Shell Dlg 2 Font Face Name Values

Windows Version	Language Version	MS Shell Dlg	MS Shell Dlg 2
Windows XP Pro SP2	English	Microsoft Sans Serif	Tahoma
Windows XP Pro SP2	Arabic	Microsoft Sans Serif	Tahoma
Windows XP Pro SP2	French	Microsoft Sans Serif	Tahoma
Windows XP Pro SP2	German	Microsoft Sans Serif	Tahoma
Windows XP Pro SP2	Japanese	MS UI Gothic	Tahoma
Windows 2000 Professional	English	Microsoft Sans Serif	Tahoma
Windows NT 4 WorkStation	Japanese	(MS Ｐゴシック) Japanese for MS PGothic	Not present
Windows 98 SE	English	Arial	Arial
Windows 98 SE	Japanese	Arial	Arial

The MS Shell Dlg font face name is intended to be used for compatibility with versions of Windows prior to Windows 2000. The MS Shell Dlg 2 font face name is intended to be used with Windows 2000 and above. However, you are free to use either font face name (where MS Shell Dlg 2 is preferred), as both names, thanks to font substitution and font mapping, work on all languages and all versions of Windows. The benefit of using one of these font face names in your application is that your application is abstracted from the problem of choosing a font directly, and this choice can be delayed until runtime. The disadvantage of using a font face name instead of a physical font name is that substituted fonts are not visible in the Properties Windows in Visual Studio and cannot be set in the Properties Window. Instead, they must be set in code:

```
public Form1()
{
    Font = new Font("MS Shell Dlg 2", 12);
    InitializeComponent();
}
```

The same comments as before about using a form base class apply equally here. An alternative to this approach is to use the `StandardPropertiesResourceManager` in Chapter 12, "Custom Resource Managers," which can assign the same value to every property (e.g., `Font`) that is loaded as a resource.

Font Linking

Font linking is a great feature introduced in Windows 2000. The basic idea is that it is unrealistic in design and performance terms for a single font to support all code points for which Unicode has a definition, but it would be useful if a single font could act as if it did. If a single font could appear to support all glyphs, an application would not have to switch fonts to display other glyphs. By default, on Windows XP Professional SP2, there are no font links, but there is nothing to stop you from adding your own. In the Registry, add new keys to `HKEY_LOCAL_MACHINE\SOFTWARE\Microsoft\Windows NT\CurrentVersion\FontLink\SystemLink`, where the key name is the name of the font and the value is the names of the fonts that it is linked to. If you install East Asian support (in the Regional and Language Options dialog, select the Languages tab, check the "Install files for East Asian languages" check box, and click OK), several entries are created (see Figure 8.7).

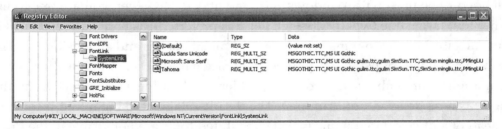

Figure 8.7   Font Linking Registry Entries on Windows XP Pro SP2 with East Asian Support Installed

Double-click the Microsoft Sans Serif key, and you will see what fonts it is linked to (see Figure 8.8). The value is exactly the same as for Tahoma. Recall that Microsoft Sans Serif and Tahoma are typically used as the values for the MS Shell Dlg and MS Shell Dlg 2 font face names, respectively.

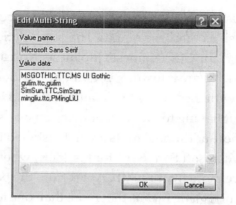

Figure 8.8   Microsoft Sans Serif Font Linking Registry Entry

You can see from this that by installing East Asian support, the Microsoft Sans Serif font has been font-linked to the MSGOTHIC, gulim, SimSun, and mingliu True-Type Collections. Table 8.4 shows a cut-down list of the Unicode code ranges that these fonts support.

Table 8.4   The Unicode Code Ranges Supported by Microsoft Sans Serif and Its Font-Linked Fonts

TrueType Font Collection	TypeType Fonts	Latin, Greek, Cyrillic	Arabic, Thai, Hebrew	CJK	Hangul	Bopomofo
N/A	Microsoft Sans Serif	Yes	Yes	No	No	No
MSGOTHIC.TTC	MS Gothic, MS PGothic, MS UI Gothic	Yes	No	Most	No	No
gulim.ttc	Dotum, DotumChe, Gulim, GulimChe	Yes	No	Some	Yes	No
SimSun.TTC	SimSum, NSimSum	Basic Latin	No	Some	No	Yes
mingliu.ttc	MingLiU, PMingLiU	Basic Latin	No	Some	No	Yes

You can see from this list that Microsoft Sans Serif has been "enhanced" to support glyphs that are outside of its base ranges. The combination of the four TrueType Collections adds support for CJK (Chinese, Japanese, Korean), Hangul, and Bopomofo glyphs. If this is such a great feature, you might wonder if Microsoft Sans Serif either should be linked with these fonts by default or should include the glyphs from these other fonts without having to link to them. The answers are flexibility and performance. By default, these additional fonts are not installed in English Windows XP Professional SP2. The Microsoft Sans Serif font is 450K, whereas the additional four TrueType Collections are more than 120Mb. Apart from the performance hit that this incurs, the method of font linking means that more than one font, can be linked to the same font. As developers, we should all appreciate this form of reuse.

In localization terms, this means that we can use a single font, such as Microsoft Sans Serif or Tahoma, and rely upon it being extended to include the glyphs that we need for other Unicode code ranges. Figure 8.9 shows a Windows Forms form that uses the Microsoft Sans Serif font to display Japanese characters on an English Windows XP Professional SP2 machine that has East Asian support installed.

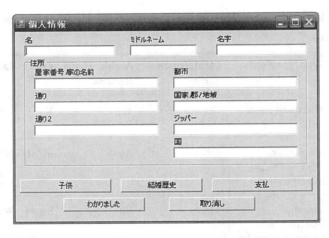

Figure 8.9   Form Using Microsoft Sans Serif on Windows XP Pro SP2 with East Asian Support

Figure 8.10 shows the same form running on English Windows XP Professional SP2 where East Asian support has not been installed.

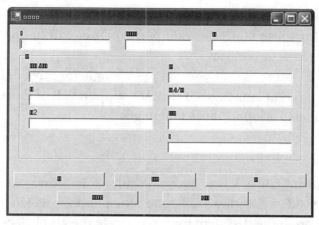

Figure 8.10   Form Using Microsoft Sans Serif on Windows XP Pro SP2 without East Asian Support

When a font does not have a glyph for a requested code point, the "not defined" glyph (a box) is displayed instead. This provides a small piece of information on the nature of the display problem (i.e., the font that is being used does not have a glyph for the code point that it is trying to display). Figure 8.11 shows the same form displayed on English Windows 98 SE.

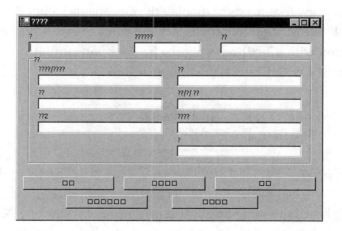

Figure 8.11   Form Using Microsoft Sans Serif on Windows 98 SE

Clearly, there is also a problem displaying some of the glyphs on Windows 98 SE, but the cause of problem is slightly different. The question marks indicate that the conversion from Unicode to the code page failed (because the code page doesn't have encodings for those Unicode code points). This will happen only on 16-bit ("code page") versions of Windows.

The moral of this story is that you can use a single font throughout your application for many different languages if it either supports all of those languages or is linked to other fonts to support those languages.

Font Fallback

Like font linking, font fallback was new in Windows 2000 and offers a similar service: When a font needs to display a Unicode code point for which it has no glyph, it can fall back to a predefined system font to provide the glyph. There are, however, several differences between font fallback and font linking. First, and most important, font fallback is implemented by Uniscribe (a layer beneath GDI+). This is important because when characters are combined in a complex script, their form can change. This is not something you see in English, for example. In English, the letter *a* is always formed the same way, regardless of what letters come before it or after it. In a complex script, the rendering of a character can be altered by many factors. Uniscribe takes care of these details without any intervention on the developer's behalf. So if the Courier New font needs to display the Devanagari letter *Aa* (U+0906) Uniscribe falls back to the Mangal font to display the letter. Figure 8.12 shows a Windows Forms application with a TextBox using the Courier New font running on Windows XP Professional SP2 with East Asian support installed.

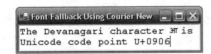

Figure 8.12　Courier New on Windows XP Pro SP2 with East Asian Support

Figure 8.13 shows the same application running on Windows XP Pro SP2 with no additional support installed. The square character indicates that the Courier New font does not have a glyph for Unicode code point U+0906 and that the fallback fonts that Courier New could fall back to are not installed.

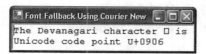

Figure 8.13   Courier New on Windows XP Pro SP2 without East Asian Support

The second difference between font fallback and font linking is that the font fall-back default fonts are hard-wired and cannot be interrogated. You can change the fallback fonts in the Registry by adding new entries to `HKEY_LOCAL_MACHINE\SOFTWARE\Microsoft\WindowsNT\CurrentVersion\Language Pack\SurrogateFallback`. Each entry has a key of "`Plane`" with a number suf-fix (e.g., "`Plane1`", "`Plane2`", etc.) and refers to a different "plane" of Unicode code points. A plane is a range of 64K code points. Each key has a string value for the font family name to use for rendering code points within that plane.

Font Names Are Sometimes Translated

The Times New Roman font can be referred to as "Times New Roman" in every lan-guage version of Windows in the world. The same is true for the majority of fonts, and this makes our lives very easy. Unfortunately, the same is not true for all fonts, especially Chinese, Japanese, and Korean fonts. For many of these fonts, the names have been localized, and this represents an additional level of consideration for your applications. Take, for example, the Japanese MS Mincho font. The following code on English Windows XP Professional SP2 sets `fontName` to "`MS Mincho`" (assuming that the MS Mincho font is installed):

```
Font font = new Font("MS Mincho", 12);
string fontName = font.Name;
```

However, the same code running on Japanese Windows XP Professional SP2 sets `fontName` to "ＭＳ 明朝". The code executes fine, but if you need to compare the font name for any reason, then your code needs to be modified. Fortunately, the `FontFamily.GetName` method has the solution. `GetName` accepts an LCID of the locale for which the font name should be returned. For the vast majority of fonts, the return value will be exactly equal to the name of the font. However, for MS Mincho, the results will differ.

```
Font font = new Font("MS Mincho", 12);
string englishFontName = font.FontFamily.GetName(1033);
string japaneseFontName = font.FontFamily.GetName(1041);
```

The LCID for `English (United States)` is `1033` and for `Japanese (Japan)` is `1041`, so `englishFontName` is set to "`MS Mincho`" and `japaneseFontName` is set to "`MS明朝`", regardless of the language version of the operating system.

It should be noted that it is also possible to specify the font name in the localized language:

```
Font font = new Font("MS 明朝", 12);
```

This font name will be recognized on both English and Japanese Windows XP Professional SP2, Windows 2000, Windows Server 2003, and also, in this case, Windows 98 SE. But this support for both the English and localized font names is limited. In Windows Server 2003, Windows XP Professional SP2, and Windows 2000, both font names should be available, but support is less complete in earlier versions. This could lead you to the conclusion that, for some fonts, you are forced to use the English name on all locales, except the locale for which the font is really needed, where the font name must be localized. Of course, if the font is required for only a single locale and all other locales use a different font anyway, the problem becomes moot because you would only ever use the translated name on the locale where the font is required.

Font Strategy

So, what does all of this mean then? It means that if your clients are using Windows 2000 or later, you can afford to use a single font throughout the application for all languages. Thanks to font linking and font fallback, a single font can supply all of the characters for all the Unicode code point ranges that you need to support. It also means that if you do nothing, then the default font chosen for you will most likely be appropriate for the machine's culture. An alternative means of delaying the choice of font until runtime is to use the MS Shell Dlg or MS Shell Dlg 2 font face names. If your clients are using a version of Windows prior to Windows 2000, they will not be able to use font linking and font fallback, and you may be forced to use a different font for each culture. In most cases, however, you should still be able to get away with a single font used throughout the application.

In ASP.NET applications, you are at the mercy of the browser and the operating system the browser is running on. The advice, however, is mostly the same: Either leave the font name alone or use a font face name (assuming that the clients are running on Windows) to delay the font choice until runtime.

Strings and String.Format

One of the most basic rules of localization is to avoid concatenating bits of text to form a sentence or phrase. For example:

```
statusBar1.Text = "Processing file " +
    fileNumber.ToString() + " of " + totalFiles.ToString() + "...";
```

This code builds up a string using English sentence rules. The result is something like this:

```
Processing invoice 3 of 15...
```

Different languages form sentences according to different rules. The same phrase in Japanese is:

15 のインボイス3 を処理する...

Notice that the 15 comes *before* the 3, not after it, as it does in English. Also be aware that this is a translator's nightmare. The translator will be presented with three strings: "`Processing file`", "`of`", and "`...`". There is no guarantee that the translator will be presented with these strings sequentially or that the translator will be aware that the three strings form a single phrase. Good translators translate meaning and not words, so this approach prevents them from providing a meaningful translation. The solution is to use `String.Format` and to use placeholders to mark the positions of the substituted text; a nonlocalized better version is:

```
statusBar1.Text = String.Format(
    "Processing file {0} of {1}...", fileNumber, totalFiles);
```

The phrase is represented by a string that has numbered placeholders (`{0}` and `{1}`). When the string is extracted from the code, moved to a resource, and sent to the translator, the translator will understand the context of the words and the relationship between them, and be able to translate the string accurately. The translated Japanese string now becomes:

｛1｝ のインボイス｛0｝ を処理する...

Notice that the placeholders are in a different order, but because they are numbered, the correct information is substituted for the correct placeholder. In the "Reintegrating Resources" section of Chapter 14, "The Translator," I show how you can ensure that translated strings have the same number and same type of placeholders as their original strings.

Text Ending with Colons

Some developers prefer to terminate strings used in labels with a full colon, whereas others prefer to leave out the colon. For the most part, localization does not play a part in your decision-making process as to which approach you should pursue. Most machine-translation facilities understand that text might be terminated with a colon and can perform their translation without the colon affecting the success of the translation. In addition, the .NET Framework's mirroring functionality (see Chapter 7, "Middle East and East Asian Cultures") in both Windows Forms and ASP.NET accounts for the colon and moves the colon from the right side of a text string to the left side of a text string.

If you are looking to create a company standard for Windows Forms user interfaces, you should take a look at Microsoft's "Official Guidelines for User Interface Developers and Designers" (http://msdn.microsoft.com/library/default.asp?url=/library/en-us/dnwue/html/welcome.asp), which includes advice on using colons in labels (open the section on Windows Interface Components, then Menus, Controls and Toolbars, and then Controls, and search on "colon").

Embedded Control Characters

This issue represents a development decision that you will need to make: Should you include embedded control characters in strings or exclude them from strings? The following code snippet has a string that contains embedded control characters ("\n"):

```
MessageBox.Show("There are 5 deliveries.\n\n" +
    "3 deliveries are suspended.\n\n" +
    "Continue with order ?",
    "", MessageBoxButtons.YesNoCancel);
```

(Ignore the fact that the string resource is hard-coded and not loaded from a resource manager, and also that the numbers are not represented by placeholders).

The "\n" control character is a new line control character. Equivalent code could be written like this:

```
MessageBox.Show("There are 5 deliveries." +
    System.Environment.NewLine + System.Environment.NewLine +
    "3 deliveries are suspended." +
    System.Environment.NewLine + System.Environment.NewLine +
    "Continue with order ?",
    "", MessageBoxButtons.YesNoCancel);
```

The question is, which is better in terms of localization? There are pros and cons with both approaches. The former approach puts formatting control in the hands of the translator. The translator is at liberty to remove or add new lines and other control characters, according to the translator's desires/needs. Whether this is necessary is probably dependent upon the complexity of the translated phrases. A single phrase or sentence almost always translates into a single phrase or sentence in any other language. A complex description made up of many sentences or paragraphs will not necessarily contain the same number of sentences (or new lines) when the entire text is translated to another language because it is the meaning that will most likely be translated. In this scenario, a translator would be trapped by the preconceptions of new lines embedded in the source code instead of resource strings. Another issue to consider is how embedded control characters are handled in machine translation. Most machine-translation facilities do not understand .NET Framework control characters, and the results of such translations can be less than successful (although you can increase your chances of success by separating control characters from other text with spaces or full stops). If you choose to put control in the hands of the developer (and, therefore, exclude control characters from strings), you should take a look at the "Control characters embedded in resource string" rule in Chapter 13, "Testing Internationalization Using FxCop," which reports embedded control characters as errors.

A variation on the theme of embedding control characters in strings is to embed placeholders in strings to mark the location of new lines and other formatting characters:

```
MessageBox.Show(String.Format("There are 5 deliveries.{0}{0}" +
    "3 deliveries are suspended. {0}{0}" +
    "Continue with order ?", System.Environment.NewLine),
    "", MessageBoxButtons.YesNoCancel);
```

In this example, the new line characters, `System.Environment.NewLine`, are passed as a string parameter to `String.Format`. The localized string can contain any number of placeholders (including zero) with the same numeric identifier (i.e., `{0}`), so the translator has complete freedom over the number of new lines in the text. Essentially, this is simply a variation of the first approach that embeds control characters in the localized string. The difference from a localization viewpoint is that the new lines are represented by placeholders instead of control characters. For some scenarios, this difference is beneficial. Some machine translators yield better results using placeholders than embedded control characters, especially when the control characters are not delimited with spaces or punctuation.

Exception Messages

Exceptions present a number of strategy questions in the internationalization story. We start by considering how exceptions gather their messages and then consider what questions you will have to answer.

In the following statement, the text is clearly hard-coded to use English:

```
throw new ArgumentException(
    "Value does not fall within the expected range.");
```

You may or may not want to localize this text. The simplest way to localize this text is to let the .NET Framework do the work for you:

```
throw new ArgumentException();
```

In the absence of a supplied message, the .NET Framework gets a message using its own `ResourceManager`. Consequently, the actual message retrieved is dependent upon `CultureInfo.CurrentUICulture` and the .NET Framework Language Packs installed on the machine. So if the `CurrentUICulture` is "de-DE" (German

(Germany)) and the German .NET Framework Language Pack is installed, the exception message will be "Der Wert liegt außerhalb des erwarteten Bereichs." Tables 8.5 and 8.6 show some examples of default exception messages for English and German, respectively.

Table 8.5   Examples of Default English Exception Messages

Exception Constructor	Message
`ArgumentException()`	Value does not fall within the expected range.
`ArgumentException(null)`	Exception of type `System.ArgumentException` was thrown.
`FileNotFoundException()`	Unable to find the specified file.
`FileNotFoundException(null)`	File or assembly name (null), or one of its dependencies, was not found.
`IOException()`	I/O error occurred.
`IOException(null)`	Exception of type `System.IO.IOException` was thrown.

Table 8.6   Examples of Default German Exception Messages

Exception Constructor	Message
`ArgumentException()`	Der Wert liegt außerhalb des erwarteten Bereichs.
`ArgumentException(null)`	Eine Ausnahme vom Typ `System.ArgumentException` wurde ausgelöst.
`FileNotFoundException()`	Die angegebene Datei konnte nicht gefunden werden.
`FileNotFoundException(null)`	Datei- oder Assemblyname '(null)' oder eine Abhänigkeit davon wurde nicht gefunden.
`IOException()`	E/A-Fehler aufgetreten.
`IOException(null)`	Eine Ausnahme vom Typ `System.IO.IOException` wurde ausgelöst.

One problem that this raises is that the localization of exception messages is clearly limited to the availability of .NET Framework Language Packs for the current culture. There is no Arabic .NET Framework 1.1 Language Pack (but there is for the

.NET Framework 2.0), for example, so .NET Framework 1.1 exception messages on Arabic Windows are in English because the fallback culture for the .NET Framework is English.

This brings us to the questions you will have to answer. The first is, what language do you want your exception messages to be in? You might feel that if your application is running on a German version of Windows, its exception messages should also be German. This may or may not be true. You might equally feel that if your developers are English, all exception messages should be in English because the exception messages are aimed at the developers, not at the users. The answer is more likely to be a combination of both approaches, where the language of the message is determined by the exception type. Consider an `ArgumentException`. This is almost certainly a programmer error and represents a fault in the application for which a software fix is required. There is no value in relaying such a message to users because they won't understand it and they won't be able to do anything about it. There is a good argument, therefore, that this message should be in the developer's language (possibly English). Now consider a `FileNotFoundException`. The English text of this exception is "Unable to find the specified file." This is something that the user might well understand and might also be able to rectify. There is a good argument, therefore, that this message should be in the user's language.

If you choose to make a distinction between exceptions that are destined for developers in one language and exceptions that are destined for users in another language, you need a way of implementing this distinction. To create exceptions with localized messages, you either use the default exception constructor or pass null for the message parameter:

```
throw new FileNotFoundException();
throw new FileNotFoundException(null);
```

The .NET Framework and the installed Language Pack provide the localized exception message. To create exceptions with English messages, you can still use the default constructor or pass null for the message parameter, but you set the `Current UICulture` before creating the exception:

```
Thread.CurrentThread.CurrentUICulture = new CultureInfo("en-US");
throw new IOException();
throw new IOException(null);
```

Good practice dictates that you would restore the `CurrentUICulture` to its former state after the exception was created, so this begs for a class to tidy up this process:

```
throw new ExceptionFactory.CreateException(typeof(IOException));
```

The `ExceptionFactory` class (next) performs this task. Its overloaded `Create-Exception` method accepts an exception type to create an exception from and, optionally, an array of parameters to pass to the exception constructor. The `CurrentUICulture` is temporarily changed to the static `ExceptionCulture` property (which, by default, is "en-US") and restored to its former state after the exception has been created. Here is the complete `ExceptionFactory` class:

```
public class ExceptionFactory
{
    private static CultureInfo exceptionCulture;
    static ExceptionFactory()
    {
        exceptionCulture = new CultureInfo("en-US");
    }
    public static CultureInfo ExceptionCulture
    {
        get {return exceptionCulture;}
        set {exceptionCulture = value;}
    }
    protected static CultureInfo oldCultureInfo;
    protected static void SetExceptionCulture()
    {
        oldCultureInfo = null;
        if (Thread.CurrentThread.CurrentUICulture.Name !=
            exceptionCulture.Name)
        {
            // change the culture to the exception culture
            oldCultureInfo = Thread.CurrentThread.CurrentUICulture;

            Thread.CurrentThread.CurrentUICulture = exceptionCulture;
        }
    }
    protected static void RestoreCulture()
    {
        if (oldCultureInfo != null)
        {
            Thread.CurrentThread.CurrentUICulture = oldCultureInfo;
```

```
            oldCultureInfo = null;
        }
    }
    public static Exception CreateException(Type exceptionType)
    {
        object exception;
        SetExceptionCulture();
        try
        {
            exception = Activator.CreateInstance(exceptionType);
            if (! (exception is Exception))
                // do not localize this
                throw new ArgumentException(
                    "exceptionType is not an Exception Type");
        }
        finally
        {
            RestoreCulture();
        }
        return (Exception) exception;
    }
    public static Exception CreateException(
        Type exceptionType, object[] args)
    {
        object exception;
        SetExceptionCulture();
        try
        {
            exception =
                Activator.CreateInstance(exceptionType, args);

            if (! (exception is Exception))
                // do not localize this
                throw new ArgumentException(
                    "exceptionType is not an Exception Type");
        }
        finally
        {
            RestoreCulture();
        }
        return (Exception) exception;
    }
}
```

Whereas this class solves this problem, its scope is limited to exceptions that your code creates. Exceptions that are thrown by the .NET Framework or by third-party code (including COM objects, for example) are outside of your control, and .NET exception messages will be localized regardless of the intended recipient of the message. For this reason, your exception-reporting facility should be sure to record the exception class name in addition to the exception message, to allow your developers to know what exception has occurred without them having to learn another language.

Hot Keys

Hot keys represent a particularly awkward problem for localization. A hot key is a key that is used with the Alt key to jump to or invoke a control on a form or Web page. Both Windows Forms applications and ASP.NET applications suffer the same problem with a similar solution, so we start by looking at the problem from the viewpoint of a Windows Forms application and then cover it again briefly for ASP.NET applications. Figure 8.14 shows a form that has hot keys (the hot keys are visible only when the Alt key is pressed). The hot keys are the underlined letters.

Figure 8.14   Windows Form with Hot Keys

Hot keys represent a localization problem, for several reasons. First, the translator will have trouble choosing a suitable key if the translation tool being used does not show the text in context. For example, if the translator is presented with the finished form as shown in Figure 8.14, the translator can make accurate guesses about the correct hot keys to assign to controls, with little fear of causing a hot key clash with another control. However, if the translator is presented with a stream of phrases out of context, the translator will have little hope of choosing unique hot keys. Second, even if the translator is presented with a visual representation of a form (for example, using WinRes), there is no guarantee that the translator is seeing the complete picture. If the form is combined with other forms or the form is modified programmatically, the translator will not be able to predict the success of the translation choices. Third, there is the problem that most machine translators do not understand that a word with an ampersand (the character used for denoting hot keys—e.g., "E&xit") is the same as the word without the ampersand (e.g., "Exit"). As such, your translations will not be successful if the original language has ampersands embedded in the text. Add to this the possibility that the translator can make honest mistakes and accidentally create duplicates (I have done this myself, all too often, even on English-only forms), and the effort involved in choosing and assigning hot keys, and the problem begs for a solution. Enter the HotkeyAssignment class.

The HotkeyAssignment class (included in the source for this book) analyzes controls and performs hot key assignments to controls at runtime according to various rules. Typically, the class would be used in a Form's constructor:

```
public Form1()
{
    InitializeComponent();
    HotKeyAssignment.AssignHotKeys(this);
}
```

To apply this solution to every form, you should create a base form, add the code to the base form's constructor, and ensure that all forms inherit from the base form.

The benefit of this approach is that the analysis and the assignment are performed at runtime: (1) after resources have been loaded and (2) after the form has been fully formed and all of its constituent components are in place. The form shown in Figure 8.14 had its hot keys assigned using the HotKeyAssignment class. The Assign-HotKeys method has a certain level of intelligence built into it. Hot keys are assigned in order of the controls' TabIndexes, with top-level menu items being assigned after all other controls have been assigned. From Figure 18.4, you can see that the "Company" label has been assigned the hot key "C" because it is an obvious choice. However, the "Contact Name" label should not have "C" (for "Contact") assigned because the "C" hot key has already been taken. In this case, the AssignHotKeys method looks at the first letter of other words until it finds an unused letter. In the "Contact Name" example, it chose "N" because it was the first letter of the second word. If an unused hot key cannot be found, it works through every letter of the text until it finds an unused hot key. If the letter "N" had already been taken, it would have chosen "o" because it is the second letter of the word "Contact". If there are no letters in the text that are unused, the next unused letter in the ValidHotKeys array is used.

The AssignHotKeys method has a second overloaded version:

```
public static void AssignHotKeys(
    Control control, bool preserveExistingHotKeys)
```

The preserveExistingHotKeys parameter allows developers to specify whether existing hot keys indicated in the controls' Text property should be preserved. This allows a combination of both approaches: The translator can make some hot key assignments that are critical, or for which the automatic assignment is unacceptable, and the remainder can be handled by the HotKeyAssignment class. So the translator simply handles the exception to the rule rather than laboriously specifying every hot key for every control. The default for this parameter is true. If you pass false for preserveExistingHotKeys, the existing hot key assignments are ignored, and are removed and replaced with new hot key assignments.

This strategy solves the problem for individual forms, but it lacks continuity. Because each form is taken in isolation and every control is processed in TabIndex order, there is no guarantee that controls that occur frequently throughout an application will always be assigned the same hot key. This can be quite irritating for a user to have to remember that a button on one form has one hot key, but the same button on another form has a different hot key. The problem is illustrated in Figure 8.14, where the "Office Occupant" check box has taken the hot key "o". A user might have expected the "OK" button to have the hot key "o", but as it occurs later in the tab order, this hot key has already been assigned and the OK button has been assigned the hot key "k". On a different form, it might have been assigned "o", and the user might anticipate this and incorrectly press Alt+O, giving a different result.

For this reason, the HotKeyAssignment class has a StandardHotKeys property and the following overloaded AddStandardHotKey methods:

```
public static void AddStandardHotKey(char hotKey)

public static void AddStandardHotKey(char hotKey, string text)

public static void AddStandardHotKey(StandardHotKey standardHotKey)
```

The `AddStandardHotKey` methods simply provide a convenient way to add new `StandardHotKey` objects to the `StandardHotKeys` array property. The `Standard-HotKeys` property allows developers to "reserve" hot keys and, optionally, their associated text, so that they are not used by other controls. The following code reserves the hot key "O" for the text "OK":

```
HotKeyAssignment.AddStandardHotKey('O', "OK");
```

Typically, this code would be executed during application startup. The result is shown in Figure 8.15, where the OK button has been assigned the hot key "O" and the "Office Occupant" check box has had to make do with "F". (Notice the knock-on effect that the Female radio button now has to use "E" instead of "F" because "F" has now been taken.)

Figure 8.15 Windows Form with Hot Keys after "O" Has Been Reserved for "OK"

A variation on this theme is that you can simply reserve various hot keys so that they are not used automatically by `HotKeyAssignments`:

```
HotKeyAssignment.AddStandardHotKey('X');
```

You would do this if you wanted to make sure that X was never automatically assigned to any control (possibly because the translator makes this assignment manually). Of course, the list of standard hot keys and their associated texts are locale specific, so you would need to load them from a resource. A simple way to achieve this is to hold the complete list as a semicolon-delimited string, like this:

```
O:OK;X;Y:;C:Cancel
```

This list contains four standard hot keys ("O" is for "OK", "X" and "Y" are simply reserved, and "C" is for "Cancel"). To load the complete list, use the HotKeyAssignment.AddStandardHotKeys method:

```
HotKeyAssignment.AddStandardHotKeys(
    resourceManager.GetString("StandardHotKeys"));
```

This assumes that you have created a resource key called StandardHotKeys and that the resourceManager variable or field can retrieve this resource.

Table 8.7 HotKeyAssignment **Static Properties**

Property	Description
CultureFormat	The format used to show the hot key in the control's text for the current UI culture
Format	The format used to show the hot key in the control's text
IgnoreAcceptAndCancelButtons	Specifies whether Accept and Cancel buttons should be ignored when assigning hot keys
StandardHotKeys	Array of StandardHotKey objects
ValidHotKeys	Array of valid hot key characters

Table 8.7 shows HotKeyAssignment's static properties. The Format property allows developers to specify how the hot key should be formatted within the control's text. It is a HotKeyFormat enumeration:

```
public enum HotKeyFormat {
    Culture, Embedded, SimpleEmbedded,
    BracketedSuffix, BracketedPrefix,
    BracketedSuffixEmbedded, BracketedPrefixEmbedded};
```

Embedded means that the hot key is embedded within the words of the control's text. This is the effect seen in Figures 8.14 and 8.15. SimpleEmbedded has the same visual effect, except that the algorithm for assigning the hot key is simpler: It does not attempt to use the first letter of each word first, and simply tries each successive letter in the string. This approach is suitable for languages that typically do not capitalize the first letter of subsequent words. For example, in Swedish, "Contact

Name" is "Kontaktens namn". Using a HotKeyFormat of Embedded, the text would be "Kontaktens &namn", giving a hot key of "n". Although this is correct in the form used in this example (because "K" and "O" have already been taken), it does not look correct in Swedish. Instead, it should be "Ko&ntaktens namn" (the underscore appears under the "n" in the first word, not under the "n" in the second word), and this is the effect achieved by SimpleEmbedded.

The Embedded and SimpleEmbedded approaches work well for languages based on a Latin alphabet. They do not work well if your language doesn't use the Latin alphabet. Such languages include Chinese, Japanese, and Korean. These languages still use alpha hot keys, but the hot keys are not normally found within the text. A common solution to this issue is to prefix or suffix the text with a bracketed hot key. The Format property can be set like this:

```
HotKeyAssignment.Format = HotKeyFormat.BracketedSuffixEmbedded;
```

Figure 8.16 shows the effect of using BracketedSuffixEmbedded on an English form. Note that the resulting text is longer than the original when the hot key is prefixed or suffixed. This may cause the text to be clipped if the controls do not autosize.

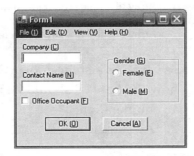

Figure 8.16   Windows Form with Hot Keys Using BracketedSuffix HotKeyFormat

The CultureFormat property is a wrapper around the Format property. The purpose of this property is to provide a culture-aware version of the Format property. If Format is Culture (which it is, by default), CultureFormat returns a value that is best suited for the CultureInfo.CurrentUICulture. So if the Current UICulture is Chinese, Japanese, or Korean, and Format is Culture, then CultureFormat returns BracketedSuffixEmbedded. If the CurrentUICulture is Swedish, then CultureFormat returns SimpleEmbedded. If the CurrentUICulture is not Chinese, Japanese, Korean, or Swedish, and `Format` is `Culture`, then `Culture Format` returns `Embedded` for Windows Forms applications.

The `IgnoreAcceptAndCancelButtons` Boolean static property allows you to ignore Accept and Cancel buttons when hot keys are being assigned. The default for this property is `false`, and the result is that these buttons are assigned their own hot keys. However, Microsoft's "Official Guidelines for User Interface Developers and Designers" states that Accept and Cancel buttons should not be assigned their own hot keys (because they already have the Enter and Escape keys assigned, respectively) so if you adhere to these guidelines, you should set this property to `true`.

ASP.NET and Hot Keys

ASP.NET applications have the same hot key issues as Windows Forms applications, with only a few differences. It is worth noting, however, that the prevalence of hot keys in Web applications is much lower than in Windows Forms applications. The requirement to provide support for hot keys in a Web application is much lower, and it is possible that this feature can simply be omitted from many Web applications. On the other hand, it should be noted that many projects (especially government projects) have accessibility requirements that demand that hot keys be available.

Although the behaviour of hot keys on a Web page is the same as for a Windows Form, their implementation differs. The ampersand character has no meaning, implied or actual, in a Web application, so the "embedded" formats (`Embedded`, `SimpleEmbedded`, `BracketedSuffixEmbedded`, and `BracketedPrefixEmbedded`) are all meaningless in an ASP.NET application. Instead, the hot key is assigned using the `WebControl.AccessKey` property. This can be set in the `.aspx` file:

```
<asp:Button id="OKButton" AccessKey="O" runat="server"
  Text="OK"></asp:Button>
```

or in code:

```
OKButton.AccessKey = "O";
```

TextBoxes also have an `AccessKey`, but in the absence of their own setting, they adopt the `AccessKey` of the `Label` immediately before them. In ASP.NET 2.0, the `Label` class has a new property, `AssociatedControlId`, which provides a more explicit link between a `Label` and its associated control instead of the somewhat vague association of "the control that follows the label."

The `HotKeyAssignment` class can be used in a similar way as for Windows Forms applications and is best placed in the page's `Load` event:

```
private void Page_Load(object sender, System.EventArgs e)
{
    HotKeyAssignment.AssignHotKeys(this);
}
```

The default for the `CultureFormat` property is `BracketedSuffix` for all cultures. `BracketedSuffix` is the same as the `BracketedSuffixEmbedded` member, seen earlier, except that no ampersand character is embedded in the text string (because it is meaningless in a Web application).

Another difference to bear in mind is that the menu is typically provided by the browser, and, like a Windows Forms application, the menu hot keys execute at the same level as hot keys on the page. So Alt+F in English Internet Explorer invokes the File menu. To avoid assigning the hot keys that are already used for Internet Explorer's menu to controls on the page, the list of valid hot keys excludes hot keys that are known to be in use. Here is the ASP.NET `HotKeyAssignment` static constructor and the `InitializeValidHotKeys` method:

```
static HotKeyAssignment()
{
    InitializeValidHotKeys();
}
protected static void InitializeValidHotKeys()
{
    ValidHotKeys = new Char[] {
        'B', 'C', 'D', 'G', 'I', 'J', 'K', 'L', 'M',
        'N', 'O', 'P', 'Q', 'R', 'S', 'U', 'W', 'X', 'Y', 'Z'
    };
}
```

You would need to set the valid hot keys for different language versions of Internet Explorer and different browsers.

Windows Forms Best Practices

This section illustrates best practices that are specific to Windows Forms applications.

Form Layout

The general wisdom on form layout for internationalized Windows Forms applications is to lay out forms so that labels are above the controls to which they refer (see Figure 8.17).

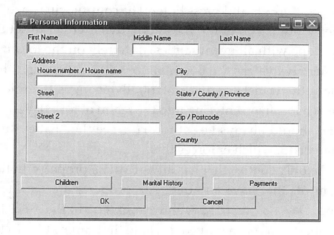

Figure 8.17 Traditional Form Layout Placing Labels above TextBoxes

The reasoning behind this approach is that text tends to expand when translated from English to other languages because English often uses fewer or smaller words. German and Welsh are typical examples of languages that occupy greater screen space than English. For this reason, Labels are placed above TextBoxes so that there is room for expansion of the text without having to move the controls on the form. Of course, there is a limit to how accommodating such a form can be. In Figure 8.17, the "House number / House name" label already occupies 75% of the room allocated to it, so it is possible that a translation would bump into the "City" label on the same line. This approach works reasonably well and is suitable for both the .NET Framework 1.1 and 2.0. It does, however, lead to forms that have room for expansion in which the room isn't always used. In an English form, for example, there may be excessive padding "just in case." As we shall see later in this section, the .NET Framework 2.0 has an alternative solution.

AutoSize

One of the most useful properties for form localization is `AutoSize`. When this property is set to `true`, the control automatically resizes to accommodate its contents. This is particularly useful for `Label` controls that are almost certain to be localized. Place a `Label` control on a form; if you are using Visual Studio 2003, set `Label1.AutoSize` to `true` (in Visual Studio 2005, this step is unnecessary); enter some text into `Label1.Text`; and press Enter. The control will resize. You don't have to use this property, but if you don't, the alternative is either to set the label size to be big enough to cope with all eventualities, or to rely on the localizer to resize the control. The former always has the potential for clipped text, and the latter pushes responsibility onto the translator and potentially changes the role from merely a translator to one of a localizer, entering into the realm of form layout. If you feel that `Label.AutoSize` should always be set to `true`, see the "Label.AutoSize must be true" rule in Chapter 13, which enforces this.

`Label` is not the only control that has an `AutoSize` property. In the .NET Framework 1.1, the controls that have an `AutoSize` property are `Label`, `RichTextBox`, `StatusBarPanel`, `TextBox`, `ToolBar`, and `TrackBar`. In the .NET Framework 2.0, the `AutoSize` property has been moved down to the `Control` base class from which all Windows Forms controls inherit. This increased availability of the `AutoSize` property is excellent for internationalization, but you should be aware of its nature. Although the `AutoSize` property is present in all controls, it is not appropriate to all controls. A `MonthCalendar`, for example, cannot realistically behave any differently if its `AutoSize` property is set to `true` than the way it behaves when its `AutoSize` property is set to `false`. For this reason, the Visual Studio 2005 Form Designer hides the `AutoSize` properties of controls for which it is inappropriate (see Table 8.8). In addition, although the default value for `AutoSize` is `false`, the Visual Studio 2005 Form Designer automatically sets the property to `true` when specific controls are added to a form (see Table 8.8). The exception to this approach is the `MaskedTextBox` control, which is new in the .NET Framework 2.0, so it does not have to maintain backward compatibility with the previous version of the framework.

Table 8.8   Windows Forms Common Controls Support for `AutoSize` **Property in Visual Studio 2005**

Control	`AutoSize` **Visible in Form Designer**	`AutoSize` **Set to** `True` **by Form Designer**
`Button`	Yes	No
`CheckBox`	Yes	Yes
`CheckedListBox`	No	—
`ComboBox`	Yes	No
`DateTimePicker`	No	—
`Label`	Yes	Yes
`LinkLabel`	Yes	Yes
`ListBox`	No	—
`ListView`	No	—
`MaskedTextBox`	Yes	**Defaults to** `True`
`MonthCalendar`	No	—
`NumericUpDown`	Yes	No
`PictureBox`	No	—
`ProgressBar`	No	—
`RadioButton`	Yes	Yes
`TreeView`	No	—
`WebBrowser`	No	—

In the .NET Framework 2.0, the `Form` class has an `AutoSize` property (because it inherits from `Control`). This is particularly helpful if a `Label` (or other control) is autosized and the form is not big enough to show the entire contents of the control. Figure 8.18 shows a simplistic form that is wide enough to contain its `Label` control. Figure 8.19 shows the same form after the label's `Text` property has changed and the label has autosized, causing the form to autosize as a consequence.

Figure 8.18   Windows Form Containing a Label that Is Smaller than the Form's Width

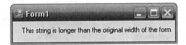

Figure 8.19   Windows Form Containing a Label that Has Autosized, Causing Its Form to Autosize

AutoSizeMode

The .NET Framework 2.0 introduces a new property, `AutoSizeMode`, which is an `AutoSizeMode` enumeration. The `AutoSizeMode` enumeration has two members: `GrowAndShrink` and `GrowOnly`. `AutoSizeMode` controls the behaviour of the `Auto-Size` property. The following controls implement the `AutoSizeMode` property:

- `Button`
- `DataGridViewColumn`
- `Form`
- `GroupBox`
- `Panel`
- `SplitterPanel`
- `TabPage`
- `ToolStripContentPanel`
- `UserControl`

The default is `GrowOnly`. When a control's contents change and `AutoSize` is `true`, the control grows to accommodate the new contents. If the new contents are smaller than the original contents, however, the control shrinks only if the `Auto-SizeMode` is `GrowAndShrink`. Using the `GrowOnly` option allows developers to lay out a form with controls that have reasonable room for expansion without leaving awkwardly large gaps. The majority of users would see a form with a common lay-out, but languages that demand larger controls would get larger controls without having to squeeze into too small of a space.

AutoEllipsis

The `Button`, `CheckBox`, `Label`, and `RadioButton` controls have a new property in the .NET Framework 2.0 called `AutoEllipsis`, which plays an active role when `AutoSize` is `false`. The purpose of this control is to provide an alternative to auto-sizing by showing an ellipsis (three periods, "…") when there is insufficient room to display the full text. Figure 8.20 shows a form with a button that has the text "This text is too long to be seen completely in this button". The text has been truncated in the display, and the remainder of the text has been replaced with an ellipsis. The full text is still available as a ToolTip.

Figure 8.20   Button with AutoEllipsis Set to True

The benefit of this approach is that the form can remain completely fixed in terms of controls and their positions and sizes, but if the controls are too small to display their text, the form remains usable, albeit in a more limited form. This approach is necessary for skinned applications in which the visual appearance of the form has been sculpted into a precise form, and autosizing and repositioning (see the next section) would destroy the form.

TableLayoutPanel and FlowLayoutPanel

One of the really useful features of HTML in terms of internationalization is that it uses flow layout by default. This means that when the text on a page changes as a consequence of localization, controls are automatically bumped out of the way. To line up controls, developers use an HTML table so that when one label bumps one control out of the way, the other controls that were lined up with it are all bumped to the same relative position. In the .NET Framework 1.1, achieving the same effect in a Windows Forms application requires a fair amount of effort. In the .NET Framework 2.0, however, you can easily achieve the same effect using a `TableLayout-Panel` control. The `TableLayoutPanel` is effectively an HTML table control for Windows Forms. The `FlowLayoutPanel` provides the same "flow layout" behaviour for Windows Forms as flow layout does for HTML (i.e., controls follow on from each other either horizontally or vertically). Although you might use `FlowLayout-Panel` less frequently than `TableLayoutPanel`, it can be invaluable in a number of UI scenarios, including providing lists and custom menu controls, auto-relocating panel-like windows, and creating custom toolbar scenarios.

Figure 8.21 shows an English and French version of the same form, with several `TableLayoutPanel` controls helping resize and reposition controls according to the different sizes of the text controls on the form.

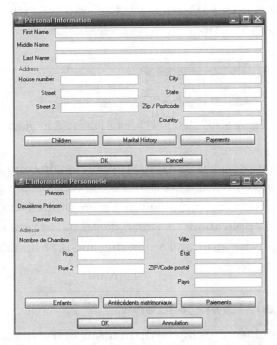

Figure 8.21   TableLayoutPanel Resizing and Repositioning Controls on Localized Forms

You can get a better idea of what's happening on this form by looking at the form in Visual Studio 2005 (see Figure 8.22).

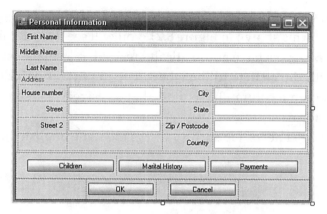

Figure 8.22 `TableLayoutPanel` **in the Form Designer in Visual Studio 2005**

There are three `TableLayoutPanels` on the form:

- One docked to the top, containing the `First Name, Middle Name,` and `Last Name` controls
- One docked to the bottom, containing the buttons
- One docked to the client of the `GroupBox` control, containing the address controls

All of the `TextBox` controls are anchored to the Left and Right sides of their cells. This means that when the cells containing them are resized, the `TextBox` controls are also resized. All of the `Label` controls are anchored to the right side of their cells so that they are always closest to the `TextBox` control to which they refer. The columns containing `Label` controls are set to `AutoSize`. For example, in the top `TableLayoutPanel`, the leftmost column is set to `AutoSize`. You can specify how columns should resize by clicking on the ellipsis in the `Columns` property of the `TableLayoutPanel` in the Properties Window. When the labels in the column automatically resize because the text has changed, the column containing them will also automatically resize. The columns containing the `TextBox` controls are all set to `Percent`. For example, in the top `TableLayoutPanel`, the rightmost column is set to `100% Percent`. This means that the rightmost column will occupy 100 percent of the remaining width of the `TableLayoutPanel` after all of the other autosize columns have been auto-sized. The `TextBox` columns of the `TableLayoutPanel` in the middle of the form are both set to 50% Percent because there are two TextBox columns. If you compare the two forms shown in Figure 8.21, you will see that the label sizes are different and the TextBoxes have automatically resized to a smaller size in the French form, to cope with the change to the labels. The important point is that all of the TextBoxes in the same column have moved and resized, thereby maintaining the symmetry of the form.

There is more good news. Figure 8.23 shows the same English form after the user has resized it.

Figure 8.23 TableLayoutPanel **Responding to the Form Being Resized**

Notice that the form is still fully functional and usable, but in this scenario, the user had a need for the form to be as small as possible. I am a big believer in letting users use their application in the way they want to use it instead of the way the developer wants them to use it. One of the most frustrating parts of using an application, for me, is to encounter a form that uses a control that should be docked when the control has not been docked. The classic example is a grid control. This control is just begging to the docked to the client of its container. The control resizes perfectly when its container is resized, so there is no reason to stifle users by not allowing them to gain the benefits of resizing the form. The point is that the TableLayout-Panel control takes this attitude to the next level; if users want a very small version of their form, the TableLayoutPanel lets them have it.

Staying on the good news theme, the TableLayoutPanel adopts its Right-ToLeft property (see Chapter 7) from its parent and mirrors its contents correctly when RightToLeft is set to Yes.

The `TableLayoutPanel` changes the Windows Forms internationalization story. The traditional approach of laying out labels above their respective controls works until the width of the labels exceeds the width allocated to them. The width allocated to them is fixed by the developer in the nature of the form. If the developer calculates this width incorrectly (and developers often use the time-honoured "try it and see" method), either the developer must change the form or the translator takes the responsibility for form layout and takes the more sophisticated role of localizer. With the `TableLayoutPanel`, developers can craft forms either using the traditional approach of laying out labels above their controls or, alternatively, laying out labels to the left of their controls. Regardless of this decision, there is no danger of overlapping controls and clipped text because the `TableLayoutPanel` will ensure that controls are moved and resized accordingly. There are several consequences of this. First, the localization effort is lower because localizers will not spend as much time changing form layouts. Second, there is a considerably higher probability of form correctness for all cultures because of the automatic resizing and repositioning. Third, the level of sophistication of the localization tools is lower because localizers may not need to redesign forms. It is still true that a better result will be achieved by allowing translators/localizers to see the form they are translating while they are translating it, just as they can with WinRes, but it strengthens the developer's argument that localizers do not need to resize and reposition controls. If you write a replacement for WinRes, the tool need not be as sophisticated because it would not have to support resizing and repositioning. Finally, the `TableLayoutPanel` control means that the localization effort is closer to that of translation than localization. The lower level of effort involved and the lower level of sophistication saves time and money, and means that the success of using a bilingual in-house employee who understands the business as opposed to software development is higher. A word of caution, though, lest you conclude that you should always use `TableLayoutPanel` controls in every scenario: `TableLayoutPanel` has been written with performance in mind, but don't underestimate the amount of effort that it goes to in order to lay out a form. If you start nesting `TableLayoutPanels` many levels deep, you can expect to see performance issues.

Where Are We?

In this chapter, we covered a collection of subjects about which you will need to make a development decision. For fonts, it may be safe to do nothing and accept the default or, alternatively, choose a font face name such as MS Shell Dlg or MS Shell Dlg 2. Strings require proper formatting using placeholders instead of concatenating bits of text. In addition, you will need to decide whether to use colons in strings and whether embedded control characters are acceptable. You will need to take a stance on the language used for exception messages and whether a distinction should be made between exceptions that are destined for the user and those that are destined for the developer. You will need to decide whether hot keys are assigned automatically at runtime, or statically in resources determined by a localizer, or whether they should be used at all. If you are writing a Windows Forms application, you will need to make various decisions regarding your form layout. These will be heavily influenced by whether you are developing using the .NET Framework 2.0 and can make use of the `TableLayoutPanel` control to move the problem from the localizer to the developer. In turn, this decision may influence whether you can perform your translation in house or whether you need to hire professional localizers.

9.
Machine Translation

W HEN IBM PC DOS WAS FIRST TRANSLATED into French, the DOS error message "Out of environment space" was translated as the French equivalent of "There is no room in the garden." I used to imagine French people looking forlornly out of the window thinking to themselves, "That may be true, but what's wrong with my computer?" The translation industry and the tools that it spawns have made great advances in the last 20 years, but the pitfalls are still the same. In this chapter, we look at how we can use machine translation (MT)—translations performed by computers. We build a translation engine that we later use in Chapter 10, "Resource Administration," to automatically translate resources and to add whole new languages to an application at the click of a button, and in Chapter 12, "Custom Resource Managers," to perform automatic translation on the fly for applications with highly dynamic content.

The journey starts with a critique of the kind of success you can expect from machine translation. We create a foundation for the translation engine upon which all translators will be based. We create a range of translators that I have arranged into groups: pseudo translators, Web service translators, HTML translators, and an Office 2003 Research Service translator. Finally, we conclude with a simple utility, Translator Evaluator, that enables you to test and compare the success, performance, and accuracy of automatic translators.

How Good Is It ?

The short answer to this question is that it's not perfect, and you wouldn't want to ship your application with a wholly machine-based translation. You should look at machine translation as a means of providing a first-cut translation. This first attempt would be handed over to a human translator (along with the original language upon which the translation was performed), who would fix the translation mistakes.

Machine translation offers a number of benefits. It significantly reduces the amount of work that the translator has to do and, therefore, reduces the cost of translation. One statistic states that the maximum number of words a translator can translate per day is 2,000. A crude estimation of the time involved in translation can be gained from adding the number of words in your resources and dividing by 2,000. The resulting time will certainly be longer than it would take a machine to translate the same text.

In addition, machine translation produces a first-cut translation that can be used for testing and demonstration purposes. The development team commonly doesn't speak the target language of the application, so, to them, a first-cut translation to the target language is indistinguishable from the final translation. The benefit, though, is that the development team and the user acceptance team can clearly see that a translation has been performed and can detect problems in the internationalization process early in the development process.

The longer answer to the question "How good is it?" requires a recognition of the problems of machine translation. Most languages are ambiguous, and English is one of the most ambiguous. If you look up a word in a dictionary, you will probably find several meanings for the same word. For example, the English word *close* can mean "to shut," "to be near," "to finish," or "to be fond of," and each meaning often has a different word. The correct meaning can be inferred only from either the surrounding words or the context in which the phrase is used. To help with the problem of context, some machine translators support a "Subject" setting that enables you to specify a genre or industry in which the words are used (e.g., Science, Sport, Accounting, Aviation, Medical). However, this doesn't always help. Often when a machine translator cannot determine the context of a word, it makes its best guess. The English phrase "Log off" seems obvious enough to an English speaker, but translated into German, it can get translated as "Plank of wood away" (*Log* is "plank of wood" and *off* is "away").

In addition, there is no one "true" translation for most words or phrases. If you translate the simple English word *Enter* into German, various translators will return "Kommen Sie herein," "Kommen Sie," "Tragen Sie ein," and "Hereingehen." If you are looking for a gauge of how accurate your translation is and you don't speak the target language yourself, try translating from your own language to the target language and back again. If you get the original text back again, the translation is more likely to be accurate (but this isn't a guarantee because it could be translated incorrectly in both directions). The reverse, however, isn't necessarily true, so if you don't get your original text back, it doesn't necessarily follow that the translation is wrong. (If you are looking for some translation-related fun, you could write a kind of translation Chinese whispers quote of the day program in which you translate a phrase through several different languages and finally back to the original language, and see what you get.) This is one of the reasons why "universal translators" that translate all languages into an intermediate language such as Esperanto and then from the intermediate language to the target language don't fare so well in terms of accuracy.

Finally, it should be pointed out that correct spelling and grammar are a prerequisite for a successful machine translation. If words are spelled incorrectly, a machine translator cannot possibly translate the word correctly (and this can affect the success of the translation of the surrounding words). See the "Resource strings should be spelled correctly" rule in Chapter 13, "Testing Internationalization Using FxCop," for details on checking the spelling of your resources.

Translation Engine

The translation engine is a library of machine translators that support one or more translation language pairs (e.g., English to French). In all but one of the translators in this chapter, the language pairs are culture neutral. The translators shown in this chapter represent examples of free translation sources, but you can add your own translator classes. Figure 9.1 shows the translators included with the code for this book.

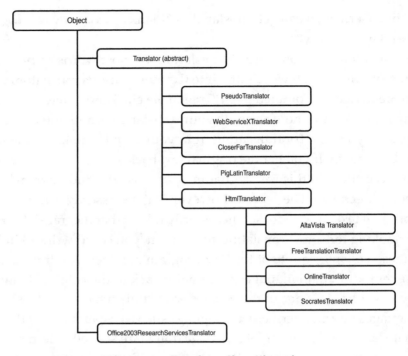

Figure 9.1   Translator Class Hierarchy

Translators implement the ITranslator interface (shown later), which has a method called Translate. In this example, we are creating a new WebServiceX-Translator object (which we cover in the section on Web service translators) and are calling the Translate method to translate "Eddies in the space time continuum" from English to German:

```
ITranslator translator = new WebServiceXTranslator();
string text = translator.Translate(
    "en", "de", "Eddies in the space time continuum");
```

Translators support a method called IsSupported so that they can be interrogated to see if they support a given language pair:

```
ITranslator translator = new WebServiceXTranslator();
if (translator.IsSupported("en", "de"))
    string text = translator.Translate(
        "en", "de", "Eddies in the space time continuum");
```

Typically, you won't use just one translator; you'll use a collection of translators. Not all translators support all possible language pairs, so a collection of translators enables you to support the sum of language pairs for many translators. In addition, not all translators are always online, so having a language pair redundancy enables you to fall back to other translators when one becomes unavailable. For this purpose, there is the `TranslatorCollection` class:

```
TranslatorCollection translators = new TranslatorCollection();
translators.Add(new PseudoTranslator());
translators.Add(new WebServiceXTranslator());
translators.Add(new CloserFarTranslator());
translators.Add(new AltaVistaTranslator());
translators.Add(new FreeTranslationTranslator());
translators.Add(new Office2003ResearchServicesTranslator());
```

In this example, we create a new `TranslatorCollection` and add a number of translators that support overlapping and unique language pairs. You can then get a translator from the collection for a given language pair:

```
ITranslator translator = translators.GetTranslator("en", "de")
string text = translator.Translate(
    "en", "de", "Eddies in the space time continuum");
```

The algorithm used to get the translator is a simple sequential search, but you could change the algorithm to be more sophisticated, to favor certain translators for certain language pairs.

The ITranslator Interface

Translators are defined by the `ITranslator` interface:

```
public interface ITranslator
{
    bool IsSupported(string inputLanguage, string outputLanguage);
    string Translate(string inputLanguage, string outputLanguage,
        string text);
    string Name {get;}
    bool Enabled {get;set;}
    string[,] LanguagePairs {get;}
}
```

You have already seen the IsSupported and Translate methods. The Name property is the name of the translator. The Enabled property specifies whether the translator is enabled. This can be used to turn off a translator. For example, the Resource Administrator (in Chapter 10) catches exceptions thrown by the Translate method and sets Enabled to false. This isn't the same as removing a translator from the collection because, in a long-running application, you might want to "resurrect" translators to give them a second chance.

The LanguagePairs property is an array of language pairs supported by the translator. The array is intended for informational purposes only. To determine whether a language pair is supported, use the IsSupported method instead of scanning the LanguagePairs array. The IsSupported method is more accurate than walking through the LanguagePairs array, mainly because the LanguagePairs array can contain wildcards ("*") to denote "any language," but also because some translators could support language pairs that can be tested only dynamically.

The Translator Class

The Translator class implements the ITranslator interface and acts as a base class for all the translators in this chapter. Of course, if you write your own translator classes, you do not need to inherit from Translator—you only need to support the ITranslator interface. The Translator class implements the basic functionality for the properties and the IsSupported method. The Translate method is left for subclasses to implement.

```
public abstract class Translator: ITranslator
{
    private bool enabled = true;
    private string name;
    private string[,] languagePairs;

    public Translator(string name)
    {
        this.name = name;
    }
    public Translator(string name, string[,] languagePairs)
    {
        this.name = name;
        this.languagePairs = languagePairs;
```

```
    }
    public string Name
    {
      get {return name;}
    }
    public bool Enabled
    {
        get {return enabled;}
        set {enabled = value;}
    }
    public virtual string[,] LanguagePairs
    {
        get {return languagePairs;}
    }
    public virtual bool IsSupported(
        string inputLanguage, string outputLanguage)
    {
        if (languagePairs == null)
            return false;

        if (inputLanguage.Length < 2 || outputLanguage.Length < 2)
            return false;

        for(int pairNumber = 0;
            pairNumber < languagePairs.GetLength(0); pairNumber++)
        {
            if ((String.Compare(inputLanguage,
                languagePairs[pairNumber, 0], true,
                CultureInfo.InvariantCulture) == 0
                || languagePairs[pairNumber, 0] == "*")
                && String.Compare(outputLanguage,
                languagePairs[pairNumber, 1], true,
                CultureInfo.InvariantCulture) == 0)
                return true;
        }
        return false;
    }
    public abstract string Translate(
        string inputLanguage, string outputLanguage, string text);
}
```

In addition, the `Translator` class supports three conversion helper methods that can be used as needed.

The TranslatorCollection Class

The `TranslatorCollection` class is a collection of objects that implement the `ITranslator` interface:

```
public class TranslatorCollection : List<ITranslator>
```

(In .NET Framework 1.1, the base class is `CollectionBase` instead of `List<ITranslator>`).

`TranslatorCollection` implements the following methods:

```
public int IndexOf(string name)
{
    for(int index = 0; index < Count; index++)
    {
        if (this[index].Name == name)
            return index;
    }
    return -1;
}
public ITranslator GetTranslator(
    string inputLanguage, string outputLanguage)
{
    int index = IndexOf(inputLanguage, outputLanguage);
    if (index == -1)
        return null;
    return this[index];
}
public ITranslator GetEnabledTranslator(
    string inputLanguage, string outputLanguage)
{
    int index = EnabledIndexOf(inputLanguage, outputLanguage);
    if (index == -1)
        return null;
    return this[index];
}
public int IndexOf(string inputLanguage, string outputLanguage)
{
    for(int index = 0; index < Count; index++)
    {
        if (this[index].IsSupported(inputLanguage, outputLanguage))
            return index;
    }
    return -1;
}
public int EnabledIndexOf(
    string inputLanguage, string outputLanguage)
```

```
{
    for(int index = 0; index < Count; index++)
    {
        ITranslator translator = this[index];
        if (translator.Enabled &&
            translator.IsSupported(inputLanguage, outputLanguage))
            return index;
    }
    return -1;
}
```

You have already seen `GetTranslator`, which gets a translator from the list when given a language pair. `GetTranslator` is based upon an overloaded `IndexOf` method, which accepts the same parameters. `GetEnabledTranslator` (based upon `EnabledIndexOf`) performs the same search as `GetTranslator`, except that it looks for only enabled translators. This method is useful if your application catches translator exceptions and "turns off" translators, or, alternatively, if you offer the user the capability to turn translators on and off.

Pseudo Translation

As part of the internationalization process, you will certainly want to test how localizable your application is. No matter how sophisticated your toolkit is, some part of the testing process must involve looking at the end result of the translation. The form in Figure 9.2 has been translated into Greek.

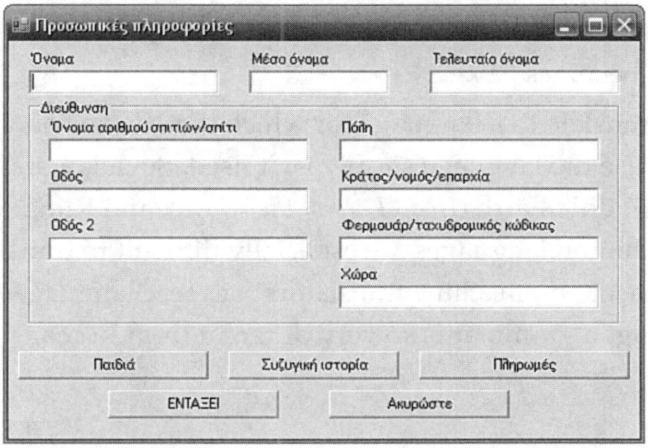

Figure 9.2 A Windows Form Localized into Greek

Although this scores 10 out of 10 for showing that the application is localizable, the user interface is very difficult to navigate if you can't read Greek. Which of the buttons in the screenshot enables the user to add payments? The user acceptance team will be unable to use the Greek version of the application to test that the application has been globalized, but if they use the English version of the application, they cannot accurately test globalization, either. You need a solution that enables the user acceptance team to read the application so that they can operate it properly, but the language and culture must be different from the development team's language and culture. Enter pseudo translation and pseudo culture.

Pseudo translation is translation that modifies the original text so that the original text can still be inferred from the translated result. You can pseudo translate your application in many different ways:

- You could capitalize the text (e.g., "Exit" becomes "EXIT"). The downside is that there is no difference when the original text is already in capitals (e.g., "OK").

- You could prefix the text with a letter (e.g., "T" for "translated"—"Exit" becomes "T Exit").

- You could prefix the text with language and culture (e.g., "Exit" becomes "fr-FR Exit").

- You could prefix the text with "xxx" and suffix with "xxx" (e.g., "Exit" becomes "xxx Exit xxx").

- You could convert to Pig Latin (e.g., "Exit" becomes "Exit-hay").

- You could convert each character to an accented version of the same character (e.g., "Exit" becomes " Ĕχĭť ").

- You could translate to a language for which there is no country. Typically, this will be because the language simply isn't used. Such languages include Latin, Esperanto, Middle Earth (from *Lord of the Rings*), and Klingon. The Middle Earth and Klingon languages are especially difficult to translate to, partly because there are no machine translators for these languages, but also because Klingon grammar is so very different from Roman grammar.

The option that I have chosen is to convert to accented characters. In this approach, each character is converted to an equivalent character that has an accent. You can find equivalent accented characters using the Character Map (Start, All Programs, Accessories, System Tools, Character Map).

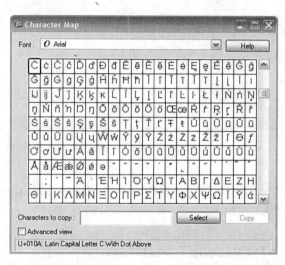

Figure 9.3   Using the Character Map to Find Accented Characters

In addition, the result needs to be padded. English is not the longest language in the world, and often only after the translation has occurred will you discover that your carefully designed forms don't allow enough room for the translated language. German and Welsh are typically significantly longer than English. If you are translating your application for the European market, target German first, in order to identify form design problems in which the translated string needs to be padded. A general rule is that, for text less than 10 characters, the text needs to be padded by an additional 400 percent; for text greater than or equal to 10 characters, the text needs to be padded by an additional 30 percent. You also need to decide whether to pad on the left, on the right, or both. The benefit of padding on both sides is that you can check for screen design problems when your forms have been mirrored (for right-to-left languages).

The form in Figure 9.4 has been translated using the `PseudoTranslator` class.

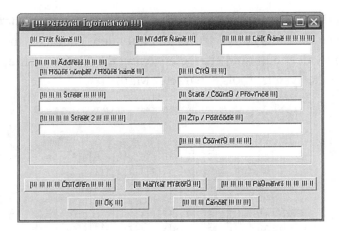

Figure 9.4   An Example of a Pseudo Translated Form

You should be able to read all the text on the form and, therefore, know which button to press to add payments.

Choosing a Culture for Pseudo Translation

To use pseudo translation, you must identify a culture that represents the pseudo language. In Chapter 11, "Custom Cultures," I show how you can create your own cultures for various reasons, including supporting a pseudo translation. Creating a custom culture is a good approach in the following circumstances:

1. You are using Visual Studio 2005 or

2. You are writing an ASP.NET application or

3. You are not using resx files for resources.

However, if you are using Visual Studio 2003 and are writing a Windows Forms application based on resx files, any custom culture that you create will not be recognized by Visual Studio 2003. See Chapter 11 for more information.

If you are unable to create a custom culture for pseudo translation, the alternative is to hijack an existing culture. In this approach, you identify a language/country that you do not expect to ever use for its real purpose and hijack it for your own purpose. This requires a certain amount of thought. First, hijacking someone else's culture could potentially offend the people of that culture (assuming that they find out). Second, you want to choose a culture that is as different from your own as possible. It should have a different date/time format, number format, currency, time zone, and as many other globalization differences as possible. So it is with great apologies to the people of Albania that I have chosen Albanian as the culture to hijack. From the Regional and Language Options page (see Figure 9.5), you can see that the Albanian culture is significantly different than that of English.

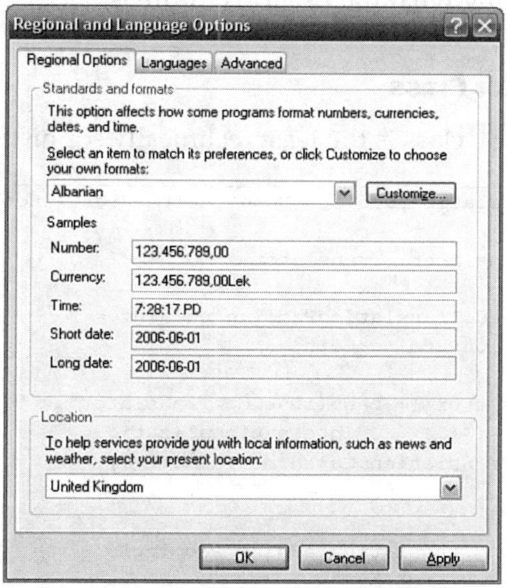

Figure 9.5   Regional and Language Options Dialog Showing Albanian Culture

The number format is different, the currency symbol is suffixed instead of prefixed, the time suffix is PD instead of AM, and the date separator is "-" instead of "/".

Regardless of whether you create a custom culture or hijack an existing culture, you need a means by which you can communicate your chosen culture to code that needs to know the pseudo culture. The following PseudoTranslation class has a static property that represents a global placeholder for your chosen pseudo translation culture ("sq" is the language code for Albanian):

```
public class PseudoTranslation
{
    private static CultureInfo cultureInfo = new CultureInfo("sq");
    public static CultureInfo CultureInfo
```

```
    {
        get {return cultureInfo;}
        set {cultureInfo = value;}
    }
}
```

Now a translator class can indicate that it supports translation to the pseudo culture without hard-coding what the pseudo culture is.

The PseudoTranslator Class

The PseudoTranslator class is the least technically sophisticated translator:

```
public enum PseudoTranslationPadding {None, Left, Right, Both};

public class PseudoTranslator: Translator
{
    private static PseudoTranslationPadding padding =
        PseudoTranslationPadding.Both;

    public PseudoTranslator(): base("Pseudo Translator",
        new string[,] {{"*",        Internationalization.
        Common.PseudoTranslation.CultureInfo.Name}})
    {
    }
    public static PseudoTranslationPadding Padding
    {
        get {return padding;}
        set {padding = value;}
    }
    public override string Translate(
        string inputLanguage, string outputLanguage, string text)
    {
        if (! IsSupported(inputLanguage, outputLanguage))
            throw new LanguageCombinationNotSupportedException(
              "Language combination is not supported",
              inputLanguage, outputLanguage);

        return PseudoTranslate(text);
    }
}
```

The constructor simply calls the Translator base class constructor and supplies its name and the array of language pairs that it supports. It supports just one language pair, which translates from "*" (meaning any language) to the pseudo translation language. The `PseudoTranslator` class has a static `Padding` property, which indicates whether padding is added on the left, the right, both sides, or not at all. The `Translate` method checks to see that the language translation is supported; if it isn't, it throws an exception. Otherwise, it performs the translation by calling the `PseudoTranslate` method:

```
protected virtual string PseudoTranslate(string text)
{
    StringBuilder stringBuilder = new StringBuilder("[");
    if (padding == PseudoTranslationPadding.Left ||
        padding == PseudoTranslationPadding.Both)
    {
        // add padding on the left
        for(int padCount = 0;
            padCount < GetPaddingOnOneSideCount(text); padCount++)
        {
            stringBuilder.Append("!!! ");
        }
    }

    bool previousCharacterIsSlash = false;
    foreach(char chr in text)
    {
        if (previousCharacterIsSlash)
            stringBuilder.Append(chr);
        else
            stringBuilder.Append(ConvertCharacter(chr));

        previousCharacterIsSlash = (chr == @"\"[0]);
    }

    if (padding == PseudoTranslationPadding.Right ||
        padding == PseudoTranslationPadding.Both)
    {
        // add padding on the right
        for(int padCount = 0;
            padCount < GetPaddingOnOneSideCount(text); padCount++)
        {
            stringBuilder.Append(" !!!");
        }
    }
    stringBuilder.Append("]");
    return stringBuilder.ToString();
}
```

It builds the translated text by adding the padding prefix (if any) and converting each character using the `ConvertCharacter` method and then adding the padding suffix (if any). Notice the references to the `previousCharacterIsSlash` variable, which is an attempt to preserve control characters embedded in the string. Refer to the section entitled "Embedded Control Characters" in Chapter 8, "Best Practices," for a discussion on the pros and cons of embedding control characters in strings. The `PseudoTranslator` class can cope with embedded control characters because it performs a translation character by character and can put embedded control characters back into the same relative position that they occupied in the original string. Other translator classes do not have the same luxury and cope with embedded control characters less successfully. (Chapter 13 includes an FxCop rule to catch resource strings with embedded control characters.) The `ConvertCharacter` method is a straight lookup, replacing character for character:

```
protected virtual char ConvertCharacter(char chr)
{
    switch (chr)
    {
        case 'A' : return 'Ă ';
        case 'B' : return 'ß ';
        case 'C' : return 'Č';
        case 'D' : return 'Đ ';
        case 'E' : return 'Ĕ ';
        case 'F' : return 'F';
        case 'G' : return 'Ğ ';
        case 'H' : return 'Ħ ';
        case 'I' : return 'Ĭ';
        case 'J' : return 'Ĵ ';
        case 'K' : return 'Ķ ';
        case 'L' : return 'Ľ ';
etc.
etc.
```

Our first translator is complete.

Static Lookup Translator

An obvious approach to translation is to keep all the phrases used in an application in a huge lookup table of some kind. This is the approach adopted by the Microsoft

Application Translator (see Appendix B, "Information Resources"). Of course, this solution doesn't help you with the actual translation process, but having found a lookup source—or, more likely, having created one yourself (or with the help of a translator)—you can save some effort on subsequent translations by keeping such words or phrases in a static lookup. Such glossaries exist. Microsoft's glossaries are at ftp://ftp.microsoft.com/developr/msdn/newup/Glossary/ (you can read these manually or use the inexpensive WinLexic (http://www.winlexic.com) to download, read, and search them in a more human interface). The Microsoft Application Translator (see Appendix B) also includes various lookup tables. However you should be aware of the following:

- The license agreement might prevent you from using the glossary in this way. (Microsoft's glossary license explicitly states this.)
- The lookups are good for only known phrases. The majority of your application text is unlikely to match existing glossary text.
- Words used in one context do not necessarily have the same translations in another context. (Welsh, for example, has many forms of "yes" and "no," which are dependent upon the question being asked.)

For these reasons, I have left this kind of translator as an exercise for the reader.

Web Service Translators

Many free and commercial machine translators are implemented as Web services. You can find Web service translators from Web service directories such as these:

- XMethods (http://www.xmethods.com)
- SalCentral (http://www.salcentral.com)

In this section, I show an example of a Web Service translator using the WebServiceX translator at http://www.webservicex.net/TranslateService.asmx. This Web service provides machine-translation services for European, Chinese, Japanese, and Korean languages. The code for this book also includes a translator for the CloserFar service, at http://www.closerfar.com/engtoarabic.asmx, which translates English to Arabic.

Start by adding a reference to the Web service (in Solution Explorer, right-click the project, select Add Web Reference..., enter the address in the URL text box, click Go, and click the Add Reference button). This is the `WebServiceXTranslator` class:

```
public class WebServiceXTranslator: Translator
{
    private net.webservicex.www.TranslateService translateService;

    public WebServiceXTranslator():
        base("WebServiceX Translator", new string[,]
        {
            {"en", "zh-CHS"},
            {"en", "fr"},
            {"en", "de"},
            {"en", "it"},
            {"en", "ja"},
            {"en", "ko"},
            {"en", "pt"},
            {"en", "es"},
            {"fr", "en"},
            {"fr", "de"},
            {"de", "en"},
            {"de", "fr"},
            {"it", "en"},
            {"es", "en"}
        })
    {
    }
    public override string Translate(
        string inputLanguage, string outputLanguage, string text)
    {
        if (! IsSupported(inputLanguage, outputLanguage))
            throw new LanguageCombinationNotSupportedException(
                "Language combination is not supported",
                inputLanguage, outputLanguage);

        if (translateService == null)
            translateService =
                new net.webservicex.www.TranslateService();

        string translatedText = translateService.Translate(
            TranslationServiceLanguage(
            inputLanguage, outputLanguage), text);

        return ConvertFromEscapedNumerics(translatedText);
    }
}
```

The constructor calls the base class, passing in the name and the list of supported language pairs. As mentioned in previous chapters, the Chinese (Simplified) language is not a simple two-letter code like most other languages. Although it is uncommon, this is not the only language that is not identified by two letters.

The `Translate` method calls the Web service's `Translate` method, passing in an enumeration that identifies the language pair and the text to translate. The `TranslationServiceLanguage` method is simply a conversion from a language pair to the required enum.

HTML Translators

Another source of translators is translation Web sites. AltaVista is one such example. Go to AltaVista and click the "Translate" link (see Figure 9.6).

Figure 9.6 AltaVista's Translation Facility

From here you can type a string into the "Translate a block of text:" box, select a language pair using the combo box, and click the Translate button; the translated text is shown on the next page. The job of an HTML translator is to automate this process and to collect the result. The result is returned somewhere in the returned HTML page and must be extracted. This process is often referred to as screen scraping and is not an ideal solution. The biggest problem is that when the HTML changes, the algorithm for extracting the string is usually broken, so the process fails. As such, it is a fragile solution; the more explicit method employed by Web services is preferable.

In the code for this book, you will find HTML translators for the following:

- AltaVista
- Free Translation
- Online Translator
- Socrates

See Appendix B for a complete list of online translators.

All the HTML translators inherit from the `HtmlTranslator` class, which uses the .NET Framework 2.0 `WebBrowser` control (in the All Windows Forms section of the toolbox). If you are using Visual Studio 2003, see the section "Visual Studio 2003 `WebBrowser` Control" for an equivalent control. Both the Visual Studio 2005 and Visual Studio 2003 projects are included in the book's source code.

The `WebBrowser` control is part of a form called `WebBrowserForm`, which is never shown. The `WebBrowser` control simply represents a way to post information to a page and to get the resulting HTML. The form has one method to wait for the completion of the page before getting the result:

```
public void WaitForBrowser()
{
    while(WebBrowser.ReadyState != WebBrowserReadyState.Complete)
    {
        Application.DoEvents();
    }
}
```

The `HtmlTranslator` class makes life easy for its subclasses. With the majority of the work performed in the `HtmlTranslator` class, the subclasses need to specify only the following:

- The translator's name
- The URL for the Web site
- The language pairs supported
- A method to format the data posted to the URL
- A method to decode the result from the Web page

This is the `HtmlTranslator` class:

```
public abstract class HtmlTranslator: Translator
{
    private string url;

    private WebBrowserForm webBrowserForm;
    private WebBrowser webBrowser;

    public HtmlTranslator(string name, string url): base(name)
    {
        this.url = url;
    }
    public HtmlTranslator(string name, string url,
        string[,] languagePairs): base(name, languagePairs)
    {
        this.url = url;
    }
    public string Url
    {
        get {return url;}
        set {url = value;}
    }
    protected virtual void InitializeWebBrowser()
    {
        if (webBrowser == null)
        {
            webBrowserForm = new WebBrowserForm();
            webBrowser = webBrowserForm.WebBrowser;
        }
    }
    public abstract string GetPostData(
        string inputLanguage, string outputLanguage, string text);
```

```
    protected string Encode(string text)
    {
        return HttpUtility.UrlEncode(text);
    }
    protected virtual string GetTranslation(string inputLanguage,
        string outputLanguage, string innerText)
    {
        return innerText;
    }
}
```

As you would expect, the action happens in the Translate method:

```
public override string Translate(
    string inputLanguage, string outputLanguage, string text)
{
    if (! IsSupported(inputLanguage, outputLanguage))
        throw new LanguageCombinationNotSupportedException(
            "Language combination is not supported",
            inputLanguage, outputLanguage);

    InitializeWebBrowser();

    string innerText = GetInnerText(GetPostData(
        inputLanguage, outputLanguage, text));
    return GetTranslation(inputLanguage, outputLanguage, innerText);
}
```

Translate initializes the Web browser and calls the subclass's GetPostData to get the data to post to the URL. GetInnerText navigates to the URL, posts the data, waits for the browser to complete the display of the page, extracts the HTML from the page, and then extracts just the text part of the HTML:

```
protected virtual string GetInnerText(string postData)
{
    string headers =
        "Content-Type: application/x-www-form-urlencoded" +
        (char) 10 + (char) 13;

    byte[] bytePostData =
        System.Text.Encoding.ASCII.GetBytes(postData);

    webBrowser.Navigate(
        new Uri(url), String.Empty, bytePostData, headers);
```

```
webBrowserForm.WaitForBrowser();

return webBrowser.Document.Body.InnerText;
}
```

The subclass's `GetTranslation` method is passed the language pair and the Web page's text, and is responsible for extracting the translated text from the page.

Visual Studio 2003 WebBrowser Control

The .NET Framework 1.1 does not have a `WebBrowser` control, but an equivalent ActiveX control can be used instead. This control is not installed in the Visual Studio toolbox by default. To install it, right-click the toolbox, select Add/Remove Items..., select the COM Components tab, click the Browse... button, enter **shdocvw.dll** from your `system32` folder, and click Open. Figure 9.7 shows the result. Click OK.

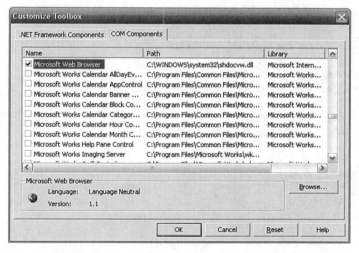

Figure 9.7   Adding the Microsoft Web Browser Control to the Visual Studio 2003 Toolbox

The ActiveX `Web Browser` wrapper control is similar to the .NET Framework 2.0 `WebBrowser` control, but you should be aware of the differences listed in Table 9.1.

Table 9.1   Relevant Differences Between the .NET Framework 2.0 `WebBrowser` **Control and the** `ActiveX Web Browser` **Control Used in .NET Framework 1.1**

.NET Framework 2.0	.NET Framework 1.1
`WebBrowserReadyState.Complete`	`SHDocVw.tagREADYSTATE.READYSTATE_ COMPLETE`
`System.Windows.Forms.WebBrowser`	`AxSHDocVw.AxWebBrowser`
`WebBrowser.Document.Body.InnerText`	`WebBrowser.Document.body.innerText`
`WebBrowser.Navigate` **accepts strongly typed params**	`WebBrowser.Navigate` **accepts objects typically passed by reference, as well as a** `Flags` **parameter (which should be** `0`**)**

The AltaVistaTranslator Class

The `AltaVistaTranslator` class uses AltaVista's translation Web page to perform translations:

```
public class AltaVistaTranslator: HtmlTranslator
{
    public AltaVistaTranslator(): base("AltaVista Translator",
        @"http://babelfish.altavista.com/tr", new string[,]
        {
            {"en", "zh-CHS"},
            {"en", "zh-CHT"},
            {"en", "nl"},
            {"en", "fr"},
            {"en", "de"},
            {"en", "el"},
            {"en", "it"},
            {"en", "ja"},
            {"en", "ko"},
            {"en", "pt"},
            {"en", "ru"},
            {"en", "es"},
            {"zh-CHS", "en"},
            {"zh-CHT", "en"},
            {"nl", "en"},
            {"nl", "fr"},
            {"fr", "nl"},
            {"fr", "en"},
            {"fr", "de"},
```

```
                {"fr", "el"},
                {"fr", "it"},
                {"fr", "pt"},
                {"fr", "es"},
                {"de", "en"},
                {"de", "fr"},
                {"el", "en"},
                {"el", "fr"},
                {"it", "en"},
                {"it", "fr"},
                {"ja", "en"},
                {"ko", "en"},
                {"pt", "en"},
                {"pt", "fr"},
                {"ru", "en"},
                {"es", "en"},
                {"es", "fr"}
        })
    {
    }
    protected virtual string DotNetLanguageCodeToLanguageCode(
        string language)
    {
        // check for a couple of adjustments to the language codes
        if (language == "zh-CHS")
            // Chinese (Simplified)
            return "zh";
        else if (language == "zh-CHT")
            // Chinese (Traditional)
            return "zt";
        else
            return language;
    }
    public override string GetPostData(string inputLanguage,
        string outputLanguage, string text)
    {
        string languagePair =
            DotNetLanguageCodeToLanguageCode(inputLanguage) + "_" +
            DotNetLanguageCodeToLanguageCode(outputLanguage);

        return "doit=done&intl=1&tt=urltext&trtext=" +
            Encode(text) + "&lp=" + languagePair;
    }
    protected override string GetTranslation(string inputLanguage,
        string outputLanguage, string innerText)
    {
        int index = innerText.IndexOf("Babel Fish Translation");
        if (index == -1)
```

```
            return String.Empty;

        innerText = innerText.Substring(index + 2);

        index = innerText.IndexOf(":");
        if (index == -1)
            return String.Empty;

        innerText = innerText.Substring(index + 3);

        index = innerText.IndexOf("Translate again");
        if (index == -1)
            return String.Empty;

        return innerText.Substring(0, index - 2).TrimEnd(
            new char[] {' ', (char) 10, (char) 13});
    }
}
```

The `GetPostData` method builds a post data string containing the language pair and the text to translate. The `GetTranslation` method looks for textual markers that are known to be immediately before the translated text and immediately after the translated text, and gets the text in between. This represents the most fragile part of this process. If the textual content of the resulting Web page changes, this code will need to be rewritten.

Office 2003 Research Services

Microsoft Office 2003 offers yet another translation opportunity. Office 2003 includes a feature called Research Services that enables you to perform various kinds of research from within an Office application. This enables you to perform the research without having to leave your Office application, but it also allows the result of the research to be pasted into your application in context. You can write your own Research Services in .NET and have Office use them just like one of its own.

But this isn't what is of most interest to us with regard to machine translation. One of the built-in Research Services is the Translation service. To see it in action, start an Office 2003 application, such as Word, and select Tools, Research…. A new pane called "Research" is added on the right side of the window. Drop down the combo box (which initially says "All Reference Books") and select Translation. In the

"Search for:" text box, enter a phrase to translate. In the two combo boxes below, enter the "From" language and the "To" language. Click the green arrow next to the "Search for:" text box; the text then is translated (see Figure 9.8).

Figure 9.8　Using the Microsoft Office 2003 Research Pane to Perform Translations (Translation Services Provided by WorldLingo.)

It is this translation facility that you can harness for your own automatic translation.

If you search on MSDN (http://msdn.microsoft.com) or the Microsoft Office Web site (http://office.microsoft.com), you will find a fair amount of information on creating your own research services and integrating them into Office. However, you won't find any information on how to consume research services. The reason behind this is that Microsoft expects that the only consumer of Office 2003 Research Services is Office 2003. However, all that you need to know is in this section. You might find it useful to download the Microsoft Office 2003 Research Services SDK, which contains some background information on the subject.

Most Office 2003 Research Services are simply Web services. As such, given the Web service's URL, its WSDL, and the format of its messages, we can use the Web service just like any other Web service. Figure 9.9 shows the list of Research Services that are contained within the Registry at `HKEY_CURRENT_USER\Software\Microsoft\Office\11.0\Common\Research\Sources`.

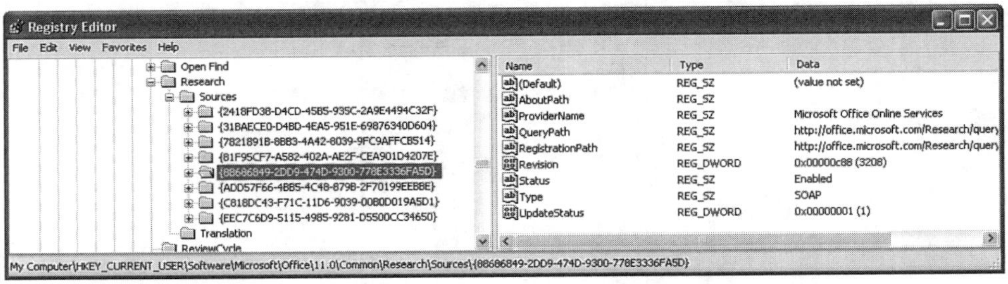

Figure 9.9   Microsoft Office 2003 Research Services Registry Entries

Research Services is an "install on demand" option, so you will need to use the translation facility once before the Registry is populated. A "source" is a provider of research information. Microsoft Office Online Services (shown in Figure 9.9) is an example of one such provider. From this entry, you can see the URL of the Web service (http://office.microsoft.com/Research/query.asmx). Providers provide services. If you expand the source's keys, you can see the list of services (see Figure 9.10).

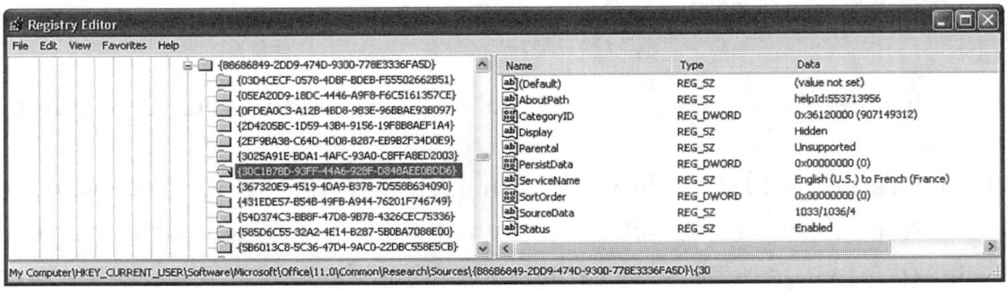

Figure 9.10   Microsoft Office 2003 Services Registry Entries

This service is a translation service that translates from "English (U.S.)" to "French (France)". The kind of service is specified in the `CategoryID`, which is

`0x36120000` (907149312) for translation services (this is the `REFERENCE_TRANS-LATION` constant in the Office 2003 Research Service SDK). Of particular interest here is the `SourceData` entry, which is in the following format:

```
<FromLCID>/<ToLCID>/<ResultType>
```

In the entry in Figure 9.10, the `FromLCID` is `1033` (which is the locale ID for "English (U.S.)"), the `ToLCID` is `1036` (which is the locale ID for "French (France)"), and the `ResultType` is `4`. The result type is "1" for keyword translators and "2" for whole-document translators; "4" is not documented but appears to be for keyword/sentence translators. For our purposes, we are interested in "1" and "4".

From this information, you could read through the list of providers collecting a list of services that have a `CategoryID` of `0x36120000` and a `SourceData` that has a result type of either `1` or `4`.

> The information contained in the Registry is simply a cache of the information returned by calling the provider's Web service's `Registration` method. If you already know the URL of the Web service and want to know the list of services that it provides, an alternative to reading through the Registry is to call the `Registration` method and read through the result.

By default, three providers of translation services are included with Office 2003:

- internal:LocalTranslation
- Microsoft Office Online Services
- WorldLingo

The "internal:LocalTranslation" provider is a set of Win32 DLLs and is not a Web service. You can find the DLLs in "`%CommonProgramFiles%\Microsoft Shared\TRANSLAT`". They are installed on demand, so they won't be present until you have translated English to/from French and/or English to/from Spanish. Because this provider is not a web service and the functions are undocumented, I have chosen to ignore this provider.

At first sight, the Microsoft Office Online Services looks like a good source of machine translation. The URL in the Registry can be used as is in Visual Studio's ASP.NET Web Service Wizard to generate a Web service reference because the Web service returns the WSDL that describes the Web service. Unfortunately, the Web service itself suffers from two problems. First, the Web service is more of a translation dictionary than a keyword translator. For example, if you translate *Stop* into German, the result (after all the HTML formatting has been removed) is this:

1. (-pp-) intransitives Verb (an)halten, stehen bleiben (auch Uhr und so weiter), stoppen; aufhören; besonders Brt. bleiben; stop dead plötzlich oder abrupt stehen bleiben; stop at nothing vor nichts zurückschrecken; stop short of doing, stop short at something zurückschrecken vor (Dativ); transitives Verb anhalten, stoppen; aufhören mit; ein Ende machen oder setzen (Dativ); Blutung stillen; Arbeiten, Verkehr und so weiter zum Erliegen bringen; etwas verhindern; jemanden abhalten (from von), hindern (from an Dativ); Rohr und so weiter verstopfen (auch stop up); Zahn füllen, plombieren; Scheck sperren (lassen); stop by vorbeischauen; stop in vorbeischauen (at bei); stop off umgangssprachlich: kurz Halt machen; stop over kurz Halt machen; Zwischenstation machen;

Clearly, this is the kind of definition that you would expect to find in a dictionary, but it is virtually useless for machine translation.

Second, it translates just single words; it cannot translate a sentence or a phrase. It is almost completely meaningless to translate words one by one and string them together, so these services have no use to us.

WorldLingo Translation Services

The third provider, WorldLingo, is the only viable option that is installed by default. The complete source code to use with this provider is included with this book. Because it is long, I focus only on the most important parts.

The first problem in using the WorldLingo services is that the WorldLingo server doesn't expose the WSDL for the Web service. You can't simply put http://www.worldlingo.com/wl/msoffice11 into Visual Studio's ASP.NET Web Service wizard; the process needs to be a little lower level. Instead, you can use an `HttpWebRequest` object to send an HTTP request to the server and read the `Web Response` object that is returned. `SendRequest` sends a SOAP request to a URL:

```
protected string SendRequest(string url, string soapPacket)
{
    HttpWebRequest httpWebRequest =
        (HttpWebRequest) WebRequest.Create(url);
    httpWebRequest.ContentType = "text/xml; charset=utf-8";
    httpWebRequest.Headers.Add(
        "SOAPAction: urn:Microsoft.Search/Query");
    httpWebRequest.Method = "POST";
    httpWebRequest.ProtocolVersion = HttpVersion.Version10;

    Stream stream = httpWebRequest.GetRequestStream();
    StreamWriter streamWriter = new StreamWriter(stream);
    streamWriter.Write(soapPacket);
    streamWriter.Close();

    WebResponse webResponse = httpWebRequest.GetResponse();
    Stream responseStream = webResponse.GetResponseStream();
    StreamReader responseStreamReader =
        new StreamReader(responseStream);
    return responseStreamReader.ReadToEnd();
}
This would be used something like this:-
string responsePacket = SendRequest(
    "http://www.worldlingo.com/wl/msoffice11", queryPacket);
```

The Web service has a method called `Query` that accepts a single parameter that is a string of XML. The XML contains the translation request, including the "from" language, the "to" language, and the text to be translated. The aforementioned Microsoft Office 2003 Research Services SDK has the structure of this XML packet. At first sight, the Research Services Class Library (RCSL, also available from http://msdn.microsoft.com) includes `QueryRequest` and `QueryResponse` classes that might help. These classes are wrappers to build and read the XML used with the `Query` method. Unfortunately, they are designed for use by developers, not consumers, of Research Services; consequently, they enable you to read the query XML and to create the response XML. This doesn't help because we want to create the query XML and read the response XML.

To create the query XML, I wrote a `GetQueryXml` method, which can be called something like this:

```
GetQueryXml("The monkey is in the tree", service.Id, "(11.0.6360)")
```

We pass the string to translate, the GUID of the service that performs the translation, and a build number. The GUID of the service identifies the from/to language pair. `GetQueryXml` then builds the necessary XML using `XmlTextWriter` according to the schema defined in the SDK.

The return result of the `SendRequest` method is the response from the Web service. Again, this is an XML string using the `QueryResponse` schema defined in the SDK. The `Response` element of this XML contains the translated text. Unfortunately, this translated text is formatted for display in an Office application, so it contains HTML formatting that must be removed first. With this done, we have our translated text.

Translator Evaluator

Now that we have completed all our translators, we can take stock and review our list. Included with the code for this book is a simple utility called Translator Evaluator. Its purpose is to enable you to experiment with different translators and compare their support, performance, and accuracy. Start `TranslatorEvaluator.exe`, enter a "from" language and a "to" language, and click the "Show Support For Languages" button (see Figure 9.11).

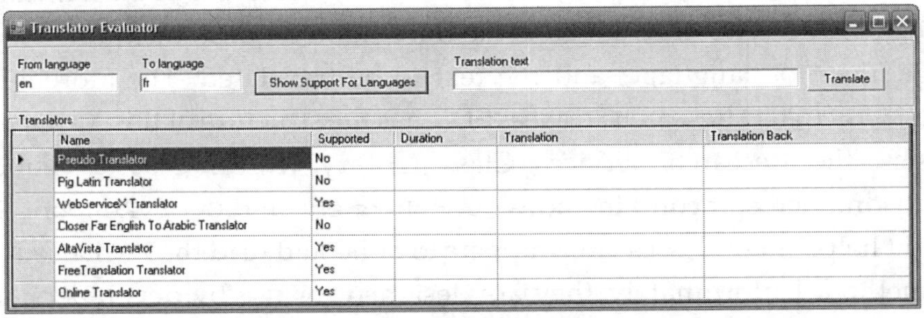

Figure 9.11   Translator Evaluator—"Show Support For Languages"

This tells you which translators support this language pair. Enter some text in the "Translation text" text box and click the Translate button. Figure 9.12 shows the result.

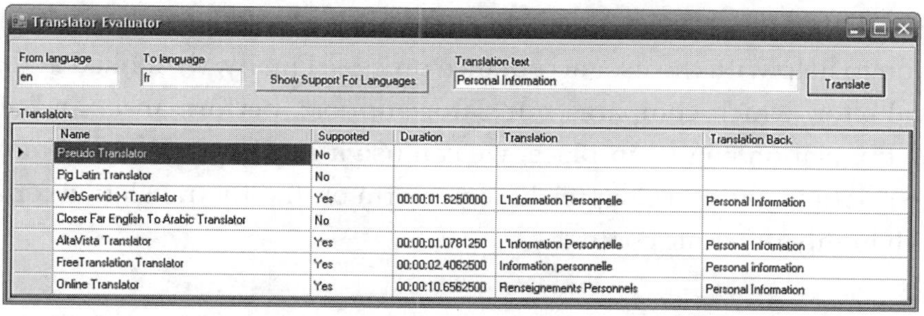

Figure 9.12 Translator Evaluator Comparing Translation Performance and Accuracy

The Duration shown is the duration for a translation from the "from" language to the "to" language only; it does not include the translation back to the original "from" language. From the duration, you can infer the relative performance of the different translators. You should run your tests several times and take a mean duration because many factors affect performance. Based on your results, you should be able to determine which translators to list first in your `TranslatorCollection` and which to list later, to be used only if the first translators fail.

The "`Translation`" column shows the translated text. Even from this example, you can see that there are differences between how the different translators translate text.

The "`Translation Back`" column shows the translation of the translated text back to its original language. You can use this to gauge the accuracy of the translation process. Remember, it is only an indication—it doesn't necessarily follow that if there are differences, the translation is wrong.

Where Are We?

In this chapter, we looked at machine translation and how we can automate it. The result of a machine translation serves as a first-cut translation (to save the translators' time and, therefore, your money), but it is also a means of helping with user acceptance testing for your application. It can also be used as a temporary fix for maintenance releases when a timely turnaround from the translator is not possible. We created a translation engine with many translators based on Web services, websites, and Office 2003 Research Services. We also looked at performing pseudo translation to help with the user acceptance process. Finally, we looked at the Translator Evaluator, which compares translator support, performance, and accuracy. With the translation engine in place, we can use it in Chapter 10 to automatically translate resources, and in Chapter 12 to perform on-the-fly translation for applications with highly dynamic content.

▪ 10 ▪

Resource Administration

S OCIETY CONSIDERS PARANOIA TO BE A bad trait but in the world of development, I have always found it to be a great asset. Walking home wondering if you thought of every angle, what if it's running in large fonts, what if it's running on Windows 2000, and so on might be bad for your blood pressure, but it's great for the software. When I see new technology demonstrated, Captain Paranoia always jumps up onto my shoulder and mutters things like, "I bet it works only in demos," "I bet it doesn't scale well," and "I bet it won't work if I use custom resource managers." Which brings us to the subject of managing resources. The Resource Editor in Visual Studio 2005 is a great step forward from the Resource Editor in Visual Studio 2003, but it obviously focuses on a single resource in a single language. Management of resources is a manual task, and in a large-scale project, the number of actions of adding, editing, and deleting resource entries and resources is large and, consequently, subject to error. This problem has two solutions:

1. Create a tool that automates many of these tasks.

2. Inspect the resulting application using static analysis to look for possible mistakes (e.g., `Form.Localizable` must be `true`).

The former is the subject of this chapter; the latter is the subject of Chapter 13, "Testing Internationalization Using FxCop."

This chapter describes two utilities that are included with the source code for this book:

- Resource Administrator
- Add Resource String Visual Studio Add-In

First I explain what the two utilities do and how to use them. Then I show the building blocks on which they were built. I don't show the complete source code for the Resource Administrator because it is considerable, but it is included with the downloadable source code.

Resource Administrator

The Resource Administrator exists to maintain a complete set of resources in all languages. The emphasis is on maintaining the complete set as opposed to individual languages. Figure 10.1 shows the main screen of the Resource Administrator for the .NET Framework 2.0. (The functionality of the Resource Administrator for the .NET Framework 1.1 is almost the same, with a few differences that exist as a result of the differences between the two frameworks.)

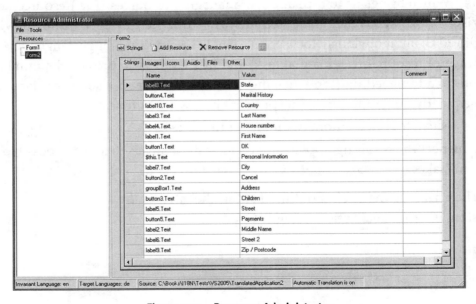

Figure 10.1   Resource Administrator

The TreeView on the left lists the base names of all of the resources. The remainder of the space to the TreeView's right should be familiar if you are using Visual Studio 2005; it is a Resource Editor control that looks and behaves similarly to the Visual Studio 2005 Resource Editor. The Resource Administrator supports the following features:

- Keeps sets of resources in synch
- Automatically translates strings, as necessary
- Is not limited to maintaining resources in resx files
- Exports resources from one project or format to another project and/or format
- Can create new resources automatically when new languages are added
- Provides reports of missing target language resources and resource strings
- Can automatically add missing target resources and strings
- Provides the functionality of Visual Studio 2005's Resource Editor to Visual Studio 2003 applications

We look at these features in the following sections.

Keeping Sets of Resources in Synch

Although the resource editor in the Resource Administrator looks and behaves like the Resource Editor in Visual Studio 2005, there are some important differences. The resource editor in the Resource Administrator maintains the complete set of resources for a given base name. So if you have `Form1Resources.resx`, `Form1Resources.fr.resx`, and `Form1Resources.es.resx` (i.e., invariant, French, and Spanish resources), when you add a new string resource to `Form1Resources`, it adds the same entry to *all* the resx files. Similarly, if you delete an entry, the same entry is deleted from all resources. In this way, you do not have to make a change to the invariant resource and then manually open the resources for every language to apply the same change to those resources.

The "set" of resources is determined by the languages specified in the Tool, Languages menu option (see Figure 10.2).

Figure 10.2   Setting the Languages in the Resource Administrator

When you add one or more languages, the Resource Administrator can create the necessary resources for those languages for you. Figure 10.3 shows a dialog box offering to add new resources after Spanish and French have been added to the list of languages to support.

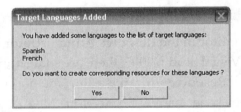

Figure 10.3   Automatically Adding New Language Resources

The Resource Administrator provides feedback on missing resources by popping up a panel on the right when one or more resources are missing (see Figure 10.4).

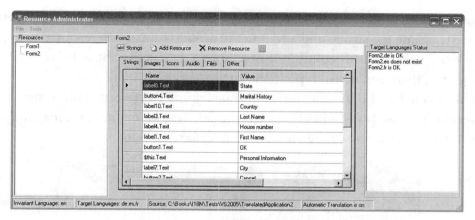

Figure 10.4   One or More Language Resources Missing

You can automatically create the missing resources by right-clicking on the resource in the resources TreeView and selecting "Create missing resource(s)" (see Figure 10.5).

Figure 10.5   Resources Context Menu for Creating Missing Resources

Automatic Translation of Strings

In Chapter 9, "Machine Translation," I created a translation engine that can be used for automatically translating resources. The Resource Administrator can use this engine when maintaining string resources. To turn automatic translation on or off, use the Tools, Automatic Translation menu item. When automatic translation is on, string resources are automatically translated before they are added to the target language resource. This occurs only when adding or editing a string resource. So if you add a new string resource with a value "Bank Account Name", then "Bank Account Name" is added to the invariant resource and "Bankkonto-Name" is added to the German resource. This is particularly useful if you are trying to maintain a pseudo translation. In this scenario, the automatic translation is always perfect because it is simply an algorithm and does not need checking by a human translator. If you were using the Visual Studio Resource Editor, you would have to first add the string to the invariant resource and then open the pseudo translation resource, pseudo translate the string, and add it to the pseudo translation resource (using the same key). This isn't difficult, but it is a human process and it will eventually go wrong (e.g., there could be a typo in the entries' key).

You can enable and disable the list of translators that the translation engine uses by selecting Tools, Translators (see Figure 10.6). Translators are automatically disabled if they fail (because they are unavailable, for example).

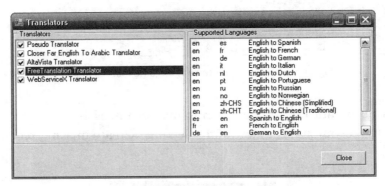

Figure 10.6   Enabling and Disabling Translators

If you want to perform an automatic translation on just the pseudo translation and leave the real languages for a human translator, you can disable all the translators except for the pseudo translator.

Resource Administrator Is Not Limited to Maintaining resx Files

In Chapter 12, "Custom Resource Managers," I introduce several new resource managers for providing additional resource manager functionality and maintaining resources in a different format (e.g., in a database). One of the drawbacks of using a format other than resx files is that support for your format is either lower or nonexistent. The Visual Studio Resource Editor maintains resources only for resx files. If you maintain resources in a database, for example, the editor cannot be used. The Resource Administrator, however, is format-agnostic. It uses the IResourcesGovernor and IResourceGovernor interfaces, explained later in this chapter, to maintain resources in any format (including a database). You can set the source that the Resource Administrator uses for resources in Tools, Resources Source (see Figure 10.7).

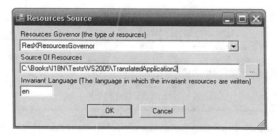

Figure 10.7   Setting the Source of Resources

The Resources Governor combo box lists three resource governors. A resource governor is a class in the downloadable source that governs or manages resources. The three choices are `ResXResourceGovernor` (for maintaining resx files), `ResourcesResourceGovernor` (for maintaining resources files), and `DbResourceGovernor` (for maintaining resources in a database). The Source Of Resources text box enables you to enter a string identifying the source of the resources. For a file-based resource governor (such as `ResXResourceGovernor` or `ResourcesResourceGovernor`), this is the name of an existing folder containing resx files. For a database-based resource governor (such as `DbResourceGovernor`), this is a valid connection string. The Invariant Language is the ISO 639 code for the language in which the invariant resources are written. This value is relevant only if automatic translation is switched on. Enter the values to find your resources and click OK; the Resource Administrator opens and maintains resources from your source.

Exporting Resources

Change is certain. One of the obstacles holding you back from using a format other than resx files might have been the lack of tools for other formats. Now with the Resource Administrator and the custom resource managers in Chapter 12, this stumbling block is removed and you might want to switch to another format. The Resource Administrator enables you to export resources in one format to another format. Select File, Export... (see Figure 10.8).

Figure 10.8   Exporting Resources to a Different Location or Format

This dialog is similar to the dialog in Figure 10.7, in that it demands a resource governor and a target string. To export to a database, select DbResourcesGovernor and enter a connection string to the database. If the target does not exist, the Resource Administrator will create it. For example, in Figure 10.8, the target is a database and the connection string is for a database called TranslatedApplication2. So a database called TranslatedApplication2 will be created, and a table called ResourceSets will be added to the database and filled with all the resources from the current source.

Another use for exporting resources is to allow WinRes to be used for localizing Windows Forms forms. WinRes supports resx and resources files only. If your resources are in a database, WinRes cannot be made to read the resources from your database. One workaround is to export the resources from the database to resx files and ship the resx files to the localizer. When the resx files are returned from the localizer, open them using Resource Administrator and export the resx files to the database.

Integrity Check

The integrity check is a comfort blanket for developers. It looks through the complete set of resources, looking for missing resources or for entries that are present in the invariant language but not in a target language. Select Tools, Integrity Check and answer Yes to the "Perform integrity check on the existence and completeness of language resources?" prompt to get a list of discrepancies (see Figure 10.9).

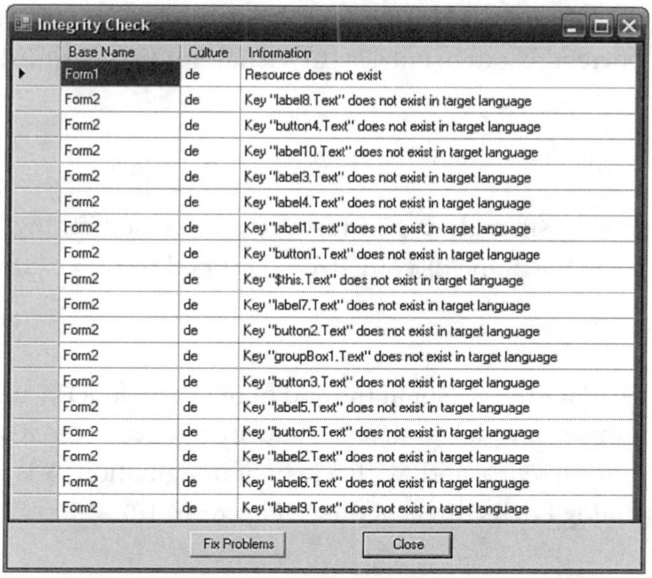

Figure 10.9   Resource Integrity Check

The Resource Administrator can automatically fix the problems listed by clicking the Fix Problems button.

Add Resource String Visual Studio Add-In

The Add Resource String Visual Studio Add-In exists as a recognition of the fact that the average brain has an eight-item stack. On average, you can hold eight new items in your working storage. If you need to remember a ninth item, either you have to commit something to longer-term storage or one item is replaced. It's a sweeping generalization, and the number 8 varies from developer to developer, but the essential idea is solid. When you're writing code, you're writing code. Anything else is a distraction. Mistakes are made when distractions occur (ask anyone with kids). Having to add a string to a resource is something that you'll do "later." And as we all know, "later" sometimes means when it is reported by the test team. Adding a resource string is often postponed when it means having to update more than one resource file because you are trying to maintain multiple languages. The Add

Resource String Add-In makes this process easier and helps reduce the number of incomplete or incorrect resource entries. In Visual Studio's Text Editor, type something like this:

```
Text = resourceManager.GetString("ProductName");
```

Or if you are using strongly typed resources, type something like this (where GlobalResources is the name of your strongly typed resource class):

```
Text = GlobalResources.ProductName;
```

For best results, place the cursor at the end of the entry label you want to add (i.e., ProductName, in this example) so that the add-in can guess the resource key. Press Alt+X, Alt+R (*R* is for *resource* and, with a leap of imagination, *X* is for *add*); the Add Resource String dialog box is displayed (see Figure 10.10).

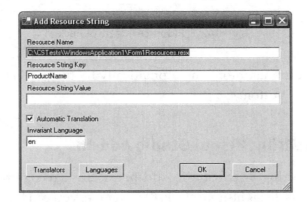

Figure 10.10   Add Resource String Dialog Box

The add-in attempts to guess the name of the resource (C:\Books\I18N\Tests\ VS2003\AddResourceStringTest\Form1Resources.resx, in this example) from the name of the open file, and also guesses the name of the key from either the text selected in the Text Editor or behind the cursor position if no text is selected. Enter a value for the resource string and click OK. The resource string is added to the resource specified in the dialog box. The Languages button brings up the same dialog as used by the Resource Administrator in Figure 10.2 and enables you to specify which languages to maintain. If you specify one or more languages, the resource string is added to those resources. If you check the Automatic Translation check box, those entries are automatically translated. The Translators button brings up the same dialog as used by the Resource Administrator in Figure 10.6, and allows you to enable or disable the translators used to perform automatic translation.

Your settings for Automatic Translation, Invariant Language, and Target Languages are all saved in the application's solution file so that you need to set these values only once for each solution.

Installing the Add-In in Visual Studio 2005

Visual Studio 2005's add-in mechanism differs from Visual Studio 2003's add-in mechanism. To install an add-in in Visual Studio 2005, you need to build the add-in assembly, copy the add-in XML file to Visual Studio 2005's add-in folder, and change the reference in the add-in file to the location of the built assembly. The add-in XML file is in the same folder as the solution file (`AddResourceString.sln`) and is called `AddResourceString.AddIn`. Copy it to `<Documents>\<User>\Application Data\Microsoft\MSEnvShared\Addins`. Open the add-in XML file and change the `<assembly>` tag to the location of the built assembly:

```
<Assembly>C:\Books\I18N\Source\VS2005\ResourceAdministration\
AddResourceString\bin\AddResourceString.dll</Assembly>
```

In Visual Studio 2005, select Tools, Add-In Manager…; check the check box next to Add Resource String and click OK. To assign a keystroke combination to the add-in, select Tools, Options (see Figure 10.11); expand the Environment node in the TreeView; select Keyboard; enter `AddResourceString` in the "Show commands containing:" text box; select "Text Editor" in the "Use new shortcut in" combo box; press Alt+X, Alt +R in the "Press shortcut keys" text box; click on the Assign button; and click OK.

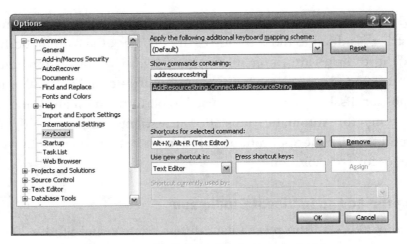

Figure 10.11   Assigning a Keystroke to an Add-In

Installing the Add-In in Visual Studio 2003

Visual Studio 2003's add-in architecture is based on COM and requires COM Registry entries. Fortunately, the Add Resource String Add-In comes with an add-in setup project to perform the necessary steps. Build the `AddResourceStringSetup` project and, in Solution Explorer, right-click the project, select Install, and follow the steps in the wizard. The add-in automatically creates an Add Resource String menu item and assigns the Alt+X, Alt+R keystroke combination to the add resource string command.

Reading and Writing Resources

With the Resource Administrator and Add Resource String utilities described, we can look at the foundation on which they are built. The starting point is the reading and writing of resources. Figure 10.12 shows the .NET Framework classes for reading and writing resx and resources files.

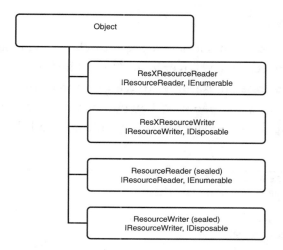

Figure 10.12   .NET Framework Classes for Reading and Writing Resources

From this diagram, you can see that there are no classes for reading and writing `.txt` or `.restext` files. The .NET Framework utilities (e.g., `ResGen`) that need to read and write `.txt` or `.restext` files do so by using `StreamReader`'s `ReadLine` and `WriteLine` methods.

> Although these classes are all part of the `System.Resources` namespace, they are not all part of the same assembly. The `ResourceReader` and `ResourceWriter` classes are part of `mscorlib.dll` and are, therefore, available to most applications by default. The `ResXResourceReader` and `ResXResourceWriter` classes, however, are part of `System.Windows.Forms.dll`, and you must add a reference to this assembly if you want to use these classes and this assembly is not referenced (in a console application, for example).

Reading Resources

The `ResXResourceReader` and `ResourceReader` classes work almost the same way (with a single difference, which I cover in the "ResX File References" section), so I use `ResXResourceReader` as an example. To read resources from a resx file, you construct a new `ResXResourceReader`, get an enumerator, and enumerate through all the `DictionaryEntry` items. The following code adds all the items to a `ListBox` called `listBox1`:

```
using (ResXResourceReader reader =
    new ResXResourceReader("Form1Resources.resx"))
{
    IEnumerator enumerator = reader.GetEnumerator();
    while (enumerator.MoveNext())
    {
        DictionaryEntry entry = (DictionaryEntry) enumerator.Current;

        listBox1.Items.Add(entry.Key.ToString() + ": " +
            entry.Value.ToString());
    }
}
```

The `DictionaryEntry` items have a key and value that correspond to the "Name" and "Value" columns you see in the Visual Studio Resource Editor.

An alternative to reading items from the source directly is to keep them in a cache in the form of a `ResourceSet`. To do this, you can supply the resource reader to the `ResourceSet` constructor (which accepts an `IResourceReader` parameter):

```
using (ResourceSet resourceSet = new ResourceSet(
    new ResXResourceReader("Form1Resources.resx")))
{
    IEnumerator enumerator = resourceSet.GetEnumerator();
    while (enumerator.MoveNext())
    {
        DictionaryEntry entry = (DictionaryEntry) enumerator.Current;

        listBox1.Items.Add(entry.Key.ToString() + ": " +
            entry.Value.ToString());
    }
}
```

Note that the `IResourceReader` (i.e., `ResXResourceReader`, in this example) is not closed until the `ResourceSet` that uses it to read from is closed. This is why the `ResourceManager.CreateFileBasedResourceManager` method mentioned in Chapter 12 keeps `.resource` files locked while the application is running.

You might have noticed from the `ResourceSet` constructors that no public constructor enables you to create an empty `ResourceSet`:

```
public ResourceSet(IResourceReader reader);
public ResourceSet(Stream stream);
public ResourceSet(string fileName);
```

You can work around this inconvenience by implementing an `IResourceReader` that enumerates through an empty `Hashtable`:

```
public class EmptyResourceReader: IResourceReader
{
    public IDictionaryEnumerator GetEnumerator()
    {
        return new Hashtable().GetEnumerator();
    }
    public void Close()
    {
    }
    IEnumerator System.Collections.IEnumerable.GetEnumerator()
    {
        return this.GetEnumerator();
    }
    public void Dispose()
    {
    }
}
```

The following code creates an empty `ResourceSet`:

```
ResourceSet resourceSet =
    new ResourceSet(new EmptyResourceReader());
```

You might argue, however, that because `ResourceSets` do not provide any means of adding new entries, there is little benefit in creating an empty `Resource-Set`. This is true for the publicly documented interface, but the protected field `Table` does allow entries to be added and deleted.

Writing Resources

To write to a resource, you use the `ResXResourceWriter` or `ResourceWriter` classes. The following `WriteResourceSet` method accepts a filename and a `ResourceSet`, and writes the `ResourceSet` to the filename:

```
private void WriteResourceSet(
    string fileName, ResourceSet resourceSet)
{
    using (ResXResourceWriter writer =
        new ResXResourceWriter(fileName))
    {
        foreach(DictionaryEntry dictionaryEntry in resourceSet)
        {
            writer.AddResource(
                dictionaryEntry.Key.ToString(),
                dictionaryEntry.Value);
        }
        writer.Generate();
        writer.Close();
    }
}
```

The `IResourceWriter` interface does not have an "append" mode, so even if you want to add a single entry to the resource, you must first add all the existing resources using `AddResource` and then add the new entry.

ResXDataNodes and Comments

If you have used the Visual Studio Resource Editor, you might be wondering how you can read and write comments. Recall that the Resource Editor enables you to store a comment against each entry in a resx file. Only resx files support comments (resources, .txt, and .restext files do not support comments), so this section is specific to resx files and the `ResXResourceReader` and `ResXResourceWriter` classes. The short answer to this apparent mismatch is that in the .NET Framework 1.1, `ResXResourceReader` does not read the comments. The Visual Studio 2003 Resource Editor gets around this limitation by reading the resx file directly using `XmlTextReader` and writing it back using `XmlTextWriter`. If you are using the .NET Framework 1.1 and want to read and write comments, you have to take the same approach: Abandon the `ResXResourceReader` and `ResXResourceWriter` classes, and use the `XmlTextReader` and `XmlTextWriter` classes instead.

The long answer is that the .NET Framework 2.0 has a more sophisticated solution. The .NET Framework 2.0 `ResXResourceReader` class has a Boolean property called `UseResXDataNodes`. By default, `UseResXDataNodes` is `false`, so `ResX-ResourceReader` behaves just as it did in the .NET Framework 1.1. If you set `ResX-DataNodes` to `true`, the value of each `DictionaryEntry.Value` read by the `ResXResourceReader` is a `ResXDataNode` object. Here is the `ResXDataNode` class:

```
public sealed class ResXDataNode : ISerializable
{
    public ResXDataNode(string name, object value);
    public ResXDataNode(string name, ResXFileRef fileRef);
    public Point GetNodePosition();

    public object GetValue(AssemblyName[] names);
    public object GetValue(ITypeResolutionService typeResolver);
    public string GetValueTypeName(AssemblyName[] names);
    public string GetValueTypeName(
        ITypeResolutionService typeResolver);

    public string Comment { get; set; }
    public ResXFileRef FileRef { get; }
    public string Name { get; set; }
}
```

You can see that it has a `Name` property (which is the same as the `DictionaryEntry.Key`) and a `Comment` property, but no `Value` property. Instead, the value is retrieved using one of the `GetValue` methods. The following code is a modified version of our first attempt to read resources, with the difference being that this code reads `ResXDataNodes` and shows the comment in the `ListBox`:

```
using (ResXResourceReader reader =
    new ResXResourceReader("Form1Resources.resx"))
{
    reader.UseResXDataNodes = true;
    IEnumerator enumerator = reader.GetEnumerator();
    while (enumerator.MoveNext())
    {
        DictionaryEntry entry = (DictionaryEntry) enumerator.Current;

        ResXDataNode dataNode = (ResXDataNode)entry.Value;

        listBox1.Items.Add(entry.Key.ToString() + ": " +
            dataNode.GetValue(
```

```
        (ITypeResolutionService) null).ToString() +
        ", " + dataNode.Comment);
    }
}
```

After the `ResXResourceReader` is constructed, `UseResXDataNode` is set to `true`. The resource entries are enumerated as before, but the `DictionaryEntry`'s `Value` is now a `ResXDataNode`. We get the value from the `ResXDataNode` using the following expression:

```
dataNode.GetValue((ITypeResolutionService) null).ToString()
```

The `GetValue` method has two overloads that tell the `ResXDataNode` how to resolve its value. We pass `null` as this value to indicate that no special steps need to be taken to resolve the value. Note, however, that we cannot simply pass `null` alone because this would match both `GetValue` overloads, so we cast null to an `ITypeResolutionService` interface to indicate which overload to use. Finally, the comment is now available simply as `dataNode.Comment`.

ResX File References

Both versions of the .NET Framework allow files such as bitmaps to be included in resources. These files are included through two methods: file embedding and file referencing. Both versions of the framework support both methods. The difference between the two methods lies solely in the packaging of the original resource source. When a file is embedded in a resource, the file's complete data stream is copied from the original file into the resx file, and the original file is no longer needed. When a file is referenced in a resource, the resource simply contains a link to the original file and both files are needed. The Visual Studio 2005 Resource Editor uses file references to add files to a resource. The Visual Studio 2003 Resource Editor has no direct support for adding files to a resource, so the method chosen depends on the approach that you take (see the "Adding Images and Files in Visual Studio 2003" section of Chapter 3, "An Introduction to Internationalization"). The following resource entry represents a bitmap that has been embedded in a .NET Framework 1.1 resx file:

```
<data name="NationalFlag" type="System.Drawing.Bitmap,
System.Drawing, Version=1.0.5000.0, Culture=neutral,
PublicKeyToken=b03f5f7f11d50a3a" mimetype="application/x-
```

```
microsoft.net.object.bytearray.base64">
  <value>
```
```
    iVBORw0KGgoAAAANSUhEUgAAABAAAAAQCAYAAAAf8/9hAAAAAXNSR0IArs4
    c6QAAAARnQU1BAACxjwv8YQUAAAAgY0hSTQAAeiYAAICEAAD6AAAAgOgAAH
    UwAADqYAAAOpgAABdwnLpRPAAAAMtJREFUOE+1ks0NwjAMhR8zeSdPwaFrd
    AFG4YDcK10CifbMwTwnVVvET1Jq6ZOjKHmxn3MQbR1dB0BIxLJu0zr4ESIU
    gDqErDPXBimCENDWXDWzFvKKoIB6EJcjs5W5EhNWUCAJAE2+FHlqJfb9MRR
    JLZwug9vNU9YwdRI1pQ8FcgVrUiVsi0J+bIosFZi7kVmQIjUxm7iMMPshFS
    OMMaPv+9eHwrgNgTSmytc+nYO1NIsf6V9wv56Ls/72H8Zx9P0tvJm4wcA4u
    ruCJ1wJmJQKMPjaAAAAAElFTkSuQmCC
```
```
  </value>
</data>
```

The following resource entry represents a bitmap that has been referenced in a .NET Framework 2.0 resx file:

```
<data name="NationalFlag"
    type="System.Resources.ResXFileRef, System.Windows.Forms">
  <value>Resources\NationalFlag.gif;System.Drawing.Bitmap,
    System.Drawing, Version=2.0.0.0, Culture=neutral,
    PublicKeyToken=b03f5f7f11d50a3a
  </value>
</data>
```

Notice that the type is no longer a `System.Drawing.Bitmap`, but a `System.Resources.ResXFileRef`. In the value element, you can see the file reference (`Resources\NationalFlag.gif`) and also the type of the contents of the file (`System.Drawing.Bitmap`). From the point of view of the resource assembly that gets compiled from these resources, there is no difference between resources that are referenced and those that are embedded because the file references are resolved before the assembly is generated, and the resulting assembly contains the complete "embedded" definition of the resource (so the referenced files do not need to be deployed and are not required at runtime). From the point of view of version control, the benefit of using file references is that you get better granularity of resource versioning. From the point of view of code that processes resx files, the distinction between referenced and embedded is important. Recall our first code snippet, which read a resx file and added the contents of each `DictionaryEntry` into a `ListBox`. This code will most likely fail if it processes a resx file with file references. The `ArgumentException` that occurs reports the problem:

```
ResX file Could not find a part of the path
'C:\Books\I18N\Tests\VS2005\WindowsApplication1\bin\Debug\
Resources\NationalFlag.gif'. Line 329, position 5. cannot be parsed.
```

Recall that the file reference is to "`Resources\NationalFlag.gif`"—i.e., a relative reference, not an absolute reference. The path is relative to the executing assembly, so it looks in the `WindowsApplication1\bin\Debug\Resources` folder and not the `WindowsApplication1\Resources` folder, where the files are. If you are using the .NET Framework 1.1, the simplest solution is to use absolute file references. If you are using the .NET Framework 2.0, you can tell the `ResXResourceReader` where to find the resource files using the `ResXResourceReader.BasePath` property:

```
ResXResourceReader reader =
    new ResXResourceReader("Form1Resources.resx");
reader.BasePath = @"..\..";
```

Alternatively, a more generic solution to the same problem is to simply set the `BasePath` to the same folder as the resx file that the `ResXResourceReader` is processing:

```
string fileName = @"C:\Apps\WindowsApplication1\Form1Resources.resx";
ResXResourceReader reader = new ResXResourceReader(fileName);
reader.BasePath = Path.GetDirectoryName(fileName);
```

The new support for file references that was added in the Visual Studio 2005 Resource Editor has an implication for code that processes resx files. As we have already seen, the code that reads entries using a `ResXResourceReader` works well in both the .NET Framework 1.1 and 2.0, as long as resources are embedded or absolute file paths are used. The Visual Studio 2005 Resource Editor, however, defaults to file references (using relative paths), so code that processes resx files that worked under the .NET Framework 1.1 will mostly likely fail when processing the .NET Framework 2.0 resx files (because the file references are relative) and must be updated to set the `ResXResourceReader`'s `BasePath` property.

Resource Governors

So far, we have seen the mechanics of reading and writing individual resource files, and the support that the .NET Framework offers for this. The .NET Framework offers no further support beyond this point. There is no abstraction from the physical nature of resources. The Visual Studio Resource Editor, for example, works solely with resx files; ResGen has different code branches to handle resx files separately from resources files and txt/restext files. Furthermore, all these resource implementations are file based and dependent upon the file system. The Resource Administrator clearly cannot make such assumptions, so a layer of abstraction from the physical implementation of resources is required. This section describes this layer of abstraction so that you can either use the same implementation to write new utilities or implement new classes to allow the Resource Administrator to work with a source of resources other than those already supported.

The resource abstraction layer is made up of Resource Governors and Resources Governors. A Resource Governor manages the physical implementation of a single resource (e.g., a resx file). A Resources Governor (*Resources* is plural) manages the physical implementation of a collection of Resource Governors. Resources Governors implement the IResourcesGovernor interface:

```
public interface IResourcesGovernor
{
    string[] GetInvariantCultureBaseNames();
    IResourceGovernor GetResourceGovernor(
        string baseName, CultureInfo cultureInfo);
    CultureInfo[] GetExistingCultures(string baseName);
    bool IsFileBased {get;}
    bool IsDatabaseBased {get;}
    bool SupportsComments { get; set; }
    bool SupportsFileReferences { get; set; }
    bool CommentsAreOptional { get;}
    bool FileReferencesAreOptional { get;}
    bool Exists { get;}
    string ResourceFileAbsolutePath { get; }
    string ResourceFileRelativePath { get; }
    void Create();
}
```

The classes that implement this interface are shown in Figure 10.13.

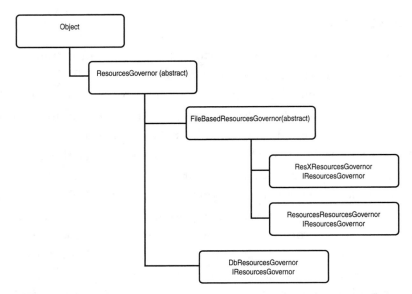

Figure 10.13   Class Hierarchy of Classes Implementing IResourcesGovernor

Resource Governors (*Resource* is singular) implement the `IResourceGovernor` interface:

```
public interface IResourceGovernor
{
    ResourceSet ReadResourceSet();
    void WriteResourceSet(ResourceSet resourceSet);
    bool ResourceExists();
    bool ResourceIsReadOnly();
    bool ResourceKeyExists(string key);
    bool AddResourceSet(ResourceSet resourceSet1,
        ResourceSet resourceSet2);
    bool ReintegrateResourceSet(
        ResourceSet flattenedMasterResourceSet,
        ResourceSet masterResourceSet,
        ResourceSet incomingResourceSet,
        AcceptResourceEntry acceptResourceEntry);
    object CreateDataNode(string name, object value);
    object CreateFileRef(string fileName, string typeName);
    object CreateFileRef(string fileName, string typeName,
        Encoding textFileEncoding);
    string BaseName {get;}
    CultureInfo CultureInfo {get;}
}
```

The classes that implement this interface are shown in Figure 10.14.

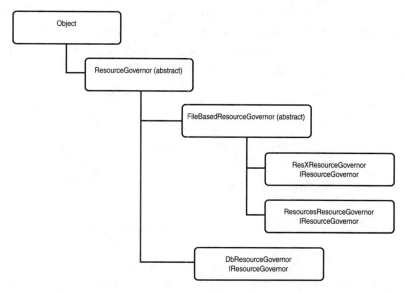

Figure 10.14 Class Hierarchy of Classes Implementing IResourceGovernor

To manipulate a collection of resources, start from an `IResourcesGovernor` (from either a `ResXResourcesGovernor`, `ResourcesResourcesGovernor`, or `DbResourcesGovernor`):

```
IResourcesGovernor resourcesGovernor =
    new ResXResourcesGovernor(@"C:\Apps\WindowsApplication1");
```

From here, you can get a list of invariant base names; the following code adds the base names to a `ListBox`:

```
string[] baseNames =
    resourcesGovernor.GetInvariantCultureBaseNames();
foreach(string baseName in baseNames)
{
    listBox1.Items.Add(baseName);
}
```

So if the `C:\Apps\WindowsApplication1` folder contained `Form1.resx`, `Form1.fr.resx`, `Form1Resources.resx`, `Form2.resx`, and `Form2.de.resx` files, the `ListBox` would contain three base names: `Form1`, `Form1Resources`, and `Form2`.

The following `listBox1.SelectedIndexChanged` event displays the invariant resource entries for the selected resource:

```
private void listBox1_SelectedIndexChanged(
    object sender, System.EventArgs e)
{
    string baseName = ((ListBox) sender).SelectedItem.ToString();

    IResourceGovernor resourceGovernor =
        resourcesGovernor.GetResourceGovernor(
        baseName, CultureInfo.InvariantCulture);

    ResourceSet resourceSet = resourceGovernor.ReadResourceSet();

    ShowResourceSet(resourceSet);
}
```

The event gets the resource base name from the `ListBox`. It calls `IResources-Governor.GetResourceGovernor` to get an `IResourceGovernor` for the given base name for the given culture. In this example using resx files, if the base name is "Form1Resources" and the culture is the invariant culture, this would create a resource governor for the "`Form1Resources.resx`" file. If the culture were German, it would create a resource governor for the "`Form1Resources.de.resx`" file. The `ShowResourceSet` method simply reads through the resources in the `ResourceSet` in the same way as shown earlier in this chapter.

You can see from the definition of `IResourcesGovernor` that the interface provides an `Exists` property to indicate whether the source of resources exists. In a file-based solution, this is whether the path exists, but in a database solution, this is whether the database exists. In addition, `IResourcesGovernor` provides a `Create` method to create the source of resources. In a file-based solution, this would simply create the path, but in a database solution, this would create the database and add the necessary tables. Similarly, the `IResourceGovernor` (*Resource* is singular) supports `ReadResourceSet` and `WriteResourceSet` methods to read and write `ResourceSet`s, `ResourceExists`, and `ResourceIsReadOnly` methods to determine whether the resource exists and whether it is read only (which is entirely possible if the resources are file based and are under the control of a version-control system).

Data Nodes, Comments, and File References

I confess that I am disappointed with the implementation of `ResXDataNodes` and `ResXFileRefs`. On the one hand, I am delighted that there is built-in support for comments and file references. But on the other hand, I am disappointed that the existing implementation is closed and aimed solely at resx files. It is true that only resx files support comments and file references as far as the .NET Framework is concerned, but the .NET Framework supports creating new `ResourceManager` classes to read and write resources in any format. Some of these formats can also support comments and file references. A database, for example, could easily support comments. Furthermore, other resource file formats such as the Oasis XLIFF XML specification have additional information that needs to be carried around with resources. The implementation of the `ResXDataNode` and `ResXFileRef` classes does not lend itself to generalization or customization. The problem is that neither class inherits from a common ancestor that could be used for generalization, nor does either class support an interface that could be used for this purpose. In addition, the `ResXDataNode` class is sealed, preventing inheritance.

To support comments and file references (and potentially additional information) in formats other than resx files, I have created two new classes: `ResourcesDataNode` and `ResourcesFileRef` (both available in the downloadable source code for this book). The `ResourcesDataNode` class is a generic counterpart to the `ResXDataNode` class and implements the `IResourcesDataNode` interface:

```
public interface IResourcesDataNode
{
    string Comment { get; set; }
    string Name { get; set; }
    object Value { get; set; }
    IResourcesFileRef FileRef { get; set; }
}
```

The `ResourcesFileRef` class is a generic counterpart to the `ResXFileRef` class and implements the `IResourcesFileRef` interface:

```
public interface IResourcesFileRef
{
    string FileName { get; set; }
    string TypeName { get; set; }
    Encoding TextFileEncoding { get; set; }
}
```

The `IResourceGovernor` interface supports the following methods to create data nodes and file references:

```
object CreateDataNode(string name, object value);
object CreateFileRef(string fileName, string typeName);
object CreateFileRef(string fileName, string typeName,
    Encoding textFileEncoding);
```

In the `ResXResourceGovernor` class, these methods return `ResXDataNode` and `ResXFileRef` objects. In other `IResourceGovernor` classes, these methods can return `ResourcesDataNode` and `ResourcesFileRef` objects. In `IResourceGovernor` classes that do not support data nodes and file references (e.g., the `Resources-ResourceGovernor` class, which manages .resources files), the `CreateDataNode` method simply returns the value of the node, and the `CreateFileRef` methods throw a `NotImplementedException`. The `IResourcesGovernor` interface has a Boolean property named `SupportsComments` that indicates whether comments are supported by the resource format and a property named `SupportsFileReferences` that indicates whether file references are supported by the resource format.

The Resource Administrator uses this infrastructure to support data nodes, comments, and file references in resource formats that support these concepts. You can use this same infrastructure in the creation of your own resource-manipulation tools.

The Resource Editor Control

If you are building your own resource-management utilities, you might be interested in the Resource Editor control. The Resource Editor used by Visual Studio is not available as a control that you can add to your own applications, so I had to write one; it is included in the downloadable source code for this book.

To use the `ResourceEditorControl`, simply add it to a form. It has a `ResourceSet` property, which is the `ResourceSet` that the control manages. The

`ResourceSet` is never saved by the `ResourceEditorControl`; this is your domain. Instead, you are notified whenever a change is made using the `Resource-SetChanging` event. You can hook into this event like this:

```
resourceEditorControl.ResourceSetChanging +=
    new ResourceSetChangingEventHandler(
    resourceEditorControlResourceSetChanging);
```

The `resourceEditorControlResourceSetChanging` method is:

```
private void resourceEditorControlResourceSetChanging(
    object sender, ResourceSetChangeEventArgs eventArgs)
{
    resourceGovernor.WriteResourceSet(eventArgs.ResourceSet);
}
```

This method assumes that there is a private field called `resourceGovernor`, which is an `IResourceGovernor` and simply saves the `ResourceSet`. The `ResourceSetChangeEventArgs` class is:

```
public class ResourceSetChangeEventArgs : EventArgs
{
    public ResourceSetChangeEventArgs(
        ResourceSet resourceSet, ResourceSetAction action,
        string resourceKey, object resourceValue ,
        string resourceComment,
        string oldResourceKey, object oldResourceValue ,
        string oldResourceComment);

    public ResourceSetAction Action { get; set; }
    public string OldResourceKey { get; set; }
    public string OldResourceComment { get; set; }
    public object OldResourceValue { get; set; }
    public string ResourceKey { get; set; }
    public string ResourceComment { get; set; }
    public ResourceSet ResourceSet { get; set; }
    public object ResourceValue { get; set; }
}
```

The `Action` property is a `ResourceSetAction` enumeration and can be `Add`, `Change`, or `Delete`. The `EventArgs` provides sufficient information for you to identify the change that the user made and respond to it appropriately.

You can modify the functionality of the `ResourceEditorControl` using three Boolean properties: `ReadOnly` enables you to disable any opportunity to modify the `ResourceSet`, `AllowComments` enables you to specify whether to allow the user to enter comments, and `UseFileRefs` enables you to specify whether files should be referenced or embedded.

Where Are We?

Visual Studio and the .NET Framework SDK provide a number of utilities for manipulating resources. Currently, they are limited to supporting file-based solutions (e.g., .resx, .resources, .txt, and .restext), and some solutions—notably, Visual Studio's Resource Editor—are aimed solely at resx files. In addition, these tools manage individual resources one at a time, which leads to a situation in which it is easy for developers to get resources out of synch with related resources. Furthermore, the effort of maintaining an up-to-date translation of resources, especially a pseudo translation, often makes this approach prohibitive. Resource Administrator solves these problems, makes the administration of resources simpler, and enables you to change resource formats more easily by allowing you to export resources in one format to resources in another format. The Add Resource String Add-In makes adding resource entries and keeping related resources in synch simpler. Finally, the resource governor architecture enables you to create new resource utilities that are format-agnostic, and to extend the Resource Administrator and Add Resource String Add-In to support new formats.

◼ 11 ◼

Custom Cultures

The `CultureInfo` class is at the heart of .NET's internationalization solution. In Chapter 6, "Globalization," you saw that in the .NET Framework 2.0, the list of available cultures is a combination of those cultures known to the .NET Framework plus those known to the operating system. In the .NET Framework 1.1, the list of available cultures is simply those known only to the .NET Framework. These cultures are fine if the country/language combination that you need is one of the available cultures and if the information for that combination is correct for your application. But there are many country/language combinations that are not available, and some of those that are available might not have the correct information for your application. For this reason, custom cultures were introduced in the .NET Framework 2.0. A custom culture is a culture that is defined by an application developer instead of Microsoft. After it is created, the .NET Framework treats it as a first-class citizen and the custom culture is just as valid as any other culture. In this chapter, we look at how to create, register/unregister, and deploy custom cultures. The story for .NET Framework 1.1 applications is not so sophisticated. It is possible to create custom cultures in the .NET Framework 1.1, but the results are less than satisfactory. This subject is covered at the end of this chapter.

Uses for Custom Cultures

Custom cultures have many uses, and it is entirely possible that free and commercial custom cultures will be downloadable from the Internet. In this section, we look at a number of reasons why you might want to create your own.

The first and simplest reason is to update an existing culture that has obsolete or undesirable information. In the section "The `CultureInfo` Class," in Chapter 6, I noted that some information, such as currency information, in existing cultures becomes incorrect over a period of time. The .NET Framework 2.0 has a new baseline of culture data to update many past inaccuracies to reflect the world at the time of its launch; (e.g., the `Turkish (Turkey)` currency has been updated from `TL (Türk Lirasi)` to `YTL (Yeni Türk Lirasi)`). In addition, culture information can be kept up-to-date by using Windows Update. In nearly all cases, the need to update culture information because of obsolete information is low. However, there will always be exceptions, and there will come a time when the existing information is undesirable (as opposed to incorrect). Custom cultures allow you to create a "replacement" culture with the same name and LCID as an existing culture, but with different property values. The first custom culture that we create here is just such a culture.

Another common reason to use a custom culture is to support a known language outside its known country of use. For example, Spanish is widely used in the United States, but the .NET Framework does not have an `es-US (Spanish (United States))` culture. Table 11.1 shows a number of examples of these cultures.

Table 11.1 Examples of Custom Cultures for Languages Outside Their Known Countries

Culture Name	Culture EnglishName	Approx. Number of Users of This Language in This Region
es-US	Spanish (USA)	22,400,000
hi-GB	Hindi (United Kingdom)	1,300,000
pa-CA	Punjabi (Canada)	300,000
zh-CA	Chinese (Canada)	870,000
zh-US	Chinese (USA)	2,000,000

It would be unfeasible for Microsoft to support the complete list of possible combinations of countries and languages, considering that there are nearly 200 countries in the world and nearly 7,000 languages. We can create "supplemental" custom cultures for these "missing" country/language combinations. The `Spanish (United`

States) custom culture in this chapter is just such a culture. This scenario applies equally to the various expatriate communities around the world. For example, there is a sizable population of British expatriates in France and Spain, generating a demand for English (France) and English (Spain) custom cultures.

A variation of this theme is to create a custom culture for which either the country and/or the language is not currently supported by the .NET Framework (or Windows). Table 11.2 shows some examples.

Table 11.2 Examples of Custom Cultures for Unsupported Countries or Languages

Culture Name	Culture EnglishName	Approx. Number of Users of This Language in This Region
bn-BD	Bengali (Bangladesh)	125,000,000
eo	Esperanto	2,000,000
fj-FJ	Fijian (Fiji)	364,000
gd-GB	Gaelic (United Kingdom)	88,892
tlh-KX	Klingonese (Klingon) ("tlh" is the ISO code assigned to "tlhIngan Hol", the name for the Klingon language)	431,892,000,000
la	Latin	?
tl-PH	Tagalog (Philippines)	14,000,000

Another equally important use for custom cultures is to support pseudo translations. In the section "Choosing a Culture for Pseudo Translation," in Chapter 9, "Machine Translation," I introduced a PseudoTranslator class that performs a pseudo translation from a Latin-based language to an accented version of the same language. The benefit is that the localization process can be tested, and developers and testers can still use the localized application without having to learn another language. In the implementation in Chapter 9, an existing culture was hijacked to serve as the pseudo translation culture. In this chapter, we create a custom culture that exists exclusively to support a pseudo translation.

Finally, another common use for custom cultures is to support commercial dialects. In this scenario, you want to ship an application in a single language, such as English, but the words and phrases used by one customer or group of customers differ from the words and phrases used by a different customer or group of customers. This is more common than it sounds. The accounting industry, for example, suffers this dilemma because the words *"practice"* and *"site"* mean different things to different people. You could create custom cultures for specific customers. For example, you could create an English (United States, Sirius Minor Publications) custom culture to serve the Sirius Minor Publications customer, and an English (United States, Megadodo Publications) custom culture to serve the Megadodo Publications customer. Both cultures would have a parent of English (United States) or just English, so that the majority of text would be common to all English customers. Sirius Minor Publications would have resources that used their own commercial dialect, and, likewise, Megadodo Publications would have resources that used their own commercial dialect. The benefit to the developers is that the application has a single code base while still catering to the needs of individual customers.

Using CultureAndRegionInfoBuilder

Creating a custom culture involves two steps:

1. Defining the custom culture
2. Registering the custom culture

Both steps are achieved using the .NET Framework 2.0 CultureAndRegion InfoBuilder class. We start with a simple example of creating a replacement culture to see the process through from beginning to end. We return to the subject later to create more complex custom cultures.

In this example, the culture is a replacement for the en-GB English (United Kingdom) culture. The purpose of this culture is to change the default ShortTimePattern to include the AM/PM suffix (just like the en-US Short-TimePattern). The ShortTimePattern is a .NET Framework property and is not part of the Win32 data, so this value cannot be set in the Regional and Language Options dialog.

The following code creates a replacement custom culture and registers it:

```
// create a CultureAndRegionInfoBuilder for a
// replacement for the en-GB culture
CultureAndRegionInfoBuilder builder =
    new CultureAndRegionInfoBuilder("en-GB",
    CultureAndRegionModifiers.Replacement);

// the en-GB's short time format
builder.GregorianDateTimeFormat.ShortTimePattern = "HH:mm tt";

// register the custom culture
builder.Register();
```

The `CultureAndRegionInfoBuilder` constructor accepts two parameters: the custom culture name and an enumeration identifying what kind of custom culture the new culture is. The replacement culture is registered using the `Register` method. Once registered, all .NET Framework 2.0 applications on this machine will use the modified `en-GB` culture instead of the original, without any change to those applications.

Installing/Registering Custom Cultures

The `CultureAndRegionInfoBuilder Register` method performs two actions:

- Creates an NLP file in the system's Globalization folder
- Adds an entry to the Registry in HKEY_LOCAL_MACHINE\System\CurrentControlSet\Control\Nls\IetfLanguage

The NLP file is a binary representation of the custom culture. No API exists for this file format, so you must treat it like a black box. The file is placed in `%WINDIR%\Globalization` and given the same name as the custom culture—e.g., `c:\Windows\Globalization\en-GB.NLP`.

The Registry entry provides the `IetfLanguage` name for the custom culture for static `CultureInfo` methods. The key is the custom culture's `IetfLanguage`, and the value is the semicolon-separated list of custom culture names that share the same

IetfLanguage. After the call to Register in the example, there will be an entry with a key of "en-GB" and a value of "en-GB", indicating that the en-GB custom culture has an IetfLanguage of "en-GB".

This approach is fine for registering the custom culture on your own machine, but it isn't very generic. If you want to create three custom cultures—say, en-GB, fr-FR, and es-ES—on your users' machines, you would have to either create one application, called, for example, CreateAndRegisterAllThreeCultures, or create three separate applications—such as Create_enGB_Culture, Create_frFR_Culture, and Create_esES_Culture. A better solution is to create a single custom culture registration program and pass it custom culture files. In the source code for this book, you will find the RegisterCustomCulture console application, which exists for this purpose. RegisterCustomCulture accepts one or more LDML custom culture files to register. LDML is the Locale Data Markup Language and is defined in Unicode Technical Standard #35 (see http://www.unicode.org/reports/tr35/). It is an extensible XML format for the exchange of structured locale data, and it is the format that Microsoft chose for importing and exporting custom cultures. Although LDML is clearly defined by the Unicode Consortium, there is wide variation in its use. If you intend to use LDML files created by sources other than the Culture AndRegionInfoBuilder, be prepared to modify the LDML before it can be consumed by a CultureAndRegionInfoBuilder. An LDML file can be created using the CultureAndRegionInfoBuilder.Save method, so the previous example could be rewritten like this:

```
CultureAndRegionInfoBuilder builder =
    new CultureAndRegionInfoBuilder("en-GB",
    CultureAndRegionModifiers.Replacement);

builder.GregorianDateTimeFormat.ShortTimePattern = "HH:mm tt";

builder.Save("en-GB.ldml");
```

This code would become part of the application's build process, resulting in the en-GB.ldml file, which would become part of the application's installation process. The file can be loaded simply by using the CultureAndRegionInfoBuilder. CreateFromLdml method:

```
CultureAndRegionInfoBuilder builder =
    CultureAndRegionInfoBuilder.CreateFromLdml("en-GB.ldml");

builder.Register();
```

The important parts of the `RegisterCustomCulture` console application are shown here:

```
static void Main(string[] args)
{
    Console.WriteLine("RegisterCustomCulture registers custom" +
        " cultures for the .NET Framework from LDML/XML files");
    Console.WriteLine("");
    if (args.GetLength(0) == 0)
        // no parameters were passed - show the syntax
        ShowSyntax();
    else if (AllFilesExist(args))
    {
        // file parameters are all good - register the cultures
        RegisterCustomCultures(args);
    }
}

private static void RegisterCustomCultures(
    string[] customCultureFiles)
{
    foreach (string customCultureFile in customCultureFiles)
    {
        if (customCultureFile.StartsWith("/u:") ||
            customCultureFile.StartsWith("/U:"))
        {
            // unregister the culture
            string customCultureName =
                customCultureFile.Substring(3);

            CultureAndRegionInfoBuilder.Unregister(
                customCultureName);

            Console.WriteLine("{0} custom culture unregistered",
                customCultureName);
        }
        else
        {
            // register the culture
            CultureAndRegionInfoBuilder builder =
                CultureAndRegionInfoBuilder.CreateFromLdml(
                customCultureFile);
```

```
            builder.Register();

            Console.WriteLine(
                "{0} custom culture registered", customCultureFile);
        }
    }
    Console.WriteLine("");
    Console.WriteLine("Registration complete.");
}
```

The `RegisterCustomCulture` application simply iterates through each of the command-line parameters. If the parameter starts with "/u:", it attempts to unregister an existing custom culture; otherwise, it attempts to load the parameters as LDML files and then register them.

It is worth noting, however, that as the `Register` method writes to the Registry and to the system's `Globalization` folder, any code that uses it requires administrator rights to execute. This means that if you intend to deploy applications that use custom cultures, the application that creates the custom cultures (e.g., `Register-CustomCulture.exe`) must obviously have administrator rights (no additional rights are required to simply create `CultureInfo` objects from custom cultures, however). If you deploy your Windows Forms applications using `ClickOnce`, you should create your custom cultures using the `ClickOnce` Bootstrapper because the `ClickOnce` application itself will not be granted administrator rights.

Uninstalling/Unregistering Custom Cultures

Custom cultures can be unregistered using the static `CultureAndRegionInfoBuilder.Unregister` method:

```
CultureAndRegionInfoBuilder.Unregister("en-GB");
```

This method attempts to undo the two steps of the `Register` method (it deletes the Registry key and attempts to delete the NLP file). The attempt to delete the NLP file might or might not be successful. The `Unregister` method looks to see if the custom culture is referenced by other custom cultures. In the process of doing so, it can open the NLP file itself and be the cause of its own failure. This is why it is possible to attempt to unregister a custom culture even after rebooting the machine and still have it fail. In this case, the `Unregister` method simply renames the file's extension to "tmp0" (e.g., "en-GB.tmp0"). There is no subsequent cleanup, so the temporary files remain in the `Globalization` folder indefinitely. This is an important point if your application registers a custom culture at startup and then unregisters as the application is shutting down. Also note that `Unregister` requires administrator rights.

Public Custom Cultures and Naming Conventions

The custom cultures that you create using the .NET Framework 2.0 are all public. This means that they are available to all users of all .NET Framework 2.0 applications on the machine on which they are installed. There is no concept of a private custom culture in functional terms. Let's consider what this means for a moment. The Registry key is public; the NLP file is placed in a public location; and the culture's name is public. This means that the cultures that you create live in the same space as the cultures that everyone else creates. We've seen this scenario before with DLLs, and it was often referred to as DLL Hell. Welcome to Custom Culture Hell.

The problem here is that when you create a custom culture and install it on a machine, you don't know if someone else has already created a culture with the same name or if in the future someone will create a culture with the same name. This is especially a problem with replacement cultures, such as the one in the first example. The new en-GB culture simply modifies the short time pattern. If someone else, possibly from another company, had already created an en-GB culture on the same machine, then your attempt to register your en-GB culture would fail because a custom culture with that name already exists. At this point, you have two choices:

- Don't install your culture. Respect the original application's en-GB culture and hope that it doesn't prevent your application from working properly.

- Go ahead and overwrite the custom culture with your custom culture.

The first approach represents the very definition of optimism. The second approach will give you the kind of reputation that was given to vendors when they overwrote existing DLLs in the DLL Hell scenario. Alternatively, consider what would happen if your application was installed on a machine first. All would be well right up until the second application overwrote your custom culture with its definition of the same culture. That application would function correctly. The best-case scenario for your application is that it would fail. The worst-case scenario is more likely: Your application would continue to function but would be incorrect.

A number of limited solutions exist, depending on whether you are creating a replacement custom culture or a supplemental custom culture. Let's start with supplemental custom cultures. A supplemental custom culture is a completely new culture that the .NET Framework and the operating system have not seen. The best solution here is to solve the problem by avoiding the problem (this is often my favorite solution to any problem). The solution lies in using a naming convention in which uniqueness is built into the name. A simple solution would be to suffix the culture name with your company's name. So if you create a supplemental custom culture for Bengali as spoken in Bangladesh (i.e., "bn-BD") and your company is the Acme Corporation, you would name the culture "bn-BD-Acme". Alternatively, you could take a more certain but completely unreadable solution of suffixing with a GUID—e.g., "bn-BD-b79a80f4-2e22-4af5-9b79-e362304b-5b10" (note that the GUID has been split into chunks of eight characters or less). The naming convention solution also has the benefit of being future-proof. Change is certain. Microsoft will add new cultures to Windows. If Microsoft adds the bn-BD culture to Windows, code that creates a custom "bn-BD" culture that used to work will throw an exception in the `CultureAndRegionInfoBuilder` constructor:

```
CultureAndRegionInfoBuilder builder =
    new CultureAndRegionInfoBuilder("bn-BD",
    CultureAndRegionModifiers.None);
```

If the culture name is suffixed to make the culture name unique, it cannot clash with new cultures or other companies' custom cultures. The downside to this naming is that it is a considerable abuse of the IETF tag that the suffix replaces. You must decide which is the lesser evil.

On the subject of supplemental custom culture names, the IETF defines a prefix ("x-" or "X-") that should be used for what are called "private" cultures (e.g., "x-bn-BD"). Don't be confused by the use of the word *private*—the cultures are still publicly available to all .NET Framework 2.0 applications. The difference is that, by prefixing the culture name with the "x-" prefix, a statement is made that the culture is for "private" use—i.e., the use of one or a limited number of applications. This prefix also solves the problem that if Microsoft introduces a culture for the same language/region, no clash will occur (because Microsoft's culture will not have the "x-" prefix). The prefix solution represents a halfway house. It solves part of the problem. Of course, if another application attempts to install a culture for the same language/region and uses the same name (including the prefix), then a clash will still occur.

If you are creating a replacement culture, such as en-GB, your options are quite limited. If it is truly to be a replacement culture, changing the name is not an option. One option is to set up or seek out a public registry on the Internet for replacement custom cultures. If such a registry exists, it could be used to track requests for changes to existing cultures and offer a "standard" replacement culture upon which well-behaved applications could agree. The "standard" replacement culture would be the sum of all agreed-upon changes. Such a co-operative solution is optimistic and not guaranteed, and can be seen as only a "gentleman's agreement." Alternatively, you could simply overwrite the opposition's replacement culture with your own. Immediately before your call to `CultureAndRegionInfoBuilder.Register`, you would add the following code:

```
try
{
    CultureAndRegionInfoBuilder.Unregister("en-GB");
}
catch (ArgumentException)
{
}
```

This code attempts to unregister any existing en-GB culture and ignores any exception that would result from an existing en-GB replacement culture. If you choose this approach, be prepared for some hate mail. The only guaranteed solution is to use a supplemental custom culture instead of a replacement custom culture, and use the previously suggested naming convention to avoid a clash. The custom culture would then be called something like "x-en-GB" or "en-GB-Acme" instead of "en-GB". The obvious downside to this solution is that the custom culture is no longer a replacement custom culture. This means that your application would need to take certain steps to ensure that the x-en-GB or en-GB-Acme culture was used instead of the en-GB culture.

Regardless of how you approach this problem, you should be aware of the limits on custom culture names. The maximum length of a custom culture name is 84 characters, and each "tag" within the name is limited to 8 characters. A "tag" is a block of letters and numbers that is delimited by a dash ("-") or an underscore ("_"). So a name of "en-GB-AcmeSoftware" is invalid because the "AcmeSoftware" tag is 12 characters long. You can work around this by delimiting words using dashes or underscores (e.g., "en-GB-Acme-Software" or "en-GB-Acme_Software").

Supplemental Substitute Custom Cultures

A "supplemental substitute" custom culture certainly sounds like a contradiction in terms. I use this term to describe a supplemental custom culture that exists to replace an existing culture without actually replacing it. In the "Public Custom Cultures and Naming Conventions" section, I discussed the problems with replacement custom cultures and suggested a solution in which, instead of creating a replacement custom culture, a new supplemental custom culture could be created that was in every way like the intended replacement custom culture. Creating a new custom culture that is like an existing custom culture is made easy with the LoadDataFromCultureInfo and LoadDataFromRegionInfo methods. This is the code for creating an en-GB-Acme supplemental substitute custom culture:

```
CultureInfo cultureInfo = new CultureInfo("en-GB");
RegionInfo regionInfo = new RegionInfo(cultureInfo.Name);

CultureAndRegionInfoBuilder builder =
    new CultureAndRegionInfoBuilder("en-GB-Acme",
    CultureAndRegionModifiers.None);

// load in the data from the existing culture and region
builder.LoadDataFromCultureInfo(cultureInfo);
builder.LoadDataFromRegionInfo(regionInfo);

// make custom changes to the culture
builder.GregorianDateTimeFormat.ShortTimePattern = "HH:mm tt";

builder.Register();
```

The `LoadDataFromCultureInfo` and `LoadDataFromRegionInfo` methods set `CultureAndRegionInfoBuilder` properties from the data in the `CultureInfo` and `RegionInfo` objects, respectively. Tables 11.3 and 11.4 show the properties set by these methods.

Table 11.3   Properties Set by CultureAndRegionInfoBuilder. LoadDataFromCultureInfo

CultureAndRegionInfoBuilder Property	Source
AvailableCalendars	CultureInfo.OptionalCalendars (specific cultures only)
CompareInfo	CultureInfo.CompareInfo (supplemental only)
ConsoleFallbackUICulture	CultureInfo.GetConsoleFallbackUICulture()
CultureEnglishName	CultureInfo.EnglishName
CultureNativeName	CultureInfo.NativeName
GregorianDateTimeFormat	CultureInfo.DateTimeFormat (specific cultures only)
IetfLanguageTag	CultureInfo.IetfLanguageTag
IsRightToLeft	CultureInfo.TextInfo.IsRightToLeft
KeyboardLayoutId	CultureInfo.KeyboardLayoutId
NumberFormat	CultureInfo.NumberFormat (specific cultures only)
Parent	CultureInfo.Parent
TextInfo	CultureInfo.TextInfo (supplemental only)
ThreeLetterISOLanguageName	CultureInfo.ThreeLetterISOLanguageName
ThreeLetterWindowsLanguageName	CultureInfo.ThreeLetterWindowsLanguageName (supplemental only)
TwoLetterISOLanguageName	CultureInfo.TwoLetterISOLanguageName

Table 11.4   Properties Set by CultureAndRegionInfoBuilder.LoadDataFrom RegionInfo

CultureAndRegionInfoBuilder Property	Source
CurrencyEnglishName	RegionInfo.CurrencyEnglishName
CurrencyNativeName	RegionInfo.CurrencyNativeName
GeoId	RegionInfo.GeoId
IsMetric	RegionInfo.IsMetric
ISOCurrencySymbol	RegionInfo.ISOCurrencySymbol
RegionEnglishName	RegionInfo.EnglishName
RegionNativeName	RegionInfo.NativeName
ThreeLetterISORegionName	RegionInfo.ThreeLetterISORegionName
ThreeLetterWindowsRegionName (supplemental only)	RegionInfo.ThreeLetterWindowsRegionName
TwoLetterISORegionName	RegionInfo.TwoLetterISORegionName

Notice that the `CompareInfo`, `TextInfo`, `ThreeLetterWindowsLanguageName`, and `ThreeLetterWindowsRegionName` properties are set by these methods only if the culture is a supplemental culture (which, in this example, it is). For replacement cultures, these properties are set in the `CultureAndRegionInfoBuilder` constructor and are considered immutable. Consequently, if you assign values to these properties for replacement cultures, they will throw an exception. This is why you can't create a replacement custom culture that simply changes the default sort order. This code attempts to create a replacement culture for es-ES (Spanish (Spain)) when the only difference is that the sort order is `Traditional` (0x0000040A) instead of the default `International`:

```
CultureAndRegionInfoBuilder builder =
    new CultureAndRegionInfoBuilder("es-ES",
    CultureAndRegionModifiers.Replacement);
```

```
builder.CompareInfo = CompareInfo.GetCompareInfo(0x0000040A);

builder.Register();
```

The assignment to `CompareInfo` throws a `NotSupportedException`. Therefore, a benefit of using a supplemental custom culture instead of a replacement culture is that these properties can have different values than those of the original culture.

In addition to the public properties in Table 11.3 the `LoadDataFromCultureInfo` method sets internal values for `DurationFormats`, `FontSignature`, and `Paper-Size`. These values are used in the LDML file created by the `Save` method. The `LoadDataFromCultureInfo` method represents the only way to set these properties.

The resulting supplemental custom culture does not have the complete functionality of the replacement custom culture. One difference lies in the behavior of the `CultureInfo.DisplayName` property. This property has a certain level of intelligence built into it. The `DisplayName` property returns the name of the culture for the `CurrentCulture` for built-in .NET Framework and Windows cultures. This means that the `DisplayName` for the `fr-FR` culture is "French (France)" when the `CurrentCulture` is "en-US", but it is "Français (France)" and "Französisch (Frankreich)" when the `CurrentCulture` is "fr-FR" and "de-DE", respectively, and the French and German .NET Framework Language Packs have been installed. Replacement cultures adopt the same functionality because the .NET Framework can identify that the culture is known. The same functionality is not available to supplemental custom cultures because the .NET Framework cannot and should not guess at the correct `DisplayName`. Consequently, the `DisplayName` of a supplemental custom culture is the same as the native name. Table 11.5 shows the difference in behavior for a `tr-TR` (Turkish (Turkey)) custom culture.

Table 11.5 CultureInfo.DisplayName Behavioral Difference for Replacement and Supplemental Custom Cultures

CurrentCulture	tr-TR Replacement Culture DisplayName	tr-TR Supplemental Culture DisplayName
en-US	Turkish (Turkey)	Türkçe (Türkiye)
tr-TR	Türkçe (Türkiye)	Türkçe (Türkiye)

The same difference in behavior is true for `RegionInfo.DisplayName`.

Custom Culture Locale IDs

Another difference between supplemental custom cultures and replacement custom cultures is their locale ID (i.e., `CultureInfo.LCID`). `CultureAndRegion InfoBuilder.LCID` is read-only. Replacement custom cultures use the same locale ID as the cultures they replace. This is helpful because it means that there is no back door to the original culture. In the following example, both lines result in the same `CultureInfo`:

```
CultureInfo cultureInfo1 = new CultureInfo("en-GB");
// The LCID for en-GB is 2057
CultureInfo cultureInfo2 = new CultureInfo(2057);
```

In almost all cases, this behavior is desirable. It does mean, however, that it is not possible to create a `CultureInfo` for the original replaced culture, even if you wanted to. If this were absolutely necessary, you would have to save the replacement custom culture to an LDML file, unregister it, create an original `CultureInfo` object, extract the information you need, and then load the LDML file and register the replacement custom culture again.

Supplemental custom cultures all have the same locale ID: `0x1000` (4096). So the "bn-BD" (Bengali (Bangladesh)) locale ID is `4096`, and the en-GB-Acme locale ID is also `4096`. Consider the following test for equality for these two cultures:

```
CultureInfo cultureInfo1 = new CultureInfo("bn-BD");
CultureInfo cultureInfo2 = new CultureInfo("en-GB-Acme");
if (! cultureInfo1.Equals(cultureInfo2))
    MessageBox.Show("CultureInfo objects are not the same");
```

The `CultureInfo.Equals` method reports that these cultures are not equal, even though their LCIDs are the same. Two `CultureInfo` objects are considered equal in the .NET Framework 2.0 if they are the same object or their `Names` and `CompareInfo` objects are the same. This contrasts to the .NET Framework 1.1 implementation, which is simply based upon a comparison of LCIDs, not object references or Names.

Also note that because all supplemental custom cultures share the same LCID, it is not possible to create a supplemental custom culture using its LCID. The following code results in an `ArgumentException` ("Culture ID 4096 (0x1000) is not a supported culture"):

```
CultureInfo cultureInfo1 = new CultureInfo(4096);
```

This is one of the reasons why you should treat LCIDs as a legacy feature or for use with Win32 APIs. You should also conclude from this that if you store the identities of cultures in a database or configuration file, your method should always be capable of storing the culture name instead of the culture LCID for custom cultures. Recall from the "Alternate Sort Orders" section of Chapter 6 that the .NET Framework 2.0 supports the creation of cultures with alternate sort orders using string identifiers (e.g., "es-ES_tradnl") in addition to LCIDs; it should be apparent that, when using the .NET Framework 2.0, you should always store culture identifiers using strings, not integers. If you want to enforce this in your applications, look at the "`CultureInfo` must not be constructed from LCID" and "`RegionInfo` must not be constructed from LCID" FxCop rules in Chapter 13, "Testing Internationalization Using FxCop."

Before we leave the subject of alternate sort orders, it is worth pointing out that because the custom culture mechanism is based upon culture names and not culture LCIDs, it is not possible to create replacement custom cultures for a culture with an alternate sort order. However, you can create a "supplemental substitute" custom culture for an alternate sort order:

```
// create the es-ES culture with the Traditional sort order
CultureInfo cultureInfo = new CultureInfo("es-ES-Tradnl");
RegionInfo regionInfo = new RegionInfo(cultureInfo.Name);

CultureAndRegionInfoBuilder builder =
    new CultureAndRegionInfoBuilder("es-ES-Tradnl-Acme",
    CultureAndRegionModifiers.None);

// load in the data from the existing culture and region
builder.LoadDataFromCultureInfo(cultureInfo);
builder.LoadDataFromRegionInfo(regionInfo);

// make custom changes to the culture
...
...

builder.Register();
```

Custom Culture Parents and Children

As you know, there is a hierarchy to `CultureInfo` objects in which specific cultures (e.g., "en-US") fall back to neutral cultures (e.g., "en"), which fall back to the invariant culture. This hierarchy manifests itself through the `CultureInfo.Parent` property. Custom cultures fit into this hierarchy, but they are not restricted to the existing pattern of just three levels of cultures, nor the idea that specific cultures have parent neutral cultures. Let's look at two examples. The first is a hierarchy of en-GB custom cultures in which the `Parent` property is not explicitly set in code and is left in the hands of the `LoadDataFromCultureInfo` method:

```
BuildCulture("English (United Kingdom) Acme"                ,
    "en-GB-Acme"         , "en-GB");

BuildCulture("English (United Kingdom) Acme Child"          ,
    "en-GB-Acme-Child" , "en-GB-Acme");

BuildCulture("English (United Kingdom) Acme Grandchild",
    "en-GB-Acme-GrandC", "en-GB-Acme-Child");


private void BuildCulture(string englishName,
    string cultureName, string loadFromCultureName)
{
    CultureInfo cultureInfo = new CultureInfo(loadFromCultureName);

    RegionInfo regionInfo = new RegionInfo(cultureInfo.Name);

    CultureAndRegionInfoBuilder builder =
        new CultureAndRegionInfoBuilder(cultureName,
        CultureAndRegionModifiers.None);

    // add data from the culture
    builder.LoadDataFromCultureInfo(cultureInfo);
    // add data from the region
    builder.LoadDataFromRegionInfo(regionInfo);
    // set the culture's English name
    builder.CultureEnglishName = englishName;

    builder.Register();

}
```

The result of this code might not be what you would expect. Figure 11.1 shows the resulting hierarchy.

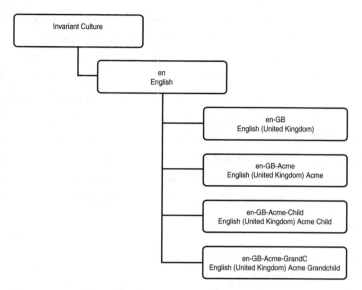

Figure 11.1 Hierarchy of custom cultures when the `Parent` **is set by** `LoadDataFromCultureInfo`

The `LoadDataFromCultureInfo` method sets the `Parent` property to `Culture-Info.Parent`, so in the first call to `BuildCulture`, `en-GB-Acme`'s parent is `en` (`English`). In the second call to `BuildCulture`, `en-GB-Acme-Child`'s parent is also `en` (`English`) because it gets `en-GB-Acme`'s parent. If you were looking to create a hierarchy in which the parent is the culture from which the data is being read, you must explicitly set `CultureAndRegionInfoBuilder`'s `Parent`. Add the following line after the call to `LoadDataFromCultureInfo`:

```
builder.Parent = cultureInfo;
```

The result is the hierarchy shown in Figure 11.2.

Now let's look at this subject from a different point of view. The `Culture-Info.CreateSpecificCulture` method creates a specific culture from either a specific culture (in which case, it simply returns the same specific culture) or a neutral culture. So if you pass the French culture to `CreateSpecificCulture`, it returns a new culture French (France); similarly, German returns German (Germany). This is of interest to custom culture developers because this behavior cannot be specified. How important this is probably depends upon whether you create a replacement custom culture or a supplemental custom culture. If you create a replacement custom culture for "en", you will not be able to change the specific culture from "en-US" to, say, "en-GB". This could have been quite a useful course of action. Consider that you are creating a Web site for Nottingham Forest Football Club in the U.K. If your users' browser language settings are "en", then it is not helpful for you to use CultureInfo.CreateSpecificCulture because it will return a culture for "en-US", which will be wrong for nearly all of your visitors (for whom "en-GB" would have been more appropriate). The same is true for the Toronto Maple Leafs Web site (in Canada), where CreateSpecificCulture would return French (France) from French instead of the more useful French (Canada).

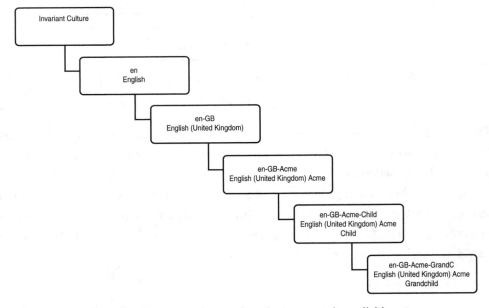

Figure 11.2 Hierarchy of custom cultures when the Parent is explicitly set

Similarly, if you create a supplemental custom culture for, say, Bengali ("bn"), you have no means of specifying what the specific culture should be (e.g., "Bengali (Bangladesh)").

Support for Custom Cultures

Custom cultures are supported not only in the .NET Framework 2.0, but also in Microsoft's .NET Framework 2.0 development tools. The .NET Framework 2.0 enables you to get a list of custom cultures using `CultureInfo.GetCultures`:

```
foreach (CultureInfo cultureInfo in
    CultureInfo.GetCultures(CultureTypes.UserCustomCulture))
{
    listBox1.Items.Add(
        cultureInfo.Name + " (" + cultureInfo.DisplayName + ")");
}
```

The `CultureTypes` value is `UserCustomCulture`. You can test a culture to see if it is a custom culture using its `CultureTypes` property:

```
CultureInfo cultureInfo = new CultureInfo("en-GB");
if ((CultureTypes.UserCustomCulture & cultureInfo.CultureTypes)
    != (CultureTypes)0)
    Text = "User Custom Culture";
else
    Text = "Not User Custom Culture";
```

The Visual Studio 2005 Form Designer also supports custom cultures. When you localize a form by setting `Form.Localizable` to `true`, the `Form.Language` combo box includes custom cultures.

> The combo box is filled using `CultureInfo.DisplayName`. Recall that, for supplemental custom cultures, `CultureInfo.DisplayName` is always `CultureInfo.Native-Name`, not `CultureInfo.EnglishName`, so your custom culture might not be where you expect it in the sorted list.

As with Visual Studio 2005, WinRes, the Windows Resource Localization Editor, supports custom cultures and allows forms resources for custom cultures to be opened and saved.

ClickOnce supports custom cultures in both Visual Studio and Mage (Manifest Generation and Editing Tool). In Visual Studio, in the ClickOnce Publish properties (in Solution Explorer, double-click Properties, and select the Publish tab), click the "Options…" button; you can set the "Publish language" (see Figure 11.3). Mage also supports custom cultures in the same way.

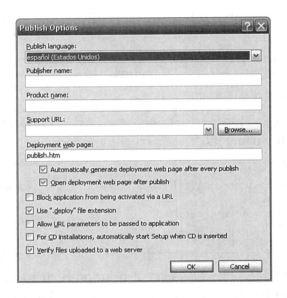

Figure 11.3   Setting the ClickOnce publish language to a custom culture

If you want the ClickOnce bootstrapper to use the language of your custom culture, you must create a new folder beneath the Bootstrapper\Engine folder with the name of your culture (e.g., "bn-BD") containing a setup.xml with translated strings. You can copy the setup.xml from the Bootstrapper\Engine\en folder to use as a starting point for your custom culture.

The support for custom cultures is limited to the .NET Framework. As a consequence, the Regional and Language Options dialog does not include custom cultures. If you use this as a means of setting the user's CurrentCulture and

`CurrentUICulture` preferences, the user will not be able to use supplemental custom cultures. Similarly, other tools that are not based on the .NET Framework 2.0 will not recognize the custom cultures, so, for example, it might not be possible to use some third-party translation tools.

ASP.NET applications can use custom cultures without any modifications. If the user sets their language preferences in the browser to a custom culture and the `Culture` and `UICulture` tags are set to `Auto`, the custom culture will be used automatically. In addition, you can easily localize the ASP.NET 2 Web Site Administration Tool for your custom culture by creating new resx files in the Web Site Administration Tool folder. See Chapter 5, "ASP.NET Specifics," for more details.

Supplemental Custom Cultures

A supplemental culture is a culture that is new to the .NET Framework and the operating system. A number of examples of supplemental custom cultures are presented in this chapter. We start with the greatest challenge: to create a supplemental custom culture from scratch without any existing `CultureInfo` or `RegionInfo` to draw from. For this example, we create a culture for Bengali (also called Bangla) in Bangladesh. The second example, which creates a supplemental custom culture from scratch, is a pseudo translation custom culture.

Bengali (Bangladesh) Custom Culture

At the time of writing, the `Bengali (Bangladesh)` culture, which we label as "bn-BD", is not known to the .NET Framework or any version of Windows. Windows Vista, however, includes the culture-neutral Bengali culture, but this is available only in Windows Vista and is not a specific culture. However, as has already been mentioned, it is entirely possible that this situation won't last and the "bn-BD" culture will arrive in some version of Windows in the future. Despite this, these future events do not invalidate this example. Consider that at such a time you will have a choice between forcing all of your users to upgrade to the new version of Windows (not necessarily possible) and using a custom culture that will work on all versions of Windows. The latter choice is the more practical choice. The same caveats regarding your culture-naming convention apply in this scenario, so although you might want to "personalize" your bn-BD culture name (e.g., "bn-BD-Acme"), I use "bn-BD" in this example for simplicity. Finally, if you run this example in any version of Windows before Windows Vista, you should install support for complex scripts to be able to see the Bengali script.

The following code creates the Bengali (Bangladesh) custom culture:

```
public static void RegisterBengaliBangladeshCulture()
{
    CreateBengaliBangladeshCultureAndRegionInfoBuilder().Register();
}
public static CultureAndRegionInfoBuilder
    CreateBengaliBangladeshCultureAndRegionInfoBuilder()
{
    CultureAndRegionInfoBuilder builder =
        new CultureAndRegionInfoBuilder("bn-BD",
        CultureAndRegionModifiers.None);

    // there is no neutral Bengali culture to set the parent to
    builder.Parent = CultureInfo.InvariantCulture;

    builder.CultureEnglishName = "Bengali (Bangladesh)";
    builder.CultureNativeName = "বাংলা (Bā Ylādesh)";
    builder.ThreeLetterISOLanguageName = "ben";
    builder.ThreeLetterWindowsLanguageName = "ben";
    builder.TwoLetterISOLanguageName = "bn";

    builder.RegionEnglishName = "Bangladesh";
    builder.RegionNativeName = "Bā Ylādesh";
    builder.ThreeLetterISORegionName = "BGD";
    builder.ThreeLetterWindowsRegionName = "BGD";
    builder.TwoLetterISORegionName = "BD";

    builder.IetfLanguageTag = "bn-BD";

    builder.IsMetric = true;
    builder.KeyboardLayoutId = 1081;
    builder.GeoId = 0x17; // Bangladesh

    builder.GregorianDateTimeFormat =
        CreateBangladeshDateTimeFormatInfo();

    builder.NumberFormat = CreateBangladeshNumberFormatInfo();
    builder.CurrencyEnglishName = "Bangladesh Taka";
    builder.CurrencyNativeName = "Bangladesh Taka";
    builder.ISOCurrencySymbol = "BDT";
```

```
    builder.TextInfo = CultureInfo.InvariantCulture.TextInfo;

    builder.CompareInfo = CultureInfo.InvariantCulture.CompareInfo;

    return builder;
}
```

The `bn-BD` parent is the invariant culture. You might want to consider creating this culture in two steps, first creating a neutral Bengali culture and then creating a specific `Bengali  (Bangladesh)` culture. There are a few values for which you should seek out a standard:

- The culture name, `bn-BD`, is obviously of critical importance, and you should seek out existing codes (if any) for this purpose. A list of language codes can be found at http://www.w3.org/WAI/ER/IG/ert/iso639.htm. Alternatively, the official ISO list can be purchased from http://www.iso.org (search for "639"). The list of country codes is available from http://www.iso.org/iso/en/prods-services/iso3166ma/02iso-3166-code-lists/list-en1.html. Alternatively, the official ISO list can be purchased from http://www.iso.org (search for "3166").

- The `GeoId` value is available from Microsoft's Table of Geographical Locations (http://msdn.microsoft.com/library/default.asp?url=/library/en-us/intl/nls_locations.asp). If your geographical region is not listed in this table, you will have to either leave the ID blank or choose a number that is not in use (of course, the number could subsequently become used for a completely different geographical region, which would invalidate your choice).

The `CultureAndRegionInfoBuilder.NumberFormatInfo` is assigned from the `CreateBangladeshNumberFormatInfo` method:

```
private static NumberFormatInfo CreateBangladeshNumberFormatInfo()
{
    NumberFormatInfo numberFormatInfo = new NumberFormatInfo();
    numberFormatInfo.CurrencyDecimalDigits = 2;
    numberFormatInfo.CurrencyDecimalSeparator = ".";
    numberFormatInfo.CurrencyGroupSeparator = ",";
    numberFormatInfo.CurrencyGroupSizes = new int[] { 3, 2 };
    numberFormatInfo.CurrencyNegativePattern = 12;
    numberFormatInfo.CurrencyPositivePattern = 2;
```

```
      numberFormatInfo.CurrencySymbol = "BDT";
      numberFormatInfo.DigitSubstitution = DigitShapes.None;
      numberFormatInfo.NaNSymbol = "NaN";
      numberFormatInfo.NativeDigits = new string[]
          { "০", "১", "২", "৩", "৪", "৫", "৬", "৭", "৮", "৯" };
      numberFormatInfo.NegativeInfinitySymbol = "-Infinity";
      numberFormatInfo.NegativeSign = "-";
      numberFormatInfo.NumberDecimalDigits = 2;
      numberFormatInfo.NumberDecimalSeparator = ".";
      numberFormatInfo.NumberGroupSeparator = ",";
      numberFormatInfo.NumberGroupSizes = new int[] { 3, 2 };
      numberFormatInfo.NumberNegativePattern = 1;
      numberFormatInfo.PercentDecimalDigits = 2;
      numberFormatInfo.PercentDecimalSeparator = ".";
      numberFormatInfo.PercentGroupSeparator = ",";
      numberFormatInfo.PercentGroupSizes = new int[] { 3, 2 };
      numberFormatInfo.PercentNegativePattern = 0;
      numberFormatInfo.PercentPositivePattern = 0;
      numberFormatInfo.PercentSymbol = "%";
      numberFormatInfo.PerMilleSymbol = "‰";
      numberFormatInfo.PositiveInfinitySymbol = "Infinity";
      numberFormatInfo.PositiveSign = "+";
      return numberFormatInfo;
  }
```

The `CultureAndRegionInfoBuilder.DateTimeFormatInfo` is assigned from the `CreateBangladeshDateTimeFormatInfo` method:

```
private static DateTimeFormatInfo
    CreateBangladeshDateTimeFormatInfo()
{
    Calendar calendar =
        new GregorianCalendar(GregorianCalendarTypes.Localized);

    DateTimeFormatInfo dateTimeFormatInfo = new DateTimeFormatInfo();

    dateTimeFormatInfo.Calendar = calendar;

    dateTimeFormatInfo.AbbreviatedDayNames = new string[]
        { "রবি.", "সোম.", "মঙ্গল.", "বুধ.", "বৃহস্পতি.", "শুক্র.", "শনি." };
    dateTimeFormatInfo.DayNames = new string[] { "রবিবার",
        "সোমবার", "মঙ্গলবার", "বুধবার", "বৃহস্পতিবার", "শুক্রবার", "শনিবার" };
    dateTimeFormatInfo.ShortestDayNames = new string[]
        { "রবি.", "সোম.", "মঙ্গল.", "বুধ.", "বৃহস্পতি.", "শুক্র.", "শনি." };

    dateTimeFormatInfo.AbbreviatedMonthNames = new string[]
        { "জানু.", "ফেব্র.", "মার্চ", "এপ্রিল", "মে", "জুন", "জুলাই", "আগ.",
```

```
                "সেপ্টে.", "অক্টো.", "নভে.", "ডিসে.", "" };
    dateTimeFormatInfo.MonthNames = new string[]
            { "জানুয়ারী", "ফেব্রুয়ারী", "মার্চ", "এপ্রিল", "মে", "জুন", "জুলাই",
            "আগস্ট", "সেপ্টেম্বর", "অক্টোবর", "নভেম্বর", "ডিসেম্বর", "" };

    dateTimeFormatInfo.AbbreviatedMonthGenitiveNames =
            new string[] { "জানু.", "ফেব্র.", "মার্চ", "এপ্রিল", "মে",
            "জুন", "জুলাই", "আগ.", "সেপ্টে.", "অক্টো.", "নভে.", "ডিসে.", "" };
    dateTimeFormatInfo.MonthGenitiveNames = new string[] {
            "জানুয়ারী", "ফেব্রুয়ারী", "মার্চ", "এপ্রিল", "মে", "জুন", "জুলাই", "আগস্ট",
            "সেপ্টেম্বর", "অক্টোবর", "নভেম্বর", "ডিসেম্বর","" };

    dateTimeFormatInfo.AMDesignator = "পূর্বাহ্ন";
    dateTimeFormatInfo.CalendarWeekRule = CalendarWeekRule.FirstDay;
    dateTimeFormatInfo.DateSeparator = "-";
    dateTimeFormatInfo.FirstDayOfWeek = DayOfWeek.Monday;
    dateTimeFormatInfo.FullDateTimePattern = "dd MMMM yyyy HH:mm:ss";
    dateTimeFormatInfo.LongDatePattern = "dd MMMM yyyy";
    dateTimeFormatInfo.LongTimePattern = "HH:mm:ss";
    dateTimeFormatInfo.MonthDayPattern = "dd MMMM";
    dateTimeFormatInfo.PMDesignator = "অপরাহ্ন";
    dateTimeFormatInfo.ShortDatePattern = "dd-MM-yyyy";
    dateTimeFormatInfo.ShortTimePattern = "HH:mm";
    dateTimeFormatInfo.TimeSeparator = ":";
    dateTimeFormatInfo.YearMonthPattern = "MMMM, yyyy";

    return dateTimeFormatInfo;
}
```

> **Note**
>
> The `Calendar` object must be assigned to the `DateTimeFormat-Info.Calendar` property before day and month names are assigned because setting the Calendar property resets these values.

The `Bengali (Bangladesh)` culture can now be used like any other .NET Framework culture.

Pseudo Translation Custom Culture

The `Pseudo Translation` custom culture is another custom culture that is created without drawing upon any existing culture or region information. The purpose of this custom culture is to provide support for the pseudo translation described in Chapter 9, in which developers and testers can use a culture other than the developer's own culture, can test that the application is globalized and localized, and still can be able to use the application without having to learn another language. The complete code for the pseudo translation custom culture is not shown here because it is identical to the previous example, except that the values are different.

The pseudo translation custom culture values themselves are important only because they must not be the same as those of an existing culture. This allows developers and testers to observe that globalization and localization are occurring. This is a little trickier than it might at first seem. The first problem is that, in choosing suitable language and region codes for the pseudo translation culture, you should avoid existing codes. You might think of using "ps-PS" (for Pseudo (Pseudo)), but the "ps" language code and "PS" region code have already been taken. Refer to the links in the Bengali (Bangladesh) custom culture to avoid choosing identifiers that are already taken. I have chosen "pd-PD" because these are still free at the time of writing. However, to ensure future safety of your choice, the safest solution is to choose a code that does not conform to the ISO specifications (e.g., "p1-P1" uses a number, which is not acceptable in these specifications). Using this approach, you can be sure that if it doesn't conform to the specification, the code will never be used by anyone else.

Many of the pseudo culture's values are easy to invent:

```
builder.CultureEnglishName = "PseudoLanguage (PseudoRegion)";
builder.CultureNativeName =
    "[!!! PšěŭďŏŁähğŭäğě (PšěŭďŏŘěğĭŏh) !!!]";
builder.ThreeLetterISOLanguageName = "psd";
builder.ThreeLetterWindowsLanguageName = "psd";
builder.TwoLetterISOLanguageName = "pd";

builder.RegionEnglishName = "PseudoRegion";
builder.RegionNativeName = "[!!! PšěŭďŏŘěğĭŏh !!!]";
builder.ThreeLetterISORegionName = "PSD";
builder.ThreeLetterWindowsRegionName = "PSD";
builder.TwoLetterISORegionName = "PD";

builder.IetfLanguageTag = "pd-PD";
```

However, you need to find the right balance: You must use values that are sufficiently different from English, to be clear that the application is not using the default culture, yet you must use values that are sufficiently understandable, to make the application still usable. Consider the following two currency strings, which were converted to a string using `123456789.123456.ToString("C")`:

```
$123,456,789.12
1'2'3'4'5'6'7'8'9@1235 ~
```

The first uses the "en-US" culture, and the second uses the "pd-PD" culture. The second clearly shows that the application is globalized, but is it still recognizable as currency? The decimal separator is "@" instead of "."; the group separator is " ' " instead of ","; the group size is 1 instead of 3; the number of decimals is 4 instead of 2; the currency symbol is "~" instead of "$"; and the currency symbol is placed to the right instead of to the left. In terms of testing globalization, this scores a 10, but is the application still usable?

I have also taken the attitude that the day and month names used in the `Date-TimeFormatInfo` should not be pseudo-ized. For example:

```
dateTimeFormatInfo.DayNames = new string[] {
    "*Sunday*", "*Monday*", "*Tuesday*", "*Wednesday*",
    "*Thursday*", "*Friday*", "*Saturday*" };
```

(The names are delimited with asterisks, however.) You might have expected the names to have been "pseudo-ized," like this:

```
dateTimeFormatInfo.DayNames = new string[] {
    "ŠŭhđäY̌", "MŏhđäY̌", "ŤŭěšđäY̌", "ŴěđhěšđäY̌",
    "ŤħŭřšđäY̌", "FřĭđäY̌", "ŠäťŭřđäY̌" };
```

The reason behind this is that I want to be able to see clearly that day and month names are taken from the appropriate `DateTimeFormatInfo` object instead of from a resource assembly. In other words, if the user is presented with "ŠŭhđäY̌", you can be sure that the application *has* been localized, but you don't know *how* it has been localized. The text could have come just as easily from a call to `Resource Manager.GetString("Sunday")`, and there is no way to make this distinction visually if the text in the `DateTimeFormatInfo` is the same as a pseudo-ized resource.

With the pseudo translation culture in place, you might want to update the `PseudoTranslation` class introduced in Chapter 9 to use the new culture instead of the previously hijacked culture:

```
public class PseudoTranslation
{
    private static CultureInfo cultureInfo =
        new CultureInfo("pd-PD");
    public static CultureInfo CultureInfo
    {
        get {return cultureInfo;}
        set {cultureInfo = value;}
    }
}
```

Culture Builder Application Sample (CultureSample)

One of the sample applications in the Visual Studio 2005 documentation is called the Culture Builder Application Sample (aka `CultureSample`) and is aimed squarely at creating custom cultures. Start the documentation and search for "Culture Builder Sample." Open either the `CultureSampleCS.sln` or `CultureSampleVB.sln` Windows Forms applications and build it; you will get `CultureBuilderSample.exe`, a UI for building new custom cultures (see Figure 11.4).

Click "New Culture." After you enter the culture's name, you can specify the culture's formatting options using a dialog (see Figure 11.5), modeled on the Regional and Language Options' Customize dialog.

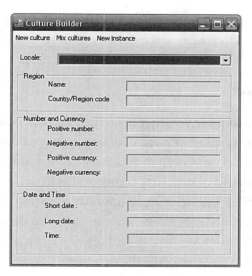

Figure 11.4   `CultureBuilderSample` application for building custom cultures

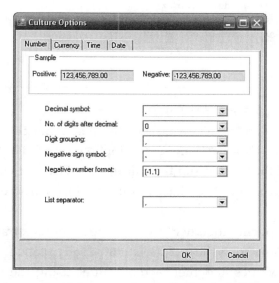

Figure 11.5   `CultureBuilderSample` application for building custom cultures

Click OK to save your custom culture. `CultureBuilderSample` can also be used to combine cultures and to create replacement cultures.

Combining Cultures

One of the common reasons for wanting to create a custom culture is to create a combination of language and region in which the language and the region are known but have not yet been paired. The benefit of creating such a combined culture is that you can refer to a language and region that is important to your target market but that is not defined in the .NET Framework or operating system. Table 11.1 shows some example combinations, with "`es-US`" (`Spanish (United States)`) being one of the most requested. The `CultureAndRegionInfoBuilderHelper` class (included with the source code for this book) performs the drudgery of combining two cultures and can be used like this:

```
CultureAndRegionInfoBuilder builder =
    CultureAndRegionInfoBuilderHelper.
    CreateCultureAndRegionInfoBuilder(
    new CultureInfo("es-ES"), new RegionInfo("en-US"));

builder.Register();
```

The `CultureAndRegionInfoBuilderHelper.CreateCultureAndRegion InfoBuilder` method creates a new `CultureAndRegionInfoBuilder` from a "language" `CultureInfo` ("`es-ES`") and a "region" `RegionInfo` ("`en-US`"). The new object is then used either to Register the culture or to Save the culture. The `Create-CultureAndRegionInfoBuilder` has various overloads to accept variations on the same theme.

The process of "splicing together" two cultures is not as straightforward as you might think. Table 11.6 shows the `CultureAndRegionInfoBuilder` properties, and the source of their values and their actual values using the `Spanish (United States)` example.

Table 11.6   CultureAndRegionInfoBuilder Properties and Values for the Spanish (United States) Culture

CultureAndRegionInfoBuilder Property	Source	es-US Value
AvailableCalendars	US CultureInfo.OptionalCalendars	
CompareInfo	Spanish CultureInfo.CompareInfo	
ConsoleFallbackUICulture	Spanish CultureInfo.GetConsole-FallbackUICulture()	
CultureEnglishName	Spanish Neutral CultureInfo.-EnglishName, US RegionInfo.-EnglishName	"Spanish (United States)"
CultureName	Spanish CultureInfo.TwoLetter-ISOLanguageName, US Region-Info.TwoLetterISORegionName	"es-US"
CultureNativeName	Spanish Neutral CultureInfo.Native-Name, US RegionInfo.DisplayName (in Spanish)	"español (Estados Unidos)"
CultureTypes	N/A (ReadOnly)	— (ReadOnly)
CurrencyEnglishName	US RegionInfo.CurrencyEnglish-Name	"US Dollar"
CurrencyNativeName	US RegionInfo.CurrencyDisplay-Name (in Spanish)	"US Dollar"
GeoId	US RegionInfo.GeoId	244 (US)
GregorianDateTimeFormat	US CultureInfo.DateTimeFormat	US DateTimeFormat (with Spanish names)
IetfLanguageTag	Spanish CultureInfo.TwoLetter-ISOLanguageName, US Region-Info.TwoLetterISORegionName	"es-US"
IsMetric	US RegionInfo.IsMetric	false
ISOCurrencySymbol	US RegionInfo.ISOCurrencySymbol	"USD"
IsRightToLeft	Spanish CultureInfo.TextInfo.Is-RightToLeft	false

Table 11.6   CultureAndRegionInfoBuilder Properties and Values for the Spanish (United States) Culture (Continued)

CultureAndRegionInfoBuilder Property	Source	es-US Value
KeyboardLayoutId	Spanish Neutral CultureInfo.KeyboardLayoutId	1034
LCID	N/A (ReadOnly)	0x1000 (4096)
NumberFormat	US CultureInfo.NumberFormat	US CultureInfo. NumberFormat
Parent	Spanish Neutral CultureInfo	"es"
RegionEnglishName	US RegionInfo.EnglishName	"United States"
RegionName	N/A (ReadOnly)	— (ReadOnly)
RegionNativeName	US RegionInfo.DisplayName (in Spanish)	"Estados Unidos"
TextInfo	Spanish Neutral CultureInfo.-TextInfo	Spanish Neutral CultureInfo.TextInfo
ThreeLetterISOLanguage-Name	Spanish CultureInfo.ThreeLetter-ISOLanguageName	"spa"
ThreeLetterISORegionName	US RegionInfo.ThreeLetterISO-RegionName	"USA"
ThreeLetterWindows-LanguageName	Spanish CultureInfo.ThreeLetter-WindowsLanguageName	"ESN"
ThreeLetterWindows-RegionName	US RegionInfo.ThreeLetterWindows-RegionName	"USA"
TwoLetterISOLanguage-Name	Spanish CultureInfo.TwoLetter-ISOLanguageName	"es"
TwoLetterISORegionName	US RegionInfo.TwoLetterISORegion-Name	"US"

The new culture is a combination of the language and the region, but many of the names used in the culture need to be localized. Whereas the new culture uses the calendar for the region, the names of the days and months of that calendar must be in the specified language (i.e., Spanish), and not the language from which the calendar has come (i.e., English). The `LoadDataFromRegionInfo` method is very helpful in this scenario, but the `LoadDataFromCultureInfo` is less so. The `CultureAnd RegionInfoBuilderHelper.CreateCultureAndRegionInfoBuilder` method is shown here:

```
public static CultureAndRegionInfoBuilder
    CreateCultureAndRegionInfoBuilder(
    CultureInfo languageCultureInfo,
    RegionInfo regionInfo,
    string cultureName)
{
    if (cultureName == null || cultureName == String.Empty)
        // the culture name is blank so construct a default name
        cultureName =
            languageCultureInfo.TwoLetterISOLanguageName + "-" +
            regionInfo.TwoLetterISORegionName;

    CultureInfo languageNeutralCultureInfo =
        GetNeutralCulture(languageCultureInfo);

    CultureInfo regionCultureInfo = new CultureInfo(regionInfo.Name);

    CultureAndRegionInfoBuilder builder =
        new CultureAndRegionInfoBuilder(
        cultureName, CultureAndRegionModifiers.None);

    builder.LoadDataFromCultureInfo(regionCultureInfo);
    builder.LoadDataFromRegionInfo(regionInfo);

    builder.Parent = languageNeutralCultureInfo;

    builder.CompareInfo = languageCultureInfo.CompareInfo;
    builder.TextInfo = languageCultureInfo.TextInfo;

    builder.IetfLanguageTag = cultureName;

    builder.RegionNativeName = GetNativeRegionName(
        regionInfo, languageCultureInfo);

    builder.CultureEnglishName =
```

```
            languageNeutralCultureInfo.EnglishName + " (" +
            regionInfo.EnglishName + ")";

        builder.CultureNativeName =
            languageNeutralCultureInfo.NativeName + " (" +
            builder.RegionNativeName + ")";

        builder.CurrencyNativeName = GetNativeCurrencyName(
            regionInfo, languageCultureInfo);

        // copy the native month and day names
        DateTimeFormatInfo builderDtfi =
            builder.GregorianDateTimeFormat;

        DateTimeFormatInfo languageDtfi =
            languageCultureInfo.DateTimeFormat;

        builderDtfi.AbbreviatedDayNames =
            languageDtfi.AbbreviatedDayNames;

        builderDtfi.AbbreviatedMonthGenitiveNames =
            languageDtfi.AbbreviatedMonthGenitiveNames;

        builderDtfi.AbbreviatedMonthNames =
            languageDtfi.AbbreviatedMonthNames;

        builderDtfi.DayNames = languageDtfi.DayNames;

        builderDtfi.MonthGenitiveNames = languageDtfi.MonthGenitiveNames;

        builderDtfi.MonthNames = languageDtfi.MonthNames;

        builderDtfi.ShortestDayNames = languageDtfi.ShortestDayNames;

        builder.KeyboardLayoutId =
            languageNeutralCultureInfo.KeyboardLayoutId;

        builder.ThreeLetterISOLanguageName =
            languageNeutralCultureInfo.ThreeLetterISOLanguageName;

        builder.ThreeLetterWindowsLanguageName =
            languageNeutralCultureInfo.ThreeLetterWindowsLanguageName;

        builder.TwoLetterISOLanguageName =
            languageNeutralCultureInfo.TwoLetterISOLanguageName;

        return builder;
    }
```

Two methods, GetNativeRegionName and GetNativeCurrencyName, make an attempt to get the native versions of the region name and currency name, respectively. They both work by changing the CurrentCulture to the language for which a native name is required (i.e., Spanish) and then getting the property. If the appropriate .NET Framework Language Pack is installed, the correct native name will be returned; otherwise, the native name will be the English name and you will need to manually update these values before registering or saving the culture. The Get-NativeCurrencyName method is shown here (the GetNativeRegionName is identical, except for the name of the property and the fact that it attempts to get the region's DisplayName because DisplayName is localized).

```
protected static string GetNativeCurrencyName(
    RegionInfo regionInfo, CultureInfo languageCultureInfo)
{
    string nativeName;
    CultureInfo oldCultureInfo =
        Thread.CurrentThread.CurrentUICulture;
    try
    {
        // attempt to change the UI culture
        Thread.CurrentThread.CurrentUICulture = languageCultureInfo;
        // get the new name (if a corresponding language pack is
        // installed then this yields a true native name)
        nativeName = regionInfo.CurrencyNativeName;
    }
    catch (Exception)
    {
        // it was not possible to change the UI culture
        nativeName = regionInfo.CurrencyNativeName;
    }
    finally
    {
        Thread.CurrentThread.CurrentUICulture = oldCultureInfo;
    }
    return nativeName;
}
```

Exporting Operating System-Specific Cultures

Another use for custom cultures is to level the playing field of supported cultures across operating systems. Recall that the list of available cultures in the .NET Framework 2.0 is determined by the operating system upon which the code is running.

Windows XP Professional Service Pack 2, for example, has many more cultures available to it than Windows 2000 Professional. If your application needs to use a culture that is available to only a more recent version of Windows, your first thought might be to upgrade your clients to that version of Windows. A simpler solution, however, would be to export the required culture from the version of Windows that has the culture to the machines that do not have the culture. For example, you could export the Welsh (United Kingdom) culture from Windows XP Professional Service Pack 2 to, say, Windows 2000 Professional (where this culture is not known). This approach becomes especially useful when newer versions of Windows are released and you covet their new cultures but don't want to upgrade your development machines.

This process is wrapped up in the CultureAndRegionInfoBuilderHelper. Export method, which can be called like this:

```
CultureAndRegionInfoBuilderHelper.Export(
    new CultureInfo("cy-GB"), "cy-GB.ldml", "en-GB", "en-GB");
```

The static Export method accepts four parameters: the CultureInfo to export, the filename to export the definition to, the text info culture that the exported culture should use, and the sort culture that the exported culture should use. The export method starts with some easily recognizable code that simply creates a new Culture AndRegionInfoBuilder object and loads its values from the existing culture:

```
RegionInfo regionInfo = new RegionInfo(cultureInfo.Name);

CultureAndRegionInfoBuilder builder =
    new CultureAndRegionInfoBuilder(cultureInfo.Name,
    CultureAndRegionModifiers.Replacement);

builder.LoadDataFromCultureInfo(cultureInfo);
builder.LoadDataFromRegionInfo(regionInfo);

builder.Save(ldmlFilename);
```

Notice that the exported culture appears at first to be a replacement culture, but this is only a ruse to allow the culture to be saved on the machine that already has the culture. The exported culture file (e.g., cy-GB.ldml) cannot be used immediately on the target machine, however. One issue needs to be addressed first. If you open the exported LDML file, you will find two lines that prevent the custom culture from being created on the target machine:

```
<msLocale:textInfoName type="cy-GB" />
<msLocale:sortName type="cy-GB" />
```

These lines define the text info and sort orders, respectively. The problem with these lines is that they refer to text info and sort definitions that the target machine does not have. These lines must be changed to a text info and sort order that the target machine does have. The remainder of the Export method does just this. The result is that these lines are changed:

```
<msLocale:textInfoName type="en-GB" />
<msLocale:sortName type="en-GB" />
```

Of course, this means that the text info and sort orders of these exported custom cultures will not be entirely correct, but because it is not possible to define new text infos and sort orders for custom cultures, this is a limitation that we have to live with.

Company-Specific Dialects

As mentioned in "Uses for Custom Cultures," at the beginning of this chapter, it can be useful to create a set of resources that use a vocabulary that is specific to a single company or group of companies. The CreateChildCultureAndRegionInfo-Builder method does just this and can be used like this:

```
CultureAndRegionInfoBuilder builder =
    CultureAndRegionInfoBuilderHelper.
    CreateChildCultureAndRegionInfoBuilder(
    new CultureInfo("en-US"),
    "en-US-Sirius",
    "English (United States) (Sirius Minor Publications)",
    "English (United States) (Sirius Minor Publications)",
    "United States (Sirius Minor Publications)",
    "United States (Sirius Minor Publications)");

builder.Register();
```

The method accepts a culture (e.g., "en-US") to inherit from, and accepts the new culture name and various strings to set various name properties to. It returns a

CultureAndRegionInfoBuilder object that can be used to register the culture. The CreateChildCultureAndRegionInfoBuilder method follows:

```
public static CultureAndRegionInfoBuilder
    CreateChildCultureAndRegionInfoBuilder(
    CultureInfo parentCultureInfo, string cultureName,
    string cultureEnglishName, string cultureNativeName,
    string regionEnglishName, string regionNativeName)
{
    RegionInfo parentRegionInfo =
        new RegionInfo(parentCultureInfo.Name);

    CultureAndRegionInfoBuilder builder =
        new CultureAndRegionInfoBuilder(cultureName,
        CultureAndRegionModifiers.None);

    // load the culture and region data from the parent
    builder.LoadDataFromCultureInfo(parentCultureInfo);
    builder.LoadDataFromRegionInfo(parentRegionInfo);

    builder.Parent = parentCultureInfo;
    builder.CultureEnglishName = cultureEnglishName;
    builder.CultureNativeName = cultureNativeName;
    builder.RegionEnglishName = regionEnglishName;
    builder.RegionNativeName = regionNativeName;

    return builder;
}
```

Extending the CultureAndRegionInfoBuilder Class

In the "Extending the CultureInfo Class" section of Chapter 6, I showed a CultureInfoEx class that extends the .NET Framework's CultureInfo class. This CultureInfoEx can be used to hold additional information about a culture; the example given added postal code format information that can be used as a mask for data entry. If you like the idea of custom cultures and you also like the idea of extending the CultureInfo class, then the natural extension is to put both together and have extended custom cultures. Unfortunately, the custom culture architecture is a closed architecture, and this scenario is not supported. A number of barriers prevent the custom culture architecture from being extended:

- `CultureAndRegionInfoBuilder` is sealed and, therefore, cannot be inherited from.
- The `CultureXmlReader` and `CultureXmlWriter` classes that read and write LDML files are both internal and sealed; therefore, they cannot be inherited from and cannot even be accessed.
- The NLP file format is binary and proprietary.

To work around these limitations, you must implement a layer on top of the custom culture architecture. The essential idea is to create a `CultureAndRegionInfoBuilderEx` class that encapsulates the `CultureAndRegionInfoBuilder` class. The new class would be a duplicate of the `CultureAndRegionInfoBuilder` class and would redirect all properties and methods from the "fake" `CultureAndRegionInfoBuilderEx` class to the `CultureAndRegionInfoBuilder` class. The `Register` method would save the additional `CultureInfoEx` information to a private area in an LDML file (e.g., "`bn-BD.ldml`"), and this file would be installed in the Windows `Globalization` folder. The `Unregister` method would delete/rename the additional file. The `Save` method would write the additional information to the LDML file, and the `CreateFromLdml` method would load the additional information from the LDML file. Finally, the `CultureInfoEx` constructor would check to see if the culture is a custom culture and, if so, would load the additional information from the associated additional information file.

Custom Cultures and .NET Framework Language Packs

The .NET Framework draws the resources it needs from both the operating system and the framework's resources. In particular resources, such as exception messages, `PrintPreviewDialog`, `CultureInfo.DisplayName`, and `RegionInfo.Display-Name` are all drawn from the .NET Framework Language Pack that matches the `CultureInfo.CurrentUICulture`. Of course, for supplemental custom cultures, no such language pack exists, so the resources fall back to English. You can do very little about this. Whereas it is technically possible to create your own .NET Framework Language Pack for your own language, there is no value in doing so because you cannot sign the assembly with the same key used to sign the .NET Framework assemblies. If your custom .NET Framework Language Pack does not use the same key, `ResourceManager` will not match your language pack satellite assemblies with the fallback assemblies in the .NET Framework. Consequently, any such custom .NET Framework Language Pack will be ignored.

This has a knock on effect if you use `ClickOnce` to deploy your Windows Forms applications because the majority of the `ClickOnce` interface is drawn from the .NET Framework Language Packs (see the "ClickOnce" section in Chapter 4, "Windows Forms Specifics"). Because you cannot create your own .NET Framework Language Packs, you cannot provide a `ClickOnce` user interface in your custom culture's language (with the exception of the `ClickOnce` bootstrapper dialogs).

Custom Cultures in the .NET Framework 1.1 and Visual Studio 2003

The story for custom cultures in the .NET Framework 1.1 is considerably more limited than for the .NET Framework 2.0, to the extent that if you are able to upgrade to the .NET Framework 2.0, I advise doing so. Assuming that this isn't possible, read on.

A custom culture in the .NET Framework 1.1 is a new class that inherits from the `CultureInfo` class and sets the necessary `CultureInfo` properties to their relevant values in the constructor. The .NET Framework SDK includes an example of such a custom culture in `<SDK>\v1.1\Samples\Technologies\Localization\CustomCulture`. To use the new custom culture, you must construct it using its own constructor. If your custom culture class is called `BengaliBangladeshCulture`, for example, you construct it using this:

```
CultureInfo cultureInfo = new BengaliBangladeshCulture();
```

It is not possible to construct it using the culture's name (e.g., "bn-BD") because the list of cultures supported by the .NET Framework 1.1 is hard-wired. Similarly, Visual Studio 2003 and WinRes 1.1 use the list supplied by the .NET Framework; therefore, it is not possible to make them aware of the custom culture, so both tools are useless for maintaining resources for the custom culture.

Where Are We?

Custom cultures in the .NET Framework represent a great leap forward and open new and exciting possibilities to developers. The new cultures are recognized by the .NET Framework as first-class citizens and, once registered, are as valid as any other culture. With this feature, we can replace existing cultures, create new cultures for previously unknown cultures or cultures that are recognized on only certain operating systems, make new language/region combinations, and support customer-specific dialects. The custom culture implementation is not without its limitations, however, and care should be taken to avoid Custom Culture Hell. Effort is required to extend the custom culture architecture, and, not unreasonably, there is no support for language packs for custom cultures. That said, the only remaining limitation is our imagination.

12.

Custom Resource Managers

S O FAR, ALL OF THE EXAMPLES THAT YOU have seen have used one of the two resource managers that are included with the .NET Framework 1.1 and 2.0—namely, `System.Resources.ResourceManager` and `System.ComponentModel.ComponentResourceManager`. In this chapter, I show how you can write your own resource managers. You might want to do this to read/write resources from a different format (e.g., a database) or to provide additional functionality to a resource manager. I start by explaining how the "file-based" resource manager embedded in the `ResourceManager` class works. This feature has been largely ignored until now, as its implementation is somewhat flawed. However, the basic idea is sound, and knowledge of what it does helps us to understand how the `ResourceManager` class works. It also paves the way for writing a replacement resource manager.

I go on to explain how the `ResourceManager` works internally, as this will help us to write our own resource managers. Our first custom resource manager reads resources from a database. This is a relatively simple and useful resource manager that we cover in two stages: reading resources from a database and, later, writing resources to a database. We follow this with two related resource managers to read/write file-based resources in `.resources` and `.resx` files. The former offers the same functionality as the file-based resource manager hidden in `ResourceManager`, but without the limitations. With these resource managers in place, we write a "translation" resource manager. This resource manager uses the translation engine that we wrote in Chapter 9, "Machine Translation," to translate missing resources on the fly. This resource manager is particularly useful for resources that frequently change where it is impractical to return to the development team for new releases whenever content changes. The last resource manager example is a resource manager to set properties such as `Font`, `ImeMode`, and `RightToLeft` on an application-wide basis.

Our job does not end with the writing of the resource managers, though. I introduce a resource manager provider class that does for resource managers what the `DbProviderFactories` class does for data providers in the .NET Framework 2.0. The last piece of the jigsaw is to use the custom resource manager. Both Windows Forms developers and ASP.NET developers have separate additional steps that must be taken to successfully use a custom resource manager. Windows Forms developers have the problem that the code generated in a form's `InitializeComponent` method includes a hard-coded reference to the `ResourceManager` or `ComponentResourceManager` classes. I show how to create a component to overcome this problem. ASP.NET developers must use ASP.NET's resource provider mechanism to get ASP.NET to adopt the new custom resource manager. Finally, we return to the subject of strongly typed resources and show how to generate strongly typed resource classes for our new resource managers.

But before we begin on our journey, a word of warning: If performance is an issue to you, you might want to stay with the `ResourceManager` or `ComponentResourceManager` classes. These classes outperform all of the solutions in this chapter, and it is unlikely that other solutions will offer better performance than the existing resource managers already do. Of course, they don't offer the same functionality as custom resource managers, so you need to weigh the benefits.

ResourceManager.CreateFileBasedResourceManager

Embedded inside the `ResourceManager` class is a second resource manager that, instead of reading resources from an assembly, reads resources from stand-alone resource files. If you have seen *Harry Potter and the Sorcerer's Stone,* you can think of this resource manager as the parasitic Lord Voldemort sharing the same body as Professor Quirrell. To make a distinction between the two resource managers that inhabit the same `ResourceManager` class, I refer to them as "assembly-based" resource managers and "file-based" resource managers. This file-based resource manager can be created using the static `ResourceManager.CreateFileBased-ResourceManager` method:

```
ResourceManager resourceManager =
    ResourceManager.CreateFileBasedResourceManager(
    "Strings", ".", null);
```

The first parameter is the base name of the resources file. This is the filename without the culture and without the file extension. The second parameter is the directory in which the file is located. The third parameter is a `Type` that is used to create new `ResourceSets`. Hereafter, this file-based resource manager is used and behaves in the exact same way as an assembly based resource manager, so to get a string, we call `GetString`:

```
MessageBox.Show(resourceManager.GetString("Hello"));
```

If the `CurrentUICulture` hasn't been set, this looks for a file called "`Strings.resources`" in the same directory as the executable. If the `CurrentUICulture` is "`fr-FR`", it looks for a file called "`Strings.fr-FR.resources`".

Of course, you need to create the resources file. If you are starting from a resx file, you can create it using the .NET Framework resgen utility:

```
resgen Strings.resx
```

This creates `Strings.resources`. You then need to move the resources file into the same directory as the executable assembly. The problem with this approach is that it requires the developer to invoke resgen manually and to copy the resulting file. It's a minor effort for a single file, but it is easily forgotten. A better solution is one that is part of the build process. The next three sections cover this process for Windows Forms, ASP.NET 2.0, and ASP.NET 1.1, respectively.

Incorporating resgen into the Build Process for Windows Forms

You can incorporate resgen into the build process so that it is run automatically. In either Visual Studio 2005 or Visual Studio 2003, right-click the project in Solution Explorer, select Properties, and click on the Build Events tab (see Figure 12.1).

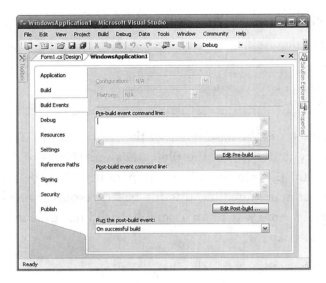

Figure 12.1   The Project's Build Events in Visual Studio 2005

In the "Post-build event command line:," you can enter a command to execute after the build process. Enter the following command (on a single line):

```
"C:\Program Files\Microsoft Visual Studio 8\SDK\v2.0\Bin\resgen"
   C:\Examples\WindowsApplication1\Strings.resx
   C:\Examples\WindowsApplication1\bin\debug\
   Strings.resources
```

(For Visual Studio 2003, use the .NET Framework SDK 1.1 `bin` folder, which is typically `C:\Program Files\Microsoft Visual Studio .NET 2003\SDK\v1.1\Bin`).

Click OK. From here on, whenever you do a successful build, this command will be run after the build has completed. Of course, this uses hard-coded paths, so a better solution is to use macros to refer to the project directory and the target directory:

```
"C:\Program Files\Microsoft Visual Studio 8\SDK\v2.0\Bin\resgen"
   $(ProjectDir)\Strings.resx
   $(TargetDir)\Strings.resources
```

This is fine if you just want to compile a single resource, but that's probably not the case for most applications. A better approach is to create a script file and put this command along with the others in the script file.

Incorporating resgen into the Build Process in ASP.NET 2.0

ASP.NET 2.0 applications do not have a project file; consequently, the solution of using Build Events cannot be used. The best option for ASP.NET 2.0 applications is to use Web Deployment Projects. Web Deployment Projects are separate projects that are added to ASP.NET 2.0 solutions. A Web Deployment Project is an MSBuild project for a Web site. Among the many additional features that Web Deployment Projects offer is the capability to add custom pre- and post-build steps. Web Deployment Projects are an add-in package for Visual Studio 2005 and can be downloaded from http://msdn.microsoft.com/asp.net/reference/infrastructure/wdp/default.aspx. To add steps to call resgen to compile resx files, install Web Deployment Projects. In Visual Studio 2005, open the Web site, select Solution Explorer, right-click the site, and select the new menu item "Add Web Deployment Project...". In the Add Web Deployment Project dialog, enter a name and location for the Web Deployment Project and click OK. The Web Deployment Project is an MSBuild file with an extension of .wdproj. To open this file, right-click it in Solution Explorer and select Open Project File. Toward the bottom of the file, you will find the following section:

```
<Target Name="BeforeBuild">
</Target>
```

By default, this section is commented out, so move it outside the commented region. Finally, you can add the GenerateResource build task to this section to compile the resources. GenerateResource is the MSBuild task that offers similar functionality to resgen.

Incorporating resgen into the Build Process in ASP.NET 1.1

Incorporating resgen into the ASP.NET 1.1 build process requires a little trickery with creating a Visual C++ project, but don't worry; there's no C++ involved in this process. Although this approach works equally well in Windows Forms application in both Visual Studio 2005 and Visual Studio 2003, I recommend using Visual Studio Build Events instead. To incorporate resgen into the build process for a solution, right-click the solution; select Add, New Project...; in Project Types, select Visual C++ Projects; in Templates, select Makefile Project; in Name, enter BuildResources (see Figure 12.2); and click OK.

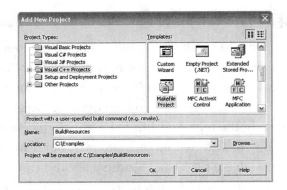

Figure 12.2   Add New Makefile Project in Visual Studio 2003

Click Finish to close the wizard. In Solution Explorer, you can delete the "Source Files", "Header Files", and "Resource Files" folders and readme.txt. Add a new text file to the project (right-click the BuildResources project; select Add, New Item...; select Text File (.txt); enter BuildResources.bat in the name; and click Open. In BuildResources.bat, add one of the following two commands, according to your version of Visual Studio:

```
call "C:\Program Files\Microsoft Visual Studio .NET 2003\SDK\
v1.1\Bin\resgen"
   C:\Inetpub\wwwroot\WebApplication1\Strings.resx
   C:\Inetpub\wwwroot\WebApplication1\bin\Strings.resources

call "C:\Program Files\Microsoft Visual Studio 8\SDK\
v2.0\Bin\resgen"
   C:\Inetpub\wwwroot\WebApplication1\Strings.resx
   C:\Inetpub\wwwroot\WebApplication1\bin\Strings.resources
```

Right-click the BuildResources project, select Properties, select NMake, and enter BuildResources.bat in the "Build Command Line" and "Rebuild All Command Line" (see Figure 12.3).

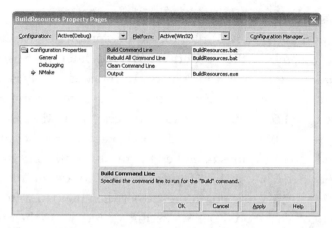

Figure 12.3   Specifying NMake Properties

Now, whenever you do a build in Visual Studio, this new make project will be built and `BuildResources.bat` will be executed, running resgen and building the resources files.

ResourceManager.CreateFileBasedResourceManager in Practice

So what the file-based resource manager gives us is the capability to read from `.resources` files instead of from an assembly. Unfortunately, there is a limitation to this approach, and that is that the `.resources` files are kept open after they have been read. This means that they cannot be updated until either the `ResourceManager.Release AllResources` method is called or the underlying `ResourceSets` get garbage collected. In a Web application, typically this means having to shut down the Web server; therefore, this file-based resource manager is impractical.

In addition to this limitation, another problem faces Windows Forms applications. Recall that when you set `Form.Localizable` to `true`, a new line of code is added to the `InitializeComponent` method to initialize a resource manager:

```
// Visual Studio 2003
System.Resources.ResourceManager resources = new
    System.Resources.ResourceManager(typeof(Form1));

// Visual Studio 2005
System.ComponentModel.ComponentResourceManager resources = new
    System.ComponentModel.ComponentResourceManager(typeof(Form1));
```

Clearly, this is initializing an assembly-based resource manager, not a file-based resource manager. There are two solutions to this problem. The first is to create a linked resource assembly; the second is covered later in this chapter in the `ResourceManagerProvider` section. A linked resource assembly is an assembly that contains links to stand-alone `.resources` file. The resource assemblies that we have seen and used so far all contain embedded resources; that is, the resources have been embedded in the assembly, and the stand-alone `.resources` files are not needed at runtime. A linked assembly doesn't embed the resource files, but instead references or "links" to them. See Chapter 14, "The Translator," for details of creating a linked assembly. Functionally, there is no difference between the two solutions, but it does solve the problem of Visual Studio hard-wiring a reference to the resource manager class. Now we can let Visual Studio write code to create a `ResourceManager/ComponentResourceManager` and have it use our linked assembly. The linked assembly still uses the stand-alone `.resources` files, but we haven't had to call the `ResourceManager.CreateFileBasedResourceManager` method to use them; therefore, Visual Studio's generated code still works. Unfortunately, using a linked resource assembly doesn't solve the problem that the resource manager still locks the `.resources` files.

ResourceManager Exposed

Before we write our custom resource managers, let's take a moment to explore how the `ResourceManager` class works internally. Armed with this knowledge, we will be better prepared to write our own resource managers. The following discussion refers equally to the `ComponentResourceManager`, as the `ComponentResourceManager` simply inherits from `ResourceManager` and adds just a single new method without modifying existing methods. See the subsequent section, "`ComponentResourceManager` Exposed," for details that are specific to the `ComponentResourceManager`.

The description of `ResourceManager` in this section is aimed at the .NET Framework 2.0. `ResourceManager` in .NET Framework 1.1 is almost identical to that of 2.0, with the exceptions that 1.1 has no concept of a resource fallback location other than the main assembly, and 2.0 includes marginally more stringent checking.

ResourceManager.GetString

Let's start our investigation from the point at which the application code wants to get a resource string. If you want to follow along very closely, you might like to decompile `ResourceManager.GetString` using Reflector (a .NET decompiler, http:// www. aisto.com/roeder/dotnet/), but this isn't necessary to understand how it works.

The `ResourceManager.GetString(string)` method calls `ResourceManager.GetString(string, CultureInfo)` and passes `null` for the `CultureInfo`. The pseudo code for this method is shown here:

```
default culture to CultureInfo.CurrentUICulture

get ResourceSet for the given culture from
ResourceManager.InternalGetResourceSet

if a ResourceSet is returned and ResourceSet.GetString returns
a string for the given key
    return the string

while (culture is not either invariant
culture or neutral resources language)
    change culture to the culture's parent

    get ResourceSet for the culture from
    ResourceManager.InternalGetResourceSet

    if the ResourceSet is null
        return null

    if ResourceSet.GetString returns a string for the given key
        return the string
end while

return null
```

`ResourceManager.InternalGetResourceSet` is called to get the `ResourceSet` for the given culture. A `ResourceSet` is a set of resource keys and values for a single culture for a single resource name. The `ResourceManager` keeps a list of resource sets that have been previously found, so the `ResourceManager` might have a list that includes resource sets for the "en-GB", "en", and invariant cultures. In practice, this list is unlikely to exceed more than three resource sets (i.e., the specific culture, the neutral culture, and the invariant culture) because most applications typically use only one language at a time.

If a `ResourceSet` is returned, the `ResourceSet.GetString(string, bool)` method is called to get the string for the given resource key name. If the returned string is not `null`, the string is returned from `ResourceManager.GetString`.

`ResourceManager.GetString` executes a `while` loop, checking that the culture is not either the invariant culture or the neutral resources culture (obtained from the `NeutralResourcesLanguageAttribute`). The culture is changed to the culture's parent. So if `ResourceManager.GetString` was passed a culture of "en-GB", then at this point, it would be checking a culture of "en". Similarly, if it was passed "en", then at this point, it would be checking the invariant culture (assuming that the `NeutralResourcesLanguageAttribute` wasn't "en"). So this loop keeps falling back through the culture hierarchy until it gets to either the invariant culture or the neutral resources language.

The loop executes a similar process as before, where it calls `Resource Manager.InternalGetResourceSet` to get a `ResourceSet` and calls `Resource Set.GetString` to get the string for the given resource key name. The only significant difference from the previous process is that if `ResourceManager.Internal-GetResourceSet` returns `null` for the `ResourceSet`, then `ResourceManager.GetString` returns `null`.

`ResourceManager.GetObject` is the exact same code as `ResourceManager.GetString`, with the sole exception that it calls `ResourceSet.GetObject` instead of `ResourceSet.GetString`.

ResourceManager.GetString Example

Suppose that we have a resource key name of "GoodMorning". In the invariant culture, we have given it the value of "Hi", in a small attempt to give the invariant culture as wide an audience as possible. In the English ("en") culture, we have given it the value of "Good Morning". In the English (United Kingdom) ("en-GB") culture, we have given it the value of "Chim chim cheroo, old chap" (which means "Good Morning"). Assume also that we have values for "GoodAfternoon" and "GoodEvening", so the complete resource listing is shown in Table 12.1.

Table 12.1 `ResourceManager.GetString` **Example Data**

Resource Key Name	Invariant	English	English (United Kingdom)
`GoodMorning`	Hi	Good Morning	Chim chim cheroo, old chap
`GoodAfternoon`	Hi	Good Afternoon	
`GoodEvening`	Hi		

If `CultureInfo.CurrentCulture` is "en-GB" and we call `Resource Manager.GetString("GoodMorning")`, the very first call to `ResourceManager.InternalGetResourceSet` gets the `ResourceSet` with the anglicized string that is returned immediately. If we call `ResourceManager.GetString("GoodAfternoon")`, the call to `ResourceManager.InternalGetResourceSet` gets a `ResourceSet` for "en-GB", but this `ResourceSet` doesn't have an entry for "GoodAfternoon", so it continues on to the `while` loop. The "parent" of "en-GB" is "en", so `Resource Manager.InternalGetResourceSet` returns a `ResourceSet` with two entries ("Good Morning" and "Good Afternoon"). The key is found and returned immediately. Finally, if we call `ResourceManager.GetString("GoodEvening")`, it gets as far as it did for "GoodAfternoon", but the "GoodEvening" key is not found in the "en" `ResourceSet`, so it goes around the `while` loop once more, getting the `ResourceSet` for the invariant culture (i.e., the parent of "en"), and returns "Hi".

ResourceManager Constructors

Before we get into the `InternalGetResourceSet` method, we need to set the scene and show how a few values used by `InternalGetResourceSet` get initialized. `ResourceManager` has three public constructors. All of these result in a resource manager that reads resources from an assembly, so I refer to these as "assembly" constructors. `ResourceManager` also has the static `CreateFileBasedResourceManager` method, which calls a private constructor to create a resource manager that reads resources from `.resources` files in a directory; I refer to this as a "file" constructor. The difference between these types of constructors is saved in two private Boolean fields called `UseManifest` and `UseSatelliteAssem`, which are `true` for the public constructors and `false` for the private constructor. As the `UseManifest` and `Use SatelliteAssem` fields are private and always hold the same values, I guess that there was once an intention to take this `ResourceManager` a little further, but it didn't happen or was undone. The `InternalGetResourceSet` method uses `UseManifest` and `UseSatelliteAssem` to determine where to initialize `ResourceSets` from.

The "assembly" constructors also set a protected `Assembly` field called `MainAssembly`. `MainAssembly` is the location of the resource. The following are two examples of invoking "assembly" constructors. The first explicitly passes an assembly that gets assigned to `MainAssembly`. The second passes a type in which the assembly that holds this type gets assigned to `MainAssembly`.

```
ResourceManager resourceManager =
    new ResourceManager("WindowsApplication1.Strings",
    Assembly.GetExecutingAssembly());

System.Resources.ResourceManager resources =
    new System.Resources.ResourceManager(typeof(Form1));
```

The "assembly" constructors also set a private `UltimateResourceFallback Location` field, `_fallbackLoc`, to `UltimateResourceFallbackLocation. MainAssembly`. This field can potentially be changed to `SatelliteAssembly` later in the `InternalGetResourceSet` method. The private `_fallbackLoc` field has a protected property wrapper called `FallbackLocation`.

The "`file`" constructor sets a private string field called "`moduleDir`" to the value passed for the path to the `.resources` files.

All of the constructors set a protected string field called `BaseNameField`, which is the name used to identify the resource without the culture suffix or resources extension. In the first example earlier, this would be "`WindowsApplication1.Strings`"; in the second example, it would be derived from the type and would be "`Windows-Application1.Form1`" (assuming that the application's namespace is "`Windows Application1`"). The constructors also set a protected `Hashtable` field called `ResourceSets`, which is a cache of `ResourceSets` that have been found and loaded. Finally, all of the constructors that accept a `Type` parameter for the `ResourceSet` type assign this value to a private `Type` field called `_userResourceSet`.

ResourceManager.InternalGetResourceSet

`InternalGetResourceSet` looks through its protected `ResourceSets Hashtable` for an entry for the given culture. If such an entry exists, it is returned. We cover the rest of this method in two stages: how it works for an assembly-based resource manager and how it works for a file-based resource manager.

Assembly-Based Resource Managers

The pseudo code for the assembly-based resource manager part of `Resource Manager.InternalGetResourceSet` is:

```
if _neutralResourcesCulture is null
    assign ResourceManager.GetNeutralResourcesLanguage to it
    set _fallbackLoc to fallback location specified in attribute

if the given culture is the neutral resources language culture
and the fallback location is the main assembly
    assign the invariant culture to the given culture

if the culture is the invariant culture
    if _fallbackLoc is Satellite
        assembly = GetSatelliteAssembly(neutral resources culture)
    else
        assembly = MainAssembly
else if TryLookingForSatellite(given culture)
    assembly = GetSatelliteAssembly(given culture)
else
    assembly = null

resource 'filename' = ResourceManager.GetResourceFileName

load a stream for the given resource 'filename'
using Assembly.GetManifestResourceStream

if this fails to load
    try loading the stream using
    ResourceManager.CaseInsensitiveManifestResourceStreamLookup

if the stream is not null
    create a ResourceSet from the stream using
    ResourceManager.CreateResourceSet

    add the ResourceSet to the Hashtable

    return the ResourceSet

return null
```

First, `InternalGetResourceSet` checks whether the private `CultureInfo` field, `_neutralResourcesCulture`, is `null` and, if it is, assigns to it the return result from `ResourceManager.GetNeutralResourcesLanguage`. The `GetNeutralResources Language` receives the `_fallbackLoc` field by reference, and if the assembly has a `NeutralResourcesLanguage` attribute and the `UltimateFallbackLocation` has been specified in the attribute, `_fallbackLoc` is set to the specified location (i.e., either `MainAssembly` or `Satellite`). This method reads the `NeutralResourc LanguageAttribute` from the main assembly. This is one of the reasons why resource managers created by `ResourceManager.CreateFileBasedResourceManager` do not respect the `NeutralResourceLanguageAttribute`. This is important if you intend to write custom resource managers because it means that, to mimic this behaviour, you need an assembly. Consequently, even if you don't intend to get resources from an assembly, you still need a reference to the assembly to get the attribute from.

If the culture passed to `InternalGetResourceSet` is the neutral resources language culture and the fallback location is the main assembly, the culture parameter is changed to be the invariant culture.

The next step is to determine which assembly the `ResourceManager` should use to find the resource. If the culture is the invariant culture, the assembly is found either from calling `GetSatelliteAssembly` or from the `MainAssembly` field, depending on whether the fallback location is `Satellite` or `MainAssembly`, respectively. `Get SatelliteAssembly` calls the internal `Assembly.InternalGetAssembly` method which is the same as the public `Assembly.GetSatelliteAssembly` method, except that it accepts a Boolean parameter indicating whether to throw an exception if the satellite assembly cannot be found. The `Assembly.GetSatelliteAssembly` method passes `true` for this parameter, whereas `ResourceManager.GetSatellite Assembly` passes `false`. (If you are having trouble loading a resource assembly that you know has the right name and is in the right place, you should examine this method; the resource assembly must have a name, location, public key, flags, and version that match the `MainAssembly`.) If the culture is not the invariant culture, it tries to look for a satellite assembly using the `TryLookingForSatellite` method. If a satellite assembly is not found, the assembly is assigned `null`.

Having decided upon the assembly, a "filename" is generated using `Resource Manager.GetResourceFileName`. The "filename" is a concatenation of the `Base NameField`, the culture name, and "resources", so if the culture is "en-GB", our earlier examples would be "`WindowsApplication1.Strings.en-GB.resources`" and "`WindowsApplication1.Form1.en-GB.resources`", respectively.

With the assembly loaded and a "filename" identified, `ResourceManager.InternalGetResourceSet` now loads the resource using `Assembly.GetManifestResource-Stream`. If this fails, it tries its own private `CaseInsensitiveManifestResourceStreamLookup` method.

If the stream is not `null` and the `createIfNotExists` parameter is `true` (which it always is when called from `ResourceManager`), it calls `ResourceManager.CreateResourceSet(Stream)` to create a `ResourceSet` from the stream, adds the `Resourc Set` to its `Hashtable`, and returns it. The `ResourceManager.CreateResourceSet` method respects the resource set type parameter, which can be passed to the `Resource-Manager` constructors, so if you specify this parameter, the resource set will be created using your resource set type. Unfortunately, and this is particularly relevant for the custom resource managers in this chapter, you cannot control the resource set creation process itself; if your resource set constructors accept different parameters to the `ResourceSet` constructors, you will not be able to use this mechanism.

File-Based Resource Managers

The pseudo code for the file-based resource manager part of `ResourceManager.InternalGetResourceSet` is:

```
assert unrestricted FileIOPermission

get the filename and path of the resource
using ResourceManager.FindResourceFile

if a file is found
    create a resource set from the file
    using ResourceManager.CreateResourceSet

    if there is not already an entry in the Hashtable for the culture
        add the ResourceSet to the Hashtable

    return the ResourceSet

if culture is the invariant culture
    throw an exception

get resource set from ResourceManager.InternalGetResourceSet
passing the culture's parent
```

```
if the resource set is not null and there is not already an
entry in the Hashtable for the culture
    add the ResourceSet to the Hashtable

    return the ResourceSet

return null
```

Fortunately, the `InternalGetResourceSet` method is a fair bit simpler for file-based resource managers. After asserting that it has unrestricted `FileIO Permission`, it calls `ResourceManager.FindResourceFile(CultureInfo)` to find the name and path of the resource file. `FindResourceFile` gets the name of the resources file using the `ResourceManager.GetResourceFileName` method discussed earlier and combines this name with the private `moduleDir` field set in the constructor. If the resulting file exists, the filename is returned; otherwise, `null` is returned.

If `FindResourceFile` returns a filename, it is loaded into a `ResourceSet` using `ResourceManager.CreateResourceSet(String)`. If there is not already an entry in the `Hashtable` for the culture, the `ResourceSet` is added to the `Hashtable` and returned to the caller.

If `FindResourceFile` returns a `null` and the `tryParents` parameter is `true` (which it always is when called from `ResourceManager`), it checks the culture. If it is the invariant culture, it throws an exception because there are no further cultures to check. If it isn't the invariant culture, it calls `InternalGetResourceSet` again with the culture's parent culture. Clearly, this will continue until either a resource file is found or we have worked our way back to the invariant culture and no resource file is found. The `NeutralResourcesLanguageAttribute` is never checked because no assembly information is passed to the `ResourceManager.CreateFileBasedResourceManager` method. This cycling through the parent cultures is, however, redundant because the `ResourceManager.GetString` method already does this. So what happens in practice is that `ResourceManager.GetString` calls `Internal GetResourceSet`, which cycles through the parents and either finds a resource set and returns it, or doesn't find a resource set and throws an exception. Either way, the steps that the `GetString` method performs to cycle through the parent cultures are not used for file-based resource managers.

ComponentResourceManager Exposed

The .NET Framework 1.1 and 2.0 both include the `System.ComponentModel.ComponentResourceManager` class. This class inherits from `ResourceManager` and adds the `ApplyResources` method used in Visual Studio 2005 Windows Forms applications. Although the class is available in the .NET Framework 1.1, Visual Studio 2003 never uses it. If you are writing Visual Studio 2005 Windows Forms applications, this section is for you.

As you know, the `ApplyResources` method uses reflection to assign all of the values in a resource to a component. To do this, it first reads all of the entries in the resource into a `SortedList` and then iterates through those entries, applying them to the given object. This section explains how it works.

The `ApplyResources` method has two overloads, in which the first calls the second and passes `null` for the `CultureInfo` parameter:

```
public void ApplyResources(object value, string objectName)

public virtual void ApplyResources(
    object value, string objectName, CultureInfo culture)
```

`ApplyResources` defaults the `CultureInfo` parameter to `CultureInfo.CurrentUICulture`. `ComponentResourceManager` has a private field called `ResourceSets`, which is a `Hashtable` of `SortedLists`. `ApplyResources` calls a private `FillResources` method to fill `ResourceSets` with data. Each entry in the `Hashtable` represents the complete "flattened" resources for a given culture for the resource. So if the culture is en-GB, for example, the `Hashtable` will contain one entry keyed on the en-GB `CultureInfo` object. The value of this entry will be a `SortedList` containing all of the resources from the fallback culture after the resources for the en culture and en-GB culture have been applied in succession. So if your form's `InitializeComponent` method calls `ApplyResources` for the `Button1` component, all of the resources for en-GB (and, therefore, the en and invariant cultures) for `Form1` will be loaded. Obviously, this is wasteful in the context of just a single component, but it is efficient if `ApplyResources` is subsequently called to initialize all of the other components on the form (which it is in `InitializeComponent`).

Having retrieved a suitable `SortedList` containing all of the flattened resources for the given culture, `ApplyResources` iterates through the entries in the `SortedList`. For each entry, it looks for a property of the given component that has the same name as the key and the same type as the value. So if the `objectName` passed to `ApplyResources` is "Button1" and the entry name is "Button1.Text", `ApplyResources` looks for a property of the given object called "Text" that is the same type as the value of the resource entry (i.e., almost certainly a string). It uses `TypeDescriptor.GetProperties` to find the property and checks its type using `PropertyDescriptor.PropertyType`. If a match is found, the value is assigned using `PropertyDescriptor.SetValue`.

The good news from the point of view of writing custom resource managers is that the `FillResources` method calls `GetResourceSet` to create and fill `Resource Sets`, and `GetResourceSet` calls `InternalGetResourceSet`, and this is the method that we override. So if you inherit from `ComponentResourceManager` and override its `InternalGetResourceSet` method, the `ApplyResources` method will behave correctly without any change.

Custom Resource Managers Examples

Before we embark on writing our first custom resource manager, you might like to look at the demo program in the source code for this book. The Custom Resource Managers Examples application (see Figure 12.4) enables you to experiment with the completed resource managers, and you may find this helpful in visualizing their operation and behavior.

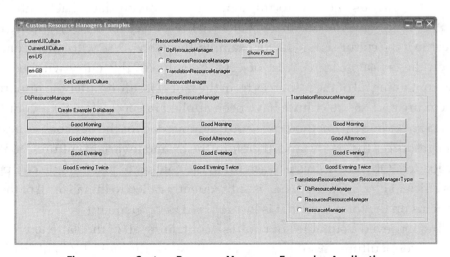

Figure 12.4   Custom Resource Managers Examples Application

To use the `DbResourceManager`, you first need to create the required SQL Server database and fill it with data. You can do this by clicking on the Create Example Database button. This creates the "`CustomResourceManagersExample`" database. You can verify that the resource manager is reading from the database by changing the contents of the `ResourceSets` table and observing the changes in the demo program. This is particularly effective when changing the entries for "`Form2`" (you can see `Form2` by clicking on the "Show Form2" button).

DbResourceManager

The first of our custom resource managers is a resource manager that loads resources from a database. We approach this resource manager in two stages: reading from the database and, later in this chapter, writing to the database. The second writing phase won't be necessary for everyone, so if you intend to maintain your resources database yourself, you can skip the writing stage.

The first decision that you need to make when writing any resource manager is which class to inherit from. If you intend your resource managers to be used in Visual Studio 2005 Windows Forms applications, you should inherit from `ComponentResourceManager` because it contains the vital `ApplyResources` method used by the `InitializeComponents` method. For all other scenarios, the `Component ResourceManager` offers nothing beyond `ResourceManager`; to avoid dragging in unnecessary baggage, you should inherit from `ResourceManager`. In this chapter, I have chosen to inherit from `ComponentResourceManager` only so that the resource managers have the broadest possible appeal, but feel free to change this decision.

The basic implementation of our `DbResourceManager` (missing one method, which we shall come to) can be seen here:

```
public class DbResourceManager: ComponentResourceManager
{
    private string baseNameField;
    private static string connectionString =
        "server=localhost;database=CustomResourceManagersExample;"+
        "trusted_connection=true";

    public static string ConnectionString
    {
        get {return connectionString;}
```

```
        set {connectionString = value;}
    }

    protected virtual void Initialize(
        string baseName, Assembly assembly)
    {
        this.baseNameField = baseName;
        ResourceSets = new Hashtable();
    }
    public DbResourceManager(string baseName, Assembly assembly)
    {
        Initialize(baseName, assembly);
    }
    public DbResourceManager(string baseName)
    {
        Initialize(baseName, null);
    }
    public DbResourceManager(Type resourceType)
    {
        Initialize(resourceType.Name, resourceType.Assembly);
    }
}
```

DbResourceManager inherits from ResourceManager. As there is no resource manager interface and no resource manager base class, we are forced to inherit from a working implementation of a resource manager. In this example, we want most of the ResourceManager methods intact, so this isn't so terrible. DbResourceManager has three constructors, which all call the protected Initialize method. These constructors match three of the ResourceManager constructors quite deliberately. I have taken the approach that the resource manager constructors should maintain as many common constructor signatures as possible. This commonality allows us to create a resource manager provider class later in this chapter. So even though the assembly parameter isn't used, it is still accepted. You might notice, though, that there is no constructor that allows us to pass a type for the resource set class. As the very purpose of this class is to change this type, it defeats the purpose of the class to pass this parameter.

The Initialize method assigns the baseName parameter to the private base-NameField field and initializes the protected ResourcesSets field (inherited from ResourceManager) to a Hashtable.

You can also see from this initial implementation that DbResourceManager has a private static string field called connectionString, which is exposed through a public static string property called ConnectionString. This is the connection string that is used to connect to the database. Strictly speaking, this should be a parameter passed to the `DbResourceManager` constructors, not a static property. If it were passed as a parameter and stored in an instance field, you would be able to have different resource managers that use different databases within the same application. I chose not to adopt this approach because (1) it would require a constructor signature that is specific to `DbResourceManager` and, therefore, would make it awkward to construct a `DbResourceManager` generically, and (2) I felt that it was unlikely that a single application would use two different resource databases simultaneously.

The only other method to implement is the `InternalGetResourceSet` method:

```
protected override ResourceSet InternalGetResourceSet(
    CultureInfo cultureInfo, bool createIfNotExists, bool tryParents)
{
    if (ResourceSets.Contains(cultureInfo.Name))
        return ResourceSets[cultureInfo.Name] as ResourceSet;
    else
    {
        DbResourceSet resourceSet =
            new DbResourceSet(baseNameField, cultureInfo);

        ResourceSets.Add(cultureInfo.Name, resourceSet);

        return resourceSet;
    }
}
```

This method looks in the `ResourceSets Hashtable` cache to see if a `Resource Set` has already been saved and, if it has, returns it. Otherwise, it creates a new `DbResourceSet` object, adds it to the cache, and returns that. The most obvious difference between this implementation and the `ResourceManager` implementation is that this implementation creates `DbResourceSet` objects, whereas the `Resource Manager` implementation, by default, creates `RuntimeResourceSet` (a subclass of `ResourceSet`) objects. Given that we know that `ResourceManager` has a constructor that accepts a `ResourceSet` type from which new resource sets can be created, you might wonder why we don't simply pass our `DbResourceSet` type to the constructor and save ourselves the trouble of overriding the `InternalGetResourceSet` method. The problem is that the `ResourceManager.InternalGetResourceSet` method performs both tasks of getting the resource stream and creating a new resource set. We don't want the `InternalGetResourceSet` method to get the resource stream, so we are forced to override it to prevent this from happening.

Note that there is no need in this class to override the `GetString` or `GetObject` methods, as they provide us with the functionality that we need.

The first implementation of our `DbResourceSet` looks like this:

```
public class DbResourceSet: ResourceSet
{
    public DbResourceSet(
        string baseNameField, CultureInfo cultureInfo):
        base(new DbResourceReader(baseNameField, cultureInfo))
    {
    }
}
```

We will be modifying this class later when we add write functionality. The constructor accepts the `baseNameField` and culture passed from the `InternalGet ResourceSet` method. The constructor calls the base class constructor and passes an `IResourceReader`, which is taken from the newly created `DbResourceReader` object. If you read through the `ResourceSet` documentation, you will find two methods, `GetDefaultReader` and `GetDefaultWriter`, which expect to be overridden and to return the `Type` of the resource reader and writer, respectively. I haven't implemented these yet because they aren't used anywhere in the .NET Framework. However, this is only to illustrate that they aren't necessary, and because you could consider this sloppy programming, I implement them in the second incarnation of this class.

The `DbResourceReader` looks like this:

```
public class DbResourceReader: IResourceReader
{
    private string baseNameField;
    private CultureInfo cultureInfo;

    public DbResourceReader(
        string baseNameField, CultureInfo cultureInfo)
    {
        this.baseNameField = baseNameField;
        this.cultureInfo = cultureInfo;
    }
    public System.Collections.IDictionaryEnumerator GetEnumerator()
    {
    }
    public void Close()
    {
    }
```

```
System.Collections.IEnumerator
    System.Collections.IEnumerable.GetEnumerator()
{
    return this.GetEnumerator();
}
public void Dispose()
{
}
}
```

The `DbResourceReader` implements the `IResourceReader` interface, which looks like this:

```
public interface IResourceReader : IEnumerable, IDisposable
{
    void Close();
    IDictionaryEnumerator GetEnumerator();
}
```

The `IResourceReader` interface allows a caller to get an enumerator for the resources and to close the resource when it is finished with it. Because these two operations are distinct, it allows the resource reader to keep the source open and to read from it as needed. This is exactly what the `ResourceEnumerator` returned from `ResourceReader.GetEnumerator` does. This is why `.resources` files are kept open by file-based resource managers. In our database implementation, it doesn't make sense to read the resource item by item, so we have no implementation for the `Close` method. The `DbResourceReader.GetEnumerator` method looks like this:

```
public System.Collections.IDictionaryEnumerator GetEnumerator()
{
    Hashtable hashTable = new Hashtable();
    using(SqlConnection connection =
      new SqlConnection(DbResourceManager.ConnectionString));
    {
        connection.Open();
        using (SqlCommand command = GetSelectCommand(connection))
        {
            SqlDataReader dataReader = command.ExecuteReader();
            while (dataReader.Read())
            {
                object resourceValue =
                    dataReader["ResourceValue"].ToString();
                object resourceType = dataReader["ResourceType"];
```

```
            if (resourceType != null &&
                resourceType.ToString() != String.Empty &&
                resourceType.ToString() != "System.String")
                resourceValue = GetResourceValue((string)
                    resourceValue, resourceType.ToString());

            hashTable.Add(dataReader["ResourceName"].ToString(),
                resourceValue);
        }
        dataReader.Close();
    }
}
return hashTable.GetEnumerator();
}
```

We create a `Hashtable` to hold the resource retrieved from the database. We do this so that we can close the connection (or at least return it to the connection pool). Of course, this approach is wasteful if you use a resource manager to retrieve a single string and then discard the resource manager, but hopefully your resource managers are used for retrieving multiple resource values.

We create a new connection passing the static `DbResourceManager.ConnectionString`. I have chosen to hard-wire the references to `SqlClient` classes in this example so that it is simple to read and work with all versions of the .NET Framework. If you are using .NET Framework 2.0, you might like to replace these classes with appropriate calls to `DbProviderFactory` methods.

The `DbResourceReader.GetEnumerator` method simply opens a connection; creates a data reader; enumerates through the result set, adding the entries to the local `Hashtable`; closes the connection; and returns the `Hashtable`'s enumerator. The `GetResourceValue` method is responsible for converting the resource's value from a string to the appropriate primitive, enum, struct, or class, according to the resource's type:

```
protected virtual object GetResourceValue(
    string resourceValue, string resourceTypeName)
{
    string className = resourceTypeName.Split(',')[0];
    string assemblyName =
        resourceTypeName.Substring(className.Length + 2);
    Assembly assembly = Assembly.Load(assemblyName);
    Type resourceType = assembly.GetType(className, true, true);
    if (resourceType.IsPrimitive)
```

```
        return Convert.ChangeType(resourceValue, resourceType);
    else if (resourceType.IsEnum)
        return Enum.Parse(resourceType, resourceValue, true);
    else
    {
        // the type is a struct or a class
        object[] parameterValues =
            StringToParameterValues(resourceValue);

        return Activator.CreateInstance(
            resourceType, parameterValues);
    }
}
```

So, for example, if the resourceTypeName is "System.Drawing.Content
Alignment, System.Drawing, Version=1.0.5000.0, Culture=neutral,
PublicKeyToken=b03f5f7f11d50a3a", then the className would be "Sys-
tem.Drawing.ContentAlignment" and the assemblyName would be "System
.Drawing, Version=1.0.5000.0, Culture=neutral, PublicKeyToken=
b03f5f7f11d50a3a". The Type, resourceType, would be loaded from the assembly, and resourceType.IsEnum would be true. The string value would then be
converted to the ContentAlignment enum using Enum.Parse.

The GetSelectCommand method is:

```
public virtual SqlCommand GetSelectCommand(SqlConnection connection)
{
    SqlCommand command;
    if (cultureInfo.Equals(CultureInfo.InvariantCulture))
    {
        string commandText =
            "SELECT ResourceName, ResourceValue, ResourceType "+
            "FROM ResourceSets WHERE ResourceSetName=" +
            "@resourceSetName AND Culture IS NULL";

        command = new SqlCommand(commandText, connection);
        command.Parameters.Add("@resourceSetName",
            SqlDbType.VarChar, 100).Value = baseNameField;
    }
    else
    {
        string commandText =
            "SELECT ResourceName, ResourceValue, ResourceType "+
            "FROM ResourceSets WHERE ResourceSetName=" +
            "@resourceSetName AND Culture=@culture";
```

```
        command = new SqlCommand(commandText, connection);
        command.Parameters.Add("@resourceSetName",
            SqlDbType.VarChar, 100).Value = baseNameField;
        command.Parameters.Add("@culture",
            SqlDbType.VarChar, 20).Value = cultureInfo.ToString();
    }
    return command;
}
```

We create a command to retrieve the resources from the database. The command string will be one of the following values, depending on whether a culture is passed:

```
SELECT ResourceName, ResourceValue, ResourceType FROM ResourceSets
WHERE ResourceSetName=@resourceSetName AND Culture IS NULL

SELECT ResourceName, ResourceValue, ResourceType FROM ResourceSets
WHERE ResourceSetName=@resourceSetName AND Culture=@culture
```

The SQL Server `ResourceSets` table is created from:

```
CREATE TABLE [ResourceSets] (
[ResourceID]         [int] IDENTITY (1, 1) NOT NULL ,
[ResourceSetName]    [varchar] (50) NOT NULL ,
[Culture]            [varchar] (10) NULL ,
[ResourceName]       [varchar] (100) NOT NULL ,
[ResourceValue]      [varchar] (200) NOT NULL ,
[ResourceType]       [varchar] (250) ,
CONSTRAINT [PK_ResourceSets] PRIMARY KEY CLUSTERED
([ResourceID]) ON [PRIMARY]
) ON [PRIMARY]
```

Figure 12.5 shows the `ResourceSets` table filled with the example data.

Figure 12.5   ResourceSets Table with Example Data

The SELECT statement simply retrieves ResourceName and ResourceValue fields for the given culture and the given resource set name. If the ResourceSetName is "CustomResourceManagersExample.Greetings" and the Culture is "en", the result set is shown in the following table.

ResourceName	ResourceValue
GoodMorning	Good Morning
GoodAfternoon	Good Afternoon

And voilà—you have a read-only database resource manager.

One downside of the DbResourceManager that you should consider is that you must decide what you should do if the resource database is unavailable. How will you report an error to the user if the text for the error is in the database that you have failed to connect to? One solution is to extend the DbResourceManager to have a fallback resource manager (preferably an assembly-based resource manager) that it could fall back to for failures in the resource manager itself.

ResourcesResourceManager and ResXResourceManager

The ResourcesResourceManager and the ResXResourceManager allow resources to be read from stand-alone .resources and .resx files, respectively. In this respect, they offer the same functionality as the ResourceManager.CreateFile BasedResourceManager method, with the exceptions that ResXResourceManager reads resx files and, more important, both resource managers read resources in their entirety into memory and, therefore, do not keep locks on the files. As such, these resource managers offer you another strategy for translating your application:

You can ship a version of your application that uses the `ResourcesResource Manager` or `ResXResourceManager` to the translator. The translator can update resources/resx files using whatever utilities you provide. The translator can immediately see the changes in the application without having to return these changes to the developers. When the translator is satisfied with the translations, the translator can ship the translated resources/resx files back to the developers, who can build a satellite assembly from the result. Everyone wins. The translator gets immediate feedback on their work, developers get to package their resources more neatly into satellite assemblies for the release version, and the users do not suffer the performance hit of a "slower" resource manager.

> It would be entirely possible to extend the `ResourcesResource Manager` class to understand `.txt` resource files or, indeed, resource files of any format. I haven't done this here, for two reasons. First, the .NET Framework doesn't include resource readers and resource writers for `.txt` files (even ResGen has its own custom code for reading `.txt` resource files). Second, I don't see a great value in supporting `.txt` files when the XML `.resx` files offer a superior text format.

The `ResourcesResourceManager` includes the whole functionality for both resource managers. The `ResXResourceManager` simply inherits from `Resource ResourceManager` and sets an "extension" field. The `ResourcesResourceManager` class is almost identical to the `DbResourceManager` class, with the following differences:

- The `ResourcesResourceManager` doesn't have a `connectionString` field or `ConnectionString` property.

- The `ResourcesResourceManager` has a private string field called `extension`, which is initialized to "`resources`".

- The `ResourcesResourceManager.InternalGetResourceSet` method creates a `ResourcesResourceSet` object instead of a `DbResourceSet` object, and passes a third parameter to the constructor—namely, the extension field.

The `ResourcesResourceSet` class is equally as simple as the `DbResourceSet` class:

```
public class ResourcesResourceSet: CustomResourceSet
{
    public ResourcesResourceSet(string baseNameField,
        CultureInfo cultureInfo, string extension):
        base(new ResourcesResourceReader(
        baseNameField, cultureInfo, extension))
    {
    }
}
```

As before with the `DbResourceSet` class, we could implement the `GetDefault Reader` and `GetDefaultWriter` methods, but as it isn't necessary for our purposes, I leave this until later.

The `ResourcesResourceReader` class also follows the blueprint laid down by the `DbResourceReader` class. Here is the `ResourcesResourceReader` class (without the `GetEnumerator` method):

```
public class ResourcesResourceReader: IResourceReader
{
    private string baseNameField;
    private CultureInfo cultureInfo;
    private string extension;

    public ResourcesResourceReader(string baseNameField,
        CultureInfo cultureInfo, string extension)
    {
        this.baseNameField = baseNameField;
        this.cultureInfo = cultureInfo;
        this.extension = extension;
    }
    protected virtual string GetResourceFileName()
    {
        if (cultureInfo.Equals(CultureInfo.InvariantCulture))
            return baseNameField + "." + extension;
        else
            return baseNameField + "." +
                cultureInfo.Name + "." + extension;
    }
    protected virtual IResourceReader GetResourceReader(
        string fileName)
    {
        if (extension == "resx")
```

```
            return new ResXResourceReader(fileName);
        else if (extension == "resources")
            return new ResourceReader(GetResourceFileName());
        else
            throw new ArgumentException(String.Format(
                "Unknown resource extension ({0})", extension));
    }
    public void Close()
    {
    }
    System.Collections.IEnumerator
        System.Collections.IEnumerable.GetEnumerator()
    {
        return this.GetEnumerator();
    }
    public void Dispose()
    {
    }
}
```

The constructor assigns the base name, culture, and extension to their respective private fields. The `GetResourceFileName` method returns the filename for the resource. The filename is constructed from the base name, culture, and extension, so in our earlier example, the name would be "`CustomResourceManagers Example.Greetings.resources`" for the invariant culture when the extension is "`resources`" and "`CustomResourceManagersExample.Greetings.en-GB .resx`" for the "en-GB" culture when the extension is "resx".

Unlike the `ResourceManager.CreateFileBasedResourceManager` method, I have assumed that the resource files are in the executable's working directory. If this doesn't follow your implementation, you can modify the `GetResourceFileName` method to support your model.

The `GetResourceReader` method gets an `IResourceReader` for the given file based upon the extension. If you wanted to support extensions other than `.resources` and `.resx`, you would modify the `GetResourceFileName` and `Get ResourceReader` methods. The `GetEnumerator` method is:

```
public System.Collections.IDictionaryEnumerator GetEnumerator()
{
    Hashtable hashTable = new Hashtable();
    string fileName = GetResourceFileName();
    if (File.Exists(fileName))
    {
```

```
        IResourceReader reader = GetResourceReader(fileName);
        try
        {
            IDictionaryEnumerator enumerator =
                reader.GetEnumerator();
            while (enumerator.MoveNext())
            {
                hashTable.Add(enumerator.Key, enumerator.Value);
            }
        }
        finally
        {
            reader.Close();
        }
    }
    return hashTable.GetEnumerator();
}
```

This simple method gets the resource filename and, if the resource file exists, gets an `IResourceReader` to read the resource file and enumerates through the whole resource, loading all the items into a `Hashtable`. Herein lies the difference between this implementation and the file-based `ResourceManager` implementation: The resource is read in its entirety and then closed, whereas the `ResourceManager` class reads the resource as necessary and leaves it open. In exchange for this improved functionality, you may take a performance hit, depending upon whether your resource managers get reused often or are created and disposed of frequently.

The `ResXResourceManager` class simply uses all of the functionality offered in the `ResourcesResourceManager` class and changes the extension to "resx":

```
public class ResXResourceManager: ResourcesResourceManager
{
    protected override void Initialize(
        string baseName, Assembly assembly)
    {
        Extension = "resx";
        base.Initialize(baseName, assembly);
    }
    public ResXResourceManager(string baseName, Assembly assembly):
        base(baseName, assembly)
    {
    }
    public ResXResourceManager(string baseName): base(baseName)
    {
    }
```

```
    public ResXResourceManager(Type resourceType) : base(resourceType)
    {
    }
}
```

Writeable Resource Managers

The custom resource managers that we have looked at so far read resources but have no capability for writing to resources. This solution is adequate if you intend to maintain the resources yourself. However, the next custom resource manager is the `TranslationResourceManager`. This resource manager performs translations on-the-fly for missing resources and needs to write back these translations to the original source. To do this our resource managers must have a write capability, and that's what this section is about.

Our first attempts at the `DbResourceSet` and `ResourcesResourceSet` classes were minimalist, to say the least. The solution to the problem of writing to resources lies in modifying these classes. In the previous discussion, I briefly mentioned that `ResourceSet` has two methods, `GetDefaultReader` and `GetDefaultWriter`, which allow us to specify which `Types` are used to create reader and writer objects for the resource. These are implemented as follows:

```
public override Type GetDefaultReader()
{
    return typeof(DbResourceReader);
}
public override Type GetDefaultWriter()
{
    return typeof(DbResourceWriter);
}
```

Unfortunately, these methods do not help us solve our problem. Nothing in the .NET Framework ever calls these methods. They exist solely to provide a means to allow generic code to create readers and writers as necessary. Certainly, this is what we want to do, but this approach isn't sufficient for our purposes. The problem with simply specifying a `Type` to create a new object from is that you are at the mercy of the caller to call the constructor signature that you want called. The following generic code illustrates the problem:

```
ResourceSet resourceSet = new ResourceSet(fileName);

Type resourceReaderType = resourceSet.GetDefaultReader();

IResourceReader resourceReader = (IResourceReader)
    Activator.CreateInstance(resourceReaderType,
    new object[] {fileName});
```

In this example, a new `IResourceReader` is being created from the resource reader type using `Activator.CreateInstance`. The generic code has determined that it will use the resource reader constructor, which accepts a single string parameter. Both of the `IResourceReader` classes that we have implemented so far (`DbResourceReader` and `ResourcesResourceReader`) do not support this constructor. Furthermore, they do not share a common constructor signature at all:

```
public DbResourceReader(
    string baseNameField, CultureInfo cultureInfo)

public ResourcesResourceReader(string baseNameField,
    CultureInfo cultureInfo, string extension)
```

It is for this reason that I have implemented a slightly more versatile solution. Both `ResourceSet` classes now inherit from a new class, `CustomResourceSet`:

```
public class CustomResourceSet: ResourceSet
{
    public CustomResourceSet(IResourceReader resourceReader):
        base(resourceReader)
    {
    }
    public virtual IResourceReader CreateDefaultReader()
    {
        Type resourceReaderType = GetDefaultReader();
        return (IResourceReader)
            Activator.CreateInstance(resourceReaderType);
    }
    public virtual IResourceWriter CreateDefaultWriter()
    {
        Type resourceWriterType = GetDefaultWriter();
        return (IResourceWriter)
            Activator.CreateInstance(resourceWriterType);
    }
    public virtual void Add(string key, object value)
    {
```

```
        Table.Add(key, value);
    }
    public new Hashtable Table
    {
        get {return base.Table;}
    }
}
```

CustomResourceSet implements two new methods: CreateDefaultReader and CreateDefaultWriter. These methods can be overridden by subclasses to create IResourceReader and IResourceWriter objects using whatever constructor the developer sees fit. You can also see a new method, Add, and a public property, Table, which we return to later. The DbResourceSet now becomes:

```
public class DbResourceSet: CustomResourceSet
{
    private string baseNameField;
    private CultureInfo cultureInfo;

    public DbResourceSet(
        string baseNameField, CultureInfo cultureInfo):
        base(new DbResourceReader(baseNameField, cultureInfo))
    {
        this.baseNameField = baseNameField;
        this.cultureInfo = cultureInfo;
    }
    public override Type GetDefaultReader()
    {
        return typeof(DbResourceReader);
    }
    public override Type GetDefaultWriter()
    {
        return typeof(DbResourceWriter);
    }
    public override IResourceReader CreateDefaultReader()
    {
        return new DbResourceReader(baseNameField, cultureInfo);
    }
    public override IResourceWriter CreateDefaultWriter()
    {
        return new DbResourceWriter(baseNameField, cultureInfo);
    }
}
```

The `DbResourceSet` constructor works as it did before, creating a new `DbResourceReader` object. In addition, it saves the parameters passed to two private fields. The `CreateDefaultReader` and `CreateDefaultWriter` methods are overridden, and the base name field and culture are passed to the `DbResourceReader` and `DbResourceWriter` constructors. The `GetDefaultReader` and `GetDefaultWriter` methods are redundant, but I have implemented them anyway for completeness. All that remains for the `DbResourceSet` class now is for us to implement the new `DbResourceWriter` class.

DbResourceWriter

`DbResourceWriter` is an implementation of the `IResourceWriter` interface:

```
public interface IResourceWriter : IDisposable
{
    void AddResource(string name, object value);
    void AddResource(string name, string value);
    void AddResource(string name, byte[] value);
    void Close();
    void Generate();
}
```

A consumer of this interface simply calls the various `AddResource` methods adding string, object, or byte[] resources. It then calls `Generate` to create the resource and finally `Close` to close the resource. You can approach this interface in one of two ways:

- You can write the resources to the target with every call to `AddResource`, and then either commit the changes when `Generate` is called or roll them back if `Close` is called without a `Generate`.

- Alternatively, you can collect all of the resources added using `AddResource` in a cache and write the resource in its entirety in the `Generate` method.

I have chosen the latter approach because we will need to open a connection to the database, and I want the connection to be open for as short a duration as possible. The `DbResourceWriter` class (without the `Generate` method) is:

```csharp
public class DbResourceWriter: IResourceWriter
{
    private string baseNameField;
    private CultureInfo cultureInfo;
    private SortedList resourceList;

    public DbResourceWriter(
        string baseNameField, CultureInfo cultureInfo)
    {
        this.baseNameField = baseNameField;
        this.cultureInfo = cultureInfo;
        resourceList = new SortedList();
    }
    public void Close()
    {
        Dispose(true);
    }
    public void Dispose()
    {
        Dispose(true);
    }
    private void Dispose(bool disposing)
    {
        if (disposing && resourceList != null)
            Generate();
    }
    public void AddResource(string name, object value)
    {
        if (name == null)
            throw new ArgumentNullException("name");
        if (resourceList == null)
            throw new InvalidOperationException(
                "InvalidOperation_ResourceWriterSaved");

        resourceList.Add(name, value);
    }
    public void AddResource(string name, string value)
    {
        AddResource(name, (Object) value);
    }
    public void AddResource(string name, byte[] value)
    {
        AddResource(name, (Object) value);
    }
}
```

The DbResourceWriter simply assigns the incoming base name and culture parameters to private fields and initializes a resourceList private field to a SortedList. The resourceList is a temporary bucket into which all of the resources are added until the Generate method is called.

As the name implies, the Generate method is responsible for generating the resource. In the case of the .NET Framework ResourceWriter and ResX ResourceWriter classes, this means writing a new .resources or .resx file. The new file overwrites the old file. In the case of a database, this means deleting all of the existing resource entries for the given resource name and inserting a new row for each resource key.

```
public void Generate()
{
    if (resourceList == null)
        throw new InvalidOperationException(
            "InvalidOperation_ResourceWriterSaved");

    using (SqlConnection connection =
        new SqlConnection(DbResourceManager.ConnectionString))
    {
        connection.Open();
        SqlTransaction transaction = connection.BeginTransaction();
        try
        {
            DeleteExistingResource(transaction);
            foreach(DictionaryEntry dictionaryEntry in resourceList)
            {
                if (dictionaryEntry.Value != null)
                    InsertResource(transaction,
                        dictionaryEntry.Key.ToString(),
                        dictionaryEntry.Value);
            }
            transaction.Commit();
        }
        catch
        {
            transaction.Rollback();
            throw;
        }
    }
    resourceList = null;
}
```

The Generate method opens a connection, creates a transaction, deletes all of the existing resources, and, for each resource that has been added to resourceList, inserts a new row into the database. Finally, the transaction is either committed or rolled back, and the connection is closed.

DbResourceManager.DeleteExistingResource and DbResourceManager. InsertResource are:

```
protected virtual void DeleteExistingResource(
    SqlTransaction transaction)
{
    // delete all of the existing resource values
    if (cultureInfo.Equals(CultureInfo.InvariantCulture))
    {
        string deleteCommandText =
            "DELETE FROM ResourceSets WHERE ResourceSetName="+
            "@resourceSetName AND Culture IS NULL";

        using (SqlCommand deleteCommand = new SqlCommand(
            deleteCommandText, transaction.Connection, transaction))
        {
            deleteCommand.Parameters.Add("@resourceSetName",
                SqlDbType.VarChar, 100).Value = baseNameField;
            deleteCommand.ExecuteNonQuery();
        }
    }
    else
    {
        string deleteCommandText =
            "DELETE FROM ResourceSets WHERE ResourceSetName="+
            "@resourceSetName AND Culture=@culture";

        using (SqlCommand deleteCommand = new SqlCommand(
            deleteCommandText, transaction.Connection, transaction))
        {
            deleteCommand.Parameters.Add("@resourceSetName",
                SqlDbType.VarChar, 100).Value = baseNameField;
            deleteCommand.Parameters.Add("@culture",
                SqlDbType.VarChar, 20).Value =
                cultureInfo.ToString();
            deleteCommand.ExecuteNonQuery();
        }
    }
}

protected virtual void InsertResource(SqlTransaction transaction,
    string resourceName, object resourceValue)
```

```
{
    string insertCommandText;
    if (cultureInfo.Equals(CultureInfo.InvariantCulture))
    {
        if (resourceValue is System.String)
            insertCommandText = "INSERT INTO ResourceSets "+
                "(ResourceSetName, ResourceName, "+
                "ResourceValue) VALUES (@resourceSetName, "+
                "@resourceName, @resourceValue)";
        else
            insertCommandText = "INSERT INTO ResourceSets "+
                "(ResourceSetName, ResourceName, "+
                "ResourceValue, ResourceType) VALUES "+
                "(@resourceSetName, @resourceName, "+
                "@resourceValue, @resourceType)";
    }
    else
    {
        if (resourceValue is System.String)
            insertCommandText = "INSERT INTO ResourceSets "+
                "(ResourceSetName, Culture, ResourceName, "+
                "ResourceValue) VALUES (@resourceSetName, "+
                "@culture, @resourceName, @resourceValue)";
        else
            insertCommandText = "INSERT INTO ResourceSets "+
                "(ResourceSetName, Culture, ResourceName, "+
                "ResourceValue, ResourceType) VALUES "+
                "(@resourceSetName, @culture, @resourceName, "+
                "@resourceValue, @resourceType)";
    }

    using (SqlCommand insertCommand = new SqlCommand(
        insertCommandText, transaction.Connection, transaction))
    {
        insertCommand.Parameters.Add(new SqlParameter(
            "@resourceSetName", baseNameField));

        if (! cultureInfo.Equals(CultureInfo.InvariantCulture))
            insertCommand.Parameters.Add(new SqlParameter(
                "@culture", cultureInfo.ToString()));

        insertCommand.Parameters.Add(new SqlParameter(
            "@resourceName", resourceName));

        insertCommand.Parameters.Add(new SqlParameter(
            "@resourceValue", resourceValue.ToString()));

        if (! (resourceValue is System.String))
```

```
        insertCommand.Parameters.Add(new SqlParameter(
            "@resourceType",
            resourceValue.GetType().AssemblyQualifiedName));

    insertCommand.ExecuteNonQuery();
    }
}
```

Writeable ResourcesResourceManager

Writing to .resources and .resx files is a fair bit easier than writing to a database, as the necessary classes (ResourceWriter and ResXResourceWriter) are part of the .NET Framework. All that we have to do is use them. The revised Resources ResourceSet class follows the same pattern as the DbResourceSet class:

```
public class ResourcesResourceSet: CustomResourceSet
{
    private string baseNameField;
    private CultureInfo cultureInfo;
    private string extension;

    public ResourcesResourceSet(string baseNameField,
        CultureInfo cultureInfo, string extension):
        base(new ResourcesResourceReader(
        baseNameField, cultureInfo, extension))
    {
        this.baseNameField = baseNameField;
        this.cultureInfo = cultureInfo;
        this.extension = extension;
    }
    public override Type GetDefaultReader()
    {
        return typeof(ResourcesResourceReader);
    }
    public override Type GetDefaultWriter()
    {
        if (extension == "resx")
            return typeof(ResXResourceWriter);
        else if (extension == "resources")
            return typeof(ResourceWriter);
        else
            throw new ArgumentException(String.Format(
                "Unknown resource extension ({0})", extension));
    }
```

```
    public override IResourceReader CreateDefaultReader()
    {
        return new ResourcesResourceReader(
            baseNameField, cultureInfo, extension);
    }
    protected virtual string GetResourceFileName()
    {
        if (cultureInfo.Equals(CultureInfo.InvariantCulture))
            return baseNameField + "." + extension;
        else
            return baseNameField + "." +
                cultureInfo.Name + "." + extension;
    }
    public override IResourceWriter CreateDefaultWriter()
    {
        if (extension == "resx")
            return new ResXResourceWriter(GetResourceFileName());
        else if (extension == "resources")
            return new ResourceWriter(GetResourceFileName());
        else
            throw new ArgumentException(String.Format(
                "Unknown resource extension ({0})", extension));
    }
}
```

Once again, the parameters passed to the constructor are saved in private fields. The GetDefaultReader, GetDefaultWriter, CreateDefaultReader, and Create DefaultWriter methods all check the extension private field and use ResourceReader/ResourceWriter or ResXResourceReader/ResXResource Writer classes, as necessary, or throw an exception for an unknown extension.

TranslationResourceManager

The resource managers that we have encountered so far all assume that the content of the application is static enough that there is time to have it translated. Whereas this will be true for many applications, it is not true for all applications. Web sites with dynamic, rapidly changing content may need a different approach. Enter the TranslationResourceManager. The TranslationResourceManager acts as a proxy for another resource manager. It accepts incoming GetString requests and forwards them to an internal resource manager to fulfill the request. If, however, the internal resource manager is unable to fulfill the request, the `TranslationRe-sourceManager` steps in to translate the string on-the-fly. The `TranslationRe-sourceManager` can optionally write back the translated string to the source of the resource, ensuring that subsequent requests (from any user) do not suffer the performance hit of translating the string. In this way, the `TranslationResourceManager` can "learn" translations. The actual translation process is performed by the `Translation` engine that we wrote in Chapter 9, and its translator classes use hard-coded algorithms or Web services, as necessary, to perform the translations.

> Before we get too excited about machine translation, the same caveats about its accuracy compared to the accuracy of human translation that were mentioned in Chapter 9 still apply.

So the important point to grasp here is that the `TranslationResourceManager` is only a conduit or a filter. It accepts requests and passes them through to another resource manager to actually do the work. It steps in only when the other resource manager cannot fulfill the request. To implement this, we need some way of getting this "internal" resource manager. You could pass this resource manager as a parameter to the `TranslationResourceManager` constructor. This would be a flexible solution and would relieve the `TranslationResourceManager` from the responsibility of this problem. I decided against this approach, for two reasons: (1) It seems unlikely to me that a single application would use different resource manager classes within the same application, so the capability to use an internal `DbResource Manager` class in one instance and a `ResourcesResourceManager` in the next is not useful, and (2) this would require a nonstandard constructor. For reasons that will become apparent in the section on the `ResourceManagerProvider` class, using a nonstandard constructor must be avoided. So the implementation uses a public static `Type` property. The consumer of the `TranslationResourceManager` specifies the resource manager `Type` at the beginning of the application:

```
TranslationResourceManager.ResourceManagerType =
    typeof(DbResourceManager);
```

From here on, the `TranslationResourceManager` creates `DbResourceManager` objects for reading and writing the resources. We also need to provide the `TranslationResourceManager` with a `TranslatorCollection` (a collection of `ITranslator` objects). You might like to refer back to Chapter 9 for a recap of the `Translator Collection` class. We provide this collection by assigning the collection to the `TranslationResourceManager`'s public static `Translators` property:

```
TranslationResourceManager.Translators = new TranslatorCollection();

TranslationResourceManager.Translators.Add(
    new PseudoTranslator());

TranslationResourceManager.Translators.Add(
    new Office2003ResearchServicesTranslator());

TranslationResourceManager.Translators.Add(
    new WebServiceXTranslator());

TranslationResourceManager.Translators.Add(
    new CloserFarTranslator());
```

This code adds a Pseudo Translator (to provide a pseudo English translation), an Office 2003 Research Services translator (to provide translations to and from numerous languages), a WebServiceX translation (to provide translation for Latin languages, Chinese, Japanese, and Korean), and a `CloserFar` translation (to provide translation to Arabic).

The `TranslationResourceManager` inherits from a `SurrogateResource Manager`, which provides the functionality of passing requests through to the "workhorse" resource manager:

```
public class SurrogateResourceManager: ComponentResourceManager
{
    private static Type resourceManagerType;
    private ResourceManager resourceManager;
    private string baseName;

    protected virtual void Initialize(
        string baseName, Assembly assembly)
    {
        if (resourceManagerType == null)
            throw new ArgumentException(
                "SurrogateResourceManager.ResourceManagerType "+
```

```
                "is null");

        this.baseName = baseName;
        MainAssembly = assembly;
        resourceManager = CreateResourceManager(baseName, assembly);
    }
    public SurrogateResourceManager(
        string baseName, Assembly assembly)
    {
        Initialize(baseName, assembly);
    }
    public SurrogateResourceManager(string baseName)
    {
        Initialize(baseName, null);
    }
    public SurrogateResourceManager(Type resourceType)
    {
        Initialize(resourceType.FullName, resourceType.Assembly);
    }
    public static Type ResourceManagerType
    {
        get {return resourceManagerType;}
        set {resourceManagerType = value;}
    }
    protected ResourceManager ResourceManager
    {
        get {return resourceManager;}
    }
    protected virtual ResourceManager CreateResourceManager(
        string baseName, Assembly assembly)
    {
        try
        {
            return (ResourceManager) Activator.CreateInstance(
                resourceManagerType,
                new object[] {baseName, assembly});
        }
        catch (TargetInvocationException exception)
        {
            throw exception.InnerException;
        }
    }
    public override object GetObject(
        string name, System.Globalization.CultureInfo culture)
    {
        return resourceManager.GetObject(name, culture);
    }
    public override ResourceSet GetResourceSet(
```

```
        CultureInfo culture, bool createIfNotExists, bool tryParents)
    {
        return resourceManager.GetResourceSet(
            culture, createIfNotExists, tryParents);
    }
    public override string GetString(
        string name, System.Globalization.CultureInfo culture)
    {
        return resourceManager.GetString(name, culture);
    }
}
```

The `Initialize` method is called by all of the constructors and calls `Create ResourceManager` to create a new resource manager from the `resourceManager Type`. `CreateResourceManager` makes the assumption that all resource managers support a constructor that accepts a string and an assembly. This is one of the reasons why the `DbResourceManager` and `ResourcesResourceManager` classes used static properties to allow nonstandard parameters to be set—to ensure that the class constructors could be called generically.

Before we move on, notice the `GetObject`, `GetString`, and `GetResourceSet` methods. These methods simply call the corresponding methods on the internal resource manager. These are the simplest examples of passing requests on to the internal resource manager. Because the `TranslationResourceManager` is concerned only with translating strings, the `GetObject` and `GetResourceSet` methods can be inherited as-is, and only the `GetString` method needs to be overridden.

Now that all of the infrastructure is in place, we can take a look at the initial implementation of the `TranslationResourceManager`:

```
public class TranslationResourceManager: SurrogateResourceManager
{
    private static TranslatorCollection translators;
    private static int translationWriteThreshold = 1;
    private CultureInfo neutralResourcesCulture;
    private int translationWriteCount = 0;

    public TranslationResourceManager(
        string baseName, Assembly assembly):
        base(baseName, assembly)
    {
    }
    public TranslationResourceManager(string baseName):
```

```
        base(baseName)
    {
    }
    public TranslationResourceManager(Type resourceType):
        base(resourceType)
    {
    }
    public static TranslatorCollection Translators
    {
        get {return translators;}
        set {translators = value;}
    }
    public static int TranslationWriteThreshold
    {
        get {return translationWriteThreshold;}
        set {translationWriteThreshold = value;}
    }
}
```

Toward the top of the class declaration there is a private static integer field called translationWriteThreshold that is initialized to 1 and a corresponding public static integer property called TranslationWriteThreshold. The translation write threshold is the number of translations that can occur before the TranslationResourceManager will attempt to write the translations back to the original resource. The initial value of 1 means that each translation will be written back to the original resource immediately. This is a heavy performance penalty but is immediately beneficial to other users who might need this resource. Setting the value to, say, 5 means that there will be five translations before the values are written back to the original resource. Setting the value to 0 means that values will never be written back to the original resource. This last setting effectively turns off the persistence of translated resources and results in a completely dynamically localized solution.

Before we move on to the meat of the class (i.e., the GetString method), let's briefly cover the NeutralResourcesCulture protected property:

```
protected virtual CultureInfo NeutralResourcesCulture
{
    get
    {
        if (neutralResourcesCulture == null)
        {
            if (MainAssembly == null)
                // We have no main assembly so we cannot get
```

```
        // the NeutralResourceLanguageAttribute.
        // We will have to make a guess.
        neutralResourcesCulture = new CultureInfo("en");
    else
    {
        neutralResourcesCulture = ResourceManager.
            GetNeutralResourcesLanguage(MainAssembly);
        if (neutralResourcesCulture == null ||
            neutralResourcesCulture.Equals(
            CultureInfo.InvariantCulture))
            // we didn't manage to get it from the main
            // assembly or it was the invariant culture
            // so make a guess
            neutralResourcesCulture = new CultureInfo("en");
        }
    }
    return neutralResourcesCulture;
}
}
```

This property initializes the `neutralResourcesCulture` private field. If the `MainAssembly` was set in the constructor, the static `ResourceManager.Get NeutralResourceLanguage` is used to get the value from the assemblies' `Neutral ResourcesLanguageAttribute`. If there is no such attribute or it is the invariant culture, `neutralResourcesCulture` is set to the `English` culture. If the `MainAssembly` was not set, we take a guess at the `English` culture. Unlike other resource managers, the `TranslationResourceManager` needs to know what language the fallback assembly uses; if it can't find out, it has to take a guess. It needs to do this because the translators, not unreasonably, need to know what language they are translating from.

The `GetString` method is:

```
public override string GetString(
    string name, System.Globalization.CultureInfo culture)
{
    if (culture == null)
        culture = CultureInfo.CurrentUICulture;

    if (culture.Equals(NeutralResourcesCulture) ||
        culture.Equals(CultureInfo.InvariantCulture))
        // This is the fallback culture -
        // there is no translation to do.
        return ResourceManager.GetString(name, culture);
```

```
// get (or create) the resource set for this culture
ResourceSet resourceSet =
    ResourceManager.GetResourceSet(culture, true, false);
if (resourceSet != null)
{
    // get the string from the resource set
    string resourceStringValue =
        resourceSet.GetString(name, IgnoreCase);
    if (resourceStringValue != null)
        // the resource string was found in the resource set
        return resourceStringValue;
}

// The string was not found in the resource set or the
// whole resource set was not found and could not be created.

// Get the corresponding string from the invariant culture.
string invariantStringValue =ResourceManager.GetString(
    name, CultureInfo.InvariantCulture);

if (invariantStringValue == null ||
    invariantStringValue == String.Empty)
    // there is no equivalent in the invariant culture or
    // the invariant culture string is empty or null
    return invariantStringValue;

// the invariant string isn't empty so it
// should be possible to translate it
CultureInfo fallbackCultureInfo = NeutralResourcesCulture;

if (fallbackCultureInfo.TwoLetterISOLanguageName ==
    culture.TwoLetterISOLanguageName)
    // The languages are the same.
    // There is no translation to perform.
    return invariantStringValue;

if (! IsOkToTranslate(fallbackCultureInfo, culture, name,
    invariantStringValue))
    return invariantStringValue;

ITranslator translator = translators.GetTranslator(
    fallbackCultureInfo.ToString(), culture.ToString());

if (translator == null)
    throw new ApplicationException(String.Format(
        "No translator for this language combination "+
        "({0}, {1})", fallbackCultureInfo.ToString(),
        culture.ToString()));
```

```
    string translatedResourceStringValue = translator.Translate(
        fallbackCultureInfo.ToString(), culture.ToString(),
        invariantStringValue);

    if (translatedResourceStringValue != String.Empty &&
        resourceSet != null)
    {
        // put the new string back into the resource set
        if (resourceSet is CustomResourceSet)
            ((CustomResourceSet) resourceSet).Add(
                name, translatedResourceStringValue);
        else
            ForceResourceSetAdd(resourceSet,
                name, translatedResourceStringValue);

        WriteResources(resourceSet);
    }
    return translatedResourceStringValue;
}
```

GetString defaults the culture to the CurrentUICulture. If the culture is the invariant culture, it calls the internal resource manager's GetString method and returns that string. (If it is the invariant culture, there is no translation to perform.) Next, we try to get a ResourceSet from the internal resource manager. The internal resource manager returns a null if there is no such resource. For example, if we ask for an Italian resource from a ResourcesResourceManager class and the relevant "it.resources" file does not exist, a null will be returned. If the ResourceSet is not null, we search it for the key that we are looking for; if it is found, we return it. This would happen if it has already been translated or if the Translation ResourceManager has previously encountered this key, translated it, and saved it back to the original resource.

If the ResourceSet was null or the key wasn't found, we have to translate it. The first step in the process is to go back to the fallback assembly and find the original string that should be translated. We can get this from the internal resource manager GetString method passing the invariant culture. If this string is empty, we don't bother going to the effort of translating it, as it will be another empty string.

Using the NeutralResourcesLanguage property, we check that the language that we are trying to translate to is different from the language of the fallback assembly by comparing the CultureInfo.TwoLetterISOLanguageName properties. If the languages are different, we can proceed with translation.

Before we perform the translation, we perform a final check to ensure that we really want to translate this key:

```
if (! IsOkToTranslate(
    fallbackCultureInfo, culture, name, invariantStringValue))
    return invariantStringValue;
```

The `IsOkToTranslate` method always returns `true`. I have included it only because you might encounter string properties of components that you do not want translated, and this represents your opportunity to filter out these properties. If this happens, you would modify the `IsOkToTranslate` method to return `false` for these properties.

The next line gets the `ITranslator`, which can handle the translation from the fallback assembly language to the language of the culture we are trying to translate to:

```
ITranslator translator = translators.GetTranslator(
    fallbackCultureInfo.ToString(), culture.ToString());
```

So an example of this line would be:

```
ITranslator translator = translators.GetTranslator("en","it");
```

This line gets a translator to translate from English to Italian. The translator then performs this translation (which might well result in a call to a Web service), and we are left with a translated string. The final piece of the jigsaw before returning the string is to keep a copy of it:

```
if (translatedResourceStringValue != String.Empty &&
    resourceSet != null)
{
    // put the new string back into the resource set
    if (resourceSet is CustomResourceSet)
        ((CustomResourceSet) resourceSet).Add(
            name, translatedResourceStringValue);
    else
        ForceResourceSetAdd(
            resourceSet, name, translatedResourceStringValue);

    WriteResources(resourceSet);
}
```

Our first challenge is to put the string back into the resource set. The second challenge is to persist the resource set. The problem with the first challenge is that the ResourceSet class lacks a public facility for adding new entries to the resource set. If you cast your mind back to the CustomResourceSet class that we wrote earlier, you will recall an Add method and a public Table property that I added to allow exactly this. So we check to see that the class is a CustomResourceSet, and if it is, we dutifully call the Add method. If it isn't, we call the rather nasty ForceResourceSetAdd method, which takes the brute-force approach of getting the protected Table field using reflection and calling its Add method. It's not nice, but it works.

The WriteResources method is as follows:

```
protected virtual void WriteResources(ResourceSet resourceSet)
{
    translationWriteCount++;
    if (translationWriteThreshold > 0 &&
        translationWriteCount >= translationWriteThreshold &&
        resourceSet is CustomResourceSet)
    {
        // the current number of pending writes is greater
        // than or equal to the write threshold so
        // it is time to write the values back to the source
        CustomResourceSet customResourceSet =
            ((CustomResourceSet) resourceSet);

        IResourceWriter resourceWriter =
            customResourceSet.CreateDefaultWriter();
        // copy all of the existing resources to the
        // resource writer
        foreach(DictionaryEntry dictionaryEntry in
            customResourceSet.Table)
        {
            resourceWriter.AddResource(
                dictionaryEntry.Key.ToString(),
                dictionaryEntry.Value);
        }
        resourceWriter.Generate();
        resourceWriter.Close();
        translationWriteCount = 0;
    }
}
```

It increments the "translation write count" and compares it with the "translation write threshold" to see if the time has come to update the original resource. If it has and the resource set is a `CustomResourceSet`, we need to write the resource. If the resource set is not a `CustomResourceSet`, the original resource doesn't get updated. This would be true if the internal resource manager was a `ResourceManager` object. The `ResourceManager` reads resources from an assembly, and I have taken the approach that writing back to the original assembly is not practical in this scenario.

The last obstacle to overcome is that `IResourceWriter` expects to write the resource in its entirety. This means that we have to load the complete resource set into the resource writer before we generate it. In other words, we can't simply save just the one new item that we have just added.

Congratulations, you are now the proud owner of a `TranslationResource Manager`.

There is one last possibility that you might like to consider. The `Translation ResourceManager` performs an "automatic" translation. That is, there is no human intervention in the translation process. An alternative to this approach would be to create a "manual" translation resource manager. This would be a variation of the automatic version, but before each string was returned, a dialog would pop up, offering a translator the original language translation and the machine translation, and allowing the translator to correct the translation and finally save the corrected translation. This manual translation resource manager would only ever be used by the translator and would be considered to be part of the permanent translation process. As such, the translator would receive a new version of the application and run the application; as the translator used the application, it would prompt for every new string that hadn't already been translated in previous translation runs. Seems like a good idea in theory, but I suspect that it would be impractical in practice, as the translator would see all of the strings out of context and would get prompted only for strings encountered during the translator's use of the application. There would be no guarantee that all strings had been encountered and, therefore, translated.

StandardPropertiesResourceManager

The `StandardPropertiesResourceManager` exists to solve a problem identified in previous chapters. Several properties (e.g., `Font`, `ImeMode`, `RightToLeft`) sometimes need to be set on an application-wide basis. That is, if you are localizing your application for Arabic, Hebrew, or Persian (Farsi), you should set the `Right ToLeft` property of each control to `Yes` (or `Inherit` for controls and `Yes` for forms). Your translator/localizer can set these values for every control or form individually, but not only is this labour-intensive, it is also error prone; it is easy to miss a few controls, especially during the maintenance phase, when new controls are added. For this reason, if your application is such that an application-wide setting is appropriate (in other words, there are no places in your application where some controls should look or behave differently from the majority of the application), the `StandardPropertiesResourceManager` offers a suitable solution.

Like the `TranslationResourceManager` in the previous section, the `StandardPropertiesResourceManager` uses a "workhorse" resource manager to perform the majority of the work of a resource manager. The part that the `StandardPropertiesResourceManager` adds to the process is that for specific properties it steps in and overrides the workhorse resource manager's value and sets its own value.

Here's how it works. Like the `TranslationResourceManager`, the `StandardPropertiesResourceManager` inherits from the `SurrogateResourceManager` to handle the job of passing requests on to the "workhorse" resource manager. The essential structure looks like this:

```
public class StandardPropertiesResourceManager:
    SurrogateResourceManager
{
    private static Font font;
    private static ImeMode imeMode = (ImeMode) -1;
    private static RightToLeft rightToLeft = (RightToLeft) -1;

    public StandardPropertiesResourceManager(
        string baseName, Assembly assembly):
        base(baseName, assembly)
    {
    }
    public StandardPropertiesResourceManager(string baseName):
        base(baseName)
    {
    }
    public StandardPropertiesResourceManager(Type resourceType):
        base(resourceType)
    {
    }
```

```
    public static Font Font
    {
        get {return font;}
        set {font = value;}
    }
    public static ImeMode ImeMode
    {
        get {return imeMode;}
        set {imeMode = value;}
    }
    public static RightToLeft RightToLeft
    {
        get {return rightToLeft;}
        set {rightToLeft = value;}
    }
}
```

There are a few static properties (`Font`, `ImeMode`, `RightToLeft`) that map onto equivalent static fields to hold the application-wide settings. You can see from this code that it would be a simple matter to add new application-wide settings to this list. The remainder of the class simply overrides the `GetObject` method to substitute requests for application-wide properties:

```
protected virtual bool SubstituteValue(string name,
    CultureInfo culture, object value, object substituteValue,
    string propertyName)
{
    if (value == null)
        return name.EndsWith("." + propertyName) &&
            substituteValue != null;
    else
        return substituteValue != null &&
            value.GetType().IsSubclassOf(substituteValue.GetType());
}

protected virtual bool SubstituteValue(
    string name, CultureInfo culture, int value,
    int substituteValue, string propertyName)
{
    return name.EndsWith("." + propertyName) &&
        substituteValue != -1;
}

public override object GetObject(string name, CultureInfo culture)
```

```
{
    object obj = base.GetObject(name, culture);
    if (SubstituteValue(name, culture, obj, font, "Font"))
        return font;

    if (SubstituteValue(name, culture,
        (int) obj, (int) imeMode, "ImeMode"))
        return imeMode;

    if (SubstituteValue(name, culture,
        (int) obj, (int) rightToLeft, "RightToLeft"))
        return rightToLeft;

    return obj;
}
```

The `GetObject` method gets the requested value from the workhorse resource manager. It then checks to see whether it is one of the application-wide values that it should substitute; if it is, it substitutes its own value.

ResourceManagerProvider

You have learned from this chapter so far that the `ResourceManager` and `ComponentResourceManager` classes provided with the .NET Framework are not the only resource managers in the world. Maybe you will choose to use one of the resource managers in this chapter, or maybe you have been inspired to write one of your own. What is a certainty, however, is that there is too much potential in this idea to live with committing your project to a specific resource manager. Furthermore, everything changes, and what is certain is that new resource managers will be written either by Microsoft or by third parties, and you will want to throw away your old, worn-out yesteryear resource managers in favour of the latest widget. This leaves us with a new problem: How can we use resource managers where we do not commit ourselves to a given resource manager class?

This is the same problem that faces ADO.NET: How can you use ADO.NET classes without committing to a given data provider? ADO.NET solves this problem in ADO.NET 2 using `DbProviderFactory` classes, and we implement a similar concept here. For ASP.NET 2.0 applications, be sure to read the section "Using Custom Resource Managers in ASP.NET 2.0," later in this chapter.

The `ResourceManagerProvider` class has only static methods, a static field, and a static property:

```
public class ResourceManagerProvider
{
    private static Type resourceManagerType =
        typeof(ComponentResourceManager);

    public static ComponentResourceManager
        GetResourceManager(Type type)
    {
        return (ComponentResourceManager) Activator.CreateInstance(
            resourceManagerType, new object[] {type});
    }
    public static ComponentResourceManager GetResourceManager(
        string baseName, Assembly assembly)
    {
        return (ComponentResourceManager) Activator.CreateInstance(
            resourceManagerType, new object[] {baseName, assembly});
    }
    public static ComponentResourceManager GetResourceManager(
        string baseName, Assembly assembly, Type usingResourceSet)
    {
        return (ComponentResourceManager) Activator.CreateInstance(
            resourceManagerType, new object[]
            {baseName, assembly, usingResourceSet});
    }
    public static Type ResourceManagerType
    {
        get {return resourceManagerType;}
        set
        {
            if (value.FullName ==
                "System.ComponentModel.ComponentResourceManager" ||
                value.IsSubclassOf(typeof(ComponentResourceManager)))
                resourceManagerType = value;
            else
                throw new ApplicationException(
                    "ResourceManagerType must be a sub class of "+
                    "System.ComponentModel."+
                    "ComponentResourceManager");
        }
    }
}
```

The public static `ResourceManagerType` property maps onto the private static `resourceManagerType` field and holds the `Type` used to create new resource managers. The private field defaults to the `ComponentResourceManager` Type, but the public property can be set like this:

```
ResourceManagerProvider.ResourceManagerType =
    typeof(DbResourceManager);
```

You would make this assignment in the application's startup process.

The remaining static `GetResourceManager` methods all create a new resource manager from the specific resource manager type and differ only in the parameters that they accept and pass on to the resource manager constructors.

So instead of writing this:

```
ResourceManager resources =
    new ResourceManager(typeof(CustomerBusinessObject));
```

you could write this:

```
ResourceManager resources =
    ResourceManagerProvider.GetResourceManager(
    typeof(CustomerBusinessObject));
```

The benefit of this approach is that you can change an entire application's resource manager classes to a different class by changing a single line of code:

```
ResourceManagerProvider.ResourceManagerType =
    typeof(TranslationResourceManager);
```

A translator, for example, could use the `ResourcesResourceManager` class during the translation process, and the live version of the application could use the `ComponentResourceManager` class.

If you like the idea of using the `ResourceManagerProvider`, you might wonder whether you have managed to track down all of the cases of creating a new resource manager object throughout your application and changed them to use `Resource ManagerProvider`, or whether you have let any fall through the net. If so, take a look at Chapter 13, "Testing Internationalization Using FxCop," and the "ResourceManager not provided by provider" rule that exists to find these rogue bits of code.

Using Custom Resource Managers in Windows Forms

The `ResourceManagerProvider` is all fine and dandy, but Windows Forms developers have an additional hurdle to overcome if it is to be used in a Windows form. The problem lies in the very first line of the form's `InitializeComponent` method when `Form.Localizable` is true:

```
// Visual Studio 2003
System.Resources.ResourceManager resources =
    new System.Resources.ResourceManager(typeof(Form1));

// Visual Studio 2005
System.ComponentModel.ComponentResourceManager resources =
    new System.ComponentModel.ComponentResourceManager(
    typeof(Form1));
```

Clearly, the Visual Studio designer doesn't respect our new `ResourceManager Provider` class and blindly uses good old `ResourceManager` or `Component ResourceManager`. This really doesn't help us much if we want to get our resources from, say, a database. What we need is for Visual Studio to generate code that uses our `ResourceManagerProvider` instead of `ResourceManager`/`Component ResourceManager`. There are two possible solutions to this problem. The first is that we can write a Visual Studio add-in that modifies or replaces the code generator for the Windows Forms designer. I decided against this approach because the second solution is much easier. The second solution is that we can resign ourselves to the fact that Visual Studio is going to write code that we don't want it to, but we can try to correct the problem before the resource manager gets used. This is the solution that we implement in this chapter.

It is not very well known that it is possible to inject completely new code into the `InitializeComponent` method. The goal of our solution, therefore, is to inject the following new line of code into the `InitializeComponent` method:

```
resources = Internationalization.Resources.
    ResourceManagerProvider.GetResourceManager(typeof(Form1));
```

("`Form1`" is the name of the form class.) This code assigns a new value to the local resources variable. It is true that the `InitializeComponent` method will first create a redundant `ResourceManager` or `ComponentResourceManager` that will not be used and will be dereferenced when we subsequently assign a new resource manager from our `ResourceManagerProvider.GetResourceManager` method, and this is wasteful. But it is also true that it solves our problem.

The secret to injecting this new code into `InitializeComponent` lies in creating a component that has custom serialization code. You can achieve this with the `DesignerSerializer` attribute:

```
[DesignerSerializer(typeof(ResourceManagerSetterSerializer),
typeof(CodeDomSerializer))]
public class ResourceManagerSetter : System.ComponentModel.Component
{
}
```

Our new `ResourceManagerSetter` class inherits from `Component` and, therefore, sits in the nonvisual area of the form designer. It has no properties, so there is nothing to serialize. Its only presence so far is that, like any component, the form class has a private field:

```
private Internationalization.Resources.ResourceManagerSetter
    resourceManagerSetter1;
```

And the field is initialized in `InitializeComponent`:

```
this.resourceManagerSetter1 =
    new Internationalization.Resources.ResourceManagerSetter();
```

The `DesignerSerializer` attribute tells the form designer to serialize this component using the `ResourceManagerSetterSerializer` class, and that this class is a kind of `CodeDomSerializer`. `CodeDom` ("code document object model") is a .NET technology that enables you to create classes from which code can be generated. It is a great technology that is used throughout Visual Studio, and although it can require a little thought to get started, it has enormous potential and is well worth mastering. The `ResourceManagerSetter` class is now complete.

All of the action occurs in the `ResourceManagerSetterSerializer` class:

```
public class ResourceManagerSetterSerializer : CodeDomSerializer
{
    public override object Deserialize(
        IDesignerSerializationManager manager, object codeDomObject)
```

```
    {
        CodeDomSerializer baseSerializer = (CodeDomSerializer)
            manager.GetSerializer(typeof(ResourceManagerSetter).
            BaseType, typeof(CodeDomSerializer));

        return
            baseSerializer.Deserialize(manager, codeDomObject);
    }

    public override object Serialize(
        IDesignerSerializationManager manager, object value)
    {
        CodeDomSerializer baseSerializer = (CodeDomSerializer)
            manager.GetSerializer(typeof(ResourceManagerSetter).
            BaseType, typeof(CodeDomSerializer));

        object codeObject = baseSerializer.Serialize(manager, value);

        if (codeObject is CodeStatementCollection)
        {
            CodeStatementCollection statements =
                (CodeStatementCollection) codeObject;

            CodeExpression leftCodeExpression =
                new CodeVariableReferenceExpression("resources");

            CodeTypeDeclaration classTypeDeclaration =
                (CodeTypeDeclaration) manager.GetService(
                typeof(CodeTypeDeclaration));

            CodeExpression typeofExpression =
                new CodeTypeOfExpression(classTypeDeclaration.Name);

            CodeExpression rightCodeExpression =
                new CodeMethodInvokeExpression(
                new CodeTypeReferenceExpression(
                "Internationalization.Resources."+
                "ResourceManagerProvider"),
                "GetResourceManager",
                new CodeExpression[] {typeofExpression});

            statements.Insert(0, new CodeAssignStatement(
                leftCodeExpression, rightCodeExpression));
        }
        return codeObject;
    }
}
```

This class overrides the `Deserialize` method, which creates a new `CodeDom Serializer` and returns it. This is a standard implementation of the `Deserialize` method, and this implementation offers nothing new. The `Serialize` method returns a collection of `CodeDom` statements. These statements can be anything. The result is placed in the `InitializeComponent` method verbatim. Our implementation simply generates a single statement. The statement is an assignment statement that invokes the `ResourceManagerProvider.GetResourceManager` method and assigns the result to a variable called "`resources`". The majority of the code in this method is `CodeDom` code; you might want to study the documentation on `CodeDom` if there is anything that you don't follow. The following line, however, is worth pointing out:

```
CodeTypeDeclaration classTypeDeclaration =
    (CodeTypeDeclaration) manager.GetService(
    typeof(CodeTypeDeclaration));
```

Recall from the line of code that we want to generate that we need to know what class we are generating the resource manager for. We need to be able to generate something like "`typeof(Form1)`", but we don't know what the name of the form class is. This line uses the `GetService` method of the `IDesignerSerializationManager` object passed to the `Serialize` method to get the `CodeTypeDeclaration` for the form.

The only caveat for the `ResourceManagerSetter` component is that it must be the first component on the form; otherwise, the assignment to the "`resources`" variable will occur too late and the "temporary" `ResourceManager`/`ComponentResourceManager` will not be so temporary, as it gets used to retrieve resources until our component kicks in. You can see the problem here where a `Button` gets created before the `ResourceManagerSetter` has had a chance to assign a new value to the "`resources`" variable:

```
System.Resources.ResourceManager resources =
    new System.Resources.ResourceManager(typeof(Form1));
this.button1 = new System.Windows.Forms.Button();
this.resourceManagerSetter1 =
    new Internationalization.Resources.ResourceManagerSetter();
this.SuspendLayout();
//
// button1
//
this.button1.AccessibleDescription =
```

```
    resources.GetString("button1.AccessibleDescription");
this.button1.AccessibleName =
    resources.GetString("button1.AccessibleName");
etc.
etc.
this.button1.Text = resources.GetString("button1.Text");
this.button1.TextAlign = ((System.Drawing.ContentAlignment)
    (resources.GetObject("button1.TextAlign")));
this.button1.Visible =
    ((bool)(resources.GetObject("button1.Visible")));
resources = Internationalization.Resources.
    ResourceManagerProvider.GetResourceManager(typeof(Form1));
```

The call to `resources.GetString` to assign the button's `Text` property will use the assembly-based resource manager.

One minor fly in the ointment with the `ResourceManagerSetter` approach is that Visual Studio spots that we have done something unusual and reports in the Task List (see Figure 12.6). You can just ignore this warning.

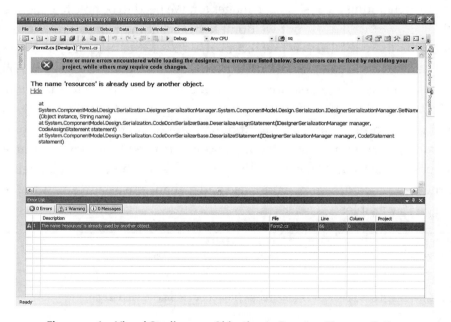

Figure 12.6   Visual Studio 2005 Objecting to ResourceManagerSetter

Finally, if you use WinRes to open forms that have a `ResourceManagerSetter`, remember that WinRes must be able to find all of the assemblies that are used by the form. So WinRes must be able to find the `ResourceManagerSetter` assembly; otherwise, it will display its unhelpful "Object reference not set to an instance of an object" error. Of course, there would be little value in using WinRes to open such forms anyway because WinRes cannot read from resources other than resx files. This limitation lends more weight to the argument to write a WinRes replacement.

Generating Strongly-Typed Resources for Sources Other Than resx Files

Way back in Chapter 3, "An Introduction to Internationalization," I introduced strongly typed resources. You might remember that they are new in .NET Framework 2.0, but as they are such a good idea, I wrote a similar utility for the .NET Framework 1.1 so that everyone could share in the joy that is strongly typed resources. You might also recall that resgen, the console application that generates strongly typed resources, accepts input only from resx files. Having spent all of this time writing custom resource managers, you might wonder how we can generate strongly typed resources from a source other than a resx file. The answer is to build our own resgen utility. In the .NET Framework 2.0, this isn't as difficult as it sounds (I return to the .NET Framework 1.1 in a moment). The .NET Framework 2.0 class `StronglyTypedResourceBuilder`, upon which resgen is built (among other classes), has overloaded `Create` methods that accept different parameters to identify resources. One overloaded `Create` clearly accepts resx files as input, and this is of no value to us. However, another overloaded `Create` accepts an `IDictionary` of resources, and it is this method that solves our problem. Here is a bare-bones implementation of `ResClassGen`, a replacement for resgen that just generates strongly typed classes from resources.

```
using System;
using System.Collections.Generic;
using System.Text;
using System.IO;
using System.Collections;
using System.Resources;
using System.Resources.Tools;
using System.CodeDom;
```

```
using System.CodeDom.Compiler;
using Microsoft.CSharp;

namespace Tools.ResClassGen
{
    class Program
    {
        static void Main(string[] args)
        {
            if (args.GetLength(0) < 1 || !File.Exists(args[0]))
                ShowSyntax();
            else
            {
                string nameSpace;
                if (args.GetLength(0) > 1)
                    nameSpace = args[1];
                else
                    nameSpace = String.Empty;

                StronglyTypedResourceBuilderHelper.GenerateClass(
                    args[0], nameSpace);
            }
        }
        private static void ShowSyntax()
        {
            Console.WriteLine("Syntax:");
            Console.WriteLine(
                "ResClassGen <ResxFilename> [<NameSpace>]");
            Console.WriteLine("Example:");
            Console.WriteLine(
                "ResClassGen Strings.resx WindowsApplication1");
        }
    }
}
```

This skeleton simply checks the parameters and calls the Strongly
TypedResourceBuilderHelper.GenerateClass method to do the work:

```
public static void GenerateClass(
    string resxFilename, string nameSpace)
{
    string[] unmatchable;
    Hashtable resources = GetResources(resxFilename);

    string className =
        Path.GetFileNameWithoutExtension(resxFilename);

    CodeDomProvider codeDomProvider = new CSharpCodeProvider();
```

```
    CodeCompileUnit codeCompileUnit =
        StronglyTypedResourceBuilder.Create(
        resources, className, nameSpace,
        codeDomProvider, false, out unmatchable);

    string classFilename = Path.ChangeExtension(resxFilename, ".cs");

    using (TextWriter writer = new StreamWriter(classFilename))
    {
        codeDomProvider.GenerateCodeFromCompileUnit(
            codeCompileUnit, writer, new CodeGeneratorOptions());
    }
}
```

The `GenerateClass` method calls `GetResources` to get a `Hashtable` of resources. (I return to `GetResources` in a moment.) It passes the `Hashtable`, which supports the `IDictionary` interface, to `StronglyTypedResourceBuilder`. `Create`. The remaining parameters to this `Create` method simply identify the name of the class, its namespace, the `CodeDom` provider used to generate the class, whether the class is internal, and a parameter into which all of the unmatchable resources are placed. The return result from the `Create` method is a `CodeCompileUnit` that contains the complete `CodeDom` graph (a tree of code instructions) from which the code can be generated. The `GenerateClass` method creates a `TextWriter` to write out the code and calls `CodeDomProvider.GenerateCodeFromCompileUnit` to output the code to the `TextWriter`.

In the .NET Framework 1.1, the `GenerateCodeFromCompileUnit` method is not available directly from the `CodeDomProvider`. Instead, you can create an `ICode-Provider` using `CodeDomProvider.CreateGenerator`, and call the same method with the same parameters from the resulting `ICodeProvider`.

The only question remaining is how to load the resources:

```
private static Hashtable GetResources(string resxFilename)
{
    ResXResourceReader reader = new ResXResourceReader(resxFilename);
    Hashtable resources = new Hashtable();
    try
    {
        IDictionaryEnumerator enumerator = reader.GetEnumerator();
        while (enumerator.MoveNext())
        {
            resources.Add(
```

```
                    enumerator.Key.ToString(), enumerator.Value);
        }
    }
    finally
    {
        reader.Close();
    }
    return resources;
}
```

This implementation simply uses a `ResXResourceReader` to read the resources from the specified resx file. Consequently, this implementation offers no benefits beyond the resgen implementation. However, you can see that by changing this method to use, say, a `DbResourceReader` instead of a `ResXResourceReader`, the `ResClassGen` utility would be able to read from your own resources.

If you are using the .NET Framework 1.1, there is no `StronglyTypedResource Builder` class, but recall from Chapter 3 that I wrote an equivalent class so that no one had to miss out. So the previous code works equally well in both versions of the framework.

Generating Strongly-Typed Resources Which Use ResourceManagerProvider

There is one more issue to attend to. If you have an excellent memory, you might remember one of the lines in the code that gets generated for the strongly typed resource class:

```
System.Resources.ResourceManager temp =
    new System.Resources.ResourceManager(
    "WindowsApplication1.strings", typeof(strings).Assembly);
```

Clearly, this line isn't very helpful to those of us who write custom resource managers because the code uses the `System.Resources.ResourceManager` class. We want it to be this:

```
System.Resources.ResourceManager temp =
    Internationalization.Resources.ResourceManagerProvider.
    GetResourceManager(
    "WindowsApplication1.strings", typeof(strings).Assembly);
```

The bad news is that the `StronglyTypedResourceBuilder` class has no facility for allowing us to specify what resource manager class to use or how to create a resource manager. If you modify the generated code, it will be overwritten the next time the resource is generated. However, all is not lost. The `StronglyTypedResource Builder.Create` method generates a `CodeCompileUnit` that, as we have seen, is a collection of all of the instructions from which the strongly typed resource class is generated. The solution lies in modifying the resulting `CodeCompileUnit` before it is passed to the `CodeDomProvider.GenerateCodeFromCompileUnit` method. To follow this code, you need a little familiarity with `CodeDom`. We start by adding a line immediately after the call to `StronglyTypedResourceBuilder.Create`:

```
ChangeResourceManager(className, codeCompileUnit);
```

This represents our point at which we start altering the `CodeDom` graph. `ChangeResourceManager` looks like this:

```
private static void ChangeResourceManager(
    string className, CodeCompileUnit codeCompileUnit)
{
    CodeNamespace codeNamespace = codeCompileUnit.Namespaces[0];
    CodeTypeDeclaration codeTypeDeclaration = codeNamespace.Types[0];
    CodeMemberProperty codeMemberProperty = GetCodeMemberProperty(
        codeTypeDeclaration, "ResourceManager");
    if (codeMemberProperty != null)
        ChangeResourceManagerGetStatements(codeNamespace,
            codeTypeDeclaration, codeMemberProperty);
}
```

We take an educated guess that the first namespace in the `CodeDom` graph contains the generated class and that the first type in the namespace is the resource class; these guesses are accurate, given the current state of `StronglyTypedResource-Builder`. We call `GetCodeMemberProperty` to get the `ResourceManager` property (`GetCodeMemberProperty` simply iterates through all of the members looking for a property called "ResourceManager"). If we get the property, we call `ChangeResourceManagerGetStatements`, which actually modifies the `CodeDom` statements for the `ResourceManager`'s get method:

```
private static void ChangeResourceManagerGetStatements(
    CodeTypeDeclaration codeTypeDeclaration,
    CodeMemberProperty codeMemberProperty)
```

```
{
    CodeTypeReference resourceManagerTypeReference =
        new CodeTypeReference(typeof(ResourceManager));

    CodeFieldReferenceExpression resMgrFieldReferenceExpression =
        new CodeFieldReferenceExpression(null, "resourceMan");

    CodeExpression ifExpression =
        new CodeBinaryOperatorExpression(
        resMgrFieldReferenceExpression,
        CodeBinaryOperatorType.IdentityEquality,
        new CodePrimitiveExpression(null));

    CodePropertyReferenceExpression typeOfExpression =
        new CodePropertyReferenceExpression(
        new CodeTypeOfExpression(
        new CodeTypeReference(codeTypeDeclaration.Name)),
        "Assembly");

    CodeExpression[] resourceManagerParameterExpressions =
        new CodeExpression[2]
        {
            new CodePrimitiveExpression(
            codeNamespace.Name + "." + codeTypeDeclaration.Name),
            typeOfExpression
        };

    CodeExpression newResourceManagerExpression =
        new CodeMethodInvokeExpression(
        new CodeTypeReferenceExpression(
        "Internationalization.Resources.ResourceManagerProvider"),
        "GetResourceManager",
        resourceManagerParameterExpressions);

    CodeStatement[] ifStatements = new CodeStatement[2]
    {
        new CodeVariableDeclarationStatement(
        resourceManagerTypeReference, "temp",
        newResourceManagerExpression),

        new CodeAssignStatement(resMgrFieldReferenceExpression,
        new CodeVariableReferenceExpression("temp"))
    };

    CodeStatementCollection statements =
        new CodeStatementCollection();

    statements.Add(
```

```
        new CodeConditionStatement(ifExpression, ifStatements));
    statements.Add(new CodeMethodReturnStatement(
        resMgrFieldReferenceExpression));

    codeMemberProperty.GetStatements.Clear();
    codeMemberProperty.GetStatements.AddRange(statements);
}
```

This code doesn't worry about what the existing CodeDom instructions are for the get method; it simply throws them away and replaces them with a new set. The new set is very similar to the previous set, with the exception that the resource manager is created from ResourceManagerProvider.GetResourceManager instead of System.Resources.ResourceManager.

Using Custom Resource Managers in ASP.NET 2.0

ASP.NET 1.1 applications have no further requirements for using custom resource managers beyond what has been covered so far. So if you are not using ASP.NET 2.0 and do not intend to upgrade to ASP.NET 2.0, you can skip this section.

As we saw in Chapter 5, "ASP.NET Specifics," Microsoft has made significant advances in ASP.NET 2.0, particularly in the area of internationalization. The issue of interest to us in this chapter is the introduction of a resource provider model. This section discusses how the existing model works and how we can write resource providers that plug into this model to use the resource managers that we have created in this chapter. We start with a description of ASP.NET's Resource Provider Model; then we implement a new resource provider that mimics the behavior of the existing provider. Finally, we implement a provider for the DbResourceManager from this chapter. From these examples, you should understand the mechanism sufficiently to write a resource provider for any of the custom resource managers in this chapter.

The Resource Provider Model

ASP.NET 2.0 uses the `ResourceManager` class, by default, for retrieving all resources from resource assemblies, both fallback and satellite. The model described in Chapter 3 is still true for ASP.NET 2.0. However, ASP.NET 2.0 allows developers to specify a resource provider that is responsible for providing localized resources. By default, the existing provider returns `ResourceManager` objects, but the model allows us to override this behavior. The essential processes that the `Resource Manager` class executes are still true for ASP.NET:

- Resources are created from resx/resources/restext/txt files.
- Resources are embedded in an assembly.
- Resources are accessed using the `ResourceManager` class.
- The ResourceManager uses the fallback process we are familiar with.

There are, however, two differences that ASP.NET 2.0 must cope with:

- ASP.NET applications are compiled to temporary directories with generated names, so code that loads resources from these assemblies needs to use these generated names.
- ASP.NET applications have both global and local resources, and these resources are placed in separate assemblies.

Before we get into the resource provider mechanism, let's put some flesh on what this means to an ASP.NET application. In Visual Studio 2005, create a new WebSite; add a button and some controls to the Default page; and select Tools, Generate Local Resource to generate local resources. Create a French version of the page by adding a `Default.aspx.fr.resx` file to the `App_LocalResources` folder and include a new entry called `Button1Resources.Text` for the French version of the button. Now add a new global resource file called `ProductInfo.resx` to the `App_Global Resources` folder. Add a key called `Name` and give it a value. Add a second resource file called `ProductInfo.fr.resx` to the `App_GlobalResources` folder, with a French value for the `Name` key. Set your browser's Language Preference to French. When the Web site runs, the resources will be compiled into resource assemblies. In our example, there will be four separate resource assemblies:

- The Global fallback resource assembly
- The Global French resource assembly
- The Local fallback resource assembly
- The Local French resource assembly

The Global resource assembly path is determined by the following formula:

```
<Temporary ASP.NET Folder>\<WebSiteName>\<GeneratedName1>\

<GeneratedName2>\App_GlobalResources.<GeneratedName3>.dll
```

So if `<Temporary ASP.NET Folder>` is "`C:\WINDOWS\Microsoft.NET\Framework\v2.0.50727\Temporary ASP.NET Files`" and the `<WebSiteName>` is "`WebSite1`", the Global fallback assembly could be something like this:

```
C:\WINDOWS\Microsoft.NET\Framework\v2.0.50727\Temporary ASP.NET
Files\website1\62a3b0ac\1072591c\App_GlobalResources.w1qus9s2.dll
```

The Global French resource assembly is placed relative to the fallback assemblies' folder in the `fr` folder and given the "`.resources.dll`" extension; in this example, it would be:

```
C:\WINDOWS\Microsoft.NET\Framework\v2.0.50727\Temporary ASP.NET
Files\website1\62a3b0ac\1072591c\fr\App_GlobalResources.w1qus9s2.resources.dll
```

The Local fallback resource assembly path is determined by a similar formula:

```
<Temporary ASP.NET Folder>\<WebSiteName>\<GeneratedName1>\

<GeneratedName2>\App_LocalResources.<FolderName>.<GeneratedName4>.dll
```

The `<FolderName>` is the name of folder where the `.aspx` files reside, where "`root`" is used for the Web site's root. So the Local fallback assembly could be something like this:

```
C:\WINDOWS\Microsoft.NET\Framework\v2.0.50727\Temporary ASP.NET
Files\website1\62a3b0ac\1072591c\App_LocalResources.root.ogd3clye.dll
```

Following the same practice as the Global satellite resource assembly, the Local French resource assembly is placed in the `fr` folder and given the "`.resources.dll`" extension; in this example, it would be:

```
C:\WINDOWS\Microsoft.NET\Framework\v2.0.50727\Temporary ASP.NET
Files\website1\62a3b0ac\1072591c\fr\App_LocalResources.root.ogd3clye.resources.dll
```

With these challenges in mind, we can look at how the ASP.NET Resource Provider model works.

The Resource Provider story starts with the `ResourceProviderFactory` abstract class. This class has a single implementation in the .NET Framework 2.0—namely, `ResXResourceProviderFactory` (see Figure 12.7).

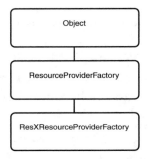

Figure 12.7   ResourceProviderFactory Class Hierarchy

`ResXResourceProviderFactory` is the default factory and is the factory that has been in use in all of the ASP.NET 2.0 Web sites in this book up to this point. The `ResourceProviderClass` has two methods that must be overridden by the subclass:

```
public abstract IResourceProvider CreateGlobalResourceProvider(
    string classKey);

public abstract IResourceProvider CreateLocalResourceProvider(
    string virtualPath);
```

These methods return an `IResourceProvider` interface. `IResourceProvider` is a simple interface:

```
public interface IResourceProvider
{
    object GetObject(string resourceKey, CultureInfo culture);

    IResourceReader ResourceReader { get; }
}
```

So the `ResourceProviderFactory` must return objects that support a `GetObject` method and a `ResourceReader` property. The `ResXResourceProviderFactory` creates a new `GlobalResXResourceProvider` object when its `CreateGlobalResource Provider` method is called and a `LocalResXResourceProvider` object when its `CreateLocalResourceProvider` method is called.

Figure 12.8 shows the class hierarchy for the classes that support `IResource Provider` in the .NET Framework 2.0.

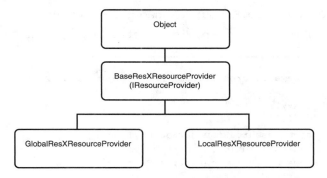

Figure 12.8   Implementations of IResourceProvider

The `BaseResXResourceProvider` implements the `GetObject` method and `ResourceReader` property required by the `IResourceReader`. The `GetObject` method calls an abstract method called `CreateResourceManager` to create a `ResourceManager` object and store it in a private field, and then calls the `Resource Manager`'s `GetObject` method. The `GlobalResXResourceProvider` and `Local ResXResourceProvider` classes both override the `CreateResourceManager` method to create a `ResourceManager`, using the correct resource name and the correct assembly. The `GlobalResXResourceProvider` overrides the `ResourceReader` property to throw a `NotSupportedException`. This doesn't affect the normal execution of a Web site because the `IResourceProvider.ResourceReader` property is not called by the .NET Framework 2.0 for global resources. The `LocalResX ResourceProvider` overrides the `ResourceReader` property to return a `Resource Reader` to read the relevant resource from the assembly.

Setting the ResourceProviderFactory

The `ResourceProviderFactory` class can be set in the `web.config`'s globalization section using the `resourceProviderFactoryType` attribute. The syntax is:

```
<globalization resourceProviderFactoryType=
    [FullClassName[, Assembly]]/>
```

So in the next example, our `ResourceProviderFactory` class is `Internationalization.Resources.Web.ResourceManagerResourceProviderFactory`, and it is in an assembly called `ResourceProviderFactories`; the complete `web.config` is:

```
<configuration
    xmlns="http://schemas.microsoft.com/.NetConfiguration/v2.0">
    <appSettings/>
    <connectionStrings/>
    <system.web>
        <globalization resourceProviderFactoryType=
            "Internationalization.Resources.Web.
            ResourceManagerResourceProviderFactory,
            ResourceProviderFactories"/>
    </system.web>
</configuration>
```

Note that the assembly name must not include the `.dll` extension, and the `Resource ProviderFactories` assembly must be available to the Web site, so it should be either installed in the GAC or added to the Web site's `bin` folder (you can do this by adding the `ResourceProviderFactories` project to the Web site's references).

Alternatively, if you include the factory class in the Web site's `App_Code` folder, you do not need to specify the assembly in the `resourceProviderFactoryType` setting.

ResourceManagerResourceProviderFactory

To see how this works in practice, we'll create a `ResourceManagerResourceProviderFactory`. This class mimics the behavior of the `ResXResourceProviderFactory` and gives us an insight into how the default provider solves its problems. In the subsequent section, we create a provider factory for the `DbResourceManager` class that we wrote in this chapter. The `ResourceManagerResourceProviderFactory` class is as follows:

```
public class ResourceManagerResourceProviderFactory:
    ResourceProviderFactory
```

```
{
    public ResourceManagerResourceProviderFactory()
    {
    }
    public override IResourceProvider
        CreateGlobalResourceProvider(string classKey)
    {
        return new GlobalResourceManagerResourceProvider(classKey);
    }
    public override IResourceProvider
        CreateLocalResourceProvider(string virtualPath)
    {
        return new LocalResourceManagerResourceProvider(virtualPath);
    }
}
```

This simple class returns a new `GlobalResourceManagerResourceProvider` object and a new `LocalResourceManagerResourceProvider` object for its two methods. The `classKey` parameter provided to the `CreateGlobalResourceProvider` method will be "`ProductInfo`" in our example. The `virtualPath` parameter provided to the `CreateLocalResourceProvider` method will be "`/WebSite1/Default.aspx`" in our example. Figure 12.9 shows the class hierarchy of the `IResourceProvider` implementations required for our `ResourceManager` and `DbResourceManager` implementations.

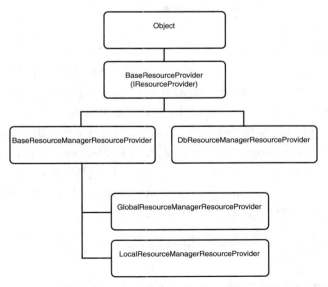

Figure 12.9   Class Hierarchy of Custom Implementations of IResourceProvider

Both of the `IResourceProvider` implementations inherit indirectly from the abstract `BaseResourceProvider` class:

```
public abstract class BaseResourceProvider : IResourceProvider
{
    private ResourceManager resourceManager;

    protected ResourceManager ResourceManager
    {
        get
        {
            if (resourceManager == null)
                resourceManager = CreateResourceManager();

            return resourceManager;
        }
    }
    protected abstract ResourceManager CreateResourceManager();

    public object GetObject(string resourceKey,
        System.Globalization.CultureInfo culture)
    {
        return ResourceManager.GetObject(resourceKey, culture);
    }

    public System.Resources.IResourceReader ResourceReader
    {
        get { throw new NotSupportedException(); }
    }
}
```

`BaseResourceProvider` has a `ResourceManager` property that initializes a private `resourceManager` field by calling the abstract `CreateResourceManager` method. It implements the `GetObject` method to call the `ResourceManager`'s `GetObject` method, and it implements the `ResourceReader` property to throw a `NotSupported Exception`. The `BaseResourceProvider` class is used in this example and also the next example to create a `ResourceProviderFactory` for the `DbResourceManager` class. The `BaseResourceManagerResourceProvider` class implements the `Create ResourceManager` method and provides a `GetInternalStaticProperty` method:

```
public abstract class BaseResourceManagerResourceProvider :
    BaseResourceProvider
{
    protected override ResourceManager CreateResourceManager()
```

```
{
    Assembly resourceAssembly = GetResourceAssembly();
    if (resourceAssembly == null)
        return null;

    ResourceManager resourceManager =
        new ResourceManager(GetBaseName(), resourceAssembly);
    resourceManager.IgnoreCase = true;
    return resourceManager;
}

protected abstract string GetBaseName();

protected abstract Assembly GetResourceAssembly();

protected static object GetInternalStaticProperty(
    Type type, string propertyName)
{
    PropertyInfo propertyInfo =
        type.GetProperty(propertyName,
        System.Reflection.BindingFlags.Static |
        System.Reflection.BindingFlags.NonPublic);

    if (propertyInfo == null)
        return null;
    else
        return propertyInfo.GetValue(null, null);
}
}
```

The `CreateResourceManager` method calls the abstract `GetBaseName` method to get the name of the resource, and the abstract `GetResourceAssembly` to get the assembly that contains the resources. These two methods represent the only differences between the "global" resource manager and the "local" resource manager. The `GetInternalStaticProperty` method is a workaround for `BuildManager` and `BuildResult` classes, hiding information from us that we need to implement this solution. It uses reflection to obtain the value of internal static properties.

With this infrastructure in place, the `GlobalResourceManagerResource Provider` class is simple:

```
public class GlobalResourceManagerResourceProvider :
    BaseResourceManagerResourceProvider
{
    private string classKey;
```

```
    public GlobalResourceManagerResourceProvider(string classKey)
    {
        this.classKey = classKey;
    }
    protected override string GetBaseName()
    {
        return "Resources." + classKey;
    }
    protected override Assembly GetResourceAssembly()
    {
        return (Assembly) GetInternalStaticProperty(
            typeof(BuildManager), "AppResourcesAssembly");
    }
}
```

The `GetBaseName` returns "`Resources`" plus the `classKey`, so if `classKey` is "`ProductInfo`", then the base name will be "`Resources.ProductInfo`". The `GetResourceAssembly` method gets the resource assembly from the `BuildManager`'s internal static `AppResourcesAssembly` property. The `BuildManager` is the class that is responsible for building the Web site when it is run.

The `LocalResourceManagerResourceProvider` class isn't quite so simple. Here is an abbreviated version of it (see the source code for the book for the complete version):

```
public class LocalResourceManagerResourceProvider :
    BaseResourceManagerResourceProvider
    {
        private string virtualPath;

        public LocalResourceManagerResourceProvider(
            string virtualPath)
        {
            this.virtualPath = virtualPath;
        }
        protected override string GetBaseName()
        {
            return Path.GetFileName(virtualPath);
        }
        protected override Assembly GetResourceAssembly()
        {
            string virtualPathParent = GetVirtualPathParent();

            string localAssemblyName =
                GetLocalResourceAssemblyName(virtualPathParent);
```

```
            Object buildResult = GetBuildResultFromCache(cacheKey);

            if (buildResult != null)
                return GetBuildResultResultAssembly(buildResult);

            return null;
        }
}
```

The `GetBaseName` method returns the base name from the virtual path. So if the virtual path is "/WebSite1/Default.aspx", the base name is "Default". The `GetResourceAssembly` method has the job of finding the local resource assembly, given that its path and part of its name has been generated on the fly. We'll take it line by line using our example. `GetVirtualPathParent` returns "/WebSite1". `GetLocalResourceAssemblyName` returns "App_LocalResources.root", assuming that the .aspx files are located in the root. `GetBuildResultAssembly` returns the `Assembly` object from the assembly name. Each of these methods is implemented in the `LocalResourceManagerResourceProvider` class. Our implementation of a `ResourceProviderFactory` and its associated classes is complete. Our class mimics the behavior of the .NET Framework 2.0's `ResXResourceProviderFactory`.

DbResourceManagerResourceProviderFactory

Our `DbResourceManagerResourceProviderFactory` solution isn't nearly as complex as the `ResourceManagerResourceProviderFactory` solution. The main difference between the two implementations lies in a decision that the `ResourceSets` table in our localization database will contain both global and local resources, so it is not necessary for us to make a distinction between the two. So in this example, we need to implement only one `IResourceProvider` class because the one class will suffice for both global and local resources. Here is the `DbResourceManager ResourceProviderFactory`:

```
public class DbResourceManagerResourceProviderFactory :
    ResourceProviderFactory
{
    public DbResourceManagerResourceProviderFactory()
    {
    }
    public override IResourceProvider
```

```
        CreateGlobalResourceProvider(string classKey)
    {
        return new DbResourceManagerResourceProvider(classKey);
    }
    public override IResourceProvider
        CreateLocalResourceProvider(string virtualPath)
    {
        string classKey = Path.GetFileName(virtualPath);
        if (classKey.ToUpper().EndsWith(".ASPX"))
            // strip off the .aspx extension
            classKey = classKey.Substring(0, classKey.Length - 5);

        return new DbResourceManagerResourceProvider(classKey);

    }
}
```

The `CreateGlobalResourceProvider` method simply returns a new `DbResource ManagerResourceProvider` object, passing in the class key (e.g., "`ProductInfo`"). The `CreateLocalResourceProvider` method needs to convert the `virtualPath` (e.g., "`/WebSite1/Default.aspx`") into a class key (e.g., "`Default`") by stripping off the path and the `.aspx` extension. The `DbResourceManagerResourceProvider` class inherits from the `BaseResourceProvider` class that we created in the previous section; therefore, it only needs to implement the `CreateResourceManager` method:

```
public class DbResourceManagerResourceProvider :
    BaseResourceProvider
{
    private string classKey;

    public DbResourceManagerResourceProvider(string classKey)
    {
        this.classKey = classKey;
    }
    protected override ResourceManager CreateResourceManager()
    {
        DbResourceManager resourceManager =
            new DbResourceManager(classKey);

        resourceManager.IgnoreCase = true;

        return resourceManager;
    }
}
```

The `CreateResourceManager` method simply creates a new `DbResource Manager` and passes it the class key. Our implementation is complete. Armed with these examples, you should be able to create a `ResourceProviderFactory` and its associated classes for any custom resource manager.

Where Are We?

In this chapter, you learned how to create custom resource managers. Simple resource managers require only a relatively small effort, but as the complexity increases and the need to create writeable resource managers arises, a greater depth of `ResourceManager` internals is required. Unfortunately, as good as these facilities are in the .NET Framework, only ASP.NET 2.0 has a concept of a resource manager provider. Windows Forms applications are unable to easily make use of custom resource managers. The code generated by Visual Studio for Windows Forms needs care and attention; there is no provider class for resource managers as there is for ADO.NET classes, and WinRes is closed beyond help. In addition, the `Strongly TypedResourceBuilder` class and resgen utility need additional work to make them viable for non-resx resources. With a little effort and trickery, we can overcome these limitations and give applications better functionality. Finally, we looked at ASP.NET 2.0's resource provider model, how it works, and how to create a custom resource provider.

13

Testing Internationalization Using FxCop

O NE OF MY GOLDEN RULES of development is:

Anything a developer has to remember to do, they will eventually forget to do.

Rather than any criticism of developers I have worked with, this is instead a simple acknowledgment of the fact that there is simply too much to remember in development and that we are all human and we will all eventually forget something important. Most development departments have a coding standard. We all know that we are supposed to adhere to this coding standard, but sometimes we forget some of the details. Sure, these get picked up in a coding review, but even the coding review is a human process and subject to error. That's where FxCop comes in and takes the hard work out of checking the tiny (and not so tiny) details.

FxCop is a static analysis tool from Microsoft. It is included with Visual Studio 2005 Team Edition for Software Developers and Visual Studio 2005 Team Edition for Software Testers, and is available for download for all versions of both Visual Studio 2003 and Visual Studio 2005 from http://www.gotdotnet.com/team/fxcop. Put simply, FxCop reads one or more assemblies and applies coding rules to them. FxCop includes a library of existing rules and enables you to write your own. Throughout this book, I have discussed many internationalization practices that will make your project viable. You may have chosen to adopt some of these ideas in your development process. Certainly, it would be a good idea to formalize these in some internationalization standards document, but documents are simply a repository of information. They are passive, not active, and developers are human and will forget the standards that they are supposed to remember. FxCop gives us the capability to ensure and enforce these standards. In this chapter, I give a brief introduction to FxCop, show how FxCop can be enabled in Visual Studio 2005 Team Edition for Software Testers, discuss the globalization and spelling rules that are included in FxCop, introduce many new globalization rules that are included with this book, and explain how these rules were written.

For the purpose of this chapter, you need either FxCop 1.35 or FxCop 1.32. The former requires the .NET Framework 2.0 and analyzes assemblies for both the .NET Framework 2.0 and 1.1; the latter requires the .NET Framework 1.1 and analyzes assemblies for only the .NET Framework 1.1. If you have Visual Studio 2005 Team System, you already have version 1.35.

A Brief Introduction to FxCop

Visual Studio 2005 introduces Team System, which is a suite of tools aimed at project managers, architects, developers, and testers, and is designed to help manage the increasingly complex Software Development Life Cycle. Team System is available in several editions, each aimed at a different role in the development process. Team Edition for Architects is aimed at architects and project managers, Team Edition for Software Developers is aimed at developers, and Team Edition for Software Testers is aimed at testers. Of particular interest to us in this chapter is Team Edition for Software Developers, which supports static analysis performed by FxCop.

FxCop has three interfaces: a GUI built into Visual Studio 2005, a stand-alone GUI (`FxCop.exe`), and a command-line interface (`FxCopCmd.exe`). This section looks at the support built into Visual Studio 2005. To follow along, create a new Windows Forms application. By default, static analysis is not included in the build process. To enable FxCop, select the project's Properties Window, select the Code Analysis tab on the left side, and check the Enable FxCop check box (see Figure 13.1).

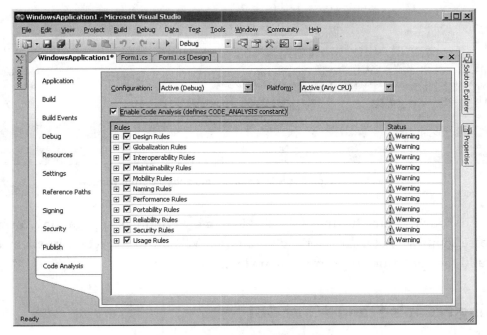

Figure 13.1   Enabling FxCop Code Analysis in Visual Studio 2005

You can also see a list of FxCop's built-in rules in this tab. One of these that should immediately catch your eye is "Globalization Rules." As you will see later, you can add new rule assemblies to this list. To see FxCop in action, add the following enum to the `Form1` class:

```
public enum CheeseEnum
    {SmokedAustrian, JapaneseSageDerby, VenezuelanBeaverCheese};
```

This enum represents a deliberate naming error; the enum name is suffixed with "`Enum`", which is contrary to Microsoft's recommended naming guidelines. When Code Analysis is enabled, FxCop is included in the build process. When you build the application, FxCop reports its errors to the Output Window just like compiler errors (see Figure 13.2).

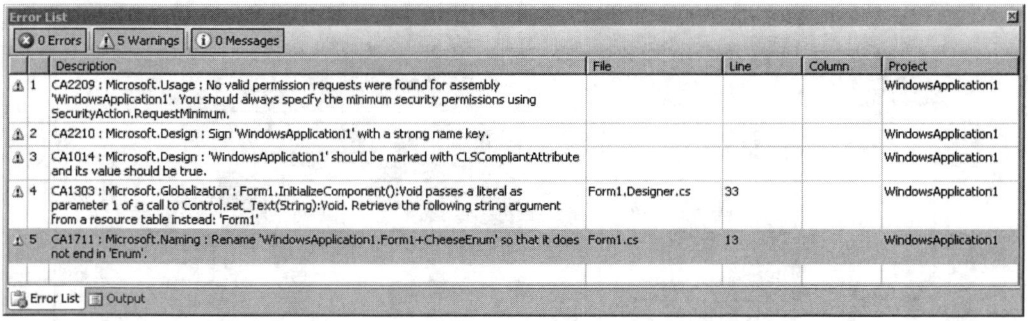

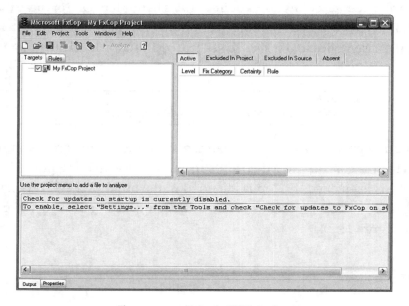

Figure 13.2   FxCop Errors in Visual Studio 2005's Output Window

The fourth item in the list is "Rename 'WindowsApplication1.Form1+ CheeseEnum' so that it does not end in 'Enum'." When you correct the problem and rebuild the application, the error will no longer be reported.

Using FxCop's Stand-Alone GUI

FxCop.exe is a stand-alone GUI that can be used with the .NET Framework 1.1 and 2.0. Run FxCop.exe, and you will see the default user interface (see Figure 13.3).

Figure 13.3   FxCop's GUI Interface

In the left pane, you can see a default FxCop project ("My FxCop Project"). FxCop projects are made up of a list of assemblies (called "Targets" in FxCop) and a list of rules. Rules are simply .NET classes that check the validity of any aspect of an assembly. If you click on the Rules tab, you will see a list of the built-in rules (see Figure 13.4).

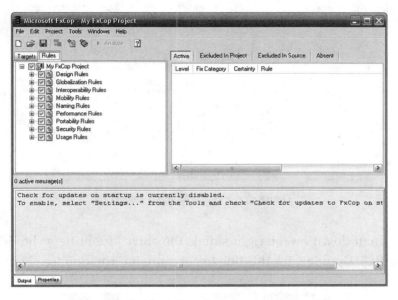

Figure 13.4   FxCop Rules

To see the stand-alone FxCop GUI in action, add the Windows Forms application created in the previous section to FxCop's list of targets (select Project, Add Targets… and select the newly built application's assembly (e.g., `WindowsApplication1.exe`). Click on the Analyze button in the toolbar. Figure 13.5 shows the result.

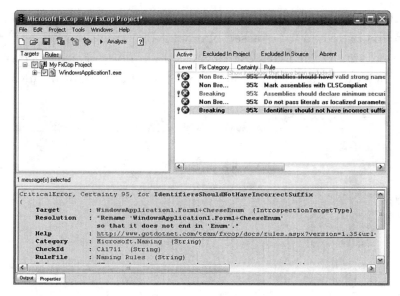

Figure 13.5   FxCop Analysis Report

The fifth item down on the right side is the entry "Identifiers should not have incorrect suffix". Double-click this line to get more information (see Figure 13.6).

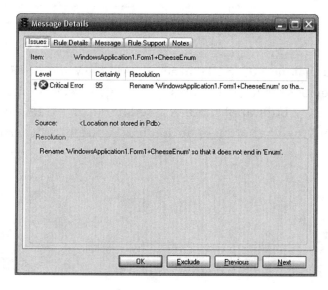

Figure 13.6   More Information

Correct the problem in the application, rebuild the application, and click Analyze again; the error is no longer reported. Clearly, there's more to FxCop than this, but now you should have an idea of what it is and how it works.

FxCop and ASP.NET

In general, using FxCop with ASP.NET applications is no different than using it with any other kind of application. You build your application and run FxCop on the generated assemblies. However, it is worth observing that FxCop can analyze code and resources only that are in an assembly. This means that if you have used the SRC attribute in your page directives, the resulting assembly will not contain your code and FxCop will be unable to analyze it. In addition, in case you needed any further justification for separating your code from your user interface, it should be obvious that any code you have in script tags in aspx files will not be included in the assembly built by Visual Studio. The solution is to move such code into a codebehind file.

Another issue for you to consider is how much of your application you want FxCop to analyze. Your aspx files make up a considerable part of your application, but these files are not compiled into the assembly built by Visual Studio (and, therefore, they are not analyzed by FxCop). These files are typically compiled at runtime. The aspx files are converted to code, and the code is compiled into an assembly. The general attitude to such code and its resulting assemblies is that it should not be analyzed by FxCop. The reasoning behind this is that a large part of the code is generated, and there is no clear distinction between the code that is generated and the HTML in the aspx files. Consequently, analyzing such assemblies generates numerous false errors and noise. For this reason, the ASP.NET 2 compiler (and other .NET Framework 2.0 code-generation tools) generates code that includes a `Generated-CodeAttribute` to show that the code is generated. FxCop ignores code that is marked with this attribute. At the time of writing, there is no way around this attribute, but this is an issue that is important to the FxCop team and a workaround might be introduced in a future release of FxCop.

If you are using ASP.NET 1.1 or a workaround for analyzing ASP.NET 2.0–generated assemblies is found, you might consider analyzing them on an occasional basis, as they do throw up FxCop errors that would not be caught otherwise. If you do want to analyze such assemblies, you will need to find them. In ASP.NET 1.1, the only way to get at the assemblies is to find them in ASP.NET's temporary folder in a series of mangled directory names. The mangling of the directory names and assembly names makes automating this process difficult. In ASP.NET 2.0, you have an alternative solution: You can precompile your Web site using the .NET Framework ASP.NET compiler. Open a .NET Framework command prompt and, from the .NET Framework folder, type:

```
aspnet_compiler -v /WebSite1 C:\WebSite1\PreCompiled -d
```

This command compiles a Web site from the `WebSite1` virtual directory and places the compiled output and debug files (PDBs) in the `C:\WebSite1\Pre Compiled` directory. This approach is marginally better than the ASP.NET 1.1 approach because the output is placed in a known location. However, the assembly names are still mangled, so there is still some work to be done. A better solution to this problem is to use a Web Deployment Project. Web Deployment Projects are MSBuild projects for ASP.NET 2 Web sites. You can find out more about Web Deployment Projects and download the Web Deployment Project add-in package at http://msdn.microsoft.com/asp.net/reference/infrastructure/wdp/default.aspx.

FxCop Globalization Rules

FxCop includes a set of rules under the heading "Globalization Rules." These rules check that your assemblies meet various internationalization standards. I briefly discuss each of these rules in turn, to highlight their pros and cons, and as a means of laying a foundation for new rules in the next section.

> To use the Globalization rules, the control flow analysis setting must be enabled, which, by default, it is. If you find that the Globalization rules are not catching errors that you suspect that they should, you should check this setting. In FxCop, select Tools, Settings…; select the Analysis Engines tab; select the Introspection engine; click the Settings button; and check the Enable Control Flow Analysis check box. This setting cannot be changed from within Visual Studio 2005.

"Avoid duplicate accelerators"

This rule is a great idea. It catches controls that use the same accelerator key in the same parent (typically a form). So if you define two labels with the texts "&Customer" and "&Contact", FxCop will catch the error and report "Define unique accelerators for the following controls in Form1 that all currently use &C as an accelerator: Form1.label1, Form1.label2". Note that the rule works by reading through the resources in the fallback assemblies, so this rule applies only if you set Form.Localizable to true. It also compares accelerator keys only on the same form, so, not unreasonably, it cannot detect clashes caused by combining forms at runtime. Also note that the rule does not apply to menu items.

> An important limitation of this rule and all FxCop rules is that FxCop's analysis engine is limited to analyzing resources in the fallback assembly only. Support for analyzing resources in a satellite assembly is planned for a future release.

"Do not hardcode locale specific strings"

This rule checks for code that contains literals that refer to culture-specific environment special folders. Special folders are folders such as "Program Files". In non-English versions of Windows, the names of special folders are localized, so if your application refers to a path by its English name, it will fail (in the German version of Windows, for example, this folder is called "Programme"). The following code results in one error (for "\System32"):

```
string windowsFolder = @"\Windows";
string systemFolder = @"\System32";
Text = "The System folder is " + windowsFolder + systemFolder;
```

The solution is to use Environment.GetFolderPath and Environment.SpecialFolder:

```
Text = "The System folder is " +
    System.Environment.GetFolderPath(
    Environment.SpecialFolder.System);
```

This rule is a good idea, but its pattern matching errs on the side of caution. The folder names cannot be even slightly disguised for the rule to apply, so the following assignments are not caught by this rule:

```
string systemDataFileName =
@"C:\WINDOWS\Microsoft.NET\Framework\v1.1.4322\System.Data.dll";

string smartTagFileName = @"C:\Program Files\Common Files\" +
    @"Microsoft Shared\Smart Tag\SmartTagInstall.exe";

string systemFolder = @"\Windows\System32";
```

I'll leave it as an exercise for you to write a more enthusiastic version of this rule after we have covered writing FxCop rules.

"Do not pass literals as localized parameters"

Here's another great idea. This rule catches literal strings that should be localizable. Here's an example:

```
MessageBox.Show("Insert the paper and press Send");
```

Clearly, this text has been hard-coded into the application and, therefore, is not localizable. The problem that this rule is trying to solve is quite a tricky one. It is trying to catch literal strings that should be localizable. In the previous example, it is easy to see that the string should be localizable. However, it is not just a simple case of mindlessly ploughing through an assembly identifying all literal strings. Assemblies are full of literal strings that are completely valid and should not be localizable. The rule has to take a more intelligent approach. The rule decides that a literal should be localized if:

- It is used as a parameter where the name of the parameter is either "caption", "message", or "text".

- It is used in an assignment to a property called either "Caption", "Message", or "Text".

- It is used in an assignment to a property that has been marked as Localizable(true).

For example, the first parameter to `MessageBox.Show()` is called "text" and, therefore, meets these requirements. The `DateTime.ToString()` method also accepts a string as a parameter, but this string is not considered to be a target for localization.

```
MessageBox.Show(DateTime.Now.ToString(
    "HH:mm:ss", CultureInfo.CurrentUICulture));
```

You can "disable" this rule at the property level by marking a property with the `Localizable(false)` attribute.

This "smart" approach to detecting literal strings ensures that there are very few false positives. The rule's heuristic also means that the vast majority of localization cases will be caught. If you have literal text that is not being caught by this rule, the best solution is to use either parameter names of "caption", "message", and "text" or property names of "Caption", "Message" and "Text", or mark properties with the `Localizable(true)` attribute. If these solutions are not suitable, for a less accurate but more open solution, look at the "Do not use literal strings" rule, which I cover later in this chapter.

Another issue that you should consider when using this rule is that it considers `Exception.Message` to be localizable. You may or may not agree with this, and you should refer to "Exception Messages" in Chapter 8, "Best Practices," for more information. In summary, messages such as "Value does not fall within the expected range" are probably intended for the developer's benefit, whereas messages such as "Access denied" might be more useful to the user. Consequently, you need a policy on whether exception messages should be localizable. If you feel that they should not be localizable, this rule will give you many false positives.

"Set locale for data types"

This rule ensures that the `DataTable.Locale` property is set on all `DataTable` objects (either directly through `DataTable.Locale` or indirectly through `DataSet.Locale`). Data that is persisted or that crosses the application boundary should use the invariant culture or a culture that is uniform throughout all uses of the data. This rule serves to remind developers of this.

"Specify CultureInfo" and "Specify IFormatProvider"

These two rules are quite similar and attempt to check for unintended results from conversions and comparisons. "Specify `CultureInfo`" checks that when you call a method that has an overloaded version that accepts a `CultureInfo` parameter, you use that overloaded version and explicitly pass a `CultureInfo` parameter. An example is `String.ToUpper()`. This method has two overloaded versions: one that accepts a `CultureInfo` parameter and one that doesn't. If you call `String.To Upper()` without a `CultureInfo` parameter, FxCop will report an error. The same is true for the "Specify `IFormatProvider`" rule, which demands that if you call a method that has an overloaded version that accepts an `IFormatProvider` parameter, you pass a value for this parameter. An example of such a method is `DateTime.ToString()`. So the following code generates a "Specify `CultureInfo`" and a "Specify `IFormatProvider`" FxCop error:

```
string greeting = "Hello";
DateTime dateTime = new DateTime(2005, 1, 31);
greeting.ToUpper();
dateTime.ToString();
```

whereas the following code does not generate these errors:

```
string greeting = "Hello";
DateTime dateTime = new DateTime(2005, 1, 31);
greeting.ToUpper(CultureInfo.CurrentCulture);
dateTime.ToString(CultureInfo.CurrentCulture);
```

If you recall our discussion of `CultureInfo.CurrentCulture` in Chapter 6, "Globalization," you will notice that there is no functional difference between these two blocks of code. If the `CultureInfo` and `IFormatProvider` parameters are excluded, they will default to `CultureInfo.CurrentCulture`. Consequently, you might ask why, then, is there a rule to ensure that the default value cannot be used? The problem is one of ambiguity. It isn't possible for a static analysis engine to determine what the purpose of the conversion is. If the purpose is to display the result in the user interface, the `CultureInfo.CurrentUICulture` should be used. Of course, if you set the `CultureInfo.CurrentCulture` to be the same as `CultureInfo.CurrentUICulture`, we are back to the situation in which passing `CultureInfo.CurrentUICulture` has no functional difference from accepting the default.

However, if the purpose of the conversion is to persist the result in a file or a database, there is a good argument that using either the `CultureInfo.CurrentCulture` or the `CultureInfo.CurrentUICulture` is incorrect. The argument would be that a persistent store should not be dependent upon a language or region so that the information is consistent across all languages and regions. In this scenario, a `CultureInfo`/`IFormatProvider` value must be passed. The problem that the rule faces is that it doesn't know when it is essential to explicitly pass a value, so it takes the approach that a value must always be passed so that the developer is forced to make a conscious decision. Unfortunately, I suspect that the majority of calls to such methods pass the default value for this parameter anyway, and the calls that use `CultureInfo.InvariantCulture` are the exception.

In the "Writing FxCop Globalization" rules section, I show you a new rule that checks for culture-specific `DateTime` format strings.

> The "Specify `CultureInfo`" rule can be reported for code that Visual Studio itself generates in a form's `InitializeComponent` method. As you are not able to change the way this code is generated, and changing the code itself is both hazardous and pointless, you should "exclude" these errors. (FxCop allows errors to be excluded so that it does not report the specific excluded cases again.)

"Specify MessageBoxOptions"

This rule ensures that all calls to `MessageBox.Show` pass a parameter for the `MessageBoxOptions`. The purpose of this requirement is to ensure that developers have considered how message boxes will behave in a right-to-left application. If you set a form's `RightToLeft` property to `true`, all of the controls will inherit this setting by default and will look and behave appropriately on a right-to-left application. However, message boxes do not inherit such look and behavior from forms, so a simple call to `MessageBox.Show("Hello")` will result in a left-to-right dialog. To fix the code, the `MessageBoxOptions` parameter must be passed. The equivalent call to `MessageBox.Show` is now:

```
MessageBox.Show("Hello", String.Empty, MessageBoxButtons.OK,
    MessageBoxIcon.None, MessageBoxDefaultButton.Button1,
    (MessageBoxOptions) 0);
```

This prevents FxCop from raising the "Specify `MessageBoxOptions`" error, because a value for `MessageBoxOptions` is passed, but it doesn't solve the problem. The solution is to pass `MessageBoxOptions.RightToLeft` and `MessageBox Options.RtlReading` for this parameter on right-to-left systems or a 0 value on left-to-right systems. See the "`MessageBox`" section in Chapter 7, "Middle East and East Asian Cultures," for more information.

FxCop Spelling Rules

In addition to FxCop's Globalization rules, FxCop includes a number of spelling rules, shown in Table 13.1.

Table 13.1   FxCop Spelling Rules

Rule Name	Category	Check Id	Description
Identifiers should be spelled correctly	`Microsoft.Naming`	CA1704	The individual words that make up an identifier should not be abbreviated and should be spelled correctly.
Literals should be spelled correctly	`Microsoft.Usage`	CA2204	Literals should consist of correctly spelled words.
Resource strings should be spelled correctly	`Microsoft.Naming`	CA1703	The individual words that make up a resource string should not be abbreviated and should be spelled correctly.

FxCop's Spelling rules are available only in the stand-alone FxCop, not in the Visual Studio 2005 Team System FxCop, because it was not possible to provide these rules for all localized versions of Visual Studio 2005.

The rule that is most relevant to internationalization is the "Resource strings should be spelled correctly" rule. This rule checks the spelling of words in the fall-back resources. Say that you have a resource string called "TheUltimateAnswer" and it has the value "Noobdy writes jokes in base 13". FxCop reports:

```
Correct the spelling of 'Noobdy' in 'TheUltimateAnswer' ==
'Noobdy writes jokes in base 13' contained in resource stream
'FxCopTest1.Form1Resources.resources'.
```

This is very useful, but there are a few things you should know. First, the spell checker requires Microsoft Office to be installed on the machine on which FxCop is running (at least one of the Office products must be version 2000 or later). If it is not installed, the rule doesn't perform any spell checking (but it doesn't cause FxCop to fail). Second, the "Resource strings should be spelled correctly rule" checks only the fallback assembly, not satellite assemblies. Third, you can add new words to the spell checker's dictionary by adding entries to CustomDictionary.xml. You can create a new CustomDictionary.xml in the same location as your FxCop project file to apply to a single FxCop project. This is the simplest option if your project is managed by a version-control system, and your FxCop project and CustomDictionary.xml are included in the version-control system. Alternatively, you can create a new CustomDictionary.xml in your user settings directory to apply to all projects for a single user. In addition, you can modify the CustomDictionary.xml in FxCop's directory to apply to all projects for all users.

You can change the dictionary that these rules use by opening FxCop.exe; selecting Project, Options...; selecting the Spelling & Analysis tab; and selecting a new language in the Dictionary Locale combo box. Note that the same language applies to all spelling rules. This represents a problem because often developers will write code using U.S. English (using U.S. English identifier names such as "color") but create fallback resources using a different language. This is even true in countries such as Australia, Canada, and the United Kingdom, where code is often written in U.S. English but fallback resources are in the countries' native English. In a future release of FxCop, it is expected that it will be possible to specify two locales for a single project (where words can match the dictionary for either locale to pass the rule) and also to specify one dictionary for code and a separate dictionary for resources. Until then, you will have to create two FxCop projects: The first would perform analysis on the code (using one dictionary), and the second would perform analysis on the resources (using the other dictionary).

Overview of New FxCop Globalization Rules

Now that we know how FxCop works and what we can expect from the FxCop Globalization rules, let's look at writing our own FxCop Globalization rules. We cover this subject in two phases. First, we look at the rules from a usage point of view. If you're just interested in adding some new globalization rules to your library of rules and you don't want to know how they work, you'll need to read only this section. Second, we look at how each rule is implemented. From this, you will learn how to write your own FxCop rules.

I have grouped the rules into three categories:

- Resource rules
- Type/Resource rules
- Instruction rules

The categories are relevant from the point of view of developing the rules, so if you intend only to consume them, then this grouping won't provide you with any benefit. Resource rules are rules that analyze the resources in an assembly. An example is:

- Control characters embedded in resource string

Type/Resource rules are rules that analyze the resources in an assembly for a given type. They are:

- `Form.Language` must be `(Default)`
- `Form.Localizable` must be `true`
- `Label.AutoSize` must be `true`

Instruction rules are rules that analyze the instructions in an assembly. They are:

- `CultureInfo` must not be constructed from LCID
- `CultureInfo` not provided by provider
- `DateTime.ToString()` should not use a culture specific format
- Dialog culture dictated by operating system

- Dialog culture dictated by .NET Framework
- Do not use literal strings
- `RegionInfo` must not be constructed from LCID
- `ResourceManager` not provided by provider
- Resource string missing from fallback assembly
- Thread not provided by `ThreadFactory`

Resource Rules

"Control characters embedded in resource string"

This simple rule walks through all of the resource string values in an assembly, looking for strings that contain embedded control characters. For example:

```
You have 5 deliveries\nPress any key
```

This string has a new line control character ("\n") in the string. For a discussion of the pros and cons of embedding control characters in resource strings, see the section entitled "Embedded Control Characters" in Chapter 8. You need to decide for yourself who should have control over control characters in your strings: the developers or the translator. If you opt for the former, you should apply this rule. If you opt for the latter, you should not apply this rule.

Type/Resource Rules

"Form.Language must be (Default)"

This rule catches forms in which the `Language` property has been set to something other than "`(Default)`". This rule doesn't correspond to a runtime problem because the form that is displayed is dependent upon `CultureInfo.CurrentUICulture`. Instead, this is a development problem. What has mostly likely happened here is that a developer has opened a form in Visual Studio and has needed to do some work on a specific culture. So the developer changed the form's language to that culture, performed the work, and then saved the form. So far, there is no problem. As usual, the problem arises during the maintenance phase. The next programmer to open the form won't necessarily check that the form's language is already "(Default)". Visual Studio 2005 is less prone to this problem than Visual Studio 2003 because it provides visual feedback of the selected culture in the Form Designer tab's text. Visual Studio allows certain changes, such as moving and resizing controls, and changing various properties, to refer specifically to the selected culture version of the form; thus, the developer is unwittingly changing only a single culture, not all cultures. Maybe I am too paranoid and this situation won't ever happen, but that's why I like FxCop—I can write rules that will never be needed 99.9 percent of the time, but I can be certain that they will always be applied.

"Form.Localizable must be true"

Here's a rather fundamental rule. This rule checks that the `Localizable` property of the form has been set to `true`. If it hasn't been set to `true`, it won't be possible to localize it. I would say that's quite fundamental, but as an application grows in size, it is sometimes possible to forget even the basics.

At the time of writing, however, this rule is appropriate only for forms developed for the .NET Framework 1.1, not for forms developed for the .NET Framework 2.0. The reason for this is that the storage of the `Form.Localizable` property changed in the .NET Framework 2.0. Here's how `Form.Localizable` is represented in a .NET Framework 1.1 resx file:

```
<data name="$this.Localizable" type="System.Boolean, mscorlib,
Version=1.0.5000.0, Culture=neutral,
PublicKeyToken=b77a5c561934e089">
```

Here's the same again, but for a .NET Framework 2.0 resx file:

```
<metadata name="$this.Localizable" type="System.Boolean, mscorlib,
Version=2.0.0.0, Culture=neutral,
PublicKeyToken=b77a5c561934e089">
```

The difference is that in the .NET Framework 2.0 `Form.Localizable` is considered to be metadata instead of data. At the time of writing, FxCop does not support the reading of metadata resources.

"Label.AutoSize must be true"

This rule checks that the `AutoSize` property of `System.Windows.Forms'` `Label` controls has been set to `true`. This applies more to .NET Framework 1.1 applications than .NET Framework 2.0 applications because Visual Studio 2005 sets `Label.AutoSize` to `true` for all new `Labels`. Clearly, this rule is dependent upon whether you feel that `Labels` should be auto-sized. Refer to the "AutoSize" section of Chapter 8 for the discussion of the pros and cons of setting `Label.AutoSize` to `true`.

Instruction Rules

"CultureInfo must not be constructed from LCID" and "RegionInfo must not be constructed from LCID"

The "`CultureInfo` must not be constructed from LCID" rule checks that the `CultureInfo` or `CultureInfoEx` constructors (or the `CultureInfo.GetCultureInfo` or `CultureInfoProvider.GetCultureInfo` methods) are not used with integers (integers are locale identifiers, LCIDs). The idea is that you should construct new `CultureInfo/CultureInfoEx` objects using a name (e.g. "en-US") and not an LCID. The reasoning behind this is that supplementary custom cultures (in the .NET Framework 2.0) all share the same LCID (`0x1000`, `4096`), which is invalid as an LCID used to construct a new `CultureInfo`. To be sure that code works as well with custom cultures as it does with regular cultures, the code should use culture names. See Chapter 11, "Custom Cultures," for more information. There is an exception to this rule, and that is when constructing a culture for an alternate sort order. For example:

```
CultureInfo cultureInfo = new CultureInfo(0x000040A);
```

This code creates the `Spanish (Spain)` culture using the alternate sort order. The rule accepts literal LCIDs as valid but instead protects against integers derived from an expression. In the .NET Framework 1.1, this exception is essential because cultures that use alternate sort orders can be constructed only using LCIDs. However, the .NET Framework 2.0 allows cultures that use alternate sort orders to be constructed using strings (e.g., "es-ES_tradnl"), so the need for the exception is minimized.

The "`RegionInfo` must not be constructed from LCID" rule is almost identical, with the exceptions that it checks for `RegionInfo` constructors and it doesn't check for calls to some `RegionInfo` equivalent to `CultureInfoProvider.GetCulture-Info` because there is no equivalent. The rule itself, however, is possibly more important because the following pattern often occurs:

```
CultureInfo cultureInfo = new CultureInfo("en-US");
RegionInfo regionInfo = new RegionInfo(cultureInfo.LCID);
```

To work with custom cultures, the second line should be changed to:

```
RegionInfo regionInfo = new RegionInfo(cultureInfo.Name);
```

"CultureInfo not provided by Provider"

In some scenarios, it is useful to ensure that all `CultureInfo` objects are created using a provider or factory instead of directly using the `CultureInfo` constructor. Two of these situations are discussed in Chapter 6 for updating out-of-date culture information and also for extending `CultureInfo` objects with additional globalization information. This rule enforces that all objects are created using the `Globalization.CultureInfoProvider.GetCultureInfo` method, so instead of writing this:

```
CultureInfo cultureInfo = new CultureInfo("en-US");
```

you should write this:

```
CultureInfo cultureInfo =
    Globalization.CultureInfoProvider.GetCultureInfo("en-US");
```

"DateTime.ToString() should not use a culture specific format"

This rule is a cousin of the "Specify IFormatProvider" rule. It checks that the format string passed to `DateTime.ToString()` is not a culture-specific format. This is not the same as checking that an `IFormatProvider` is passed. Here's an example that breaks the rule:

```
DateTime dateTime = new DateTime(2005, 1, 5);
string dateTimeString = dateTime.ToString("MM/dd/yyyy");
```

The `"MM/dd/yyyy"` format is culture-specific. A date displayed in this format in Germany would not be interpreted as the same date displayed in the U.S. If you include an `IFormatProvider`, it changes only the formatting of the string; the order is dictated by the string parameter. So the following amendment changes only the slashes to periods:

```
string dateTimeString =
    dateTime.ToString("MM/dd/yyyy", new CultureInfo("de-DE"));
```

All of the single-character string format parameters (e.g., "d", "D") are quite acceptable because they are simply shorthand for a culture-sensitive setting. For example, `DateTime.ToString("D")` is the same as `DateTime.ToLongDateString()`, which is culture sensitive. These single-character formats are not raised as an error.

"Dialog culture dictated by operating system" and "Dialog culture dictated by .NET Framework"

These two rules provide reminders about various Windows Forms dialogs. Recall from Chapter 4, "Windows Forms Specifics," that many of the .NET Framework controls (e.g., `OpenFileDialog`) take their localized resources from the operating system and that one control takes its localized resources from the .NET Framework Language Pack. If you have written an application that allows the user to change the UI culture of your application (either through the "Regional and Language Options" or through a manual approach), the change will affect all of the resources over which your application has control, but it won't affect these dialogs because they are not influenced by your application's settings. As a consequence, your application's user interface will have a split personality.

"Do not use literal strings"

This rule is related to the "Do not pass literals as localized parameters" rule. The latter rule aims for correctness, and the number of false positives that it generates is very low. Necessarily, its scope is narrow. This new rule has a much wider approach and generates a significant number of false positives. I start by explaining the rule and then I talk about how we can overcome the large number of false positives.

The "Do not use literal strings" rule mindlessly ploughs through assemblies looking for strings. It ignores all strings in the `InitializeComponent` method of `Form` classes, as these will already have been handled by setting `Form.Localizable` to `true` (and the "`Form.Localizable` must be `true`" rule ensures that it is true). It also ignores all strings that are parameters to:

- Exception constructors (because these are handled by other rules)
- `ResourceManager` constructors (because these are never localizable)
- `ResourceManagerProvider` constructors (because these are never localizable)
- `DateTime.ToString()` (because these are never localizable)
- `Debug.WriteLine` (because these are used for debugging)
- `Trace.WriteLine` (because these are used for debugging)

It also ignores strings that are single characters (after all of the white space has been removed). The result is a "suspect" string. The first time you run this rule, all suspect strings will be reported. They will also be written to a file called `Literal-Strings.xml`, which will be used later. The list will include a significant number of false positives. The developer should then look at each error and decide which are genuine reports and fix them (by putting the string in a resource). This leaves us with a whole bunch of false positives. We need a way to say that these are okay and that they shouldn't be reported on again. For this purpose, I wrote the Literal String Manager. When you start the Literal String Manager, it looks for the `Literal-Strings.xml` file and displays it like this:

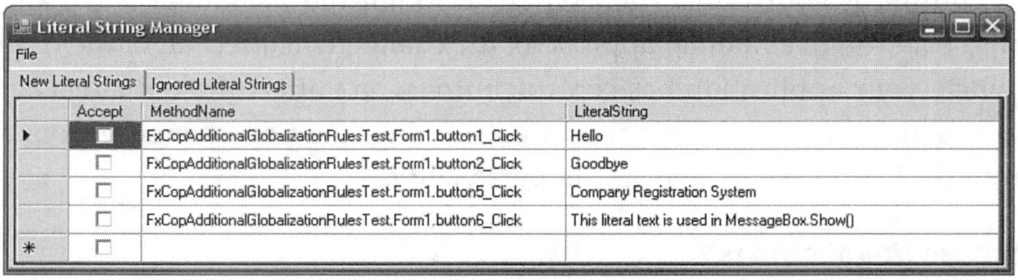

Figure 13.7   Literal String Manager Showing Suspect Strings

The idea is that you go down the list accepting all of the strings that you don't want to see again (it's a bit like a spam filter for localizability). The list of accepted strings is written to `IgnoredLiteralStrings.xml`. This file is read by the "Do not pass literal strings" rule so that you don't get told about these false positives the next time you run FxCop.

As such, this rule represents a fine balance between the benefit of being told about strings that you have forgotten to make localizable and the additional effort of maintaining the list of ignored literal strings. My experience of this is that it catches many more strings than I want to admit to, and, as such, I have to live with the inconvenience of keeping the ignored list up-to-date.

"ResourceManager not provided by provider"

This rule is useful if you write custom resource managers (see Chapter 12, "Custom Resource Managers"). It checks to see if a resource manager is created from the `ResourceManager` class or a descendant of it. The approach recommended in Chapter 12 is to create all resource managers using the `ResourceManagerProvider` class written in the same chapter. The `ResourceManagerProvider` class, therefore, does to `ResourceManagers` what the ADO.NET 2 `DbProviderFactories` class does to connection classes; it provides a level of indirection between the application and the exact `ResourceManager` class that is used. This rule ensures that developers stick to the approach of using the `ResourceManagerProvider` class and don't stray back into creating resource managers using an explicitly named class.

"Resource string missing from fallback assembly"

This rule checks that all resource names used in `ResourceManager.GetString()` exist in an equivalent resource in the fallback assembly. In this code snippet, the `Resource-Manager.GetString()` method is being called with a resource name of "Hello":

```
string hello = resourceManager.GetString("Hello");
```

This rule looks through the corresponding resource for a key called "Hello", and if the key doesn't exist, the rule identifies it as an error. It makes no difference whether you use strongly-typed resources or not, as the strongly-typed resources simply map a property name onto a string and, hence, will be checked in the same way. Hence, this rule epitomises the value of FxCop; recall my maxim from the beginning of the chapter, "Anything a developer has to remember to do, they will eventually forget to do." One of the things that a developer has to remember to do is to add the keys that they use to the fallback resource. My experience is that this is very easily forgotten, and this rule exists to catch those times.

Of course, this does raise the question of how the rule finds the correct resource to locate the key. Herein lies a bit of an assumption. The assumption is that you have adhered to the naming convention suggested in Chapter 3, "An Introduction to

Internationalization." To recap briefly, I suggested that each source file have a corresponding resource file with the same name, but suffixed with "Resources". So "Form1.cs" would normally have an associated resource file "Form1.resx", which is maintained by Visual Studio; your own resources under your own control would go in a file called "Form1Resources.resx". If this convention is maintained, the rule will be able to find the associated resource. If the convention is not maintained, you will need to modify the rule to locate the associated resource.

"Thread not provided by ThreadFactory"

This rule enforces the recommendation made in Chapter 3 that threads should be created using a thread factory instead of the System.Threading.Thread constructor. This ensures that all new threads have their CurrentCulture and Current UICulture properties set, so instead of writing this:

```
Thread thread = new Thread(new ThreadStart(Work));
```

developers should write this:

```
Thread thread = ThreadFactory.CreateThread(new ThreadStart(Work));
```

Writing FxCop Globalization Rules

Now that we know what all of the new rules are, we can turn our attention to implementing them. In earlier versions, FxCop used an analysis engine that was based upon reflection. Since v1.30, FxCop has supported a new engine that is based upon introspection, and the reflection engine has now been dropped. All of the rules in this section are based on the introspection engine. Introspection is a reflection-like technology that is multithreaded, provides faster analysis of assemblies, works with different versions of the .NET Framework, and, unlike reflection, does not lock those assemblies.

Getting Started Writing FxCop Rules

As I mentioned earlier, we look at the rules in order of their categories. We start our journey with a resource rule—that is, a rule that analyzes resources. This rule is "top heavy" because we use it as an example of how to write FxCop rules in general.

FxCop introspection rules are .NET classes that inherit from `BaseIntrospection Rule`. They are placed in a class library and must have an associated entry in an embedded XML resource. Start by creating a new class library. I called my project and solution "`GlobalizationRules`", but to avoid a clash with FxCop's own DLLs, I set the output assembly to "`I18NBook.GlobalizationRules`". Add references to `FxCopSdk.dll` and `Microsoft.Cci.dll` (both are in the `FxCop` folder). We will create an abstract globalization rule base class from which all of our globalization rules will inherit. This gives us a point at which we can add more functionality later:

```
public abstract class BaseGlobalizationRule: BaseIntrospectionRule
{
    protected BaseGlobalizationRule(string name):
        base(name, "GlobalizationRules.RuleData",
        typeof(BaseGlobalizationRule).Assembly)
    {
    }
}
```

The constructor accepts a string that represents the rule's name. This string is critical to binding the rule to its rule data, as we shall see in the first rule. The `BaseGlobalizationRule`'s constructor calls the `BaseIntrospectionRule`'s constructor and passes the rule name, a fully qualified XML resource name, and an assembly where the fully qualified XML resource can be found. The XML resource is an XML file that contains essential property values of each rule. Because we will use the same XML file for all of our rules, we can specify this here in the base class and not bother our descendants with this problem or the problem of where this XML resource can be found. We will see an implementation of the XML resource in the first rule.

Add a new XML file to the project (in Solution Explorer, right-click the `Globalization Rules` project; select Add, New Item...; and select XML File). Name the file "`RuleData.xml`". The name of the file is important. The second parameter passed to the `BaseIntrospectionRule` constructor must identify this XML resource by name. If the file is called "`RuleData.xml`" and the project's default namespace is "`GlobalizationRules`", the fully qualified name of the `RuleData` resource is "`GlobalizationRules.RuleData`". Finally, in the Properties Window of `RuleData.xml`, set Build Action to Embedded Resource so that the `RuleData.xml` file is embedded into the `GlobalizationRules` assembly as a resource.

"Control characters embedded in resource string"

To create a rule, we need to write a new class and inherit from our `BaseGlobalizationRule`:

```
public class ControlCharactersEmbeddedInResourceString:
    BaseGlobalizationRule
{
    public ControlCharactersEmbeddedInResourceString():
        base("ControlCharactersEmbeddedInResourceString")
    {
    }
}
```

The constructor calls the `BaseGlobalizationRules` constructor and passes the name of the rule. This name must exactly match the entry in the XML rules file. This brings us to adding the entry in the XML rules file. The XML rules file is a simple XML file with a `<Rules>` element containing zero or more `<Rule>` tags. Each `<Rule>` must have an attribute called `TypeName` that exactly matches the string passed to the `BaseGlobalizationRule` constructor. The `Rule` elements provide more information about the rule. Here's an XML document, including the definition of the `ControlCharactersEmbeddedInResourceString` rule:

```
<?xml version="1.0" encoding="utf-8" ?>
<Rules>
    <Rule TypeName="ControlCharactersEmbeddedInResourceString"
    Category="Globalization" CheckId="G0007">
        <Name>Control characters embedded in resource string
        </Name>
        <Description>Resource string has control characters embedded in
        it. Strings should not contain control characters because they
        represent functionality and not text
        </Description>
        <Owner>Guy Smith-Ferrier</Owner>
        <Url>http://www.dotnet18n.com/fxcop</Url>
        <Resolution>Break up the string in "{0}" into separate strings
        and use Environment properties instead of control characters or
        hard code the control character strings. The string is "{1}".
        </Resolution>
        <Email></Email>
        <MessageLevel Certainty="95">Warning</MessageLevel>
        <FixCategories>NonBreaking</FixCategories>
    </Rule>
</Rules>
```

The Name element is shown in the error list. If you are using the stand-alone FxCop GUI, you can see most of the other elements in the Rule Details tab of the Message Details dialog (see Figure 13.8).

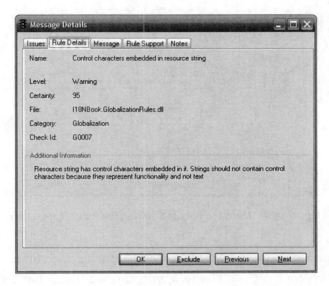

Figure 13.8   Rule Details Tab Showing the Use of A Rule's XML Information

Perhaps the most important element is the Resolution, which, in this rule, is:

```
Break up the string in "{0}" into separate strings and use
Environment properties instead of control characters or hard
code the control character strings. The string is "{1}".
```

It is important because it is shown in the Issues tab of the Message Details dialog, which is the first thing the developer sees when double-clicking the error (see Figure 13.9).

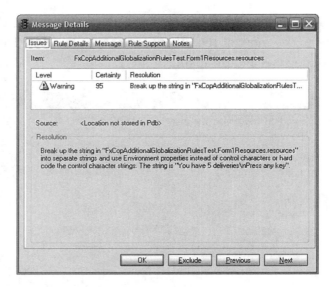

Figure 13.9   Message Details Showing the Rule's Resolution

What is important about it is that it contains information about the specific error in question. In the `Resolution` element, you can see that it has two placeholders: `{0}` and `{1}`. In the Issues tab, you can see that these placeholders have been substituted with values "`FxCopAdditionalGlobalizationRulesTest.Form1 Resources.resources`" and "`You have 5 deliveries\nPress any key`". When we implement the rule, you will see how these placeholders are filled.

Visual Studio 2003 has an excellent gotcha that you should be aware of when modifying the XML rules file. If you modify the XML file, the change is not considered to be important enough to rebuild the XML resource (even if you save the XML file after making your change). This means that you can add new rules to the XML rules file and build your rules assembly, only to find that FxCop doesn't see your new or modified rules. To get the change noticed, you must do a rebuild (Build, Rebuild Solution). This behavior is the same for all embedded resources.

To implement the rule, you override one of the `BaseIntrospectionRule.Check` methods:

```
public virtual ProblemCollection Check(Member member);
public virtual ProblemCollection Check(Module module);
public virtual ProblemCollection Check(Parameter parameter);
public virtual ProblemCollection Check(Resource resource);
public virtual ProblemCollection Check(TypeNode type);
public virtual ProblemCollection Check(string namespaceName,
    TypeNodeList types);
```

The strategy is to look through the list of possibilities, find the one that matches the entity that you want to analyze, and override that method. In our case, we want to analyze resources to see if they contain control characters, so we override the `Check(Resource)` method. Here's our implementation:

```
public override ProblemCollection Check(Resource resource)
{
    ResourceReader reader = new ResourceReader(
        new System.IO.MemoryStream(resource.Data));
    try
    {
        IDictionaryEnumerator enumerator = reader.GetEnumerator();
        while (enumerator.MoveNext())
        {
            if (ResourceStringHasEmbeddedControlCharacters(
                enumerator.Value))
            {
                Resolution resolution = GetResolution(
                    new string[] {resource.Name.ToString(),
                    enumerator.Value.ToString()});
                Problems.Add(new Problem(resolution));
                return Problems;
            }
        }
    }
    finally
    {
        reader.Close();
    }
    return base.Check(resource);
}
```

Our method is called iteratively for every resource in the fallback assembly. The resource is loaded from `resource.Data` using a `MemoryStream`. We read through each item in those resources using a `ResourceReader`. For each item, we call `ResourceStringHasEmbeddedControlCharacters`, which is implemented like this:

```
protected virtual bool ResourceStringHasEmbeddedControlCharacters(
    object resourceObject)
{
    if (resourceObject is string)
    {
        string resourceString = (string) resourceObject;
        int startIndex = 0;
        int foundCharacter;
        while ((foundCharacter =
            resourceString.IndexOf('\\', startIndex)) > -1)
        {
            if (foundCharacter < resourceString.Length &&
                resourceString[foundCharacter + 1] != '\\')
                return true;
            startIndex = foundCharacter + 1;
        }
    }
    return false;
}
```

This test checks that the value is a string and that it contains a "\", which is not the last character and is not followed by another "\" (two "\" characters indicates a literal "\" and not a control character). If the string is identified to contain a control character, we need to report this problem back to FxCop. We do this by creating a new `Problem` object, adding it to the `Problems` collection, and returning it from the method:

```
Resolution resolution = GetResolution(
    new string[] {resource.Name.ToString(),
    enumerator.Value.ToString()});

Problems.Add(new Problem(resolution));

return Problems;
```

`GetResolution` is a `BaseIntrospectionRule` method that gets the `Resolution` element of the rule as specified in our `RuleData.xml` file. Recall that our resolution string has two placeholders. These placeholders are replaed by the two parameters passed to `GetResolution`, which are the name of the resource and the value of the resource string. Finally, the resolution is converted to an array of `Problem` objects. Our rule is complete.

Type/Resource Rules

"Form.Language must be (Default)"

This rule represents the first of our Type/Resource rules. These are similar to the Resource rule that we have just looked at, but they allow us to iterate through resources of a given type. In the case of the "`Form.Language` must be `(Default)`" rule, the type is "`System.Windows.Forms.Form`". Because this functionality is shared across several rules, I have written a new base class, `BaseTypeResourceRule`, to encapsulate this functionality:

```
public abstract class BaseTypeResourceRule: BaseGlobalizationRule
{
    private string typeName;

    public BaseTypeResourceRule(string name, string typeName):
        base(name)
    {
        this.typeName = typeName;
    }
    public override ProblemCollection Check(TypeNode type)
    {
        if (TypeIsSubClassOf(type, typeName))
        {
            Resource resource;
            if (GetResource(type, out resource))
                return CheckResource(type, resource);
        }
        return base.Check(type);
    }
    public abstract ProblemCollection CheckResource(
        TypeNode type, Resource resource);

    protected virtual void ResourceToList(
        Resource resource, IList list)
    {
        ResourceReader reader = new ResourceReader(
```

```
            new MemoryStream(resource.Data));
        try
        {
            IDictionaryEnumerator enumerator =
                reader.GetEnumerator();
            while (enumerator.MoveNext())
            {
                list.Add(new DictionaryEntry(
                    enumerator.Key, enumerator.Value));
            }
        }
        finally
        {
            reader.Close();
        }
    }
}
```

The `BaseTypeResourceRule` overrides the `Check(TypeNode)` method and checks that the type matches the type specified by the subclass ("`System.Windows.Forms.Form`", in our example). If the type matches, it calls the `BaseGlobalizationRule.GetResource()` method to get the resource that corresponds to the type (if any). It then calls `BaseTypeResourceRule.CheckResource()` to check the resource. This is the method that the subclass overrides to implement its own rule. (I chose to call this method `CheckResource` instead of `Check` to avoid clashing with the existing `Check(Resource)` method signature.)

The `ResourceToList` method is a helper method that exists to read the list of resource entries into an `IList`. This method is useful when you need bidirectional navigation through the list.

The `FormLanguageMustBeDefault` rule is implemented like this:

```
public class FormLanguageMustBeDefault: BaseTypeResourceRule
{
    public FormLanguageMustBeDefault(): base(
        "FormLanguageMustBeDefault",
        "System.Windows.Forms.Form")
    {
    }
    public override ProblemCollection CheckResource(
        TypeNode type, Resource resource)
    {
        ResourceReader reader = new ResourceReader(
            new System.IO.MemoryStream(resource.Data));
```

```
try
{
    IDictionaryEnumerator enumerator =
        reader.GetEnumerator();
    while (enumerator.MoveNext())
    {
        string key = (string) enumerator.Key;
        if (key == "$this.Language")
        {
            if (enumerator.Value != null &&
                enumerator.Value is CultureInfo &&
                ((CultureInfo) enumerator.Value).
                Equals(CultureInfo.InvariantCulture))
                return null;
            else
            {
                Resolution resolution = GetResolution(
                    new string[] {type.Name.Name});
                Problems.Add(new Problem(resolution));
                return Problems;
            }
        }
    }
    return null;
}
finally
{
    reader.Close();
}
}
}
```

The constructor ensures that the `CheckResource` method is only ever called for resources of `System.Windows.Forms.Form`. We override the `CheckResource` method and iterate through all of the items looking for the "`$this.Language`" entry. We cast the corresponding value to a `CultureInfo` and check that it is `Culture-Info.InvariantCulture` (i.e., "`(Default)`"). If it isn't, we return a problem.

"Form.Localizable must be true"

This rule is almost a carbon copy of the last rule. The difference is that we are looking for an entry that is "`$this.Localizable`", and we are checking that it is `true`. Recall, however, from the earlier explanation of this rule that this rule does not work with forms developed for the .NET Framework 2.0, and this is because the implementation of the `Form.Localizable` resource changed from being data to metadata. In the previous `CheckResource` method, the `ResourceReader` reads only the resource data and not the metadata:

```
ResourceReader reader = new ResourceReader(
    new System.IO.MemoryStream(resource.Data));
```

At such time as FxCop includes metadata in its `Resource` class, this line could be modified for analyzing .NET Framework 2.0 forms.

"Label.AutoSize must be true"

This rule needs to be slightly smarter than the previous two Type/Resource rules. It needs to look for controls that are of type "`System.Windows.Forms.Label`" and then check their corresponding `AutoSize` property (if any). When writing a rule like this, it helps if you take a look at the resx file from which the resource is compiled. Add a label to a form and open the form's resx file with a text editor. Look for an entry similar to the following:

```
<data name="&gt;&gt;label1.Type">
  <value>System.Windows.Forms.Label, System.Windows.Forms,
    Version=1.0.5000.0, Culture=neutral,
    PublicKeyToken=b77a5c561934e089
  </value>
</data>
```

This is the type definition of the label. We need to find these entries to identify which controls are `Label` controls. "`&gt;&gt;`" is the way that "`>>`" is represented in XML, so the name attribute in this example is "`>>label1.Type`". Consequently, we are looking for entries that start with "`>>`" and end with "`.Type`", and whose value element begins with "`System.Windows.Forms.Label, `". Notice that I don't check the remainder of the type definition because I don't want the rule to be limited to a specific version of the .NET Framework.

Having found a type definition for a label, we can extract the label's name (i.e., "`label1`"). From this, we can look for the `AutoSize` property, which, in the resx file, will be:

```
<data name="label1.AutoSize" type="System.Boolean, mscorlib,
  Version=1.0.5000.0, Culture=neutral,
```

```
PublicKeyToken=b77a5c561934e089">
   <value>False</value>
</data>
```

From here, we need only check that the value element is `true`. This kind of checking requires us to have bidirectional access to the entries in the resource. As such, we will make use of the `ResourceToList` method implemented in our `BaseType-ResourceRule` class. With our strategy in place, we can look at the implementation of our `CheckResource` method:

```
public override ProblemCollection CheckResource(
    TypeNode type, Resource resource)
{
    StringCollection badControls = new StringCollection();
    ArrayList list = new ArrayList();
    ResourceToList(resource, list);
    foreach(DictionaryEntry dictionaryEntry in list)
    {
        string key = (string) dictionaryEntry.Key;
        if (key.StartsWith(">>") && key.EndsWith(".Type"))
        {
            string entryType = (String) dictionaryEntry.Value;
            if (entryType.StartsWith("System.Windows.Forms.Label, "))
            {
                // This is a label. Now check its AutoSize property.
                // If the key is ">>label1.Type" then the control
                // name is "label1".
                string controlName = key.Substring(2, key.Length -7);
                int labelAutoSizeIndex = IndexOfDictionaryEntry(
                    list, controlName + ".AutoSize");
                if (labelAutoSizeIndex == -1 ||
                    ! (bool) ((DictionaryEntry)
                    list[labelAutoSizeIndex]).Value)
                    badControls.Add(controlName);
            }
        }
    }
    if (badControls.Count == 0)
        return null;
    else
    {
        StringBuilder badControlNames =
            new StringBuilder(badControls[0]);
        for(int badControlNumber = 1;
            badControlNumber < badControls.Count; badControlNumber++)
```

```
        {
            badControlNames.Append(
                ", " + badControls[badControlNumber]);
        }
        Resolution resolution = GetResolution(new string[]
            {type.Name.Name, badControlNames.ToString()});
        Problems.Add(new Problem(resolution));
        return Problems;
    }
}
```

You can see from this method that when a problem is found, it is not reported immediately. Instead, a list of offending controls is built up, and when the check is complete, the list is converted to a single string.

Instruction Rules

"DateTime.ToString() should not use a culture specific format"

The "DateTime.ToString() should not use a culture specific format" rule is the first of the instruction rules that we will look at. These rules work by looking at the IL instructions of the code in the assembly. We override the Check(Member) method and iterate over the instructions of every method, looking for a given pattern. This requires you to appreciate the problem from the perspective of IL instead of your chosen development language, but if you aren't intimate with IL, this isn't quite as difficult as it may seem. The skeleton of the Check method is:

```
public override ProblemCollection Check(Member member)
{
    Method method = member as Method;
    if (method == null)
        return null;

    for(int instructionNumber = 1; instructionNumber <
        method.Instructions.Length; instructionNumber++)
    {
        Microsoft.Cci.Instruction instruction =
            method.Instructions[instructionNumber];
        // Perform some analysis on the instruction
    }
    return base.Check(method);
}
```

This code simply iterates through each instruction. In this rule, we start at the second instruction (i.e., instruction 1) because we need to look at each instruction's previous instruction, and the first instruction obviously doesn't have a previous instruction. Having obtained each instruction, the most likely action to take is to check what kind of instruction you have, and you can do this with the `Instruction.OpCode` property. This is where life isn't quite as difficult as it may seem. If you are wondering how to decipher the IL in an assembly without having to learn IL first, use `ILDasm`. In the case of our `DateTime.ToString` rule, the simplest solution is to write a piece of code with the offending line in it and then decompile it. Here's an offending snippet of source code:

```
public virtual string GetDate()
{
    DateTime dateTime = new DateTime(2005, 31, 1);
    return dateTime.ToString("MM/dd/yyyy");
}
```

If you decompile this with `ILDasm`, you get:

```
.method public hidebysig newslot virtual
        instance string  GetDate() cil managed
{
  // Code size       32 (0x20)
  .maxstack  4
  .locals init ([0] valuetype [mscorlib]System.DateTime dateTime,
           [1] string CS$00000003$00000000)
  IL_0000:  ldloca.s   dateTime
  IL_0002:  ldc.i4     0x7d5
  IL_0007:  ldc.i4.s   31
  IL_0009:  ldc.i4.1
  IL_000a:  call       instance void [mscorlib]
                   System.DateTime::.ctor(int32, int32, int32)
  IL_000f:  ldloca.s   dateTime
  IL_0011:  ldstr      "MM/dd/yyyy"
  IL_0016:  call       instance string
                   [mscorlib]System.DateTime::ToString(string)
  IL_001b:  stloc.1
  IL_001c:  br.s       IL_001e
  IL_001e:  ldloc.1
  IL_001f:  ret
} // end of method Form1::GetDate
```

The important point to grasp here is that when you iterate over the instructions in the method, they will come out in the order in which you can see them in ILDasm. Furthermore, the Instruction.OpCode will either exactly match or closely resemble the IL instruction name that you can see for each line. So, in this example, the first instruction will be a "ldloca.s" instruction and the second will be a "ldc.i4" instruction.

In the case of our DateTime.ToString rule, we are looking for the following pattern:

```
IL_0011:   ldstr      "MM/dd/yyyy"
IL_0016:   call       instance string [mscorlib]
                      System.DateTime::ToString(string)
```

The ldstr instruction loads a literal string, and the call instruction calls a method on an object. We can see the class name and method from the call instruction (System.DateTime::ToString(string)), and we can see the literal string that is loaded "MM/dd/yyyy". So our rule must look for a call to the System.DateTime.ToString method that is immediately preceded by a ldstr instruction, and check that the string is not culture specific.

Here's the implementation:

```
public override ProblemCollection Check(Member member)
{
    Method method = member as Method;
    if (method == null)
        return null;

    for(int instructionNumber = 1; instructionNumber <
        method.Instructions.Length; instructionNumber++)
    {
        Microsoft.Cci.Instruction instruction =
            method.Instructions[instructionNumber];
        if (instruction.OpCode == OpCode.Call &&
            instruction.Value is Microsoft.Cci.Method)
        {
            Microsoft.Cci.Method instructionMethod =
                (Microsoft.Cci.Method) instruction.Value;
            if (instructionMethod.FullName ==
                "System.DateTime.ToString(System.String)")
            {
                // This is a call to DateTime.ToString. Check
```

```
            // to see if the previous instruction is a ldstr.
            Microsoft.Cci.Instruction previousInstruction =
                method.Instructions[instructionNumber - 1];
            if (previousInstruction.OpCode == OpCode.Ldstr)
            {
                // This instruction is a "load string".
                string loadString =
                    previousInstruction.Value.ToString();
                if (DateTimeFormatStringIsCultureSpecific(
                    loadString))
                {
                    Resolution resolution = GetResolution(
                        new string[] {loadString});
                    Problems.Add(new Problem(resolution));
                    return Problems;
                }
            }
        }
    }
}
return base.Check(member);
}
```

Having identified the string parameter to `DateTime.ToString()`, it then calls the `DateTimeFormatStringIsCultureSpecific` method:

```
protected virtual bool DateTimeFormatStringIsCultureSpecific(
    string format)
{
    if (format.Length == 1)
    {
        string[] cultureSensitiveFormats = new string[]
        {"d", "D", "f", "F", "g", "G", "m", "M", "r", "R",
        "s", "t", "T", "u", "U", "y", "Y"};
        foreach(string cultureSensitiveFormat in
            cultureSensitiveFormats)
        {
            if (format == cultureSensitiveFormat)
                return false;
        }
    }
    return true;
}
```

This method verifies that the format is not one of the culture-aware formats and concludes that, if it isn't, it must, therefore, be culture specific.

"Dialog culture dictated by operating system" and "Dialog culture dictated by .NET Framework"

These rules simply check for the creation (or "instance initialization," in FxCop-speak) of new objects from specific classes. They are different from previous rules, however, in that they utilize FxCop's "visit" methods. The `BaseIntrospection-Rule`, from which all of the rules in this chapter inherit, inherits from FxCop's `StandardVisitor` class.

> You should be aware that although this inheritance chain is correct at the time of writing, it may change in a future release of FxCop, and these rules might need a corresponding change at that time.

`StandardVisitor` implements approximately 140 methods that start with the word "Visit" (e.g., "VisitMethodCall", "VisitAssignment", "VisitExpression"). Each method "visits" a node (a fragment of code) of a different type, so `VisitMethodCall` visits method calls. FxCop rules begin the process of visiting nodes by calling a visit method with a wide scope. For example, the rules in this section begin the visiting process by calling `VisitMethod`. This fires calls to numerous "visit" methods in `StandardVisitor` (e.g., `VisitAssignment`, `VisitMethodCall`), according to what code is in the method that has been passed to the `Check` method. As the implementer of a rule, you need only override the visit method or methods that interest you. In the classes in this section, we override the `VisitConstruct` method that is called for each invocation of a constructor. Although all of the other visit methods will also be fired as necessary, we can remain oblivious to this fact and simply focus on the instructions that are of interest to us (i.e., the construction of new objects). This approach significantly reduces the amount of code you have to write and saves us from manually iterating through every instruction in a method. The two classes are:

```
public class DialogCultureDictatedByNETFramework: NewObjectRule
{
    public DialogCultureDictatedByNETFramework():
        base("DialogCultureDictatedByNETFramework",
        new string[] {"System.Windows.Forms.PrintPreviewDialog"})
    {
    }
}

public class DialogCultureDictatedByOperatingSystem: NewObjectRule
{
    public DialogCultureDictatedByOperatingSystem():
        base("DialogCultureDictatedByOperatingSystem",
        new string[]
            {
                "System.Windows.Forms.OpenFileDialog",
                "System.Windows.Forms.SaveFileDialog",
                "System.Windows.Forms.FolderBrowserDialog",
                "System.Windows.Forms.FontDialog",
                "System.Windows.Forms.ColorDialog",
                "System.Windows.Forms.PrintDialog",
                "System.Windows.Forms.PageSetupDialog",
                "System.Windows.Forms.MessageBox"
            })
    {
    }
}
```

As you can see, they simply pass an array of class names to the `NewObjectRule` base class. Here's the `NewObjectRule` with the all-important `Check` and `Visit` methods missing:

```
public abstract class NewObjectRule: BaseGlobalizationRule
{
    private string[] searchClassNames;
    private StringCollection foundClassNames;
    public NewObjectRule(string name, string[] searchClassNames):
        base(name)
    {
        this.searchClassNames = searchClassNames;
    }
}
```

The `Check(Member)` method checks that the member is a `Method` and initializes the private `foundClassNames` field to a new `StringCollection`. You cannot pass your own parameters to "visit" methods, so you have to declare fields, initialize them in the `Check` method, set them in the "visit" method, and then check their values upon return to the `Check` method.

```
public override ProblemCollection Check(Member member)
{
    Method method = member as Method;
    if (method == null)
        return null;

    foundClassNames = new StringCollection();
    VisitMethod(method);
    if (foundClassNames.Count == 0)
        return base.Check(member);
    else
    {
        StringBuilder classNames =
            new StringBuilder(foundClassNames[0]);
        for(int classNameNumber = 1;
            classNameNumber < foundClassNames.Count;
            classNameNumber++)
        {
            classNames.Append(", ");
            classNames.Append(foundClassNames[classNameNumber]);
        }
        foundClassNames = null;
        Resolution resolution = GetResolution(new string[]
            {method.Name.Name, classNames.ToString()});
        Problems.Add(new Problem(resolution));
        return Problems;
    }
}
```

Notice the call to `VisitMethod`. This starts the whole visiting process going. We are uninterested in the majority of the nodes that get visited, with the exception of calls to instance initializers. To zero in on these instructions, we override the `VisitConstruct` method:

```
public override Expression VisitConstruct(Construct cons)
{
    if (cons != null)
    {
```

```
        MemberBinding memberBinding =
            cons.Constructor as MemberBinding;
        if (memberBinding != null)
        {
            InstanceInitializer instanceInitializer =
                memberBinding.BoundMember as InstanceInitializer;
            if (instanceInitializer != null)
            {
                foreach(string searchClassName in searchClassNames)
                {
                    if (instanceInitializer.DeclaringType.FullName ==
                        searchClassName &&
                        foundClassNames.IndexOf(searchClassName)
                        == -1)
                        foundClassNames.Add(searchClassName);
                }
            }
        }
    }
    return base.VisitConstruct (cons);
}
```

The `VisitConstruct` method compares the class name being used to construct a new object with the array of class names it is looking for. When a match is found that isn't already in the private `foundClassNames` field, it is added to the list. Upon return to the `Check` method, the list is turned into an FxCop Problem if the list is not empty.

"Do not use literal strings"

From the earlier description of this rule, you can guess that it has quite a lot to do. It has to identify literal strings, ensure that they are not used in situations that are known not to be localizable, ensure that they are not already in the list of ignored literal strings, and finally save the newly identified literal strings to a file that can be read by the Literal Strings Manager. Let's get started.

We need a few private fields to keep track:

```
private string ignoredLiteralStringsFilename;
private DataSet ignoredLiteralStringsDataSet;
private ArrayList literalStrings;
private StringCollection assemblyPaths;
```

ignoredLiteralStringsFilename is the filename and path of the ignored literal strings file. ignoredLiteralStringsDataSet is the DataSet that gets loaded from the ignored literal strings file. literalStrings is a list of LiteralString objects representing the literal strings that we find and the methods in which they were found. assemblyPaths is a collection of all of the paths of the assemblies that get analyzed. We need this later for finding a common directory in which to put the file containing the newly identified literal strings.

Now for the executable code. First, this rule overrides the Check(Method) method. We look at what it does in pieces. The first line ensures that we perform our test only if the method is not the InitializeComponent method of a System. Windows.Forms.Form descendant:

```
if ( ! (method.Name.Name == "InitializeComponent" &&
    TypeIsSubClassOf(method.DeclaringType,
    "System.Windows.Forms.Form")))
```

Then we iterate over all of the instructions looking for a load string instruction. We check that the string is a candidate for localizability and isn't already in our list of ignored strings:

```
string loadString = instruction.Value.ToString();
if (IsSuspectString(method, loadString))
```

The IsSuspectString method checks that there is more than one character after the white space has been removed and that the string isn't in the ignored LiteralStringsDataSet. We will see where this is initialized in a moment.

```
protected virtual bool IsSuspectString(
    Method method, string stringFound)
{
    if (! StringContainsMoreThanOneCharacter(stringFound))
        return false;

    if (ignoredLiteralStringsDataSet != null)
        return ! IsStringIgnored(method, stringFound);

    return true;
}
```

We read the next instruction and check that it isn't one of our excluded cases using DoNotUseLiteralString's IsInstructionNewObject and IsInstruction SpecificMethodCall helper methods:

```
Microsoft.Cci.Instruction nextInstruction =
    method.Instructions[instructionNumber + 1];
if (! (IsInstructionNewObject(nextInstruction, "System.Exception") ||
    IsInstructionNewObject(nextInstruction,
    "System.Resources.ResourceManager") ||
    IsInstructionNewObject(nextInstruction,
    "Internationalization.Resources.ResourceManagerProvider") ||
    IsInstructionSpecificMethodCall(nextInstruction,
    "System.DateTime.ToString") ||
    IsInstructionSpecificMethodCall(nextInstruction,
    "System.Diagnostics.Debug.WriteLine") ||
    IsInstructionSpecificMethodCall(nextInstruction,
    "System.Diagnostics.Trace.WriteLine")))
{
```

If we've gotten this far, it is a candidate for localizability, so we need to make a record of it in the literalStrings private field and report it as a problem:

```
literalStrings.Add(new LiteralStringInformation(
    method.DeclaringType.FullName + "." + method.Name.Name,
    loadString));

Resolution resolution = GetResolution(new string[] {loadString});

Problems.Add(new Problem(resolution));

return Problems;
```

Finally, we need to learn a new trick that enables us to see when an analysis run starts and stops. For this, we override the obviously named BeforeAnalysis and AfterAnalysis:

```
public DoNotUseLiteralStrings(): base("DoNotUseLiteralStrings")
{
}
public override void BeforeAnalysis()
{
    assemblyPaths = new StringCollection();
    literalStrings = new ArrayList();
    InitializeIgnoredLiteralStringsDataSet();
```

```
    base.BeforeAnalysis();
}
public override void AfterAnalysis()
{
    base.AfterAnalysis();
    WriteLiteralStrings();
}
```

You can see here that instead of initializing our information about the ignored literal strings in the constructor, we wait until `BeforeAnalysis` is called. The strings are written back only after the analysis is complete. The only part that is missing is how to get the names of the assemblies that are being analyzed. We can get these from overriding the `Check(Module)` method:

```
public override ProblemCollection Check(Module module)
{
    string path =
        module.ContainingAssembly.Directory.ToString().ToUpper();
    if (assemblyPaths.IndexOf(path) == -1)
        assemblyPaths.Add(path);
    return base.Check (module);
}
```

When the analysis is complete, we write out the list of literal strings that we carefully gathered into our `literalStrings` list to a new "`LiteralStrings.xml`" file ready for the Literal Strings Manager to process it.

"CultureInfo not provided by Provider", "ResourceManager not provided by provider", and "Thread not provided by ThreadFactory"

These simple rules inherit from the abstract `ObjectNotProvidedByProvider` class, which overrides the `Check(Member)` method and looks for the creation of objects that inherit from a given class:

- "`CultureInfo` not provided by Provider" looks for the `System.Globalization.CultureInfo` class
- "`ResourceManager` not provided by provider" looks for the `System.Resource.ResourceManager` class
- "Thread not provided by `ThreadFactory`" looks for the `System.Threading.Thread` class

It ensures that all methods of the `Globalization.CultureInfoProvider`, `Internationalization.Resources.ResourceManagerProvider`, or `Interna-tionalization.Common.ThreadFactory` classes are ignored, as these methods are the only code that can legitimately create new `CultureInfo`, `ResourceManager`, or `Thread` objects. Like the `NewObjectRule` shown earlier, the `ObjectNotProvided-ByProvider` abstract class looks for the creation of new objects by overriding the `VisitConstruct` method. Here's the `ObjectNotProvidedByProvider` class with the all-important `Check` and `Visit` methods missing:

```
public abstract class ObjectNotProvidedByProvider:
    BaseGlobalizationRule
{
    private string className;
    private string providerClassName;
    private bool classFound;

    public ObjectNotProvidedByProvider(string name,
        string className, string providerClassName): base(name)
    {
        this.className = className;
        this.providerClassName = providerClassName;
    }
}
```

The `ObjectNotProvidedByProvider` class has a Boolean field called `class-Found` that is initialized to `false` by the `Check` method and potentially set to `true` by the `VisitConstruct` method:

```
public override ProblemCollection Check(Member member)
{
    Method method = member as Method;
    if (method == null)
        return null;

    if (! TypeIsSubClassOf(method.DeclaringType, providerClassName))
    {
        classFound = false;
        VisitMethod(method);
        if (classFound)
        {
            Resolution resolution = GetResolution(
                new string[] {method.Name.Name});
            Problems.Add(new Problem(resolution));
```

```
            return Problems;
        }
    }
    return base.Check(member);
}

public override Expression VisitConstruct(Construct cons)
{
    if (cons != null)
    {
        MemberBinding memberBinding =
            cons.Constructor as MemberBinding;
        if (memberBinding != null)
        {
            InstanceInitializer instanceInitializer =
                memberBinding.BoundMember as InstanceInitializer;
            if (instanceInitializer != null &&
                instanceInitializer.DeclaringType.FullName
                == className)
                classFound = true;
        }
    }
    return base.VisitConstruct (cons);
}
```

The "`CultureInfo` not provided by Provider" class inherits from `ObjectNot-ProvidedByProvider` and is representative of all three rules:

```
public class CultureInfoNotProvidedByProvider:
    ObjectNotProvidedByProvider
{
    public CultureInfoNotProvidedByProvider(): base(
        "CultureInfoNotProvidedByProvider",
        "System.Globalization.CultureInfo",
        "Globalization.CultureInfoProvider")
    {
    }
}
```

"Resource string missing from fallback assembly"

This rule looks for instructions that load a string, sees if the string is used by `ResourceManager.GetString`, and ensures that the string key is in the fallback resource that corresponds to the type in which the string was found.

The rule overrides the `Check(Member)` method. The check for load string instructions should be getting obvious by now:

```
for(int instructionNumber = 0; instructionNumber <
    method.Instructions.Length; instructionNumber++)
{
    Microsoft.Cci.Instruction instruction =
        method.Instructions[instructionNumber];
    if (instruction.OpCode == OpCode.Ldstr &&
        instructionNumber + 1 < method.Instructions.Length)
    {
        string loadString = instruction.Value.ToString();
```

Then we check that the next instruction is `ResourceManager.GetString()`:

```
Microsoft.Cci.Instruction nextInstruction =
    method.Instructions[instructionNumber + 1];
if (nextInstruction.OpCode == OpCode.Callvirt &&
    nextInstruction.Value is Microsoft.Cci.Method)
{
    Microsoft.Cci.Method nextInstructionMethod =
        (Microsoft.Cci.Method) nextInstruction.Value;
    if (nextInstructionMethod.FullName ==
        "System.Resources.ResourceManager." +
        "GetString(System.String)")
```

Then we check that the associated fallback resource has the required string and, if not, report it as a problem:

```
Resource resource;
if (GetResource(method.DeclaringType, out resource, "Resources"))
{
    if (! KeyExistsInResource(resource, loadString))
    {
        Resolution resolution = GetResolution(
            new string[] {method.Name.Name, loadString});
        Problems.Add(new Problem(resolution));
        return Problems;
    }
}
```

We have seen the `BaseGlobalizationRule.GetResource()` method before, but in this example, we are passing a resource suffix, "`Resources`". This allows the

`GetResource` method to search for resource names that are deliberately suffixed with "Resources". The `KeyExistsInResource` method is a simple scan of the resource:

```
protected virtual bool KeyExistsInResource(
    Resource resource, string keyName)
{
    ResourceReader reader = new ResourceReader(
        new System.IO.MemoryStream(resource.Data));
    try
    {
        IDictionaryEnumerator enumerator = reader.GetEnumerator();
        while (enumerator.MoveNext())
        {
            if (enumerator.Key.ToString() == keyName)
                return true;
        }
    }
    finally
    {
        reader.Close();
    }
    return false;
}
```

Where Are We?

In this chapter, you learned that the decisions that you have made throughout this book can be enforced using FxCop. You can write a document detailing all of the practices that your developers should follow, but such a document is passive and not easily enforceable. With FxCop, you can enforce your standards using the existing Globalization rules, using the new Globalization rules in this chapter, or using new Globalization rules that you are now able to write.

14

The Translator

I T GOES WITHOUT SAYING THAT THE TRANSLATOR or localizer plays a fundamental role in the internationalization process. Even if you use machine translation, a human will still be needed to review and fix the result of the machine's translation. Your translator/localizer could be a professional agency, a freelance translator, or, indeed, a bilingual, business-aware employee working in the same country as or a different country than the development team. Regardless, the role of the translator/localizer is critical, and the success of the internationalization of the project is dependent to some extent on how well this role is integrated into the development process. In this chapter, we explore strategies for including the translator/localizer in the development process and how to reintegrate this work with the project's source. Your options are dictated by whether your application is a Windows Forms application or an ASP.NET application, by whether it is a .NET Framework 1.1 application or a .NET Framework 2.0 application, and also by your perception of the translator/localizer's scope in the localization process.

The Translation Process

The essential steps in the translation process are not particularly surprising:

1. The developers package up the resources and ship them to the translator/localizer.

2. The translator/localizer updates the resources and returns them to the developers.

3. The developers reintegrate the resources into the application source.

Though these steps are easily recognizable, it is worth highlighting a couple points. First, and most important, there is a time delay between when the resources are shipped to the translator/localizer and when those resources are returned to development for reintegration into the application. During this time, the development of the application will continue, and it is unrealistic to treat the resources as "locked" during this period. Consequently, you should consider that development maintains the "master" copy of resources and that the resources that are returned from the translator/localizer must be reintegrated into the master copy (as opposed to replacing the master copy). We return to this subject in the "Reintegrating Resources" section.

Second, it should be recognized that translation/localization is a part of the development process. This means that if development is an iterative process, translation/localization is likely to be an iterative process, too. Translation/localization might not follow the same iterations as development, but it is highly likely that it will be performed in iterative steps. So whereas you might strive to complete a considerable part of the application before translation/localization occurs, and even use pseudo translation to catch as many translation/localization errors as possible before engaging the translator/localizer, the application is unlikely to be frozen after translation/localization has occurred. Instead, as each bug is fixed and as each form is modified, new text is used. Your translation/localization process could well consist of a large translation/localization phase, but it will be followed up with smaller iterative phases. This means that your translator/localizer needs a way of finding all the new text and resources to translate. Without this, the translator/localizer will need to manually search the application for new resources to translate, and this is a labor-intensive and error-prone approach.

Translator or Localizer?

Before you engage the services of a translator or localizer, you should be sure what role you expect this person to play. A translator simply translates all the text in the application. A localizer also does this but has a wider scope. A localizer considers the size and position of controls, the assignments of hotkeys, the use of images and colors, the assignment of right-to-left properties and IME modes, and the correctness of globalization; in general, a localizer has an understanding of the appropriateness of the resulting application in the chosen culture. The choice between these roles is dependent, to a large extent, on the technology you have used to build your application. For example, if you have written a Windows Forms 1.1 application, the controls' positions (and, to some extent, their sizes) are most likely fixed. In this scenario, you might want to give the translator/localizer the opportunity to move and resize controls for a given culture. If, however, you have written a Windows Forms 2.0 application and used `TableLayoutPanels` and `FlowLayoutPanels`, the positioning and sizing of the controls will probably already be handled by the .NET Framework, and such changes would be unwanted. Similarly, an ASP.NET application might rely on the essential nature of HTML for positioning and sizing, and again such changes to positions and sizes would be unwanted. You need to make similar decisions on issues such as hotkey assignments, fonts, right-to-left settings and IME modes, to determine whether these are handled within the application logic (and, therefore, by developers) or within resources (and, therefore, by a localizer). With these decisions in place, you are better able to give your translator/localizer an accurate scope of his or her role.

Your decision on the translator/localizer's role might have an impact on how you process the resources when they return. If the translator/localizer's role is solely one of translation, your reintegration process will only reintegrate text strings into the master copy. All other resources (e.g., `colors`, `Size`, `Location`, `Font`, `RightToLeft`, `ImeMode`) will be ignored. In this scenario, your translation/localization tool should disable or hide these resources to avoid unnecessary frustration on your translator's part. Unfortunately, this is not possible if you use the Windows Forms Resource Editor (`WinRes.exe`) because it does not support customization. This lends more weight to the argument to write your own WinRes.

Translation/Localization Strategies

The approach that you take to translation/localization depends partly on the role that your translator/localizer takes, partly on what format you use to store your resources, and partly on whether your application is a Windows Forms or ASP.NET application. We start by considering the translator/localizer's role. At the minimalist end of the scale, your translator could simply translate all the text in your resources and return them to you. The tool used to perform the translation could even be NotePad if the resources are resx files. This is, of course, possible but not desirable. The problem with this minimalist approach is that there is no feedback process. The translator translates the text out of context. This means that the translator does not see the context in which the translation is used. A vital part of this process is that the translator must see the result of the translation in context. The context in which a phrase is used often changes the vocabulary or grammar used in a translation. If the translator does not see this until the changes are reintegrated into the product, the number of round-trips between the developers and the translators will be unnecessarily high. For this reason, we need to employ a translation/localization strategy in which the translator/localizer is given feedback before the resources are returned to the developers. In an ideal world, this would mean allowing the translator/localizer to make changes in context. WinRes is an excellent tool for this purpose in Windows Forms applications (assuming that the user interface is static and not dynamically generated at runtime), and we return to WinRes later.

The second factor that has a significant impact on your translation/localization strategy is what format you use to store your resources. Some formats are read directly by an application, and others require processing before they can be read. For example, if you store your resources in a database, the translator need only change the database, and the application will use the updated text. However, if you use resx files, Windows Forms applications and ASP.NET 1.1 applications do not directly read resx files. Instead, they read resources from resource assemblies. Consequently, any change to a resx file needs to be propagated to its resource assembly before the change can be seen.

The third factor that has a significant impact on your translation/localization strategy is whether your application is a Windows Forms application, an ASP.NET 1.1 application, or an ASP.NET 2.0 application. We cover the issues concerning each over the next sections.

ASP.NET 2.0 Translation/Localization Strategies

ASP.NET 2.0 has the simplest translation/localization strategy. ASP.NET 2.0 applications compile resx files to resource assemblies when a page is first requested. This process is handled by the `ResXBuildProvider` and is part of the nature of ASP.NET 2.0; you need take no steps to ensure that this happens. More important, when a resx file is changed, ASP.NET 2.0 unloads the application domain, rebuilds the resource assembly, and continues to process the request. Any changes made by the translator/localizer can be seen immediately by refreshing the page. This kind of immediate feedback improves the quality and speed of the translation/localization. The downside to this approach is that when the application domain is unloaded, all state is lost unless the state is held in a separate location. This affects the behavior of the application, so translators/localizers might need to retrace their path through the application. The solution to this problem is to store the state in a separate process using the `Web.config sessionState` element (set the `mode` attribute to either `StateServer` or `SQLServer`).

Windows Forms and ASP.NET 1.1 Translation/Localization Strategies

To some extent, Windows Forms (1.1 and 2.0) applications and ASP.NET 1.1 applications have the same translation/localization problems with the same solutions. The problem is that if your resources are stored in resx files, your application will not, by default, see any changes made by the translator/localizer to those resx files because the application reads its resources from its resource assemblies. This section is about solving this problem.

ResXResourceManager

In Chapter 12, "Custom Resource Managers," I wrote a `ResXResourceManager` class that reads resources directly from resx files instead of from assemblies. In addition, unlike `ResourceManager.CreateFileBasedResourceManager`, these resx files are not locked, so they can be updated while the application is running. This is a relatively easy solution to the problem, with only a few drawbacks. First, you would need to modify your application to use a `ResXResourceManager` instead of a regular `ResourceManager` or `ComponentResourceManager`. The best approach here would be to use the `ResourceManagerProvider` class, also introduced in Chapter 12. In addition, in a Windows Forms application, you would need to use the `Resource ManagerSetter` component (also in Chapter 12) to change the resource manager in Windows Forms. Second, you would be advised to create two versions of your application: one for production and one for translation/localization. The former would use either `ResourceManager` (Windows Forms 1.1, ASP.NET 1.1) or `Component ResourceManager` (Windows Forms 2.0), and the latter would use `ResXResource Manager`. In this way, the production version uses the resource managers that are optimized for performance, and the translation/localization version uses the resource manager that provides the necessary functionality for translating the application.

Linked Satellite Resource Assemblies

A less intrusive but less effective solution to the same problem is to use linked satellite resource assemblies. A linked satellite resource assembly is a satellite resource assembly in which the resources have been linked to the assembly instead of being embedded in the assembly. The satellite resource assemblies that have been discussed throughout the majority of this book have all used embedded resources—that is, the resources have been embedded inside the assembly. The resulting assembly is a single file that contains all the resources for a single culture. A linked satellite resource assembly, on the other hand, is an assembly that has links to separate .`resources` files in the same directory. The benefit of this solution is that it is unobtrusive. The application source code is not modified in any way; the solution is simply a packaging/deployment issue. The application continues to use the same `ResourceManager` or `ComponentResourceManager` as before. The difference between the production version and the translation/localization version is that the former uses embedded assemblies and the latter uses linked assemblies. There are two disadvantages to this solution. The first is that the translation/localization version must include some facility to convert the updated resx files to resources files (i.e., the only format recognized by linked resource assemblies). The second is that the `ResourceManager` class locks the resources files when it reads them, preventing them from being written to (i.e., when the resx file is converted to a resources file) until the `ResourceManager`'s application domain is unloaded (which is typically when the application is closed) or the resources files are unlocked using `Resource-Manager.ReleaseAllResources`.

Building a Linked Satellite Resource Assembly Using the .NET Framework SDK

Visual Studio builds satellite resource assemblies with embedded resources, so to build a satellite resource assembly with linked resources, you have to use either the .NET Framework SDK tools or the .NET Framework classes. The former is suitable for inclusion in a build process, and we cover it in this section. The latter is suitable for inclusion in custom utilities, and we cover it in the next section.

In this example, we build a French (fr) satellite resource assembly. To convert a resx file to a resources file, use resgen.exe. Assuming that you have a resx file called Form1.fr.resx, open a Visual Studio command prompt and, in the same folder as your resx file, type this:

```
resgen Form1.fr.resx
```

The result is a new binary resource file called Form1.fr.resources. The .NET Framework SDK includes a tool called Assembly Linker (al.exe), which exists to create assemblies. The following command creates a French linked satellite resource assembly from the Form1.fr.resources file:

```
al /target:library
/link:Form1.fr.resources,WindowsApplication1.Form1.fr.resources
/culture:fr /out:WindowsApplication1.resources.dll
```

The /target switch specifies the output type (library, exe, or win). The /link switch tells Assembly Linker to add a linked resource. The "Form1.fr.resources" part is the name of the file to link, and the "WindowsApplication1.Form1.fr. resources" part is the name that the resource is given inside the assembly. The resource name must be fully qualified, so it must include the application's default namespace (e.g., "Windows-Application1"). To create a "normal" resource assembly where resources are embedded, replace the /link switch with the /embed switch. To specify more than one resource to include in the assembly, you specify multiple /link or /embed switches. The /culture switch specifies the culture of the assembly and is essential. Simply placing the assembly in a directory with the culture name is not enough to identify its culture. Finally, the /out switch specifies the output assembly filename.

Building a Linked Satellite Resource Assembly Using .NET Framework Classes

The .NET Framework includes a class called AssemblyBuilder (in System. Reflection.Emit) that exists to build assemblies in code. To achieve the same result as the Assembly Linker in the previous example, I have written a method called `BuildLinkedSatelliteResourceAssembly`. It is called like this:

```
BuildLinkedSatelliteResourceAssembly(
    new string[] {"Form1.fr.resources"},
    "WindowsApplication1",
    new CultureInfo("fr"),
    "WindowsApplication1.resources.dll");
```

The first parameter is an array of resources files to link. The second parameter is the default namespace. The third parameter is the `CultureInfo`. The fourth parameter is the resource assembly output filename. The method is implemented like this:

```
public static void BuildLinkedSatelliteResourceAssembly(
    string[] resourceFileNames, string defaultNamespace,
    CultureInfo cultureInfo, string outputFilename)
{
    AssemblyName assemblyName = new AssemblyName();

    assemblyName.CultureInfo = cultureInfo;

    assemblyName.Name =
        Path.GetFileNameWithoutExtension(outputFilename);

    AssemblyBuilder assemblyBuilder =
        System.Threading.Thread.GetDomain().
        DefineDynamicAssembly(assemblyName,
        AssemblyBuilderAccess.RunAndSave,
        Path.GetDirectoryName(outputFilename));

    foreach(string resourceName in resourceFileNames)
    {
        assemblyBuilder.AddResourceFile(
            defaultNamespace + "." + resourceName, resourceName);
    }

    assemblyBuilder.Save(assemblyName.Name + ".dll");
}
```

The `AssemblyBuilder` class does not have a public constructor. Instead, you construct new `AssemblyBuilder` objects using the `AppDomain.DefineDynamic Assembly` method. This method accepts an `AssemblyName` object, which represents the full name of the assembly (name, culture, version, public key). `DefineDynamic Assembly`'s second parameter specifies that the assembly can be executed and also saved to disk. The third parameter specifies the location of the new assembly.

The `AssemblyBuilder.AddResourceFile` method represents one of a tiny minority of methods in the .NET Framework that is poorly named. The name implies that it will add a resource file, but it does not do this. Instead, it adds a *link* to a resource file instead of embedding the resource in the assembly (to embed a resource, use the `ModuleBuilder.DefineResource` method). Finally, note that the `AssemblyBuilder.Save` method accepts a simple filename. It must not contain a path. The path is set in the original call to `AssemblyBuilder.DefineDynamicAssembly`.

Rebuilding Satellite Resource Assemblies

A variation on the previous theme is to rebuild the satellite resource assembly entirely using embedded resources. In this scenario, the translator/localizer gets the same production version of the application as everyone else. In addition, the translator/localizer gets the original resx files plus a utility to rebuild the satellite resource assemblies from those resx files. The benefits of this approach are that it is unobtrusive and you do not have to create a separate version of the application for the translator/localizer. There are several drawbacks to this approach, though. The first is that the satellite resource assembly is opened by the application, which means that it cannot be written to until the application is closed. Another potential drawback is that the new satellite assembly is not identical (excluding the resources) to the original satellite assembly. Information such as version information, public key, custom attributes, and `AssemblyName.Flags` is not transferred from the original assembly to the new (you see how to do this in the next section). Whether this is a problem depends upon whether your application needs this information. The final drawback is that the new assembly contains resources only for which resx files exist. If the original assembly contains resources for which no resx file is present (because not all of the original resx files used to build the assembly were deployed to the translator's machine), the new assembly will not contain that resource. Again, you learn how to overcome this in the next section.

To rebuild a satellite resource assembly from resx files, I have written a method called `BuildEmbeddedSatelliteResourceAssembly`, which is called like this:

```
BuildEmbeddedSatelliteResourceAssembly(
    new string[] {"Form1.fr.resx"},
    "WindowsApplication1",
    new CultureInfo("fr"),
    "WindowsApplication1.resources.dll");
```

The parameters are the same as for the `BuildLinkedSatelliteResource-Assembly` method, shown earlier, with the exception that the filenames are resx files and not resources files. The method is implemented like this:

```
public static void BuildEmbeddedSatelliteResourceAssembly(
    string[] resourceFileNames,
    string defaultNamespace,
    CultureInfo cultureInfo,
    string outputFilename)
{
    AssemblyName assemblyName = new AssemblyName();
    assemblyName.CultureInfo = cultureInfo;
    assemblyName.Name =
        Path.GetFileNameWithoutExtension(outputFilename);

    AssemblyBuilder assemblyBuilder =
        System.Threading.Thread.GetDomain().
        DefineDynamicAssembly(
        assemblyName,
        AssemblyBuilderAccess.RunAndSave,
        Path.GetDirectoryName(outputFilename));

    ModuleBuilder moduleBuilder =
        assemblyBuilder.DefineDynamicModule(
        assemblyName.Name + ".dll",
        assemblyName.Name + ".dll",
        false);

    foreach(string resourceFileName in resourceFileNames)
    {
        string resourceName = Path.ChangeExtension(
            Path.GetFileName(resourceFileName), ".resources");

        IResourceWriter resourceWriter =
            moduleBuilder.DefineResource(
            defaultNamespace + "." + resourceName,
            resourceName, ResourceAttributes.Public);

        WriteResourceFromResXToResourceWriter(
            resourceWriter, resourceFileName);
```

```
    }

    assemblyBuilder.Save(assemblyName.Name + ".dll");
}
```

The first part of the `BuildEmbeddedSatelliteResourceAssembly` method is the same as the previous `BuildLinkedSatelliteResourceAssembly` method. The differences start with the call to `AssemblyBuilder.DefineDynamicModule`, which defines a new module and enables us to add resources to the module using the `ModuleBuilder` return result. What is not obvious from this code is the importance of `DefineDynamicModule`'s name parameter (i.e., its first parameter). For the resources to be embedded in the assembly, this parameter must exactly match the assemblies' filename (without the path).

The `ModuleBuilder` enables us to create new embedded resources using its `DefineResource` method. We do this in the `foreach` block, where we iterate through each of the resx files. `DefineResource` does not allow us to embed a resx or resources file wholesale in a single operation. Instead, it returns an `IResourceWriter`, which we use in `WriteResourceFromResXToResourceWriter` to add each entry in the resx file one by one:

```
private static void WriteResourceFromResXToResourceWriter(
    IResourceWriter resourceWriter, string resourceFileName)
{
    using (ResXResourceReader reader =
        new ResXResourceReader(resourceFileName))
    {
        foreach(DictionaryEntry entry in reader)
        {
            resourceWriter.AddResource(
                entry.Key.ToString(), entry.Value);
        }
    }
}
```

Rebuilding Satellite Resource Assemblies from Original Assemblies

The solution to two of the drawbacks in the previous approach is to load missing information (e.g., resources, version information, public key, custom attributes) from the original assembly. To load this information, the original assembly must be loaded using reflection. This introduces a new drawback. When you load an assembly, it cannot be written to because it is already open. You could create a new application domain that could be unloaded before the new assembly is written, but satellite assemblies cannot be loaded into any domain other than the current domain (a `SerializationException` occurs). Microsoft's Introspection Engine (as used in FxCop), also called the Common Compiler Infrastructure (CCI), can solve this problem; however, at the time of writing, it is not part of the .NET Framework SDK and has little documentation, so I have chosen not to use it. However, it might become part of the .NET Framework SDK in the future, so this is a potential solution to remember. A workaround is to begin by copying the assembly to a temporary location, loading it from the temporary location, and then writing the new assembly to the original location. This works if the operation occurs once within an application domain, but thereafter the assembly is still loaded from the first attempt and subsequent attempts will fail. With this limitation in mind, I have written `BuildEmbeddedSatelliteResourceAssemblyFromAssembly`, which is called like this:

```
BuildEmbeddedSatelliteResourceAssemblyFromAssembly(
    new string[] {"Form1.fr.resx"},
    "WindowsApplication1",
    new CultureInfo("fr"),
    "WindowsApplication1.resources.dll");
```

`BuildEmbeddedSatelliteResourceAssemblyFromAssembly` is implemented like this:

```
public static void
    BuildEmbeddedSatelliteResourceAssemblyFromAssembly(
    string[] resourceFileNames,
    string defaultNamespace,
    CultureInfo cultureInfo,
    string outputFileName)
{
    string inputFileName;
    string tempPath = Path.GetTempPath();
    if (tempPath.EndsWith(Path.DirectorySeparatorChar.ToString()))
        inputFileName = tempPath + Path.GetFileName(outputFileName);
    else
        inputFileName = tempPath + Path.DirectorySeparatorChar +
            Path.GetFileName(outputFileName);
```

```
if (File.Exists(inputFileName))
    // there is already a version of the input file
    // in the temporary folder
    File.Delete(inputFileName);

// move original assembly to a temporary location
File.Move(outputFileName, inputFileName);

Assembly inputAssembly = Assembly.LoadFrom(inputFileName);
AssemblyName inputAssemblyName =
    AssemblyName.GetAssemblyName(inputFileName);

AssemblyName assemblyName = new AssemblyName();
assemblyName.CultureInfo = inputAssemblyName.CultureInfo;
assemblyName.Name =
    Path.GetFileNameWithoutExtension(outputFileName);
assemblyName.CodeBase = inputAssemblyName.CodeBase;
assemblyName.Version = inputAssemblyName.Version;
assemblyName.SetPublicKey(inputAssemblyName.GetPublicKey());
assemblyName.Flags = inputAssemblyName.Flags;

AssemblyBuilder assemblyBuilder =
    System.Threading.Thread.GetDomain().
    DefineDynamicAssembly(assemblyName,
    AssemblyBuilderAccess.RunAndSave,
    Path.GetDirectoryName(outputFileName));

AddVersionInfoResource(assemblyBuilder, inputAssembly);

ModuleBuilder moduleBuilder =
    assemblyBuilder.DefineDynamicModule(
    assemblyName.Name + ".dll",
    assemblyName.Name + ".dll", false);

string[] resourceNames =
    inputAssembly.GetManifestResourceNames();
foreach(string resourceName in resourceNames)
{
    string fixedName = resourceName.Substring(
        resourceName.IndexOf(".") + 1);

    IResourceWriter resourceWriter =
        moduleBuilder.DefineResource(
        resourceName, fixedName, ResourceAttributes.Public);

    WriteResourceToResourceWriter(
        inputAssembly, resourceWriter, defaultNamespace,
        resourceName, resourceFileNames);
```

```
    }

    assemblyBuilder.Save(assemblyName.Name + ".dll");
}
```

This method follows a similar pattern to previous methods, with some notable differences. It starts by attempting to move the original assembly to a temporary location, and the "input" assembly is loaded from the temporary location (making the original location available to write the new assembly to). It loads its assembly name information (name, version, culture, public key) from the input assembly. It copies the input assembly's Version Information resource to the output assembly using `AddVersionInfoResource`. Previous methods in this chapter have iterated through all of the input resource files, adding them to the assembly. In this method, however, the driving force is not the input file list, but the resources that exist in the input assembly. `Assembly.GetManifestResourceNames` gets an array of resource names in the assembly. We walk through this list looking for matching input
resource files. Where an input resource file is found, the resources are loaded from the input resource file. Where a matching resource file is not found, the resources are loaded from the input assembly. This process occurs in the `WriteResourceToResourceWriter` method:

```
private static void WriteResourceToResourceWriter(
    Assembly inputAssembly,
    IResourceWriter resourceWriter,
    string defaultNamespace,
    string resourceName,
    string[] resourceFileNames)
{
    string resourceFileName = GetResourceFile(
        defaultNamespace, resourceName, resourceFileNames);
    if (resourceFileName != null)
        WriteResourceFromResXToResourceWriter(
            resourceWriter, resourceFileName);
    else
        WriteResourceFromAssemblyToResourceWriter(
            inputAssembly, resourceWriter, resourceName);
}

private static string GetResourceFile(
    string defaultNamespace,
    string resourceName,
```

```
        string[] resourceFileNames)
{
    foreach(string resourceFileName in resourceFileNames)
    {
        string resourceFileNameWithResourcesExtension =
            Path.GetFileName(Path.ChangeExtension(
            resourceFileName, ".resources"));

        if (String.Compare(resourceName,
            defaultNamespace + "." +
            resourceFileNameWithResourcesExtension,
            true,
            CultureInfo.InvariantCulture) == 0)
            return resourceFileName;
    }
    return null;
}
```

WriteResourceToResourceWriter uses the GetResourceFile method to determine whether the resource should be loaded from the resource file or the assembly. The WriteResourceFromResXToResourceWriter method is the same method as shown earlier in this chapter. The WriteResourceFromAssemblyToResourceWriter method is this:

```
private static void WriteResourceFromAssemblyToResourceWriter(
    Assembly inputAssembly,
    IResourceWriter resourceWriter,
    string resourceName)
{
    Stream resourceStream =
        inputAssembly.GetManifestResourceStream(resourceName);
    try
    {
        ResourceSet resourceSet = new ResourceSet(resourceStream);

        IDictionaryEnumerator dictionaryEnumerator =
            resourceSet.GetEnumerator();
        while (dictionaryEnumerator.MoveNext())
        {
            object resourceValue = resourceSet.GetObject(
                dictionaryEnumerator.Key.ToString(), true);

            resourceWriter.AddResource(
                dictionaryEnumerator.Key.ToString(), resourceValue);
        }
```

```
    }
    finally
    {
        resourceStream.Close();
    }
}
```

The `Assembly.GetManifestResourceStream` gets a resource `Stream` from the assembly, given a resource name. The `ResourceSet` constructor accepts a stream as a source of resources, so iterating over the entries in this stream is straightforward.

Rebuilding Satellite Resource Assemblies from Original Assemblies Without Resx Files

One last option that you might consider is to not ship your resx files to your translator/localizer at all. At first, this might not seem like such a great idea because, without resx files, how will your translator/localizer translate the resources? However, consider that the previous example could draw on resources from the original assembly when resx files were missing. If all the resx files were missing, the satellite resource assembly would become the complete source of resources. Clearly, there is not much point in rebuilding an assembly that is exactly the same as the original (you would be better off simply copying the file), but if your translation tool could read resources directly from the assembly, you would not need to ship resx files to the translator/localizer. The resx files are, after all, just an intermediary file that allows the resources to be modified as XML. If you write your own translation tools, the need for XML files disappears. The benefit to this approach is that the translator gets exactly the same version of the application as everyone else. In addition, no special preparation is needed to add resources files to the translator's copy. When the translator has finished translating/localizing, it simply sends back the satellite resource assemblies. One disadvantage to this approach is that when the assemblies are returned to development, they have to be processed to be converted back into resx files. You might argue, however, that this reintegration step is a necessary step, regardless of whether files are returned from the translator/localizer as resx files, satellite resource assemblies, or a database. Another disadvantage to this approach is that it makes using WinRes a little more difficult; resources must be copied out from the satellite resource assembly to a temporary resx file because WinRes can read only resx files. This is another justification for writing a WinRes alternative.

Signed Assemblies

The translation/localization strategies for rebuilding assemblies offered in this chapter are less suitable if you sign your assemblies. The problem is that you need to rebuild the satellite resource assemblies, but you don't want to release your private key for these assemblies to be re-signed. If you do sign your assemblies, you need to ship a separate version of your application to your translator/localizer. The production version of your application would use signed assemblies, and the translator/localizer's version would either use delay-signed assemblies or would use an alternative solution altogether (e.g., `ResXResourceManager`).

WinRes Translation/Localization Strategies

In Chapter 4, "Windows Forms Specifics," I introduced the Windows Resource Localization Editor (`WinRes.exe`). To recap, WinRes is part of the .NET Framework SDK and allows localizers to localize Windows Forms using an editor that closely resembles the Visual Studio Windows Forms Designer. As such, the translator/localizer must install the .NET Framework SDK to use WinRes. WinRes is covered in depth in Chapter 4, so you should refer back to this chapter if you are unfamiliar with it. In this section, we look at issues that are specific to the translation/localization process.

Invoking WinRes from Within an Application

WinRes can be used by the translator/localizer simply by running `WinRes.exe` and selecting a relevant resource file. However, this process will rapidly become tedious in a large application, and developers can provide a little help in this area to simplify this process. WinRes can be invoked from within the application itself. The idea is that the translator/localizer uses the application as is, and whenever he wants to translate/localize a form, he presses some key or performs some action that invokes WinRes for the current context. This speeds up the translation/localization process and reduces the translators/localizer's need to manually map forms to files. It is not a panacea, however, because the translator/localizer might well want to invoke WinRes manually, but automating the process will save some time and aggravation.

The essential process of invoking WinRes is achieved using `System.Diagnostics.Process.Start`:

```
Process.Start("WinRes.exe", "Form1.fr-FR.resx");
```

This passes "Form1.fr-FR.resx" as a parameter to WinRes.exe. This assumes that WinRes.exe and Form1.fr-FR.resx are in the same directory as the application, which is unrealistic, so a little more work is required. The InvokeWinRes class included in the downloadable source for this book solves the problem with a little more polish. We start with the problem of deciding upon an action that the translator/localizer should use to invoke WinRes. I have chosen a keystroke of F10 (simply because I don't use F10 very often in Windows Forms applications). To use it, I set the Form's KeyPreview to true and add a KeyUp event:

```
private void Form1_KeyUp(
    object sender, System.Windows.Forms.KeyEventArgs e)
{
    InvokeWinRes.CheckInvoke(e.KeyCode, this);
}
```

This is best set up in some form base class from which all forms inherit. The InvokeWinRes.CheckInvoke method checks the key pressed against the keystroke designated to invoke WinRes and attempts to invoke WinRes for the given form. InvokeWinRes has the following fields, which have corresponding property wrappers:

```
private static bool enabled = true;
private static string resourceExtension = ".resx";
private static string resourcePath = @"resources\";
private static Keys invokeKey = Keys.F10;
private static string winResPath;
```

The enabled field and corresponding property allow developers to turn off InvokeWinRes. You would turn it off in the production version. The resourceExtension field and corresponding property enable you to switch to another extension (which, given the current functionality of WinRes, could be only ".resources"). The resourcePath field and corresponding property enable you to specify where the resx files are. The invokeKey and corresponding property specify the keystroke used to invoke WinRes. The winResPath field is the path to the WinRes executable (and required DLLs). The corresponding property initializes winResPath by looking for WinRes.exe in the application's path and falling back to the location of the .NET Framework SDK. It is important that it looks first in the application's path because WinRes 2.0 is typically placed in the application's path to locate the application's assemblies in order to load forms that use form inheritance (see the "WinRes and Visual Form Inheritance" section of Chapter 4). Here is the `WinResPath` property:

```
public static string WinResPath
{
    get
    {
        if (winResPath == null)
        {
            string applicationPath = Path.GetDirectoryName(
                Application.ExecutablePath);
            if (File.Exists(applicationPath +
                Path.DirectorySeparatorChar + "WinRes.exe"))
                winResPath = applicationPath;
            else
            {
                string frameworkSdkPath = GetFrameworkSdkPath();
                if (frameworkSdkPath != null &&
                    frameworkSdkPath != String.Empty)
                    winResPath = frameworkSdkPath + "bin";
            }
        }
        return winResPath;
    }
    set {winResPath = value;}
}

protected static string GetFrameworkSdkPath()
{
    string sourcesKeyName = @"Software\Microsoft\.NETFramework";

    RegistryKey frameworkKey =
        Registry.LocalMachine.OpenSubKey(sourcesKeyName);

    if (frameworkKey == null)
        return null;

    string frameworkVersion =
        System.Environment.Version.Major.ToString() + "." +
        System.Environment.Version.Minor.ToString();

    object sdkValue = frameworkKey.GetValue(
        @"sdkInstallRootv" + frameworkVersion);

    if (sdkValue == null)
        return null;
```

```
    return sdkValue.ToString();
}
```

The `GetFrameworkSdkPath` method gets the location of the .NET Framework SDK that corresponds to the version of the .NET Framework that the application is using. So if the application is a Windows Forms 1.1 application running on a development machine, the key would be `HKey_Local_Machine\Software\Microsoft\.NETFramework\sdkInstallRootv1.1` and the value would be something like `C:\Program Files\Microsoft Visual Studio .NET 2003\SDK\v1.1\`. The `WinResPath` property then appends "bin" to the folder name to get to the SDK's binaries.

The `InvokeWinRes.CheckInvoke` method is a convenient wrapper around the `InvokeWinRes.Invoke` method:

```
public static void CheckInvoke(Keys key, Form form)
{
    CheckInvoke(key, form.GetType().Name);
}

public static void CheckInvoke(Keys key, string baseName)
{
    if (key == invokeKey)
    {
        Invoke(baseName);
    }
}
```

After the keystroke is checked, `Invoke` is called with the `baseName` of the form (e.g., "Form1"). `InvokeWinRes.Invoke` is this:

```
public static void Invoke(string baseName)
{
    if (enabled)
    {
        string winResPath = WinResPath;
        if (winResPath == null || winResPath == String.Empty)
            MessageBox.Show("WinRes path is not found");
        else
        {
            string winResProgram = winResPath + @"\WinRes.exe";

            if (! File.Exists(winResProgram))
                MessageBox.Show(String.Format(
```

```
                        "WinRes ({0}) not found", winResProgram));
            else
            {
                bool isFileFound = false;
                CultureInfo cultureInfo =
                    Thread.CurrentThread.CurrentUICulture;

                string resxFileName = resourcePath + baseName +
                    "." + cultureInfo.Name + resourceExtension;

                StringBuilder resxFileNamesBuilder =
                    new StringBuilder(resxFileName);

                while (true)
                {
                    if (File.Exists(resxFileName))
                    {
                        Process.Start(winResProgram, resxFileName);
                        isFileFound = true;
                        break;
                    }

                    if (cultureInfo == cultureInfo.Parent)
                        break;

                    cultureInfo = cultureInfo.Parent;
                    if (cultureInfo.Equals(
                        CultureInfo.InvariantCulture))

                        resxFileName = resourcePath + baseName +
                            resourceExtension;
                    else
                        resxFileName = resourcePath + baseName + "."
                            + cultureInfo.Name + resourceExtension;

                    resxFileNamesBuilder.Append(", " + resxFileName);
                }
                if (! isFileFound)
                {
                    MessageBox.Show(String.Format(
                        "No resx files ({0}) found to translate"
                        , resxFileNamesBuilder.ToString()));
                }
            }
        }
    }
}
```

The `Invoke` method cycles through `CultureInfos` looking for a corresponding resource file. So if the `CurrentUICulture` is "`fr-FR`", then it first looks for "`Form1.fr-FR.resx`". If this is not found, it then looks for the parent ("`Form1.fr.resx`") and then its parent ("`Form1.resx`"), until there are no more parents. Notice that the error messages are not localized. I have taken the attitude that these messages are intended for the translator/localizer, and working on the principle that the vast majority of translators/localizers read English, it is not necessary to localize these messages.

Using WinRes with Formats Other than Resx and Resources

One of the limitations of WinRes is that it can read and write only resx and resources files. If you have used another format (such as a database), WinRes cannot be made to read your format. The workaround is to export the resources from their original format to a temporary resx file, run WinRes, and then import the resources from the resx file into the original format. Whether this export/import process occurs on the fly or whether it is part of the setup process on the localizer's machine is a matter of preference. However, if the modified resources are not immediately reimported after the localizer has made changes, the application will not immediately reflect those changes.

To export the resources from their original source to resx files, we use the `IResourcesGovernor` interface and `ResourcesGovernor` classes created in Chapter 10, "Resource Administration." The `InvokeWinRes resourcesGovernor` field and corresponding `ResourcesGovernor` property are as follows:

```
private static IResourcesGovernor resourcesGovernor;

public static IResourcesGovernor ResourcesGovernor
{
    get {return resourcesGovernor;}
    set {resourcesGovernor = value;}
}
```

These allow the application to specify what the original source of the resources is. Typically, this would be specified at the same time that the `IResourcesGovernor` is initially created (i.e., at application start up):

```
public Form1()
{
    InvokeWinRes.ResourcesGovernor = new DbResourcesGovernor(
        "server=localhost;database=InvokingWinRes;" +
        "trusted_connection=true");

    InitializeComponent();
}
```

The `InvokeWinRes.Invoke` method needs a couple lines added to export the resource immediately before WinRes is invoked. The following two lines are added immediately inside the `else` block, which has determined that WinRes can be invoked:

```
if (resourcesGovernor != null)
    ExportResources(baseName);
```

So if a `ResourcesGovernor` has been set, the resources must be exported from that `ResourcesGovernor` to resx files. This is what the `ExportResources` method does:

```
protected static void ExportResources(string baseName)
{
    if (resourcesGovernor != null)
    {
        IResourcesGovernor outputResourcesGovernor =
            new ResXResourcesGovernor(resourcePath);
        CultureInfo cultureInfo =
            Thread.CurrentThread.CurrentUICulture;
        ArrayList resourceSets = new ArrayList();
        ArrayList cultureInfos = new ArrayList();
        while (true)
        {
            IResourceGovernor inputResourceGovernor =
                resourcesGovernor.GetResourceGovernor(
                baseName, cultureInfo);

            ResourceSet resourceSet =
                inputResourceGovernor.ReadResourceSet();
            resourceSets.Add(resourceSet);
            cultureInfos.Add(cultureInfo);

            if (cultureInfo == cultureInfo.Parent)
                break;
```

```
            cultureInfo = cultureInfo.Parent;
        }
        for(int cultureInfoNumber = cultureInfos.Count - 1;
            cultureInfoNumber >= 0; cultureInfoNumber--)
        {
            ResourceSet resourceSet =
                (ResourceSet) resourceSets[cultureInfoNumber];

            cultureInfo =
                (CultureInfo) cultureInfos[cultureInfoNumber];

            if (resourceSet != null)
            {
                IResourceGovernor outputResourceGovernor =
                    outputResourcesGovernor.GetResourceGovernor(
                    baseName, cultureInfo);

                outputResourceGovernor.WriteResourceSet(resourceSet);
            }
        }
    }
}
```

This method exports all resources for the given base name (e.g., "Form1") from the original source to resx files. The algorithm that the ExportResources method uses is not as straightforward as you might have imagined for solving this problem. Indeed, if you were to refactor this code, you would probably end up with a slicker solution to the problem. ExportResources takes two passes through the culture hierarchy, and at this stage in the problem, there is no justification for taking these two passes. However, this approach will become necessary in the next section, so, for now, take it on trust that this is necessary.

ExportResources cycles through the culture hierarchy from the CurrentUICulture (e.g., "Form1.fr-FR") through all of its parents (e.g., "Form1.fr" and "Form1"), getting a ResourceSet from the "input" source (using IResourceGovernor.ReadResourceSet()). The CultureInfo and its corresponding ResourceSet are stored in lists. The subsequent for loop traverses these lists in the reverse order, so the invariant culture is processed first, then the neutral culture, and then the specific culture, each writing the ResourceSet to the "output" source (using IResourceGovernor.WriteResourceSet()). Again, at this point, there is nothing to be gained in traversing the list in one direction, so this additional effort is not yet necessary.

WinRes 1.1 and Single File Mode

In Chapter 4, you learned that the WinRes included in the .NET Framework 2.0 supports two file modes: Visual Studio File Mode and Single File Mode. Unfortunately, the WinRes included in the .NET Framework 1.1 supports just Single File Mode. This means that the resx files created by Visual Studio 2003 are incompatible with WinRes 1.1, and vice versa. The distinction between the two modes is that Visual Studio maintains resx files using inheritance, whereas WinRes's Single File Mode does not use inheritance and "flattens" resx files. That is, WinRes 1.1 resx files must be wholly contained and self-sufficient. In this section, we work around this limitation so that WinRes 1.1 can be used with Visual Studio 2003's resx files.

The solution is straightforward: We must "flatten" the resx files that WinRes uses. This means that the resx files must contain all their own resources, plus the resources of their parents and their grandparents, etc. So `Form1.fr.resx` should contain all its own resources, plus all the resources of `Form1.resx`. Similarly, `Form1.fr-FR.resx` should contain all the resources of `Form1.fr.resx` (which now includes all the resources of its parent, `Form1.resx`).

The flattening process is achieved using `IResourceGovernor.AddResource-Set`, which is implemented in the `ResourceGovernor` base class:

```
public void AddResourceSet(
    ResourceSet resourceSet1, ResourceSet resourceSet2)
{
    Hashtable resourceTable1 = GetResourceSetTable(resourceSet1);

    IDictionaryEnumerator resourceSet2Enumerator =
        resourceSet2.GetEnumerator();

    while (resourceSet2Enumerator.MoveNext())
    {
        DictionaryEntry entry =
            (DictionaryEntry) resourceSet2Enumerator.Current;

        if (! resourceTable1.ContainsKey(entry.Key))
            resourceTable1.Add(entry.Key, entry.Value);
    }
}
```

This method accepts two `ResourceSets`. The entries of the second `ResourcSet` that do not already exist in the first `ResourceSet` are added to the first `ResourcSet`.

So the first `ResourceSet` might represent `Form1.fr-FR`, and the second `Resource Set` might represent `Form1.fr`.

The point in time at which the flattening should occur is dependent upon the original source of the resources. If the original source is not a resx file format (e.g., it is a database), the resources must be flattened when they are exported. This requires a change to the `ExportResources` method shown in the previous section. The `for` loop now looks like this:

```
for(int cultureInfoNumber = cultureInfos.Count - 1;
    cultureInfoNumber >= 0; cultureInfoNumber--)
{
    ResourceSet resourceSet =
        (ResourceSet) resourceSets[cultureInfoNumber];

    cultureInfo = (CultureInfo) cultureInfos[cultureInfoNumber];

    if (resourceSet != null)
    {
        IResourceGovernor outputResourceGovernor =
            outputResourcesGovernor.GetResourceGovernor(
            baseName, cultureInfo);

        if (System.Environment.Version.Major == 1 &&
            cultureInfoNumber != cultureInfos.Count - 1)
        {
            ResourceSet parentResourceSet = (ResourceSet)
                resourceSets[cultureInfoNumber + 1];

            outputResourceGovernor.AddResourceSet(
                resourceSet, parentResourceSet);
        }
        outputResourceGovernor.WriteResourceSet(resourceSet);
    }
}
```

The difference lies in the innermost `if` statement. It checks the major version of the .NET Framework, and if it is `1`, it knows that the resx files must be flattened. At this point, the reasoning behind walking through the list cultures twice should be clearer. This `for` loop starts with the invariant resources and then proceeds to the neutral resources. The neutral resources must be flattened before the specific resources so that the specific resources contain the resources of both the neutral *and* the invariant resources.

If the original source of resources is resx files, a better solution would be to perform this flattening process when the resx files are prepared for translation and sent to the translator/localizer.

Resource Translation Manager

We have looked at using WinRes to allow the translator/localizer to edit Windows Forms' forms, but this approach covers only part of the localizable resources in an application and is applicable only to Windows Forms applications. A significant number of resources cannot be maintained using this approach, and the .NET Framework does not include a translator/localizer tool for editing resources directly. Translators/localizers might already have their own (preferred) tools for translating resx files that use Translation Memories (TMs) or other translation technologies; if so, you are well advised to leave this decision in their hands. However, if you are using a bilingual, business-aware employee or your resource format is not resx, you might need to provide a tool for editing resources. In the downloadable source code for this book, you will find the Resource Translation Manager. Figure 14.1 shows the Resource Translation Manager being used to maintain the German resources for a Windows Forms application.

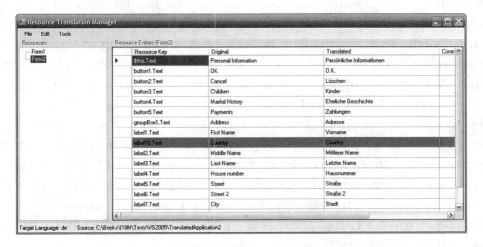

Figure 14.1 The Resource Translation Manager

The Resource Translation Manager shows the translator/localizer a tree view of all the resources. Clicking on a resource base name (e.g., "Form2") in the tree view shows the list of resource entries for both the original (invariant) language and the selected target language (and their comments, if the resource source supports them). The translator/localizer can edit the target language entries. Untranslated entries are shown in red so that the translator/localizer can easily identify entries that need attention. The translator/localizer can mark a resource entry as translated (by right-clicking the entry and selecting "Mark As Translated") so that entries that are the same in both the original language and the target language do not continually show up as untranslated. The list of entries specifically marked as translated is maintained in a separate XML file so that when the next translation iteration occurs, the list does not have to be remarked.

The translator/localizer can change languages or the source of the resources by selecting Tools, Resources Source. Settings are stored in `ResourceTranslation Manager.exe.config`.

Reintegrating Resources

At the beginning of this chapter, I pointed out that there is a time delay between sending the resources to the translator/localizer and getting them back, and that during this time it is unrealistic to stop development. The solution described assumes that the development department has the "master" copy of resources and is free to modify forms as it sees fit. Thus, the incoming resources from the translator/localizer cannot simply be copied back to the master copy. Instead, they must be reintegrated with the original copy.

The process of reintegrating resources is a little involved, so we start with an overview of the process. The essential goal is to add back to the original "master" resources any resources that have been changed by the translator/localizer. It is more complicated than you might imagine because of the fact that Visual Studio form resources use inheritance. Assume that we are using the .NET Framework 2.0. If we send a French resx file (`Form1.fr.resx`), for example, to the translator, it will contain only those differences from the invariant resx file (`Form1.resx`). If the translator/localizer makes a change to the French form by translating the Form's title, this

new item will be different than the invariant resource, and the French resx file will
contain a new entry:

```
<data name="$this.Text">
  <value>L'Information Personnelle</value>
</data>
```

Thus, the incoming French resx file contains more entries than the original master French resx file.

Alternatively, if we are using the .NET Framework 1.1, we have to flatten the Form
resx files so that WinRes 1.1 can read them. In this case, the incoming French resx file
will also contain more entries than the original master French resx file. So regardless
of the version of the .NET Framework you are using, the incoming resources will contain more entries than the original master resources. However, to reintegrate these
resources, we cannot simply copy all "new" resource entries from the incoming
resources to the master resources. If the form has been updated since its release to the
translator/localizer and a control has been deleted, adding back all "new" entries
would mean that the deleted control would be added back to the project. In addition,
if you are using the .NET Framework 1.1, adding back all "new" entries would mean
that the master resx files would be converted from Visual Studio File Mode to Single
File Mode. This is why the reintegration process is more complicated than you might
imagine. In addition to this, you might want to perform some filtering of changes.
Recall that you might or might not want to allow your translator/localizer to redesign
your forms. If you want to leave form design in the hands of developers, you would
reject any changes that are not strings or images. Still further, you might want to reject
any incoming change if the incoming invariant resource value is not the same as the
current "master" invariant value. This situation would indicate that the resource
value has been changed by the development team since it was sent to the translator.
In this case, you should reject the incoming translation because it is a translation of a
different string and is no longer correct.

So the strategy is this: For each incoming set of resources (where a set is all the
files related to a single base name e.g., `Form1.resx`, `Form1.fr.resx`, `Form1.
fr-FR.resx`), a flattened `ResourceSet` for the master resources is created. This con-
tains the complete set of the resources for the given base name. For each incoming
resource, we compare the incoming resource entries against this flattened

ResourceSet to see if the entry's key already exists. If it does already exist, the entry is one that existed at the time that the resources were sent to the translator/localizer and that still exists in master copy now. If the entry's value is different, the translator/localizer has changed this value, so we need to update our resources. If the incoming resource key exists in the master "unflattened" resource, this is a value that already existed but has now been changed, so we simply change our copy of it. If the resource key does not exist in the master "unflattened" resource, this is a value that had no previous translation but does now, so we add the new entry to the master "unflattened" resource.

With the problems and solutions outlined, let's proceed to the code. The IResourceGovernor has a method called ReintegrateResourceSet that is implemented in the ResourceGovernor base class. This method accepts the flattened master ResourceSet, the master ResourceSet to be updated, and the incoming ResourceSet:

```
public bool ReintegrateResourceSet(
    ResourceSet flattenedMasterResourceSet,
    ResourceSet masterResourceSet,
    ResourceSet incomingResourceSet,
    AcceptResourceEntry acceptResourceEntry)
{
    bool changesMade = false;
    Hashtable flattenedMasterResourceTable =
        GetResourceSetTable(flattenedMasterResourceSet);

    Hashtable masterResourceTable =
        GetResourceSetTable(masterResourceSet);

    IDictionaryEnumerator incomingResourceSetEnumerator =
        incomingResourceSet.GetEnumerator();

    while (incomingResourceSetEnumerator.MoveNext())
    {
        DictionaryEntry incomingEntry = (DictionaryEntry)
            incomingResourceSetEnumerator.Current;

        if (incomingEntry.Value != null &&
            flattenedMasterResourceTable.ContainsKey(
            incomingEntry.Key) && !
            flattenedMasterResourceTable[incomingEntry.Key].Equals(
            incomingEntry.Value))
        {
```

```
        if (acceptResourceEntry == null ||
            acceptResourceEntry(incomingEntry,
            flattenedMasterResourceTable[incomingEntry.Key]))
        {
            if (masterResourceTable.ContainsKey(
                incomingEntry.Key))
                masterResourceTable[incomingEntry.Key] =
                    incomingEntry.Value;
            else
                masterResourceTable.Add(
                    incomingEntry.Key, incomingEntry.Value);

            changesMade = true;
        }
    }
  }
  return changesMade;
}
```

The method updates the master `ResourceSet` with changes from the incoming `ResourceSet`. To call `ReintegrateResourceSet`, we iterate through each of the incoming base names (using `IResourcesGovernor.GetInvariantCultureBase-Names()`):

```
IResourcesGovernor incomingResourcesGovernor =
    new ResXResourcesGovernor(@"C:\CustomerCare\Incoming");

IResourcesGovernor masterResourcesGovernor =
    new ResXResourcesGovernor(@"C:\CustomerCare");

foreach(string baseName in
    incomingResourcesGovernor.GetInvariantCultureBaseNames())
{
    ResourceSet flattenedMasterResourceSet =
        GetFlattenedResourceSet(masterResourcesGovernor, baseName);

    foreach(CultureInfo cultureInfo in
        incomingResourcesGovernor.GetExistingCultures(baseName))
    {
        IResourceGovernor incomingResourceGovernor =
            incomingResourcesGovernor.GetResourceGovernor(
            baseName, cultureInfo);

        IResourceGovernor masterResourceGovernor =
            masterResourcesGovernor.GetResourceGovernor(
            baseName, cultureInfo);
```

```
    if (incomingResourceGovernor.ResourceExists() &&
        masterResourceGovernor.ResourceExists())
    {
        ResourceSet incomingResourceSet =
            incomingResourceGovernor.ReadResourceSet();

        ResourceSet masterResourceSet =
            masterResourceGovernor.ReadResourceSet();

        if (masterResourceGovernor.ReintegrateResourceSet(
            flattenedMasterResourceSet, masterResourceSet,
            incomingResourceSet, null))

            masterResourceGovernor.WriteResourceSet(
                masterResourceSet);
    }
  }
}
```

So the base names might be "Form1", "Form1Resources", "Form2", and so on. We get the flattened master ResourceSet using GetFlattenedResourceSet, which we return to in a moment. We get an array of CultureInfo objects for which resources exist for the given base name, so if "Form1.resx", "Form1.fr.resx", and "Form1.fr-FR.resx" exist, the array will contain the invariant CultureInfo, the "fr" CultureInfo, and the "fr-FR" CultureInfo. We see if both the incoming resource exists and a corresponding master resource exists (a form could have been deleted in its entirety since the translator/localizer was sent the original files). Finally, we call IResourceGovernor.ReintegrateResourceSet; if this returns true, indicating that changes were made, we call IResourceGovernor.WriteResourceSet to make the changes permanent.

Notice that we pass null as the fourth parameter to IResourceGovernor.ReintegrateResourceSet. This parameter enables us to control which entries are accepted as valid updates. It is an AcceptResourceEntry delegate:

```
public delegate bool AcceptResourceEntry(
    DictionaryEntry entry, object originalValue);
```

By passing null for this parameter, we accept all updates. If you have taken the approach that your translator/localizer is simply a translator and all other changes (such as moving and resizing controls) should be rejected, you would pass a delegate for this parameter:

```
if (masterResourceGovernor.ReintegrateResourceSet(
    flattenedMasterResourceSet,
    masterResourceSet,
    incomingResourceSet,
    new AcceptResourceEntry(AcceptStringAndImageResourceEntry)))
```

The `AcceptStringAndImageResourceEntry` method is shown here:

```
private bool AcceptStringAndImageResourceEntry(
    DictionaryEntry entry, object originalValue)
{
    return entry.Value is string || entry.Value is Image;
}
```

This method rejects changes to all entries that are not strings or images. You could also use this approach to strip out hotkeys if you are using an automated runtime solution (see the Hotkeys section of Chapter 8, "Best Practices"). Another possibility is to compare the number of parameters in the original string with the number of parameters in the new string. So "`Welcome, {0}`" has one parameter, but "`Bienvenue`" has none, and this could be perceived as a translation error. A variation on the same theme is to check that the type of parameters in the new string is the same as in the original string. So if the original string was "`Your goods will be delivered on {0:D}`" (where "`D`" is being used as a long date format) and the parameter was changed to "`{0:C}`" (where "`C`" is a currency format), a runtime error would occur and this problem could be caught here.

The final piece is the `GetFlattenedResourceSet` method. The purpose of this method is to return a completely flattened `ResourceSet` from all the `ResourceSets` for a given base name:

```
private ResourceSet GetFlattenedResourceSet(
    IResourcesGovernor masterResourcesGovernor, string baseName)
{
    CultureInfo[] masterCultureInfos =
        masterResourcesGovernor.GetExistingCultures(baseName);

    if (masterCultureInfos.GetLength(0) == 0)
        return null;

    Array.Sort(masterCultureInfos, new CultureInfoParentComparer());

    IResourceGovernor masterResourceGovernor =
```

```
        masterResourcesGovernor.GetResourceGovernor(
        baseName, masterCultureInfos[
        masterCultureInfos.GetLength(0) - 1]);

    ResourceSet flattenedMasterResourceSet =
        masterResourceGovernor.ReadResourceSet();

    for(int cultureInfoNumber =
        masterCultureInfos.GetLength(0) - 2;
        cultureInfoNumber >= 0; cultureInfoNumber--)
    {
        CultureInfo cultureInfo =
            masterCultureInfos[cultureInfoNumber];

        masterResourceGovernor =
            masterResourcesGovernor.GetResourceGovernor(
            baseName, cultureInfo);

        masterResourceGovernor.AddResourceSet(
            flattenedMasterResourceSet,
            masterResourceGovernor.ReadResourceSet());
    }
    return flattenedMasterResourceSet;
}
```

This method gets a list of existing cultures (e.g., invariant, "fr", "fr-FR") and sorts them in parental order so that the invariant culture is first, then the neutral culture ("fr"), and then the specific culture ("fr-FR"). It creates a new ResourceSet from the most specific culture (e.g., "fr-FR") and then adds in new resource entries from each of the "parent" cultures using IResourceGovernor.AddResourceSet. The IComparer class used to perform the sorting in Array.Sort is as follows:

```
public class CultureInfoParentComparer : IComparer
{
    int IComparer.Compare(Object x, Object y)
    {
        CultureInfo cultureInfoX = ((CultureInfo) x);
        CultureInfo cultureInfoY = ((CultureInfo) y);
        if (cultureInfoX.Equals(CultureInfo.InvariantCulture) &&
            cultureInfoY.Equals(CultureInfo.InvariantCulture))
            return 0;
        else if (cultureInfoX.Equals(CultureInfo.InvariantCulture))
            return -1;
        else if (cultureInfoY.Equals(CultureInfo.InvariantCulture))
```

```
            return 1;
        else if (cultureInfoX.IsNeutralCulture &&
            cultureInfoY.IsNeutralCulture)
            return 0;
        else if (cultureInfoX.IsNeutralCulture)
            return -1;
        else if (cultureInfoY.IsNeutralCulture)
            return 1;
        else if (! cultureInfoX.IsNeutralCulture &&
            ! cultureInfoY.IsNeutralCulture)
            return 0;
        else if (! cultureInfoX.IsNeutralCulture)
            return -1;
        else
            return 1;
    }
}
```

The `IComparer.Compare` method returns -1 if x is before y, 0 if x is the same as y, and +1 if x is after y.

Where Are We?

This chapter proposes many strategies. Your choice of strategy is determined to some extent by the technology behind your application (i.e., Windows Forms or ASP.NET, .NET Framework 1.1 or 2.0), but also by your choice of resource format. Clearly, the .NET Framework favors using resx files: WinRes 2.0 reads and writes Visual Studio File Mode resx files directly, and ASP.NET 2.0 automatically detects changes to resx files. However, other formats, such as a database, can ease the translation/localization process: Changes to a database are recognized immediately (if the resource is not cached by a `ResourceManager`), and there is no need to rebuild resource assemblies. The reintegration of resources returned by the translator/localizer is a critical part of the internationalization process, and consideration should be given to the fact that the application might well have changed since the resources were sent to the translator/localizer, and not all of the translator/localizer's changes will necessarily be accepted.

Where are we in terms of this book? I sincerely hope that you are standing on top of the mountain and enjoying the view.

▪A▪

New Internationalization Features in the .NET Framework 2.0 and Visual Studio 2005

This appendix contains a list of the new features in the .NET Framework 2.0 and Visual Studio 2005 that are relevant to internationalization. The appendix is useful if you already have a good knowledge of internationalization in the .NET Framework 1.1 and Visual Studio 2003 and want to get up to speed as quickly as possible. It is also useful if you are trying to decide whether to start a new project in your familiar .NET Framework 1.1 and Visual Studio 2003 or make the leap to the more recent version. The appendix is mostly a list of pointers to sections of this book where the relevant features are covered in more detail.

If you are looking for a complete list of changes between any two versions of the .NET Framework, download `LibCheck.exe` from http://www.microsoft.com/downloads. This tool compares two versions of the .NET Framework and lists every difference.

Compatibility

This section covers the compatibility between the two versions of the .NET Framework and Visual Studio.

Windows Forms Compatibility

Visual Studio 2005 serializes components on a form using a model called Property Reflection (see Chapter 4, "Windows Forms Specifics"). Visual Studio 2003, however, serializes components using a model called Property Assignment. When you open a Visual Studio 2003 solution in Visual Studio 2005, it prompts you to convert the solution, giving you an opportunity to back up the old solution. The forms files (i.e., the .cs, .resx, and culture-neutral and culture-specific .resx files) are all initially unchanged and remain compatible with Visual Studio 2003. However, after a form has been changed, the source and resx files are written out using Visual Studio 2005's Property Reflection model. The resulting code and resx files are now different. Although Visual Studio 2003 doesn't use the Property Reflection model, the resulting code and resx files are recognizable and can be opened and compiled using Visual Studio 2003 (assuming that the form contains only components and code that both platforms recognize). Unfortunately, Visual Studio 2003 fails to understand that the form's Localizable property should be true and sets it to false. When you set it to true again, Visual Studio 2003 naturally rewrites the source file and resx file, and the form returns to Visual Studio 2003's Property Assignment model.

The upshot of all this is that both versions of Visual Studio can read each other's form files (as long as you use components that are present in both versions of the framework). However, when you make any change to a form, the version of Visual Studio you are using writes out the form again using the model that it uses to write forms. Because Visual Studio 2003 doesn't understand Visual Studio 2005's serialization of the form's Localizable property, you must set this to true again; this constitutes a change, which, therefore, means that the form is converted back to Visual Studio 2003's model. You should also be aware that the scenario of opening Visual Studio 2005 forms in Visual Studio 2003 is not an officially supported model, so although this is often possible, you are on your own with regard to support.

Windows Forms Designer

The Visual Studio 2005 Windows Forms Designer adds many enhancements beyond the Visual Studio 2003 Windows Forms Designer, but it also removes one area of functionality. In the Visual Studio 2003 Windows Forms Designer, you can add new controls to any language version of a form. For example, with the French version of a form selected in the designer, you can add a new button to the form and it will be added to all forms. The Visual Studio 2005 Windows Forms Designer, however, requires that you first change back to the default language before adding new controls. Instead of viewing this as a step backward in Visual Studio 2005, you should understand that Visual Studio 2003 should not have allowed new controls to be added to forms other than the default language form, but this practice was not explicitly prevented.

CultureInfo.DisplayName and CultureInfo.EnglishName with Scripts

The format of the text returned by the `CultureInfo DisplayName` and `English-Name` properties for some cultures with scripts has changed. The format used in the .NET Framework 1.1 is to delimit the script entirely in its own parentheses. For example, the culture for the Azeri language in Azerbaijan using the Latin script ("`az-AZ-Latn`") has this `EnglishName`:

```
Azeri (Latin) (Azerbaijan)
```

However, the .NET Framework 2.0 includes the script in the same parentheses as the country:

```
Azeri (Latin, Azerbaijan)
```

If you have logic that parses the name to extract its component information, you need to update this logic. Note that this change does not apply to new cultures with script suffixes that were introduced in the .NET Framework 2.0. For example, the "`sr-BA-Latn`" culture's `EnglishName` is "`Serbian (Latin) (Bosnia and Herzegovina)`".

CultureInfo.GetCultures Order

The order of the cultures returned from the `CultureInfo.GetCultures` method is different between the two versions of the framework. The order in both versions of the .NET Framework is unsorted and unspecified, but they are nonetheless different.

Control.DefaultFont Logic

The logic used to determine the DefaultFont property of System.Windows.Forms. Control is slightly more sophisticated in the .NET Framework 2.0. Because Control is the base class for all Windows Forms controls, this affects all controls. The difference is that on Arabic Windows, Control.DefaultFont now defaults to Tahoma, 8 point.

CultureInfo.Equals Logic

The logic used in the CultureInfo.Equals method has changed. In the .NET Framework 1.1, CultureInfo.Equals tests equality with another CultureInfo by comparing their locale IDs (LCIDs). In the .NET Framework 2.0, this comparison does not work because custom cultures all share the same LCID. Thus, a Spanish (United States) custom culture has the same LCID as a Bengali (Bangladesh) custom culture. In the .NET Framework 2.0, the CultureInfo.Equals method assumes that two cultures are equal if they have the same name and the same CompareInfo objects. (A test based simply on a name would be incorrect because alternate sort orders have the same culture name but different sort orders.) I have not found any circumstance in which this difference causes an incompatibility.

CultureInfo.OptionalCalendars Has New Calendars

The .NET Framework 2.0 introduces new calendar classes. These new calendars classes are available to the cultures for which they are relevant through the CultureInfo.OptionalCalendars array property. Consequently, the lengths of these arrays and, perhaps more important, the order of the elements of these arrays are different in some cultures (e.g., Arabic (Saudi Arabia)).

Base Data Has Changed for Some Cultures

The month and day names returned by the DateTimeFormatInfo, MonthNames, and DayNames array properties have changed for the Arabic (Morocco), Divehi (Maldives), Kannada (India), and Norwegian (Nynorsk) (Norway) cultures (i.e., ar-MA, div-MV, kn-IN, and nn-NO).

In addition, the currency symbols have been updated for several cultures, including Turkish (Turkey) (i.e., tr-TR), for which the currency symbol in the .NET Framework 1.1 is "TL" (Türk Lirasi); however, in the .NET Framework 2.0, the currency symbol is "YTL" (Yeni Türk Lirasi), regardless of the version of Windows and whether Windows Updates is turned on.

ResX Relative File References Break Code That Uses ResXResourceReader

The Visual Studio 2005 Resource Editor includes support for adding files such as bitmaps to resx resource files. The resulting entry in the resx file is of type ResX-FileRef. The ResXFileRef class is supported in both the .NET Framework 1.1 and 2.0. The problem (from the point of view of code that reads resources), however, is that the Visual Studio 2005 Resource Editor uses relative paths (see the "ResX File References" section in Chapter 10, "Resource Administration"). If you process resx files using the ResXResourceReader class, in most cases your code that reads resx files will fail if it tries to read a .NET Framework 2.0 resx file because it won't know where to find the referenced files. A number of solutions exist, but the simplest is to set the ResXResourceReader.BasePath property to the path where the referenced files are located.

ResX Changes Break Code That Uses ResXResourceReader

The serialization of the Form.Localizable property to resx files has changed. In the .NET Framework 1.1, this property was represented as data in the resx file like this:

```
<data name="$this.Localizable" type="System.Boolean, mscorlib,
Version=1.0.5000.0, Culture=neutral,PublicKeyToken=b77a5c561934e089">
  <value>True</value>
</data>
```

In the .NET Framework 2.0, however, the same property is represented like this:

```
<metadata name="$this.Localizable" type="System.Boolean, mscorlib,
Version=2.0.0.0, Culture=neutral, PublicKeyToken=b77a5c561934e089">
  <value>True</value>
</metadata>
```

The difference is that the `Form.Localizable` property is now treated as metadata instead of data. This has an impact on any code that reads resx files using the `ResXResourceReader.GetEnumerator()` method. The following code adds all the entries in a resx file to a `TextBox`:

```
ResXResourceReader reader =
    new ResXResourceReader(@"..\..\Form1.resx");

IDictionaryEnumerator enumerator = reader.GetEnumerator();
while (enumerator.MoveNext())
{
    DictionaryEntry entry = enumerator.Entry;
    string value = String.Empty;
    if (entry.Value != null)
        value = entry.Value.ToString();

    textBox1.Text += entry.Key.ToString() + ", " + value +
        System.Environment.NewLine;
}
```

In the .NET Framework 1.1, this code includes the `$this.Localizable` entry. In the .NET Framework 2.0, it does not. To read this entry in the .NET Framework 2.0, you need to use the new `ResXResourceReader.GetMetadataEnumerator` method:

```
ResXResourceReader reader =
    new ResXResourceReader(@"..\..\Form1.resx");

IDictionaryEnumerator enumerator = reader.GetMetadataEnumerator();
while(enumerator.MoveNext())
{
    DictionaryEntry entry = enumerator.Entry;
    textBox1.Text += entry.Key.ToString() + ", " +
        entry.Value.ToString() + System.Environment.NewLine;
}
```

This code results in just a single entry (i.e., `$this.Localizable`).

In addition, the change from data to metadata affects any FxCop rule that reads resource data looking for the `Form.Localizable` property. See the "`Form.Localizable` must be `true`" rule in Chapter 13, "Testing Internationalization Using FxCop," for an example.

.NET Framework Redistributable

The deployment story for the .NET Framework has improved. In both .NET Framework 1.1 and 2.0, the .NET Framework redistributable (`dotnetfx.exe`) installs an `English (United States)` version of the framework. This has not changed. However, the packaging of the user interface used during the installation process has. In the .NET Framework 1.1, you could distribute different language versions of the .NET Framework redistributable. So if you distributed the German .NET Framework redistributable, the setup user interface would be in German, and the English version of the framework would be installed. In the .NET Framework 2.0, however, there is just a single .NET Framework redistributable that contains the localized user interface for all supported languages. The user interface used during installation is determined by the language version of the operating system. In addition to the installation languages supported by the .NET Framework 1.1, the .NET Framework 2.0 supports Arabic and Hebrew.

If you download the .NET Framework 2.0 redistributable from http://www.microsoft.com/downloads, be aware that the combo box that offers you a choice of languages simply refers to the language of the Web page from which the redistributable can be downloaded. The `dotnetfx.exe` on each and every page is 100 percent identical.

.NET Framework Language Packs

Arabic and Hebrew have been added to the list of .NET Framework Language Packs. The list of language versions for Visual Studio 2005 is the same as for Visual Studio 2003.

.NET Framework

This section describes enhancements to the .NET Framework classes, paying particular attention to the `System.Globalization` namespace.

New IdnMapping Class

The IdnMapping class provides support for international domain names. See the "International Domain Name Mapping" section of Chapter 6, "Globalization."

String Identifiers for Alternate Sort Orders

Some cultures support more than one solution for sorting data. The .NET Framework 1.1 allows these alternate sort orders to be specified when a new CultureInfo is created by providing the locale ID (LCID), which represents the language, region, and sort order. The following code creates a CultureInfo object for Spanish in Spain using the traditional sort order:

```
CultureInfo cultureInfo = new CultureInfo(0x0000040A);
```

This is still supported in the .NET Framework 2.0, but the .NET Framework 2.0 supports an alternative solution when the language, region, and sort order can be specified as a string:

```
CultureInfo cultureInfo = new CultureInfo("es-ES_tradnl");
```

You can see from this example that the sort order ("tradnl") is a suffix of the region ("ES"). The sort order can be specified for only alternate sort orders—in other words, you cannot specify the Spanish default International (Modern) sort order using "es-ES-Intl". The complete list of alternate sort order identifiers is listed in the "Alternate Sort Orders" section of Chapter 6.

This enhancement is an important one because it enables developers to support a single data type (i.e., string) for storing and transmitting culture identifiers. Without this enhancement, developers must support both string and integer data types to be able to represent all cultures with all sort orders.

CultureInfo.GetCultures and CultureTypes Enumeration

The CultureTypes enumeration has four new members: FrameworkCultures, ReplacementCultures, UserCustomCulture, and WindowsOnlyCultures, which are used in CultureInfo.GetCultures. See the "CultureInfo.GetCultures and CultureTypes Enumeration" section in Chapter 6.

New CultureInfo Properties

`CultureInfo` has a new property, `IetfLanguageTag`, which gets the RFC 3066(bis) standard identification for a language.

New CultureInfo Methods

`CultureInfo` has a new method called `GetCultureInfo`, which provides caching support for `CultureInfo` objects. The first call to `CultureInfo.GetCultureInfo` creates a `CultureInfo` method as normal, but subsequent calls for the same `CultureInfo` get the cached copy. The benefit is better performance. However, all cached cultures are read-only and, more important, do not accept user overrides (accepting user overrides is a recommended practice); if you want to accept user overrides, you should not use this method. `CultureInfo` has a similar method called `GetCultureInfoByIetfLanguageTag` that performs the same operation but accepts an IETF language tag instead of a culture name.

String.Compare and StringComparison Enumeration

The `String.Compare` method has a new overload, `String.Compare(string, string, StringComparison)`, which accepts a `StringComparison` enumeration. This provides a more convenient way of specifying how a string comparison should be performed instead of having to remember what `String.Compare` or `String.CompareTo` overload to call.

New DateTime Properties

`DateTime` has a new property called `Kind`, which is a `DateTimeKind` enumeration. This enables developers to specify whether the `DateTime` is local time, coordinated universal time (UTC), or unspecified (the default). This is used in conjunction with the new "K" `DateTime` format specifier, and it provides developers with control over the serialization of dates that include time zones.

New DateTimeFormatInfo Properties

`DateTimeFormatInfo` has two new properties, `AbbreviatedMonthGenitiveNames` and `MonthGenitiveNames`, which surface the names of months when they are used in their genitive form (see the "Genitive Date Support" section in Chapter 6). The .NET Framework 1.1 supports genitive month names but does not expose the names for you to use for your own purposes.

`DateTimeFormatInfo` also has a new `ShortestDayName` property, which returns an array of the shortest day names (e.g., "Su", "Mo", "Tu", "We", "Th", "Fr", "Sa").

New DateTime Methods

Two new methods, `TryParse` and `TryParseExact`, are siblings of the `Parse` and `ParseExact` methods. They enable you to attempt to parse a date without throwing an exception. Both methods return a Boolean indicating the success of the parsing operation.

New Calendars

The .NET Framework 2.0 adds eight new `Calendar` classes: `EastAsianLunisolar-Calendar` (abstract), `ChineseLunisolarCalendar`, `JapaneseLunisolar Calendar`, `KoreanLunisolarCalendar`, `TaiwanLunisolarCalendar`, `Jalaali Calendar`, `PersianCalendar`, and `UmAlQuraCalendar`. See the "Calendars" section in Chapter 6.

New Calendar Properties

`Calendar.AlgorithmType` is a read-only property that enables you to determine whether the calendar is a solar calendar, a lunar calendar, or both. `Calendar.IsReadOnly` is a read-only property indicating whether the calendar's properties are read-only.

`Calendar.MaxSupportedDateTime` and `Calendar.MinSupportedDateTime` are read-only properties indicating the upper and lower bounds of the calendar.

New Calendar Methods

`Calendar.GetLeapMonth` returns a month number of the leap month in a given year and, optionally, an era. The month number is 0 if the year does not have a leap month. `Calendar.ReadOnly` is a static method that returns a read-only calendar object.

New CompareInfo Properties

CompareInfo has a new Name property, which provides a string identifier for the CompareInfo. Typically, this name is the same culture string used to identify a CultureInfo (e.g., "es-ES" for Spanish (Spain) international sort), but for alternate sort orders, this includes the sort suffix (e.g., "es-ES_tradnl" for Spanish (Spain) traditional sort).

New CompareInfo Methods

CompareInfo has a new static method, IsSortable, which returns true if a character or string is sortable. A character or string is sortable if all its characters are known to the .NET Framework's sort tables. In this situation, String.Compare compares all characters in the string. However, if a string contains characters that are not known to the .NET Framework's sort tables, String.Compare simply ignores those characters. In this situation, a more accurate test for equality can be achieved using String.CompareOrdinal, which compares the Unicode code points of all characters, regardless of their presence or absence in the .NET Framework's sort tables.

New RegionInfo Properties

RegionInfo has new properties to help with internationalizing currency names: CurrencyEnglishName and CurrencyNativeName. RegionInfo.GeoId is a numeric geographical identifier for the region. It is useful for uniquely identifying a region and also for use with the Win32 GetGeoInfo function. See the "Geographical Information" section in Chapter 6. RegionInfo.NativeName returns the name of the region that is used in that region.

New TextInfo Properties

TextInfo.CultureName returns the name of the culture to which the TextInfo is attached. TextInfo.IsReadOnly indicates whether the TextInfo object is read-only. TextInfo.IsRightToLeft indicates whether the associated language is a right-to-left language (in the .NET Framework 1.1, this is achievable only by hard-coding a known list of right-to-left cultures). TextInfo.LCID is the locale ID of the associated language.

New TextInfo Methods

`TextInfo.ReadOnly` is a static method that returns a read-only `TextInfo` object.

New NumberFormatInfo Properties

`NumberFormatInfo` has two new properties, `DigitSubstitution` and `Native Digits`, which provide information about the digit systems used for formatting. `DigitSubstitution` is a `DigitShapes` enumeration that is either `None`, `Context`, or `NativeNational`. `NativeDigits` is an array of strings of the digits used for number formatting. Both properties are purely informational and have no effect in the .NET Framework 2.0. They exist for you to use for your own purposes and in expectation of better support in a future version of the .NET Framework. The following code shows their values for `English (United States)` and `Arabic (Saudi Arabia)`:

```
CultureInfo cultureInfo = new CultureInfo("en-US");
textBox1.Text +=
    cultureInfo.NumberFormat.DigitSubstitution.ToString() +
    ":- " +
    ArrayToString(cultureInfo.NumberFormat.NativeDigits) +
    System.Environment.NewLine;

cultureInfo = new CultureInfo("ar-SA");
textBox1.Text +=
    cultureInfo.NumberFormat.DigitSubstitution.ToString() +
    ":- " +
    ArrayToString(cultureInfo.NumberFormat.NativeDigits) +
    System.Environment.NewLine;
```

(`ArrayToString` is a simple custom method to convert an array to a string.) The result is this:

```
None:- 0, 1, 2, 3, 4, 5, 6, 7, 8, 9
Context: ٠, ١, ٢, ٣, ٤, ٥, ٦, ٧, ٨, ٩
```

`DigitSubstitution` is `None` for all cultures except for Arabic, Kyrgyz, Mongolian, and Persian-specific cultures.

New ResourceReader Methods

ResourceReader has a new method called GetResourceData, which reads a resource as an array of bytes. The purpose of this method is to allow data of *any* type to be read from a .resources file. The problem that it solves is that it is not normally possible to read data from a .resources file if the data cannot be deserialized. Typically, data cannot be deserialized if the type is unknown to the application that is deserializing the data. So if one application stores, say, a BusinessObject type in a .resources file and the application reading the file does not have a reference to the assembly containing the BusinessObject type, the attempt to deserialize the BusinessObject will fail. However, the GetResourceData method allows the data for this resource to be retrieved as an array of bytes. The following example retrieves a resource entry called "String1" from "Form1Resources.resources":

```
ResourceReader reader =
    new ResourceReader("Form1Resources.resources");

string resourceType;
byte[] resourceData;

reader.GetResourceData(
    "String1", out resourceType, out resourceData);

textBox1.Text +=
    "ResourceType: " + resourceType + System.Environment.NewLine +
    "ResourceData: " +
    System.Text.Encoding.UTF8.GetString(resourceData);
```

The result is this:

```
ResourceType: ResourceTypeCode.String
ResourceData: &This is the resource value for String1
```

Of course, this particular exercise is unnecessary because the string type can always be deserialized, but it shows the method's behaviour.

New ResXResourceReader Properties

ResXResourceReader has a new property, BasePath, which specifies the path where files referenced in relative file references can be found. ResX file references exist in both the .NET Framework 1.1 and 2.0, and are described in the "ResX File

References" section in Chapter 10. Another new property, `UseResXDataNodes`, is a Boolean value indicating whether the resource entries' values are the simple values that they are in the .NET Framework 1.1 or are `ResXDataNode` objects. The default is `false`, so it is compatible with the .NET Framework 1.1. The benefit of the `ResX-DataNode` objects is that they contain comments and file references. See the "ResX-DataNodes and Comments" section in Chapter 10.

New ResXResourceReader Methods

`ResXResourceReader` has a new method called `GetMetadataEnumerator`. This method returns an enumerator for a resx's metadata. The `Form.Localizable` property is treated as data in the .NET Framework 1.1 but as metadata in the .NET Framework 2.0. The `GetMetaDataEnumerator` method provides a means by which these metadata values can be retrieved. See the "ResX Changes Break Code That Uses `ResXResourceReader`" section of this appendix for more details.

New ResXResourceWriter Methods

`ResXResourceWriter` has a new method called `AddAlias`, which adds an assembly alias to the resx file. After `ResXResourceWriter.Generate` is called, the resx file contains a corresponding assembly element:

```
<assembly alias="System.Windows.Forms" name="System.Windows.Forms,
Version=2.0.0.0, Culture=neutral, PublicKeyToken=b77a5c561934e089" />
```

Subsequent entries in the resx file need to refer to only the alias instead of the full assembly name:

```
<data name="button1.ImeMode"
type="System.Windows.Forms.ImeMode, System.Windows.Forms">
  <value>NoControl</value>
</data>
```

The result is a smaller resx file.

In addition, `ResXResourceWriter` has a new method called `AddMetadata`, which adds metadata entries to a resx file. Such entries are intended to be used for design-time properties such as `Form.Localizable`. Metadata entries are read using the new `ResXResourceReader.GetMetadataEnumerator` method.

New String and StringInfo Methods

String has two new methods, `Normalize` and `IsNormalized`, which are used to normalize strings. The problem that they solve comes from the fact that some Unicode characters can be represented in more than one way (by using several combined Unicode characters). The binary representations are different, but the characters that they represent are the same. If their binary representations were compared, they would appear to be different, even though they result in the same character. Unicode supports a concept called normalization that resolves these representations to a simpler form, and the `Normalize` and `IsNormalized` methods implement this process.

The `String` and `StringInfo` classes also have a new property, `LengthInText-Elements`, and a method, `SubstringByTextElements`, which together enable you to process strings in terms of their text elements instead of their characters. Many scripts (e.g., Japanese Hiragana) combine characters to form text elements, and it is often meaningless to process individual characters in such scripts.

The `String.Compare` method has several new overloads that accept a new `StringComparison` enumeration that simplifies string comparisons. For example, calling `String.Compare` with the `StringComparison.Ordinal` value is the same as calling `String.CompareOrdinal`. Microsoft now recommends using ordinal comparisons for culture-insensitive comparisons. See the "Sort Orders" section of Chapter 6 for more details on ordinal comparisons.

New CharUnicodeInfo Class

The .NET Framework 2.0 introduces a new class, `CharUnicodeInfo`, which provides information about a Unicode character. The information is drawn from the Unicode Character Database for Unicode 4.1. It has four static methods (`GetDecimalDigitValue`, `GetDigitValue`, `GetNumericValue`, and `GetUnicodeCategory`) to retrieve various kinds of information about a character. Putting aside the 0 to 9 digits that we already know about, Unicode defines numerous code points for characters that have a numeric meaning. For example, the Unicode character $1/2$ (U+00BD) is one half, so `CharUnicodeInfo.GetNumericValue` returns 0.5 for this character. A similar effect is true for Roman numerals (e.g.,"I" is 1), Tamil characters (e.g., U+0BF2 is 1000), and Tibetan characters (e.g., U+0F32 is half nine).

resx Files and File References

resx files in both the .NET Framework 1.1 and 2.0 support file references. This means that a file can be referred to instead of being embedded in the resx file. The resulting resource in the resource assembly is exactly the same as for a resource that is embedded, however, so this is simply a development issue. The important point here is that file references are now the default for the Visual Studio 2005 Resource Editor, so any file that you add to a resource, by default, simply has a reference to the file. A copy of the file is added to a local `Resources` folder (in a Windows Forms application) or the `App_GlobalResources` or `App_LocalResources` folder (in an ASP.NET application), and the reference is to the file in this folder instead of the original file. In addition, the file reference is a relative reference instead of an absolute reference.

New ResourceManager Methods

`ResourceManager` has a new method called `GetStream`, which returns an `UnmanagedMemoryStream` for a resource given the name of that resource. The method is not CLS compliant.

Customizing the Fallback Process

The .NET Framework 2.0 enables you to specify that the location of the fallback resources is a satellite assembly. In the .NET Framework 1.1, the only choice was that fallback resources were in the invariant or fallback assembly. The downside to this approach is that there is no separation between resources and code. See the "`NeutralResourcesLanguageAttribute` and `UltimateResourceFallback Location`" section in Chapter 3, "An Introduction to Internationalization."

ResView and ResExtract (Managed Resource Viewer)

The Base Class Library Samples includes two new utilities for manipulating resources, which are collectively referred to as the Managed Resource Viewer. Although they are not specific to the .NET Framework 2.0, they were released during the same time period, so I have included them in this appendix. `ResView` is a resource viewer, and `ResExtract` extracts resources from a resource assembly. See http://msdn.microsoft.com/netframework/downloads/samples/bclsamples/ for more details.

Strongly Typed Resources

The .NET Framework 2.0 and Visual Studio 2005 support a concept of strongly typed resources. So instead of writing this:

```
MessageBox.Show(resourceManager.GetString("InsufficientFunds"));
```

You can write this:

```
MessageBox.Show(Form1Resources.InsufficientFunds);
```

You gain several benefits from this. The resource entry name is checked at design time instead of runtime, so typos are eliminated. The property is strongly typed, which gives compile-time type checking. The resource class (`Form1Resources`, in this example) encapsulates the `ResourceManager`, so it is not necessary to manage it yourself. Strongly-typed resources are initially covered in Chapter 3 but are also covered again in several other chapters. If you are staying with the .NET Framework 1.1, see the "Strongly-Typed Resources in the .NET Framework 1.1" section in Chapter 3 for an equivalent solution.

Custom Cultures

The .NET Framework 2.0 supports a concept of custom cultures. This concept existed in the .NET Framework 1.1, but it was primitive and difficult to gain any real benefit from. This improved implementation is recognized by the .NET Framework 2.0, the .NET Framework 2.0 SDK, and Visual Studio 2005. A custom culture is a culture that you define. It can be a modification of an existing culture, a combination of existing cultures, or a completely new culture in its own right. This idea has huge potential, which is why this book includes a whole chapter on this subject: Chapter 11, "Custom Cultures."

Visual Studio's Resource Editor

Visual Studio's Resource Editor has had an overhaul for Visual Studio 2005. Apart from its visual appearance, the main feature is that it does not handle all resources as strings. It enables you to manage bitmaps, icons, audio, and other files as resources.

Windows Forms

This section details the .NET Framework 2.0 and Visual Studio 2005 enhancements which are specific to Windows Forms applications.

Property Reflection Model

Visual Studio 2005 supports a model for serializing Windows Forms called property reflection. Instead of properties being serialized one by one as they are in Visual Studio 2003's property assignment model, properties are loaded using reflection by searching for resources with names that match the control and its properties. The end result is no different from the end result of Visual Studio 2003 in terms of functionality. The difference lies in the performance of forms that have large numbers of controls, so property reflection is said to scale better than property assignment. See Chapter 4.

Control.AutoSize

In the .NET Framework 1.1, several controls have an `AutoSize` property, but many do not. In the .NET Framework 2.0, the `AutoSize` property has been moved to the `System.Windows.Forms.Control` base class, meaning that all controls now have an `AutoSize` property. You will find that a few controls (e.g., `ListBox`) hide their `AutoSize` property in the Form Designer, but putting these controls aside this means that significantly more controls in Windows Forms 2.0 have an `AutoSize` property. See the "`AutoSize`" section in Chapter 8, "Best Practices."

Label.AutoSize Default

The default for `Label.AutoSize` remains unchanged in the .NET Framework 2.0 and is still `false`. However, Visual Studio 2005 treats this control differently from Visual Studio 2003: When a `Label` control is added to a form, its `AutoSize` property is automatically set to `true`. The effect is that it appears that the default has changed from `false` to `true`. This is helpful because it is more usual to want `Label` controls to be autosized on a localized form. Note that the `LinkLabel` control inherits from `Label`, so the same change applies to `LinkLabel` controls.

A similar effect can be seen for `CheckBox` and `RadioButton` controls. These controls do not have an `AutoSize` property in the .NET Framework 1.1. In the .NET Framework 2.0, the default value for `AutoSize` for `CheckBoxes` and `RadioButtons` is `false`, but Visual Studio 2005 automatically sets it to `true`.

AutoSizeMode Property

Some controls (`Button`, `DataGridViewColumn`, `Form`, `GroupBox`, `Panel`, `Splitter-Panel`, `TabPage`, `ToolStripContentPanel`, `UserControl`) have a new property called `AutoSizeMode` that can be set to determine whether the control should automatically grow and shrink as necessary or grow only as necessary. See the "`Auto-SizeMode`" section in Chapter 8.

AutoEllipsis Property

Some controls (`Button`, `CheckBox`, `Label`, `RadioButton`) have a new `AutoEllip-sis` property, which automatically displays an ellipsis in the text when there is insufficient room to display the whole text. This is useful for controls that must be localized but whose size must not change (such as controls on a sculpted form). The full text is still available as a ToolTip. See the "`AutoEllipsis`" section in Chapter 8.

RightToLeftLayout Property

The `Form` control, together with a number of other Windows Forms controls, now has a `RightToLeftLayout` property. This Boolean property is used in conjunction with the `RightToLeft` property and takes effect only when `RightToLeft` is `Yes`. Its purpose is to relocate controls within the form so that the controls appear as if they have been laid out correctly for a right-to-left language instead of a left-to-right language. In addition, it correctly mirrors a form's title bar so that the System Menu, Close, Maximize, and Minimize buttons are repositioned correctly. See the "Right-to-Left Languages and Mirroring in Windows Forms Applications" section of Chapter 7, "Middle East and East Asian Cultures," for more details.

TableLayoutPanel and FlowLayoutPanel Controls

The .NET Framework 2.0 includes two new controls, `TableLayoutPanel` and `FlowLayoutPanel`, which bring the power of HTML's table and flow layout to

Windows Forms. These are significant controls and can have a considerable impact on the way you design your forms for localization and the subsequent role that a translator/localizer might take. Using these controls means that your forms can automatically adapt to controls that resize as a consequence of their text changing size. Well-designed forms, therefore, do not need to be redesigned for different cultures, and a single form can fit all cultures. This drastically reduces the localization effort. See the "TableLayoutPanel and FlowLayoutPanel" section in Chapter 8.

BackgroundWorker

Windows Forms 2.0 introduces a new component called BackgroundWorker, which simplifies moving work to a background thread. This control is relevant to internationalization because, unlike the primitive Thread class that it replaces, BackgroundWorker does not provide you with direct access to the background thread upon which it is based. You can still set the BackgroundWorker's Thread's CurrentCulture and CurrentUICulture, but these must be set in the DoWork event handler:

```
public void BeginBackgroundWorker()
{
    BackgroundWorker backgroundWorker = new BackgroundWorker();
    backgroundWorker.DoWork +=
        new DoWorkEventHandler(backgroundWorker_DoWork);
    backgroundWorker.RunWorkerAsync();
}

void backgroundWorker_DoWork(object sender, DoWorkEventArgs e)
{
    Thread.CurrentThread.CurrentCulture = new CultureInfo("de-DE");
    Thread.CurrentThread.CurrentUICulture = new CultureInfo("de-DE");
    // do some work
}
```

WinRes

WinRes in the .NET Framework 1.1 SDK is difficult to use, for several reasons. WinRes in the .NET Framework 2.0 SDK is considerably improved, so if you rejected this tool previously, you should take a fresh look at it in 2.0 for small to medium-sized projects (for large projects, consider using one of the commercially available tools).

First and foremost, WinRes now understands the resx files that Visual Studio 2005 creates. It supports two file modes: Visual Studio File Mode and Single File Mode (the only mode used in WinRes 1.1). This means that you can read and write resx files in both Visual Studio 2005 and also WinRes 2.0 without having to commit to one tool.

WinRes 2.0 has significantly better error reporting. WinRes 1.1 had a handful of cryptic and unhelpful error messages, which lead to a lot of thrashing around trying to identify the real problem. WinRes 2.0 has more descriptive error messages.

WinRes 2.0 is more resilient than its predecessor. WinRes 1.1 refused to load a form if it found a single fault on the form. WinRes 2.0 loads all that it can load and reports the problems about the failed components.

WinRes 2.0 supports loading forms that inherit from other forms when the controls on those other forms have public visibility. Although this support is not absolute, it is considerably better than WinRes 1.1's nonexistent support.

Finally, WinRes 2.0 offers many of the same design and productivity improvements that you see in Visual Studio 2005's Forms Designer (e.g., snap lines).

See the "Windows Resource Localization Editor (WinRes)" section in Chapter 4.

ASP.NET

Visual Studio 2005 is a quantum leap beyond Visual Studio 2003 in terms of internationalization of ASP.NET applications. As with so many features in the .NET Framework 2.0 and Visual Studio 2005, this subject alone justifies the upgrade.

Localizability

Visual Studio 2005 enables you to localize forms with the same kind of productivity and efficiency that Visual Studio provides for Windows Forms applications. Select Tools, Generate Local Resources from Visual Studio 2005's menu; all the `Localizable` property values are moved to an associated resx file, and a "`meta:resourcekey`" attribute referring to those resources is added to the control. See the "Localizability in Visual Studio 2005" section in Chapter 5, "ASP.NET Specifics."

Web.config <globalization> culture and uiCulture Attributes

The `<globalization>` section of `Web.config` has always had `culture` and `uiCulture` attributes, which enable you to specify the `CurrentCulture` and `CurrentUICulture` of an entire Web site or folder. In ASP.NET 2.0, however, these attributes can be set to "`auto`" to automatically pick up the user's preferred settings from the HTTP header. See the "Application-Wide Automatic Culture Recognition" section in Chapter 5.

New Page Culture and UICulture Attributes

The `Page` class now supports `Culture` and `UICulture` attributes, which work in the same way as the `<globalization>` element's `culture` and `uiCulture` attributes, except that they apply to a single page. See the "Automatic Culture Recognition for Individual Pages" section in Chapter 5.

New Page.InitializeCulture Method

The `Page` class has a new method called `InitializeCulture`, which can be overridden to set the culture. This method is called before all the page's events so that it occurs early in the pipeline. You would use this method if the "`auto`" settings did not provide the functionality you are looking for. See the "Manual Culture Recognition for Individual Pages" section in Chapter 5.

Web Control Properties Are Marked as Localizable

In ASP.NET 1.1, no properties of any control are marked with the `Localizable` attribute. This is because Visual Studio 2003 does not offer any localization support for ASP.NET applications, so the presence or absence of the `Localizable(true)` attribute makes no difference. In ASP.NET 2.0, you will find that many properties of Web controls are marked as `Localizable(true)`, and this is how Visual Studio 2005 can localize pages. What is important to note here is that only a few HTML control properties are marked as `Localizable(true)`. In general, this means that if you want to localize your ASP.NET applications, you must use Web controls instead of HTML controls.

New Localize Control

The `Localize` control inherits from the `Literal` control and adds no new properties, methods, or events. At runtime, the `Localize` control is identical to the `Literal` control. The difference between the two controls lies in Visual Studio 2005's handling of these controls at design time. The `Localize` control uses the `Localize Designer`, whereas the `Literal` control uses the `LiteralDesigner`. The purpose of both the `Localize` control and the `Literal` control is to allow text to be placed in a control that can be localized—your choice between the two controls is determined by your preference of design-time support.

Automatic resx File Change Detection

By default, ASP.NET 2 applications monitor their associated resx files at runtime. When one of their associated resx files changes, ASP.NET unloads the application domain, rebuilds the associated resource assemblies, and reloads the application. This means that translators can modify resx files and see their changes immediately. In addition, the resources used in Web sites can be updated without needing to manually rebuild the application. Of course, this unloads the application domain, and any state in that domain will be lost. See the "ASP.NET 2.0 Translation/Localization Strategies" section in Chapter 14, "The Translator."

◼ B.

Information Resources

THIS APPENDIX IS A COLLECTION OF RESOURCES that I have found useful or that I think you might find useful in the course of internationalizing a .NET application. It is a subjective list, and no meaning should be attached to the omission of any particular resource.

On the Web site for this book (http://www.dotneti18n.com), you will find the complete source code for this book, as well as additional code examples and utilities, a list of errata, and news of the latest editions.

Books

Developing International Software, Second Edition. Dr. International. Microsoft Press: 2002.

This is a great book. Now that you have bought *.NET Internationalization*, you should rush out and buy *Developing International Software*. The first edition of this book, *Developing International Software for Windows 95 and Windows NT*, by Nadine Kano, is more different than you would expect from simply changing from first edition to second edition. The first edition is available online at http://www.microsoft.com/globaldev/ dis_v1/disv1.asp. Large parts of the second edition are also available online in various pages at http://www.microsoft.com/globaldev.

Resources

This section is a list of resources that are themselves a collection of resources.

Multilingual Computing Annual Resource Directory. http://www.multilingual.com. (Look for "Resource Directory" in the "Resources" menu.) A free downloadable PDF reference guide of language technology products and services.

I18N Gurus. http://www.i18ngurus.com. "The open internationalization resources directory."

Webb's World. http://www.webbsnet.com. Technical resources and translation services.

opentag.com. http://www.opentag.com. "A place for localization tools and technologies." Includes an XML FAQ.

Tex Texin's Web site at http://www.i18nguy.com. A considerable internationalization resource.

Magazines

Multilingual Computing & Technology. http://www.multilingual.com. It might be a stretch to say that this is the focal point of the industry, but it is certainly worth reading.

Localisation Focus. http://www.localisation.ie/publications/locfocus/index.htm.

Translation Journal. http://www.accurapid.com/journal. "A Publication For Translators by Translators about Translators and Translation."

Machine Translation. http://www.springeronline.com/journal/10590/about.

Web Sites and FTP Sites

Forums and newsgroups: At the time of this writing, Microsoft is replacing its newsgroups with forums. At some point in the near future, the internationalization newsgroup (microsoft.public.dotnet.internationalization at msnews.microsoft.com) will be replaced with an equivalent forum at http://forums.microsoft.com/msdn. This newsgroup/forum is an excellent source of internationalization answers.

Dr. International. http://www.microsoft.com/globaldev/DrIntl/default.mspx. Various resources, FAQ, and "Ask Dr. International," which allows you to ask internationalization questions.

The Unicode Consortium. http://www.unicode.org. All the facts on Unicode.

The World Fact Book. http://www.odci.gov/cia/publications/factbook/index.html. A great source of information about countries, regions, and languages.

Ethnologue. http://www.ethnologue.com. Comprehensive statistics and descriptions of languages by country and "a whole lot more." Available free online and also for purchase in book and CD-ROM versions.

Localization Glossary. ftp://ftp.microsoft.com/developr/msdn/newup/Glossary/. Translations in more than 40 languages of textual phrases used in various Microsoft products.

Postal Code Formats of the World. http://www.magma.ca/~djcl/postcd.txt. An analysis of postal code formats used in various countries.

Frank's Compulsive Guide to Postal Addresses. http://www.columbia.edu/kermit/postal.html. An analysis of address formats and postal codes used in various countries.

The Global Source-Book for Address Data Management. http://www.grcdi.nl/book2.htm. A commercial, comprehensive analysis of address formats and information from 242 countries.

Country Codes. http://www.statoids.com/wab.html. A listing of a wide variety of codes (ISO, ITU, IOC, etc.) used in 240 countries.

Microsoft Typography Fonts and Products. http://www.microsoft.com/typography/fonts/default.aspx. Information on what products supply what fonts, and also what fonts are supplied by what products. You can use this to determine whether a user is likely to have a font you need.

Ranking of Top 20 Translation Companies. http://www.commonsenseadvisory.com/members/res_cgi.php/050701_QT_top_20.php. A list of the top 20 largest suppliers of translation services.

The Savvy Client's Guide to Translation Agencies. http://www.bytelevel.com/reports/savvy/2005.html. An annually up-dated commercial review of translation agencies and how to choose one.

Greatranslations. http://www.greatranslations.com. A Web site for translators. You can find translators and links to many free localization resources here.

Foreign Word. http://www.foreignword.com. A wealth of free language tools and resources.

The Translation Guide. http://mason.gmu.edu/~aross2. A searchable collection of 520 links to online machine translators, dictionaries, and word lists.

100 Links to Online Translators and Machine Translation Software. http://www.bultra.com/mtlinks.htm.

The Calendar Zone. http://www.calendarzone.com. An extensive collection of links to numerous calendar types.

Shtick! http://www.shtick.org/Translation. A collection of machine translations that have resulted in less than perfect but fairly amusing results.

Lost in Translation. http://www.tashian.com/multibabel. Mindless "Chinese Whispers" translation fun.

Online Machine-Translation Web Sites

Table B.1   Online Machine-Translation Web Sites

Name	Address	Number of Language Pairs	Comments
AltaVista	http://www.altavista.com	36	Roman languages, plus Chinese, Korean, Japanese, and Russian
Bowne Global	http://itranslator.bowneglobal.com	18	Roman languages

Name	Address	Number of Language Pairs	Comments
Dictionary.com	http://www.dictionary.com	24	Roman languages, plus Chinese, Korean, Japanese, and Russian
FreeTranslation	http://www.freetranslation.com	16	Roman languages, plus Russian
Google	http://www.google.com	18	Roman languages, plus Chinese, Korean, and Japanese
Infoseek	http://www.infoseek.co.jp/Honyaku	6	English, Chinese, Japanese
LinguaTec	http://www.linguatec.net/online/ptwebtext/index_en.shtml	18	Roman languages, plus Chinese, Korean, Japanese, and Taiwanese
Online Translator	http://www.online-translator.com	16	Roman languages, plus Russian
LingvoBit	http://www.poltran.com	2	English to/from Polish only
Reverso	http://www.reverso.net/text_translation.asp	10	Roman languages
Socrates	http://www.rustran.com	2	English to/from Russian only
Systran	http://www.systranbox.com	42	Roman languages, plus Arabic, Chinese, Korean, Japanese, Russian, and Swedish
WorldLingo	http://www.worldlingo.com	13 languages	Roman languages, plus Chinese, Korean, Japanese and Russian
@nifty	www.nifty.com/globalgate	2	English to/from Japanese only

Blogs

Table B.2   Blogs

Name	RSS
Jesper Holmberg	http://blogs.msdn.com/jesperh/Rss.aspx
Dr. International	http://blogs.msdn.com/drintl/rss.aspx
Michael Kaplan	http://blogs.msdn.com/michkap/rss.aspx
Christian Nagel	http://weblogs.asp.net/cnagel/Rss.aspx
Brian Pepin	http://www.urbanpotato.net/Rss.asmx/GetRss?document=970
Raghavendra Prabhu	http://blogs.msdn.com/rprabhu/rss.aspx
Achim Ruopp	http://blogs.msdn.com/achimr/Rss.aspx
Guy Smith-Ferrier	http://www.guysmithferrier.com/rss.aspx
Shawn Steele	http://blogs.msdn.com/shawnste/rss.aspx

Conferences

The Internationalization and Unicode Conference. http://www.unicode.org/conference/about-conf.html.

Microsoft Global Development and Deployment Conference. http://www.microsoft.com/globaldev/gdc/gddchome.mspx.

The Annual Internationalisation and Localisation Conference. http://www.localisation.ie.

The Annual International Workshop on Internationalisation of Products and Systems. http://www.iwips.org.

Localization World. http://www.localizationworld.com.

TRANSDEX and The Internationalization and Unicode Conference, two co-located conferences hosted by Global Meeting Services, Inc.

Translating and the Computer. http://www.aslib.com/conferences.

Organizations

Localization Industry Standards Association. http://www.lisa.org. Nonprofit organization for the globalization, internationalization, localization, and translation business community.

Association of Translation Companies. Although this is an actual name of an association (in the U.K.), it is a commonly used phrase in many countries. For example, there is the Spanish Association of Translation Companies, the Hellenic Association of Translation Companies (Greece), and the Association of Hungarian Translation Companies. If you are looking for such an association in a specific country, try searching for the same combination of words and insert the language name somewhere in the phrase (e.g., "Association of Finnish Translation Companies").

European Union of Associations of Translation Companies (EUATC). http://www.euatc.org.

The Localization Institute. http://www.localizationinstitute.com. Providers of training, seminars, conferences, and internationalization resources.

The Globalization and Localization Association (GALA). http://www.gala-global.org. News, events, resources, and membership to GALA.

International Association for Machine Translation (IAMT). Publishes a newsletter, organizes workshops and conferences, and compiles a resource listing. The association is an umbrella for the following more local branches:

> Association for Machine Translation in the Americas (AMTA). http://www.amtaweb.org.
>
> Asian-Pacific Association for Machine Translation (AAMT). http://www.aamt.info.
>
> European Association for Machine Translation (EAMT). http://www.eamt.org.

The Translation Automation User Society. http://www.translationautomation.com. A networking community for users of translation and localization technologies and services. As the name implies, TAUS is focused on the automation of translation.

Commercial Machine-Translation Products

TranSphere. http://www.apptek.com/products/transphere.html. Applications Technology, Inc. (AppTek). Includes an API for programmatic control of translation engines.

Direct-API. http://www.worldlingo.com/products_services/development_tools.html. WorldLingo Translations, LLC. Has an HTTP-based API for programmatic control of a translation engine. It works by sending an HTTP GET request (which includes your password parameter) to the WorldLingo server, which returns an HTTP HTML response. It is much like the HTML screen scraping examples in Chapter 9, "Machine Translation," except that the interface is much leaner and WorldLingo has a duty to maintain compatibility.

e-Translation Server. http://www.linguatec.de/products/firm/index_en.shtml. Linguatec Language Technologies. Has an HTTP-based API for programmatic control of a translation engine.

LEC TranslateDotNet and LogoMedia. http://www.lec.com. Language Engineering Company. Provides various machine-translation solutions.

Transparent Language, Inc. http://www.transparent.com. Transparent. Provides a range of translation solutions.

Alternatives to .NET Framework Internationalization

I sincerely hope that if you have read this far, you have learned enough to internationalize your .NET applications yourself. However, if this is not the case, Table B.3 shows a few third-party products that handle part or all of the internationalization process.

Table B.3   Third-Party Alternatives to .NET Framework Internationalization

Product Name	Web Site
Catalyst	http://www.alchemysoftware.ie
Language Studio	http://ls.atia.com/
Lingoware	http://www.lingoware.com

Product Name	Web Site
Localizer	http://www.lingobit.com
Multilizer	http://www.multilizer.com
Passolo	http://www.passolo.com
RC-WinTrans	http://www.schaudin.com
SDL Insight	http://www.sdl.com
Software Translator for Windows	http://www.eurocitysoftware.com
Visual Localize	http://www.visloc.com

You might also like to know that Microsoft might release a similar tool into the fray. In May 2004, Microsoft announced Microsoft Application Translator (MAT). At the time of this writing, the product is on hold, but it might (or might not) be released after the publication of this book. MAT is an on-the-fly user interface translator. It intercepts Windows applications and translates their text as it is rendered in the user interface. It uses lookup tables to perform the translations. These lookup tables are included in MAT, and you can edit them and add new tables.

This innovative product has pros and cons. The pros are that the original application does not need to be modified in any way, and the source code for the original application is not required. In addition MAT is expected to be free to ISVs, developers, and users. The cons are that it simply translates bits of text—no other part of the internationalization process is handled. For example, all globalization issues are not handled; sort orders, the formatting of dates, currencies, and numbers all remain unchanged and use the original developer's preconceptions. In addition MAT runs only on Windows XP, Windows Server 2003, and later releases. If MAT does get released, you will probably find references to it at http://www.microsoft.com and http://www.microsoft.com/globaldev.

Index

Symbols

100 Links to Online Translators and Machine Translation Software, 600

: (colon), strings terminating with, 274

== (equality) operator, 177

@__BuildControlform1 method, 143-144

@__BuildControlTree method, 147

A

AAMT (Asian-Pacific Association for Machine Translation), 603

AbbreviatedMonthGenitiveNames property (DateTimeFormatInfo class), 581

absolute positioning, 238-240

accelerators, duplicate, 495

AcceptStringAndImageResourceEntry method, 569

AcquireRequestState method, 134

Add Input Language dialog box, 243

Add Resource String Visual Studio Add-In, 341-343

   installing in Visual Studio 2003, 344

   installing in Visual Studio 2005, 343

AddAlias method, 586

AddMetadata method, 586

AddResourceFile method, 545

AddResourceSet method, 561

AddStandardHotKey method, 283-285

AddVersionInfoResource method, 550

administration (resource), 11, 333

   Add Resource String Visual Studio Add-In, 341-343

     installing in Visual Studio 2003, 344

     installing in Visual Studio 2005, 343

comments, 348-350

reading resources, 346-347

Resource Administrator, 334-335

   adding resources to, 335-336

   automatic translation of strings, 337-338

   exporting resources, 339-340

   integrity checks, 340-341

   missing resources, 336-337

   Resource Governors, 338-339, 353-358

Resource Editor control, 358-360

.resx file references, 350-352

ResXDataNode class, 348-350

writing resources, 348

AltaVistaTranslator class, 322-324

alternate sort orders, 182-190

   AlternateSortOrders class, 185-186

   cultures with alterate sort orders, 184

   GetAlternateSortOrders method, 186

   InitializeCulture method, 189-190

   Internet Explorer Language Preferences, 188

   specifying in Regional and Language Options dialog, 186-187

AlternateSortOrders class, 185-186

alternatives to .NET Framework internationalization, 604-605

American Standard Code for Information Interchange (ASCII) character set, 15

AMTA (Association for Machine Translation in the Americas), 603

Annual International Workshop on Internationalization of Products and Systems, 602

J-K

L

THIS BOOK IS SAFARI ENABLED

INCLUDES FREE 45-DAY ACCESS TO THE ONLINE EDITION

The Safari® Enabled icon on the cover of your favorite technology book means the book is available through Safari Bookshelf. When you buy this book, you get free access to the online edition for 45 days.

Safari Bookshelf is an electronic reference library that lets you easily search thousands of technical books, find code samples, download chapters, and access technical information whenever and wherever you need it.

TO GAIN 45-DAY SAFARI ENABLED ACCESS TO THIS BOOK:

- Go to **http://www.awprofessional.com/safarienabled**
- Complete the brief registration form
- Enter the coupon code found in the front of this book on the "Copyright" page

If you have difficulty registering on Safari Bookshelf or accessing the online edition, please e-mail customer-service@safaribooksonline.com.

Addison
Wesley